Farrar's Funeral Home Dandridge

The Funeral Home Records

Of

Farrar's Funeral Home Records

Jefferson County Tennessee

Dandridge

Transcribed from the original records
by Wayne Shaw

To my Grand children

Kiera, Bonnie and Allen

2013

Farrar's Funeral Home Dandridge TN

Farrar's Funeral Home Dandridge

Legend

M- Married

S-Single

W- Widowed

FBLOC-Fathers Birth Location

MBLOC- Mothers Birth Location

By- Who Paid For Funeral

Farrar's Funeral Home Dandridge

NAME	DATE	DLOCAT	BLOCAT	BDATE	AGE	SPOUSE	FATHER	FRLOCAT	MOTHER	MRLOCAT	BY	BURIAL	VET	SON	DAUG	BROTHER	SISTER
Abernathy, Winnie Atchley	May 9, 1985	Jeff Co	Tn	Apr 15, 1902	83	W	Atchley, Albert		Finchum, Josie		Charles, Mrs. Laverne Greenwood - Knoxville,	Woodlawn - Knoxville,					
Acuff, Billy	Jan 1, 1964	Tn	Tn								Acuff, Jo Ann	Greenwood - Knox Co					
Acuff, Ellis Vida	Mar 24, 1959	Jeff Co	Tn	Mar 20, 1877	82	W	Northern, William L.		Hawkins, Matilda		Acuff, Mrs. Raymond	Mill Springs					
Acuff, Lillie Pearl	Jan 17, 1966	Jeff Co	Tn	Mar 20, 1887	68	W	Acuff, Raymond		Northern, Cornelius		Acuff, Mrs. Raymond	Mill Springs					
Acuff, Ora Raymond	Feb 2, 1980	Andrew Johnson Hwy.	Tn	Jan 6, 1899	81	W			Acuff, Hadley		Whitaker, Mrs. Albert [Lorene]	Mill Springs					
Acuff, William	Apr 15, 1966	Jeff Co	Tn	Jun 25, 1930	35		Acuff, Raymond	Indiana	Carroll, Lillie Pearl		Acuff, Mrs. William [Lorene]	Mill Springs					
Adams, Frank	Sep 26, 1939	Jeff Co	Indiana	Jan 3, 1900	39	Ng			Brady, Martha	Indiana	Adams, Mrs. Minnie	Lebanon					
Adams, Mabel Lena	Dec 4, 1987	Talbott, Tn	Rockwood, Ky	Jan 20, 1924	73		Godwin, William Pascal		Harp, Ida		Wilson, Sharon Sue [Daug] - Tri City F.H. Benham, Ky	Crouch					
Adams, Omer	Jun 28, 1987	Jeff City	Brinkley, Ky	Feb 24, 1935	62	W	Fields, Loretta		Fignon, Lonnie			J.M.G.	army		Riley, Dianna - Vance, Kristy		Tolliver, Wilma
Adcock, William Eddie	Aug 16, 1992	J.M.H.	Welch, W. Va.	Aug 16, 1992	70		Adams, William		Lester, Sara K.		Wife	Woodlawn - Bluewell, Va.	unk				
Adcock, Bernice Loretta	Oct 3, 1946	Jeff Co	Tn	Apr 8, 1924	22	S	Adcock, M.L.	Tn	Cantwell, Leona C.	Tn	Adcock, M.L.	Pleasant Grove					
Alley, Alma Gertrude	Sep 11, 1987	Knoxville, Tn	Tn	Nov 17, 1909	77	W	Alley, Arville		Cox, Minnie		Alley, Arville	J.M.G.					
Alley, Arvilla Randolph	May 1, 1990	Jeff Co	Jeff Co	Jan 10, 1911	79	W			Carris, Mollie		Alley, Robert E.	J.M.G.					
Alley, Dorman Howard	May 22, 1995	Jeff City	Tn	Jan 28, 1931	64		Emory, Virginia		Alley, James Fletcher		Bolotite, Minnie		Wife		Wesley H. & Susan [G] Joshua		
Alley, Edna																	
Alley, Henry Houston	Oct 16, 1982	Jeff City	Tn	Mar 13, 1981	81	Ng	Alley, William		Newman, Lidisha		Ferrar F.H. [Dandridge, Tn] Denton, Ida - Large, Mrs. - Burchfield, Mrs. - Bell, J.V.V. - Crville - Wiley, Alfreda - [Children]	Memorial Gardens					
Alley, Laura	Feb 2, 1971	Jeff City	Tn	May 18, 1867	83	W	Newman, Nip		Bettis, Kate		Lawrence, Jack - Alley, A.C.Grobert & Crville	Holston View - Knox Co					
Alley, Minnie [F]	Apr 21, 1971	Jeff Co	Tn	Mar 6, 1887	84	W	Colletin, Thomas A.		Long, Amanda C.		Alley, Damon - [Daug] Shannone, Sd.	Mt. Pleasant					
Alley, Mary Carrey	Oct 18, 1990	Jeff Co	Tn	Dec 17, 1887	74	W	Carey, James		Burchfel, Junie		Denton, Mrs. Ida Rimmler, Butch	Memorial Garden					
Alley, Oscar W.	Oct 21, 1982	Jeff Co	Jeff Co	May 21, 1907	85	W	Alley, Arnold		Newman, Laura		Elmore, Beulah	Alley - Jeff Co	42-45			Robert-Curtis	
Akard, Bessie Elvena	Aug 13, 1979	Jeff Co	Tn	Feb 17, 1904	75	W	Grogan, W.S.		Harris, Polly		Blevins, Mrs. & Gene	Shiloh					Lawrence, Ruby
Akard, Rollo Ketron	Mar 4, 1975	Jeff Co	Tn	Oct 26, 1911	63	W	Akard, Ephraim		Senns, Eliza		Akard, Bill	Shiloh - Grainger Co					
Albaugh, Fannie	May 30, 1990	Jeff Co	Tn	May 20, 1901	88	W	Bishop, Jacob G.		Milligan, Eva		Hodge, Doris	Lebanon Baptist					
Albertson, Curtis J.	Mar 2, 1995	Knoxville, Tn	Lima, Ohio	May 7, 1939	55	Patricia L.	Albertson, Charles K.		Young, Louise		Wife	Veterans - Knoxville, Tn	62-68				
Albright, Frank N.	Apr 11, 1966	Jeff Co	Tn	Dec 26, 1920	45	Ng			Nicols, Nellie		Albright, Mrs. Katherine - Bill						
Albright, Infant	Feb 15, 1927	Jeff Co	Tn	Feb 15, 1927	0		Albright, W.D.				Albright, Mrs. Katherine						
Albright, Katherine	Dec 3, 1992	Waverly, Tn	Jeff Co	Nov 8, 1923	69	W	Zirkle, Joseph		Long, Cora		McClaren, Helen [Daug] Shannone, Sd.	West View		Charles Z.			
Albright, Nellie Nichols	Oct 19, 1981	Tn	Muncie, Indiana	Dec 27, 1898	72	W			Swann, Victoria		Albright, Frank & Bill	West View					
Albright, Wallace Daniel	Oct 11, 1944	Jeff Co	Nov 13, 1893	Nov 13, 1893	50	Ng	Albright, Frank	Ohio	Wallace, Maude	Ohio	Albright, Mrs. W.D. & Nellie	West View	WW 1				
Alexander, Dora V.	Apr 13, 1987	J.M.H.	Dec 20, 1897	Dec 20, 1897	89	Alexander, Michael [D]	Volbe, Jackson		McWilliams, Nancy		Bernard-Crane, Mrs. [Russell Spring, Ky] Bernard F.H.	J.M.G.					
Alexander, George Scott	Dec 18, 1948	Utrica Co., Tn	Ky	Jan 22, 1871	77-10-26	W	Allen, Robert	Tn	McIntanit, Sarah	Tn	Allen, Robert	Shiloh					
Allen, Jackie Clark [M]	Sep 7, 1995	Knoxville, Tn	Tn	Mar 15, 1965	30	S	Allen, Jack A.		Clark, Shirley		Allen, Jack A.	Jefferson Memorial					
Allen, John C.	Mar 5, 1981	Jeff City	Tn	Aug 11, 1892	88		Allen, George		Bryant, Oufill		Cox, Terry	Jefferson Memorial					
Allen, Lorene L.	Jul 24, 1983	Knoxville, Tn	Middlesboro, Ky	May 19, 1917	66		Godwin, Bessie K.		Lynch, Mary V.		Baldwin, Iva & Cancer[Sister]	Duncan-Baldwin - Jeff Co					Tommie & Tommie-Haskell & Shirley-Dennel & Dorothy
Allen, Minnie	Mar 14, 1956	Jeff Co	Tn	Aug 30, 1878	77		Allen, Charles		Henderson, Sam		Tatler, Mrs. C.W. Bernard	Wesley Chapel					Bri-Lexif Poorn, Donnel & Dorothy
Allen, Pearl	Apr 30, 1978	At Home	Tn	Sep 20, 1888	89	Allen, Mabel [D]	Poore, Bessie		Hicks, Orpha		Catfell, Mrs. W.H.	West View					Bri-Lexif Poorn, Donnel & Isaac

NAME	DDATE	DLOCAT	BLOCAT	BDATE	AGE	SPOUSE	FATHER	FRLOCAT	MOTHER	MTRLOCAT	BY	BURIAL	VET	SON	DAUG	BROTHER	SISTER
Allen, Sandra Lucille	Jul 3, 1981	Jeff City	Tn	Jul 11, 1953	27	Allen, Robert Wayne Sr.	Hill, Andrew		Davis, Lucille		Allen, Robert W. Sr.	Jefferson Memorial					
Allen, Virginia	Jan 28, 2000	Jeff City	Ga	Jan 23, 1909	90	W	Williamson, Emory		Lees, Rayworth		Allen, Anton (Son)	Summerville - Agusta, Ga					
Allsup, Lena	Jan 11, 1960	Jeff City	Nc	Aug 3, 1876	83	Ng	Case, Henry				Allsup, M.H.	Valley View (Cedar Grove)					
Allsup, Marshall H.	Nov 28, 1961	Jeff Co	Tn	Jun 11, 1874	87	W					Whitaker, Enos	Cedar Grove - Jeff Co					
Allsup, W.L.	Apr 3, 1956	Rutledge	Ng	Apr 17, 1856	79	Ng					Allsup, Ray	Sunrise					
Allton, Cillie	Dec 3, 1983	Care Inn	Tn	Jan 30, 1897	86	Allton, Thomas Ralph	Newman, Arthur		Sawyers, Maggie		Allton, Thomas Ralph	Greenwood - Knoxville, Tn					
Allton, James J.	Nov 24, 1964	Knox Co	Tn		82	S	Allton, W. Frank		Maddox, Nellia		Allton, Ralph-Porter-Arthur & T.R. (Brothers)	Buffalo Grove					
Allton, Juanita	Nv 15, 1971	Knox Co	Tn	Oct 8, 1891	80/86	Allton, Reese (D)	Talley, William		Ballinger, Sarah		Allton, Rosa Jewell	West View					
Allton, Mary Ella	Apr 2, 1981	Jeff Co	Tn	Nov 22, 1880	80	S	Maddox, Nellia		Maddox, Nellia		Allton, J.J.	Buffalo Grove					
Allton, Reese J.	Jan 6, 1980	Jeff Co	Tn	Jan 27, 1885	74	Ng	Allton, W. Frank		Maddox, Nelly		Allton, Mrs. & Jewell	Buffalo Grove					
Allton, William Fred Sr.	Mar 8, 1974	Knoxville, Tn	Tn	Jul 28, 1920	53	Henry, Connie	Allton, Ralph		Newman, Cillie		Allton, Mrs. Fred Sr.	Jefferson Memorial					
Anderson, Aaron C.	Dec 22, 1975	J.M.H.	Tn	Jul 16, 1892	83	W			Link		Anderson, Jobert	Jefferson Memorial					
Anderson, Ada	Apr 25, 1981	Jeff Co	Tn	May 3, 1904	56	Anderson, Gus	Chuck, Richard		Richard, Tronia		Anderson, Gus	Buffalo Grove					
Anderson, Claude Oakley	Oct 21, 1951	Jeff Co	Tn	Jul 8, 1883	68	Ng			Kidwell, Mollie		Kidwell, Mollie	Ebenezer					
Anderson, Eliza Vida	Jul 31, 1943	Jeff Co	Ga	Oct 1 1871	71	Anderson, Sam [Age-84]	Snodgrass, William H.		Dillard, Louise	Ga	Anderson, Sam	Buffalo Grove					
Anderson, Elizabeth Pauline	Mar 13, 1943	Kingsport	Jeff Co			Anderson, J. Tom		Jones, Maude	Tn	Anderson, J.T.	Buffalo Grove						
Anderson, Eula Smelcer	May 26, 1979	Knoxville, Tn	Tn	Jul 21, 1915	63	W	Smelcer, E.S.		Cobble, Nellie		Jefferson Memorial						
Anderson, Hobert P.	Apr 7 1993	Jeff Co	Tn	Dec 5, 1918	74	Ng	Robertson, Lydia		Robertson, Lydia		J.M.G.	navy					
Anderson, Horace Eugene	May 2, 1945	Jeff Co	Jeff Co	Jun 27, 1908	36	S	Anderson, Sam T.	Tn	Snodgrass, Lydia	Nc	Anderson, Robert & Shirley (Son)	J.M.G.		Eugene & Norma			
Anderson, James Augustus	Mar 14, 1981	Jeff City	Tn	Apr 18, 1901	79	Ballinger, Mary Ducan	Allton, Ralph		Snodgrass, Lydia		John & Frank	Buffalo Grove					
Anderson, James Thomas	Feb 25, 1952	Jeff Co	Tn	Nov 30, 1873	78	Ng	Anderson, Caleb		Douglas, Catherine		Anderson, Mary B.	Buffalo Grove					
Anderson, John Pleasant	Mar 29, 1964	J.M.H.	Tn	Mar 2, 1894	90	S	Anderson, Samuel T.		Snodgrass, Vida		Mc Carter, Mrs. James-Johnson, Ruth-Katherine [Daug]	Buffalo Grove					
Anderson, Katherine Reece	Jun 18, 1957	Jeff Co	Tn	Jun 6, 1902	55	Anderson, W. C.	Chuck, Richard		Rockard, Fronia		Hutton, Mrs. Agnes Anderson, Billy June	Buffalo Grove					
Anderson, Lena Belle	Jan 12, 1964	T.B. Hospital	Tn	Jan 13, 1922	41	Anderson, Fred L. [Doc]	Hall, Lou		Melone, Mary Ann		Anderson, F-L-[Pueblo, Colo]- Wycouff, Mrs. Albert [Colo]	Buffalo Grove					
Anderson, Liddie Margarite	Jul 28, 1971	Knox Co	Tn	Feb 13, 1886	82	Anderson, Aaron	Robinson, Matthew		Rinchard		Jefferson, Aaron	Jefferson Memorial					
Anderson, Lula	Mar 30, 1991	Oak Ridge, Tn	Sevier Co	May 26, 1908	82	W	Mc Carter, Thomas L.		Proffitt, Martha		Thomas, Agnes [Daug]	Buffalo Grove					
Anderson, Maude Jones	May 26, 1959	Knox Co	Tn	Oct 1, 1881	77	Anderson, J.T.	Jones, Nelson				Mc Carter, Mrs-James-Johnson, V.L.- Sharp, Ruth-Frances-Charlotte-Maude	Buffalo Grove					
Anderson, Mildred Ann	Oct 21, 1960	Jeff Co	Tn	Oct 9, 1960	12d		Anderson, Caleb		Douglas, Kathryn	Tn	Anderson, J.H.	Strawberry Plains					
Anderson, Nelson Newman	Mar 12, 1940	Morristown	Tn	May 6, 1861	76	Ng	Purkey, Robert		Palmer, Eunice		Willie	Jernigan					
Anderson, Pearl Margaret	Sep 19, 1982	J.M.H	Jeff City	Dec 17, -82	74	Anderson, Hobert	Anderson, Robert M.		Mc Carter, Lula		Hubbard	J.M.G.					
Anderson, Robert Audrey	May 30, 1990	Harriman City	Tn	Oct 25, 1934	55	Div					Thomas, Agnes	Buffalo Grove					
Anderson, Robert Mack	Nov 8, 1984	Oak Ridge, Tn	Tn	Dec 21, 1908	75	Ng	Anderson, James T.		Jones, Maude		Anderson, Mrs. Jula-Thomas, Mrs Leonard	Buffalo Grove					
Anderson, Samuel F.	Feb 12, 1935	Jeff City	Tn	Sep 20, 1934	4m		Anderson, Fred L.	Tn	Hall, Letha	Tn	Anderson, Sam	Buffalo Grove					
Anderson, Samuel Frank	Nov 2, 1951	Jeff Co	Tn	Feb 27, 1904	47	Ng	Anderson, S.A.		Snodgrass, Vida		Anderson, Mrs. Myrtle	Buffalo Grove					
Anderson, Samuel Thompson	May 22, 1946	Jeff City	Tn	Dec 28, 1859	86	W	Anderson, Caleb	Va	Douglas, Catherine	Jeff Co	Anderson, John [Son]	Buffalo Grove					
Anderson, William Caleb	Feb 21, 1982	Jeff Co	Tn	Jun 9, 1899	82	W	Anderson, Samuel		Snodgrass, Villa		Cross, Billie A.	Buffalo Grove					

NAME	DDATE	DLOCAT	BLOCAT	BDATE	AGE	SPOUSE	FATHER	FBRLOCAT	MOTHER	MFBLOCAT	BY	BURIAL	VET	SON	DAUG	BROTHER	SISTER
Andres, Kia Rachelle	Mar 4, 1996	Knoxville, Tn	Knoxville, Tn	Mar 4, 1996			Andres, William Patrick		Mc Neil, Angela S.		Mother - Edmonds, Lillian [G-Mother]	Wills					
Anzai, Irma	Sep 6, 1996	Miami, Fl	Newark, NJ	Aug 12, 1920	76	W			Williams, Clara		Hill, (Ginny (Dlng - FL) Hicks, Mrs. Chester - Ayden, John	Lenoir City			Barber, Carol		
Auden, Nancy Kate	Nov 30, 1948	Shaw Plains	Monroe Co., Tn	Jul 8, 1871	77,4-22	W	Lattimore, John	Tn	White, Mary								
Arnold, Jason Matthew	Aug 16, 1993	Rutledge, Tn	Clarksville, Tn	Sep 11, 1976	16		Arnold, Kenneth D.		Berry, Trina	Tn	Mother - Brunner, Jane Berry, Clyde & Ed [Parents], Russell, Mandy [G-Mother]	J.M.G.		Jon-Josh			[Aunt] Mansell, Kathy
Arnold, Marshall R.	May 15, 1993	Jeff City	Austinville, Va	Jun 20, 1919	73	Thacker, Edith	Arnold, Newell B.		Walter, Linnie		Wills	West View		Jerry & Trish & Wendy		Kenneth [Flo]-Newell [Val]-Emory [Cal]	
Arnold, Mrs. Will	Nov [22], 1959										Northern, Earl - Hayworth Horace [New Market]						
Arwood, Katherine	Aug 1, 1952	Hamblen Co	Tn		28-3 25	Ng	Rector, George		Clevenger, Ola		Conklin, Mrs. Rhonda [Rick]	Will - Hamblen Co					
Ashburn, Reea Ieona	May 4, 1986	LI.T.H.	Tn	Jun 20, 1937	48	Div	Rimes, Ronda		Mc Nish, Gladys			West View					
Ashcraft, Harold Dean	Feb 14, 1989	Pine Bluff Ar		Jan 5, 1940	39	W	Ashcraft, Harold Ray		Fuels, Marilyn Erle		Schuknecht, Carolyn [Sister]	Pine Ridge - Grapevine, Tn					
Ashley, Lenina	Jul 3, 1977	Jeff Co	Va	Nov 28, 1894	82	W	Cox, H.F.	Tn	Mitchell, Armunda	Tn	Cox, [Pres & Ed] Brinner, Mrs. Oma	West View					
Ashmore, Lyda Edgar	Feb 6, 1942	Jeff City	Tn	Feb 20, 1874	67	W	Edgar, Robert M.	Tn	Renelus, Martha	Tn	Archley, Mrs. - Atchley, Press - Bates, Mrs.	West View					
Ashley, B.R.	Dec 10, 1932	New Market			84	Ng	Atchley, Ben	Tn	Lyon, Sue	Tn	Wills	Piedmont					
Ashley, Fred E.	Oct 13, 1980	Knoxville, Tn	Tn	Jun 24, 1915	65	Elder, Joyce	Atchley, Robert H.		Elder, Zenna		Atchley, Mrs. Joyce	Hillcrest					
Ashley, J.P.	Jan 28, 1931	Dandridge	Tn	Aug 8, 1859	71	W	Atchley, J.C.	Tn	Lyle, Emma	Tn		Cate					
Ashley, Mrs. P.M.	May 15, 1936				65												
Ashley, P.M.	April 30, 1935																
Ashley, Pixie A.	Sep 14, 1983	Jeff Co	Tn	Sep 28, 1895	87	Watson, Marie	Atchley, Rush		Franklin, Nancy		Marie & Irene	Nance's Grove					
Atchley, Virginia Irene	Jul 23, 1971	Oak Ridge, Tn	Tn	Jan 26, 1895	76	Atchley, Pixie [D]	Wilson, Alton		Mc Ghee, Alice		Arthur, Gladys	Nance's Grove					
Atkins, Sarah B.	Oct 25, 1959	Tn	Tn	May 13, 1866	92	W	Hodges, Jim		Smith, Margaret		Hodges, Mary	Hodges, Jeff Co					
Auth, Abbie H.	Oct 18, 1958	Tn	Tn	Jul 29, 1858	87	Ng	Hodge, Jim	Nc	Mc Knight, Grace		Auth, H.B. - Hudson, L.H.	Friends Station					
Auburn, Carl O.	Jan 28, 1940	New Market	Tn	Nov 30, 1893	46	Ng	Auburn, Charles Andrew	Tn	Painter, Maggie	Ga	Auburn, Mrs.	New Market					
Austhus, William Hobert	May 14, 1977	Jeff Co	Tn	Apr 6, 1914	63	Yeary, Lillie	Austhus, John D.		Ellison, Sarah		Yeary - Clairborne Co	Elmwood -					Beeson, Anna Belle
Austin, Flado Eloise	Apr 8, 1989	Alabama		May 9, 1899	89	W	Hobbridge, William Timothy		Mackey, Mollie Eliza		Albright, Jane	Birmingham, Ala.					
Adell, Cora Dorothy	Mar 30, 1994	Minneapolis, Mn	Mn	Oct 23, 1892	101	Aztell, Warren Fess [D]	Stamms, Leonard Eldon		Miller, Dorothy A. & Howard [Dawg]		Miller, Dorothy A. & Howard [Dawg]	West View	Alan & Betty			
Adell, Warren Fess	Mar 24, 1961	Jeff Co	Illinois	Jul 12, 1882	78	Ng	Adell, Nathan H.		Trim, Ellen		Adell, Mrs. W.F.	West View					
Bacon, Ada Jo	Jul 12, 1956	Knoxville, Tn	Tn	May 23, 1956	19	S	Bacon, James F.		Richard, Mrs. Hunner - Bayless, Ralph		Richard, Mrs. Hunner - Bayless, Ralph	Mt. Pleasant - Talbott, Tn					
Bacon, Geneva Naomi	Sep 13, 1972			Oct 19, 1921	50	Bacon, Ada [De]	Bayless, C.P.		Collett, Ida		Bacon, Ada Jr.	Mt. Pleasant	Walter T.			Bryan	
Bacon, Ollie B.	Dec 10, 1985	New Market, Tn	New Market, Tn	May 2, 1903	92	Bishop, Glass	Milligan, Eva		Hodge, Doris [Daug]		Hodge, Doris [Daug]	J.M.G.					
Bacon, Ruby Grace	Feb 2, 1994	Jeff City	Jeff Co	Jul 2, 1912	81	Anderson, Claude	Mills, Viola		Page, Jean "Suzie" [Daug]		Page, Jean "Suzie" [Daug]	Ebenezer	Charles E. - [Br-Law] Nelson, Clarence - Pegs, Ron	Nelson, Doris - [Br-Law] Bacon, Nina		Lixon [D]	
Behner, Walter S.	Sep 13, 1987	J.M.H.	Tn	Dec 10, 1901	85	Bishop, Ollie	Baer, Samuel		Masser, Anna		Blevins, Gall Baer, Mare & Mrs.	J.M.G.					
Baer, Joseph William	Sep 29, 1954	Knox Co	Tn	Oct 29, 1885	78	W	Baer, W.F.		Brooks, Mary Jane		Morgan Baer	Sunderland					
Baer, Mary Jane	Aug 21, 1954	Jeff Co	Tn	May 10, 1883	91	W	Brooks, George		Price, Margaret		Morgan, Louise	Sunderland					
Baer, Minnie J.	Apr 1, 1960	Jeff Co	Tn	May 5, 1881	79	Ng	Moody, Hugh		Baer, J.W.		Baer, J.W.	Sunderland					
Baer, Mollie Mae	Oct 20, 1965	Jeff Co			82	S	Brooks, Mary Jane		Morgan, Mrs. R.C. - Raymond		Morgan, Mrs. R.C. - Raymond	Sunderland					
Behner, Mary Catharine	Nov 15, 1992	Batesville, Ark.	Batesville, Ark.	Sep 18, 1908	84	Behner, Carl Tabb [Dr.]	Garrott, E.P.J.		Mayfield, Edis		Junsland	West View	T. Mayfield	Day, Mary B. - Hendricks, Frances B.			

NAME	DDATE	DLOCAT	BLOCAT	BDATE	AGE	SPOUSE	FATHER	FELLOCAT Y	MOTHER	MFELOCAT Y	BY	BURIAL	VET	SON	DAUG	BROTHER	SISTER
Behner, Maxford Tabb	Oct 3, 1983	Union City, Ga.	Charlottesville, Va	Sep 17, 1959	34		Behner, T. Maxford		McIntyre, Sara		Father - Behner, Carl [Uncle] - Hendricks, James & Frances - Clay, James [3-Parents]	West View					Lancaster, Susan & Frank H. - Margaret Catherine
Bailey, Mollie	Apr 13, 1953	Jeff Co	Tn	Jul 1, 1879	73	W	Hodge, Charles		Parrott, Polly		Bailey, Mrs. Claude	Pleasant Grove					
Bailey, Beatrice Lyle	Oct 29, 1969	Jeff Co	Tn	Sep 19, 1900	69	Ng	Lyle, Mathis		Lyle, Mollie E.		Bailey, Claude	Piney					
Bailey, Claude	Mar 16, 1978	Jeff City	Tn	Nov 25, 1898	79	W	Perrin, James		Frazier, Mrs. James		Bailey, Wallace	Pleasant Grove					
Bailey, Clyde Ernest	Apr 16, 1957	E. S. Hospital	Tn	Mar 31, 1912	45	S	Bailey, Noah		Gilbert, Eliza		Pratt, Mrs. - Clarence & Troy Jones, Mrs. Nancy - Fritts, Mary C.	West View					
Bailey, Danny Ray	Jul 21, 1977	Morristown, Tn	Tn	Feb 17, 1958	19	Lee, Margaret	Bailey, J.R.		Bernard, Mary Catherine		Bailey, J.W. & Mrs.	Strawberry Plains					
Bailey, David Marion	May 13, 1941	Straw Plains	Jeff Co		86-2-25	Bailey, Earle			Sessoms, Hannah	Jef Foo	Bailey, Manuel [Son]	Piney					
Bailey, Dewitt Talmadge	May 18, 1971	Lenoir City, Tn	Nc	Feb 1, 1898	73	Pendergrass, Gertrude [D]	Bailey, Joe		Bailey, Nancy		Bailey, Wallace [Marion, Ind.]	West View					
Bailey, Donna Jean	Aug 11, 1984	Knoxville, Tn	Manistee, Mich.	Nov 8, 1933	60	Bailey, Raymond D.	Carlson, Gordon		Carlson, Dorothy		Husband	J.M.G.		Merr S. [ind]- David M. [ind]- Scott W.- Joseph G. [Fa]			[Niece] Breeden, Barrie
Bailey, Dorothy Christine	Mar 14, 1984	Jeff City	Knox Co	Mar 4, 1913	81	W	Haun, Erastus		Burkhart, Iva		Gann, Wilma [G-Daug]	Pleasant Grove					Lenear, Edna
Bailey, Eva Clark	Apr 17, 1984	Jeff Co	Tn	Aug 29, 1906	55	W	Clark, William		Atchley, Hattie E.		Roderick, Mrs. D.A. Jr.- Hinchey, Mrs. Charles- Georgia-Shirley-Paul-Mack [Children]	Piney					
Bailey, Flora E.	Jul 13, 1954	Strawberry Plains, Tn	Tn	May 30, 1886	68	Ng	Seals, George		Vaughn, Nina		Bailey, Rev. Manuel	Piney					
Bailey, Gertrude	Dec 5, 1959	Hamblen Co	Tn		54	Bailey, Dewitt	Stinnett, James C.		Pendergrass, Mary		Bailey, Dewitt	Piney					
Bailey, Gregory Wayne	Oct 31, 1977	Jeff Co		Oct 31, 1977		Bailey, Dewitt	Bailey, Jerry Allen	Tn	Carroll, Judy	Tn	Bailey, Mrs. Dewey	West View					
Bailey, Hugh S.	Sep 16, 1953	Jeff Co	Tn	Mar 21, 1903	50	Div	Bailey, Sam		Perrin, Mollie		Roderick, Mrs. D.A.- Mack - Georgia -Betty, Shirley	Pleasant Grove - Piney					
Bailey, J.R.	Oct [?], 1957	Shreveport, La	Tn	Dec 21, 1872	39	Ng	Bailey, Sam		Gibbs, Ann		Bailey, Sam - Farrell, Grunge	Strawberry Plains					
Bailey, Joseph William	Jun 20, 1945	Jeff Co	Mitchell, Nc	Dec 21, 1872	72	Ng	Bailey, Mack	Nc	Bailey, D.T.	Nc	Bailey, D.T.	Lebanon - Mt. Horeb					
Bailey, Julia Emmaline	Oct 28, 1981	Knox Co	Tn	Jun 20, 1873	68	W	Helton, John		Breeden, Margaret		Lauderdale, Mrs. Vallie [Saginaw, Mich.]	Piney					
Bailey, Luther H.	Nov 9, 1952	Straw Plains	Tn	Aug 14, 1876	76	Ng	Bailey, Charlie		Dalton, Lucinda		Bailey, Mrs. Eva [Wife]- Paul-Mark-Hack-L.H. Jr [Sons]	Strawberry Plains					
Bailey, Mack	Mar 29, 1998	Knoxville, Tn	New Market, Tn	Oct 3, 1933	64	Jones, Rosemary	Bailey, Hugh		Clark, Eva		Wife	Strawberry Plains		Tracy	Bailey, Alicia Leigh		Roderick, Willis- Bailey, George- Johnson, Betty - Graham, Shirley
Bailey, Manuel [Rev.]	May 25, 1965	Strawberry Plains	Tn	Jun 24, 1891	73	Dorothy	Bailey, Marion		Lyles, Sarah		Bailey, Mrs. Dorothy	Piney					
Bailey, Marvin Arthur	Dec 29, 1949	Mt. Home V.A.	Tn	Oct 27, 1921	28	S	Bailey, Sam		Blackson, Shiina		Bailey, Mrs. Dorothy	Piney	WW 2				
Bailey, Mary Sylvia	Oct 22, 1985	J.M.H.	Tn	Oct 18, 1921	64	S	Bailey, William P.		French, Minnie Belle		Snodderly, Mrs. Frank	Piedmont					
Bailey, P.I.	Dec 1, 1928		Tn	Jul 10, 1885	63-4-21	Ng	Bailey, J.W.		Bailey, N.A.	Nc	Bailey, J.W. & Mrs. R.P.	Pleasant Grove					
Bailey, R.P.	Feb 11, 1955	Jeff City	Ng	Sep 29, 1896	38	Nc	Bailey, J.W.		Bailey, N.A.	Nc	Bailey, J.W. & Mrs. R.P.	New Gray- Knoxville					
Bailey, Shina	Jul 31, 1954	Knox Co	Va	Apr 17, 1894	60	Ng	Blackson, Andy		Blackson, Mary		Bailey, Sam	Strawberry Plains					
Bailey, William Troy	Jan 11, 1958	Jeff Co	Tn	Jul 1, 1922	35	S	Bailey, Noah		Gilbert, Eliza		Bailey, Noah - Pratt, Mrs.	Piney	WW 2				
Baker, Bessie Ellen	Aug 17, 1966	Jeff City	Tn	Feb 11, 1896	70	Baker, George	Dyke, Dewitt		Roach, Mary Jean		Baker - Earl - Ray & George	Jefferson Memorial					

NAME	DDATE	DLOCAT	BLOCAT	BDATE	AGE	SPOUSE	FATHER	FBLOCAT	MOTHER	MFBLOCAT	BY	BURIAL	VET	SON	DAUG	BROTHER	SISTER
Baker, Charles Taft	Jul 7, 1998	New Market, Tn	Union Co, Tn	Oct 19, 1908	89	Kiek, Myrtie	Baker, Solomon B.		Nicely, Martha Catherine		Wife	J.M.G.		Warren-C.L.	Ballinger, Jean		
Baker, George	Mar 7, 1972	Jeff Co.	Union Co, Tn	May 8, 1892	79	W	Baker, James		Bailey, Hulda		Baker, Earl-Ray	Memorial Gardens					
Baker, Georgia Wood	Sep 5, 1971	New Market, Tn	Tn	May 22, 1889	82	W	Palmer, Ben		Lowery, Susan		Wood, Lloyd	Flat Gap					
Baker, Harrison Benjamin	Sep 21, 1956	Tn	Tn	Jan 4, 1892	64	Ng	Baker, James		Gaddis, Elizabeth		Baker, Leon	Mt. View					
Baker, Helen Louise	Aug 9, 1954	Mt. Horeb	Tn	Jun 6, 1926	16-10-17		Baker, Harrison	Tn	Lunce, Mary		Baker, Harrison	Mt. View					
Baker, Jake Lunce	Oct 22, 1949	Jeff Co	Tn		8		Baker, Harrison		Lunce, Mary	Tn	Baker, Helen, M.	Mt. View					
Baker, James Earl	Dec 22, 1985	J.M.H.	New Market, Tn	May 6, 1918	67	Miller, Helen	Baker, George		Dye, Bessie		Baker, Helen, M.	Jefferson Memorial	WW 2				
Baker, James Edmund	Aug 25, 1983	Jeff Co	Union Co, Tn	Feb 26, 1911	42	Div	Baker, Blaston		Nicely, Martha C.		Baker, Charles	Grovestown - Union Co					
Baker, Josephine	Aug 31, 1979	De Paul, Fla	Tn	May 23, 1939	40	Ng	Cox, Taylor					Jefferson Memorial					
Baker, Louise M.	Sep 12, 1951	Jeff Co	Tn	Nov 17, 1871	79	W	Massengill, William H.		Gibbons, Mary		Moore, Jessie B. - Large, Mrs.	Mt. Horeb					
Baker, Martha Catherine	Aug 25, 1943	Friends Station	Union Co, Tn	Mar 26, 1868	75	Baker, Samuel Boston		Nc	Whitted, Merita	Tn	Charles - Roebia	Groves - Union Co					
Baker, Pauline	Feb 17, 1999	Morristown, Tn	Jeff Co	Mar 11, 1914	84	Smith, William Jackson			Gibbons, Marth Jane		Sartain, Violet Dwane & Bill Diaug	Ebenezer		[G] Sartain, Emily-Summer		
Baker, Preston L.	Jan 16, 1987	J.M.H.	Tn	Sep 10, 1899	87	S			Nicely, Martha C.		Baker, Charlie	New Market					
Baker, Richard	Jan 28, 1940	Dandridge		Jan 8, 1926	8		Baker, Solomon B.				Baker, Jake	Pleasant Hill					
Batch, Anne Ellison	Mar 4, 1978	Knoxville, Tn		Nov 19, 1922	55		Ellison, Thaddeus S.		Huff, Ethel		Batch, Charles D.	Union - Newport					
Batch, Charles D. Jr.	Nov 30, 2000	Jeff City	Tn	Aug 23, 1919	81	Ann	Batch, Charles D. Sr.		Easterly, Emma J.		Wife	Union - Newport, Tn	unk				
Blackburn, Glenn D.	Dec 11, 1996	Jeff City	Jeff City	Oct 2, 1903	93	Katie C.	Blackburn, Charles A.		Franklin, Georgia Inez		Wife	J.M.G.	William	Corbett, Barbara - Blackburn, Glenda	[1/2] Blackburn, Leland	
Belding, Lena	Dec 15, 1985	J.M.H.	Tn	Mar 21, 106	79	Belding, J.A.	Reeser, Robert D.		Jordan, Lydia		Belding, J.A. A[bk]	Chucky - Chucky, Tn					
Baldwin, Addie	Mar 17, 1946	Hamblen Co	Tn	Oct	92	W	Unk		Unk		Taylor, Paul - England, Mrs.	Presby - New Market					
Baldwin, Oliver	Feb 27, 1946	Tazewell, England		Dec 25, 1867	78	W	Unk				Hale, J.D. (Guardian)						
Bales, Arlie E.	Feb 24, 1941	Sevier Co		Mar 24, 1902	97	Bales, D.H.	Thornton, T.A.		Gibson, Elizabeth	Tn	Lawson, Alma Bales & Russell C. (Daug)						
Bales, Bertha	Sep 5, 1899	Dandridge, Tn	Christnal Hill, Tn		77-0-19				Bales, Mary		Shackelford, Mrs. Beulah (Daug)	Pleasant Grove					
Bales, Burrell W.	Dec 30, 1992	Eldorado, Ill.	Jeff Co	Aug 21, 1910	82		Bales, Roy R. Sr.		Frazier, Blanche		Willard, Hazel (Sister)	Trentville					Roy R. Jr - [In-Law] Lawj Bales, Dorothy
Bales, Callie M.	Oct 26, 1933	Friends Station	Tn	Apr 27, 1907	26	Bales, P.R.	Humbard, T.M.	Tn	Green, Florence	Tn	Bales, P.R.	Piney					
Bales, Carl A.	Feb 24, 1934	New Market	Tn	Apr 2, 1897	36	S			Dinwiddie, Bertie	Tn	Bales, W.D.	J.M.G.					
Bales, Carroll F.	Nov 16, 1996	Jeff Co	Tn	Jan 15, 1927	69	Kidwell, Lema	Bales, William		Elmore, Reba		Wife	Friends Station				Cartland-Jim-T.J.	Bennett, Wand - Foreley, Catherine
Bales, Charlie V.	Mar 25, 1940	Friends Station	Tn	Oct 10, 1887	52	W	Bales, W.T. Sr.	Tn			Children	Friends Station					
Bales, Driel Hicon	Jan 7, 1946	Knox Co	Tn	Apr 6, 1863	82	W	Bales, Tom		Bales, Patricia	Tn	Bales, Roy-Harry-Myrtie-Lola	Piney Grove					
Bales, Ellen M.	Dec 28, 1964	Knox Co	California	May 29, 1907	57	Eckel, Ocrtie	Mellen, Ida M.				Bales, Pryor & Children	Piney Grove					
Bales, Floyd E.C.	Dec 14, 1972	Tn	Tn	Sept 19, 1893	79	Elmore, Reba & Mary	Arnold, Angie		Arnold, Angeline			Jefferson Memorial					
Bales, Rufus Paul [Rvd]	Mar 11, 1989	Hillhaven, Tn	Jeff Co	Jul 25, 1904	84	Sellers, Pauline	Bales, William T.		Arnold, Angie		Bales, Pauline-Nathan	Friends Station					
Bales, Helen, Elizabeth	Jul 8, 1941	Clairbourne Co	Jeff Co		28-5-26	S	Bales, Roy R.		Frazier, Blanche	Jeff Co	Bales, Roy R. & Miss Leona	New Market					
Bales, Herman E.	May 19, 1987	Jeff Co	Tn	Sep 20, 1900	36	Ng	Bales, Paul		Sellers, Pauline		Bales, Pauline	Friends Station	WW 2				
Bales, James Edward Jr.	Oct 6, 1989	J.M.H.	Fort Huchauca, Az	Jul 9, 1959	30	Div	Bales, James E. Sr.		White, Mary		Bucis, Mrs. Mary	Zion Luthern - Knox Co					
Bales, Lee Houck	Apr 17, 1950	Knox Co	Tn	Jul 1, 1890	59	W	Bales, W.T.				Haworth, William T.	Friends Station					

NAME	DDATE	DLOCAT	BLOCAT	BDATE	AGE	SPOUSE	FATHER	FBLOCAT	MOTHER	MFBLOCAT Y	BY	BURIAL	VET	SON	DAUG	BROTHER	SISTER
Bates, LaHonne	Jan 7, 1984	At Home	Tn	Sep 8, 1903	80	S	Forsyth, Will		Underwood, Mattie Elizabeth		Blanton, Betty D. - French, Doris E. - Bates, W.F. Jr. - [Children]	Piney					
Bates, Lula	Jan 28, 1959	Meritous Gap, Ky	Tn		18	S	Bates, Dan				Bailey, Roy Sr. - Jones, Mrs.	Piney					
Bates, Lydia Louisa Moore	July 28, 1942	New Market	Tn	Jun 5, 1897	45	Bates, Lee					Bates, Lee & Daughter	Friends Station					
Bates, Margaret Ann	Feb 15, 1955	Tn	Tn	Nov 4, 1954	3m	Ng	Bates, J.R. Jr.	Tn	Cox, Sylvia	Tn	Bates, J.R. Jr.	Friends Station					
Bates, Mary Bernice	Sep 22, 1946	Jeff Co	Sevier Co	Jul 17, 1908	38	Ng	Huffaker, S.N.		Griffey, Anna Belle	Tn	Bates, J.R.	Friends Station					
Bates, Maude Mai	Nov 9, 1928		Tn		21-7-20		Wilson, John	Tn	Brooks, Ellen		Will, Dan						
Bates, Minonza Henry	Mar 2, 1940	New Market	Tn	Aug 15, 1890	49	Bates, Charlie	Henry, William J.	Tn	Hodge, Amanda	Tn	Bates, Charlie	Friends Station					
Bates, Paulee	May 28, 1989	J.M.H.	Jeff Co	Oct 13, 1909	79	W	Salters, Thomas P.		Newman, Daisy		Bates, L.N. - Thomas - Robert - Inez	Friends Station					
Bates, Pryor Lee	Oct 6 1981	Morristown, Tn	Tn	Jun 17, 1904	77	W	Bates, James P.		Russell, Julia		Denny, Mrs. Geraldine	Friends Station					
Bates, Reba	Jun 7, 1979	Knoxville, Tn	Tn	May 15, 1895	84	W	Elmore, Joel A.		Lewis, Cordie		Bates, Carroll E.	Jefferson Memorial					
Bates, Roy R. Sr.	Feb 3, 1984	Jeff Co	Tn	Jan 30, 1888	78	W	Bates, Dan		Cotis, Ester		Bates, Leona - Roy L. - Evelyn - William, Mrs.	New Market					
Bates, Ruth	Mar 16, 1979	Cave-In-Rock, Illinois	Knox Co.	Aug 31, 1894		Trent, James Robert	Martin, Jennie		Gates, E.W.		Gates, E.W.	Trentville - Knox Co					
Bates, Sallie A.	Sep 16, 1950	Knox Co	Tn	Jun 19, 1878	72	W	Atchley, Ben J.		Franklin, Nancy		Carroll, Mrs. J.A.	New Market Freddy					
Bates, Thomas Paul	Aug 26, 1991	U.T.H.	Ga	Nov 6, 1928	62	Ng	Bates, Rufus		Cates, Pauline		Bates, Alice H.	J.M.G.					
Bates, Violet	Aug 21, 1992	F.S.H.	Eudia, Ky	Jul 20, 1941	51	Bates, Jimmy L.	Miller, Walter		St. John, Helen		Husband	J.M.G.					
Bates, Walter Emmerson	May 2, 1946	Jeff Co	Greene Co	Jun 12, 1884	61	Ng	Bates, Harry	Tn	Marshall, Margaret M.	Tn	Bates, Mrs. Walter	Piney Grove					
Bates, William Alex	Oct 28, 1961	Knox Co	Tn	Oct 6, 1897	64-0-18	Ng	Bates, W.T.		Arnold, Angie		Bates, Mrs. Sallie H.	Jefferson Memorial					
Bates, William Franklin Sr.	Jul 2, 1957	Jeff Co	Tn	Mar 22, 1891	66	Ng	Bates, John A.		Templeton, Sarah E.		Bates, William F. Jr. - Wallace T. - Howard, Willis, Mrs. Roy B.	West View					
Bates, William Thomas	Nov 13, 1947	Jeff Co	Jeff Co	Mar 2, 1864	83-8-11	W	Bates, W.A.	Tn	Hatcher, Nancy	Tn	Bates, Floyd E.	Friends Station					
Bates, Leslie	May 30, 1959	New Market	Tn	Mar 1, 1882	66	Bates, Roy R. Sr.	Henry, Robert A.		Moore, Mattie		Bates, Roy	New Market West View					
Batew, Frank L.	May 9, 1935		Ga	Jan 19, 1893	42	Ng	Batlew, Tom		Mc Allister, Sarah		New Market West View					
Batew, Louis Frank	Nov 20, 1982	J.M.H.	Tn	May 29, 1919	63	Div	Batlew, Frank		Bisgom, Marie Edna		Lawson, Peggy (Utah)	Vernal Memorial - Vernal, Utah					
Batew, Roy W.	Jan 19, 1957		Ga	Nov 1, 1910	56	Ng	Batlew, Frank				Batlew, Mrs. Roy	Jefferson Memorial					
Batew, Ruby Geneva	May 13, 1998	Dandridge, Tn	Jeff Co	Dec 8, 1912	85	Miller, Clifford Eugene	Frank, Elizabeth		Cox, Cellfaj (Dana)		Cox, Cellfaj (Dana)	J.M.G.			Moore, Donna		
Batew, Bobbie Gisen	Oct 12, 1935		Tn	Oct 12, 1935	3d		Batlinger, C.H.	Tn	Young, Linia	Tn	Batlinger, C.H.	Batlinger					Baker, Helen
Batlinger, Frank L.	May 28, 1961	Jeff City	Tn	Mar 10, 1911	50	Mc Swain, Mary	Batlinger, Frank				Batlinger, Mrs. Mary - Grd.	New Market	unk.				
Batlinger, Franklin, Delane	Sep 5, 1970	Jeff Co	Tn	Oct 29, 1933	36	Barlow, Shirley	Batlinger, Frank		Duncan, Mary		Batlinger, Mrs. Franklin D.	Mt. View					
Batlinger, James Allen	May 7, 1937	Mill Springs	Tn	Apr 9, 1860	77	W	Batlinger, P.M.	Tn	Hopkins, Carolyn	Tn	Batlinger, Rose-Swan - Don-Starrman - Luckington, Mrs. Ia [Crawfordville, Indiana]	Mill Springs					
Batlinger, James Ulyses	May 16, 1980	At Home	Tn	Jul 29, 1936	43	Ng	Batlinger, Frank		Duncan, Mary		Batlinger, Mrs. Ann Faye Hickey	New Market					
Batlinger, Jimmy Dean	Jul 28, 1983	Spring City, Tn	Tn	Jun 12, 1963	20	S	Batlinger, James Ulyses		Walker, Nettie		Strange, Mrs. Nettie	West View					
Batlinger, Laura Viola	Aug 16, 1946	Jeff Co	Grainger Co	May 2, 1874	72	W	Daniel, James				Mc Curry, Edith - Batlinger, Frank	New Market					
Batlinger, Cissie G. (F)	Apr 30, 1973	Akron, Ohio	Tn	Feb 17, 1958	78	W	Batlinger, Doyle & Elmer		Batlinger, Mary		Batlinger, Joe	Mill Springs					
Batlinger, Rickey Leon	Feb 17, 1958	Jeff Co	Tn	Feb 17, 1958			Batlinger, Doyle & Elmer		Batlinger, Mary		Batlinger, Doyle	Mill Springs					
Batlinger, Shirley Rhea	Nov 10, 1967	J.M.H.	Tn	Feb 25, 1934	32	W	Barlows, Clark		Brooks, Vadna		Mother - E.J. Fielding	Mt. View					
Belonick, Lauren Amanda	Jul 6, 1998	Jeff City	Chicago, Ill.	Dec 3, 1983	13		Belonick, Larry B.		Ward, Terri		F.H. [Covington, La]	First Baptist Folcom					

NAME	DATE	BLOCAT	BLOCAT	BDATE	AGE	SPOUSE	FATHER	FBRLOCAT	MOTHER	MRBLOCAT	BY	BURIAL	VET	SON	DAUG	BROTHER	SISTER
Banks, Kizzie	Jan 25, 1929	Knox Co	Tn	May 26, 1891	54	Ng	Dockins, Jim	Tn	Glendenon, Mary	Tn	Banks, Eddie & Perry	Oakland					
Banks, Nancy	Oct 26, 1945	Knox Co	Tn	Nov 11, 1882	89	W	Dockins, Jim		Elliott, Margaret		Banks, E.R.	Oakland					
Banner, John H.	Jul 18, 1972	Jeff Co	Va	Apr 17, 1901	67	W	Banner, Harvey		Carman, Louisa		Purkett, Mrs. G.C.	Piedmont					
Barber, Beecher Smith	Jun 26, 1998	Jeff Co	Va	Jun 12, 1903	81	Ng	Barber, Harvey		Colley, Emma		Barber, Robert	Mt. View					
Barber, George Clint	Apr 12, 1990	J.M.H.	W	Dec 15, 1907	82	W	Barber, Harvey		Carman, Louisa		Barber, Dale - Louise	Mt. View					
Barber, Harold Smith	Nov 10, 1983	J.M.H.	Tn		60	Brooks, Vadney	Barber, Beecher Smith		Brooks, Edna		Barber, Mrs. Robert	Mt. View					
Barber, James Donald	Feb 18, 1999	Jeff Co	Tn	Nov 10, 1923	60	S	Barber, Clark		Brooks, Vadney		Barber, Randy [Son]	Mt. View	52-54	Timothy-Gregory			
Barber, Lou	Jun 7, 1983	Tn	Tn	May 29, —	80-0-8	W					Templeton, Mrs. Larry	Mt. Horeb			Gerald-Dale-Lania		
Barber, Sanford Barnett	Jan 18, 1987	Jeff Co	Tn	Aug 3, 1903	83	W	Barber, Harvey R.		Cannon, Louisa		Barber, Mayford	Mt. Horeb					
Barding, Jarvis Chester (Jud)	Aug 20, 1984	J.M.H.	Tn	Apr 5, 1917	67	Haun, Ina	Barding, Frank		Swift, Cindy		Barding, Mrs. Ina H.	Jefferson Memorial					
Barker, Infant Male	May 31, 1946	Jeff Co	Tn	May 31, 1946	Sm		Barker, Thomas Click	Ga	Hughes, Estis Mae	Dandson, Tn	Barker, T.C.	Roseberry					
Barkley, Phillip Michael	May 23, 2000	Hamblen, Tn	Tn	May 22, 1947	53	Hogan, Sheila Jean	Barkley, William		Satterfield, Lucille		Wife	Cremated					
Barkley, Ellis Lillie Mc Daniel	Jul 15, 1981	Hancock Co., Tn		Apr 5, 1915	75	Barnard, Buford			Bell, Minnie		Mc Daniel, Randy [Son]	J.M.G.					
Barnard, Infant	Jun 18, 1956										Barnard, Perry [Shaw Plans]						
Barnes, Ben Bradford	Feb 6, 1981	Knox Co	Tn	May 12, 1956	2		Barnes, Ben W.	Ga	Sjolem, Patricia	Tn		Jefferson Memorial					
Barnes, Gaylord Winton Jr.	Feb 8, 1996	Morristown, Tn	Cleveland, Ohio	Apr 11, 1922	65		Barnes, Gaylord Winton Sr.		Lawrence, Mary Irene		Bolden, Frank R. [Friend]	Plott Mt. - Landing, Tn	55-57	Gaylord W. 3rd [Ad] -George [Ga]-Thomas J. [Tn]	Bolden, Evelyn [Ad] - Strickley, Mary [Ind.]		
Barnes, Laura	Sep 7, 1974	Jeff City	Tn	Jul 8, 1893	81	W	Purkey, George W.		Green, Nancy Katherine		Green, Dorothy - Shelton, Jean - Elmore, Mae - Hardy, Linda	West View					
Barnes, Mary Bellinger	Aug 18, 1984	Knoxville, Tn	Tn	Jun 29, 1913	71	W	Duncan, Bert		Kerr, Sally		New Market	New Market					
Barnett, Agnes Marie	Aug 31, 1985	Jeff City	Tn	Feb 10, 1910	75	Div	Ingram, James Louie		Husband, Jennie		Barnett, Earl - Robinson, Sylvia [Mich]	West View					
Barnett, Nancy	Jan 19, 1996	Phila., Pa	Pulaski, Va	Aug 10, 1913	82		Barnett, Unk		Forney, Unk		Forney, James [Gerald]	West View					
Barnett, Mary Alice	Jul 4, 1980	New Market, Tn	Ky	Apr 3, 1902	78	Barkley, Rea [DI]	Barchett, William		Unk		Barkley, Mrs. Donald	Mt. Sleens - Big Branch, Ky		W. Sleens - Big Branch, Ky			
Barton, Lucy Mae	Nov 21, 1951	Jeff Co	Tn	Mar 10, 1905	46	Barton, John	Mc Ghee, Joe		Davis, Elizabeth		Winstead, Mrs. W. Charles - Long, Mrs. Coy - Barton, C.E.	Wooden					
Basden, Willie Glenn	Jul 22, 1993	Morristown, Fl.	Tn	Mar 7, 1931	62		Basden, Glenn L.		Brackman, Lillie J.		Lunell, Glendell [Sister] Holly Hill - Knoxville, Tn						
Baskett, James Dean	Oct 11, 1952	Hamblen Co	Tn	Apr 28, 1916	36	Ng	Baskett, John T.		Keys, Ethel		Baskett, Mrs. J.D. [Pauline]	Shiloh			Grover	Miller, Orma	
Basketter, Cecil Ralph	Sep 27, 1995	Talbott, Tn	Greene Co., Tn	Jun 15, 1912	83	Shacklefield, Ina	Basketter, John Taylor		Keys, Laura Ethel		Wife	Sunderland		C.R. [Gid]	Williams, Barbara [Vri] - Mellon, Susie [Gid] - Shoun, Donna [Gid]		
Bass, Elsie B.	Mar 3, 1958	Jeff Co	Greene Co., Tn	Jun 15, 1912	80	W	Pelton, Margaret		Unk		Wills	Sunderland					
Bass, Frank Lee	Nov 28, 1960	Jeff City	Wilson Co., Tn	Oct 4, 1977	78	Frances	Bass, William		Pelton, Margaret		Myers, Mrs. Albert - Bass, W.W.	Mt. View					Litton, Edna [In-Law] Myers, Katherine & Albert
Bass, Madeline	Feb 3, 1998	Trade, Tn	Atl, Georgia	Oct 25, 1912	92	Bass, W.W.	Bass, William		Bass, Mellie		Bass, Frances	J.M.G.					
Bass, Bryce Lowery	Mar 27, 1944	Jeff City	Jeff Co	Oct 25, 1943	Sm	Walsh, George Thomas	Garland, Catherine	Tn	Winstead, Frances		Husband	Ebenezer		Tom [Gid] - Charles [Gid]			
Bass, William Wilson (Dr.)	Feb 23, 1998	Warren Co., Tn	Jeff City	Jul 7, 1908	89		Bass, Frank L.		Bryan, Elsie		Bass, Thomas & Mandi [Son]	Ebenezer		Charles & Vicki Groves		Myers, Katherine & Dr. Albert	
Bassett, Elizabeth	Feb 25, 1989	Knox Co	Tn	Nov 11, 1916	72	W	Jones, Charles E.		Lyon, Julia		Bass, Magnus Thomas	J.M.G.					
Bassett, Louis (Black)	Nov 10, 1991	J.M.H.	Jeff Co	Jun 22, 1884	107	W	Unk		Peck, Josephine		Treece, Florence [Dau]	West View					

NAME	DDATE	DLOCAT	BLOCAT	BDATE	AGE	SPOUSE	FATHER	FELLOCAT	MOTHER	MFRLOCAT	BY	BURIAL	VET	SON	DAUGH	BROTHER	SISTER
Bateman, Anna Lee	Dec 29, 1994	Morristown, Tn	Jeff Co	Aug 24, 1914	80	Kerr, Hugh	Kerr, Hugh	Tn	Wilson, Ellis		Bateman, James F. [Son]	J.M.G.			Howard, Patricia - Hicks, Carolyn - Whitehead, Mary - Kilby, Jewell		Hodge, Mrs. John - Shisworth, Mrs. Jack
Bateman, Barbara Gail	Mar 6, 1945	Jeff Co	Jeff Co	Mar 6, 1945		Ng	Bateman, Theo James, J.H.		Williamson, Ruby	Tn	Bateman, Marion						
Bateman, Carrie James	Aug 21, 1952	Jeff Co		Jul 18, 1888	64	Ng			Smith, Viola		Bateman, Marion	Shiloh					
Bateman, Catherine M.	Nov 1, 1991	Talbott, Tn	Streator, Ill.	Jan 30, 1902	64	W	Gaydos, Joseph		Buns, Catherine		Heifner, Little [Daug]	Calvary - Terre Haute, Ind.					
Bateman, Chester Theodore	Jul 29, 1955	Jeff Co	Tn	May 12, 1906	42	Ng			Quinn, Mrs. F.M.		Calvary, Mrs. F.M.	Shiloh					
Bateman, James Dud	Sep 14, 1988	Morristown, Tn	Tn	Feb 24, 1910	78	Ng	Bateman, Marion		James, Carrie		Bateman, James Fain	J.M.G.					
Bateman, Marion	Mar 17, 1961	Hamblen Co	Tn	Jan 2, 1888	73	W	Bateman, Marion		Farrow, Marion		Bateman, Marvin - Silvers, Marvin - Bateman, Dud - Underwood, Mrs.	Shiloh					
Bateman, R.W. [M]	Dec 28, 1987	Hamblen Co	Tn	Feb 22, 1896	91	W	Unk		Hemsley, Jane		Leonard F.H. Bugan, Oh] Bateman, Leland - [Dau]	Oak Grove - Logan, Oh	WW 1				
Bates, Claude	Jan 10, 1987	J.M.H.	Nc	Aug 24, 1923	63	Ng	Bates, Lafayette		Hampton, Catherine		Bates, Mrs. Claude & Children	Memorial Gardens		James Calvin - Reba [Mich] Charles Edwin [Fla]-Bobby [Fla]	Elker, Polly - White, Jennie - Killion, Catherine [Ohio]		
Bates, Florence Maybelle	Aug 31, 1993	Dandridge, Tn	Culberson, Nc	Aug 20, 1902	91	Ng	Jenkins, Charles		Hawkins, Patsy		Heifmaker, Patsy [Daug]	J.M.G.				Shields, Jessie	
Bates, Peatrina May [Black]	Jul 12, 1987	Jeff City	Little Rock, Ar.	Feb 22, 1929	68		Todd, H.J.		Linest, Maggie		Rutiford, Patricia A. [Daug]	Cremated			Nelson, Donna - Bates, Regina-Pam		
Bayless, James Thomas	Dec 28, 1994	Peteraburg, Va	Jeff Co	Jun 11, 1910	84		Bayless, Charlie P.		Colley, Ida		Bayless, Miss Grace	J.M.G.					Brabson, Frances - Bayless, Annie - Bertha - Richard, Ellie
Bayless, Jerry Wesley	Nov 14, 1989	Knox Co	Tn	Apr 25, 1969	22	S	Bayless, Ralph		Woods, Ina		Bayless, Ralph	Hillcrest - Dandridge, Tn					
Bayless, Ralph Hunter	Nov 7, 1986	J.M.H.	Tn	Oct 2, 1913	76	Woods, Ina	Bayless, Charlie P.		Collett, Ida Belle		Bayless, Ina Woods	Hillcrest	WW 2				
Bayless, Vida	Sep 1, 1975	Hamblen Co	Tn	Jul 20, 1917	58	Bayless, James T.	Ward, Henry Cray		Brogan, Mary		Bayless, James T. & Ray	Jefferson Memorial					
Bayless, William Charles	May 28, 1926		Tn	Mar 27, 1862	80	W	Peck, Willie H.	Tn	Milligan, Thelia	La.	Milligan, Henderson	New Market					
Baysinger, Infant Female	Dec 10, 1942	Knox Co	Tn	Dec 9, 1942		Ng	Baysinger, Lloyd		Hickey, Daisy	Sevier Co	Baysinger, Lloyd	West View					
Baysinger, Lloyd William	Nov 1, 1986	Knoxville, Tn	Tn	Jul 25, 1917	69	Div	Baysinger, Ernest		Warren, Julia		Harpes, Mrs. John Wolfenbarger, Mildred [Daug]	Oakland - Jeff Co					
Beard, Okla M.	Aug 12, 1984	Jeff City	Newport, Tn	Oct 13, 1906	67	W	Austin, Sam		Brady, Mary		Beard, Mrs. Flora [Daug]	Lynnhurst - Knoxville,	Rueck, Sam				
Beard, William Arley	May 8, 1948	Jeff Co	Washington Co, Tn	Jun 12, 1888?	61	Ng	Beard, Richard A.	Tn	Mc Clanahan, Artemisa	Tn	Beard, Mrs. Flora [Wife]	New Market					
Beard/James Lowornes	Jan 8, 1995	Dndridge, Tn	Winston-Salem, Nc	Jan 24, 1970	24		Beard, Shershen		Miles, Marie		Mother [Rel]	Evergreen					
Beason, Frances G.	Feb 7, 1996	Strawberry Plains	Jeff Co	Jul 28, 1912	86		Woods, John		Fine, Myrtle		Lusk, Catherine B. [Daug]	Strawberry Plains			Lawson, Agnes - Langston, Mary - Smith, Joyce		
Beason, Luther C.	Aug 15, 1976	J.M.H.	Tn	Aug 22, 1908	67	Wood, Frances	Beason, Pearl		Ketner, Mary		Holden Memorial [Service]	Holden Memorial [Service]					
Beever, Ralph	Sep 13, 1981	Jeff Co	Nc	Apr 13, 1911	70	W	Taylor, Bolden		Moss, Mary		Jefferson Memorial	Jefferson Memorial					
Beeler, Eliece	Jan 8, 1971	Jeff Co	Nc	Jul., 1917	53	Beever, Ralph	Murphy, Margaret		Higdon, Effie		Memorial Gardens	Memorial Gardens					
Beevers, James E.	May 5, 1949	Jeff Co		Jan 1, 1907	42	Ng	Bedgood, Biscomi		Rose		Beever, Mrs. Ada	West View					
Bedgood, Aubrey	Oct 17, 1956	Hancock Co	Alabama	Jul 8, 1908	48	Ng	Bedgood, Aubrey J.		Rose		Bedgood, Mrs. Aubrey [Betty Jean]	Alabama					
Beeler, Adelaide	Jan 15, 1927				84	W	Hicks, Calvin	Va	Newchum, Winifred Faye	Va	Beeler, M.L.	Baptist					
Beeler, Cynthia Ann	Jul 3, 1999	Jeff City	Madisonville, Tn	Apr 21, 1947	52	W	Robinson, William Kermit				Mother	Hiwasee - Madisonville, Tn			Beeler, Tracy Michelle	John-William M.	Kerin, Susan

NAME	DDATE	DLOCAT	BLOCAT	BDATE	AGE	SPOUSE	FATHER	FELOCAT	MOTHER	MFELOCAT	BY	BURIAL	VET	SON	DAUG	BROTHER	SISTER
Beeler, Lois Mae	Oct 8, 1983	Jeff Co		Oct 22, 1872	76	W	Brown, ---		Hicks, Adelaid		Choris, Alva's Grandson	Baptist - Jeff Co					
Beeler, Martin Luther	Oct 11, 1949	Jeff Co	Tn	Jul 2, 1952	76	Ng	Beeler, Joseph C.		Marcus, ---		Beeler, Dr. E.R.	West View [Black Section]					
Beeler, Claudion Louise	Jul 3, 1952	Knox Co					Beeler, Earl R.				Peck, Joh R.	West View [Black Section]					
Beg, Nellie Christmas Peck	Apr 25, 1988	Chicago, Ill.		Mar 5, 1906	74	W					Bell, Mrs. Hattye	Jefferson Memorial					
Bell, Bruce Holman	Dec 17, 1983	J.M.H.	Jeff Co	Aug 30, 1909	74	W	Bell, James Walter		Parker, Mattie		Smith, Joye Bell [Dang]	Jefferson Memorial					
Bell, Gertrude	Apr 5, 1981	Jeff Co		Apr 14, 1915	75	W	Nelson, Daniel Ottis		Huff, Josephine		Smith, Joye Bell [Dang]	J.M.G.					
Bell, Hattye E.	Jul 18, 1984	Jeff City	Caliborne Co, Tn	Apr 26, 1914	80	W	Soul, Tilman		Hall, Bertie		Edmonds, Mitzi [Ene]	J.M.G.				Henry	
Bell, Hugh Lynn	May 17, 1981	Jeff City		Dec 23, 1915	65	Nelson, Gertrude	Parker, Mary		Bell, Gertrude		Bell, Gertrude	Jefferson Memorial					
Bell, James C.	Oct 4, 1991	J.M.H.	Crockett Co, Tn	Jan 5, 1977	74	W	Bell, Elmer C.		Grear, Loraitta		Mercier, Merene [Sister]	J.M.G.	unit				
Bell, James Howard	Feb 8, 1961	Jeff City	Washington	Apr 26, 1943	17	S	Bell, James C.		Colley, Dorothy		Bell, Dorothy	Memorial Gardens					
Bell, James Walter	Feb 16, 1967	Jeff Co	Tn	Apr 2, 1882	88	Ng	Bell, James W.		Walker, Mary		Bell, Mrs. James-Hugh-Bruce	Oakewood, Richmond, Tn					
Bell, Maggie	Mar 10, 1951	Jeff Co	Tn	Apr 2, 1882	68	Ng	Smith, Jim		Walker, Mary		Thompson, Arthur - Williams, Male	West View					
Bell, Margaret Easley	Jul 16, 1980	Jeff Co	Tn	Oct 25, 1902	77	Bell, Ralf Rudolph	Godwin, Oscar E.		Bell, Nora B.		Bell, Mrs. Catherine [daug]	White Pine					
Bell, Richard Dennis	Sep 14, 1975	Jeff Co	Tn	Oct 16, 1955	19	S	Bell, Lester		Collins, Ocla Vee		Heavin, Mrs. Ocla Ve- Collins, Jennie V.	Jefferson Memorial					
Bell, Ralf R.	Jun 28, 1981	Jeff City	Tn	Sep 6, 1880	90	W	Bell, Samuel Biddle		Blackburn, Emma K.		Fields, W.H. - Tinsley, Earl	White Pine					
Bellamy, John Powell [Black]	Mar 18, 1983	Knoxville, Tn	Jeff Foity		51		Bellamy, John L.		Jennie		Mother	Cremated			[Niece] Slaughter, Dawn	Michael W.	
Bellamy, Maybell	Feb 23, 1979	Jeff City		Aug 28, 1941	78-4 12	W	Collins, Elizabeth		Chamberlain, Lewis & Barbara		Mother	Mill Springs					
Bellamy, William Thomas	Apr 3, 1975	Tn		Feb 14, 1896	77	Ng	Bellamy, Thomas W.		Collins, Elizabeth		Bellamy, Mrs. Maghill C.- Chamberlain, Barbara	Mill Springs					
Bellamy, Robert Cecil	Aug 11, 1956	Jeff City	Tn	May 26, 1936	20	Young, Alice	Bellamy, G.H.		Hickton, Ninah		Bellamy, G.H.	New Market					
Bender, Elizabeth Maud	Sep 14, 1971	Jeff City	Germany	Apr 16, 1889	82	W	Bender, Martin, Carl				Bender, Ernest	Berlin, N					
Bender, Ernest	Oct 19, 1982	J.M.H.	Germany	Jan 24, 1916	66	Farrell, Kathryn	Bender, Karl M.		Mund, Elizabeth		Bender, Mrs. Kathryn F.	Jefferson Memorial	1032				
Bender, Kathryn	Feb 8, 1995	Farragut, Tn	Birtingham, Alabama	Jul 9, 1923	71	Farrell, Kathryn	Farrell, Joel E.		Riley, Claudine		Bagpott, Kathy & Phil [Daug]	J.M.G.		[G] Mc Closley, Heath		Robert	
Bennett, Charles A.	Aug 18, 1970	Jeff Co	Seminole, Oklahoma	Jul 22, 1911	59	Ng	Bennett, James A.		Yandell, Minnie		Bennett, Edwin C. & Ruth A.	Maple Grove - Seminole, Oklahoma					
Bennison, Trennor	Feb 27, 1995	Gaffiney, Sc	Tn	Jul 31, 1900	94	Sunny, Margaret	Bennison, William D.		Glover, Sarah		Willie	J.M.G.	Allen. T.				
Beeners, Franklin D.	Jan 16, 1945	Knox Co	Knox Co	Mar 20, 1933	10	S	Beeners, James	Ga	Guy, Ada Mae	Tn	Beeners, Jim	West View			[G] King, Patricia- Goodman, Caryl		
Berry, Ben F.	Jan 28, 1955	Knox Co	Union Co, Tn	Apr 8, 1889	65	W	Berry, Pryor L.		Lynch, Sadie		Berry, Clyde & Willard	New Market					
Berry, Clyde Ernest Sr.	Mar 13, 1999	Sharp Chapel, Tn	Union Co, Tn	Jul 10, 1919	79	Billie R.	Berry, Benjamin F.	Tn	Berry, Dora		Willie	J.M.G.	42-46	Johnnie-Ernest	Becky		
Berry, Dora L.	Oct 10, 1948	Jeff Co		Nov 20, 1895	52-16 20	Ng	Broden, Andrew C.		Ellison, Elizabeth	Tn	Berry, B.F.	New Market					
Berry, Imogene	Jun 25, 1988	New Market, Tn	Tn	Mar 27, 1912	73	W	Lowe, Grover		Marph, Cleo		Neath, Robert	Oakland - Grainger Co					
Bettis, A.C.	Nov 7, 1932	Jeff City	Tn	Jan 4, 1883	49	Ng	Bettis, J.A.	Tn	Hodge, Emy	Tn	Bettis, Mrs.	Lebanon					
Bettis, Andrew B.	May 7, 1942	Jeff Co	Tn	Feb 16, 1859	83	W	Lyle, Theresay	Tn			Bettis, J.E. & Mary	West View					
Bettis, Andrew T.	Jun 18, 1945	Jeff Co				Ng	Bettis, G.A.	Tn			Bettis, Raymond - Shoun, Kyle						
Bettis, Cecile Gertrude	May 9, 1977	Jeff Co	Tn	Jun 12, 1903	73	W	Bible, Andrew Shields		Thomas, Amanda		Bales, Mrs. Roy R. Jr. - Murphy, Mrs. Georgia - Hickman, Mrs. Ross	Jefferson Memorial					Thomas, Donna - Johnson, Elizabeth
Bettis, Celia	Jan 3, 1976	Knoxville, Tn	Tn	Oct 27, 1900	75	W					Murphy, Mrs. Katherine - Hickman, Mrs. Ross	Jefferson Memorial Gardens					
Bettis, Curtis Edward	Oct 20, 1993	Jeff Co		Jun 26, 1930	73	Lowe, Nina	Bettis, Edward		Wiggins, Reba		Willis - Moore, Thelma [Aunt]				Mc Gedetck, Linda & George - Norman, Jill & Ralph		Stambaugh, Alma - Breeden, Ruth
Bettis, Cynthia Ann	Mar 28, 1955	Tn		Nov 10, 1955	81-5 19	W	Moore, H.H.		Cate, Rebecca		Moore, Joe	West View					

NAME	DDATE	DLLOCAT	BLLOCAT	BDATE	AGE	SPOUSE	FATHER	FBLLOCAT	MOTHER	MFBLLOCAT	BY	BURIAL	VET	SON	DAUG	BROTHER	SISTER
Bettis, Dale Keith	Jan 26, 1998	Jeff City	Knoxville, Tn	Sep 9, 1924	73	Holloway, Dolores	Bettis, Guy	Tn	Phillips, Martha	Tn	Glass, Ernest	West View		Norris-Don	Woodbcol, Debra Holly; Bettis, Dixie Lynn		Lynch, Bonnie - Landom, Janey - Swicegood, Joyce
Bettis, Dan H.	May 6, 1928	Jeff City	Tn		70-1-29	S	Bettis, Anderson				Glass, Ernest	Wesleys Chapel					
Bettis, Edd C.	May 5, 1963	Tn		Dec 15, 1887	75	W	Bettis, Caswell		Chaney, Amanda		Bettis, Curtis, Stambaugh, Alma - Cross, Lula - Cyrl. (Alice)	West View	unk				
Bettis, Emma Catheryn	Sep 9, 1944	Jeff Co	Tn	Feb 23, 1861	83	S	Bettis, Emsley	Tn	Lyle, Thursey	Tn	Bettis, Mrs. Neil	West View					
Bettis, Frank Eugene	Jun 17, 1963	Jeff City	Tn	Jun 5, 1884	79	Ng	Bettis, Charlie		Douglas, Alta		Marks, Annette - Jones, Carroll - Luke & Francis	Hopewell					
Bettis, Frank Owen	Mar 25, 1950	Jeff Co	Tn	Mar 12, 1877	73	W	Bettis, John		Williams, Mary		Carmichael, Robert	New Market					
Bettis, George Thomas	Sep 2, 1965	Knox Co	Tn	May 12, 1865	80	W	Bettis, Cas		Chaney, Amanda		Bettis, Mrs. G.T. & Children	Jefferson Memorial					
Bettis, Gertrude Ann	Jul 27, 1941	Jeff Co			53-8-1	S	Bettis, Emmett		Dunwoodie, Ella	Jeff Co	Bettis, Emmett & Leon	Oakland					
Bettis, Guy	Aug 20, 1977	Morristown, Tn	Tn	Feb 5, 1897	80	Pate, Pearl			Rimmer, Maude		Gotts, Mrs. Guy - V.A.	Jefferson Memorial	WW 1				
Bettis, Hazel H.	Oct 10, 1982	Jeff City	Tn	Jul 10, 1909	83	Riley, Jennie			Largo, Nellie		Moore, Georgia (Daug)	Lebanon Presby.				Kerr, Jewell	
Bettis, Infant Doug	Feb 2, 1942	Jeff Co				Ng	Bettis, H.H.		Phillips, Elizabeth	Jeff Co	Bettis, H.H., Howard, Mrs. Rod (Alice)	Wesleys Chapel					
Bettis, J.A.	Mar 1, 1934	Mt Horeb	Tn	Aug 12, 1851	82	Ng	Bettis, A.C.		Riley, Jennie Thelma		Bettis, Mrs. A.C.	Wesleys Chapel					
Bettis, John Calvin	May 4, 1944	Talbott	Tn	Jul 9, 1875	68	Ng	Bettis, William W.	Tn	Riggs, Mary A.	Tn	Bettis, Mrs. John C. (Alice)	Sunderland					
Bettis, Leon Cass	Aug 17, 1977	Jeff Co	Tn	Jun 23, 1909	68	Wilkerson, Ray	Bettis, Emmett		Howard, Gertie		Bettis, Mrs. Leon	West View					
Bettis, Lora M.	May 2, 1964	Jeff Co	Tn	Oct 14, 1884	79	W	Morgan, Newton		Johnson, Lillie M.		Marks, Annette - Jones, C.W. - Bettis, E. Luke	Hopewell					
Bettis, Lol Mae	Aug 24, 1948	Jeff Co	Tn	Aug 4, 1924	24	Bettis, Claude F.		Riley, Lula	Tn	Bettis, Claude	Pleasant Grove					
Bettis, Luther Emmett	Jan 4, 1966	Knox Co	Tn	Apr 18, 1883	84		Bettis, Cas		Chaney, Amanda		Bettis, Leon	Lebanon					
Bettis, Martha Walker	Jul 19, 1942	Jeff Co	Tn	Jul 12, 1865	77	Bettis, Porter C.			Walker, Billie	Tn	Wort, Mae-Ward, Orle	Sunderland					
Bettis, Mrs.	Mar [19], 1932		Tn		53-9-1		Bettis, Emmett				Bettis, Elizabeth		Talbott				
Bettis, Marie Bowers	Sep 3, 1976	Jeff City	Tn	May 21, 1919	59	Div	Bowers, Thomas G.		Bowers, Eula		Finchum, Mrs. Patricia (William) - Bettis, Michael	Jefferson Memorial	WW 2				
Bettis, Nell	Sep 12, 1948	Jeff Co	Tn	Aug 1, 1865	63-1-11	Ng	Hayes, Sarah	Tn			Bradley, Mrs. Mary - Henderson, Julia	West View					
Bettis, Nettie Ann	Nov 2, 1948	Blount Co	Tn	Aug 22, 1883	65-2-10	W	Largo, Frank	Tn			Bettis, Hazel	Lebanon					
Bettis, Ola Rhea	Dec 2, 1996	Jeff Co	F.S.H.	Dec 9, 1911	74	Bettis, Leon [X]	Wilkerson, Oscar		Chambers, Tolby		Bettis, Tommy L.	West View					
Bettis, Pearl Helen	Mar 15, 1993	Jeff City	Spiceland, Indiana	Apr 10, 1901	91	W	Pate, Issac		Adams, Helen		Bettis, Dale K. [Son]	J.M.G.			Swicegood, Joyce - Landess, Janeel - Lynch, Bonnie		Schiveri, Evelyn - Hamilton, Dorothy
Bettis, Reba Kate	Aug 29, 1954	Tn		Jul 17, 1883	61	Ng	Wiggins, John M.		Bryan, Ruth		Moore, Mrs. Dexter - Bettis, E.C.	West View					
Bettis, Richard E.	Jan 23, 1941	New Market			76-6-21	W			O'Dell, Anna F.	Jeff Co	Bettis, H.H.- Davis Mrs. Sam	Jeff - Jeff, Oklahoma					
Bettis, Rue	Mar 6, 1976	Jeff Co	Tn	Jul 17, 1899	76	Bettis, Cecil			Rimmer, Maud Ray		Bettis, Mrs. Rue	Jefferson Memorial					
Bettis, S.O.	Jan 21, 1935	Dandridge	Tn	Feb 8, 1865	69	Ng	Bettis, D.L.	Tn	Edgar, Unk	Tn	Bettis, Walter G. & Rue (Son)	Dandridge					
Bettis, Walter B.	Mar 20, 1941	Jeff City	Tn		30-8-24	Ng	Bettis, Emmett		Howard, Gertrude	Jeff Co	Bettis, Emmett & Leon	West View					
Bettis, William A.	Jun 9, 1948	Jeff Co		Sep 14, 1868	79-3-25	W	Bettis, Pryor C.		Chaney, Amanda A.	Tn	Bettis, Tom	Jeff - Jeff, Oklahoma					
Bewley, James Oscar Sr.	Sep 29, 1948	Jeff Co	Hamilton Co	Jan 27, 1884	64-8-2	W	Bewley, Jacob M.	Tn	Parvin, Martha Jane	Tn	Bewley, Mrs. Lillie (Wife)	West View					
Bible, Altige Wesley	Oct 18, 1947	Hamilton Co	Greene Co, Tn		73-9-3	Ng	Bible, Joe A.		Freshour, Malvina	Tn	Bible, Keel	Bible					
Bible, Andrew S.	Mar 9, 1941	Jeff Co	Cocke Co		71-1-1	Bible, Amanda			Reed, Anny Jane	Tn	Bible, B.A. [Son]	Bible					

NAME	DDATE	DLOCAT	BLOCAT	BDATE	AGE	SPOUSE	FATHER	FELOCAT	MOTHER	MFELOCAT	BY	BURIAL	VET	SON	DAUG	BROTHER	SISTER
Bible, Cleo	Jan 25, 1954	Jeff Co	Tn	Oct 19, 1970	73	Mc Claren, Klieba	Bible, Andrew Shipley		Bettis, Louisa		Shipley, Mrs. Ted	West View					
Bible, Elbert Lyman	Apr 24, 1983	U.T.H.	Tn	Jan 22, 1910	73	Mc Claren, Verba	Bible, Clarence		Thomas, Amanda		Bible, Mrs. Klieba	Jefferson Memorial					
Bible, Helen	Oct 8, 1954	Tn	Tn	Aug 6, 1919	35	Bible, Ronald Jr.	Hicks, Clarence		Holton, Ada		Bible, Ronald Jr.	White Pine					
Bible, Irene	Jan 22, 1979	Jeff City	Tn	Sep 2, 1909	69	W	Nov, Alexander Jasper		Mc Crary, Mary V.		Harper, Mrs. Jerry & Brothers	Mt. Pleasant					
Bible, Jackson Lytelle	Aug 9, 1972	New Market, Tn	Greene Co., Tn	Feb 22, 1906	64	Nox, Irene	Bible, Abigo		Bible, Nora		Bible, Mrs. J.L.	Mt. Pleasant					
Bible, Jonathan David	Nov 21, 1942	Jeff Co	Tn	Oct 9, 1863	79	Ng	Bible, Elbert	Tn	Reed, Anny	Tn	Shipley, Mrs. & Clark, Mrs.	West View					
Bibler, Mary Catherine	Mar 30, 1978	Jeff City	Indiana	Jul 18, 1896	81	S	Bibler, Travetis M.		Folk, Mary H.		Jester, Mrs. Harold	Star Of Hope - Huntington, Ind.					
Biddle, Nettie Pearl	Nov 27, 1990	Jeff City	Grainger Co.	Jan 7, 1898	92	S	Dalton, Gilbert		Cochrum, Laura E.		Biddle, Clarence [Son]	Greenwood - Knoxville, Tn					
Biddle, James S.											Biddle, Panther?						
Bird, J.W.	Feb 15, 1935	Jeff City	Tn	Feb 5, 1896	69	S	Bird, J.M.	Tn	Weier, Martha	Tn	Bird, Ruby - Moore, Mrs. George	West View					
Bird, Non	Mar 30, 1951	Jeff Co	Tn	Feb 10, 1876	74	S	Bird, James M.		Wenn, Margaret		Bird, Mrs. Ruby	West View					
Bird, Newton L.	Nov 15, 1952	Jeff Cith	Tn	Feb 19, 1871	81	W	Bird, James M.		Tinsley, Francis		Gray, Sue - Cline, Duane [Cousins]	West View					
Bird, Ruby	Jul 10, 1963	Jeff City	Jeff City	Oct 13, 1904	86		Bird, Newton		Leslie		Bird, Mrs. Ruby	West View					
Birdwell, Ida	Dec 22, 1931	Jeff City	Tn	Sep 26, 1873	48	Birdwell, J.F.	Trenthain, L.A.	Va	Collins, Mary	Va	Birdwell, J.F.	Shady Grove					
Birkle, R.T.	Nov 8, 1939	Shady Grove	Tn	Nov 29, 1859	79	Ng	Birkle, William		Glaut, Mary		Birkle, Mrs. & George	Shady Grove					
Bishop, Fannie H.	Apr 26, 1948	Jeff Co	Tn	Mar 20, 1872	76-1-8	W	Holston, H. Willey	Tn	Mc Elhaney, Julia		Bishop, Jesse H. [Son]	Lebanon					
Bishop, Anthony Ray	Sep 27, 1981	Hamblen Co	Tn	Sep 8, 1961			Hurst, Henry				Bishop, Jesse H. [Son]	Lebanon					
Bishop, Bertha Mae	Apr [11], 1991	Hamblen Co	Tn		87	W	Hurst, Henry		Mc Elhaney, Julia		Bishop, Jesse H [Son]	Lebanon					
Bishop, Bryan	Dec 18, 1996	Jeff Cith	Hamblen Co	Sep 18, 1896	100	S	Bishop, Jacob		Milligan, Eva		Young, Ruth B. [Daug]	J.M.G.					
Bishop, Buena Juanita	Jan 19, 1997	Knoxville, Tn	Washington Co, Tn	Aug 1, 1907	89	W	Parker, John		Murray, Pearl		Bishop, Helen [Daug]	Lebanon Baptist			Patterson, Lorene		
Bishop, Darrell Allen	Mar 4, 1997	Knoxville, Tn	Hamblen Co	Jun 2, 1957	39				Richard, Evelyn		Mother	Pleasant Ridge			Snyder, Julie B.& S. Dick	John R.	Bailey, Eula - Woodruff, Lillian
Bishop, Eva E.	Feb 9, 1929	Tn	Tn		62	W						Lebanon					
Bishop, George D.	Oct 18, 1959	Jeff Co	Tn	Feb 27, 1870	89	Ng	Bishop, Robert				Bishop, Mrs. Wanda - Pines, Alice - Bishop, Mary Ellen - Morgan, Elizabeth [Jim] - Paschal, Virginia	West View					
Bishop, Georgia Helen	Mar 15, 1990	J.M.H.	Tn		69	Ng	Ellison, James		Hammer, Georgia	Tn	Bishop, Wayne	Lebanon					
Bishop, Leila Mae	Mar 17, 1928	Ga		Aug 1, 1920	38-9-3	Bishop, Wayne	Daughtry, Jake	Ga			Bishop, Jess	Lebanon Baptist					
Bishop, Mary Jane	Nov 4, 1984	Morristown, Tn		Sep 25, 1898	86	Bishop, William Tate [D]	Turner, William		Cox, Harriet		Walker, Mrs. L.C.	West View					
Bishop, Mrs. Jessie	Jan 12, 1927	Tn	Tn		88	W	Jowerd, W.N.	Tn	Bollinger, Martha	Tn	Bishop, Q.M.	West View					
Bishop, Naomi	Dec 13, 1928		Tn			W	Bishop, Felle	Tn	Turner, Mary	Tn	Lebanon	Lebanon Church					
Bishop, Wallace Clifford	Sep 27, 1991	F.S.H.	Jeff Co	Apr 17, 1909	82	Painter, Beune	Bishop, George D.	Tn	Hill, Lucinda	Tn	Bishop, C.D. - Rines, Snyder, Julia [Daug]	Lebanon Church					
Bishop, William Tate	Nov 14, 1942	Hamblen Co	Tn	Jan 1, 1887	45	Ng	Bishop, George D.	Tn	Hill, Lucinda	Tn	Bishop, Max	West View					
Bivens, Charlie Taylor	Nov 9, 1956	Knox Co	Tn	1895		Div					Bivens, John	West View					
Bivens, Martha Jane	Jun 22, 1996		Tn			Div	Bivens, C.W.				Bivens, C.W.	West View					
Black, Reuben Clay	Sep 16, 1989	London, Ky	Cocke Co, Sevierville, Ala.	May 31, 1961	28		Black, Clay		Mc Nish, Catherine		Black, Lola	West View	army				
Black, Robert Douglas	May 23, 1991	U.T.H.	Tn	Sep 21, 1952	38	Munsey, Freda	Black, Clarence W.		Bennett, Lola		Black, Frida J. Munsey	Cremated	unk				
Blackburn, Bess	Jun 3, 1972	U.T.H.	Tn	Aug 14, 1887	84	W	Newman, John E.	Tn	Everhart, Mennie		Blackburn, Donald N. [Son]	Hebron					
Blackburn, Charles Alexander	Oct 18, 1947	Jeff Co	Tn	Nov 27, 1873	73-10-21	Ng	Blackburn, William E.	Tn	Hoffmeister, Funnie		Blackburn, Glenn	Hebron					
Blackburn, Eliza Jane	May 1, 1960	Knox Co	Tn	Sep 2, 1873/74	86-7-29	S	Blackburn, John F.		Rankin, Sarah Jane	Tn	Blackburn, Glenn	Cedar Hill - Washington D.C.					
Blackburn, Grace Ann	Oct 8, 1952	Mexico	W	Jul 27, 1882	70	W	Saunders, John		Ecker, Julia		Hale, J.D.	Hebron		Albert	Brown, Jean		
Blackburn, Harriette	May 12, 1998	Dandridge, Tn	Jeff Co	Sep 29, 1917	80	Blackburn, Donald N.	Mc Marry, Ben W.		Blackburn, Eva		Husband	Hebron					Rankin, Mildred - Felknor, Elizabeth

NAME	DDATE	DLOCAT	BLOCAT	BDATE	AGE	SPOUSE	FATHER	FELLOCAT	MOTHER	MERLOCAT	BY	BURIAL	VET	SON	DAUG	BROTHER	SISTER
Blackburn, Ida Adaline	Nov 23, 1942	Shady Grove	Jeff Co	Nov 22, 1872	70	W	Harrison, John	Va	Rankin, Mary	Tn	Blackburn, W.E. & Tom [Children]	Hopewell		Nelson Lacy			
Blackburn, Katherine Eve	Jan 11, 1968	Jeff Co	Tn	May 30, 1906	61-7-11	Ng	Cata, William Joel		Jernigan, Racheal		Blackburn, Glen	Memorial Gardens					
Blackburn, Mary Leola	Jan 19, 1927		Tn		41-9-22	Blackburn, Charles	Martin, W.K.	Tn	Rankin, Addie	Tn	Blackburn, Edd	Mt. Hebron					
Blackburn, Peter Samuel	Jun 7, 1950	Jeff Co	Tn	Nov 16, 1887	62	S	Blackburn, John F.	Tn	Eckel, Julia	Tn	Blackburn, Eliza Billie - Strat, Mrs.	Eckel - Jeff Co					
Blackburn, Sarah Jane	Dec 14, 1925	Jeff Co	Tn		80-6-14	W	Rankin, P.M.		Lockhart, Martha	Tn	Blackburn, Edd	Hebron					
Blackburn, William Edward	Jan 25, 1951	Jeff Co	Tn	Sep 27, 1877	73	Ng	Blackburn, John		Rankin, Sara Jane		Blackburn, Mrs. Bess	Hebron					
Blair, Marie Elaine	May 8, 1959	Kox Co	Tn		3m 6d	Ng	Blair, Paul		Cannon, Frances		Blair, Paul	Piney					
Blair, Paul Edward	Apr 7, 1980	Jeff Co	Tn	Apr 6, 1980	1d		Blair, Paul Edward Sr.		Cannon, Frances		Blair, Paul	Piney					
Blanc, Henry Daniel	Jun 18, 1998	Knoxville, Tn	Knoxville, Tn	Apr 29, 1928	70	Wadden, Betty Gay	Black, Adrian		West, Freda		Wife	U.T. Medical (Memphis, Tn)			Malone, Jenny - Barnett, Linda Gay		
Blane, Adron	Jan 29, 1954	Knoxville, Tn	Jeff Co	Dec 14, 1899	54	Ng	Blane, Henry D.		Hinton, Biggie		Blane, Mrs. Freda W.	West View				Adrian	
Blanton, Clarence	Mar 6, 1947	Mt. Home, Tn	Tn	May 22, 1911	55-9 14	S	Bible, Mary Jane	Tn	Blanton, J.D.	Greene Co, Tn	Blanton, J.D.	West View					
Blanton, Esther E.	Sep 22, 1990	Jeff City	Tn	Feb 5, 1903	77	S	Blanton, J.D.		Bible, Mary Jane		Blanton, Louise-Ray	West View					
Blanton, Rebecca Lynn	Dec 12, 1994	Knoxville, Tn	Nichsville, Ind.	Nov 9, 1974	20	Blanton, Nelson Lee	Wilson, Herman G.		Pruitt, Sharon		Blanton, Louise-Ray, Husband - Blanton, Nelson (Parents) - Brewster, Evella & Shirley, Betty [G- Mother]	Greenland - Novelaktiond, Ind.				Brewster, Greg	
Blaszczyk, Mary Irene	Apr 8, 1991	J.M.H.	Elmhurst, Illinois	May 14, 1942	47	Ng	Kleck, John		Murry, Kathleen M.		Blaszczyk, Robert [Husband]	Cremated					
Blazier, Paul Columbus	Jan 13, 1998	New Market, Tn	Pennellville, Tn	Apr 8, 1904	91	Phillips, Agnes	Blazier, Robert Campbell		Bagsinger, Mary		Wife	Woodlawn - Wadsworth, Ohio					
Blecher, Muriel	Mar 27, 1999	Morristown, Tn	Earlville, Il	May 14, 1908	57	Elsie M.	Peterson, Nillson		Schneider, Gien [Daug]		Schneider, Gien [Daug]	Oak Ridge - Sandwick, Il		J. Kent & Jeanette			
Bledsoe, David East	Mar 9, 1982	V.A.- Mt. Home		Jul 2, 1932	49	Div	Bledsoe, Samuel E.		Harkimond, Bessie		Kendall, Mrs Bessie	Jefferson Memorial					
Blevins, Anna Kate	Jun 24-27, 1943	Ohio	Va			W					Blevins, H.W. [Middletown, Ohio]	Jefferson Memorial					
Blevins, Fonnie Elizabeth	Feb 23, 1981	Jeff City	Va	Nov 22, 1902	78	W	Gilbert, Grant		Vance, Renda		Haga, Clyde & Lorraine	Jefferson Memorial					
Boatman, Avrile Lee	Sep 24, 1965	Jeff Co		Apr 8, 1908	57	W	Boatman, Reed		Harbin, Ida		Glann, Jessie Ray & Betty Kate- Cotton	Jefferson Memorial					
Boatman, Elsie Lillian Cotton	Oct 7, 1990	Greene Co, Tn	Greene Co, Tn	May 3, 1910	80	W	Jones, Oliver		Pinkston, Nancy E.		Brinkley, Gemma B. [Daug] - Betty & Jessie	J.M.G.					
Boatman, John Louis	Jul 18, 1980	Knoxville, Tn	Tn	Jul 14, 1920	60	W	Boatman, Reed		Harbin, Ida		Boatman, Stella Mae	West View					
Boatman, Rayford Dean	Feb 7, 1999	Rutledge, Tn	Rutledge, Tn	Jul 14, 1938	60	Lee, Frances	Hunt, Eulah Mae		Hurst, Eulah Mae		Wife	J.M.G.		Donnie		Sonny-Billy-Mike	
Bolden, Carolyn Joyce	Mar 22, 1950	Jeff City	Tn	Mar 18, 1950	60	W	Bolden, Alice		Bolden, Alice		Mc Daniel, Mrs. George	Shiloh					
Bolden, Deborah Jane	Feb 9, 1946	Jeff City	Tn	Dec 24, 1872	73	Ng	Brooks, Alex		Ross, Mary		Miller, Pauline - Bolden, Mrs. Horace	Welsey Chapel					
Bolden, Kathryn	May 31, 1992	J.M.H.	Tn	Nov 4, 1909	82	W	Line, Nelson		Williams, Marjorie Emma	Tn	Rogers, Opal [Sister]	Mt. View					
Bolden, Robert E.	Feb 3, 1975	Jeff Co	Tn	Jul 3, 1914	60	Bolden, Anna K.	Bolden, Henry Green		Newman, Mary Emma		Bolden, Anna K.	Mt. View					
Bolden, Sandra Louise	Jul 26, 1982	S.M.M.C.	Nov 4, 1951	Sep 29, 1937	54	Bolden, Earl E.	Bolden, Claude		Boatman, Peggy J.		Bolden, Claude	West View					
Bolden, Shirley Jean Donahue Jenkins	Mar 16, 1992	Knox Co, Tn	Tn	Jun 1, 1924	62	Div	Murphy, Claude		Strout, Georgia		Husband	Cremated					
Bolden, Virginia E.	Mar 13, 1987	J.M.H.	Tn	Jan 3, 1876	76	S	Cox, Otha		Combs, Blanche		Bolden, Donald	J.M.G.					
Bolding, David F.	Aug 29, 1952	Jeff Co	Nc			S	Bolding, W (D).L.		Smart, Rhoda J.		Haynes, Don	Oakland					
Bolding, Marcus L.	Jul 7, 1974	Jeff Co	Nc	Apr 19, 1890	84	Johnson, Rilta L.	Bolding, James D.		Robin, Betty E.		Bolding, J.A. - Jaynes, Kate	Chuckey - Chuckey, Tn					Reed, Eva - Owens, Ann - Dobson, Shirley

NAME	DDATE	DLOCAT	BLOCAT	BDATE	AGE	SPOUSE	FATHER	FBLOCAT	MOTHER	MFBLOCAT	BY	BURIAL	VET	SON	DAUG	BROTHER	SISTER
Bolding, Retta Johnson	Sep 19, 1974	Jeff City		Apr 18, 1890	84	Bolding, M.L. [D]	Johnson, John D.		Ellis, Rhoda		Jaynes, Kate	Chuckey - Greene Co, Tn					
Bolding, Robert Henry	Jan 19, 1945	Jeff City	Nc	Aug 25, 1945	71+4 24	S	Bolding, Lafayette	Nc	Smart, Rhoda Jane	Nc	Bolding, D.F. - Haynes, Mr.	Oakland					
Bolin, Ben F.	Apr 30, 1970	Knoxville, Tn	Tn	Jan 7, 1896	73	W	Bolin, Josh		Snyder, Mattie		Bolin, Lynn	Piney					
Bolin, Berry Leon	Apr 7, 1946	Jeff Co	Tn	Apr 7, 1946	24		Bolin, Lynn Burley	Tn	Sanford, Myra	Alabama	Bolin, L.B.	Piney					
Bolin, Bruce M.	Feb 10, 1987	Knoxville, Tn	Tn	Feb 2, 1906	79	W	Bolin, Andy				Bolin, L.B.	Pleasant Grove					
Bolin, Emma Louise	Jan 31, 1960	Jeff Co	Tn	Oct 23, 1920	39	Ng	Franklin, Jim		Jernigan, Martha		Bolin, Wayne & Earl - Woods, Mr.	Lebanon - Greenbriar					
Bolin, Ferrum Allard	Oct 12, 1973	Jeff Co	Tn	Jul 12, 1935	38	Cannon, Evelina	Bolin, Burchell		Bolin, Allie M.		Bolin, Dexter	Piney					
Bolin, Gladys Annetta	Feb 28, 1970	Strawberry Plains	Tn	Dec 28, 1933	66	Bolin, Ben		Palmer, Alice		Bolin, Evelina	Piney						
Bolin, James Elbert	Feb 28, 1950	Jeff Co	Tn	Jul 12, 1867	82	W	Kuni, Ixd ?		Kuni, Doris		Bolin, Lynn [Son]	Piney					
Bolin, Jesse E.	Aug 28, 1970	Knox Co	Tn			W	Bolin, Joshua		Snyder, Mattie		Bolin, Bruce & Children - Miller, Mrs. Hugh - Horace-Pauline-Sons [Illinois]	Pleasant Grove [Piney]					
Bolin, Lattie	Dec 30, 1969	Strawberry Plains	Tn			W	Carr, George		Brooks, Ellen		Bolin, Howard - Jones, Mary Katie	Piney					
Bolin, Laura Lorene	Feb 12, 1985	Knoxville, Tn	Tn			Ng	Pratt, Wiley				Bolin, Bruce & Children - Earl	Pleasant Grove					
Bolin, Melvin Baxter	Aug 15, 1980	Knox Co	Tn	Oct 8, 1911	73	Bolin, Bruce				Connett, Mrs. - Rainwater, Mrs. Chester - Bolin, Howard & Ben [Seiverville]	Piney						
Boling, Mrs. W.L.	Dec 24, 1933	Jeff City		Nov 30, 1915	18	Boling, W.L.	Boling, W.L.	Tn	Anderson, Susie	Tn	Boling, Howard	Piney					
Boling, N.L.	Dec 24, 1933	Jeff City		Apr 4, 1898	35	Ng	Boling, M.W.		Mantis, Mary	Tn	Boling, Howard	Piney					
Bolton, Frank Elgin	Aug 18, 1977	Knoxville, Tn	Ga	Feb 14, 1910	67	Shaver, Jessie	Bolton, Benjamin		Willingham, Hattie		Bolton, Mrs. Jessie	Rehoboth - Atlanta, Ga					
Bonds, Addie	Dec 29, 1931	Jeff Co		Nov 16, 1932	68	Ng	Franklin		Yates, Lucy	Tn	Bonds, John	Piedmont					
Bonds, Charles Everett	Dec 13, 1934	Jeff Co		Sep 20, 1934	3d		Bonds, Franklin		Yates, Lucy	Tn	Bonar, Elmer	Lockhart					
Bonds, Charotate	Dec 29, 1992	Seiverville, Tn	Jeff Co	Dec 7, 1934	58	Moore, Billy Joe	Moore, James P.		Lyle, Ruth		Bonds, Mike [Son]	D.M.G.		Moore, James	Harold		
Bonds, Ivan Reece	Jun 1, 1950	Jeff Co	Sc	Sep 7, 1855	94-B 24	W					Bonds, Miss Allie	Piedmont			[G] Bonds, Christine-Jennifer		
Bonner, Virginia Myrtle	Apr 10, 1954	Mo	Sc	Apr 3, 1885	79	Bonner, Rev. J.H.	Dist, D.W.		Roach, Jo Anne		Puckett, Clifford - Bonner, J.H.	Piedmont					
Boswell, Mack Sr.	Sep 2, 1974	Jeff Co	Alabama	Apr 15, 1907	67	Ng	Boswell, James		Taylor, Lizzie		Boswell, Mrs. Gladys	West View					
Bounds, Laura Cornelia	Sep 7, 1986	J.M.H.		May 23, 1923	63	W	Arp, Joe		Graham, Lillie		Finchum, Mrs. Roy - Dawn	Highland Memorial - Knox Co					
Bouton, Martha Jane	Apr 27, 1981	Jeff City	Tn	Dec 18, 1896	84	S	Bouton, Daniel A.		O'Dell, Fannie G.		Finchum, Mrs. Roy [Artist]	Jefferson Memorial					
Bowen, Helen	Apr 20, 1998	Richmond, Va	Jeff City	Mar 26, 1920	78	Kinder, William	Helm, William		Helm, Luie Beatrica		Tarr, Mrs. W.T. (Mary B.)	West View	army				
Bowen, John T.	Dec 27, 1949	Hamblen Co.	Tn	Jan 13, 1867	88	Ng	Bowen, William A.		Pitt, Sherry B. [Niece]		Piedmont						
Bowen, William Allen	Aug 20, 1972	Bristol, Tn	Tn	Apr 29, 1918	54	Kinder, Helen	Bowen, William A.		Thornhill, Emma		Bowen, Mrs. Alice	West View					
Bowling, Joseph Wesley	Oct 8, 1983	Jeff City	Nc	Jan 8, 1912	71	W	Vollies, Roy		Roberts, Leona		Bowen, Mrs. W.A.	West View					
Bowling, Lillie Cordelia [Dee]	Apr 30, 1997	Jeff City	Tn	Dec 22, 1929	67	Weatherly, Carol	Bryant, Violet		Burchell, Mrs. Ina Lee		Phillip - Greene Co, Tn	Army					
Bowman, Elmer William	Jul 18, 1981	Jeff Co	Tn	May 2, 1903	78	Ng	Bowman, William M.		O' Neal, Helen		Willis	Cremated					
Bowman, Infant	Jan 6, 1937	J.M.H.							Grills, Kitty Jane		Bowman, Elmer	Jefferson Memorial					
Bowman, Lucy Emmaline	Nov 10, 1998	J.M.H.	Tn	Jun 29, 1905	83	W	Franklin		Huskins, Sally M.		Bowman, Lon E.	J.M.G.					
Bowman, Mrs. Elmer	Aug 3, 1932	Jeff Co	Tn	Jun 6, 1863	69	W	Grills, Will	Tn	Willis, Lizzie	Tn	Bowman, Douglas	Piedmont					
Bowman, Omer Russell	Sep 25, 1954	Lebanon, Indiana	Tn	Aug 26, 1906	48	Ng	Bowman, William		Grills, Catherine		Bowman, Elmer	Union-Washington Co, Tn					
Bowman, Phebe	Sep 25, 1954	Lebanon, Indiana		Sep 23, 1911	43	Ng	Story, -				Bowman, R.C.	Union - Washington Co, Tn					
Boyle, Helen C.	Feb 26, 1997	Jeff Co	Jeff Co	Mar 22, 1920	76	Cameron, J.W.			Cox, Bertie		Boyle, Jim [Son]	J.M.G.	Mike				Massengall, Elsie - Bishop, Virginia - Gibbons, Marcella

NAME	DDATE	DLOCAT	BLOCAT	BDATE	AGE	SPOUSE	FATHER	FELOCAT	MOTHER	BY	BURIAL	VET	SON	DAUG	BROTHER	SISTER
Brabson, Joan Joyce	Mar 6, 1994	Knoxville, Tn	Jeff City	Oct 24, 1931	62	Brabson, J.B.	Mills, John		Swann, Katherine	Husband	Gillette - Jeff Co		Paul & Delilah	Dobson, Rhonda - Copeland, Deborah & Terry - Jeffries, Paulette & Quinan		Sheets, Jean & Cunningham, Tom - Dorris & Willie - Brabson, Mary Alice & Earl
Brabson, Parnott H.	Sep 17, 1952	Jeff Co.	Tn	Apr 15, 1952			Brabson, Will		Roberts, Amanda	Helton Spring - Grainger Co	Helton Spring - Grainger Co					
Bradford, Anderson	Dec 4, 1936	Jeff City	Alabama	Dec 26, 1896	39	Ng	Anderson, Joe		Swann, Mrs. Carl	Anderson, Mrs. - Gardner, Dan -	Shiloh					
Bradford, Mary E. (Black)	Jul 26, 1995	Dayton, Oh	Jeff City	Jan 5, 1922	73		Mills, William Anderson		Tate, Alice	Langston, Fred (Son - Dayton, Oh)	West View		Hollis Lee	Reynolds, Carolyn		
Bradford, Orson B.	Mar 15, 1959	Tn	Tn	Jun 11, 1915	24	Ng	Bradford, Thomas	Tn	Elza	Myers, Sam P.	Shiloh					
Bradley, Carolyn Sue	Apr 23, 1989	Talbott, Tn	Morristown, Tn	Aug 11, 1952	36	Bradley, David E.	Hannah, Clifford		Wixler, Nancy	Bradley, David E.	Mt. View					
Bradley, Cloyce Flowers	Jan 22, 1994	Nashville, Tn	Powell Station, Tn	May 30, 1908	85	Jernigan, Mary	Bradley, Alfonso Clay		Flowers, Edith Elizabeth	Wife	West View		Cloyce F. Jr. - William Mc Pheeters-Clay Jernigan	Williams, Leah (Neb.) - Shraub, Mary I (Nati)	David (G) David Jr.-Shannon	
Bradley, Edna Ruth	Jul 28, 1995	Jeff City		Nov 17, 1935	59	Bradley, Edward	Miller, Robert		Reneau, Allie	Husband	Mt. View			Charles-Ray Curtis		
Bradley, Holland E.	Mar 1, 1965	Jeff Co		Jan 4, 1898	67	Mary	Talbott, Mary		Collins, Mary	Mary & Sons - Ord.	Sunderland					
Bradley, Holland Jr.	Oct 17, 1933	Jeff Co.					Bradley, Holland E.				Sunderland					
Bradley, John Shannon	Oct 1, 1984	Jeff Folby	Tn	Jul 11, 1924	60	Gilliam, Thelma			Collins, Mary	Bradley, Mrs. Thelma G.	Garden Of Gethsemane - J.M.G.	WW 2				
Bradley, Joseph Harrison	Oct 30, 1966	Knox Co	Ga	Jan 14, 1889	77	Trent, Mattie		Unk		Bradley, Mrs. Mattie	Holston View - Knox Co					
Bradley, Lucy Herrell	Sep 21, 1975	Knoxville, Tn	Tn	Nv 21, 1924	51	Div	Herrell, Willis S.		Parkey, Beulah	Herrell, Harry	Lynnhurst					
Bradley, Mary Viola	Jun 14, 1987	J.M.H.	Tn	Feb 1, 1906	81	W	Collins, Deadrick		Clark, Emma	Bradley, James	Sunderland					
Bradley, Mattie T.	Aug 9, 1979	Jeff City	Tn	Dec 18, 1902	76	W	Trent, K.T.		Green, Alice Jane	Coleman, Mrs. Inez	Highland Memorial - Knox Co					
Bradley, Rhonda Gay	Sep 20, 1958	Jeff Co	Indiana	Feb 11, 1958	2		Bradley, Edward Eugene		Linghiatter, Alice D.	Bradley, Alice	Sunderland					
Bradshaw, Elizabeth G.	Dec 17, 1949	Jeff Co	Tn	Jan 25, 1964	85	W	Cline, Joseph		Newman, Mary	Bradshaw, John	Shraw Plains					
Bradshaw, Infant	Apr 18, 1927		Tn		0		Harfknondt, Sam	Tn	Harknondt, Bessie	Bradshaw, Sam	Sunderland					
Bradshaw, John P.	Jul 18, 1953	Jeff Co	Tn	Feb 9, —		Gregory, Mattie	Bradshaw, W.H.		Cline, Elizabeth	Bradshaw, Mattie	Strawberry Plains					
Bradshaw, Mary L.	Aug 7, 1936		Tn	Mar 12, 1846	90	W	Lyle, Cliborn		Cannon, Polly	Bradshaw, E.C. & Henry R.	Mt. Horeb					
Bradshaw, Mattie Katherine Gregory	Jul 26, 1990	Morristown, Tn	Tn	Aug 12, 1892	97	W	Jackson, Andrew		Fon, Letha	Hale, J.D.	Strawberry Plains					
Bradshaw, William P.M.	Mar 6, 1928		Tn	Jan 8, 1910	80+- 21	Ng	Bradshaw, John	Tn	Hall, Ng	Bradshaw, E.C.	Mt. Horeb					
Bradshaw, Bertha Jones	Aug 13, 1957	Jeff City	Tn	Apr 4, 1883	74	W	Travis, Lemuel		Martin, Carrie	Jones, Jr.-Alvin-Hubart - Bobby - Carathers, Harold-Harley	Pleasant View					
Brady, Doris	Nov 8, 1942	Knox Co	Rutherford Co, Tn		32	Brady, Leland	Harris, John	Tn	Shofar, Ruth	Brady, Leland	Murfeesboro					
Brady, Harvey Thomas	Jun 5, 1946		New Market, Tn	Jun 3, 1946	2d		Brady, James Thomas	New Market, Tn	West, Pauline	Brady, James	Pleasant Grove					
Brady, Infant Male & Female	Nov 12, 1946	New Market	New Market	Nov 12, 1946			Brady, James Alex		Mondy, Jennie	Brady, James A.	Pleasant Grove					
Brady, James Thomas	May 5, 1946	Jeff Co.	Tn	Feb 22, 1924	22	Ng	Brady, James A.	Tn	Woolard, Little Mae	Brady, William C. & Pauline	Pleasant Grove					
Brady, Pauline	Feb 26, 1967	Knox Co	Tn	Feb 17, 1925	42	W	West, William R.		Cate, Amanda	Drake, Mrs. Ronald H. (Nancy) (Fla) Madden, Katherine - Williamson, Rachel (Nieces)	Pleasant Grove					
Bragg, Hazel (Black)	Feb 25, 1994	Jeff City	Dandridge, Tn	Sep 4, 1895	98		Marshall, William		Elliott, Susan		J.M.G.					
Bragg, Julia [Col]	May 10, 1926		Jeff Co	Feb 29, 1865	81	Ng	Sædhom, Powell	Tn		Bragg, Josie	Poor House					
Bragg, Rutus M. [Col]	Jun 23, 1946	Harrison Co				Ng	Unk			Bragg, Josie	Flat Gap					

NAME	DDATE	BLOCAT	BLOCAT	BDATE	AGE	SPOUSE	FATHER	FBLOCAT	MOTHER	MFBLOCAT	BY	BURIAL	VET	SON	DAUG	BROTHER	SISTER
Bramlet, Homer T.	Jul 19, 1995	Jeff City	Georgia	May 9, 1908	87	Howard, Mary	Bramlet, Wesley		Whitlock, Hannah		Wife	Piedmont					Herbison, Phebe - Miller, Ruby
Bramlet, Mary Ruth	Jan 25, 1997	Jeff City	Jeff Co	Oct 23, 1913	83	S	Howard, Sherffie		Pyle, Fan & Tom [G-Child]			Piedmont				William & Helen	
Brannen, Maggie C.	Apr 14, 1954	Jeff Co	Tn	Jan 27, 1872	87	S	Brannen, Beverage		Colletts, Vina K.		Wife	West View					
Branner, George R.	Nov 14, 1928		Tn [D. Florida]	Jan 27, 1872	37	Ng	Brannen, S.M.	Tn	Helm, Debbie			Brenner					
Brannom, Deborah	Jan 7, 1925		Tn		78-3-25	W	Helm, William T.	Tn	Lewis, Margaret	Tn		West View					
Brashear, John Cripps	Dec 27, 1977	Jeff City	Lyndon, Ky	May 9, 1908	69	S	Brashear, Paul B.		Gray, Verna			Redheaven - Louisville, Ky					
Braud, Lionel R.	Apr 25, 1996	Morristown, Tn	Claremont, N.H.	Nov 4, 1923	74	Betts, Irene	Braud, Silas		La Petra, Florence - Toney		Wife	Cremated	41-60	Tony	Cole, Debra - Wells, Cathy [Tn]		Powell, Rita - Wheeler, Jeanie - Rivers, Clara
Brazelton, Amanda [Col]	May 7, 1948	Jeff Co		Jun 12, 1892	55-10-25	S	Unk		Brazelton, Alex - Mitchell, Mrs. Odell [Chicago, Illinois]	Tn		Zion M.E.					
Brazelton, Anna	Mar 19, 1940	Mill Springs	Tn		93	W	Martin, David	Tn	Manley, Caroline - Brazelton, Agnes	Tn		Mill Springs Colored					
Brazelton, Leon [Col]	Apr 27, 1943	New Market	Tn		93	S		Tn		Tn		Colored					
Brazelton, Mack Almeda [F]	May 21, 1973	Knoxville, Tn	Alabama	Jun 30, 1891	71	Brazelton, Samuel T.	Tucker, Oscar		Shields, Ella Jane	Tn		Friends Station					
Brazelton, Mary Comfort	Nov 18, 1950	Knox Co	Tn	Mar 4, 1878	72	W	Pats, Edward		Goins, Amanda			Mt. Zion M.E.					
Brazelton, Samuel C.	Apr 14, 1954	Knox Co	Jeff Co	Jan 14, 1887	67	Ng	Brazelton, Walter		Loy, Hazel			Strawberry Plains					
Breeden, Ada Mae [Annie]	Jul 4, 1988	Knoxville, Tn	Tn	Jan 1, 1922	66	S	Richardson, Nannie		Breeden, James			Friends Station					
Breeden, Agnes Roberta	Aug 26, 1944	Jeff Co	Tn	Oct 15, 1920	23	Ng	Patterson, George A.	Tn	Monroe, Josie	Tn	Patterson, G.A.	Shady Grove					
Breeden, Annie	Jan 2, 1970	Jeff Co	Tn	Feb 28, 1888	82	W	Breeden, James Lewis		Kimbrough, Lucilla		Welch, Mrs. Franklin - Strange, John D. [Va]	Community Chapel					
Breeden, Bobby Max	Apr 22, 1988	Jeff City	Jeff Co	Mar 31, 1935	53		Betts, Lena Ruth		Breeden, Darrin [Son]			Strawberry Plains		Jeff-Tony			Nichols, Judy
Breeden, Bruce	Jun 23, 1934	Jeff City			72	Ng	Breeden, Thomas O.		Breeden, Mrs. Bruce			Jefferson Memorial					
Breeden, C.M.	Nov 18, 1988	Jeff Co		Nov 9, 1896	63	Ng	Breeden, Thomas O.		Breeden, Mrs. Bertha			Jefferson Memorial					
Breeden, Ethel Oliver	Sep 18, 1962	Mc Minn Co, Tn	Tn	Dec 3, 1887	74	Ng	Breeden, Thomas O.		Rice, Tennessee V.		Breeden, Clarence - Eunice - Compton, Mrs.	Mt. Pleasant					
Breeden, Geneva	Mar 8, 1951	Jeff Co	Tn	May 18, 1926	24	Ng	Brooks, Robert		Rice, Virginia		Breeden, Ervin	West View					
Breeden, Harrison Benjamine	Dec 27, 1988/86	Tn	Tn	Aug 21, 1896	71	W	Brooks, B.A.		Kitts, Myrtle		Lyle, Mrs. Bessie	Friends Station					
Breeden, James Louis	Sep 17, 1993	Talbott ,Tn	Tn	Sep 30, 1910	82	Betts, Lena Ruth	Breeden, Elthue		Watt, Susie		Nichols, Judy & J. Hood [Daug]	J.M.G.		Bobby	Kerr, Judy		Lee, Mamie - Bowman, Eunice
Breeden, Lena Ruth	Jul 27, 1999	Jeff City	Jeff Co	May 19, 1915	84	Betts, E.C.		Wiggins, Robie K.				J.M.G.					Stanbaugh, Alma
Breeden, Lula Templin	Apr 21, 1956	Jeff Co	Tn	Nov 1, 1895	60	Breeden, Harvey	Templin, John		Cox, Ella		Chambers, Mrs. J.T. - Breeden, Harvey	Balch					
Breeden, Ray O.	Sep 25, 2000	Port Orange, Fl	Tn	Apr 7, 1920	80	Lee, Anna	Miller, Bertha				Wife	J.M.G.	unk				
Breeden, Thomas O.	Jun 8, 1928	Jeff City	Tn		72-8-14	Ng	Breeden, Ng	Tn		Tn	Sons	Mt. Pleasant					
Breeden, Thomas Walker	Aug 11, 1983	V.A. - Nashville, Tn	Tn	Oct 28, 1917	65	Layman, Ruth	Breeden, Howard E.		Walker, Mattie		Mt. Pleasant - Jeff Co	Mt. Pleasant					
Brewer, Margaret Jane	Jul 29, 1946	Knox Co	Sevier Co	Jan 3, 1872	74	W	Hensley, Isom	Va	Mc Coulfay, Prudent	Tn	Baker	Buffalo Grove	WW 2				
Brewer, Freeman E. [Zeke]	Jul 3, 1993	Jeff City	Sevierville, Tn	Dec 9, 1918	74	Garrett, Sue		Byrd, Viola Gann		Bradley, Brenda [Niece] - Gann, Cuittie [Uncle] - Gibson, Myrtle [Aunt]	Buffalo Grove	43-46			Fred [1/2] Jenkins, Ronald	[1/2] Hodge, Delati Jenkins - [In-Law] Garrett, Genevie
Brewer, Mary Sue	Jan 13, 1996	Jeff City	Jeff Co	Jul 7, 1907	88	W	Garrett, Edwin		Johnson, Lura L.		Bradley, Brenda [Niece]					Fred	

NAME	DDATE	DLOCAT	BLOCAT	BDATE	AGE	SPOUSE	FATHER	FBLOCAT	MOTHER	MFBLOCAT	BY	BURIAL	VET	SON	DAUG	BROTHER	SISTER
Brewer, Other Jenning	May 23, 1967	Knox Co	Tn		37	Ng	Brewer, Ollie James		Scribner, Mildred		Brewer, Mrs. Phyllis J.	Memorial Gardens					
Brickman, John Spencer	Nov 29, 1995	New Market, Tn	New Jersey	Jun 26, 1932	63	Fassel, Florence	Brickman, John H.		Stephens, Elizabeth		Purkey, Gail & Ginsheweister, Neb & Lawrenceburg, Tn	J.M.G.	62-65				
Bridges, Ada	Mar 18, 1972	Hamblen Co	Alabama	Jul 24, 1885	86	W	Pullen, Andrew J.		Stephens, Elizabeth		Monroes – Lawrenceburg, Tn					George-Clarence	Pierson, Ethel - Von Horn, Adelia
Briggs, Lee Robert	Mar 25, 1991	J.M.H.	Mt. Carmel, Illinois	Feb 16, 1962	29	Hills, Joanna	Griggs, Doyle		Stone, Dora		Briggs, Joanna H. - Barbett F.H. (Cairo, Illinois)		unk				
Briggs, William Melrose	May 10, 1974	U.T.H.	Nova Scotia, Canada	Jan 9, 1901	73	Durgin, Doris		Briggs, Edward		Cameron, Christine	Briggs, Mrs. Doris	Jefferson Memorial					
Brimer, Dora V.	Apr 3, 1989	J.M.H.	Dandridge, Tn	Dec 3, 1902	86	S	Brimer, Houston		Denton, Elizabeth		Fountain, Maxine	New Market					
Brimer, Jacob Rhoden	Dec 21, 1981	J.M.H.	Tn	Sep 2, 1891	90	W	Brimer, Robert		Reneau, Julia		Brimer, Mrs. Gladys R.- Walter R.	Hills Union					
Brimer, John Raymond	Mar 1, 1972	Knox Co	Tn	Oct 22, 1955	16	S	Brimer, Walter [Buster]		Guess, Darlene		Brimer, Buster	Memorial Gardens					
Brimer, Katie Belle	Mar 11, 1981	Hamblen Co				W	Alby, W. W.		Strelcher, Minnie		Brimer, J.R.	Hills Union					
Brimer, Lara Wooten Cable	Mar 24, 1978	Jeff City	Tn	Sep 24, 1885	92	W	Wooten, Joseph A.		Parrott, Catherine		May, Mrs. Lloyd - Miller, Mrs. Frank	West View					
Brimer, Walter R.	Feb 11, 1986	Talbott, Tn	Dandridge, Tn	May 6, 1924	73	Brimer, Darlene G.	Brimer, Jacob		Alley, Katie		Wife	J.M.G.		Robert William Richard	Foust, Linda - Saylor, Donna		Brimer, Gladys Ruth
Brinkley, Bazzie Ernest	Sep 22, 1958	Hamblen Co	Tn	Aug 3, 1899	64	W			Brinkley, Malinda		Brinkley, J.C.- Earl- Raymond	Lebanon					
Brinkley, David K.	Aug 18, 1993	Indianapolis, Ind.	Indiana	Nov 16, 1954	38		Brinkley, Kenneth		Hill, Isa		Blankenship, Jackie (Sister - Indiana)	Lebanon Baptist					
Brinkley, Isa Hill	Jan 29, 1985	Indianapolis, Ind.	Indiana	Jun 4, 1926	58	W	Hill, James H.		Williams, Bertha		Blankenship, Jackie B. (Greenwood, Ind)	Lebanon					
Brinkley, Kenneth	Oct 28, 1981	V.A. Hosp- Indiana	Tn	Mar 15, 1918	63	W	Brinkley, Ernest		Jackson, Iola		Brinkley, Mrs. Isa Hill	Lebanon (Greenbrier)	WW 2				
Brinkley, Nancy Izel	Jan 30, 1959	Hamblen Co	Tn	Oct 23, 1898	59	Brinkley, Ernest	Jackson, William		Mooney, Annie		Brinkley, Ernest	Lebanon					
Brinkley, Raymond	Feb 22, 1987	F.S.H.	Tn	Jul 2, 1922	64	Brinkley, Mrs. Geneva	Jackson, Ernest		Jackson, Nancy		Brinkley, Geneva	Hamblen Memorial	WW 2				
Bronheim, Cunnie [F]	Feb 27, 1970	Jeff City	Va		91-11-29	W	Temple, Roy		Cosby, Nellie		Odor, Mrs. Charles	Clinlef - Albermarla, Va					
Bronner, Alice	Oct 9, 1926	Tn			77-2-26	W	Elevins, John		Kyle, Minerva	Tn	West View	West View					
Bronner, Will [Cdf]	Dec 26, 1939	Jeff Co	Tn	Mar 1, 1891	48	Ng	Bronner, Abraham L.	Tn	Stewart, Ida	Tn	Bronner, Daphne [Oak Grove]	Belmont					
Bronnon, Infant Male	Apr 17, 1947	Jeff Co		Apr 17, 1947	w	W	Bronner, Charles Clifton	Tn	Pruitt, Agness Delcie	W. Va	Clifton, Charles	Sunderland					
Brooks, Bessie Ruth	Jun 11, 1988	Dandridge, Tn	Tn	Apr 8, 1920	w	W	Crane, Robert		Ramines, Mary		Brooks, Loomia-Jimmy	Wesley Chapel - Jeff Co					
Brooks, Blanche	Nov 22, 1985	Care Inn	Tn	Dec 26, 1895	89	Brooks, Charlie J. [D]	Shurmate, Even		Hill, Margaret		Wisecarver, Margaret B.	West View					
Brooks, Blanche	Jul 12, 1990	Hilltween	N. Whitesboro, Nc	Dec 7, 1903	86	W	Absher, S.E.	Tn	Gray, Dora	Tn	Brooks, Jack	J.M.G.					
Brooks, Charles Jackson	Feb 3, 1947	Jeff Co	Jeff Co	Oct 13, 1889	57-3-20	Ng	Brooks, A.I.	Tn	Churchman, Betty	Tn	Brooks, Mrs. C.J.	West View	unk				
Brooks, Conard Leo	Jun 21, 1964	Knox Co	Jeff Co	Oct 28, 1917	46	Ng	Brooks, Floyd		Herbin, Fannie		Brooks, Mrs. Catherine Holston View - Knox Co	West View					
Brooks, David Clyde	May 10, 1985	J.M.H.	Va	Jul 12, 1915	69	Div	Brooks, William		Colley, Emma		Young, Mrs. Daniel L., Culver, Mae (Lincoln, Ohio) - Downy, Ruth (Atlanta, Ne) - Clem [LA, Cal]	Mt. View					
Brooks, Floyd Ellar	Nov 18, 1956	Knox Co	Nc	Dec 29, 1898	57	W	Eller, David C.		Swift, Zelda		Peleutte - Brunswick, Ga	Mt. View					
Brooks, Floyd Omar	Mar 18, 1948	Jeff Co	Tn	Jun 19, 1897	50-9-21	Ng	Brooks, Will		Bolin, Celia		Brooks, Mrs. Fannie [Mother]	Roseberry					
Brooks, Guy Adan	Nov 4, 1991	F.S.H.	Tn		80	Ng	Brooks, William		Colley, Emma		Walker, Shirley [Cousin]	Mt. View	unk				
Brooks, Harry K.	Nov 23, 1933	Dumplin		Jan 13, 1921	12	S	Brooks, Walter		Callis, Ollie		Brooks, Walter	Dumplin					
Brooks, Hazel Alimea	Apr 27, 1965	Jeff Co	Va	Sep 22, 1910	54	W	Couns, Tula M.	Tn	Southerland, Vada	Tn	Brooks, Halcion	Mt. View					

NAME	DDATE	DLOCAT	BLOCAT	BDATE	AGE	SPOUSE	FATHER	FELOCAT	MOTHER	MFRLOCAT	BY	BURIAL	VET	SON	DAUG	BROTHER	SISTER
Brooks, J. Allen	Apr 30, 1966	Grainger, Co	Tn	Aug 3, 1939		Ng	Brooks, Ferris L.		Morgan, Mamie		Walker, Mrs. Mossie - Brooks, Mrs. Betsy Carol	New Blackwell Branch - Grainger Co					
Brooks, Jimmy Ray	Apr 20, 1966	Jeff City			1d		Brooks, Jay Allen	Tn	Lumpkin, Betsy Carol		Brooks, Jay	New Blackwell					
Brooks, Katherine Lashes	Dec 20, 1993	Jeff City	Worchester, Mass.	Sep 13, 1993	3m		Brooks, Roy Edward Jr.		Craustein, Christine		Mother - Graustein, Arthur & Jean - Brooks, Betsy (G-Parents) Taylor, Trudy Bell, Paul & Audrey (G-G-Parents)	Mill Springs				Graustein, Jonathan	
Brooks, Lyafatte	Jul 12, 1947	Jeff Co	Jeff Co		abt 68		Brooks, Marion	Tn	Riley, Mancy	Tn	Brooks, Albert & Ernest	Piedmont					
Brooks, Mary Ellen Crooke	Jul 1, 1980	Jeff City	Tn	Dec 25, 1921	58	Brooks, David	Jett, Ethel Pearl				Wollenbarger, Mrs. Catherine - Crooke, Shannon	Shiloh - Grainger Co					
Brooks, Mrs.	Oct 10, 1933	Morristown, Tn									Newman, Mrs. - Brooks, Mrs. R.A.	Jeff City					
Brooks, Perry Halron	Sep 8/8, 1966	Tn	Va	May 4, 1907	59-4-4	W	Brooks, William		Colley, Emma		Carr, Jeanette	Mt. View					
Brooks, Ray Larry	Jan 3, 1994	Monroe Co, Tn	Va	Mar 19, 1912	81	Inman, Lillian	Brooks, David C.		Calhoun, Vinnie		Wife	Eastview Memorial - Koxilla, Tn		[Step] Brogdan, Arthur	[Step] Patty, Phyllis June - Reever, Wanda - Etheridge, Robin - Burkett, Shirley - Orthman, Kathy		[Nioca], Writ, Janet
Brooks, Rebecca	Sep 3, 1940	New Market	Tn	Jun 14, 1884	56	Brooks, Fayette	Miller, James	Tn	Willcoxs, Mary	Tn	County	Piedmont					
Brooks, Rex Alexander	Oct 10, 1984	Carr Inn	Tn	Jan 12, 1893	91	Asther, Blanch	Brooks, J.T.		Mewman, Arthlee		Brooks, Mrs. Rex	Deep Springs	WW 1				
Brooks, Rau W.	Apr 30, 1965	Jeff Co	Tn	Oct 28, ----	66-	Ng	Brooks, William A.		Bolden, Celia Ann		Shipley, Joyce & Jack	Mill Springs					
Brooks, Roy Monroe	Mar 1, 1988	J.M.H.	Tn	Feb 13, 1918	70	Div	Brooks, Uhyssa M.		Housewright, Grace A.		Brooks, Everette Jenkins	Hillcrest					
Brooks, Samuel Saggel	Mar 26, 1982	Knox Co	Tn	7 22, 1918	44	Jenkins, Everette	Brooks, Charles E.		Saffell, Nora		Brooks, Franklin						
Brooks, Sharon Darlene	Nov 6, 1957	Milligan Clinic	Tn			S	Brooks, Franklin		Norton, Charlotte		Brooks, Franklin	Woodard					
Brooks, Sina Ruth	Apr 29, 1985	Jeff City	Vonore, Tn	Jul 25, 1914	80	Ng	Sheets, T.F.		Jones, Sarah E.		Witt, Janet & Bill[Doug]	Fair - Jeff Co		Tom & Laura	James, Becky & Danny Crosby, Carol & Jim	Gifford	
Brooks, W.A.	Jun 23, 1953	Jeff Co	Tn	Nov 4, 1872	80	W	Brooks, Marion F.		Elder, Adiline			Fair - Jeff Co					
Brooks, William Lee	Feb 18, 1950	Knox Co	Tn	Feb 9, 1884	86	W	Brooks, Marion F.		Riley, Martha			Piedmont					
Brookshire, Jennetta	Jan 27, 1931	Strawberry Plains	Tn	Apr 2 1926	4	S	Brookshire, R.L.	Tn	Lerkson ?, Alice	Tn	Brookshire, R.L.	Oak Grove					
Brophy, Corinne	Dec 3, 1980	Jeff City	Mo	Dec 17, 1887	82	W	Sutton, Joseph		Norris, Bessie		Brophy, Roger-Richard* Corinne	West View					
Brophy, Frank B.	Mar 22, 1971	Jeff Co	California	Mar 21, 1891	79	Sutton, Corinne	Brophy, Francis		Johnson, Mary		Brophy, Corinne	West View	WW 1				
Brotherton, Alfreds	Sep 27, 1992	Maryville, Tn	Jeff Co	Sep 27, 1992	102	W	Hill, Alfred O.		Carter, Mary		Brotherton, Sarah Dwen [Daug-in-Law]	Buffalo Grove					
Brotherton, Carroll C. (F)	Feb 8, 1982	Jeff City	Jeff Co		85	W	Cole, Isaac		Brotherton, David [Son]			Jarrigan					
Brotherton, Cora Cornelia	Nov 17, 1977	At Home	Tn	Sep 22, 1884	93	W	Brotherton, Richard P.		Kidwell, Lillian		Brotherton, Grace	Mt. Horeb					
Brotherton, George L.	Feb 16, 1986	Clarksville, Tn ?	Tn		54	Ng	Brotherton, Richard P.		Kidwell, Lillian		Brotherton, Mrs. Trudy R. (Clarksville, Tn)	Mt. Horeb					
Brotherton, George Lee	Nov 23, 1950	Green Co, Tn	Green Co, Tn	Oct 21, 1896	54	Ng	Brotherton, Richard P.		Kidwell, Lillian		Brotherton, Mrs. Julia (Wife)	West View					Abbott, Mrs. Clinton - Kirkpatrick, Mildred & Howard [Br- & Lewis] Sheets, Georgie-Naomi-Ella
Brotherton, Grace	Apr 26, 1994	Dandridge, Tn	Jeff Co	Mar 28, 1900	94		Brotherton, Richard P.		Kidwell, Lillian		Brotherton, David-Joel [Nephew]	Mt. Horeb					

NAME	DDATE	DLOCAT	BLOCAT	BDATE	AGE	SPOUSE	FATHER	PBLOCAT	MOTHER	MTBLOCAT	BY	BURIAL	VET	SON	DAUG	BROTHER	SISTER
Brotherton, Grover H.	Dec 1, 1951	Jeff Co	Tn	Nov 5, 1889	62	Ng	Brotherton, Richard P.		Kidwell, Lillian		Brotherton, Mrs. G.H. - Roger & Alfred	Buffalo Grove	WW 1				
Brotherton, James Lynn	Sep 1, 1983	Jeff Co	Tn	Apr 13, 1930	33	S	Colis, Carroll				Jarrigan	Jarrigan					
Brotherton, Allie Mae	Jan 15, 1961	Cocke Co	Tn	Sep 1, 1898	62	W			Reneau, Louriene			West View					
Brotherton, Quince David	Feb 15, 1967	Jeff Co	Tn	Apr 25, -94	72-9- 68-6- 18	Ng	Brotherton, Richard F.		Kidwell, Lillian		Brotherton, Mrs. Coral	Jarrigan					
Brotherton, R.P.	Aug 24, 1928		Tn		20	Brotherton, R.J.	Kidwell, J.H.	Tn	Couch, E.	Tn	Brotherton, R.J.	Mt. Horeb					
Brotherton, Ada Ethene	Aug 27, 1933	Jeff City	Tn	May 26, 1851	82	Brotherton, James	Brotherton, James	Nc	Bradley, Synthia	Tn	Family	Mt. Horeb					
Brown, Allie Mae	Oct 13, 1958	Jeff City	Tn	Oct 26, 1942	15	S	Brown, Henry		Jones, Mae		Brown, Mae	Mt. View - Jeff Co					
Brown, Charles Brabty	Nov 25, 1947	Jeff Co	Tn	May 6, 1908	33-1- 10	Div		Va	Crozier, Bertie	Va	Brown, Mrs. George (Mabel)						
Brown, Curtis R.	Aug 14, 1981	Jeff Co	Tn	Jan 4, 1947	13	S	Brown, Frank	Tn	Ellison, Lucy		Brown, Frank	New Market					
Brown, Elvin Harrison	Sep 18, 1979	Jeff City	Tn	Mar 22, 1948	67	Brannam, Mary Jane	Miller, Rudolph		Brown, Mary Jane		Brown, Mary Jane	Mt. View					
Brown, Emily	Jan 12, 1962	Knox Co	Tn	Nov 27, 1911	90	Brown, Jim (D)	Brown, James E.		Dobson, Nora Peralee		Brown, Mrs. Elvin	Jefferson Memorial					
Brown, Frank Raymond	Apr 2, 1982	J.M.H.	Tn	Feb 8, 1871	65	Ellison, Lucy	Case, Henry		Presely, Rachael		Pomlinex, Lawrence - Brown, Hugh	Fain - Jeff Co					
Brown, G.I.	Dec 22, 1933	Tn	Tn	Jun 1, 1916	55	Ng	Brown, James E.		Dobson, Nora P.	Tn	Brown, Lucy C.E.	Mt. View					
Brown, Hattie Lucinda	Apr 10, 1988	Jeff Co	Tn	Dec 14, 1878	86	W	Brown, John	Tn	Buckalher, Marice	Tn	Brown, Mrs. G.I.	West View					
Brown, Hazel Elizabeth	Mar 20, 1947	Tn	Tn	Apr 10, 1882	10	W	Wilson, Bill		Lunsford, Mary		Brown, John-Claud & Sister	Balch					
Brown, Horace Clayton (Col)	Sep 5, 1954	Jeff Co	Tn	Jan 2, 1936	9		Miller, Claude	Tn	Brown, Claude	Tn	Brown, Claude	Chestnut Grove					
Brown, Howard William	Nov 16, 1970	Jeff Co	Tn	Aug 23, 1895	69	Ng	Cox, Augusta		Cox, Augusta		Brown, Mattie	West View Colored					
Brown, Ida Cameron	Feb 3, 1984	J.M.H.	Tn	Oct 14, 1907	63	W	Dobson, Jim		Dobson, Nora		Brown, Wayne	Buffalo Grove					
Brown, James	Oct 18, 1985	New Market	Tn	Dec 25, 1904	75	W	Easley, Mary		Knowling, Elizabeth		Cannon, Dee	Piedmont					
Brown, James Andrew	Aug 14, 1996	Pulaski, Tn	Tn	Dec 5, 1933	1	Brown, Virginia	Brown, J.H.	Tn	Kerr, Julia	Tn	Brown, J.H.	Mt. View					
Brown, James Elmore	Sep 10, 1949	Jeff Co	Tn	Feb 15, 1995	91		Brown, John		Wife		City - Athens, Al.		[Step] Hart, Ed				
Brown, James Henry	Nov 20, 1949	Knox Co	Tn	Dec 10, 1882	66	Ng	Link		Edwards, Rachael		Brown, Elvin	Lebanon Presby					
Brown, James Minnie	Dec 6, 1998	Jeff Co	Tn	Jan 14, 1946	3	Paxton, Edith			Brown, Ida Belle		Brown, Ida	Oak Grove - Greenville, Tn					
Brown, Janie Love	Feb 6, 1983	Tn	Tn	May 4, 1909	79	Huffaker, James	Brown, James F.		Caldwell, Mary		Brown, Edith Paxton	Beech Springs - Sevier Co	WW 2				
Brown, Jeanette Alice	Oct 30, 1948	Claiborne Co	Tn	Nov 20, 1870	77	W	Huffaker, Mary		Johnson, Melinda		Southerland, Mrs. Katherine						
Brown, Leon	Jan 16, 1995	Tn	Tn	Oct 23, 1923	77-11- 10	W	Ousley, James	Tn	Edwardson, Mary	Tn	Brown, Ella	Campbell					
Brown, Mattie Moore	Nov 9, 1978	Detroit, Mich.	Tn	Aug 16, 1889	tn	W	Brown, Immanuel		Lunsford, Hattie		Brown, William F. - Morris, Mrs. Ruby K.	Gethesmane - J.M.G.					
Brown, Mildred Love	Oct 4, 1981	Jeff Co	Tn	May 31, 1931	69	Brown, Leon	Brown, Bill				Probert, Mrs. Nancy - Brown, William F.	West View					
Brown, Mitchell William Sr.	Nov 4, 1981	Jeff Co	Tn	Sep 30, 1916	50	Div	Parrott, Francis M.		Jones, Elizabeth		Jefferson Memorial	Jefferson Memorial					
Brown, Nancy E.	Jan 1, 1927	Tn	Tn	Feb 26, 1909	65	W	Brown, Tom		Free, Susie		Brown, Mitchell W. Jr.	Mt. View					
Brown, Nancy Mae	Aug 25, 1996	J.M.H.	Tn	Feb 26, 1909	85-0- 10	W	Raskin, Joe	Tn	Glass, Unk	Tn	Bettis, Thelos	Mt. Horeb					
Brown, Nora	Nov 21, 1974	Tn	Tn	Jun 1, 1889	77	W	Jones, William H.		Comte, Vidole		Combs, Jim	Mt. View					
Brown, Rachael Elizabeth	July 10, 1948	Jeff Co (Res. Green Co)	Tn	May 11, 1930	85	W	Dobson, Wedley		Holt, Julia		Brown, Elvin-Henry- Frank-Jim (Sons)	Lebanon - Mt. Horeb					
Brown, Rena Mae	May 10, 1966	Jeff City	Tn	Feb 15, 1976	18	Ng	Carr, George W.	Tn	Roach, Bessie K.	Tn	Carr, Mrs. George	Sunderland					
Brown, Roberta Viola	Nov 14, 1953	Jeff Co	Tn	Feb 15, 1944	24	S	Brown, Henry		Jones, Anna		Brown, Mae	Mt. View					
Brown, Ruth Jane	Mar 10, 1952	Tn	W. Va	Apr 10, 1888	65	W	Crozier, Lewis P.		Shines, Belle		Mulder, Mrs. C.P. (Saulsbury, Nc) - Brown, Stanley (Miami), Fij - Mc New, Mrs.	West View					
Brown, William Ranslow Sr.	Oct 16, 1997	Sioux City, Ia	Jan 14, 1924	73		Ng			Hart, Melissa		Brown, Arthur	Grants Chapel					
Brown, William Robert	Feb 8, 1946	Tn	Tn	Jan 12, 1894	62	Ng		Tn	Smith, Helen	Tn	Newman, Will	Newman, Will	Brown, Carl Ranslow					
									Edwards, Rachael		Edwards, Rachael	Arlington National - Va	68-70	Brown, W.R. Jr. (Son) - Claude & Leon	Brown, Mrs. Nellie -	Balch	Lund, Betsy - [Step] Corsett, Fredina

NAME	DDATE	BLOCAT	BLOCAT	DDATE	AGE	SPOUSE	FATHER	F/B LOCAT	MOTHER	M/B LOCAT	BY	BURIAL	VET	SON	DAUG	BROTHER	SISTER
Brownlow, Euphew Evelyn	Mar 25, 1991	Greenville, Tn	Tn	Aug 20, 1905	85	W	Brownlow, Joe	Tn	Lane, Minnie Belle	Tn	Brownlow, Robert E. (Son)	West View					
Brownlow, J. Foster [Col]	Aug 5, 1928		Tn		60-9-6	W	Brownlow, Foster	Tn	Fugatt, Ruth	Tn	Brownlow, Clodie & Father	Colored					
Brownlow, Nancy Meriah Manny	Oct 19, 1925	Tn				W	Ng	Tn	Chandlotte	Tn	Brownlow, Father	Colored					
Brownlow, Paul [Col]	Oct 28, 1944	Jeff Co	Jeff Co	Aug 1, 1892	52	S	Brownlow, Foster		Murray, Nancy		Brownlow, T.C.	Colored					
Brownlow, Robert Eugene Sr. [Black]	May 2, 1991	Green Co, Tn	Va	Apr 12, 1932	59	Div	Brownlow, Thurman E.	Tn	Murray, Evelyn		Nance, Beulah - Brownlow, T.C.	Cremated	unk				
Brownlow, Thurman C. [Col]	Jul 15, 1971	Vet Hosp. Mt. Home	Tn	Sept 27, 1896	74	Ripley, Evelyn	Brownlow, J.F.		Murray, Nancy		Brownlow, Evelyn	West View	WW 1				
Boyles, Minnie Lucretia	Oct 1, 1944	Jeff Co	Ky	Apr 27, 1862	82	W	Whittenburg, William	Tn	Campbell, Mary Ann	Tn	Creswell, J.O.	Greenwood - Chattanooga, Tn					
Bruce, Garland Eugene	Jul 6, 2000	Jeff City	Ky	Oct 1, 1926	73	Martin, Ruth	Bruce, Benjamin		Williams, Ruth		Wills	J.M.G.					
Bruce, Glenn	Dec 4, 1977	N.C. Baptist	Tn	Mar 21, 1924	53	Clapp, Mary	Bruce, Everett		Mullins, Lula		Mc Swain - Glenn	Jefferson Memorial	WW 2				
Bruce, Mary Jane [Col]	Feb 20, 1931	Jeff City		Sept 15, ---			Ng				Colored	Colored					
Bruner, Yolan Mary	Jul 13, 1991	J.M.H.	Allouna, Pa	Oct 20, 1913	77	W	Baliagh, Andrew		Yariga, Barbara		Capp, Susan (Daug)	Cremated					
Bruner, R. W.	Jul 13, 1940	Anderson Co	Va	Jan 3, 1876	64	Ng	Bruner, Sam	Va	Armstrong, Mary	Va	Baker	Baker					
Bryant, Julia A.	Feb 8, 1953	Jeff Co	Ky	Nov 10, 1856	96	W	Atchison, Thomas		Money, Cortine		Young, Mrs. Guy	Bellinger - Jeff Co					
Bryon, Wyatt Jennings	May 11, 1983	Jeff Co	Fla	Nov 9, 1909	95	Stone, Mamie					Bryon, Mrs. Evelyn	Memorial Gardens	WW 2				
Bull, Floyd Reed	Oct 27, 1957	Jeff Co	Tn	Dec 23, 1899	61	Ng	Bull, Rev. William Sr.	Tn	Woolard, Martha		Bull, Mrs. Magnie & Children	Hillcrest					
Bull, Kenneth	Dec 28, 1922	New Market	Tn	Jan 9, 1932	11m		Bull, F.E.	Tn	Gettis, Magnie	Tn	Bull, F.E.	Friends Station					
Bull, Marshall Gaddis Jr.	Nov 26, 1946	Jeff Co	Tn	Nov 24, 1946		Trd	Bull, M.G. Sr.	Trd	Roderick, Mary Ruth	Tn	Bull, M.G. Sr.	Friends Station					
Bull, Martha Elnora	Jun 26, 1965	Jeff Co	Tn	Sep 22, 1880	84	W	Wolland, Joseph		Hatcher, Mary		Wilson, Mrs. Earl - Bull, Wilma	Valley View - Jeff Co					
Bull, Mary Magnie	Sep 16, 1988	Jeff Co	Tn	Aug 11, 1899	90	W	Gaddis, John J.		Rhess, Dora		Bull, Ettis	Hillcrest					
Bull, William G.	Jul 22, 1925	Tn	Tn		74-11-20	W	Bull, Elijah		Reed, Unk	Tn	Bull, J.C.	Wesleyan Chapel					
Bull, William M. Sr.	Dec 19, 1960	Tn	Tn	Jun 26, 1879	81	Ng	Bull, Melvin		Cotter, Adelia		Bull, Rein - Chambers, Mary - Wilson, Kate - Doyal, Constance	Cedar Grove - Jeff Co					
Bullen, Audrey	Jun 26, 1994	Jeff City	Grainger Co	Oct 20, 1934	59	Bullen, Johnny Claude	Hodge, Coy Clayton		Berley, Sue Etta		Husband	J.M.G.				Jim - Robert - Eugene - Lewis - Cecil	Hodge, Evelyn (In-Law) Hodge, Hazel - Juanita - Carolyn
Bullen, Ruby	Jun 17, 1988	Hilltower	Tn	Aug 26, 1911	79	W	Farmer, John		Farmer, Hattie		Bullen, Gail	Mc Ginnis - Harrell - Grainger Co					
Bullion, Imogene	Mar 18, 1991	Nashville, Tn	Hamblen Co	Sep 16, 1928	62	Div	Puntkey, Lawrence		Garrison, Kate		Bullion, Eugene (Sr.) - Copp, Diane - Phillips, Paul (Daug)	J.M.G.					
Bunch, Amanda	Nov 4, 1933	Knox Co	Ohio	Dec 13, 1930	55	S	Bunch, Paris		Kirkland, Sue		Jackson, Mrs. Cleo	New Market					
Bunch, Betty Marie	Dec 25, 1985	Ohio	Jeff Co	Dec 5, 1945	1d	Sd	Bunch, Lawrence	Tn	Jones, Bonnie Edith	Jeff Co	Bud/Neh Lawrence	Cedar Grove - Grainger Co					
Bunch, Bonnie Jean	Oct 28, 1941	Jeff Co	Tn		4m		Bunch, L.E.			Tn	Bunch, L.E.	Mill Springs					
Bunch, Lenos Wayne	May 2, 1946	Jeff Co		Dec 16, 1889	82	Ng			Flora, Cynthia		Burchell, Flora	Mill Springs					
Burchell, John M.	Feb 11, 1972	Jeff Co	Tn			Mc Gill, Johann	Burchell, John				Burchell, Flora - Roy - Luther - Morrell, Ray - Mc Ghee, Pearl - Betsy, Betty - Tolliver, Glady - Wilkin, Forest	Narrow Valley - Grainger Co					
Burchell, Josie Ellen	Oct 28, 1975	Hamblen Co	Tn	Nov 26, 1975	83	W	Burchell, James Robert		Green, Sarah Jane		Burchell, Flora	Jefferson Memorial					
Burchell, Lloyd William Sr.	Sep 8, 1997	Knoxville, Tn	Tn	Apr 30, 1940	57	Georgia A.	Burchell, Lloyd		Lawless, Pearlie		Wills	Community Chapel		Junior - Terry - Herbie			
Burchell, Samuel P.	Sep 16, 1995	Talbott, Tn	Tn	Mar 27, 1923	72	Raby, Betty	Burchell, George		Northern, Flora		Wills	East View Memorial - Knox Co	Dennis & Cathy				
Burchell, James Curtis	Mar 12, 1967	Knoxville, Tn	Tn	Jun 21, 1900	46	S	Burchell, J.H.		Underwood, Effie		Burchell, J.H.	Mill Springs					
Burchell, James Harvey	Feb 28, 1979	Knoxville, Tn		Mar 18, 1885	93	W	Burchell, Joseph A.		Moore, Mary E.		Burchell, Helen	Sunderland	WW 2		Smith, Phyllis - Steph, Vickie & Roy	
Burcfield, James Paul	Sep 8, 1989	J.M.H.	Jeff Co	Mar 13, 1923	66	S	Burcfield, James H.		Underwood, Geneive		Burcfield, Helen	Sunderland					

NAME	DDATE	DLOCAT	BLOCAT	BDATE	AGE	SPOUSE	FATHER	FRLOCAT	MOTHER	MFRLOCAT	BY	BURIAL	VET	SON	DAUG	BROTHER	SISTER
Burchfiel, Mattie Sue	Aug 24, 1976	Jeff City	Tn	Sep 2, ---	84	Burchfiel, C.O. [D]	Stilson, Sam		Pollard, Viola		Williford, Anna Ruth (Pony) - Addison, Virginia - Gass, Mrs. Frank - Etherton, Mrs. Dewey	Flat Gap					
Burchfiel, William Cecil	Mar 16, 1948	Knox Co	Jeff Co	Mar 21, 1911	36	Ng	Burchfiel, J.H.	Tn	Underwood, Geneva	Tn	Burchfiel, J.H.	Sunderland					
Burchfiel, Cleophas O.	Sep 7, 1971	Jeff Co	Tn	May 1, 1894	77	Stilson, Mattie	Burchfiel, Russ		Hughes, Edith		Burchfiel, Mattie - Gass, Bobby - Williford, Perry - Mallicoct, James - V.A.	Flat Gap	WW 1				
Burchfiel, Gurland A.	Sep 27, 2000	Knoxville, Tn	Tn	Feb 20, 1918	82	W	Burchfiel, Jim		Kilmer, Lockie		Sellars, Hal (Nephew)	J.M.G.	unk				
Burchfield, Shirley Isabelle Purkey	May 17, 1952	Jeff Co	Jeff Co	May 8, 1941	11	S	Burchfield, J.L.	Jeff Co	Messengill, Yvonne	Jeff Co	Burchfield, M.I.	Sutherland					
Burchfield, Wanda Faye	Sep 1, 1999	Whitesburg, Tn	Whitesburg, Tn	Jun 29, 1944	55	Burchfield, Fred	Bentley, George Vency		Condray, Easter		Jhuband	Sunderland					
Burk, Major Lee	Nov 28, 1959	Bedford Co	Tn	Nov 6, 1894	65	Ng	Burk, J.C.	Tn	Hickle, Addaid	Tn	Burk, Mrs.	Willow Mount - Bedford Co	WW 1				
Burnett, Alice	Apr 24, 1925	Tn	Tn			Burnett, J.J.	Beeler, J.C.		Beeler, Luther		Beeler, Luther	Baptist					
Burnett, Calvin Keith	Mar 9, 1929	Tn	Tn		4-5-0	S	Burnett, Loyd	Tn	Roberts, Ruril	Tn	Burnett, Loyd	Sunderland					
Burnett, Clifford Theodore [Zack]	Jun 13, 1981	Morristown, Tn	Tn	Mar 31, 1907	74	Div	Burnett, T.C.		Carter, Myrtle		Bryant, Beely & Harry - Marysville, Tn - Tarver, Marjorie - Burnett, Harold [Fla]	Sunderland					
Burnett, J.S.	Sept 7, 1933		Strawberry Plains														
Burnett, Jean Beatrice	Feb 1, 1996	Jeff City	Strawberry Plains	Apr 26, 1929	66	Within, William Floyd			Mills, Lucy		Henry, Kathy (Daug) - Leonard [Son]	Trentville		David		4	5
Burnett, John Bewley	Apr 12, 1956	Strawberry Plains	Tn	Jun 16, 1878	77	Ng					Nunnell, J.B.-Claude-Leonard [Sons]	Strawberry Plains					
Burnett, Lloyd Thomas	Jan 20, 1977	Morristown, Tn	Tn	Jan 26, 1902	74	Roberts, Ruril	Burnett, Thomas C.	Tn	Carter, Myrtle	Tn	Burnett, Mrs. Lloyd T. - Burnett, Mrs. Rural	Sunderland					
Burnett, Lois Alice	Nov 12, 1931	Straw Plains Hamblen Co	Tn	Nov 15, 1930	11m	Burnett, Kirk [DM]	Burnett, John		Roach, Stella		Burnett, Mrs. John	Sunderland					
Burnett, Myrtie	Sep 1, 1969	Tn	Tn	Dec 22, 1882	86	Colbach, Hassledene	Burnett, T.C.		Lloyd, Mary Frances		Burnett, Mrs. Alleen	Sunderland					
Burnett, Robert Keith	Jul 27, 1981	Jeff City	Tn	May 26, 1905	56	Colbach, Hassledene	Burnett, T.C.		Carter, Myrtle L.		Burnett, Hassledene	Sunderland					
Burnett, Rural Grace	Oct 4, 1980	Atlanta, Tn	Jeff Co	Jul 27, 1903	87	W	Roberts, Herbert		Linn, Betty		Burnett, Lloyd E. [Son]	Sunderland					
Burnett, Sarah Jean [Tootsie]	Feb 11, 1971		Tn	Aug 27, 1928	42	S	Burnett, Robert Keith		Cobbach, Hansieteen		Burnett, Hansieteen	Sunderland					
Burns, Mary Janette	Jul 28, 1981	Knoxville, Tn	Tn	Sep 19, 1981	67-10-9	W	Franklin, Benjamin		Maples, Lular		Maples, Jennie	Straw Plains					
Burns, Pleas Thomas	Feb 11, 1980	Knoxville, Tn	Ky	Dec 23, 1907	72	Moles, Mary	Burns, Judson Isaac		Paddy, Hannah Elizabeth		Cole, Willa Dean - Moles, Jennie - Alfred	Hill Grove - Leitchfield, Ky					Hudson, Bobby Lee
Burton, Charles Wayne	Feb 7, 1991	S.M.M.C.	Tn	Mar 16, 1940	50	Div	Burton, Dorasy		Ealy, Evelyn		Burton, Evelyn E. [Mother]	J.M.G.	unk				
Burton, Henry Lyman	Jun 22, 1980	Jeff Co	Ga	May 5, 1990	60	W	Burton, W.T.		Brannan, Laura		Burton, W.H. - Hudson, Robbie Lee [Otts]	Coolsville, Ga					
Burton, Hugh Dorsey	Nov 14, 1975	Jeff City	Ga	Jun 29, 1916	59	W	Burton, Charlie		Ellenburg, Cornelia		Burton, Mrs. Dorsey	Jefferson Memorial					
Burton, William Henry	Oct 30, 1994	Jeff City	Cattersville, Ga.	Nov 30, 1924	69	Gass, Helen	Burton, Henry Lyman		Tomlison, Lucille		Wife	J.M.G.	43-46	Harry Steven-William Berry			
Bussell, Victoria	Jun 6, 1955	Granger Co.	Tn	May 3, 1852	83	Bussell, John	Morley, Wilson	Tn	Watson, Tamer		Bussell, John-Stalnworth, H.P.	Sunrise					
Butcher, Harold Edgar	Jun 13, 1954	Campbell Co, Tn	Tn	Nov 6, 1924	29	S	Butcher, Hebert E.		Davis, Lillis	Tn	Butcher, Mrs. H.E.	Pleasant View					
Butcher, Hubert Edgar	Aug 24, 1951	Knox Co	Union Co, Tn	Mar 20, 1893	58	Ng	Butcher, Daad		Jessee, Rebecca		Butcher, Mrs. H.E.	Pleasant View	WW 1				
Butcher, Lillie Nola	Feb 19, 1988	Breckenridge, Texas		Dec 2, 1898	89	W					Jones, Marion Butcher [TX] - Mershan F.H. [TX]	Pleasant View - Maynardville, Tn					
Butler, Eula	Apr 15, 1980	New Market, Tn	Tn	Mar 16, 1899	91	W	Otey, John M.		Hale, Margaret M.		Mc Kinney, Margaret - Ousriook, Dean	West View					

NAME	DDATE	BLOCAT	BLOCAT	BDATE	AGE	SPOUSE	FATHER	FBLOCAT	MOTHER	MFBLOCAT	BY	BURIAL	VET	SON	DAUG	BROTHER	SISTER
Butler, George Otis	Apr 5, 1982	Jeff Co	Tn	Jan 10, 1890	72	Ng	Butler, George G.		Robertson, Emma Lee		Butler, Mrs. George (Elsie)	West View					
Butler, Janis Gayle [F]	Jan 25, 1946	Jeff Co		Dec 15, 1945	1m		Butler, Betheil Hardin	Ky	Kennedy, Martha Louisa	Tn	Butler, Mrs. B.H.	Strawberry Plains					
Buedner?, James H.	Sep 6, 1925				55-10-17	W	Buedner, R.B.	Tn		Tn	Russell, L.F - Luttrell, Unk.	Greenwood					
Byers, Steven Andrew	Sep 19, 1987	Phillipines		Jul 28, 1968	19	S	Byers, James		Stotzfus, Irene		Stotzfus, Agnus E - Byers, Irene (St. Pete, Fla.)						
Byram, James Merton Jr.	Nov 4, 1983	J.M.H. (Rsle Ne)	Nc	Jan 15, 1935	48	Lowry, Cserolyn	Byram, James M. Sr.		Brooks, Virginia		Byram, Carolyn - Grace F.H. (Asheville, Nc)	Haruing Baptist - Chandler, Nc	none				
Byrd, Ada Rae Anderson	Aug 18, 1983					Byrd, Bill					Boyer-Van Worner-Scott F.H. (Toledo, Ohio) - Byrd, Bill - Van Worner, Roger	West View					
Byrd, Eula Frances	Mar 14, 1985	Humana Hosp.	Tn	July 8, 1917	67	S	Byrd, John Joe		Newman, Leona		Byrd, Kenneth L. (Indianapolis, Ind.)	West View					
Byrd, John Ellis	Nov 3, 1968	New Orleans, La	Tn	Jan 25, 1911	57	Div	Byrd, Newton		Leslie, Francis		Byrd, Ruby	West View	WW 2				
Byrd, John Joe	Mar 9-19, 1947	Grainger Co	Tn	Oct 9, 1889	77-5-9	Div	Unk		Unk		Newman, Leona						
Byrd, John Milton	Sep 26, 1983	Hamblen Co	Tn	Jul 17, 1911	52	Div	Byrd, John Joe		Newman, Leona		Byrd, Kenneth	West View					
Byrd, Lola	May 23, 1956	Jeff Co	Tn	Jul 17, 1911	72	Byrd, John Joe [J]	Byrd, John Joe				Roach, Mrs. Horace-Milton-Mc Craig-Kennett-Frank-Ruth-Frances	West View					
Byrd, Nelson T.	Feb 13, 1987	Ridgeview Terrace N. Home	Tn	Feb 13, 1904	83	W	Byrd, Dave		Mc Daniel, Jane		Byrd, Glenda L.	Buffalo Baptist					
Byrd, Ruth Irene	Feb 7, 1975	Cook Co.	Tn	July 16, 1914	61	S	Byrd, John Joe		Newman, Leona	Tn	Byrd, Frances	West View					
Byrd, Sarah	Jan 10, 1932	Grainger Co	Tn	Jan 8, 1929	2		Byrd, Jim	Tn	Phillips, Hattie		Byrd, Jim L.	Shiio					
Byrd, Victor Mc Coy	Apr 27, 1987	Durham, Nc	Tn	Dec 23, 1920	46	Div	Byrd, John Joe		Newman, Leona		Crockett, Jim & Francis (Patricia)	West View	WW 2				
Cabbage, Loran Paris	Jan 10, 1948	Grainger Co	Tn	Jul 1, 1902	45	Ng	Cabbage, J.L.	Tn	Capps, Ollie	Tn	Cabbage, Mrs. Harriet	West View					
Cadle, Alfred James	Sep 20, 1971	Jeff Co	Tn	Mar 17, 1915	56	Herron, Ruth	Cadle, James T.		Herzt, Melissa		Cadle, Mrs. Ruth H. - Cameron, George - ???ton, Wendell	Memorial Gardens					
Cadle, Darrell Glenn	Jun 14, 1959	Knox Co	Tn		3		Cadle, Billy		Bible, ---		Cadle, Billie	Memorial Gardens					
Cadle, Hattie	Aug 18, 1979	Jeff City	Ky	Mar 2, 1909	70	W	Cox, Elijah		Brock, Lula		Cadle, Mrs. Willard - Cadle, Billy	Jefferson Memorial					
Cadle, Willard H.	Jun 11, 1959	Jeff Co			64	Hattie C.	Cadle, Walter				Cadle, Mrs. Willard - Feror, Walter	Jeff Memorial					
Cain, Carl Edgar	Feb 21, 1966	Mascot, Tn	Tn	May 19, 1910	57	Ng	Cain, Jacob		Oxidier, Cora		Cain, Mrs. Hazel Bailes	Nanci's Grove	WW 2				
Cain, Evelyn Ann	May 15, 1946	Jeff Co	Jeff Co	Jan 7, 1942	S		Cain, Roy	Tn	Sellers, Irene	Tn	Cain, Irene & Edd	Friends Station					
Cain, Gary	May 15, 1946	Jeff Co	Jeff Co	Sept 2, 1940	S		Cain, Roy	Tn	Sellers, Irene	Tn	Cain, Irene & Edd	Friends Station					
Cain, Innis Edd	Aug 8, 1946	Knox Co	Corbin, Ky	Oct 5, 1871	64	Ng	Cain, Dan	Ky	Hall, Jennie	Ky	Cain, Mrs. Rebecca	Friends Station					
Cain, Jacob Willis	Jan 29, 1947	Jeff Co		Jul 19, 1928	18-6-10	S	Oak Paul		Davis, Nellie	Tn	Cain, Irene & Edd	Trent					
Cain, Judy Cornelia	Feb 28, 1957	Straw Plains		Dec 23, 1956	2m		Cain, Ralph Jr.		Young, Lula Mae		Cain, Ralph Jr.	Love					
Cain, Rebecca Jane	Apr 4, 1989	New Market, Tn	Tn	Sep 6, 1862	86	W	Elmore, Mitchell		Tucker, Lula Ann		Cain, Ruby						
Cain, Roy	May 15, 1946	Jeff Co	Tn	Jul 20, 1916		Ng	Cain, Edd	Tn	Elmore, Rebecca	Tn	Friends Station	West View					
Calhoon, Noah	Feb 14, 1928	Jeff Co	Va			Ng	Calhoon, L.?	Tn	Hapner, Barby	Va	Calhoon, T.A & Harold (Son)	West View					
Caldwell, Mauda Wagner	Oct 20, 1954	Knoxville, Tn	Tn	Dec 23, 1893	70		Caldwell, Dr. J.M.		Hawkins, Susan E.		Caldwell, Dr. T.A.	West View					
Caldwell, Adra Cate	Jul 21, 1943		Tn	Feb 25, 1860	87	W	Cate, ---		Johnson, Mary		Caldwell, David M.	New Market					
Caldwell, Fred C.	Nov 17, 1957	Knox Co	Tn	Feb 25, 1880	72		Caldwell, Anderson		Chincrlow, Margot		Caldwell, Ralph	Lebanon					
Caldwell, James W.	Oct 2, 1935		Tn	Jul 22, 1863	72		Caldwell, Fred		Chincrlow, Margot		Garrett	New Market					
Caldwell, Mrs. Fred	May 6, 1957	Knoxville	Tn	May 21, 1883	53	Caldwell, Fred	Cooper, T.F.	Tn	Gillis, Mary	Tn		New Market					

NAME	DDATE	BLDCAT	BLDCAT	DDATE	AGE	SPOUSE	FATHER	FBLOCAT	MOTHER	MFBLOCAT	BY	BURIAL	VET	SON	DAUG	BROTHER	SISTER
Caldwell, Stella	Dec 19, 1965	Jeff Co	Tn	Apr 8, 1885	80	Ng	Blackburn, W.W.		Miller, Harriet		Caldwell, T.A.-Ralph-Fred C.	New Market					
Caldwell, Turner Anderson	Nov 14, 1970	Jeff Co	Tn	Jun 28, 1892	77	W	Caldwell, John M.		Cate, Adra		Caldwell, John D. & Harold	Beaver Creek					
Caley, Maude Minniebelle	Oct 30, 1941	Jeff Co			41-5-16	Caley, Henry				Jeff Co	Caley, James- Smith, Mary Elizabeth	Buffalo Grove					
Callies, James	Oct 8, 1948	Jeff Co [Res-NJ]	New Jersey		9m	Ng	Callies, James Sr.	Tn	Smith, Mary Elizabeth		Callies, Mrs. James - Smith, M.C.	Buffalo Grove					
Callihan, Roy Lee	Dec 29, 1987	J.M.H.	Ky	Feb 10, 1915	72	Ng	Callihan, Daniel Boone		Aldridge, Ethel		Callihan, Barbara Ann-Vandek F.H. [Corbin, Ky]	Buffalo Grove					
Calloway, Lucy M.	Jul 31, 1931	New Market	Tn	May 24, 1908	23	S	Calloway, William	Tn	Byrley, Ida E.	Tn	Calloway, William	Narod's Grove					
Callette, J.A.	Aug 8, 1955	Talbotts	Tn	Jul 1, 1897	58	Ng	Callette, J.W.	Tn	Moore, Mary Mollie	Tn	Callette, J.W.	Mt. Pleasant					
Callies, Louise	May 19, 1936	Jeff Co	Augusta, Ga	Oct 11, 1874	51-7-8	Ng	Moore, Isaac	Va	Reed, Emmahiah	Va	Calley, Julia Howell, Mrs. Edward - Calloway, Bill	Mt. Horeb					
Calloway, Idis E.	Mar 8, 1956	New Market	Tn	Jul 21, 1872	83	W	Byerly, James		Stripe, Mary	Tn	Calloway, W.F.-Joe-Hugh-John - Winyard, Mrs. P.E. [Children]	Narod's Grove					
Calloway, Lissie	Oct 10, 1945	Grainger Co	Grainger Co	May 11, 1865	80	W	Mitchell, Isaac	Tn			Calloway, Sokor-John & Alma, Allie - Children	Indian Ridge					
Calloway, Mary Edna	Feb 14, 1966	Jeff Co	Tn	Apr 10, 1866	69	Ng	Davis, Homer T.		Byrley, Lois			Memorial Gardens					
Calloway, Annie Lou	Feb 25, 1976	Jeff Co	Tn	Aug 22, 1902	73	S	Cameron, War E.		Knowling, Lizzie		Gann, Amanda	Mt. View					
Cameron, Bertie Mae	Nov 11, 1983	Tn	Tn	Aug 23, 1889	94	W	Cox, La Roy		Bates, Allsia		Gibbons, Mrs. Marcella	Jefferson Memorial					
Cameron, Clara	Jan 27, 1982	J.M.H.	Tn	May 16, 1925	56	W	Cox, Joseph E.		Barbee, Louella		Maw, Laura Belle - Cameron, Bobby	West View					
Cameron, Clarence Calloway	Nov 19, 1948	Jeff Co	Tn	Nov 16, 1948		Ng	Cameron, Hugh	Tn	Howell, Eula Mae	Tn	Rick, Mrs. W.	New Market					
Cameron, Dale A.	Mar 6, 2000	Dandridge, Tn	Tn	Mar 5, 1941	59	Div			Whitaker, Claren [Doug]		Whitaker, Claren [Doug] Wife	J.M.G.	unk				
Cameron, Dee	Apr 6, 2000	Talbott, Tn	Tn	Mar 14, 1933	67	Lancaster, Opal L.	Cameron, Charles		Cameron, Ida		Sartain Springs		Army				
Cameron, Grace	Feb 5, 1929	Tn	Tn		20-4-19	Cameron, A.C.	Walker, Noble	Tn		Tn	Cameron, ?	West View					
Cameron, Harmon Lindy [M]	Mar 17, 1957	Tn	Tn	Jul 18, 1935	21	S	Cameron, Thurman				Cameron, T.H.	Ebenezer					
Cameron, Harold Gene	Jan 4, 1996	Jeff City	Grainger Co	Sep 28, 1942	52	Cline, Mary Ruth	Cameron, Roscoe		McElhiney, Elsie		Wife	J.M.G.	709	[Step] Kelley, Wesley	Greentree, Patty - Burnett, Cindy [Colo.] - Dockins, Sandra	Robert-Miller	Roach, Nancy - Greentree, Marine
Cameron, Infant Male	Jul 27, 1948	Jeff Co	Tn	Jul 26, 1947	12 hours	Ng	Cameron, Simmie	Tn	Newman, Elizabeth		Cameron, Porter	Mt. Pleasant					
Cameron, J.W.	Oct 11, 1935	Jeff Co	Tn	Oct 30, 1883	51	W	Miller, James		Cameron, Esther		Cameron, Simmie	Mt. Pleasant					
Cameron, James Miller	Aug 28, 1950	Jeff Co	Tn	Nov 25, 1948	11	Ng	Cameron, Frank	Tn	Cameron, Esther		Hammer, Mrs. Dennis [Myra]	Mt. Pleasant					
Cameron, James Nelson	Feb 15, 1990	Morristown, Tn	Jeff Co	Jun 30, 1941	48	Div	Cameron, Robert F.		Senter, Rosa Lee		Hammer, Mrs. Dennis [Myra]	Lebanon Church					
Cameron, Jessie Margaret	Oct 21, 1965	Jeff Co	Tn	Sep 26, 1901	64	W	McClenaham, Robert		Pendergrass, Martha		Prince, Mrs. Gordon - Stinnett, B. - Newman, Carol - Phelgar, Mrs.	West View					
Cameron, Joseph T.	Aug 8, 1948	Jeff Co	Grainger Co	Sep 9, 1879	68-10-10	Ng	Cameron, Alexander		McGee, Elizabeth	Tn	Cameron, Mrs. Jessie	West View					
Cameron, Lon C.	Mar 7, 1957	Jeff Co	Tn	Apr 12, 1895	60-10-25	W	Cameron, Robert Franklin		Newman, Betty		Edwards, Mrs. Hrbert [Wanda]	Mt. Olive	WW 1				
Cameron, Lydia Loraine	Aug 23, 1926	Tn	Tn		4-4-28	S	Cameron, J.W.	Tn	Cameron, J.W.	Tn	Cameron, J.W.	Mt. Pleasant					
Cameron, Lyntberg	May 16, 1931	Jeff Co	Tn	Jun 22, 1900	104	Cameron, Porter [D]	Cameron, Porter		Gilbert, Martha	Va	Cameron, Porter	Mt. Pleasant					
Cameron, Martha	Apr 30, 1999	Jeff Co	Tn	Jul 18, 1896	82	Cameron, Porter [D]	Gilbert, Simmie		Duty, Margaret		Gionne, Mrs. Amanda - Cameron, Simmie	Ebenezer					
Cameron, Mary Lusty	Jul 29, 1969	Jeff Co	Tn	Dec 10, 1898	70	Cameron, W.E. [D]	Boruff, Mack Henry		Bellinger, Sarah	Tn	Cox, Mrs. Hall	Mt View					
Cameron, Nannie Mai	Apr 19, 1996	Tn	Tn	Feb 10, 1879	57	Cameron, J.L.	Barbee, T.		Nolen, Elizabeth		Cameron, J.T.	Mt Springs					
Cameron, Porter Jarragan	Oct 17, 1951	Jeff Co	Tn	Feb 5, 1882	69	Ng	Cameron, William E.		Cameron, Rosa		Cameron, Thurman	Ebenezer					
Cameron, R.B.	Jul 25, 1975	Jeff Co	Tn	Jun 3, 1932	43	S	Cameron, Lee		Cameron, Rosa		Quinn, Willy Mae	Mt. Pleasant					

NAME	DDATE	DLOCAT	BLOCAT	BDATE	AGE	SPOUSE	FATHER	FBLOCAT	MOTHER	MFBLOCAT	BY	BURIAL	VET	SON	DAUG	BROTHER	SISTER
Cameron, Raymond Sr.	Aug 25, 1983	U.T.H.	Tn	Jul 18, 1919	64	Virginia	Cameron, Joseph		Livingston, Pearl		Cameron, Mrs. Virginia	Jefferson Memorial					
Cameron, Robert [Ted]	Jul 7, 1989	Morristown, Tn	Tn	Oct 31, 1914	74	Senter, Rosie	Cameron, William		Cox, Bertie		Cameron, Rosie S.	J.M.G.					
Cameron, Ross	Mar 16, 1976	Jeff Co	Tn	Mar , 1895		W	Cameron, Ward E.		Oulin, Mrs. Willie Mae		Knowling, Lizzie	Mt. Pleasant					
Cameron, Thurman H.	Apr 24, 1981	Morristown, Tn	Tn	Jun 21, 1914	66	Mc Millian, Marie	Cameron, Porter J.		Gilbert, Martha J.		Cameron, Lawrence	Ebenezer					
Cameron, War Edgar	Jan 1, 1971	Jeff Co	Tn	Ay 5, 1900	70	W	Cameron, War Sr.		Nolen, Elizabeth		Cox, Hal - Dody, George - Foster, Thelma - Cameron, J.M. & Edward	Mt. View					
Cameron, William Ben	Sep 18, 1949	Jeff Co	Tn	Jun 12, 1884	65	Ng	Cameron, Ward		Smith, Sadie		Cameron, S.G. - L.J. - Hugh - Vaughn - Mrs. W.B. (Hessie)	Flat Creek - Knox Co					
Campbell, Andrew Joshua	Dec 14, 2000	Knoxville, Tn	Md	Dec 12, 1982	38	Ng	Campbell, James		Auer, Florine		Mother	Cremated	unk				
Campbell, Beulah	Apr 18, 1947	Oak Ridge, Tn	Jeff Co	1911	36	Ng	Pitts, Charlie	Tn	Murry, Mattie	Tn	Campbell, Porter (Husband)	Flat Gap					
Campbell, Edgar Scott	Jun 14, 1986	S.M.H.	Tn	Jul 22, 1913	72	Odom, Christine	Campbell, Mech H.		Mills, Lillie		Campbell, Mrs. Edgar	Everlasting Life - J.M.G.					
Campbell, Eva Delora	Dec 18, 1998	New Market, Tn		Oct 5, 1910	88	Ng	Campbell, Mech H.		Weidner, Nancy		Underwood, Jean (Niece)	Piedmont					
Campbell, Frank M.	Apr 30, 1965	Jeff Co	Ga	Oct 18, 1914	50	Ng	Campbell, W.L.		Reinhardt, Madge		Campbell, Mrs. Frank - J.D.-Wallis - Williams, Anderson - Ringold, Ga	Lynnhurst	WW 2				
Campbell, Howard Washington	Sep 2, 1945	Jeff Co	Jeff Co	May 4, 1874	71	Ng	Campbell, Jess	Tn	Bales, Nancy	Secker Co	Campbell, Hodge	Lynnhurst					
Campbell, Jay C.	Jan 31, 1985	Jeff Co	Knox Co	Feb 7, 1915	79	Quinn, Lula	Campbell, William		Parks, Alta		Campbell, Wayne (Son)	New Market					
Campbell, Jeremy Scott	Feb 22, 1994	Morristown, Tn	Morristown, Tn	Feb 22, 1994			Campbell, Hence Edward		Bowling, Yolanda		Father - Bowling, Denver - Campbell, Hence & Phyllis [G-Parents], Campbell, Wr [Son]	West View				Blythe, David Jr.	Barnett, Brittany McNelle
Campbell, Lula Irene	Jan 4, 2000	Jeff City		Feb 10, 1910	89	W	Widener, John	Va	Ferris, Wayne	Va	New Market	Piedmont					
Campbell, Nancy Jane	Sep 16, 1943	Va Washington Co, Tn		Jul 11, 1874	69	Campbell, S.A.	Basletin, John	Tn	Rogers, Lillian	Tn	Campbell, R.K.	Fairview - Washington Co					
Campbell, Ruby Nell	Apr 14, 1944	Jeff Co		Jun 21, 1904	39	Campbell, Russell K	Campbell, Hugh		Mack, Link		Campbell, Edgar-Earl-Eva - Jarnigan, Mrs. Ora	Piedmont					
Campbell, Sanford A.	Jan 18, 1964	Jeff Co	Nc	Aug 17, 1873	92	W	Campbell, Hugh		Mack, Link		Campbell, E.C.- Bailey, Gertie - Morgan, Judy	Piedmont					
Campbell, William P.	Sep 1, 1958	Jeff Co	Tn	May 6, 1873	85	Ng	Campbell, Joe		Sellers, Mary		Bailey, Gertie - Morgan, Judy	Trentville - Knox Co					
Campbell, Benjamin F.	Jul 17, 1979	Jeff City	Tn	Jul 23, 1979	87-11-24	Div	Cameron, Thomas		Newman, Margaret		Bacon, Mildred - Cameron, Charles	Lebanon					
Cannon, Charles W.	Feb 28, 1996	Knoxville, Tn	Jeff Co	Feb 24, 1917	79	Franklin, Mary Violet	Cannon, Benjamin F.		Grant, Hulda		Nanney, Charlotte [Daug]	Lebanon Presby.		Gary	Province, Mary - Florence - Burnette, Joy - [In-Law] Ogle, Ann		
Cannon, Clifford	Jun 19, 1941	Alpha, Tn	Hamblen Co	23-6-18		Hale, Francis			McGitauney ?, Willie Belle	Tn	Cannon, Mrs. John S.						
Cannon, Daisy Mills	Feb 15, 1973	Jeff Co	Tn	Jul 2, 1906	67	Cannon, Tommy	Mills, Doc		Strange, Thera		Cannon, Tommy	Lenoir					
Cannon, Earl Tommie	Aug 30, 1983	J.M.H.	Tn	May 10, 1910	73	Cannon, Margie	Cannon, Arthur		Lindrum, Mary		Cannon, Mrs. Margie	Lebanon Presby.					
Cannon, Floyd John	Dec 18, 2000	Talbott, Tn	Tn	Jan 7, 1954	46	Div	Cannon, William Buford		Hill, Lorraine		Warren, Rena [Sister]	J.M.G.					
Cannon, Frank Marion	Apr 25, 1947	Knox Co	Texas	Jun 4, 1899	47-10-21	Ng	Cannon, Frank	New Mexico	Link		Cannon, Mrs. Frank - Newman, John T. - Hensley, T.L. - Cannon, Ray H. - Johnson, Everett	Piney Grove			Providence, Mary - Florence - Burnette, Joy - [In-Law] Ogle, Ann		
Cannon, Geraldine	Jun 7, 1982	J.M.H.	Jeff City	Mar 17, 1939	53	Cannon, Ralph	Glass, Frank L. Sr.		Colley, Donna		Cannon, Mrs. Frank	Lebanon Presby.					
Cannon, H.A.	Dec 21, 1983	Jeff City	Tn	Jun 13, 1982	57	Ng					Husband - J.O.V.	Johnson					
Cannon, Newman A.	Mar 20, 1940	Eastern State			34	S	Cannon, Thomas	Tn	Newman, Tn		Cannon, Tommy	Mt. Hareb					

NAME	DDATE	DLOCAT	BLOCAT	BDATE	AGE	SPOUSE	FATHER	FBLOCAT	MOTHER	MFBLOCAT Y	BY	BURIAL	VET	SON	DAUG	BROTHER	SISTER
Cannon, Hubert Carl	Dec 2, 1950	Mt. Horne, Tn	Tn	July 25, 1915	35	Ng	Cannon, Ben F.		Grant, Hulda		Cannon, Mrs. Violet	Lebanon	WW 2				
Cannon, Mary V.	Jul 20, 1996	Strawberry Plains	Mc-Minn Co.	Mar 19, 1920	76		Franklin, Mack B.		Webb, Annie Victoria		Manley, Charlotte [Daug]	Lebanon Presby.		Gary Wayne & Ann Ogle	Providence, Mary - Burnette, Joy		Mt. Spurdeon, Lorena - Hubbell, Gladys - Cline, Lucille
Cannon, Minnie Virginia	Feb 21, 1981	Jeff Co	Va	Jul 6, 1899	81	W	Lawson, Bob		Pruitt, Jenny		Cannon, Roy Harold- Frankie	Piney Grove					
Cannon, Raymond Carl	Aug 19, 1948	Jeff Co	Jeff Co.	Jan 20, 1935	13		Cannon, Earl Tommy	Tn	Mills, Daisy	Tn	Mills, Daisy	Lebanon	715				
Cannon, Roxie Lee	Jan 16, 1948	Hamblen Co.	Hamblen Co	Jun 10, 1922	25	S	Cannon, Ben F.	Tn	Grant, Hulda	Tn	Cannon, Ben F.	Lebanon - Mt. Horeb	658				
Cannon, Tommie Frank	May 15, 1998	Knoxville, Tn	Jeff City	Aug 10, 1958	39		Cannon, Ralph Henry		Gass, Geraldine		Father	Lebanon Presby.		Jackson	Jessika	Joseph - [Step] Creatiive, Mitch	Peoples, Ruth
Cannon, Velma G.	Dec 22, 1988	S.M.H.	Tn	Nov 1, 1919	69	Cannon, Roy H.	Frazier, Fred	Tn	Reed, Sallie	Tn	Cannon, Roy H.	Blue Springs - Straw Plains, Tn					Douglas, Ruth
Cannon, William Buford	Sep 12, 1998	Knoxville, Tn	Niagara Falls, Canada	Mar 12, 1920	68	Ng	Cannon, Carl		Bishop, Nellie B.		Cannon, Lorraine	Jeff Mem					
Card, Robert Howard	Feb 9, 1995	Knoxville, Tn	Tn	Apr 27, 1940	54	Card, Betty	Card, John		Puttick, Nettie		Card, Mary Ann [Daug]	Cremated				Victor [Ontario]	
Cardwell, Pauline M.	Apr 19, 1996	Murry Co, Ga		Apr 9, 1918	78		Kendrick, Sam		Stafford, Della		Cardwell, Robert [Son]	East View- Knox Co.			Branch, Doris		Burton, Donna [Ontario]
Cardwell, Margaret Jo Luttrul	Jul 2, 1998	Hilhaven	Tn	Nov 2, 1921	66	Cantwell, J.L. [DH]	Mullins, William Silas		Mullins, Olive Verena	Tn	Luttrell, William J.	J.M.G.				Glenn-F.M.-Houston	Sherrod, Betty- Bowman, Rosine - Coffey, Jennie Mae - Moore, V.I.
Capps, Hazel Annette	Jul 18, 1944	Jeff Co	Bluff City, Tn	Mar 22, 1910	34	Capps, E.O.	Brewer, Wiley		Stanford, Ellis	Tn	Capps, E.O.	Narod's Grove					
Carathers, George Holley	Nov 22, 1989	J.M.H.		Dec 15, 1913	75	Jones, Ida Mae	Carathers, Newton C.		Malone, Lorma		Carathers, Ida Mae Jones	J.M.G.					
Carathers, Pamela Gail	Feb 18, 1959	Jeff Co	Tn	Feb 18, 1959		S	Carathers, Harold		Ballinger, Helen Lorene		Carathers, Harold	Ballinger					
Carback, Lila H.	Jun 14, 1975	Morristown, Tn	Tn	Sep 27, 1890	84	S	Carback, Oscar W.		Vineyard, Mary Ellen		Lambdin, Mrs. J. Carl	West View					
Carl, Roland H.	Oct 4, 1996	Lewisburg, Pa	Tn	Jan 30, 1910	86	S	Carl, Lee		Coup, Mary		Lambdin, Mrs. J.F.H. [Milton, Pa]	Ballinger	army				
Carlton, Orvilla	Jul 18, 1987	Anchorage, Alaska	Northumberland, Pa	Feb 13, 1920	67	Grace	Carlton, Donnie R. & Grace		Dale Rance F.H.		Carlton, Donnie R. & Grace	J.M.G.					
Carmichael, A.A.	Feb 3, 1931	Jeff City	Tn	Sep 11, 1852	78	Ng	Carmichael, Lemuel	Tn	Miller, Susan	Tn	Carmichael, E.W.	West View					
Carmichael, Ada Lee	Feb 6, 1975	Knoxville, Tn	Tn	Mar 24, 1899	75	S	Carmichael, Thomas A.		Douglas, Lillie		Frazier, Mrs. Inez	West View					
Carmichael, Harry Douglas	Jul 22, 1974	Knoxville, Tn	Tn	Apr 15, 1909	65	Purkey, Ethel	Carmichael, Thomas A.		Douglas, Lillie H.		Carmichael, Mrs. Ethel	Jefferson Memorial					
Carmichael, Lillie H.	Jun 28, 1956	Jeff City	Tn	Mar 21, 1956	80-3-8	Carmichael, T.A. [?]	Douglass, Bollner		Chambers, Nancy		Frazier, Mrs. Frank Carmichael, F.E. [Knoxville]	West View					
Carmichael, Lou	Aug 22, 1936	Jeff City	Tn			Ng	Webb, Jessie		Mullins, Nancy		Carmichael, W.E.- Carmichael, Edd [Knoxville]	West View					
Carmichael, Mary S.	Jul 31, 1931	Jeff City	Tn	May 6, 1859	72	W	Trotter, Mary	Tn	Fagan, Julia	Tn	Crabtree, Mrs. W.E.- Carmichael, W.F.R.	West View					
Carmichael, Mary Vester	Jul 31, 1983	Knoxville, Tn	Tn	Aug 20, 1903	29	S	Carmichael, W.R.	Tn	Yarborough, Celina	Tn	Carmichael, W.F.R.	Sunderland					
Carmichael, Nellie	Nov 15, 1980	Hamblen Co	Tn	May 14, 1887	73	Carmichael, Olen	Britton, George W.		Campbell, Nannie		Britton, Jay	Sunderland					
Carmichael, Olen Alpha [M]	Apr 20, 1955	Jeff City	Tn	Aug 1, 1890	64	Ng	Carmichael, Thomas	Tn	Underwood, Ng	Tn	Carmichael, Mrs. Nellie	Sunderland					
Carmichael, Ruia	Jun 16, 1928		Tn		15-6-28	S	Carmichael, Clas	Tn	Houser, Sallie	Tn	Carmichael	Piedmont					
Carmichael, T.A.	Oct 1, 1928	Tn	Tn	Jul 6, 1868	67	W	Carmichael, William		Bishop, Martha		Carmichael, Kindred	West View					
Carmichael, William	Nov 15, 1935	Piedmont	Tn	Jun 30, 1903	92	W	Carmichael, Kindred	Tn	Eager, Mollie	Tn	Sons	Piedmont					
Carnahan, Cleo [F]	Sep 22, 1995	Jeff City	Harlan, Ky	Jun 30, 1903	92	W	Irvin, Bill		Lassiter, Martha		Lassiter, Opal J. [Daug]	Resthaven - Harlan, Ky					
Carpenter, David L.	Jan 6, 1996	Morristown, Tn	Pine River, Mn	Dec 31, 1922	73	S	Carpenter, Calvin J.		Parks, Minnie		Wille	City - Hunter Town, In.	42-46	Michael-Ron-Dan-Denny-D. Scott-Paul			
Carpenter, Elmer Allen	Jun 16, 1988	J.M.H.	Missouri	Feb 12, 1919	69	Davis, Mary	Carpenter, John		Miller, Ruth		Bales, Lorna	Hebron	WW 2				
Carpenter, Mary	Feb 25, 1984	Knoxville, Tn	Jeff Co	Aug 17, 1926	67	Davis, Ben			Rankin, Estis		Carpenter, Lorna [Daug]	Hebron					Murphy, Betty - Bales, Jackie - [In-Law] Stills, Los

NAME	DDATE	BLOCAT	BLOCAT	BDATE	AGE	SPOUSE	FATHER	FBLOCAT	MOTHER	MBLOCAT	BY	BURIAL	VET	SON	DAUG	BROTHER	SISTER
Carr, Freda Blanc	Mar 3, 1998	J.M.H.	Tn	Jan 1, 1900	96	W			Blanc, Adrian Jr. [Son] Bessie - Robert-Nellie-Jones, Mary-Christman, Sarah [Children]		Carr, William	West View					
Carr, George Bill	Oct 24, 1985	Jeff Co	Tn	Jun 21, 1890	75	Bessie	Carr, Robert		Yoakley, Mary	Granger Co	Sundarland	Sundarland					
Carr, infant	Jan 6, 1942	Ridgeview N.C.		Feb 28, 1892	92	Blanc, Freda West	Kear, Marion		Roach, Bessie		Carr, William	West View	WW 1&2				
Carr, Isaac Newton [Dr.]	Jul 5, 1984	Jeff Co	Indiana	Aug 12, 1942	58	S	Carr, Samuel		Oliver, Bertha		Carr, Marion T. [Columbia, Sc] Miller, Janet [Sister]	Cremated					
Carr, Judith Delnea	Oct 18, 2000	Jeff City		Jul 22, 1999	1	S	Carr, Frank D.		Blanchett, Beatrice		Carr, Frank	Sundarland					
Carr, Lisa	Jul 26, 1956	Jeff City	Tn	Jun 20, 1916	83	W	Corbett, Earnest		Gilliam, Nellie		Carr, Lisa C. [Son]	Mt. View					
Carr, Mary E.	Jan 20, 1951	Jeff Co		Nov 12, 1920	19		Yoakley, Noah		Staffel, Martha		Carr, Bobby E. [Son] Glass, Mrs. Scott	Sundarland					
Carr, Mattie Louise	Aug 25, 1971	Jeff Co	Tn	Feb 16, 1920	50		Riley, George		Riley, Mary C.		Mt. View	Mt. View					
Carr, Otis	Dec 28, 1993	J.M.H.	Swelar Co	Feb 16, 1913	77		Carr, Nicholas		Owsley, Lillis		Carr, Erin B.	Mt. View					
Carr, Robert Lee	Aug 15, 1986	U.T.K.	Tn	Feb 11, 1911	75	Corbett, Lillis		Kear, Nicholas				Carr, Lisa C.	Mt. View				
Carr, Tom	Jan 30, 1982	Jeff Co		Jan 1, 1900	82	Ng	Carr, John		Gilbert, Martha Ann		Carr, Mary W.	State Hill - Hamilton Co					
Carroll, Claude Hammond	Dec 8, 1985	Knoxville, Tn	Tn	Jan 11, 1911	74	W	Carroll, George W.		Simpkins, Ida		Bexler, Margaret - Stansfield, Catherine	Mill Springs					
Carroll, Dudley A.	Jul 15, 1967	Jeff Co	Tn	Dec 24, 1892	84	Ng	Carroll, Dudley A.		Cordia		Carroll, Mrs. D.A. - Jenkins, Ida	Mill Springs					
Carroll, Ida Simpkins	Dec 4, 1974	Knoxville, Tn	Tn	Jan 11, 1892	82	W	Simpkins, Tom		Clevenger, Cordelia		Parker, Mary Lou	Mill Springs					
Carroll, Mae Bessie	Nov 23, 1949	Jeff Co	Tn	Apr 14, 1904	45	Ng	Ballinger, Marrie		Carroll, Clarence		Pleasant Grove					
Carroll, Ross	Apr 22, 1957	Jeff Co	Tn	Apr 16, 1897	60	Ng	Carroll, George W.		Northern, Cordelia		Carroll, Mrs. Pearl	Mill Springs					
Carson, Edward	Jun 27, 1941	Talbott	Tn		1-10	S	Carson, Waywood		Walker, —		Carroll, Capwood	Sundarland					
Carson, Rhonda Michelle	Jul 3, 1971	Talbott, Tn	Tn	Nov 8, 1965	5		Carson, William Roy		Finse, Anna Mae		Carson, William Roy	Sundarland					
Carson, Alice	Aug 18, 1988	Knox Co	Tn	Dec 23, 1892	75	Cate, Edd	Wollensanger, John W.		Nash, Duck		Cate, Clarence & Edd	Memorial Gardens					
Carter, Allen L.	Jun 15, 1996	Granger Co	Tn	Jan 10, 1949	47	Foster, Wanda			Kidwell, Gladys		Wife	New Blackwell Church		Tim & Jamie [Step] Gondrea, Adam & Vickie	Owens, Angali & Don-Shepley, Cox, Vanessa & Darrell		
Carter, Betty Ann	Jan 29, 1940	Talbot Morristown, Tn	Tn	Jul 10, 1951	28	Doele, Linda	Carter, Pryor Lee Sr.	Tn	Elder, Mattie		Carter, Linda	Carter					
Carter, Charles Roger [Black]	Jul 21, 1979	Morristown, Tn	Tn		4		Carter, Jessie					Jefferson Memorial					
Carter, Connedline Alexander	Jul 30, 1947	Jeff Co	Tn	Dec 12, 1924	42	Ng	Carter, Alfred Jackson [Boone]	Monroe Co., Tn	Newman, Sarah		Carter, Paul R.	Wesleya Chapel					
Carter, David Crockett [Col]	Jan 25, 1957	Jeff Co	Tn	Sep 19, 1942		S	Carter, Erlie [Boone]	Alabama	Marris, Mrs. Nellie	Alabama	Carter, Erlie	West View Colored					
Carter, David Erb	Sep 19, 1942	Jeff Co	Tn	Sep 19, 1942	31-8+	S	Carter, E.H.	Tn	Gilliam, Willie Anne	Tn	Carter, Erlie	West View					
Carter, Dorothy	Aug 8, 1925		Tn		16		Carter, Pitch		Gilliam, Ida		Carter, Mrs.	Mt. Pleasant					
Carter, E.H.	Feb 5, 1928	Jeff Co	Tn	Jan 19, 1903	69		Carter, Harvey		Franklin, Julia		Carter, E.H.	Mt. Pleasant					
Carter, Edith Ragel	Mar 4, 1973		Tn	Jan 7, 1929	45	Carter, Harvey	Ragel, W.B.		Harris, Lillie		Carter, Harvey	Mt. Pleasant					
Carter, Ernestine [Negro]	Apr 24, 1974	Morristown, Tn	Tn				Hodge, Carter				Carter, Pryor	Jefferson Memorial					
Carter, Ethel	Jan 18, 1994	Jeff City	Jeff Co	May 28, 1913	80	Carter, Pryor	Pleis, Phess		Wadkins, Carrie		Pleis, Kenneth Edward [Son]	J.M.G.		James Dan-Court-John William	Butler, Marcellite James	[in-Law] Carter, Przyc-Nellie-[Or], Carter, Garris [W, Va]	
Carter, Ethel Minnie	Feb 23rd, 1985	Jeff City	Tn	Jan 17, 1899	96	W	Dills, De Witt		Snyder, Mrs. Maude Carter, Mrs. Floyd [Alice]		Snyder, Mrs. Maude Carter, Mrs. Floyd [Alice]	Piedmont					
Carter, Floyd Monroe	Feb 17, 1951	Knoxville, Tn	Oklahoma	Jan 28, 1913	38	W	Carter, William S.		Strait, Vina		West View	West View					
Carter, Harvey R.	Feb 23, 1977	Hillcrest Home	Tn			Ng			Carter, Zelma		Carter, Zelma	Mt. Pleasant					
Carter, Hannalda	Aug 25, 1936		Hillcrest Home	Apr 13, 1853	83		Graham, George W.	Tn	West, Elizabeth	Tn	Yates, J.E. & George	Shiloh					
Carter, James Bataan [Negro]	Sep 18, 1976		Tn	Jul 8, 1913	63	Div	Carter, Silvester		Tatle, Willie		Brown, Jane	West View					
Carter, John [Black]	Jul 10, 1979	Jeff City	Tn	Feb 4, 1915	65	Pitts, Carrie Ellen	Carter, Silvester		Tatle, Willie		Carter, Mrs. Carrie	West View					Edwards, Shelby

NAME	DDATE	DLOCAT	BLOCAT	BDATE	AGE	SPOUSE	FATHER	FELLOCAT	MOTHER	MFSLOCAT	BY	BURIAL	VET	SON	DAUG	BROTHER	SISTER
Carter, John Sr. [Col]	May 12, 1956	Jeff Co	Carter Co., Tn	Sep 25, 1840	115-7-17	W	Unk		Unk		Carter, J.B. Jr.	West View Colored					
Carter, John William	Apr 13, 2000	Knoxville, Tn	Tn	Jul 1, 1951	48	Div	Carter, James B.		Pate, Ethel		Carter, Johnna S. [Daug]	Cremated					
Carter, L.C.	Feb 23, 1998	Jeff City	Ky		abnt 33	Ng					Universal Mines	Mineral Bluff, Ga					
Carter, Lavina Ellen	Dec 19, 1984	Jeff Folly	Tn	Dec 5, 1891	93	W			Johnson, C.B.		Nelson, Mrs. Verna	West View					
Carter, Mack Ernest	Jul 25, 1956	Jeff Co	Tn	Oct 2, 1892	63	S	Carter, George M.		Newman, Sarah C.		Carter, Mrs. G. -Roy - Smith, Mrs.	Wesleys Chapel Colored	WW 1				
Carter, Melonda [Col]	Apr 30, 1934	Jeff City										Colored					
Carter, Melodore Duncan [M]	Apr 16, 1966	Tn	Tn	Jul 14, 1872	93	Ng	Carter, Henry		Wright, Mary		Carter, Paul - Kitn, Mrs. - Purkey, Mrs.	Jefferson Memorial					
Carter, Mattie Roger [Col]	Apr 6, 1955	Jeff Co	Tn	Feb 7, 1928	27	Ng	Ehlers, Charlie		Smith, Gertrude		Carter, Pryor	West View Colored					
Carter, Minnie Florence	Aug 5, 1970	Jeff Co	Tn	Sep 17, 1877	92	W	Marr, John		Harmon, Mary		Carter, Paul-Claudule - Purkey, Willie	Memorial Gardens					
Carter, Ossie	Apr 27, 1967	Jeff City	Greene Co, Tn	Dec 10, 1906	88	Ng	Carter, M.D.		Marr, Minnie		Purkey, Willis Belle [Sister]	J.M.G.		1		Byrl	
Carter, Paul Isaac	Jan 26, 1982	Morristown, Tn	Tn	Aug 31, 1919	62	Ng	Carter, M.D.		Marr, Minnie		Carter, Mrs. Lois Smith	Jefferson Memorial					
Carter, Pryor Lee [Black]	Feb 9, 1998	Jeff City	Jeff City	Apr 2, 1919	78		Carter, Sylvester		Tate, Willis		Bowen, Willie Elizabeth Ann	J.M.G.		Jackie			Morris, Nellie
Carter, Sylvester [Col]	Aug 5, 1983	J.M.H.	Tn	Feb 27, 1950	33	Carter, Willie	Etter, Mattie Roger	Tn	Carter, Mrs. Tawana A.	veteran	Jefferson Memorial	veteran				
Carter, William S.	Mar 19, 1954	Jeff Co	Tn	Jul 5, 1883	70	Ng	Carter, George M.		Newman, Sarah C.		Carter, Mrs. W.S. [Lavina]	West View					
Carter, Willis [Col]	Oct 28, 1944	Jeff Co	Tn	Oct 1, 1890	54	W	Tate, John	Tn	Moore, Jane	Tn	Morris, Nellie	Colore					
Carter, Sarah Katherine	Sep 26, 1956	Tn	Tn	Dec 14, 1859	97	W	Newman, Aaron		Puckett, Nancy		Miller, Mrs. G.C. [Ruth]	Wesleys Chapel					
Cart, Gary	Dec -, 1979	Jeff City [Ree Ky]			45						Justice F.H. [Pikeville, Ky]						
Carver, Terry Wayne	Jan 25, 1996	Greer, Sc	Wayensville, Nc	Sep 17, 1951	44	W	Carver, Jack		Reagan, Pearl		Wife	Karr-Loveday					
Carver, Allie Ruth	Oct 30, 2000	Jeff City	Tn	Nov 23, 1929	70	Scates, Brenda	Henderson, Jasper		Mills, Lillie Mae		Husband	Hills Union-Dandridge, Tn					
Case, Charlie	N	Mar 2, 1982	Nashville, Tn	Tn	77	Case, John Henry	Pressley, Rachael		Pressley, Rachael		Case, Edward [Nashville, Tn]	Friends Station					
Case, John Henry	Nov 19, 1958	Jeff Co	Tn	Jun 15, 1911	47	Ng	Riley, Elbert		Pressley, Rachael		Case, John Henry	Riley, Elbert					
Case, Johnny Ray	Jan 3, 1944	Jeff Co	Tn	Jan 3, 1944			Case, Raymond	Tn	Riley, Sarah A.	Tn	Corbett, Mary Lillie	Case, Raymond J R.	West View				
Case, Mary Lillie	Oct 13, 1983	Knoxville, Tn	Tn	Dec 2, 1904	98	W	Corbett, John		Knight, Onnie		Case, Raymond	West View					
Case, Raymond Riley	Jan 28, 1993	Knoxville, Tn	Jeff Co	Aug 3, 1917	75	Case, Brenda	Case, Luther		Riley, Sarah		Walker, Agnes [Daug]	West View	Army	Dale		Paul-Bob-Bill	Boatman, Stella - Rinehart, Mary
Case, Sarah Ann	Sep 16, 1971	Jeff Co	Tn	Aug 16, 1892	79	W	Riley, Nathan		Murray, Rachael		Rinehart, Mary - Boatman, Mrs. - Stelle - Mary-[Song] Raymond - Paul-Bill-Robert	West View					
Case, Vivan Bernice	Sep 17, 1972	Hamblen Co		Sep 17, 1972		Ng	Case, Floyd William		Lofland, Helen Beckey		Case, Lloyd	Franklin - Jeff Co					
Case, William Luther	Dec 17, 1983	Jeff City	Tn	Jun 19, 1888	75	Ng	Case, Henry		Pressley, Rachael		Case, Mrs. Sarah Riley	West View					
Case, Jewel Dean	Dec 11, 1942	Jeff City	Tn	Jul 22, 1942			Case, Raymond	Tn	Stallings, Lillie	Tn	Case, Raymond & W.L.	West View					
Cate, Alice Elizabeth	Apr 29, 1976	Jeff City	Tn	Oct 19, 1891	84	W	Langston, John Wesley		Shellings, Arie		Smith, Willis E. Jr.	Pleasant Grove					
Cate, Alma Luzernia	Dec 22, 1944	Spartanburg Co, Sc		Nov 1, 1907	37	Cate, Hollis	Steele, M.W.		Purkey, Bertha B.		Cate, Hollis - Steele, M.W. - Smith, Mrs. Edd - Smith, Harmer - Cate, Mrs. William	Beaver Creek					
Cate, Barbara Jean	Mar 5, 1956	Jeff City	Tn	Mar 5, 1956		Cate, Hollis	Cate, Roy H.	Hancock Co	Mc Campbell, Vennie	Claiborne Co	Cate, Roy H.	Mc Campbells Chapel					

NAME	DDATE	DLOCAT	BLOCAT	BDATE	AGE	SPOUSE	FATHER	FELOCAT	MOTHER	MFELOCAT	BY	BURIAL	VET	SON	DAUG	BROTHER	SISTER
Cate, Beryl Genome	Jan 20, 1939	Jeff Co	Tn	Aug 30, 1918	20	Ng	Cate, William M	Tn	Lindsey, Mien Leona	Tn	Cate, William & Mrs. Grace F.	Pleasant Grove					
Cate, Charles Tilman (Fuzz)	Nov 10, 1985	Orlando, Fla.	Tn	Dec 31, 1951	33	Morrison, Debbie	Cate, Tilman Jr.		Hancock, Helen		Cate, Tilman S. Jr.	Cate - Jeff Co					
Cate, Earl	Jul 10, 1983	Knoxville, Tn	Tn	Mar 18, 1890	93	W	Cate, George Alvin		Young, Mrs. Mary Ruth Cate		Young, Mrs. Mary Ruth Cate	Jefferson Memorial					
Cate, Edith Gertrude	Jan 28, 1990	E.T.B.H. Humana Hosp.	Knox Co, Tn	May 2, 1904	85	W	Reed, James		Hunt, Elizabeth Augusta		Reed	Pleasant Grove (Piney)					
Cate, Euia B.	Sep 5, 1988	Tn	Tn	Sep 27, 1905	82	W	Bisko, John D.		Richard, Elzieah Cate		Jones, Mary Cate	Buffalo Grove					
Cate, George Zinkle	Jun 28, 1956	Jeff Co	Tn	Aug 12, 1909	46	S	Cate, W.J.		Jernigam, Rachael		Phillips, Mrs. Ivei Mae - Hall, Mrs. Esther T.; Phillips, Mrs. Ivei Mae -	Buffalo					
Cate, Hallie Freeman	Mar 8, 1983	Jeff Co	Tn	Sep 18, 1905	57	W	Cate, Sam		Underwood, Crillie		Cate, Hugh E.	Beaver Creek					
Cate, Horace	Nov 4, 1934	Tn	Tn	Mar 3, 1882		S	Cate, W.L.	Tn	Underwood, Cattie		Stansberry, George	West View					
Cate, Hugh Edward	Mar 22, 1993	Jeff City	Tn	Dec 9, 1929	63	Silver, Clara	Cate, Hollis		Saul, Anna		Stansberry, George	J.M.G.		Martin Hugh	Frisir, Sharon - Snodgrass, Bethany	
Cate, I.M.	Aug 15, 1934	Jeff City	Tn	May 13, 1850	84	Ng	Cate, Perry	Tn	Underwood, Sallie	Tn	Family	West View					
Cate, Infant Mae	Jul 10, 1987	Knox Co	Knox Co	May 10, 1987		W	Cate, Clarence H.		Floyd, Joyce		Cate - Jeff Co	Cate - Jeff Co					
Cate, James Floyd	Feb 28, 1981	U.T.H.	Tn	Sep 12, 1893	87	Howard, Nettie Mae			Hamilton, Mrs. Mary-Knox Co		Hamilton, Mrs. Mary- J.F. Knox Co	Highland Memorial - Knox Co	890				
Cate, Jason Howard	Nov 1, 1974	U.T.H.		Oct 28, 1974	18 h		Cate, Kenneth		Howard, Alice Ann		Cate, Mrs. J.F.	Jefferson Memorial					
Cate, Lydia Mae	Aug 5, 1926				18-1-20	S		Texas	Atchley, Nettie	Tn	Cate, Kenneth	Alder Branch					
Cate, Martin Hugh	Oct 13, 1988	Jeff City	Jeff City	Jun 22, 1956	32	Holt, Melissa	Cate, Hugh E.		Silver, Clara		Wife	J.M.G.					Frisir, Sharon & Tom - Snodgrass, Bethany & Scott
Cate, Millie	Apr 11, 1936	Jeff City	Tn	May 26, 1851	84	W	Thomas, J.	Tn	Dexton, Mary		Wife	Jeff City					
Cate, Narcissus Ellis	Aug 30, 1906		Tn	Apr 9, 1832	74	W	Ellis, Samuel L.		Randle, Nancy Angeline		West View	West View					
Cate, Nettie Mae	Feb 5, 1983	U.T.H.	Tn	Oct 28, 1893	89	W	Howard, Napoleon		Bellinger, Ida		Hamilton, Mrs. Mary C. - Knox Co	Highland Memorial - Knox Co					
Cate, Ruby	Dec 19, 1990	Hilltaven	Tn	Oct 18, 1907	83	W	Bisley, William P.		Groech, Minnie		Snodsmly, Mildred (Sister)	Piedmont					
Cate, Shana Le Ann	Jun 29, 1983	J.M.H.	Tn	Jun 29, 1983		Ng	Cate, Christopher		Shelton, Doris		Cate, Christopher	Cate - Jeff Co					
Cate, W.L.	May 31, 1931	Jeff City	Tn	Aug 12, 1856	75	W	Cate, Nelson	Tn	Scruggs, Margaret Ann	Tn	Shanks, Eugene	West View					
Cate, William Joel	Apr 20, 1954	Jeff Co	Tn		87	W	Cate, William C.		Phillips, Emmaline		Sheldon, Mrs. Lois	Buffalo Grove					
Cate, Hugh Johnson	Jul 15, 1949		Tn	Oct 18, 1886	49-5-27	Ng	Cate, Wm J.		Jernigam, Rachael	Tn	Cate, Mrs. Euia Blanton	Buffalo Grove					
Cates, Charles T.	Jan 7, 1953	Durham, Nc	Tn	Mar 8, 1896	56	Div.	Cates, Will J.		Franklin, Mrs. Tom		Franklin, Mrs. Tom	Buffalo Grove					
Cates, Elizabeth	Apr 11, 1953	Durham, Nc	Tn		54	W	Bettis, Wade		Jernigam, Rishcpeld		Cates, Charles L Jr.	West View					
Cates, John H.	Jan 12, 1972	Jeff Co	Tn	Aug 5, 1893	78	W	Cates, Allen		Cate, Mrs. Lila		Cate, Mrs. Pearl L. - Cate, Mrs. Pearl L. -	West View	WW 1				
Cates, Tilman Swain	Jan 12, 1950	Jeff Co	Tn	Nov 10, 1897	52	Ng	Cates, Jesse T.		Odoms, Martha		Cate, Mrs. Eva G.	Bethem Cate					
Cattlet, Barbara Louise	May 3, 1990	Greenville, Tn	Tn	Nov 10, 1911	78	Ng	Denton, E.A.		Chappell, Millie		Farrar, Ruth Denton	J.M.G.					
Cattlet, Ben S.	Apr 16, 1964	Jeff Co	Tn	Oct 31, 1912	51	Denton, Louise	Cattlet, William Henry		Cattlet, Louise		Cattlet, William Henry	Memorial Gardens	WW 2				
Cattlet, Charles A.	Jul 10, 1949	Jeff Co	Sevier Co. Tn	Jan 2, 1898	51	Ng	Cattlet, James M	Tn	Mullendom, Willie		Cattlet, Mrs. Ruby	White Pine					
Cattlet, Dorothy Green	Feb 24, 1925	Danidson Co. Tn	Nov 19, 1890		34	S	Cattlet, W.H.		Munro, Bertie	Tn	Cattlet, C.A.	West View					
Cattlet, Jennifer Leigh	Sep 2, 1982	Jeff City	Jeff City	Aug 9, 1893	10 m	W	Cattlet, C.A. Jr.		Rupp, Betty		Jefferson Memorial	Jefferson Memorial					
Cattlet, Katherine	Sep 28, 1998	U.T. Hospital	Morgan Co. Tn	Sep 18, 1911	87	Ng	Mc Goddrick, George W.		Melhom, Mary		Cattlet, C.A. Jr. (Nephew) Woodlam - Knoxville, Tn	Woodlam - Knoxville, Tn					
Cattlet, Lady Kate	Oct 12, 1999	Jeff City	Sep 25, 1918		81		Allen, Mode		Davis, Pearl		Cattlet, Charles A. Jr. (Cousin); Litton, Ted - Richard (Nephew) - Stanley, Ann Whitney (Niece)	J.M.G.					In-Law] Litton, Mattie Belle - Revello, Julia Cattlet
Cattlet, Mattie H.	Jun 15, 1957	Sevier Co	Nov 14, 1893		74	W	Cattlet, Jim		Mullendom, Willie		Cattlet, Ben S. & Bill	West View					
Cattlet, Rotolyre B. [F]	Nov 12, 1992	Jeff City	Feb 23, 1917		69	W	Ballard, Edwin		Munro, Bertie		Cattlet, Charles A. (Son)	West View				Peck, Bobbie C.	Brantley, Birdie - Cottrell, Ruby
Cawood, Alvis Garfield	Sep 11, 1984	At Home	Tn	Aug 31, 1910	74	Hamlin, Margaret	Cawood, William H. Sr.		Ferguson, Asrah Jane		Cawood, Mrs. A.G.	Jefferson Memorial	WW 2				

NAME	DDATE	DLOCAT	BLOCAT	BDATE	AGE	SPOUSE	FATHER	FBLOCAT	MOTHER	MFBLOCAT	BY	BURIAL	VET	SON	DAUG	BROTHER	SISTER
Chadwick, Edna Asie	Sep 18, 1944	Jeff Co	Granger Co	May 27, 1904	40	W	Neal, Herbert	Ky	Collins, Sarah Ann	Grainger Co T	Neal, Mrs. Sarah & Ellie	Roseberry					
Chamberlain, Lewis Claude	Apr 3, 1963	Knox Co	Tn	Oct 4, 1900			Chamberlain, Lewis Trent		Collins, Barbara		Chamberlain, Lewis T., Bilisy, Bill - Maivert, Lorraine	Mill Springs			Braxton, Shirley - Smith, Betty & Barney		
Chambers, Bryan Jr.	Sep 10, 1939	Jeff Co	Tn	Feb 16, 1926	13	S	Chambers, Bryan Sr.		Gilbert, Alice	Va	Chambers, Bryan Sr.	Lebanon (Greenbrier)					
Chambers, Charles Lee Jr.	Jul 22, 1969	Hamblen Co.	Tn	Jul 23, 1947	21	S	Chambers, Charles Sr.		Cameron, Shenice		Chambers, Charles	Lebanon - Greenbrier					
Chambers, Clarence A.	Jul 18, 1984	Knoxville, Tn	Blount Co., Tn	Jun 27, 1913	81	W	Chambers, Ollie		Stilson, Julia		Wife	Mt. View			Braxton, Shirley - Smith, Betty & Barney	Henry-Robert - W.T.	Wells, Mozelle - Colby, Belle
Chambers, H.C.	Mar 4, 1939	Dandridge	Tn	Mar 3, 1859	80	W	Chambers, Henry	Tn			Chambers, P.L.	Shady Grove					
Chambers, Johnnie Edward	Aug 17, 1932	New Market	Tn	Aug 17, 1932	0		Chambers, G.A.	Tn	Dutton, Minnie Gray	Tn	Chambers, G.A.	Mt. Olive					
Champ, Ashby Gray	Apr 17, 2000	Knoxville, Tn	Tn	Mar 2, 1928	72	Vales, Imogene	Champ, Ashby Lee		Gray, Lexie M.		Wife	J.M.G.	unk				
Champion, Infant Female	May 1, 1960	Morristown, Tn		May 1, 1960			Champion, Rickie		Champion, Rickie		Champion, Rickie	Community Chapel - Talbot, Tn					
Chandler, James Morris	Nov 14, 1985	Talbott, Tn	Indiana	Feb 15, 1919	66	Heeg, Lydia M.	Chandler, Luther		Chandler, Mrs. Lydia		Wife	West View					
Chandler, Mary Ruth [Negro]	May 4, 1974	Jeff Co	Tn	Mar 15, 1909	65	W	Mc Farland, William		Messengill, Nannie		Haynes, Mary Kolle & Brue	West View					
Chandler, Nannie Susan	Jun 29, 1983	Milligan Clinic	Blount Co		86	S	Chandler, Richard		Taylor, Amanda		Kfaine, Mildred - Mae & Rae	Magnolia - Blount Co					
Chandler, William James	Apr 13, 1998	Jeff City	Blount Co., Tn	Jan 21, 1912	86	Drennon, Betty	Chandler, Robert		James, Geneva		Sharp, Sarah Jane [Dau]	J.M.G.					Tilley, Lillian
Chapman, Brenda Kay	Aug 8, 1955	Hamblen Co	Tn	Sep 16, 1954	0		Chapman, Arlie R.		Spink, Nina R.		Chapman, A.R.	Mt. Olive					
Chapman, Eva May	Jan 2, 1996	Jeff City	Hamner, Ny	Jul 6, 1917	78		Card, Charles		Vivrue, May		Sager, Christine & Harry [Bragi]	Hopewell Dandridge, Tn					
Chapman, Frances	Feb 8, 1983	Jeff City	Flag Pord, Tn	Dec 31 1919	73	Chapman, Joe	Blankenship, Horace F.		Sims, Mary F.		Husband	J.M.G.		Harold Joe- John		Harold	
Chapman, George Le Roy	Mar 21, 1984	Knoxville, Tn	Mass.	Jul 4, 1906	77	W	Chapman, Frank		Renovell, Jennie		Chapman, Robert - Bolden, Earl E. - Wallace, D.M. - Chapman, J.S.	Weymouth, Mass.	WW 2				[Aunts] Anderson, Estelle - Cornett, Jessie
Chapman, James S.	Sep 6, 1936	New York	New York	Jan 14, 1855	81	Ng	Chapman, —	New York	Hogri, Siaryihia	New York	Jarnigan						
Chapman, Joe A (Dr.)	Jul 21, 1983	Jeff City Westpoint, Tn		Oct 23, 1919	73		Chapman, F.D.		Irwin, Lena Mee		Chapman, John L. [Son]	J.M.G.	44-46	Harold Joe		Carl	Lewis, Ruby
Chapman, Meba	Dec 10, 1983	J.M.H.	Ky	Jan 16, 1908	75	Chapman, George L.	Chapman, F.D.		Clark, Grace		Chapman, George	UT Medical - Memphis, Tn					
Charles, Ruth	Dec 21, 1973	Hamblen Co	Tn	Jun 27, 1895	78	W	Coheer, William A.		West, Mollie		Franklin, Odney - Huff, Mrs. Eliza [Crm, Ohio]	West View					
Charlton, Elizabeth Jane	Jun 5, 1925		Tn		88-4 27	W	Jett, Edward T.	Tn	Maxofield, Malinda	Tn	Charlton, J.J.	Charlton, J.J.					
Charlton, Ina	Mar 7, 1979	Knoxville, Tn	Tn	Apr 16, 1895	83	W	Collier, W.L.		Carter, Mary		Bright, Mrs. Velma - Perton, June - Turpin, Agnes	Mt. Horeb					
Charlton, Jessie J.	May 13, 1963	Knoxville, Tn	Tn	Sep 23, 1878	74	Ng	Chariton, Joseph E.		Jett, Elizabeth		Chariton, Mrs. Ina	West View					
Cherry, Robert Clarence	Sep 12, 1994	Knoxville, Tn	Davenport, Iowa	Oct 25, 1929	64	Lundquist, Evelyn	Cherry, Gerald Newton		Cole, Annette Margaret		Wife	Davenport Memorial - Davenport, Iowa	51-53	Todd & Amy Jo-Tim & Bonnie	Owens, Susan & Keith		
Chesher, Lucy L.	Jun 16, 1953	Grainger Co	Tn	Aug 11, 1875	77	W	Lambdin, Dempsey		James, Victoria		Chesher, Beulah	West View					
Chesher, Thomasgal S. 1947	Jul 5, 1947	Knox Co	Tn	Aug 7, 18--	77		Lambdin, Dempsey				Beulah	West View					
Childress, Catherine	Aug , 1959	Jeff Co	Tn			Ng					Childress, L.K.	Strawberry Plains					
Chin, David Yi-Min	Nov 5, 1977	Knoxville, Tn	China	Aug 24, 1920	57	Wang, Mary C.	Chin, James Sha		Chin, Mary C. & Sons		Chin, Mary C. & Sons	Jefferson Memorial					
Choate, Elsie Clyde	Nov 29, 1972	Jeff City	China	Oct 27, 1919	53	Bundte	Choate, Milton		Knight, Mary		Choate, Bunnie	West View					
Chrisley, Ella Mae	Oct 1, 1982	Atlanta, Ga	Tn	Apr 25, 1907	75	W	Walker, D.E.		Dixon, Callie		Walker, Raymond-John	West View					
Churchman, Charlie	May 25, 1957	Jeff Co		Nov 12, 1895	61	S	Churchman, Rufus J.		Hodge, Martha		Churchman, S.G. [Brother]	West View					
Churchman, Chyjo Leonard	May 15, 1995	Knoxville, Tn	Tn	Oct 6, 1897	98	Silvers, Edna	Churchman, R.J.		Hodge, Martha		Churchman, Mrs. Dan [Helen] & Bruce	West View	18-19	Lowell-John R.		George	
Churchman, Dan H.	Dec 4, 1966	Jeff Co	Tn	Mar 3, 1898	68	Ng	Churchman, John		Alexander, Paralee		Churchman, Mrs. Dan [Helen] & Bruce	West View					Volies, Mary K.

NAME	DDATE	DLOCAT	BLOCAT	BDATE	AGE	SPOUSE	FATHER	FBLOCAT	MOTHER	MFBLOCAT	BY	BURIAL	VET	SON	DAUG	BROTHER	SISTER
Churchman, Frances Grace	Jan 18, 1992	U.T.H.	Jeff City	Jun 16, 1928	64	S	Churchman, James Hodge		Heck, Loma		Jett, Mary C. [Sister]	West View					
Churchman, James Hodge	Aug 15, 1954	Jeff Co	Tn	May 6, 1899	55		Churchman, R.J.		Hodge, Martha Blanche		Fenish, Mrs. Blanche	West View					
Churchman, Lona	Sep 4, 1987	Morristown, Tn	Virginia	Aug 10, 1903	84	W	Churchman, James H. [D]		Dyson, Iva Lee		Churchman, James	West View					
Churchman, Rufus Jackson	Nov 28, 1956	Jeff Co	Tn	Jul 22, 1862	94	W	Churchman, William		Kinder, Sarah		Churchman, Clyde-George-S.B.	Piedmont					
Clinat, Steve	Jul 25, 1975	Morristown, Tn	Tn	Aug 12, 1913	62	W	Clinat, Paul		Chla, Bertha		Clinat, Hazel	Jefferson Memorial					
Clark, Alonzo	Feb 17, 1983	Newport, Tn	Tn	May 16, 1913	69	Price, Gladys	Clark, Samuel .		Blaise, Ariiecla		Clark, Joe-Mrs. Gladys P.	Manes Chapel [Service]	WW 2				
Clark, Elizabeth Frances	Feb 28, 1929		Tn		69	W	Moore, John	Tn	Moore, Mary	Tn		Friends Station					
Clark, Freddie [F]	Sep 2, 2000	Dandridge, Tn	Al	Sep 1, 1916	83	W	Womnack, Fred		Willis, Minnie	W	Bishop, Rose Marie [Niece - Huntsville, Al]	Riverdale - Columbus, Ga					
Clark, Gladys M.	Jul 17, 1985	Jeff City	St. Louis, Mo	Sep 19, 1908	86	Clark, William Paul	Middlebohnert, Herbert Lee		Westbrook, Priscilla Estelle		Husband	J.M.G.					
Clark, Jerry Richard Jr.	Nov 20, 1984	Jeff Co		Nov 18, 1984			Clark, Jerry Richard Sr.	La	Jones, Wilma Dianna	La	Clark, Jerry Sr.	Mer Rouge - Gasirop, La					
Clark, Judy Lee	Jun 22, 1987	J.M.H.	Tn	Feb 18, 1945	42	Clark, Jay	Lee, James D.		Aufr, Mt Diarlie		Clark, Jay	J.M.G.					
Clark, Luther	Nov 9, 1932	Grainger Co	Tn	Oct 9, 1858	74	S	Clark, James	Tn	Young, Elizabeth	Tn	Clark, Tom & Kidwell	Shilo					
Clark, Nell H.	Apr 28, 1985	Knox Co	Tn	Jul 11, 1907	57	W	Hams, John E.		Hayes, Dollie		Ellis, -J.W.	Jarriogian					
Clark, Vivian	May 2, 1985	Jeff City	Tn	May 21, 1932	52	Ng	Bowiin, Sid		Hyden, Edith		Clark, B.K.	Lebanon					
Clark, William Paul Sr.	Nov 10, 1998	Hickman, Ky	Apr 18, 1904		94	W	Clark, Eddie Calvin		Bellew, Ellis		Clark, B.K.	J.M.G.		William Jr.			
Clarkston, Billy H.	Jul 10, 1984	Knoxville, Tn	Ky	Jun 28, 1934	50	Div	Clarkston, Mc Yatiely Garfield		Henderson, Judy A- Tom - Clarkston, Sidney		Henderson, Judy A- Tom - Clarkston, Sidney	Wesleys Chapel		William Jr.			
Clear, William Phillip Sr.	Sep 7, 1994	Knoxville, Tn	Apr 20, 1921		73	Bond, Polly	Clear, F. Wheeler		Dickenson, Ossie L.		Wells, Minnie	J.M.G.	43-46				
Clevenger, D.P.	Feb 7, 1931	Knoxville	Tn	Aug 2, 1858	72				Young, Susie	Tn	Marney, Elvia & Mrs. George - Clevenger, Mrs. D.P.	Shilo					
Clevenger, G.W.	Dec 25, 1934	Grainger Co	Tn	May 28, 1860	74	W		Tn	Clevenger, Will	Tn	Clevenger, G.W. & J.P. [Prepaid]	Shilo					
Clevenger, Hattie Lillie	Aug 31, 1974	Jeff City	Tn	Aug 31, 1974	87-3-12		Clevenger, Joe C.		Bnannam, Laura		Northern, Stanley - Shockley, D.C.	West View					
Clevenger, Joe Cannon	Jul 28, 1983	Jeff Co	Tn	Jan 1, 1896	77	Solomon, Hattie	Clevenger, George H.		Clark, Mehrala		Clevenger, Hattie	West View					
Clevenger, Katherine Scott	Nov 25, 1965	Fortress Co, Tn	Tn	Feb 3, 1925	65	W	Clevenger, Milton		Scott, Lucy & Cecil		Scott, Lucy & Cecil	Mt. View					
Clevenger, Mary Catherine	Mar 13, 1990	Jeff Co					Breeden, Charles M.		Miller, Bertha		Burnett, Grace	J.M.G.					
Clevenger, Melvin Clifford	Jun 21, 1998	Jeff Co	Huntsville, Ala.	Jan 7, 1952	46	Dittrich, Ingrid	Clevenger, Howard		Clevenger, Lillie		Wife	Cremated		Timothy		William	
Clevenger, Raffial	Dec 29, 1998	Jeff Co	Tn	Mar 1, 1917	51	Clevenger, Ruben	Norton, John		Bozeman, Maria		Clevenger, Ruben R.- Norton, John - Henry, Shirley	Roseberry - Knox Co			William	Pam Ruth	
Clevenger, Ruben Rudolph	Jan 7, 1981	Jeff City	Tn	Jun 22, 1909	71	W	Clevenger, Charlie		Walker, Rosa		Brooks, Helen - Henry, Shirley	Breitwen					
Clevenger, Samuel Joseph	Sep 30, 1944	Grainger Co	Feb 13, 1872		72	S	Clevenger, William		Byrd, Nancy	Tn	Roach, Mrs. Minnie C.	Shiloh					
Clevenger, Virginia Tennessee	Nov 2, 1936		Dec 6, 1861		74	W	Young, George		Smith, Betsy		Manely, Miss Elvie [Kzonville]	Shiloh					
Clevenger, William Columbus [Ozzie]	Mar 5, 1974	Knox Co [Rea Scott Co]	Tn	Jul 9, 1917	56	W	Clevenger, Edward		Clevenger, Hattie		Clevenger, Mrs. William C. [Oneida]	Jefferson Memorial					
Click, Sharon	Feb 6, 1996	Jeff City	Harrisonburg, Va	May 12, 1969		Click, William C.		Dove, Faye		Husband [Charotte, Nc]	Harrisonburg, Va					
Climer, Clarence Tex L.	Oct 23, 1993	Knoxville, Tn	Greene Co, Tn	Nov 30, 1919	73	Pettigrew, Sylvia	Climer, Henry		Cobbs, Ethel		Wis - Crittenden, Lynndale [Aunt]	J.M.G.		Charles Lee Ray-Robert W.	Lannon, Shirley Ann - Mullins, Debra E- Deering, Melissa	Claude	Doulhd, Lois

NAME	DDATE	DLOCAT	BLOCAT	BDATE	AGE	SPOUSE	FATHER	FBLOCAT	MOTHER	MFBLOCAT	BY	BURIAL	VET	SON	DAUG	BROTHER	SISTER
Cline, Anna	Sep 16, 1903	Jeff City	Jeff Co	Dec 19, 1908	84	Mowry, William Sidney	French, Virginia		Early, Virginia [Daug - Wagnonville, Nc]		Cline, Charles A - Raoul, Bill	West View					
Cline, Anna D.	Feb 26, 1989	U.T.H.	Tn	May 20, 1919	69	Cline, Charles A.	Hopkins, Bill	Tn	McClanahan, Lizzie	Tn	Cline, Roger Dale	J.M.G.					
Cline, Charles A.	Sep 25, 1989	J.M.H.	Garisille, Arkansas	Aug 6, 1920	69	w	Cline, Charles B.	Hinkle, Eula		Cline, Roger Dale	Oak Grove	WW 2				
Cline, Cora	Feb 7, 1949	Jeff Co.	Claiborne Co, Tn	Mar 20, 1881	67	w	Brown, Alfred		Underwood, Ellen	Tn	Cline, J.V. 3rd [Son]	West View					
Cline, Eula Mae [Dunn]	Apr 18, 1991	Jeff City	Jeff Co	Sep 27, 1914	76	w	Fongus, Will		Ogle, Una		Cline, Neff [Son]	West View					
Cline, Frontis Cecil Neff Jr.	Aug 31, 1985	Washington, Usa		Nov 15, 1941	43	Div	Cline, Frontis C.N. Sr.		Neff Sr.- Helen		Everlasting Life - J.M.G.						
Cline, Frontis Grayden [Major]	Jan 6, 1982	Jeff City	Tn	Feb 16, 1907	74	Bond, Margaret	Bond, Fred Lee		Cline, Fred G. [Dayton, Ohio]		West View					
Cline, Frontis Neff	Dec 26, 1998	Jeff City	White Pine, Tn	Sep 16, 1909	89	s	Bettis, Viola		Cammack, Mary Ruth [Daug]		J.M.G.		Nov, Louise & Jack		D.P.	
Cline, J.V. Jr.	Jun 30, 1984	J.M.H.	Tn	Jul 8, 1910	73	Fongub, Eula Mae	Cline, J.V. Sr.		Bird, Susie		Cline, Mrs. Eula M.-J.V. 3rd	J.M.G.					Collins, Ruth
Cline, James Phillip	Sep 26, 1988	J.M.H.	Tn	Apr 27, 1937	51	Ausmus, Zella	Cline, Phillip L.		Mowry, Anna		Cline, Zella [Marelle]	J.M.G.					
Cline, James V. Sr.	Mar 8, 1947	Jeff Co.	Tn	Feb 5, 1871	76-1-3	w	Cline, Phillip B.	Va	Neff, Amanda E.	Va	Cline, Phil	West View					
Cline, Janet Suzanne	Dec 1, 1939	Jeff City	Tn	Jun 4, 1909	4m		Cline, Walter V.	Tn	Brown, Cora A.	Tn	Cline, Phil	West View					
Cline, Jessie Kyle [Buck]	May 31, 1982	J.M.H.	Tn	Jul 20, 1909	72	w	Cline, Walter V.		Brown, Cora A.		Cline, Dyke	Community Chapel - Talbott, Tn					
Cline, Jo Ella	May 22, 1988	Talbott, Tn	Tn	Nov 2, 1914	51	Cline, Buck	Hagg, Frank		Cline, Buck		Community Chapel					
Cline, Lucy	Dec 21, 1950	Knox Co	Tn	May 19, 1874	76	w	Martin, Robert		Colbech, Mary		Martin, W.R.	Strawberry Plains					
Cline, Margaret	Oct 14, 1982	Dayton, Ohio	Athens, Ga	May 23, 1928	64	Cline, Frontis G.	Bond, Fred Lee		Grimes, Ann Low		Cline, Fred G.	West View					
Cline, Pearl Elizabeth Virginia	Jul 22, 1985	J.M.H.	Tn	Sep 20, 1903	81	s	Cline, Walter V.		Brown, Cora A.		West, Kylene - Cline, Lucille	West View					
Cline, Philip Bird	Feb 17, 1979	Morristown, Tn	Tn	Apr 5, 1903	74	Mowrey, Ann	Bird, James V.		Bird, Susan		Cline, Mrs. P.B.	Seahorn Chapel					
Cline, Rex Bedford	Mar 17, 1981	Jeff Co	Tn	May 12, 1924	56	Ng	Cline, Walter		Brown, Cora		Cline, Mrs. Lucille F.	West View					
Cline, Susie M.	Jan 15, 1947	Blount Co	Tn	Jan 24, 1873	73-11-21	Ng	Bird, James N.	Tn	Weir, Marthes	Tn	Cheatnes, Mrs. Z.L.- Cline, Grady	West View					
Cline, Una	Aug 29, 1982	J.M.H.	Tn	Feb 4, 1915	67	Ng	Ogle, Henry		McCarter, Eva		Cline, Neff	Jefferson Memorial					
Cline, Viola	Nov 1, 1981	Jeff Co	Tn	Jan 15, 1888	93	w	Bettis, Jake		Sims, Ellen		Line, Mrs. Inez	West View					
Cline, Walter Von	Aug 18, 1950	Jeff Co	Tn	Jun 15, 1872	78	w	Cline, Phillip L.		Neff, Amanda		Cline, Pearl - Buck & Rex	Seahorn Chapel					
Cloninger, Raymond Vondas	Nov 13, 1981	Sevier Co	Tn	Dec 27, 1935	55	Helton, Helen	Cloninger, Rome		Flenniken, Anocidhel		Cloninger, Helen Helton	J.M.G.					
Clowers, Mary Eliza	Mar 17, 1987	Humana Hosp.	Tn	Aug 9, 1902	84	w	Johnson, William		Jarnigan, Therlie		Cates, Donna	National - Knoxville, Tn					
Cloyd, Maud	Feb 25, 1979	Jeff City	Tn	Apr 10, 1887	91	w	Hixson, William H.		Campbell, Eliza H.		Cloyd, Will J.	Oak Grove - Greenville, Tn					
Cluck, Mary C.	Oct 25, 1927	Tn			72-8-11	w	Johnson, Calloway	Tn	Phillips, Emily	Tn	Cates, Will	Sunderland					
Cluck, Mary Isabelle	Nov 25, 1949	Knox Co	Tn	Feb 26, 1871	78	w	Walker, Martha		Ebenezer							
Cochran, Barbara	Nov 19, 1983	Jeff City	Claiborne Co, Tn	Aug 2, 1909	84		Satterfield, Tilman R.		Herrell, Mary Susan		Anderson, Norma & Eugene[Daug]	Mill Springs		[G] Roberts, Eddie	[G] Roberts, Pam		
Cochran, Charles Paul	Jul 28, 1983	Abilene, Texas	Nov 27, 1968	24		Cochran, Charles R. [?]		Thornhill, Wanda		Cochran, Jean Rapass Mother - Breeden, Blanche Thornhill - [G-Mothers]	Grants Chapel - Dandridge, Tn					
Cochran, Chester C.	Apr 15, 2000	Jeff City	Tn	Oct 7, 1912	87	Calloway, Ruby	Pattes, David		Anderson, Bill - Flynn, Mrs. - Williford ?	Tn	Anderson, Bill - Flynn, Mrs. - Williford ?					
Cochran, Delilah	Apr 20, 1954	Jeff Co	Tn	Jul 22, 1899	84	W	Ng		Link		Cochran, W. Bruce	Mill Springs					
Cochran, Hasbell George	Sep 5, 1988	J.M.H.	Tn	May 6, 1915	73	Ng	Cochran, Maynard T.		Carroll, Cora		Cochran, Barbara S.	Mill Springs	WW 2				
Cochran, Helen Louise	Mar 24, 1992	J.M.H.	Campbell Co, Tn	Feb 28, 1932	60	w	Cochran, Beecher				Husband	Sunderland					
Cochran, Lila Ann	Jun 25, 1928		Tn		66-4-19	w	Prater, U.E.		Hatmaker, Bonnie		Mill Springs Church					

NAME	DATE	B.LOCAT	B.LOCAT	D.DATE	AGE	SPOUSE	FATHER	F.B.LOCAT	MOTHER	M.F.B.LOCAT	BY	BURIAL	VET	SON	DAUG	BROTHER	SISTER
Cochran, Loraine Clark	Apr 23, 1994	Knoxville, Tn	Pikeville, Ky	Jun 20, 1934	59	Cochran, Don	Maden, William	Tn	Cox, Mabel		Husband	J.M.G.		Clark, Gary & Monica-Larry W. & Kathy (Step) Cochran, Jeff & Kim - Nick & Cheri	[6] Clark, Stephanie-Crystal - Cochran, Amy	Haworth, Ruby - [1/2] 5	
Cochran, O.R.	May 14, 1994	Jeff City	Tn	Mar 29, 1893	41	Ng	Hodges, F.P.	Tn	Cochran, Mrs. O.R. Cochran, Beecher	Tn	Cochran, Mrs. O.R.	Mill Springs					
Cochran, Sallie Carroll	Nov 12, 1973	Jeff Co	Tn	Apr 29, 1885	88	W	Hodges, Mary				Cochran, Beecher	Mill Springs					
Cochran, Thomas Maynard	Jan 18, 1951	Jeff Co		Aug 9, 1885	65	Ng	Cochran, F.P.P.		Hodge, Mollie		Cochran, Mrs. Cora J. (Wife)	New Market					
Cochran, Virginia Katherine	Jan 15, 1981	Strawberry Plains	Tn	Jun 3, 1926	54	Cochran, Henry T. Sr.	Cowden, William Anderson		Thompson, Nannie C.	Tn	Cochran, Henry T. Sr.	Pleasant Grove					
Cochran, Boyd Helm	Mar 14, 1942	Granger Co	Granger Co	Sep 28, 1915	26	S	Cochran, Robert W.	Tn	Helm, Nora	Tn	Nora-Kathleen-George [Family]	Shiloh					
Cochran, Cora	Aug 29, 1984	Granger Co	Tn	Jan 11, 1890	74	Cochran, T.M.	Northern, Cordelia				Cochran, Christine-Hazkell-Talley Hollie-Collingsworth, Elverta-Deathridge, Dorothy-Tipton, Naomi	Mill Springs					
Cochran, William Bruce	Jun 17, 1981	Jeff Co	Tn	Sep 29, 1961	69	Ng	Cochran, Mordisa		Potter, Dellia E.		Cochran, Bruce & Sallie	Mill Springs					
Cochran, Ida Mauley	Feb 28, 1946	Jeff Co	Granger Co	Jul 1, 1865	80	Cochran, A.O.	Mauley, Wilson	Tn	Watson, Tumar	Tn	Cochran, Guy - Clevenger, Mrs.	West View					
Cochran, M.M.	Sep 1, 1934	Mill Springs	Tn	May 30, 1907	77	Ng	Jarnigan, Thenia Stubblefield, —	Tn	Cochran, Lloyd	Tn	Cochran, W.R.	Mill Springs					
Cochran, James Earl	May 1, 1985	J.M.H.	Tn			Mc Clane, Hazal	McClane, Hazal		Shubblefield, —		Cochran, Mrs. Hazal	Mill Springs					
Cochran, James Floyd	Sep 2, 1981	Hamblen Co	Tn	May 24, 1923	88	Talley, Elizabeth	Cochran, Robert F.		Helm, Nora		Cochran, Elizabeth	J.M.G.	unk				
Cochran, Joe Clark	Apr 5, 1978		Tn			D	Clark, Ella		Comba, Mrs.		Talley	Oakland					
Cochran, John Guy	Apr 7, 19996	Knoxville, Tn	Granger Co	Aug 15, 1905	90	Cochran, Albert O.			Manley, Ida		Skeen, Helen [Daug]	West View					
Cochran, Lee M.	Oct 28, 1988	E.T.B.H.	Tn	Sep 28, 1916	72	S	Cochran, Millard Patton		Talley, Willie		Turley, Margaret	Shiloh			Blanche - Scroggins, Connie & Rick	
Cochran, Lula	Aug 13, 1985	Jeff City	Tn	Jun 4, 1904	81	Cochran, Guy	NeedHam, Porter		Hodge, Elizabeth		West, Roscoe-Edgar	West View					
Cochran, Millard Patton	Oct 6, 1951	Tn	Tn	Mar 15, 1873	78	Ng	Cochran, Bradford		Cheatten, Eliza	Tn	West, Roscoe-Edgar - Gray, Bedford - Cochran, Claude - Cochran, Mrs. M.P. - Albert	Shiloh					
Cochran, Nora Olin	Aug 21, 1987	J.M.H.	Tn	Nov 15, 1894	92	Ng	Cochran, Bradford		Ward, Kathryn	Tn	Henry, Agnes L.	J.M.G.					
Cochran, Willie Katie	Oct 27, 1977	Jeff Co	Tn	Jul 27, 1885	92	W	Trawie, Nick		Long, Carrie		Turley, Mrs. Margaret-West, Roscoe & Edgar	Shiloh - Granger Co					
Cochran, Albert Orlando	Nov 21, 1945	Jeff Co	Granger Co	Aug 18, 1870		W	Cochran, J.K.	Tn	Myers, Elizabeth	Tn	Cochran, Guy & Reta	West View					
Cochran, Mary L.	Nov 11, 1932	Tn	Tn	Aug 20, —	2		Cochran, John	Tn	Jones, Gladys	Tn	Cochran, John	Lebanon					
Cochran, Thelma Oline	Sep 14, 1948	New Market	Tn	Oct 5, 1901	44	Cochran, Charles	Ballinger, Masanic ?	Tn	Hill, Elva	Tn	Cochran, Charles	Lebanon					
Cody, Albert H.	Aug 6, 1986	Jeff Co	Tn	Jun 6, 1942	6	Ottinger, Mary Louise [D]	Hill, Tiney	Tn	Hill, Elva	Tn	Cochran, Elva H.	Open Door - Newport, Tn	WW 2				
Cody, George M.	Aug 19, 1994	Jeff Co	Dekunak, Springs, Fla.	Jul 12, 1916	79	Cody, Mary Louise	Cody, James Boyd		Helm, Tina		Lawnie, Ruby Cody [Niece]	Open Door - Newport, Tn					
Cody, Mary Louise	Aug 6, 1986	Jeff Co	Boyle Creek, Tn	Dec 21, 1916	71	Cody, Albert H. [D]	Ottinger, Albert L.	Tn	Trentham, Arcie Chiora		Lawnie, Ruby	Open Door - Newport, Tn					
Cody, Millie Lee	May 19, 1993	Jeff City	Talbott, Tn	Jul 21, 1911	81	Cody, George	Pollard, Hardin		Chuck, Ola		Husband	Sardein Springs - Jeff Co				Richard-Emory	Hodge, Maude
Cody, Rubie	Jul 27, 1935	Tn	Tn	Jan 25, 1936		Cody, Albert	Pollard, Hazel	Tn	Cody, Albert [White Pine]		Cody, Albert [White Pine]	Pleasant Ridge					
Cody, T.J.	Jan 11, 1987	Jeff City	Amanda S.	Nov 24, 1977	19	Cody, Tommy C.			Mc Kinney, Gladys N.		Wife	Cottage Hill - New Market				Tina-Tommy-Carol	
Cody, Tommy Carroll	Mar 27, 1980	Jeff City	Tn	Mar 15, 1940	40	Div	Cody, Albert H.		Pollard, Hazel		Cody, Albert H.	Pleasant Ridge					Huff, Tina
Cody, Wild Bill	Aug 6, 1988	U.T.H.	Tn	Jan 13, 1971	17	S	Cody, Tommy Sr.		Mc Kinney, Gladys		Whitley, Gladys	Pleasant Ridge					
Colie, Clarence Jones	Jan 4, 1950	Jeff Co	Tn	Dec 24, 1894	55	Ng	Jones, Dan J.		Jones, Elizabeth		Colie, Mrs. Clarence [Maude]	Buffalo Grove					

NAME	DDATE	DLOCAT	BLOCAT	BDATE	AGE	SPOUSE	FATHER	FBLOCAT	MOTHER	MFLOCAT	BY	BURIAL	VET	SON	DAUG	BROTHER	SISTER
Collis, Florence	Mar 14, 1999	Jeff Co	Tn	May 30, 1882	86	Collis, Roy V. [D]	Franklin, Benjamin		Walker, Elizabeth		Collis, Mildred	Jarnigan					
Collis, Helen	Oct 12, 1966	J.M.H.	Tn	Jul 8, 1899	87	W	Nance, John Robert		Loy, Martha E.		Collis, Miss Martha Low	Hebron					
Colie, J.J.	Nov 27, 1928		Tn		82-11-27	W	Coll, John L.	Tn	Bettis, Mary	Tn		Lebanon					
Colie, John Andrew	Aug 17, 1975	Tn	Tn	Apr 7, 1894	81	Nance, Helen	Colie, Isaac A.		Newman, Loella		Colie, Mrs. John A.	Hebron					
Colie, Julia R.	Apr 9, 1992	J.M.H.	Jeff Co	Sep 23, 1936	55	Colie, Robert	Colie, Pauline				Husband	Hebron					
Colie, Martha Lou	Feb 24, 1999	Jeff City	Jeff Co	Apr 2, 1931	67	W	Colie, John		Nance, Helen		Colie, Robert [Brother]	Hebron				John Nance & Claudine	
Colie, Maude	Nov 13, 1981	Knoxville, Tn	Tn	Apr 2, 1893	88	W	Hill, A.O.F.		Carter, Mary		Newman, Mrs. Jack - Colie, C.J. Jr. - Watson, Mary	Buffalo Grove					
Coker, Katherine	Jan 20, 1992	Hilliwen	Talbott, Tn	Mar 25, 1906	85	S	Colie, Roy V.		Franklin, Florence		Blackburn, G.D. Elizabeth [Cousin]	Jarnigan					
Colie, Mildred Inez	Mar 8, 2000	Tn	Tn	Nov 15, 1935	64	S	Colie, Roy V.		Franklin, Florence		Colie, Julianne	Jarnigan					
Colie, Robert Anderson	May 27, 1963	Tn	Tn	Jul 13, 1884	78	W	Colie, Isaac		Newman, Louella M.		Colie, Mrs. Florence & Mildred	Jarnigan					
Colemous, John	Aug 1, 1957	Jeff Co	Tn	May 1, 1876	90	Ng					Colemous, Mrs. Rhona H.	West View					
Coker, John William	Jun 12, 1976	Knoxville, Tn	Alabama	Aug 8, 1908	67	Zara, Katherine Jones	Coker, William S.		Butt, Shugg		Coker, Mrs. Katherine [Gladys]	West View			Gregg, Juanita [Br-Law] Cole, Anna Mae		
Coker, Katherine	May 22, 1999	Jeff City	Jeff City	Apr 25, 1916	83	W	Jones, Clint		Jones, Dora		Thacker, Jamie & Bobby [Daug]	Mill Springs		Young, Bill & Linda [AL]			Barbee, Shirley & Troy
Colbach, Infant Female	Sept 1, 1944	Jeff Co		Sept 1, 1944	72-7-10		Colbach, Bruce	Tn	Unk	Jeff Co	Colbach, Mrs. Ras	West View					
Colbach, Josie	Feb 6, 1941	Jeff Co	Tn		85	W	Colbach, William		Unk	Tn	Colbach, Sarah [Daug]	West View					
Colbach, Sarah Lou	Jun 12, 1950	Jeff Co	Tn	Aug 26, 1901	48	S	Colbach, Noah		Cole, Sarah		Burnett, Mrs. Robert - Hasseltine - Charlie	West View					
Colbach, Fannie	Feb 11, 1991	Morristown, Tn	Jeff Co	May 1, 1900	90	W	Hinchey, Robert Sr.		Wright, Josephine H.		Colbach, Mrs. Naomi Peck - Godfrey, Mrs.	West View					
Colbach, Wylie Ras	Aug 18, 1981	Tn	Tn	Oct 9, 1903	77	Hinchey, Fannie	Colbach, Noah		Wright, Josephine		Colbach, Bruce [Son]	Wesleya Chapel					
Cole, Alan Pauline	Jun 12, 1993	Knoxville, Tn	Knoxville, Tn	Apr 7, 1906	85	Smith, Charles H.			Parker, Linnie		Colbach, Mrs. Fannie - Bruce - Lawrence, Gladys	Beaver Creek				Ralph-Ed	
Cole, James	Apr 3, 1986	Jeff Co	Tn	May 3, 1932	21	Div	Cole, William		Cole, Almeda		Dalton, Christine [Daug]	Lockney - Texas	WW 2				
Cole, Johnny F.	Apr 25, 1950	Jeff Co	Texas	Apr 14, 1865	85	Ng	Cole, Henry		Brewster, Mildred		Cole, Mrs. Naomi Peck - Godfrey, Mrs. Miller, Lizzie - Frank, Curtis	Shiloh					
Cole, King	Jun 16, 1947	Jeff Co	Ky	Apr 14, 1865	82-8-28	Ng	Frank, W.A.	Ky	Frank, Ida	Ky	Cole, Henry	West View					
Cole, Pearl	Jul 18, 1965	Jeff Co	Tn	Mar 5, 1898	67	Div	Backles, A.J.		Wood, Ida		Wright, Elizabeth	J.M.G.					
Cole, Sarah J.	Apr 30, 1934	Jeff City	Tn	Dec 16, 1874	59	Cole, A.R.	Coleman, Gus Taylor	Tn	Francis, Martha Jane	Tn	Cole, A.R. - Cole, M.M. - Cole, Flora - Cole, E.L.	Beaver Creek					
Coleman, Mary	Aug 3, 1989	Jeff Co	Tn			S	Unk			Tn	Charles, Dorothy	Chestnut Hill Church					
Coley, Jane	Jun 7, 1932	Jeff City	Jeff Co	Jun 10, 1901		Ng	Collins, Gentry		Unk			Beaver Creek					
Coley, Lula Nichols	Jul 1, 1964	Knox Co	Tn	May 29, 1907	57	Ng	Unk		Smith, Rose		Smith, Rose	Beaver Creek					
Collins, Luther Arvillo	Jun 14, 1955	Knox Co	Grainger Co	Jan 4, 1890	66	S	Collins, Gentry		Alexander, Amelia		Collins, Fred -Charlie- Smith, Rose	Shiloh					
Colbach, Charles Henry	Mar 25, 1958	Jeff Co	Tn	Jul 31, 1891	66	Turpin, Alice	Colbach, Nooch		Hurst, Susan		Colbach, Alice	West View					
Collett, Bonnie Jane	Dec 13, 1992	Knoxville, Tn	Kettle Island, Ky	Oct 29, 1947	45	Collett, William	Lefevers, Walter Sr.		Clarke, June		Husband	Mt. Pleasant			Carolanna	Charles Vernon- Walter Jr -Billy Joe	Brown, Paulette - Denton, Shella
Collett, James W.	Jan 19, 1949	Jeff Co	Tn	Aug 31, 1886	45	W	Collett, Thomas	Tn	Smith, Amanda	Tn	Collett, T.A.	J.M.G.	WW2	Mt. Pleasant			
Collett, Mrs. T.A.	May 4, 1932	Jeff City	Tn	May 12, 1871	77-8-7	Collett, T.A.	Brunner, Beveridge		Richard, Mrs. Mel		Mt. Pleasant	West View					
Collett, Robert Dee Arnold [Red]	Mar 31, 1968	Jeff Co	Jeff Co	Apr 1, 1909	58	Div	Collett, Joe		Hendrix, Mrs. Ruby		Collett, T.A.	West View		William Vernon- Walter Lee			
Collette, Kenneth Lee	Dec 4, 1959	Dublin, Va	Tn	Jun 15, 1915	44	S	Collette, T.A.		Brannen, Verdie		Collette, Wm Kate	West View	WW 2	Charles Vernon- Walter Jr -Billy Joe		Brown, Paulette - Denton, Shella	

NAME	DDATE	DLOCAT	BLOCAT	BDATE	AGE	SPOUSE	FATHER	FBLOCAT	MOTHER	MFBLOCAT	BY	BURIAL	VET	SON	DAUG	BROTHER	SISTER
Collins, Lloyd Alvin	Feb 2, 1941	Jeff Co	Jeff Co		1m-1d	S	Collins, K.H.		McMillian, Margaret Lee	Knox Co	Collins, K.H.						
Collins, Mellie Moore	Mar 20, 1948	Jeff Co	Jeff Co	Jul 24, 1874	73-6-26	Ng	Moore, James	Tn	Moore, Mollie		Richard, Mrs. Mell - Ingram, Mrs. H.A. [Talbott]	Mt. Pleasant					
Collins, Martha Chewe	Sep 24, 1946	Jeff Co	Jeff Co	Mar 6, 1900	46	S	Collins, James W.	Sevier Co	Moore, Mollie	Jeff Co	Collins, Mrs. James W. [Talbott]	Mt. Pleasant - Jeff Co					
Collins, Tom Arvilla	Dec 7, 1946	Knox Co	Granger Co Dandridge, Tn	Apr 10, 1880	66	W					Vina Kate & Kenneth [Sister] Wells, Mozelle C.	West View					
Collins, Belle Chambers	Dec 25, 1996	Jeff City	Jeff Co	Nov 5, 1915	81	W	Chambers, Otha		Shiska, Julia		Wells, Mozelle C. [Sister]	Mt. View				Bud-Harry-Robert	
Colley, James Taylor	Jan 13, 1993	Cocke Co	Tn	Jan 4, 1929	24	Ng	Colley, Peyton K.		Fields, Kate		Dunn - Cocke Co	Mt. View	Korea				
Colley, James W.	Aug [19], 1970	Jeff Co	Va	Sep 27, 1901	68	Chambers, Bell	Colley, James H.		Ramsey, Cora		Colley, Bell	Mt. View					
Colley, Julia	Oct 29, 1956	Jeff Co	Va	Nov 7, 1891	64	S	Colley, David		Moore, Dulcima		Cox, Janette- Carr, Jeanita - Colley, Sam	Mt. Hereto					
Colley, Kristie Dee Ann	Mar 6, 1974	Knoxville, Tn	Tn	Dec 25, 1968	5		Colley, Ronald		Patterson, Nicia		Colley, Ronald	West View					
Colley, Patton K.	Jan 25, 1957	Jeff Co	Va			W			Moore, Dulcima		Colley, Dora - Lurone, Mrs.	Batch					
Colley, Ruby E.	Aug 8, 1987	Jeff City	Jeff Co	Dec 13, 1931	65		Miller, Paul		Hubbard, Coria		Colley, Melinda [Dang]	J.M.G.		Terry [Dd.] - [Step] Colley, Ronnie			
Colley, Sam	Dec 26, 1982	Knoxville, Tn	Jeff Co	Jan 24, 1917	75	Ruby	Colley, Pat		Fields, Katie E.		Colley, Mike [Son]	J.M.G.		Samuel Ronald	[Step] Alvie, Darlene - Colley, Malinda	Willis	
Colley, Willis Daisy	Jul 3, 1952	Knoxville, Tn	Tn	May 5, 1926	26		Elder, Dick		Richard, Julia		Colley, Mrs. Letha	Mt. Pleasant					
Colley, Andrew	Nov 10, 1952	Jeff Co	Tn			W						Ebenezer					
Collier, Emma Lee	Mar 14, 1972	Jeff Co	Tn	Jul 23, 1904	67	Collier, E.O.	Woods, Lizzie		Carter, Mary		Collier, E.O.	Ebenezer					
Collier, Estel Dell	Oct 4, 1975	Talbott, Tn	Tn	May 6, 1902	73	W	Grant, Huse				Collier, Jim	Lakewood - Jackson, Miss.					
Collier, Guy Coldwell	Jun 27, 1978	Jeff Co	Miss.	Aug 26, 1898	77	Ng	Collier, W.H.		Phillips, Maggie		Collier, Mrs. Guy						
Collier, Jennie Forrest	Jul 8, 1944	Jeff Co		Jul 22, 1874	69	W	Simpson, Andrew Jackson	Va	Link	Nc	Collier, J.A. & W.H. - Smith, Mrs. R.N. [Children]	Shiloh					
Collier, L.D.	Jan 15, 1933	Talbott, Tn		Dec 29, 1858	74	Ng	Collier, Sam	Tn	Betts, Celline [Children]	Tn	Collier, Mrs.	Ebenezer					
Collier, Lottie Mae	Jul 17, 1992	Morristown, Tn	Tn	May 26, 1908	84	W	Hanson, Pleas L.		Messengill, Roberta F.		Betts, Ruby [Dang]	Ebenezer					
Collier, Lowell Dean	Oct 31, 1979	Tn		Oct 1, 1936	43	Hicks, Benda	Collier, James		Haynes, Lelah		Collier, Family	Ebenezer	Korea				
Collier, Mary Catherine	Jul 23, 1956	Knox Co	Tn	Oct 1, 1938	17	S	Collier, Este Ovd		Grant, Emma Lee		Collier, E.O.	Ebenezer					
Collier, William Howard	Sep 18, 1957	Jeff Co	Tn	Jun 14, 1909	48	Ng	Collier, L. Dowl		Sawyers, Jennie		Collier, Mrs. Lettie & Children	Ebenezer					
Collier, Alricia Ruth	Oct 31, 1982	Jeff Co	Tn	Oct 27, 1982		Ng	Collier, Harold F.		Lowe, Merry C.		Collier, Harold	Memorial Gardens					
Collier, Anna Mae	Jan 5, 1987	J.M.H.	Tn	May 23, 1919	67	Collier, George Kinder	Parker, Decatur		Simpson, Eva		Collier, George Kinder	J.M.G.					
Collier, Arthur Bruce	May 25, 1995	Jeff Co	Tn	Jan 19, 1903	92	Warren, Clara	Collins, Billy		Owens, Susan		Stile	New Market	42-43		[Nieces] Smith, Barbara - Hall, Lorene		
Collins, B. Frank	Nov 12, 1987	Jeff Co	Tn	Feb 7, 1894	73	W	Collins, James		Owens, Susan		Collins, James & Ben - V.A.	New Market	unk				
Collins, Betty Marie	Nov 12, 1979	Jeff City	Tn	Mar 4, 1979		W			Collins, Sherry Lynn		Collins, Donna	County - Jeff Co					
Collins, Billy Edward Jr.	Mar 3, 1995	Knoxville, Tn	Knox Co	Sep 2, 1966	28	Staiano, Tammy	Collins, Billy Edward Sr.	Tn	Katherine		Wills	Pleasant Grove		T.J. Mitch		Virgil-Johnny-Joe	
Collins, Eliza	Jun 2, 1944	Granger Co		Jan 31, 1852	92	S	Clark, John A.	Cochran, Nancy	Owens, Susan	Tn	Collins, Ernish	Pleasant Grove					
Collins, Emma Clark	May 22, 1944	Jeff City		Jun 1, 18[8]84	59	W	Clark, John A.	Tn	Owens, Susan	Tn	Collins, Ernish	Pleasant Grove					
Collins, Ethel Etter	Jul 8, 1970	Jeff Co	Tn	Jul 5, 1906	68	Collins, Rev.	Etter, Charlie		Carmichael, Little J.		Carroll-Fred-Mrs. Bishop-Bradley-Gregson-Pascal [Children]	West View					
Collins, Eva	Jul 14, 1970	Jeff Co	Indiana	Oct 9, 1889	80	Ng	Simpkins, Tom		Colvenger, Cordia		Collins, Treator	Mill Springs					
Collins, Florence	Aug 9, 1943	Jeff Co	Tn	Oct 1, 1896	46	Collins, James	Foster, J.T.	Tn	Bowers, Lewis	Tn	Collins, James - Foster, J. Shade	Mill Springs					
Collins, Fred M.	Oct 4, 1990	J.M.H.		Sep 13, 1908	82	W	Collins, John D.		Clark, Emma		Turpin, Nancy E. [Dang]	J.M.G.					
Collins, George K.	Jun 20, 1992	Humana Hosp.		Jul 21, 1915	76	W	Collins, William		Huff, Hazel [Dang]			J.M.G.					
Collins, Greely Willard [Black]	Mar 12, 1993	Thornhill, Tn	Aug 25, 1905	87					Owens, Bessie		Dean, Barbara [Friend]	West View				Vincent-Howard-Paul	
Collins, Henry C.	Aug 4, 1948	Granger Co	Oct 14, 1891	56-9-20	Ng		Collins, Perrin	Tn			Collins, Mrs. Hettie	Lebanon					Riley, Nellie

NAME	DDATE	BLOCAT	BLOCAT	BDATE	AGE	SPOUSE	FATHER	FBLOCAT	MBLOCAT	MOTHER	BY	BURIAL	VET	SON	DAUG	BROTHER	SISTER
Collins, Hattie	Jul 30, 1977	Jeff Co	Tn	Oct 10, 1894	82	W	Collins, Rice			Hipsher, Martha	Hands, Mrs. Woodrow	Lebanon					
Collins, Hiram (Jacks)	Jan 3, 1969	Jeff Co	Tn	Apr 5, 1905	63	Div	Collins, Hiram			Miser, Maggie	Collins, Mrs. Edith & Sons	West View					
Collins, Infant	Feb 20, 1957	Jeff Co	Tn	Feb 20, 1957						Witts, Shirley Darline	Collins, Hiram Jr.	West View					
Collins, J. Dedrick	Aug 22, 1943	Granger Co	Tn	Jul 5, 1880	63	Ng	Collins, Gentry	Tn		Alexander, Arbolia	Collins,Carroll-Fred-J.D.Jr.-Paschal; Sam-Bishop, Eura & Bryan-Green, Euna & Collins, B. Frank	West View					
Collins, James Ernest	Nov 13, 1954	Jeff Co	Tn	Nov 3, 1888	66	S	Collins, James A.		Tn	Owens, Susan E.	Wife	Pleasant Grove	unk				
Collins, John Dedrick	Feb 6, 2000	Jeff City	Tn	Nov 3, 1913	86		Collins, Marshall			Hubbard, Elizabeth	Wife	West View		Johnny	Collier, Virginia & Estel Gann, Jane & Eddie	
Collins, John James	Jul 2, 1952	Jeff Co	Tn	Nov 3, 1903	49	Ng	Collins, Marshall			Mc Spadden, Katherine	Collins, Fred	West View					
Collins, King George	Jul 18, 1965	Jeff Co	Tn	Aug 28, 1938	26	S	Collins, Fred			Collins, Fred	Jefferson Memorial	West View					
Collins, Martha Miran	Jan 28, 1972	Knox Co		Aug 28, 1938	81		Turner, Thomas			Thomas, Mae - Collins, Eugene - Edith-Lillian-Margaret	West View	West View					
Collins, Mary Katherine Mc Spaddon	Jul 27, 1986	J.M.H.	Tn	Feb 27, 1907	79		Collins, Fred			Fox, Georgia E.	Collins, Donnie	J.M.G.					
Collins, Mrs.	Jul 7, 1933									Bellamy, Mrs. Will							
Collins, Nancy E.	Aug 1, 1954	Knox Co	Tn	Oct 13, 1900	53	Ng	Jones, G. Lee			Swang, Jessie	Collins, Frank B (Rev)	West View					
Collins, Nina Myrtle	Jan 22, 1965	Knox Co	Tn	Mar 27, 1917	48	Collins, Paro	Edmonds, James			Russell, Lookie	Collins, Paro	Blue Springs - Jeff Co					
Collins, Odell	Jul 25, 1928	Jeff Co	Tn		10	S	Collins, Bill	Tn	Tn	Collins, Elizabeth	Bellamy, Bill	Mill Springs					
Collins, Paul	Jul 10, 1980	Jeff Co	Tn	Jun 3, 1921	39	Ng	Collins, Marshall			Hubbard, Elizabeth	Collins, Mrs. Paul	Memorial Gardens					
Collins, Pearl Amber	Mar 22, 1967	Hill Haven	Tn	Mar 9, 1904	63	Collins, Robert M. [D]	Andrews, Griff			Johnson, Rachel	Collins, Dorsey [Son]	West View					
Collins, Ralph	Dec 28, 1984	Morristown, Tn	Tn	Feb 3, 1926	58	Free, Dorothy	Turner, Fannie			Collins, Mrs. Dorothy	Mt. View						
Collins, Robert Manard	Sep 22, 1955	New Market, Tn	Tn	Jan 13, 1907	48	Ng	Hubbard, Jim			Collins, Eliza	Collins, Mrs. Pearl	West View					
Collins, Ronald Steven	Feb 5, 1956	Jeff City	Tn	Sep 23, 1948	47		Collins, William Fred Jr.			Layman, Bonnie	Collins, Mike [Brother]	J.M.G.	69-75			[In-Law] Collins, Janet-Wilma	
Collins, Ruth Elizabeth	Apr 24, 1956		Tn		78	W				Hubbard, -	Father - Jarnigan, Sarah Alice [G-Mother]	West View					
Collins, William Pierder	Jan 7, 1955	Knoxville, Tn		Feb 5, 1950	34		Collins, William Fred			Collins, Betty-Jean	Godfrey, Ellie G. (Greensboro, So) - Collins, Paul-Charles-Arthur (Marion, Nc)	J.M.G.		David		Fouty, Lura & Joe	
Collins, William Earl	Nov 12, 1995	Jeff City	Tn	Jun 10, 1951	44	Lawrence, Wilma	Collins, William Fred			Collins, Betty-Jean	Wife	J.M.G.		William Andrew			
Collins, William Fred	Feb 5, 1996	Jeff Co	Tn	Sep 5, 1924	41	Layman, Bonnie	Turner, Marion			Bonnie	Jefferson Memorial	West View		Steve-Mike		[In-Law] Collins, Janet	
Collins, William Fred	Jun 5, 1959	Jeff Co	Tn	Jun 13, 1962	86	Ng	Collins, Gentry			Alexander, Billie	Collins, Mrs. Miriam	West View					
Collins, William Henderson	May 16, 1948	Hawkins Co., Tn			abt 97	W	Unk			Unk	Mill Springs	Mill Springs					
Collins, Wilma Geraldine	Dec 5, 1944	Jeff Co	Tn	Dec 14, 1937	6		Collins, John D.	Tn		Walker, Nora	Collins, J.D.	West Range					
Collins, Charlie W.	May 4, 1970	Grainger Co	Tn		83	Ng	Couch, John		Tn	Shafer, Isabella	Hughes, Georgia	Richland					
Collins, Clesson Elbert	Jun 11, 1969	Knox Co	Tn	Dec 3, 1894	74	Ng	Couch, John			Shafer, Isabella	Combs, Kenneth	Shiloh					
Combs, Delia	Mar 9, 1928		Tn		59-7-21		Combs, P.N. [D]		Tn	Smith, Belle	Sons	Shiloh					
Combs, Emma M.	Jan 15, 1960	Jeff Co	Va	Dec 22, 1881	79	Ng	Moore, Sam			Tipton, Rebecca	Haworth, Mrs. Raymond - Tallay, Mrs. Basil - Hasley, Mrs. - Cox, Mrs.	West View					
Combs, Gladys Rita	Jul 11, 1991		Tn		83	Combs, Frank	Clark, Thomas C.			Shafer, Belle	Combs, Allen [Son] Combs, Mrs. J.J. (Georgia)	Shiloh					
Combs, Haskell Alexander	Sep 3 1969	V.A. Hospital	Grainger Co	Oct 25, 1892	76	W	Combs, Thomas John			Hughes, Mary J.J.	National - Knoxville, Tn	Shiloh	WW 1				
Combs, Hollis Maynard	May 16, 1959	Grainger Co	Tn			Ng	Combs, Phillip N.			Young, Mary	Combs, Mrs. Willie Mae	Shiloh - Grainger					

NAME	DDATE	DLOCAT	BLOCAT	BDATE	AGE	SPOUSE	FATHER	FERLOCAT	MOTHER	MFRLOCAT	BY	BURIAL	VET	SON	DAUG	BROTHER	SISTER
Combs, J. Ralph	Jan 20, 1987	Sevier Co	Tn	Oct 3, 1947	19	Ng	Combs, J.C.		Seals, Augusta		Combs, Mr. J. Ralph [Alice E.]	Memorial Gardens					
Combs, J.N.	Apr 23, 1932	Granger Co	Tn	Dec 12, 1855	76	Ng	Combs, James	Tn	Duncan, Margarette		Combs, Mrs. J.W.	Shiloh					
Combs, James Arthur	Jun 2, 1972	Rutledge, Tn	Tn	Sep 13, 1901	70	Satterfield, Lillian	Combs, George W.		Cameron, Rachael		Combs, Mrs. James [Doug]	Oakland - Granger Co					
Combs, John [Doug]	May 12, 1969	Jeff Co	Tn	Feb 18, 1877	92	W	Combs, Tom		Talley, Mrs. Basil [Doug]		Combs, Mrs. Augusta [Wife]	West View					
Combs, John Chester	Jul 11, 1953	Jeff Co	Tn	Jan 22, 1915	38	Ng	Combs, John		Moore, Emma		Combs, Mrs. Augusta	West View					
Combs, Lincis Ruth	Apr 6, 1995	Jeff City	Knoxville, Tn	Dec 31, 1947	47	Combs, Roger Dale	Cox, Alger		Lamberton, Ruth		Husband & Lamberton, Phillip [Step-Father]			Brian & Jennifer-David & Tonya			
Combs, Margie B.	Nov 1 1931	Granger Co	Tn	Jan 6, 1875	56	W	Curl, J.?		West, Addie	Tn	Curl, A.B.	Shiloh					Tony
Combs, Martha Lillian	Jan 15, 1919	J.M.H.	Jeff Co	Nov 8, 1911	79	W	Satterfield, Horace		Hodge, Aurelia		Combs, Max [Son]	West View					
Combs, Minnie Ollie	Dec 8, 1951	Granger Co	Va	Aug 24, 1892	59	Div.	Lester, Johnson		Boyd, Virginia		Robinson, Mrs. Marshall [Bevois, Ky] - Hollis, C.W.-Hampton, Estel-Fred Lew Jr. [Children]	West View					
Combs, Phillips N.	Sep 8, 1926				65-6-28	Ng	Combs, James	Tn	Duncan, Martha	Tn	Combs, A.V.	Shiloh					
Combs, Rachel	Mar 3, 1932		Tn	Jan 14, 1865	90	Combs, G.W.	Combs, J.A.	Tn	Lee, Sallie	No	Combs, J.A. [Son]	Shiloh					
Combs, William Frank	Dec 18, 1984	Granger Co	Tn	Apr 30, 1908	86	W	Combs, Phillip		Young, Cordelia		Combs, Robert E. [Son]	Shiloh	Allen				
Combs, William Lester	Aug 12, 1972	Knoxville, Tn	Tn	Dec 19, 1910	61	S	Combs, George W.		Cameron, Rachael		Combs, Mrs. J.A.	Shiloh					
Combs, Willie Mae	Apr 22, 1978	Jeff City	Tn	Feb 20, 1901	77	W	Northam, Dudley A.		Talley, Mary Etta		Mc Claire, Mrs. Billie - Murph, James A.- Betty	Shiloh - Granger Co					
Compton, Sarah Cora	Mar 2, 1947	Jeff Co	Washington Co, Tn	Apr 21, 1869	77-10-11	Ng	Moore, Landon T.		Longyeow, Mary E.	Tn	Trent, Mrs. J.A. [Ohio]	West View					
Compton, T.B.	Jun 27, 1954	Atlanta, Ga Sc		Sep 25, 1866	67	W			Hodge, Mrs. Pauline			West View					
Congdon, Ann Leedy	Jul 1, 1981	Colorado	Tn			Congdon, C.P. [D]			Leedy, Xan		Leedy, Xan	Jefferson Memorial					
Conklin, Elizabeth	Amr 27, 1955	Jeff City	Indiana	Jan 14, 1865	90	W	Brown, John		Smith, Mary		Conklin, R.M. - J.B.	Jarnigan					
Conklin, Francis Merle [F]	Mar 28, 1959	Jeff Co	In Office	Nov 26, 1907	61	Conklin, J.B.	Johnson, J.E.		Merrick, Anna		Conklin, J.B.	Jarnigan					
Conklin, John Robert	Feb 25, 1962		Tn	Jun 3, 1929	92	Longmire, Joan	Conklin, John Buford		Johnson, Marie F.		Jarnigan	Jarnigan					
Conklin, John Buford	Apr 27, 1971	Bean Station, Tn	Tn	Dec 3, 1901	69	W	Conklin, J.E.		Brown, Elizabeth		Conklin, John Robert	Jarnigan					
Connelly, Howard Don	Apr 28, 1978	Youngstown, Ohio		Jun 8, 1936	41	Poore, Geneva	Connelly, Frank		Fox, Mary Catherine		Connelly, Geneva	Connelly - Youngstown, Ohio					
Conner, Maude	Jul 16, 1974	Knoxville, Tn	Tn	May 17, 1886	88	W	Darfield, J.W.		Poore, Mary		Childress, Mrs. Mary	West View					
Conwell, James O'Theil	Jul 10, 1986	J.M.H.	Tn	Aug 12, 1905	82	W	Conwell, Scott		Unk		Clements, Mary-Jo	West View Cremated					
Conwell, Bobby Dean	Dec 1, 1947	Jeff Co	Sevier Co	May 10, 1943	4		Conwell, Andrew		Winkler, Doyle	Okla	Winkler, Doyle	Piney					
Conwell, Carrie Lou	Aug 3, 1944	Jeff Co	Jeff Co	Jul 13, 1944			Cook, William C.	Union Co	Ninomdsy, Ettis	Knox Co	Monday, Andy	New Market					
Cook, Edgar Marion	Apr 27, 1983	Jeff City	Ga	Jul 16, 1897	85	Grey, Lillie	Cook, Frank		Muff, Dallas		Cook, Mrs. Lillie	Jefferson Memorial					
Cook, Ellis	Jul 18, 1946	Knox Co		May 5, 1913	33	Ng	Monday, S.H.				Cook, William - Monday, A.H.	New Market					
Cook, Grace	Nov 18, 1966	Jeff Co	Tn	Sep 18, 1866	70	Cook, Bill	Wilkerson, Oscar		Chambers, Fabby		Hodgson, Mrs. Charles Lindsey, Mrs. Mable - Battle, Rhea - Moreland, Harold	West View					
Cook, Infant	Sept 29, 1939	New Market	New Market	Sep 29, 1939			Cook, Bill		Cook, Andrew		Cook, Andrew & Brothers	New Market					
Cook, Lillis Grey	May 29, 1996	Cleveland, Tn	Turledge, Tn	Aug 14, 1896	99	W	Hodge, Joseph		Moody, Ester		Cook, Marion [Son]	J.M.G.	Clarence [Va]				
Cook, Richard	Oct 17, 1944	Jeff Co	Union Co, Tn	1890	84	W	Cook, Marcus	Tn	Powell, —	Tn	Cook, O.D.-Wylie & H.B.	New Market					
Cook, Tommy Dean	Aug 11, 1974	Knoxville, Tn	Tn	Dec 30, 1953	20	S	Cook, Albert T.		Brooks, Helen		Cook, Albert & Solomon, Betty - Cook, Albert	Pleasant Grove - Union Co					
Cook, William C.	Dec 12, 1964	Jeff Co	Tn	Jul 30, 1905	59	Grace	Cook, Thomas		Keck, Savanah		Seals, Mrs. Albert & Grace	New Market					
Cookes, David O'Conner	Dec 26, 1950	Union Co, Tn	Tn	Nov 11, 1884	66	Ng	Cooke, R.C.		Miller, Sarah		Cooke, Mrs. D.O. [Martha]	Lynnhurst					Collins, Amy Cox - Collins, Angel Cox
Cooper, Alice	Jan 23, 1933	Jeff City	Tn	Mar 6, 1860	72	W	Hodge, Liggon		Mc Daniel, Mary	Tn	Cooper, D.H.	West View					

NAME	DDATE	DLOCAT	BLOCAT	BDATE	AGE	SPOUSE	FATHER	FRLOCAT	MOTHER	MFRLOCAT	BY	BURIAL	VET	SON	DAUG	BROTHER	SISTER
Coppedge, John Ceideman	Apr 13, 1989	Jeff Co	Florida	May 24, 1904	84	W	Breeden, Howard				Goebl, Rev. Guy	Evergreen - Jacksonville, Fla					
Corbett, Cora Mae	Feb 12, 1976	Knoxville, Tn				W	Corbett, J.R.		Walker, Martha		Corbett, J.R.	Jefferson Memorial					
Corman, Almeda Roberts	Sep 27, 1948	Hope, Kansas	Tn	Jun 7, 1920	55	Corman, J. Porter	Breeden, Howard Roberts, Joseph Andrew	Tn	Cole, Catherine	Tn	Satterfield, Mrs. Ralph	New Market					
Corman, James Porter	Nov 28, 1954	Jeff Co	Tn	Jan 9, 1948	76	W	Corman, Shields		Harper, Mary Frances		Satterfield, Mrs. Ralph	New Market					
Cornwell, Martha Jean	Aug 16, 1953	Hamblen Co	Jeff Co	Apr 16, 1878		W	Cornwell, Ross		Young, Johnnie Jane Ellison, Margaret Faye		Cornwell, Ross	Sunderland					
Cornwell, Vanessa Faye	Oct 10, 1960	Hamblen Co	Tn	Aug 11, 1953			Cornwell, Lowell				Cornwell, Lowell	Sunderland					
Corum, Arthur Hood	Jan 27, 1947	New Market	Greinger Co	Jul 21, 1990	21m	Ng	Corum, Solomon	Greinger Co	Forrester, Katherine	Greinger Co	Corum, Mrs. Arthur	New Market					
Corum, Daisy Lee	Sep 19, 1959	New Market		Mar 9, 1883	76-4-19	Corum, Hood [D]					Corum, Dorothy Lee & A.H.	New Market					
Corum, Lon	Dec 5, 1928		Tn	Mar 8, 1882	56-8-27	W	Corum, Sam	Tn	Fowler, Ng	Tn	Corum, Mrs & Dorothy	Friends Station					
Corum, Mary Catherine	Nov 29, 1944	Jeff Co	Tn	Oct 18, 1914	30	S	Corum, A. Hood	Tn	Newman, Daisy Lee	Tn	Corum, Mrs & Dorothy	New Market					
Cotner, Mamie Elizabeth [Cel]	Nov 4, 1957	Jeff City	Tn	1923	34	Cotner, Wilson			Unk		Cotner, Wilson	West View Colored					
Cotner, Wilson D. Jr. [Cel]	Nov 2, 1960	Jeff City	Tn	Jun 6, 1955	5		Cotner, Wilson D. Sr.		Williams, Maxie		Cotner, Wilson Sr.	West View Colored					
Cotter, Clarence B.	Apr [15], 1945	Park Ridge, Ill.		Jul 31, 1951	40						Cotter, K. [Jeff City] Cotter, Robert E. [Brother]						
Cotter, Gary Lee	Oct 16, 1981	Dandridge, Tn	Jeff Co	Apr 10, 1907	90	Cotter, Eugene			Mary		Cotter, Robert E.	Lebanon Cumberland	unk	Manning, Mary E.			
Cotter, Lelo C.	Jan 27, 1998	Dandridge, Tn	Jeff Co		90	Cameron, W. E.			Knowling, Lizzie K.		Seale, Elizabeth [Daug]	Mt. View					
Cotter, Roy Mack	Oct 29, 1977	Jeff Co	Tn	Mar 29, 1912	65	Cameron, Lelo	Cotter, Clarence D.		Miller, Elizabeth		Cotter, Mrs. Roy M.	Mt. View					
Cotter, Willie H. [M]	Oct 27, 1960	Jeff Co	Tn	Dec 13, 1904	55	Klepper, Edith	Cotter, William H.		Cotner, Alice M.		Cotter, Edith	Lebanon - Mt. Horeb					
Couch, Allie Elizabeth	Apr 26, 1965	Knox Co	Tn	Aug 8, 1892	72		Peoples, David A.		Couch, Harriet		Couch, Lloyd-Robert [Sons], H????, Helen [Va]	Memorial Gardens					
Couch, Anna Beryl	Jun 4, 1981	J.M.H.	Tn	Apr 25, 1918	63	Couch, Lloyd	Craig, Felix G.		Dillard, Ella		Couch, Lloyd	West View					
Couch, Bertram Eugene	Feb 24, 1951	Hamblen Co	No	Sep 16, 1883	67	Ng	Couch, Josh		Mem, Marg		Couch, Mrs. B.E. [Ollie]	Jarnigan					
Couch, Beulah	Jan 10, 1957	Jeff Co	Tn	Jan 15, 1877	79	Ng	Hill, A.O.P.		Carter, Mary		Lupee, R.J. Jr. - Couch, G.N.	Buffalo Grove					
Couch, Gilbert N.	Apr 6, 1963	Jeff Co	Tn		83	W	Couch, William		Tucker, Martha		Leeper, Mrs. R.J. Jr. - Couch, Earl - Denton, Mrs. D.C.	Buffalo Grove					
Couch, Horace A.	Aug 7, 1964	Jeff Co	Tn	Nov 1, 1916	47	S			Peoples, Allie		Couch, Robert-Lloyd - Rich, Mrs. - Beason, Mrs. - Murrell, Mrs. [Va]	Jefferson Memorial	WW 2				
Couch, John P.	Jul 30, 1951	Hamblen Co	Tn	Aug 27, 1951	72-11-3	W	Couch, William S.		Peoples, Allie		Redman, Rebecca	Mt. Pleasant					
Couch, Lloyd F. [Harpor]	Sep 12, 1987	J.M.H. Morristown, Tn	Tn	Apr 11, 1911	76	W	Couch, Bertram P.		Malcom, Sallie		Couch, Janette - Rudder, Hazel - Malcom	West View					
Couch, Malcolm Thomas	Sep 6, 1999	Hamblen Co	Tn	Mar 20, 1911	88	Quarles, Margaret	Couch, John P.		Adams, Charles E.		Adams, Charles E.	J.M.G.					
Couch, Robert Clarence	May 2, 1983	Knoxville, Tn	Jeff City	Aug 1, 1923	69	Messengill, Jamel	Peoples, Allie		Willie		Willie	J.M.G.		John Edward & Beth			
Courtney, Hugh H. Sr.	Aug 21, 1983	J.M.H. Birmingham, Ala.	Tn	Dec 30, 1904	78	Witt, Mary Lynn	Courtney, Thomas		Carmichael, Ida		Courtney, Mrs. Hugh	Jefferson Memorial					
Courtney, John Thomas	Feb 21, 1986	Tn	Tn	Mar 29, 1913	72	May, Mary	Courtney, Thomas		Carmichael, Sarah		Courtney, Mary Mary	Sunderland					
Courtney, Mary Lynn	Feb 16, 1993	Jeff City	Knoxville, Tn	May 22, 1909	83		Witt, J.P.		Harmon, Bonie		Courtney, Hugh Jr. [Son]	J.M.G.			Carolyn		
Courtney, Robert Franklin Jr.	Nov 25, 1975	Dumas, Ark	Jeff City	Mar 27, 1934	41	Crawford, Sarah	Courtney, Robert F.		Johnson, Shirley		Johnson, F.H. [Dumas, Ark.]	Jefferson Memorial					Merrick, Helen - Couch, Blanche - Beason, Merian - Rich, Claurila
Courtney, Thomas	Jul 9, 1960	Jeff Co	Tn	Mar 12, 1878	82	W	Courtney, Tom		Thomas, Annie		Courtney, Hugh H. - James, Mrs. Frank [On Flyleaf]	Sunderland				Jim	Lilea, Janet
Cousaubury, John	Feb 25, 1926	Jeff Co	[D.?, KY]														

NAME	DDATE	BLOCAT	BLOCAT	BDATE	AGE	SPOUSE	FATHER	FRELOCAT	MOTHER	MRELOCAT	BY	BURIAL	VET	SON	DAUG	BROTHER	SISTER
Codd, Chris	May 22, 1943	Jeff Co					Codd, Joe				Maudie, Mrs. W.M. - Hunter, Mrs. Gene	Kingsport, Texas / Sarah Swann					
Cowan, Annie	Nov 26, 1932	Jeff City	Tn	Jan 20, 1886	33	Cowan, John	Ballard, Tyson H.		Brown, Maggie	Tn	Cowen, Mrs. Margaret	Jefferson Memorial					
Cowen, Hugh L.	Apr 6, 1970	Miami, Fla.	Tn		63	Purifoy, Margaret											
Cowan, James Robert	Oct 3, 1978	Jeff City	Tn	Dec 14, 1921	56	S	Cowan, John	Tn	Ballard, Annie	Tn	Cocate, Ted - Curtis, Leslie (1 sisa)	West View	WW 2				
Cowan, Joel Walter	Feb 23, 1946	Dandridge	Tn	Dec 22, 1855	90	Ng					Cowan, J.B. - Ridgeway, Mrs. William	Presby - Dandridge	WW 2				
Cowen, Walter Edward	Oct 25, 1944	Jeff Co	Jeff Co	Aug 1, 1899	45	S	Cowan, A.W.	Tn	Harris, Ewis Mae	Tn	Harris, Mrs. W.R. - Widower, Cox, Mrs. A.W.	West View					
Cox, A.W.	Feb 26, 1955	68		Mar 28, 1866	In	W	Cox, Roscoe		Pierce, Rindy		Cox, James Tom - Artie-White, Mrs. Glen - Tatin, Clarence	West View					
Cox, Adaline	Jan 25, 1959	Jeff City	Tn	Apr 5, 1882	77	Ng	Knight, James		Gardens, Adaline Ann			Mt. Horeb					
Cox, Adon Kern	Jun 16, 1953	Jeff Co	Tn	Feb 14, 1879	74	S			Ferguson, Clarissa Ann			West View					
Cox, Allen	Oct 6, 1952	Knox Co	Tn	Nov 26, 1880	71	W	Cox, William K.		Hunter, Hattie		Hunt, Clarice	West View					
Cox, Alger Earl	Jul 16, 1975	Jeff City	Tn	Aug 12, 1925	49	Mc Gough, Ruth	Cox, Luther		Varnell, Stella		Cox, Susan - Turner, Mrs. Donnie - Cox, Augusta - V.A.	Jefferson Memorial	WW 2				
Cox, Charley James	Jun 3, 1973		Tn	Aug 5, 1920	52	Div	Cox, James R.		Finley, Della		Cox, Susan - Turner, Mrs. Donnie - Cox, Augusta - V.A.	Jefferson Memorial	WW 2				
Cox, Cleva	Nov 3, 1987	Jeff City	Jeff Co	Mar 8, 1920	77		Rankin, Fate		Ward, Grace		Cox, Terry [Son]	J.M.G.		Curry, Shelba - Gregory, Judy	Curry, Shelba - Gregory, Judy	
Cox, Curtis Haskell	Sep 8, 1987	Greene Co. / Tn	Tn	Oct 24, 1915	81	Rankin, Cleva	Cox, George Walter	Tn	Carter, Martha E.	Tn	Wife	J.M.G.	navy	Terry		Ralph [Ohio]	
Cox, Edna	Dec 31, 1982	New Market	Tn	Oct 14, 1875	57	W	Forrest, M.L.	Tn	Parrott, Mary E.	Tn	Sexton, Walter	New Market					
Cox, Etsb Maude	Jan 4, 1929		Tn		0-3-7		Cox, James	Tn	Travis, Nellie		Cox, James	West View					
Cox, Florida	Mar 2, 1934	Jeff City	Tn	Jan 14, 1881	73	W	Gass, M.	Tn	Randies, Nina	Tn	Oakland	Oakland					
Cox, Flossie M.	Oct 2, 1958	Jeff Co	Tn	May 28, 1891	67	Cox Joe Ralph [0]	Mc Intosh, John S.		Reese, Eliza		Tinsley, Mrs. Elenor Jr.-Willard, Daine & Joe-Tate, Betty - Dobbins, Patsy - Hatcher, Sylvia	Mill Springs					
Cox, George David	Sep 20, 1959	Jeff Co	Tn	Nov 23, 1912	62	Wells, Margaret	Cox, Joseph		Barlow, Louella		Cox, Mrs. Margaret-White, Nancy - Ingram, Bertine - Cox, Tom -	West View	WW 2				
Cox, George Washington	Sep 20, 1959	Jeff Co	Tn	Aug 26, 1975	84	W	Cox, James		Lline, Nancy		Cox, Mrs. Elizabeth - Hartman, Mrs. Faye [Dang]	Mt. Horeb					
Cox, Howell	Mar 28, 1979	Jeff City	Cameron, Elizabeth	May 4, 1905	73	Cox, Jessie Barton			Ingram, Mary Jane		Jefferson Memorial	Jefferson Memorial					
Cox, Ida Pauline	Feb 18, 1989	J.M.H.	Tn	May 1, 1908	80	W	Reneau, William O.		Carson, Matilda		Cox, John Jr.	Mt. View					
Cox, Ira	Mar 26, 1925		Tn [0.No]		26	S	Cox, Hugh F.		Cox, Mary E.		Cox, H.F.	West View					
Cox, Inert	Jul 3, 1935		Tn				Cox, Offis	Va	Cox, Offis		Cox, Offis	Oakland					
Cox, Inert Mae	Sep 30, 1968		Tn	Jul 3, 1935			Combs, Hugh F.		Roach, Estel Mae		Cox, H.F.	Piedmont					
Cox, James Garfield	Dec 26, 1980	J.M.H.	Jeff Co	Apr 10, 1920	70	Underwood, Helen	Cox, George Washington		Knight, Adaline		Cox, Helen U. - V.A.	Mt. View	unk				
Cox, James Rufus	Jan 7, 1964	Ft. Worth, Tx	Tn	Jan 10, 1891	73	W	Cox, Ross		Brinser, Charlie		Cox, Charlie - Gist	West View	WW 1				
Cox, Jeffery Patton	Apr 6, 1982	Jeff Co	Tn	Apr 6, 1982			Cox, Riley		Hufrfellow, Lourise		Cox, Riley	Jefferson Memorial		Roscoe-Riley-Gerald	Johnson, Betty	
Cox, Jessie Pearl	Jan 9, 1986	Ft. Worth, Tx	Tn	Nov 27, 1911	86		Gallyon, William Luther		Conruth, Bessie		Herron, Gladia [Dang]	J.M.G.					
Cox, Joe Frank	Sep 10, 1977	J.M.H.	Tn	Jun 22, 1907	70	Ng	Cox, William Luther		Newman, Emeline		Jefferson Memorial Gardens	Jefferson Memorial Gardens					
Cox, John Anderson	Sep 2, 1966	Morgan Clinic	May 8, 1922		46	Walters, Nannie B.	Cox, Luther		Varnell, —		Cox, R.T. - Edgar, Ann - Cox, Mrs. John A.	Jefferson Memorial Gardens					
Cox, John Jr.	Jun 5 1998	Jeff Co	Tn	Dec 16, 1925	72		Cox, John Sr.		Reneau, Pauline		Cox, Johnny E. [Son]	Mt. View		Robert-Stanley-Leroy-Albert & Naone		
Cox, John Ralph	Feb 22, 1927		Tn		0-10-0		Cox, Joe Ralph	Tn	Mc Intosh, Flossie	Tn	Mc Intosh, Mary - Cox, J.R.	Mill Springs			Knight, Mary & Tommy Johnson, Pauline & Steve - Miller, Betty	Gregory, Judy	

NAME	DDATE	DLOCAT	BLOCAT	BDATE	AGE	SPOUSE	FATHER	FELLOCAT	MOTHER	MFLOCAT	BY	BURIAL	VET	SON	DAUG	BROTHER	SISTER
Cox, John Raymond	Sep 25, 1945	Jeff Co	Jeff Co	Feb 23, 1907	38	Brannen, Edna Mae [Age 33] Ng	Cox, Joseph Daniel	Tn	Collins, Ollie	Tn	Cox, Mrs. Raymond	Balch	WW 1				
Cox, John Sr.	Feb 28, 1976	Dandridge, Tn	Tn	May 16, 1896	79		Cox, George		Love, Fannie		Cox, Mrs. John Sr.	Mt. View					
Cox, John Tate	Aug 18, 1995	Jeff City		May 22, 1922	73	Young, Marvis	Cox, Joseph E.		Barbee, Lou Ellis		Wife	Renfhaven - Newport, Tn	41-64	John M. [Non]- Stephen J. [Ste]- Gregory B. [?]			
Cox, Lenial Brown Sr.	Aug 31, 1990	Jeff City	Tn	Mar 6, 1906	74	W	Cox, Joseph		Lawson, Louella		Barbee, Judy	West View					
Cox, Lon	Jul 26, 1962	Jeff Co	Tn	Mar 4, 1890	72	Ng	Cox, Jess		Ingram, Jane		Cox, Grace & Glenn	Sunderland					
Cox, Lona K.	Jun 27, 1969	Knox Co		May 9, 1902	67	Cox, Tom [D]	Mc Danille, E.K.		Turner, Celia		Howard, Mrs. -	Memorial Gardens					
Cox, Louella	Nov 16, 1969	Jeff Co	Tn	Aug 23, 1883	86	W	Barbee, William		Patton, Margaret Isabella		Cameron, Clara - Cox, J.T. & Marvin	Pleasant View					
Cox, Luther Filoy	Jan 29, 1982	Jeff City	Tn	Oct 2, 1982	69	Ng	Cox, John A.		Miller, Cordelia Ann		Cox, Algin	Jefferson Memorial Dandridge					
Cox, Margaret Catherine	Jan 11, 1983	Jeff Co	Tn	Jul 15, 1898	74	W	Henderson, Samuel		Northern, Elmer		Northern, Elmer	Dandridge					
Cox, Margaret Grace	Apr 8, 1947	Jeff Co	Sevier Co	Aug 19, 1867	59-7-19	S	Cox, William K.	Tn	Ferguson, Clarissa Ann	Tn	Cox, Luia	West View					
Cox, Mary Jane	Sep 21, 1949	Jeff Co	Tn	Sep 14, 1865	85	W	Unk		Ingram, Emma		Cox, Howell - Lou - Frank	Pleasant View					
Cox, Mildred Allene	Dec 15, 1987	Arkansas	Tn	Aug 11, 1913	74	W	Lockhart, Milburn, H.		Miller, Grace P.		Cox, Dale [Son]	J.M.G.					
Cox, Nancy Jane	May 13, 1966	J.M.H.	Tn	May 14, 1942	43	S	Cox, Taylor		Baxter, Roxie		Nance, Mrs. Harold	Jefferson Memorial					
Cox, Oitha Houston	Oct 25, 1983	Jeff City	Jeff Co	Oct 26, ----	56-11-29	Ng	Cox, Robert		Henderson, Margaret		Cox, Blanche & Children	West View					
Cox, Paul Anderson	Nov 20, 1966	Jeff Co	Tn	Nov 9, 1904	62	Ng	Cox, Anderson		Brimmer, Cordelia		Memorial Gardens	West View					
Cox, Porter Ann	May 10, 1966	Jeff Co	Tn	Apr 25, 1915	54	Ng	Cox, Ale		Barbee, Louella		Cox, Mrs. Jessie	Mt. View					
Cox, Ray W.	Nov 25/27, 1978	Jeff City		Sept -, 1896	82	S	Cox, H.F.		Mitchell, Armanda		Cox, Dorothy	West View	WW 2				
Cox, Reuben Elsworth [Col]	Feb 15, 1941		Yazoo, Miss.		abr 35		Gadsberry, Sarah		Nox, Jack T.	Yazoo, Miss.	Booth, W.P. [Brother]	Gary, Indiana					
Cox, Robert Earl	Jun 14, 1997	Jeff City	Tn	Jan 7, 1944	53	Ragain, Judith	Cox, John Anderson Sr.				Wife	J.M.G.	66-72	Dusty-Chad	Maruk, Stacy	John Anderson Jr.	
Cox, Rosie Erma	Oct 17, 1995	J.M.H.	Tn	May 27, 1922	63	Cox, Taylor	Trent, Nancy Jane				Wife	J.M.G.					
Cox, Stella	Jun 28, 1996	J.M.H.	Tn	Sep 26, 1896	89	W	Varnell, John R.		Magalis, Martha		Ronnie-Jim, Helen, Harold - Tharp, Mrs. Herbert - Fielden, Mrs. Cleda [Daug]	Everlasting Life - J.M.G.					
Cox, Taylor F.	Apr 1, 1988	Hillhaven	Tn	Dec 3, 1915	72	W	Cox, Robert		Henderson, Margaret		Cox, Taylor Frances - Nance, Judy	J.M.G.	WW 2				
Cox, Temple Ingram	Nov 28, 1987	Jeff Co	Tn	Jul 14, 1889	98	W	Ingram, Lavatta		Henderson, Margaret		Brown, Mrs. Grace Cox	Sunderland					
Cox, Thomas F.	Feb 2, 1988	Milligan Clinic	Tn	Dec 12, 1904	83	Mc Daniel, Lena	Cox, William		Newman, Emma		Sheddan, Mrs. Albie - Cox, Mullin-Jane & Howell	Memorial Gardens	WW 2				
Cox, Wendell Oliver	May 24, 1948	Hamblen Co	Tn	Aug 28, 1937	10		Cox, Howell	Tn	Richard, Ida F.	Tn	Cox, Mullin-Jane & Howell	Mt. Yale					
Cox, William Le Roy Sr.	Sep 1, 1983	J.M.H.	Tn	May 15, 1910	73	Div	Cox, Joseph		Barbee, Louella		Myers, Mrs. Lois Howell	Flat Gap	WW 2				
Cox, William Anderson	Aug 3, 1984	J.M.H.	Tn	May 30, 1929	55	S	Cox, Paul A.		Gellison, Jessie Pearl		Cox, Jessie	Jefferson Memorial					
Cox, William K.	Aug 15, 1935	Jeff Co	Tn		83-1-5	Ng	Couch, William W.	Tn	Couch, Eliza	Tn	Sons	West View					
Cox, Willie Mai	Nov 26, 1933		Tn	Jan 26, 1902	31	Ng	Martin, Clarrie		Couch, Eliza		Cox, Jim	West View					
Cozart, Mattcal Jane	Jun 4, 1987	J.M.H.		Feb 1, 1911	76	Cozart, Robert [D]	Leonnard, William H.	Tn	Martin, Carrie	Tn	Cozart, Billy Joe - Doughlas, Nelda - World, Latty	J.M.G.					
Cozart, Robert	Jul 6, 1977	Jeff Co		May 17, 1903	74	Ng	Cozart, James		Allen, Susie		Cozart, Mrs. Robert Howell	Jefferson Memorial					
Craig, Ella Kate	Dec 23, 1950	Jeff Co	Tn	Feb 22, 1888	62	Craig, Feilie	Dillard, Bud		Davis, Katherine		Couch, Mrs. Bele - Couch, Mrs. Lloyd	West View					
Craig, William Desmund Jr.	Jun 22, 1941	Polk Co		Aug 25 1941	25-8-28	S	Craig, F.G.	Tn	Dillard, Ella	Polk Co	Craig, F.G.	Mill Springs					
Craustein, Arthur William Jr.	Jul 23, 1998	Knoxville, Tn	Tn	Apr 17, 1896	56	Craustein, Hugh D.	Craustein, Arthur W. Sr.	Nc	Cook, Audrey Belle	Polk Co	Wife	Jefferson Memorial			Smith, Ann		Smith, Barbara Jean - Lowe, Nancy - Jackson, Sue
Crawford, Anna	Oct 5, 1982	J.M.H.	Tn			Munn, Benjamin			Hurt, Minnie		Manley, Mrs. Nell - Crawford, Charles-Thomas	Jefferson Memorial					Mtser, Laura Belle

NAME	DDATE	BLOCAT	BLOCAT	BDATE	AGE	SPOUSE	FATHER	FBLOCAT	MOTHER	MFBLOCAT	BY	BURIAL	VET	SON	DAUG	BROTHER	SISTER
Crawford, Doyle	Oct 18, 1998	Jeff City	Greeneville, Tn	May 4, 1915	83	S	Unk		Unk		Harris, Gina [Fillmore Admin.]	Oakland - Grainger Co					
Crawford, Harry	Feb 10, 1998	Humana Hosp.	Sullivan Co., Tn	Mar 7, 1913	75	S	Unk		Unk		Eggers, Stacey [Guardian]	Hopewell					
Crawford, Hugh Daniel	May 30, 1975	Jeff Co	Tn	Jun 25, 1892	82	Mann, Annil	Crawford, William M.		Killion, Margaret		Crawford, Mrs. Hugh Daniel [Wife]	Jefferson Memorial					
Crawford, Jane King	May 22, 1976	Keeton, Va	Tn	Oct 19, 1902	73	W	King, William Felix	N.I.	Halfacer, Anna M.		Crawford, Charles J. & Jack & Johnny	West View					
Crawford, Louie Irene	Apr 24, 1942	New Market	Cordonia, Illinois	Apr 8, 1868	74	Crawford, Charles J.	Johnson, Joseph J.		Cook, Sarah	Illinois	Crawford, Charles J. & Jack & Johnny	West View					
Crockett, Charles Gordon	Sep 4, 1980	Troy, New York	Tn	Mar 26, 1929	51	S	Crockett, Floyd V.		Turner, Mrs. Jean B. [Mr.]		Turner, Mrs. Jean B. [Mr.]	West View	Korea				
Crockett, Cinelus Nile	Nov 21, 1998	Strawberry Plains	Maheny, Tn	Apr 28, 1922	76	Stewart, Nell	Crockett, Charles Nell		Cobbins, Gaynell		Wife	East View Memorial					Berry, Jan - Cantrell, Nan
Crook, Gertrude A.	Jul 19, 1905	No		Apr 25, 1907	28	S	Crook, F.A.	Indiana	Grattan, Lillie	Indiana	Crooks, F.A.	West View					Varble, Bea
Crooks, Frank Abraham	Jul 31, 1945	Jeff Co	Lawrence Co, Indiana	Jul 20, 1872	73	Ng	Crooks, Newton	Indiana	Osborn, Sallie	Bedford, Indiana	Crooks, David N.	West View					
Crooks, Frank Edward	Dec 23, 1999	Jeff Co	Tn	Mar 4, 1915	54	Ng	Crooks, Walter		Osborn, Sallie	Indiana	Crooks, Mary E.	Shiloh - Grainger Co					
Crooks, Grace Lillie	Aug 18, 1944	Indiana	Indiana	May 7, 1881	63	W	Draper, Joseph		Draper, Grace		Crooks, Ruth-Fred-Fern [Children]	West View					
Crooks, May	May 12, 1947	Morgan Co, Tn	Bedford, Indiana	Apr 5, 1876	71-1-7	S	Crooks, Newton	Indiana	Osborn, Sallie	Indiana	Crooks, Daniel N. - Ott, Glenna [Wurtburg]	West View					
Crooks, Sudie	Aug 17, 1949	Jeff Co	Tn	Oct 22, 1878	69-9 / 25	W	Myreatt, Hanibal	Tn	Renfro, Susan Ann	Tn	Crooks, Franklin	West View					
Cross, Abie	Dec 27, 1927	Tn	Tn		80	W	Unk		Unk		Cross, W.J.	Brenner					
Cross, Charlie Wesley	Apr 9, 1946	Tn		Jul 30, 1885	60	W	Cross, Abe	Tn	Unk	Tn	Cross, Sam C.	Shiloh					
Cross, Della Gertrude	Jan 26, 1942	Grainger Co		Aug 4, 1905	49-9 / 25	Cross, Charles	Cross, William J.	Tn	Cook, Sienna	Th	Cross, Charles						
Cross, Fannie Florence	Oct 2, 1940	Jeff City		Aug 4, 1905	35	Ng	Spiver, James	Tn	Cook, Sienna	Th	Cross, Bill	Shiloh					
Cross, Harvey F.	Jan 21, 1990	U.T.H.	Jeff City	Apr 2, 1926	63	Div	Cross, William J.		Cook, Sienna	Tn	Cross, John D. - V.A.- Jerry Carmichael, Ethel -Manby, Nell- Brown, Mrs. J.M.	Shiloh	WW 2				
Cross, Hattie E.	Apr 5, 1972	Tn		Mar 22, 1915	57	W	Phillips, Nora	Tn	Morris, Maude		Cross, Fred & Daughs	West View					
Cross, James Roy	Mar 3, 1966	Tn		Apr 11, 1914	52	Ng	Cross, J.J.		Morris, Maude	Tn	Cross, Mrs. Lois & Children	Jefferson Memorial					
Cross, John	Oct 1, 1927	Tn		Jul 30, 1885	60	Ng	Cross, Abe		Cross, Alta		Cross, Alta	West View					
Cross, John David	Oct 22, 1987	Knoxville, Tn	Jeff City	Dec 26, 1927	59	W	Cross, William J.	Tn	Spencer, Fannie		Cross, Jerry [Son] Cross, Louise- Raymond T.-C.A.- Maude-Roy	Shiloh	52-54	Lynn	Frazier, Kelly		
Cross, John J.	Oct 15, 1959	Knox Co				Ng	Stansbury, John	Tn	Cross, Nancy		Cross, J.D. - V.A.- Raymond T.-C.A.- Maude-Roy	Piedmont					
Cross, Maggie	Mar 28, 1928	Tn				Cross, John	Stansbury, John		Young, Mattie	Tn	Cross, J.D.- Morrison, Lucille [Rel.]	West View					
Cross, Raymond Lewis	Aug 23, 1974	Tn		Jul 24, 1924	50	S	Cross, Sam		Spencer, Fannie		Cross, Mrs. Lois & County- Walker, Edd	Shiloh - Grainger Co					
Cross, Sam	Feb 11, 1947	Jeff Co		Apr 12, 1888	85	S	Cross, Ab		Newman, Margaret		Cross, J.D. & Raymond	Poor Farm					
Cross, William J.	Aug 18, 1973	Jeff City	Tn	Sep 3, 1905	77	W	Cross, Ab		Walker, Lura		Cross, J.D. & Raymond	Shiloh - Grainger Co	WW 1				
Crossing, Elmo French [M]	Feb 21, 1983	V.A.- Mt. Home		Jul 7, 1921	72	Div	Crowell, Floda		Crossing, Anna		Crossing, Anna	Jefferson Memorial	WW 1				
Cross, James A.	Oct 14, 1993	Rowan Co., Nc			72	S	Watts, Sam		Curse, Patricia A.		Cross, Catherine [Daug]	Cremated					
Culberson, Maude R. [Black]	Mar 27, 1989	J.M.H.			91	Culberson, Thomas	Culberson, William M.		Elliott, Sarah		Meadon, Catherine [Daug] - Williamson, Rachel	West View					
Cunningham, Keneth	Sep 29, 1933	Talbott		Apr 26, 1920	13	S	Cunningham, John	Tn	Crisjer, Frankie	Tn	Dyer, E.W., Jarnigan, Martha [Sister]	Tellico Plain					
Cunningham, Clifford [Col]	Feb 16, 1941	Jeff Co			33	S	Unk		Tate, Mollie		Martha Davis Baptist	Martha Davis Baptist					
Cunningham, George [Col]	Apr 17, 1947	Knox Co			36	Davis, Mary	Unk		Hodge, Lula	Jeff Co	Mary & Ross	New Market					
Cunningham, Irene [Col]	Mar 1, 1928				2	S	Cunningham, William		Hodge, Lula	Tn	Cunningham, William	New Market Colored					
Cunningham, Jim [Col]	Dandson Co, Tn		May 23, 1926		20	S	Cunningham, Will	Tn	Anderson, Mary	Tn	State Pen - Smith, Bonnie	New Market					
Cunningham, James [Col]	Aug 25, 1946	Jeff City	Tn	Sep 30, 1872	68	S	Cunningham, William	Tn	Anderson, Mary	Tn	Cunningham, Ross	New Market					

NAME	DDATE	DLOCAT	BLOCAT	BDATE	AGE	SPOUSE	FATHER	FBLOCAT	MOTHER	MFBLOCAT	BY	BURIAL	VET	SON	DAUG	BROTHER	SISTER
Cunningham, Luther Roger [Col]	May 27, 1940	Jeff Co.	Tn	May 27, 1940	4m		Cunningham, Buford	Tn	Cunningham, Clara	Tn	Cunningham, Buford	Colored					
Cunningham, Mary Mollie [Col]	Aug 16, 1963	Jeff Co.	Tn	Sep 12, 1888	74.5	W	Tate, John		Jane		Bradford, Martha - Jennie-Erna-Boe- William-Buford	West View Colored					
Cunningham, Roger Taylor [Col]	Nov 18, 1953	Jeff Co.	Tn			S	Cunningham, William		Hodge, Lula		Cunningham, Ross- Lloyd-Mary - Buford, Delly & Curtis	Youngs Memorial					
Cupp, Edgar Earl	Nov 4, 1995	Jeff City	Hamblen Co	Aug 24, 1913	82		Cupp, Jake		Vaughn, Martha E.		Cupp, Fern [Nephew] - Mc Kenzie, Suana - Rowe, Rosie - Hilbert, Joyce [Niece]	Pleasant View					William Martha [TX]
Cupp, Fern W.	Nov 18, 1995	Knoxville, Tn	Hamblen Co.	May 10, 1935	60		Cupp, James Houston		Carroll, Grace [Friend]		Cureton, Charles - Justice, Mrs. J.E.	J.M.G.					
Cupp, Martha Elizabeth	Jul 1, 1953	Jeff Co.	Tn	Oct 24, 1892	60	W	Vaughn, James H.		Weaver, Mary		Cupp, Mary Lee-Nelson	Pleasant View					
Cupp, Mary Lee	Apr 17, 1918	Jeff Co.	Tn	Sep 6, 1918	58	S	Cupp, Jake		Wraght, Martha		Cupp, Edgar E- Fern	Pleasant View					
Cureton, Charles B.	Apr 2, 2000	Jeff City	Tn	Aug 23, 1917	82	W	Cureton, Charles		Thomas, Ellie		Cureton, Charles B Jr.- Rutledge, Tn	Central Pt. Church - Rutledge, Tn					
Cureton, Clara M.	Feb 18, 1995	Jeff City	Green Co., Ky	Apr 23, 1912	82		Simpson, Charles Edward		Kent, Nettie Mae		Doughty, Nelda & Charles [Daug]	J.M.G.		Charles [Ind]-Oakley- Vice, Lorenna [III] - Proud, Genevie [ON]			
Cureton, Thomas Radford	Aug 26, 1941	Jeff Co	Tn		16-9- 13	S	Cureton, Charles		Thomas, Ellie		Cureton, Charles -						
Cureton, William Ray	Oct 3, 1995	Jeff City	Jeff City	Aug 18, 1922	73	W	Cureton, Charles		Wells		Cureton, Charles -	J.M.G.		John Ray-Gary Lynn-Dennis Allen		Charles Burnett- James-Gene-Roger	Nelson, Kathleen Mills [Ga]
Curl, Jennie A.	Jul 12, 1926	Jeff City	Tn		75-0- 28	W	Welch, E.		Walker, Sarah		Curl, A.B.	Shilo					
Curl, Jessie Loretta	Jun 7, 1993	Granger Co	Granger Co	Jun 8, 1914	78	Curl, John T.	Mc Ginnis, Oral		Farmer, Elizabeth		Husband	Oakland - Grainger Co		Marvin-Delmas A.		Wiley-Bill-Herman- Ethred	Surfington, Pauline
Curl, John Terry Sr.	Apr 29, 1945	Granger Co	Tn	Feb 19, --45	66-2- 10	Ng	Curl, J.D.		West, Jane A.	Tn	Curl, A.B.	Shiloh					
Curl, John Terry	Mar 27, 1995	Jeff City	Granger Co	Jun 23, 1916	78	Ogle, Wanda	Curl, John		Moody, Tinny		Curl, Marvin & Pastry [Son]	Oakland - Grainger Co	2319	Delmas & Sherry - [Step] Wagner, Gilbert - Ogle, Dewey			Hensley, Ads - Williams, Estelle - Duck, Helen - Staines, Leola - Duck, Eva
Curl, Julia Tina	Jan 11, 1958	Grainger Co	Tn	Nov 16, ---	71-1- 25	W	Moody, Samuel		Gray, Jerusha		Williams, Mrs. Lewis [Daug]	Shiloh - Grainger Co					
Curl, Michael Eugene	Dec 8, 1998	White Pine, Tn	Knoxville, Tn	Aug 7, 1966	32	Curl, Eugene Franklin	Duhon, Shirley Elizabeth			Father	Oakland					
Curry, Callie	Oct 16, 1982	Jeff Co.	Tn	Jan 6, 1882	70	Curry, Bruce C.	Helin, Richard S.	Tn	Smith, Sara		Curry, B.C.	Hillcrest					Myers, Jill - Ripple, Sherry
Curry, William Bennett	Oct 13, 1941	Talbott	Cocke Co		20-3- 28	S	Hout, Clarence		Farmer, Queenie	Cocke Co	Curry, Paul	Flat Gap					
Curry, Zona Cass	Oct 14, 1952	Jeff Co	Tn	Sep 22, 1964	88	W	Glass, John C.		Dimwoodie, Melinda		Curry, R.C.- Edd- Burley, Mrs. Lillie - Wagner, Mrs. Fred	Wesleys Chapel					
Curtis, Helen G.	Feb 4, 1998	Dandridge, Tn La Cross, Wi	Jun 2, 1998	99	Tobin, William	Shanks, Margaret		Curry, Neil [Son]		Cremated		Curtis, Malcolm - Edfield, Ruth		Mosher, Margaret - Edfield, Ruth		
Dackclona, Glenda Faye	Mar 9, 1998	Knoxville, Tn	Eden, Nc	Jun 20, 1975	22	Howell, Early Glen	Hughes, Mary			Mother	West View		Curtis, Malcolm Terry Scott 3			Leon & Missie - Jeff & Townsend, Debbie & Dean
Dall, Beulah Faye	Apr 16, 1982	Knoxville, Tn	Tn	Feb 26, 1998	Dackdona, Terry Scott 2nd	W	Gaines, Iva				Highland Memorial - Knox Co		Terry Scott 3 Rd		Felicia-Early-Daniel	
Dale, Imogene	Mar 2, 1940	Mill Springs	Tn	Jan 27, 1940	1m	Dall, Martin L.	Dall, Clarl		Dall, Martin L.		Dale, Curtis	Mill Springs					
Dale, James C.	Feb 3, 1971	Jeff Co.	Tn	Apr 22, 1907	63	Ng	Dale, Meck		Dale, Curtis	Tn	Dale, Glenn-Jay-Ezra - Simmons, Bell - Lyons, Georgia	Pleasant Grove					
Dalton, Eliza Francis	Feb 11, 1932	New Market	Tn	May 20, 1899	32	Ng	Brabson, A.W.		Ellie		Dale, Martin L.	Hillcrest					
Dalton, Ruby Irene	Jul 28, 1988	Jeff City	Tn	Sep 4, 1919	68	W	Seaton, Solomon		Watson, Jannie	Tn	Dalton, Raymond - Gann, Brenda	Limestone - Grainger Branch - Grainger Co					
Dance, Bessie Lou	Oct 14, 1988	J.M.H.	Tn	May 24, 1899	89	W	Goble, Daniel M.		Tate, Mary		Lawrence, Mary	Blackwell Branch - Piedmont					

NAME	DDATE	DLOCAT	BLOCAT	BDATE	AGE	SPOUSE	FATHER	FRLOCAT	MOTHER	MFRLOCAT	BY	BURIAL	VET	SON	DAUG	BROTHER	SISTER
Dance, Earl Harding	May 7, 1935		Tn	Oct 8, 1920	14	S	Dance, Roy	Tn	Enckley, Dorothy	Tn	Dance, Bessie G. & Carolyn - Gwen, Betty - Sisgis, Mrs. Robert [Sissgi]	Rocky Valley	Rocky Valley Baptist				
Dance, Horace Beecher	Oct 23, 1961	Jeff Co	Tn	Feb 8, ---	77-7-25	Ng	Dance, James		Jed, Texanna		Hickman, Sylvia - Riley, Jim	Pleasant Grove					
Dance, Nora Hickman	Dec 8, 1966	New Market, Tn		Jul 18, 1895	91	W	Cate, George B.		Dalton, Louie		Dance, W.H.	Piedmont					
Dance, Texanna Elizabeth	May 31, 1950	Jeff Co	Tn	Jan 21, 1864	86	W	Jed, R.E.		Carter, Mary C.		Dance, W.H.	Piedmont					
Dance, Walter Herbert	Oct 25, 1950	Jeff Co	Tn	Jun 2, 1887	63	Ng	Dance, James		Jed, Texie		Dance, Kathleen - Calloway, Laura	Piedmont					
Daniel, Curtis Hoover	Jan 30, 1929	Jeff Co	Tn		2m-23d	S	Daniel, Garret	Tn	Wilmoth, Emma	Tn	Hodge, J.J.	Sunrise					
Daniel, Frank	Apr 24, 1950	Jeff Co	Tn	Mar 18, 1867	83	S	Daniel, Will				Alltup, Roy	Sunrise - Grainger Co					
Daniel, Martha	Jul 31, 1998	Morristown, Tn	Gardner, Me	Dec 9, 1946	51	Daniel, Fred	Donaldson, Fred		Murdock, Ethel		Daniel, Jose-John-Louise	J.M.G.		Jason-Barry	Danette	Fred-Ernest	Engelking, Patricia
Daniels, Charles A.	Apr 16, 1972		Tn								Roseberry - Knox Co	Roseberry					
Daniels, Herbie Lytle	Nov 3, 1993	Morristown, Tn	Illinois	Sep 25, 1906	87		Lytle, Brazelton		Cox, Elizabeth		Daniels, Charles [Son]	West View		Herbert-Lytle [Snooke]	Seals, Peggy		
Daniels, Hubert Aubrey	Nov 4, 1983	Jeff Co	Ga	Oct 23, 1903	60	Daniels, Charlie	Daniel, Charles		Freeman, Lenora		Daniels, Mrs. Hardie	West View					
Daniels, Infant Male	Oct 7, 1947	Jeff Co		Oct 7, 1947	nc		Daniels, Hubert					West View					
Daniels, Joseph Bolin	Aug 15, 1990	Jeff City	Tn	Apr 15, 1919	71	Morbett, Mary F.	Daniels, Charles A.		Guy, Rufina		Daniels, Mary F.	J.M.G.	Army				
Daniels, Julia B Etter	Mar 2, 1994	Jeff City	Talbott, Tn	Dec 3, 1905	88		Rickard, William J.		Byrd, Mattie		Parker, Jo Ann [Daug]	Mt. Pleasant		Eller, Joe P. [In-Law] Woodard, Afton - Maxie - Chris - Hazel - Coley, Willie [D]	McMurtury, Mary - Looney, Bonnie - Delucker, Bessie [Step] Atkins, Hazel - Ashley,	Marshall	
Daniels, Louise	Apr 12, 1998	Jeff City	Knox Co	Nov 17, 1924	73		Daniels, Charles A.		Guy, Rufina Mae		Ebert, Patricia [Niece - ALU]	Roseberry					
Daniels, Rufina Mae	Nov 25, 1943	Knox Co	Ga	Jun 19, 1895	48	Daniels, Charlie	Gray, John E.	Ga	Robinson, Lydia E.	Ga	Daniels, Charlie [Clinton]	Roseberry - Knox Co					
Dannenhold, Cyril Roger	May 30, 1999	Knoxville, Tn	Jeff City	Jun 23, 1943	55		Dannenhold, Cyril O.		McCown, Jean		Daniels, Mrs. Eula - Mother	Cremated					
Dambach, William Harmon	Aug 13, 1982	Jeff Co	Tn	Oct 11, 1905	56	Ng	Dambach, Robert		Gidden, Julia		Dambach, Mrs. William H.	Nance's Grove					
Davidson, Virard Samuel	Apr 12, 1985	Morristown, Tn	Jeff Co	Jul 13, 1910	84		Davidson, Ben		McGhee, Martha		McCapnhook, Margaret [Daug]	Narcos Grove - New Market, Tn					
Davies, Randee H.	Jan 8, 1997	Battleboro, Vt		Jul 13, 1947	49	Davies, Edward J.	Herbert, Thomas L.		Hurley, Frances		Husband	Cremated			Arthur-Curtis- Jerry	Murphy, Peggy - Hubbard, Marcie	
Davis, Ada Belle	Mar 23, 1985	Knoxville, Tn		Nov 8, 1918	66	W	Shipley, David A.		Russell, Nora Jane	Tn	Davis, Ira Chris	Hebron				Bingsworth, Jodee	
Davis, Anna Taylor [Col]	Aug 27, 1996	New Market	Tn	Feb 2, 1921	15	S	Davis, John	Tn	Davis, Mollie	Tn	Mother	Hebron					
Davis, Benjamin Franklin	May 27, 1955	Jeff Co	Tn	Sep 9, 1879	75	Ng	Davis, James B.		Rankin, Grace		Davis, Mrs. Eula - Carpenter, Mrs.	Hebron					
Davis, Bernice	Nov 19, 1996	J.M.H.	Tn	Jan 24, 1903	83	S	Davis, C.A.		Franklin, Grace		Greeden, Mrs. Ruth - Wisecarver, Bice	Hebron					
Davis, Bessie	Dec 22, 1927	J.M.H.			25-6-3	S	Davis, C.L.	Tn	Allen, Hanna	Tn	Allen, Mode	West View					
Davis, Carl Melvin	Apr 12, 1973	Knoxville, Tn	Tn	Feb 24, 1894	79	Cooper, Mamie	Davis, Frank		Kinder, Lucy		Davis, Eula - Hodges, Mrs. Mary - Davis, Frank	Shiloh - Grainger Co					
Davis, Charles B.F.	Dec 26, 1985	J.M.H.	Tn	Sep 30, 1892	93	Cassady, Grace	Davis, E.M.		Loope, Mary		Snodderly, Mrs. Louise D.	Highland Memorial - Knox Co	WW 1				
Davis, Christopher Alexander	Mar 25, 1957	Jeff Co	Tn	Feb 15, 1874	83	W	Davis, J.B.		Rankin, Martha Jane		Davis, Ira M. - Bernice	Hebron					
Davis, Dora G.	Dec 13 1986	Hill Haven N. Home		Mar 15, 1884	102	W	Gilley, Jess		Blevins, Dora		Davis, Ralph [Kingsport, Tn] - Badgere F.H. [Nc] - Dunaway, W.L. [Bernice]	Davis - W. Jefferson, Nc					
Davis, Elsie N.	Apr 9, 1981	Jeff City	Tn	Jan 8, 1898	83	Div	Davis, J.R.		Bowers, Margaret			Chilhowee - Seymour, Tn					

NAME	DDATE	DLOCAT	BLOCAT	BDATE	AGE	SPOUSE	FATHER	FELOCAT	MOTHER	MFELOCAT	BY	BURIAL	VET	SON	DAUG	BROTHER	SISTER
Davis, Eliza [Col]	Feb 19, 1946	Jeff Co	Jeff Co	Jan 5, 1865	81	W	Thomas, Press	Tn	Unk		Cunningham, Glennie- Mollie-Ross - Kelly, Ida	Mt. Zion Colored					
Davis, Eliza Arican	Mar 19, 1962	Strawberry Plains		Apr	73-10- 28	W	Ausbran, John		Mays, Marilda		Davis, Jas [Son] - Smith, J.W. & Jack - Plaunt, W. William	Chinquipin - Hancock Co					
Davis, Elizabeth E.	Oct 12, 1966	Jeff City	U.S.A.	Apr 26, 1903	93	W	Baker, Walter		Hunt, Mary		Santen, Violet Dean [Niece] - Smith, Eanoe [Nephew]	Ebenezer					
Davis, Eitis Catharine	May 30, 1965	Jeff Co		Feb 23, 1886	77	Davis, B.F. [D]	Franklin, Lon		Looney, Josephine		Bolack, Mrs. Sarah J. - Murphy, Mrs. Betty - [Niece]	Hebron					
Davis, F.M.	Jan 3, 1941	Straw Plains	T		84-1-	W					Davis, J.J. & Chas B.F. [Sons] -	Hickory Valley					
Davis, Frank D.	Aug 11, 1950	Hamblen Co	Tn	Mar 16, 1877	73	Ng	Davis, William		Rickels, Ann		Ely, Hubert & Anna	Laurencsburg, Tn ?					
Davis, Grace Cassady	Feb 10, 1968	J.M.H.		Apr 25, 1897	88	Davis, Charles B.F. Cassady, Gordon Will		Snodderly, Mary Alice		Snodderly, Louise D.	Highland Memorial - Knox Co					
Davis, Hubert	Dec 1, 1941	Rogersville, Hawkins Co	Tn		16-4- 19			Tn		Tn		Shaula					
Davis, Ira M.	Feb 10, 1977	Jeff Co	Sevierville, Tn	Apr 2, 1913	63	S	Davis, Christopher A.		Alvin, Addis		Davis, Mrs. Ira M.	Hebron Presby.	WW 2				
Davis, J. Fred	Mar 15, 1973	Brunswick, Ga.		Oct 31, 1910	62	Ng			Snodderly, Ann		Davis, Mrs. J. Fred	Straula					
Davis, James Franklin Sr. [Col]	Apr 18, 1957	J.M.H.	Tn	Mar 6, 1917	40	Pate, Louise	Davis, John			Tn	Davis, Louise - Crit.	St. Luke	unk				
Davis, James Mack	Feb 22, 1955	Blount Co	Tn	Jul 27, 1887	67	Ng	Hitch, Jennie		Rankin, Grace		Davis, Mrs. Anna Lynn Byrd	Sunderland					
Davis, Jasper Judson	Sep 8, 1979	Jeff City	Tn	Dec 19, 1901	77	Grubb, Alberta	Loope, Mary Jane		Davis, Mrs. J.J.		Highland Memorial - Knox Co					
Davis, John	Apr 16, 1983	Knox Co	Tn	Jan 10, 1916	47	Edwards, Ruth	Davis, J. Wiley Lee		Autrican, Eliza		Davis, John & Ruth	Hillcrest					
Davis, Karen Ann	Jun 19, 1964	Granger Co	Tn	Oct 6, 1961	2	Ng	Davis, Frank		Miller, Mary Ruth		Davis, Frank	Shiloh					
Davis, Lawrence Horner Jr.	Jul 17, 1975	St. Louis, Mo		Mar 14, 1925	50	Poehncke, Catherine	Davis, Lawrence H. Sr.		Frick, Cornelia		Davis, Larry [Me]	Calvary - St. Louis, Mo					
Davis, Lela Frances	Oct 20, 1984	Knoxville, Tn	Oregon	Jul 7, 1922	62	S			Cassady, Grace		Snodderly, Louise - Davis, Grace	Highland Memorial East - Knoxville, T					
Davis, Lucy N.	Sep 13, 1983	Tn		Oct 3, 1895	67	S	Davis, J.R.		Bowers, Margaret		Davis, Ersa	Chillhowee - Sevier Co					
Davis, Mollie T.	Jun 10, 1927	Tn		Jan 3, 1874	72	W	Davis, James M.		Margaret		Davis, Lucy [Daug]	Trentville					
Davis, Margaret Bowers	Jan 8, 1946	Sevier Co	Tn	Feb 7, 1857	77	Ng	Bowers, James M.	Tn	Jarnagin, Thenia	Tn	Davis, J.W.	Chilhowee - Sevier Co					
Davis, Mira	Aug 28, 1934	Granger Co	Tn	May 8, 1872	82	W	Cochran, Loyd	Tn			Davis, J.W.	Shilo					
Davis, Norvesta Leah	Dec 9, 1954	Union Co, Tn		May 9, 1872	82	W	Jesson, John T.	Tn	Kelley, Louisa E.		Jadon ?, Union Co, Tn					
Davis, Orpha Hicks	Jul 19, 1946	Cocke Co		Sep 15, 1855	90	Davis, John Wesley [D]	Hicks, James	Tn	O' Dell, Orpha	Tn	Allen, Mrs.	West View					
Davis, Paul Thomas	Jun 12, 1981	Jeff Co		Jun 12, 1981	1	Fonda	Davis, Phillip Milton	Florida	Will, Carolyn Mae	Tn	Davis, Phillip M.	Jefferson Memorial					
Davis, Robert [Col]	Jun 15, 1944	U.T.H.	Tn	Aug 15, ----	80	W	Davis, Dave	Tn	Thompson, Eliza	Ohio	Davis, Alberta & Arthur	New Market					
Davis, Sarah Elizabeth	Oct 22, 1927	Jeff Co	Tn	Jun 11, 1870	64	W	Neace, Noah	Tn	Beavins, Jane	Tn	Grenison, Mrs.	West View					
Daugh, T.M.	Jul 1, 1934	Ng	Tn	May 1, 1900	74	W	Davis, John T.	Va	Jackson, Mary E.	Va	Davis, Mrs. T.M.	West View					
Davis, Thomas Andrew	Mar 6, 1975	Jeff Co	Tn	May 1, 1900	74	W	Davis, Thomas		Marshall, Lucy		Profitt, Lillian	Lebanon					
Davis, Thomas Christapher	Apr 28, 1985	J.M.H.		Aug 2, 1983	1		Davis, Ira Christopher		Davis, Ira		Davis, Ira	Hebron					
Dawdy, Kristen Roberta	Jan 31, 1985	U.T.H.	Michigan	Nov 24, 1966	18	S	Dawdy, James	Tn	Carpenter, Barbara Williford, Aline	Tn	Neal, William L.	Trufant - Trufant, Mich.					
Dawson, Leonard	Jun 27, 1937	Jeff Co		Jun 27, 1937		Dawson, Leonard	Williford, Aline		Day, Mrs. J. Alvin & Sons			Ebenezer					
Day, James Alvin	Jun 23, 1974	Strawberry Plains, Tn		Jun 24, 1899	75	Lewis, Sally	Day, William Newton		Perkey, Sarah		Day, Mrs.	Holston View - Knox Co	WW 1				
Day, James L.	Feb 1, 1928				44-3- 21	Ng	Day, Felix				Day, Mrs.	Greenbriar					
Day, Mary C.	Nov 6, 1961	Mill Springs	Tn		86	W					Day, Mrs.	Mill Springs					
Day, Sallie	Mar 1, 1993	Jeff Co	Lone Mt. Tn	Sep 15, 1904	88	W			Lewis, William		Kelley, Eula Mae [Junior]	Highland Memorial		James- Samuel Edwin	Edith		
Day, William	Nov 28, 1935	Straw Plains	Tn			W	Lewis, William		Shumate, Mary Ann		Day, William N. [Son]	Piney					
De Marco, Andrew William Sr.	Sep 16, 1986	Jeff City	New Jersey	Jun 24, 1946	40	W	De Marco, Angelo J.		Capolla, A. Marcella		De Marco, Carol E. Rainwater, C.S.	Buffalo Grove					

NAME	DDATE	DLOCAT	BLOCAT	BDATE	AGE	SPOUSE	FATHER	FBLOCAT	MOTHER	MBLOCAT	BY	BURIAL	VET	SON	DAUG	BROTHER	SISTER
De Vore, Peter Mann	Mar 21, 1947	Crossville, Tn	Ohio	Jul 25, 1856	90-7-25	W	De Vore, Daniel	Ohio	Shepard, Caroline	Ohio	Underwood, Mrs. N.T. - Zirkle, Lewis (Idaho) - De Vore, Frank & Ralph	Lebanon					
De Witt, Doyle	Oct 25, 1994		Tn														
Dean, Miliz Jane	Jan 3, 1975	Alabama	Tn	Dec 1, 1975			Mullins, Laura		Mullins, Laura		Dean, Edwin J.	West View					
Deathenage, Alvin Earl	Oct 22, 1973	Nashville, Tn	Mo	Jul 14, 1909	64	Payne, Mary	Deathenage, William C.		Yarberry, Catherine		Deathenage, Mrs. Alvin E.	West View					
Deathenage, Catherine Elizabeth	Mar 7, 1947	Jeff Co	Mo	Jan 31, 1889	58-2-6	Ng	Yarberry, Henry	Mo	Cook, Mary	England	Deathenage, W.C. [Husband]	West View					
Deathenage, Dean O.	Oct 29, 1933	Jeff Co	Mo	Jun 25, 1866	67	W	Deathenage, William J.		Cook, Tennessee		Milligan, F.L.	West View					
Debos, Charles [Col]	Feb 2, 1935	Jeff City								Tn	Narcie, Alice	Colored					
Debos, Emily [Col]	Nov 7, 1927		Tn					Tn	Narcie, Alice		Narcie, Alice						
Debos, Ulyes	Dec 9, 1986	Jeff City			66	Debos, Charlie	Rogan, Joe		Killies, Alice		Wife	J.M.G.					
Denney, Louie Earl Sr.	Mar 1, 1987	Howard Co, Ga	Jeff City	May 15, 1910	89	Russell, Freddie Mae	DevilSous, Otis		Merryweather, Ida		Wife	City - Franklin, Ga					
Denney, Robert Roy	Mar 3, 1948	Wayne Co, Ky	Sep 23, 1905	91		Lawrence, Jessie	Denney, Joseph Benjamin		Test, Dovie		Wife	City - Franklin, Ga		[Nephew] Cole, Ernest O. [Nieces] Denison, Myra - Greene, Harbin, Shirley Robert				
Dennis, Mack	Jan 24, 1978	Jeff City	Tn	Jul 31, 1895	52-7-24	Div	Denney, Reuben	Ky	Lain, Mary Ellia	Ky	Morgan, Mrs. Lula	Demsey - Ky		Donald L -L Earl Jr.	Muller, Sarah Lynn [Preg?] & John S - Tarr, Deidre D. & William L.		
Dennis, Mary Rita	Mar 25, 1980	J.M.H.	Grainger Co	Nov 26, 1931	76	Kinder, Mary	Dennis, William Wiley		Tate, Mary T.		Dennis, Mrs. Mack-Mrs. W.E.-Mary - Homer, Dorothy - Behanon, Mary D.	Jefferson Memorial					
Dennis, Minnie M.	Jul 30, 1927	Tn		May 9, 1909	79	W	Kinder, Edward		Moody, Augusta	Tn	Honorali, Mrs. Dorothy - Dennis, Joan	J.M.G.					
Dennis, W.W.	Aug 19, 1971	Knox Co	Tn	Aug 26, 1888	64-5-18	Dennis, Link	Tate, Davis	Tn	Raisley, Mary Jane		Dennis, Link	Shilo					
Dennison, Bessie May	Mar 18, 1931	Jeff City	Tn	Jan 23, 1852	82	W	Galpyn, Scott		Nox, Charles - Dalton, Delia		Dennis, Link	Shilo					
Dennison, Hugh Preston	Feb 4, 1986	St. Mary's Hosp.	Tn	Jul 29, 1927	79	Dennis, Willey		Link			Dennis, Mack	Shilo					
Dennison, Jessie M.	Jun 26, 1996	Jeff Co	Tn		58	Dennison, Orville	Newcomb, James		Breeden, Bessie		Dennison, Orville	Piney Grove					
Dennison, Orville	Apr 18, 1967		May 16, 1866	69		Ng	Dennison, Preston		Warren, Marth		Dennison, Mrs. Jossie M. - Curtis-Lewis- Runnie - Pruitt, Mrs. Boy - Shaw, Mrs. Bobby	Cates - Jeff Co					
Dennison, Alma Lee	Jul 25, 1994	Strawberry Plains					Dennison, Hugh P.		Rodder, Jessie M.		Dennison, Luthur [Son]	Pleasant Grove					
Denton, Angelia Mee	May 24, 1957	Knoxville, Tn	Knox Co	Mar 27, 1930	64		Headless, Maude		Dennison, Margie & C.O.	Orvill	Denton, Margie & C.O.	Piedmont				Runnie	
Denton, Charles Orville	Apr 3, 1960	Hamblen Co	Tn	May 4, 1911	46	Denton, C.O.	Lee, John H.		Williford, Mary Evelyn		Denton, John	Jefferson Memorial					West, Ellen
Denton, Dean O.	Dec 1, 1972	Knoxville, Tn	Tn	Apr 2, 1960	1d		Denton, John E. Jr.		Inman, Julia		Denton, Clark - Franklin, Shirley	Piedmont					
Denton, David Crockett	Aug 16, 1894	Tn	Dec 18, 1910	61	W	Denton, Johnathan		Goins, Emma		Denton, Edd-Fred W - Denton, Mrs. Dorothy	Caldonia - Knox Co					
Denton, Debra Dawn	Nov 14, 1988	U.T.H.	Tn	Aug 16, 1894	77	W	Denton, Jake				Denton, David N. [Columbia, Sc]	J.M.G.					
Denton, Donnie Alan	Jan 3, 1979	Madison Jackson Hosp.	Tn	Nov 25, 1898	89	Couch, Mildred	Denton, George W.		Denton, Nancy Ann		Denton, Roger-Mrs. Bette [Columbia, Sc]	Jefferson Memorial					
Denton, Ellen	Jun 19, 1977	Morristown, Tn	Tn	Sep 23, 1967	11		Denton, James Clark		Shauck, Joelene		Denton, James C.	Jefferson Memorial					
	Mar 12, 1976	Jeff Co	Tn	Oct 2, 1958	18	S	Denton, James C.		Shauck, Joelene		Denton, James C.	Jefferson Memorial					
			Tn	May 15, 1898	77	W	Lewis, James		Fox, Mercy		Fincham, A.H. & Sammy	Fox - Sevier Co					

NAME	DDATE	DLOCAT	BLOCAT	BDATE	AGE	SPOUSE	FATHER	FELLOCAT	MFRLOCAT	MOTHER	BY	BURIAL	VET	SON	DAUG	BROTHER	SISTER
Denton, Evan Earl	Apr 27, 1976	Knoxville, Tn	Tn	Feb 12, 1923	53	Ng	Patterson, Lanston O.			Denton, Susie Mae	Denton, Mrs. Earl	Clapps Chapel - Knoxville, Tn			Gels, Ruby - Faulkner, Margaret - Winger, Betty - Hermitage, Nancy - Estey, Mattie - Expectation, Lola - [Step] 2	3	
Denton, Florence	Oct 14, 1979	Jeff City	Tn	Sep 14, 1909	70	Denton, Clyde A.	Humphrey, David			Scott, Mattie	Denton, Jake A.	Caledonia - Knox Co					
Denton, Florence K.	Apr 10, 1987	J.M.H.	Tn	Aug 9, 1926	60	Denton, Clyde E.	Mc Claff, Frank			Snyder, Hattie	Denton, Clyde E.	Caledonia - Knox Co					
Denton, George Mitchell	Jul 17, 1966	Morristown, Tn	Tn	May 1, 1891	75	W	Denton, Neal			Fox, Julia	Denton, G. Jr.	West View					
Denton, Hugh W.	Mar 28, 1940	Dandridge	Tn	Apr 30, 1858	81	W	Denton, John B.	Tn		Baker, Martha	Denton, Mattie - Chambers, Ada	Dandridge					
Denton, Ida Leona	Jan 24, 1966	Jeff City	Jeff Co	Oct 21, 1906	89	W	Alley, Henry H.			Cary, Mary	Alley, Fredia [Sister]	J.M.G.				Vincent, Charles	
Denton, Isaac	Apr 4, 1940	County Farm		abt 70		s	Denton, —	Tn		Denton, —	Northern, E.A.	Swannylvania					
Denton, J. Henry	Oct 10, 1946	Jeff Co		Jun 18, 1877	69	Ng	Denton, William M.	Tn		Fox, Martha	Hill, Mrs. Laura E.	New Market					
Denton, Jake A.	May 22, 1995	Joelton, Tn	Jeff Co	Oct 12, 1912	82	Reeder, Dorothy	Denton, Dan			Mc Ginnis, Jane	Wife (Joelton, Tn)	Caledonia		Clarence - [Step] 1			3
Denton, James Clark	Dec 31, 1978	Savannah, Tn	Tn	Jun 27, 1920	58	Strauds, Jostene	Denton, Mel M.			Hicks, Frances	Denton, Roger - Mrs. James Denton - V.A.	Jefferson Memorial	unk				
Denton, Jimmie Darel	Jan 7, 1981	Jeff City	Tn	Oct 24, 1980		Ng	Denton, James C.	Tn		Shrauds, Jostene	Denton, James & Jostene	Jefferson Memorial					
Denton, Joe M.	Nov 7, 1952	Newport	Tn	Dec 20, 1858	73	Ng	Denton, David			Plarman, Mary J.	Denton, Jake	Reed Town					
Denton, John Arthur	Apr 23, 1984	Jeff City	Tn	Nov 11, 1902	81	Ng	Denton, J.C.			Brimmer, Sarah	Denton, Mrs. Aileen M. & Son	Dandridge					
Denton, John Dukes	Dec 7, 1983	Fresno, Calif	Tn	Aug 28, 1914	69	Div	Denton, Daniel O.			Mc Ginnis, Melinda Jane	Denton, Thomas S.	Caledonia - Knox Co					
Denton, Julia	Nov 12, 1932	Jeff City	Tn	Mar 5, 1906	66	W	Inman, R.			Denton, Mell	Denton, Mell	Dandridge					
Denton, Melinda Jane	Feb 24, 1957	Anderson Co., Tn	Tn	1896	59		Mc Ginnis, William H.			Collins, Sarah	Denton, Dan & Clyde- Howard-C.E.-Tom-John-Mary-Fred - Mc Guinnis, John	Caledonia - Knox Co					
Denton, Margaret	Sep 8, 1933	Jeff City	Tn	Feb 2, 1880	53	Denton, W.J.	Brinner, Robert	Tn	Tn	Reneau, Julia	Denton, N.J.	Hill Chapel					
Denton, Mattie	Sep 21, 1931	Jeff City	Tn	Aug 16, 1882	49	Denton, J.E.	Hill, A.O.P.	Tn	Tn	Carter, Mary	Denton, J.E.	Dandridge					
Denton, Mel M.	Dec 20, 1966	Jeff Co	Tn	Dec 5, 1914	75-6-14	Hicks, Frances	Denton, Jonathan Y.	Tn		Inman, Julia	Denton, Mrs. Frances	Memorial Gardens					
Denton, Mildred	Nov 19, 1984	Knoxville, Tn	Tn	Dec 5, 1914	69	Div	Phillips, Joseph Arthur			Anderson, Katherine Ruth	Denton, Roger	Hillcrest					
Denton, Mildred C.	Jul 27, 1995	Morristown, Tn	U.S.A	Feb 15, 1910	85	W	Couch, Gilbert N.			Couch, Martha Lindy	Denton, David N. & Rita [Son]	J.M.G.			Clark, Joan & Morris		
Denton, Millie C.	May 18, 1961	Jeff Co.	Indiana	Mar 26, 1881	80	W	Chappell, Abram			Easton, Lucinda	Denton, Ruth - Catlett, Mrs.	Oak Grove - Greene Co				Lesger, Mrs. R.J.	
Denton, Nina Sellers	Jun 28, 1933	Dandridge	Tn	Jun 22, 1910	23	Denton, D.E.	Sellers, Fred		Tn	Brewden, Ellen	Denton, D.E.	Chestnut Grove					
Denton, Paris Mae	Jul 12, 1982	Knox Co	Tn	May 29, 1897	85	Lathou, Nathaniel		Tn		Blair, Laura	Denton, George M.	West View					
Denton, Robert Wilson	Mar 20, 1977	Knoxville, Tn	Greene Co, Tn	Sep 17, 1909	67	Brantley, Gladys	Chappell, E.A.			Chappell, Millie	Catlett, Mrs. Louise D. Joplene M.	Oak Grove - Greene Co, Tn					
Denton, Trula M.	Jul 23, 1991	J.M.H.	Sevier Co, Tn	Mar 24, 1923	68	W	Johnson, Arthur			Long, Myrtle	Denton, Donald [Son]	Hillcrest					
Denton, Wartley	Sep 20, 1936	Tn	Tn	Jun 15, 1876	40		Denton, Jonathon	Tn		Inman, Julia	Churchman, Bruce	Dandridge					
Denton, William D. Jr.	Feb 3, 1959	Hamblen Co	Tn	Feb 3, 1959			Denton, W.D. Sr.			Denton, W.D. Sr.	Denton, W.D. Sr.	Russellville - Hamblen Co					
Denton, William Durman	May 30, 1963	Jeff Co	Tn	Dec 15, 1934	28	Bentley, Mary Lee				Bentley, Mary Lee	Denton, Mary Lee - Alley, Mrs. V. - Get.	Memorial Gardens	Korea				
Denton, William Eli	Dec 16, 1939	Oak Grove	Tn	Nov 9, 1873	66	Ng	Denton, William	Tn		Hicks, Rachel	Denton, Mrs. E. - Denton, Mrs. V. - Children	Seaborn Chapel					
Depew, William Junior	Oct 27, 1959	U.Y. Hospital	Tn	Jun 24, 1892	67	W	Depew, George			Fox, Rachel	Depew, Leonard & Sister	Walters Ford - Sullivan Co					
Derryberry, Geneva T.	May 9, 1992	Forsyth, Ga	Tn	Jun 3, 1916	75	W	Tipton, Zonal			Bicknell, Myra	Denton, D.E.	West View					
Derryberry, Lynda Ann	May 5, 1957	F.S.H.	Jeff Co	Jun 3, 1942	54	W	Derryberry, Claud			Tipton, Geneva	Derryberry, Lynda [Daug]	Tipton, Tn					
Dewdle, Floyd J.	Sep 5, 1992	Jeff City	Jeff City	Jun 24, 1934	56	Patterson, Carolyn	Dewdle, George W.			Payne, Garble Ethel	Porter, Winnie [Sister]	West View - J.M.G.					
Di Giacomo, Angelo Charles	May 28, 1997	Jeff City	Brooklyn, Ny	Sep 22, 1920	76	Volpe, Susan	Di Giacomo, Peter			Fiorella, Lillian	Wife	Veterans - Knoxville, Tn	1997				

NAME	DDATE	BLOCAT	BLOCAT	SDATE	AGE	SPOUSE	FATHER	FBLOCAT	MOTHER	MFBLOCAT	BY	BURIAL	VET	SON	DAUG	BROTHER	SISTER
Diamond, Oscar R.	Dec 15, 1971			May 22, 1907	64	Kelemen, Glenna	Diamond, James	Nc	Andriulonis, Laura	Tn	Carr, Linda [Daug] Husband	Straw Plains Cremated		Tom-Mike			
Dickenson, Mary Elizabeth	Jul 2, 1999	Knoxville, Tn	Tn	May 4, 1923	76	Dickenson, Henry	Drumheller, Tom		Loeb, Betsy		Husband	Cremated					
Dickenson, Mrs. R.M.	Dec 13, 1931				16												
Dietz, Frank		New Market	Nc	Dec 19, 1914	16	St	Dickson, Richard	Nc	Baumister, Maria	Tn	Dickson, Maud	Stilo					
Dietz, Inga Marie	Jul 19, 1979	J.M.H.	Germany	Mar 24, 1936	43	Dietz, Erich	Welker, Anton		Travis, Maud	Tn	Stelz, Erich	Ashelawn - Asheville, Nc					
Dillard, Katie Davis	Jan 3, 1940	Jeff Co.	Ga	Jun 3, 1857	82	W	Davis, Elisha	Ga	Lynn, —	Ga	Craig, F. G. [Jeff City]	Copperhill, Tn					
Dillon, Cynthia Lauren	May 9, 1990	S.M.M.C.	Knoxville, Tn	May 7, 1990	2m	Ng	Dillon, Timothy Scott		Asbury, Tam	Ga	Dillon, Mrs. Retta [Sister]	J.M.G.					
Dillon, Merd	Apr 28, 1951	Strawberry Plains	Va	1882	69	Ng					Dillon, Timothy	Strawberry Plains					
Dillon, Zachary Scott	Jun 16, 1987	S.M.H.	Va	Jun 16, 1987	1m		Dillon, Timothy Scott		Asbury, Tamie D.		Dillon, Mrs. Retta [Sister]	J.M.G.					
Dinsdale, James Ranklin	Nov 16, 1945	California	Tn	1867	2m		Dinsdale, James H.		Rankin, Sally			West View					
Dinsmore, Donald E. Sr.	Feb 3, 2000	Morristown, Tn	Tn	May 11, 1941	58	Div.	Dinsmore, Fayne		Bailey, Wanda Randall		Dinsmore, Donald E. Jr. [Son]	Community Chapel		Andrew		Spellmeir, Deborah & Jack	Joe [Ohio]
Dinwiddie, Francis Trout	Oct 11, 1935			Mar 23, 1857	78		Trent, James				Bailey, Mrs. W.H.	Piney Flats					
Dirt, Mary [Col]	Oct 4, 1936			Oct 2, 1936	act 0-5				West, Margaret								
Dirt, Thomas Calvin [Col]	Mar 21, 1940	Jeff City			act 70		Unk		Unk		Hendricks, C. [Citira]	Colored					
Disher, Christopher Alan Robert	Sep 8, 1986	Indiana		Oct 1, 1964	21	Moore, Kelly	Disher, R. Robert		Perry, Elizabeth		Disher, Kelly M. - Moore, Kelly	J.M.G.					
Dixon, Doshia	Feb 5, 1974	Jeff Co		Jul 19, 1885	88	W	Prince, George		Morgan, Rose			Jefferson Memorial					
Dixon, Elory Pyatt [M]	Jul 15, 1965		Tn	Nov 29, 1895	60	Ng	Dixon, Alvin		Bowden, Minnie Ann		King, Ruby- Newman, Martha, Mrs. Ruby- Newman, Mrs. Jewell	Memorial Gardens					
Dixon, Robert Earl	Aug 11, 1997	Maroot, Tn		Apr 22, 1926	71	Frances	Dixon, Luther		Travis, Maude		Wife - Pithey, Virginia - Richard, Hazel	Shiloh					
Dixon, Sarah Lucy	Jul 11, 1948	Mc Minn Co. Tn		Jul 28, 1871	76-11-15		Dobson, Jesse	Tn	Newman, Albie	Tn	Tarbutt, Rhea	Cochran - Englewood					
Dixson, Hobert Doyle	Nov 24, 1985	Knoxville, Tn	Tn	Apr 20, 1923	62	Furness, Cheryl	Dixson, Samuel		Johnson, Leon		Dixon, Mrs. Scheryl F.- Trabue, [Tn]	Mt. Horeb					
Doane, Bertha	Feb 13, 1975	Jeff Co	Tn	Aug 12, 1975	95	W	Cox, John N.		Marshall, Sarah		Doan, J.N.L.	Friends Station					
Doane, Georgia French	Aug 29, 1974	Washington Co, Va	Washington Co, Va	Feb 28, 1874	69	S	Doane, William	Tn	Keller, Muehia J.	Va	Doan, R.H. & W.E.	Friends Station					
Doane, Jessie N.	Aug 13, 1986	Knoxville, Tn		Apr 15, 1924	72		Doane, William E.		Cox, Bertha		Dobyns, Carol Ann & John [Daug - Montgomery, Ala.]	West View					
Doane, Robert H.	Aug 21, 1945	Knox Co	Peorisburg, Va	Nov 7, 1869	75	Cowell, Addie	Doane, William P.	Tn	Doane, Nola	Va	Doane, Mrs. Addie C. & Mrs. Robert H.	Friends Station		Moore, Sharon & Sammy			
Doane, Emma Lois	May 25, 1979	Jeff City	Tn	Jul 17, 1912	66	Dockery, Ava	Bales, Walter		Perry, Elizabeth		Dockery, Mrs. Addie & Children	Valley View - Jeff Co					
Dockery, Florence	Nov 15, 1950	Jeff City	Tn	Apr 4, 1883	67	W	Bailey, Golden		Derrick, Pleahima		Dockery, Artis	Beaver Creek					
Dockery, Mary Lou	Oct 6, 1981	Knoxville, Tn	Jeff Co	Sep 8, 1907	84	W	Love, H. Marshall		Collier, Callie B.		Dockery, Mike [Son]	Mt. Horeb					
Dockery, Mitchell Garrett	Dec 19, 1948	Jeff Co	Sevier Co	Mar 24, 1881	67-8-25	W	Unk		Unk		Dockery, Artis	Beaver Creek					
Dockins, Clarence Raigh	Dec 17, 1992	Knox Co	Tn	Sep 22, 194	38	Ng	Dockins, Charlie		Casa, Lona	Tn	Dockins, Mrs. Cille - Dockins, John L. [Mother] - Dockins, Clyde	Union Hill - Jeff Co					
Dockins, James	Apr 28, 1934	New Market	Tn	May 17, 1858	75	Ng	Dockins, Thomas	Sc	Bailey, Hester	Tn	Dockins, John L. [Mother] - Dockins, Clyde	Hills Chapel					
Dockins, Theofa Louise	Dec 29, 1946	Knox Co	Knox Co	Dec 19, 1946	1m		Dockins, Alonzo	Tn	Dance, Nola	Tn	Dockins, Alonzo	Nanceh's Grove					
Dockins, Tammy Denise	Oct 31, 1966	Knox Co	Tn		6		Farrow, Carolyn Mee		Dockins, Rex. James	Nc	Dockins, Rex. James	West View					
Dockson, Charles W.	Dec 3, 1940	Jeff City	Tn		66-5-21	Dockson, Rachael G.					Nc	Dockson, Mrs. Rachael		span am			
Dockson, J.W.	Jan 12, 1925	Jeff City	Tn		83	W	Dockson, Walter					Dockson, Rescoe	Mt. Horeb				
Dockson, Rachael	Apr 14/17, 1963	Jeff Co	Tn	May 15, 1881	81-11-2	W	Godwin, Reece		Mc Daniel, Maggie		Allen, Mildred [J.- Clifford]	West View					
Dodson, Ruby	Jul 31, 1928				31-10-14	Dockson, Herbert			Messengill, Will		Messengill, Hannah	Messengill					
Doll, Lillie Viola	Sep 8, 1980	Jeff Co	Tn		40-9-2	Doll, James C.			Mesley, Hannah		Doll, James C.	Tn	Pleasant View				
Doll, Eugene	Jan 1, 2000	Morristown, Tn		Sep 21, 1915	84	Ng	Doll, Edgar		Agnes		Blevins, William [Step-Son]	New Market					
Donelson, Joseph P.	Feb 17-19, 1925																

NAME	DDATE	DLOCAT	BLOCAT	BDATE	AGE	SPOUSE	FATHER	FBLOCAT	MOTHER	MFBLOCAT	BY	BURIAL	VET	SON	DAUG	BROTHER	SISTER
Donahue, Lenore M.	Apr 27, 1965	Jeff Co	Illinois	Sep 25, 1909	55	Donahue, Francis J.	Bussen, Andrew Z.		Kuhl, Julia		Donahue, Francis	St. Michaels - Galena, Illinois					
Donaldson, Alice B. [Col]	Mar 29, 1947	Jeff Co				Ng	Bartley, John	Tn	Unk		Donaldson, Hugh -Bill & Frank	Colored					
Donaldson, Charles Frank [Col]	Oct 22, 1959	Jeff City			82	Ng	Donaldson, S.R.		Watkins, Laura		Donaldson, Laura	West View Colored	WW 1				
Donaldson, Charlie [Col]	May 16, 1953	Jeff Co	Tn	Feb 2, 1870	83	W	Donaldson, Sam		Unk		Donaldson, Ralph - Mable-Ruth-Carl B. - Rogers, Lee	West View Colored					
Donaldson, Dora [Col]	Apr 1 1927	Jeff Co			19-1-23	S	Donaldson, S.M.	Tn	Watkins, Laura	Tn	Donaldson, S.M.	Colored					
Donaldson, Harry W. [Col]	Jun 14, 1970	Jeff Co	Tn	Jun 2, 1924	46	Div	Donaldson, Frank		Kgie, Louise		Peck, Allie - Donaldson, Phyllis	West View					
Donaldson, Infant	Nov 29, 1945	Jeff Co	Tn	Nov 29, 1945		Div	Donaldson, James		Young, Ruby	Tn	Donaldson, Family - Grainger Co.	Colored					
Donaldson, John Clayton [Col]	Apr 1, 1940	Jeff City	Tn	Jun 17, 1934	5	S	Donaldson, Ralph	Tn	Tate, Nellie	Tn	Donaldson, Ralph	Colored					
Donaldson, Lee [Col]	Apr 19, 1928	Tn				S	Donaldson, S.M.	Tn	Watkins, Laura	Tn	Donaldson, S.M	Colored					
Donaldson, Louise [Col]	Nov 9, 1983	Jeff Co		Sep 22, 1900	83	Donaldson, Frank	Kyle, John		Mary Alice		Donaldson, Phyllis [Chicago] - Louise & Carl B. - Charles	West View Colored					
Donaldson, Margie [Col]	Jul 13, 1946	Jeff Co	Jeff Co				Donaldson, Frank		Donaldson, Helena		Rogers, Tom (Ontario)- Neal (Sig)- Carl William - Sue - Bill - Donaldson, Carl B.- Charles - Ramsey	Colored					
Donaldson, Nathaniel Elder [Black]	Apr 7, 1988	V.A. - Mt. Home	Tn	May 18, 1922	65	Div	Donaldson, Frank		Kyle, Louise		Donaldson, Helena	West View	WW 2				
Donaldson, Nellie [Col]	Oct 29, 1936	V.A. - Mt. Home	Tn	Jul 8, 1897	39	W	Tate, John		Tate, Jane		Donaldson, Ralph	Jeff City					
Donaldson, Ralph M. [Col]	Jun 26, 1965	Jeff Co	Tn	Jul 14, 1897	67	W	Donaldson, Charlie		Watkins, Georgia Ann		Langston, Margaret - Donaldson, Ralph M. (Dayton, OH)-James C.- Smith, Jane	West View Colored					
Donaldson, Richard Ivan [Black]	Apr 13, 1983	V.A. - Mt. Home	Tn	Jul 27, 1935	47	S	Donaldson, Charles F.		Kyle, Louise		Donaldson, Phyllis - Rayne, A.A. & Sons	West View	kansa				
Donaldson, Samuel M. [Bick] [Col]	Apr 9, 1947	Jeff Co	Tn	Feb 2, 1870	77-2-7	W	Donaldson, Sam Sr.	Tn	Unk		Donaldson, Phyllis - Hugh-Ed-Claude-George	West View Colored					
Donaldson, Willie B. [Col]	Jan 31, 1970	Tn		Sep 21, 1878	91	Donaldson, Johnn W. [D]	Gour, William		Kidd, Carrie		Landreth, Clara & Wilma - Brown, Margaret- Donaldson, Lucille	West View					
Donohue, Francis John	Mar 4, 1972	La Crosse, Wisconsin	Tn	Jun 17, --		Bettis, Luis	Donohue, Jeffery M.		Moher, Adelaide		Donohue, David-Luis	Galena, Illinois			Brewer, Glenda- Brown, Sandra - Malone, Sharon - Jones, Mary	Ray-Lyle-Carl-Clifford-George	Cox, Jen - Smith, Hattie
Dotson, Agnes Kathleen	Apr 14, 1995	Knoxville, Tn	Jeff City	Nov 18, 1925	70		Woods, Carl		White, Rosa		Nolen, Bill [Son]	J.M.G.		Eddie			
Dotson, Austin	Jun 29, 1998	Tn	Tn	Feb 2, 1910	78	Mildred Arlene	Dotson, John		Hayes, Mary	Tn	Dotson, Mildred Arlene	Mt. View					
Dotson, Beulah Augusta	Oct 28, 1995	Knoxville, Tn	Silver Co., Tn	Feb 10, 1920	75	Dotson, Ephrim	Loveday, Greene		Hurst, Bethena		Husband	Mt. View		George-Carroll	Standlfer, Lorene - Jarnigan, Mildred Moorehead, Sandra Jones (Step) Lowe, James (Step) Lowe, Brenda Ann		Otella - Lineberry, Mabel - Trent, Peggy
Dotson, Paul Edward	Jul 3, 1984	Jeff City	Rutledge, Tn	Feb 24, 1927	67	Mason, Ethel	Dotson, Ray Herman		Roberts, Virgila Mae	Tn	Wife	J.M.G.	45-46	[G] Lowe, Paul W. Sr.			
Dotson, Sylas Gertrude	Apr 1, 1946	Jeff Co	Jeff Co	Mar 31, 1946	1	Ng	Dotson, James	Tn	Holloclaw, Edith Gertrude	Tn	Dotson, James	Mt. View					
Dotson, William Robert	Jan 17, 1951	New Market	Tn	Jun 2, 1881	79	Ng	Dotson, Wickey		Holt, Julia		Dotson, Mrs. Dora	Mt. View					
Dotson, Willie Francis [F]	Jan 27, 1965	Mascot, Tn	Tn	Sep 9, 1892	72	W	Scott, Sam		Riley, Mary Ellen		Dotson, James & Trela	Mt. View					
Doutin, James Halstead	Oct 30, 1990	Morristown, Tn	Talbott, Tn	Sep 24, 1908	72	Mc Elwen, Margaret	Doutin, Jack		Halstead, Lena		Doutin, Mrs. Margaret	Sunderland					
Doughty, Cynthia Lynn	Jun 30, 1996	Greenville, Tn		Jun 6, 1957	39		Doughty, Charles		Mc Kinney, Nelda		Father	J.M.G.				Steven	Jones, Marilyn

NAME	DDATE	DLOCAT	BLOCAT	BDATE	AGE	SPOUSE	FATHER	FRLOCAT	MOTHER	MFRLOCAT	BY	BURIAL	VET	SON	DAUG	BROTHER	SISTER
Doughty, Nelda Irene	May 24, 2000	Jeff City	Ky	May 6, 1930	70	Doughty, Charles	Mc Kinney, William T.	Nc	Cureton, Clara Simpson	Nc	Hazard	J.M.G.					
Douglas, Annie	Jun 16, 1927		Nc		56-5-6	Douglas, Dr. J.I.	Rumey ?, Deward	Nc		Nc	Clayton, J.H. - Jarnigan, Frank	Wooesboro, Nc					
Douglas, Bess E.	Apr 8, 1928		Tn		24-4-2	S	Douglas, George W.	Va	Perry, Mary Elizabeth		Douglas, N.O.	Piedmont					
Douglas, Carroll Alexander	Jul 3, 1925		Tn		37-7-21	S	Douglas, S.W.	Tn	Dukes, Sarah J.	Tn	Douglas, S.W.	Piedmont					
Douglas, Eliza	May 28, 1927	Rocky Valley	Knox Co	Jul 6, 1863	73	W	Privette, I.	Nc	Vaughn, Jane	Nc	Douglas, George	Strawberry Plains					
Douglas, Infant Female	Feb 24, 1950	Morristown, Tn	Tn	Feb 24, 1950			Douglas, Richard		Gaylor, Elizabeth		Douglas, Mrs. O.L.	Sunset - Madisonville, Tn					
Douglas, Orlando L.	Nov 7, 1975	Hamblen Co	Tn	Aug 10, 1889	86	Lovin, Rillis	Dukes, ----		Taylor, Mrs. W.J.		Douglas, Mrs. O.L.	Piedmont					
Douglas, Sallie	Sep 21, 1951	Hamblen Co	Tn								Cope, Lillian	Piedmont					
Douglas, Scott W.	Feb 18, 1927		Tn		64-3-0	Ng	Douglas, Edward	Tn	White, Sarah	Tn		Piedmont					
Downs, Joe R. Sr.	Jan 12, 1989	J.M.H.	J.M.H.	Sep 25, 1926	62	Holmes, Geraldine	Downs, Frank		Vaughn, Leona	Tn	Downs, Joe R. Jr. - V.A.	Hermitage Memorial - Nashville, Tn	44-65				
Downten, James 9th	Jul 21, 1991	Covington, Ky	Hendersonvill le, Tn	Apr 1 1915	76	Brewer, Helen	Downton, James 4th	Tn	Scanlon, Catherine		Downten, John (Son)	Hamblen Memorial					
Doyle, George Ray	May 3, 1989	J.M.H.	Jeff Co	Jul 4, 1912	76	Kinder, Pearl	Doyle, Austin	Tn	Newman, Little Mae		Doyle, Mrs. Pearl	J.M.G.					
Doyle, Lillis Mae	Apr 6, 1967	Jeff Co	Tn		47-7-12	W	Newman, George		Hupon, Mollie		Newman, Carroll	West View					
Drake, Charlotte M.	Feb 10, 1964	J.M.H.	La	Jan 11, 1913	71	W	Neison, Charles		Sprayger, Maude		Breeden, Mrs. Molly	Hopewell - Dandridge, Tn					
Drinnen, Grover Carmack	Jul 10, 1948	Hamblen Co	Hancock Co, Tn	Apr 4, 1906	42	Ng	Drinnen, John J.	Tn	Buttry, Zouria	Tn	Dixon, Dana E.	Middlesboro - Ky					
Drinnon, Jason Glenn	Oct 20, 1973	Jeff Co	Tn	Feb 26, 1925	48	Denton, Eula	Drinnon, Robert R.				Drinnon, Mrs. Glenn & Sons	Jefferson Memorial					
Drinnon, Nellie Harrison	Dec 1, 1972	Jeff City	Tn	Nov 15, 1888	84	W	Amis, Tom		Dodson, Lula		Drinnon, Glenn	Bertrade - Hamblen Co					
Drinnon, Vera Ianitha	Feb 14, 1958	Jeff Co	Tn	Jun 28, 1913	44	W	Drinnon, Kimbrough		Amos, Nellie		Chandler, Mrs. Bill	Bertrade - Hamblen Co					
Drumheller, Roberta L.	Jun 11, 1981	Jeff City	Nc	Sep 23, 1902	78	Drumheller, Thomas O.	Leib, R.C.		Capps, Hattie		Dickerson, Mrs. Mary	Greenwood - Knoxville, Tn					
Duck, Jesse Ervin	Aug 14, 1960	Granger Co	Nc	Jun 29, 1874	86	Ng	Duck, William Henry		Buckner, Anne		Duck, Mrs. O.C.- Tom-One-Clyde - Robinson, Mrs. [Nc]	Shiloh					
Duck, Lydia	Dec 29, 1971	Knox Co	Tn		84-6-8	Duck, J.C. [Ð]	Briggs, Marcus		Robinson, Margaret		Duck, One-Tom-Clyde	Shiloh					
Duggan, Willie C.	Aug 19, 1971	Knox Co	Sc	Jul 6, 1895	88	Duggan, A.M.					Duck, Archie M.	Piney					
Dugger, Paul Edward	Dec 20, 1999	New Market, Tn		Dec 25, 1930	69	Howard, Virgie	Dugger, Raymond	Tn	Walkins, Rosslee	Tn	Dugger, Archie M.	Pleasant Grove	Korea				
Dugger, Richard A.	Apr 9, 1979	Jeff Co	New, Market, Tn	Apr 9, 1979	80	Ng	Dugger, Paul E.	Tn	Howard, Virgil Mae	Tn	Dugger, Paul E.	Pleasant Grove					
Dugman, Charlie H.	Dec 19, 1959	Knox Co	Tn		80	W	Dugman, Mike		Stipes, Ann		Dugman, Mrs. C.H.	Strawberry Plains					
Dugman, Jennie	Jul 31, 1982	Knox Co	Tn	Mar 14, 1879	83	Ng	Rudder, Samuel	Tn	Frye, Nancy	Tn	Dugman, H.M.	Strawberry Plains					
Dukes, Dr. N.M.	Jun 6, 1933	Straw Plains	Tn	Sep 2, 1961	71	Ng	Dukes, A.P.		Dukes, Mary		Dukes, Mrs. N.M.	Piedmont					
Dukes, J.M.	May 10, 1941	Piedmont	Jeff Co	Jun 20, 1863	74	W			Colin, Mary	Jeff Co	Dukes, Alex (Sn)	Piedmont					
Dukes, Martha Ann	May 28, 1954	Jeff Co	Tn		90	W	Colin, Mathew		Underwood, Martha	Tn	Dukes, Alex - Cope, Pearl	Piedmont					
Dukes, Mary Alice	Feb 8, 1926	Jeff Co	Tn		s	Colin, Mathew		French, Kate	Tn	Dukes, J.M.	Piedmont						
Dukes, Morgin M. [M]	Jun 18, 1957	Jeff Co	Tn	Jul 23, 1892	64	Ng	Dukes, Joe		Erwin, Lizzie	Tn	Dukes, Bessie & James - Coats, Morna - Ott	Nance's Grove	WW 1				
Dukes, Noa Monroe	Jan 25, 1932	Knoxville	Tn	Apr 30, 1871	10-9-23	s	Dukes, George A.	Tn	Colin, Mary		Dukes, N.M.	Piedmont					
Dukes, W.T.	Mar 27, 1926	Jeff Co	Tn		69	Ng	Dukes, A.p.P.		Link	Tn	Puckett, S.B.	Piedmont					
Duncan, Bert	Oct 4, 1947	Jeff Co	Tn		76-6-24	Ng	Duncan, Taylor	Tn	Unk		Me Swain, Mae - Dunca, Frank	New Market					
Duncan, Mary Candice	Nov 7, 1996	Greene Co., Tn	Mar 17, 1920	76			Carter, Manlove D.		Harmon, Minnie F.		Murphy, Carolyn [Dung] Frank	New Market					
Duncan, Noah	Aug 4, 1960	Ky	Tn		51	S	Duncan, John		Kerr, Sallie		Me Swain, Mrs. Jess - Frank	New Market					

NAME	DDATE	BLOCAT	BLOCAT	BDATE	AGE	SPOUSE	FATHER	FBLOCAT	MOTHER	MFBLOCAT	BY	BURIAL	VET	SON	DAUG	BROTHER	SISTER
Duncan, Sallie	Jul 11, 1959	Jeff City	Tn	Nov 27, 1879	79	W	Kerr, R.C.		Clendenon, Elizabeth		Duncan, Frank -Arville - Ballinger, Mrs., Frank	New Market					
Dunlap, Robert Michael	Dec 19, 1991	U.T.H.	Knoxville, Tn	Oct 4, 1955	36	W	Dunlap, B.C.		Barrier, Dorothy		Willie	J.M.G.					
Dunn, Floyd Harrison Jr.	May 29, 1950	Jeff Co.	Jeff Co.	May 29, 1950	Sn		Dunn, Floyd H.		Sanders, Marion		Dunn, F.H.	Friends Station					
Dunn, Johnnie Marie	Jul 1, 1949	Knox Co.	Tn	Jun 10, 1931	18	Ng	Vance, Ernest		Sellers, Ruth		Vance, Wilma & Ernest	Woodlawn					
Dunsmore, James William	Mar 19, 1931	New Marker	Tn	Nov 25, 1930	Sn		Dunsmore, Allison	Tn	Bewins, Ola	Tn	Home (Service)						
Dunwoody, Ethel [Col]	Jul 13, 1926		Tn		S		Dunwoody, Carl		Webb, Dora	Tn	Welsh, Dora	Colored					
Dunwoody, James Carl Jr.	Sep 28, 2000	Jeff City	Tn	Feb 26, 1922	78	S	Dunwoody, James C. Sr.					J.M.G.	unk				
Dupsley, Jeanne Merrie	Mar 4, 1986	J.M.H.	Algiers, Algeria	Dec 8, 1906	91	W	Ingram, Sylvia Inez		Unk		Dickerson, Louise	West View					
Durance, Barbara Jean	Jan 14, 1946	Jeff Co.	Tn	Oct 15, 1937	8		Durance, J.W.	Ga	Underwood, Helen	Ga	Underwood, Ruth	West View					
Durland, Frances	Nov 23, 1984	J.M.H.	New York.	Dec 26, 1906	77	W	Stanford, William E.		Rich, Hazel		Durland, William F. [Monrok, Nd.]	Buffalo Grove					
Dyer, Anne	Feb 12, 1981	Knoxville, Tn	Weakly Co, Tn	May 30, 1925	65	Dyer, Jack M.	Whitewington, Clarence		Warren, Grace		Dyer, Jack M.	J.M.G.					
Dyer, Bessie Belle	Mar 18, 1984	Hamblen Co.	Tn	Feb 18, 1893	71	Dyer, W.E.	Smith, James P.		Moore, Sarah		Dyer, W.E. & Children	Jefferson Memorial Gardens					
Dyer, Ernest Smith	Jun 27, 1976	Jeff Co.	Tn	Nov 11, 1917	58	W	Dyer, W.E.		Smith, Bessie B.		Dyer, Mrs. Smith West View	West View					
Dyer, Henry C. [Col]	Mar 5, 1968	Jeff City	Tn	Jul 4, 1899	Ng		Dyer, Sally		Dyer, Mrs. Lucille & Children		West View Colored						
Dyer, James [Col]	Feb 18, 1925		Tn	Nov 9, 1934	90	W					Galbraith, Flo	Jefferson City Colored					
Dyer, John Clayton [Col]	May 14, 1940	Jeff Co	Tn		15	S					Dyer, Ruth	M.E. (Colored)					
Dyer, Michael Clayton (Black)	May 10, 1992	Muskegon	Tn	Jan 27, 1946	47	Div	Dyer, Henry		Treece, Lucille		Dyer, Lucille Tn.	J.M.G.					
Dyer, Rickey Gene	Dec 5, 1989	Jeff Co	Tn	Dec 5, 1989			Dyer, Sammie Oscar		Sowey, Jeanette Elizabeth		Thorngrave - Knox Co						
Dyer, Sallie	Dec 22, 1927		Tn		69	Ng					Taylor F.H.	West View					
Dyer, Sophia Died	Feb 29, 1976	Pittsburg, Pa	Tn	Dec 1, 1906	69	W					Dyer, James Walker	West View					
Dyer, William Ernest	Aug 19, 1966	Talbott, Tn	Tn	May 15, 1896	69	W	Dyer, Lafayette		Huff, Livonia		Dyer, Jack	Everlasting Life - J.M.G.					
Easley, Ella	Jul 9, 1960	Jeff City	Tn	Apr 1, 1868	92	W	Clark, John B.		Stanford, Hannah		Easley, Zinda-J.E.-Clifford	West View					
Easley, Lillie Frances	Mar 23, 1984	Jeff City	Tn	Mar 29, 1898	85	W	Flowers, Addison		Black, Mary L.		Weinman, Martha Bill - Johnson F.H. [Newbern, Tn]	Jefferson City Colored					
Easley, Linda	Jun 29, 1965	Jeff Co.									Easley, J.E.						
Easterday, Zelda Ruth	Jan 23, 1998	Jeff City	Sterling, Ohio	Nov 23, 1917	80		Eby, Henry		Belcher, Goldie		Easterday, Terry [Son - Fontana Dam, Nd] - Murray F.H. [Creston, Oh]	Maple Mound					
Easterly, Kitty June	Feb 14, 1973	Knoxville, Tn	Tn	Jan 24, 1887	86	Easterly, Reuben (D)	Cox, Samuel		Cooper, Mary Ann		Easterday, Terry [Son - Keaton, Mrs. Irene	Memorial Gardens					
Easterly, Ruben T.	Dec 19, 1984	Jeff City	Tn		81	Ng	Easterly, Laylette		Hamilton, Virginia A.		Seals, Virginia - Maddox, Annie	Memorial Gardens					
Eaves, Elizabeth [Col]	Jan 5, 1952		Tn	Feb 19, 1883	68	W	Price, Dan		Howell, Monnie		Easterly, Mrs. R.T.	West View Colored					
Ebert, Robert F.	May 1, 1987	Alexandria, Alabama	New York	Jan 7, 1949	38	Daniise, Patricia A.	Ebert, Foster Fredrick		Dawen, Ella Mae		Ebert, Patricia [Alexandria, Ala.] - V.A.	J.M.G.	army				
Eckert, Fritz Otto	Feb 15, 1981	Jeff City	Germany	Jul 12, 1904	76	Shutz, Paula Ella	Eckert, Paul		John, Minna		Perkins, Mrs. Rita L.	Cremated					
Eckert, Paula Ella	Mar 2, 1985	J.M.H.	Berlin, Germany	Jan 14, 1905	80	W	Shutz, Herman		Unk		Perkins, Mrs. Richard						
Edds, Rachel	Dec 7, 1993	Talbott, Tn	Tn	Jan 22, 1901	92	W	Chance, Hugh C.		Mink, Elizabeth		Edds, Sidney [Son]	Fairview - New Tazewell, Tn		Hull, Andrew		Housley, Henry	
Eddy, Susan Elizabeth	Sep 21, 1997	Jeff City	Tn	Jul 12, 1961	36	Eddy, Garth	Housley, Charles		Elizabeth		Husband - Housley, Iris [Step-Mother]	J.M.G.		Hull, Andrew	Hull, Mallory	Housley, Henry	
Edgar, Ellen	Jul 11, 1951	Jeff City	Fayetteville, Nc.	May 7, 1882	69	W	Kyle, William		Morris, Evelyn		Murphy, Mrs. John - Ruby & Eula	West View					
Edgar, James D.	Mar 24, 2000	Knoxville, Tn	Tn	Oct 30, 1917	82	Styles, Thelma	Edgar, James Patton Howard		Henry, Alice		Willie	West View	WW 2	Jim & Mizi	Householder, Janet & Gary		

NAME	DDATE	BLOCAT	BLOCAT	DDATE	AGE	SPOUSE	FATHER	FELOCAT	MOTHER	MFELOCAT	BY	BURIAL	VET	SON	DAUG	BROTHER	SISTER
Edgar, James Howard	Jan 3, 1947	Jeff Co.	Tn	Feb 2, 1877	69-11-3	Ng	Edgar, Robert	Tn	Reneau, Martha	Tn	Dugar, Mrs. Alice (Edgar, Henry)	West View					
Edgar, Johnnie Alice Henry	Feb 21, 1985	Cara Inn	Tn	Feb 2, 1884	101	W			Green, Nancy Katherine		Anderson, Mrs. La Roy (Katherine) - Ellison, Annie	West View					
Edgar, Lucile Albenia	Mar 18, 1953	Jeff Co	Tn	Mar 9, 1953	62-0-9	W	Purley, George W.		Green, Nancy Katherine		Anderson, Mrs. La Roy (Katherine), Sr)	West View					
Edgar, Mack	Feb 5, 1953	Jeff Co	Tn	Apr 7, 1887	66	Ng	Edgar, Abtanort		Newman, Serepta		Edgar, Tom - Mc Glamory, Hood	West View					
Edgar, Thomas H.	Apr 28, 1945	Jeff Co	Tn	Apr 19, 1880	65	Cox, Dollie	Edgar, Robert	Tn	Reneau, Martha	Tn	Edgar, Lola	West View					
Edgar, Trdal E.	Aug 12, 1942	Jeff City		Mar 14, 1914	28	S	Edgar, Howard	Tn	Henry, Alice	Tn	Edgar, Lola	West View					
Edgar, W.A.	Feb 25, 1929	Jeff City	Tn			Ng						West View					
Edmonds, Adie Julie	May 8, 1957	Jeff City	Tn			W	Kilgore, George		Ellis, Mary		Lowery, Mrs. Moxie - Mrs. Floyd - Henderson, James R. - Edmonds, Mrs. Floyd - Dixon, Mrs. Ann - Harris, Ruth - Manning, Mrs.	West View					
Edmonds, Billy Thomas	Mar 28, 1980	Jeff Co	Tn	Jan 31, 1939	21	Ng	Unk		Edmonds, Ruth		Edmonds, John-Glenn - Cherry, Prairie - Barnes, Condar	Roseberry - Knox Co					
Edmonds, Carrie Elizabeth	Jan 1, 1966	Jeff Co	Tn	May 29, 1899	66	W	Sutton, Sam		Mc Gaha, Jane		Edmonds, W.A.	Beaver Creek					
Edmonds, Eugene	May 14, 1931	Strawberry Plains	Tn	Jul 2, 1904	26	S	Edmonds, W.A.	Tn	Kilgore, Adie	Tn	Edmonds, W.A.	West View					
Edmonds, Helen Ruth	Jan 21, 1962	Tn		Jul 24, 1946	15	Ng	Unk		Edmonds, Mary Ruth		Davis, Mrs. Mary R.	Hillcrest					
Edmonds, James William	Jan 14, 1981	Knox Co	Tn	May 28, 1873	98	Ng					Manning L.G. - Davis, John - Paul (Jewal) - Clyde - Ross, Bertha	Hillcrest					
Edmonds, John Jennings Junior	Dec 28, 1992	Knoxville, Tn	Tn	Jul 6, 1922	70	Stapleton, Nola	Edmonds, Ted R.		Sutton, Carrie E.		Wife	J.M.G.	43-45		Ellison, Gail		
Edmonds, Johnny Melvin	Nov 17, 1990	Knoxville, Tn	Tn	Nov 13, 1931	59	Div	Edmonds, Robert		Hale, Nancy		Edmonds, Orvetel L. (Son)	Burchfield - Sevier Co					Cherry, Pauline
Edmonds, Larry Thomas	Jun 17, 1945	Jeff Co	Tn	Jan 10, 1939	6		Edmonds, Von		Collins, Nan	Tn	Edmonds, Nan	West View					
Edmonds, Nola G.	Jan 3, 1995	New Market, Tn	Hawkins Co, Tn	Mar 31, 1925	69		Stapleton, Robert C.		Green, Bertie J.		Stapleton, J.A. (Brother)	J.M.G.			Ellison, Gail E & Mitch	Dane-Luke-Kyle	Russell, Eula [md.] - Templin, Emma - Lyle, Chesley - Walker, Dorothy
Edmonds, Ted	Dec 29, 1936	Straw Plains	Tn	Jan 1, 1986	38	Ng	Edmonds, ???	Tn	Celia, Ellora	Tn		Beaver Creek					
Edmonds, Trdia	Jan 2, 1936	Tn	Tn	Jul 18, 1874	61		Edmonds, George		Griffin, Matilda			Piney					
Edmonds, Virginia Marcella	March 13, 1975	Knoxville, Tn	Tn	Apr 24, 1927	47	W	Collins, Sam	Tn	Free, Edith	Tn		Burchfield - Knox Co					
Edmonds, Vn R.	Jan 4, 1975	Knoxville, Tn	Tn			Collins, Nan	Edmonds, W.A.		Kilgore, Adie		Edmonds, Nan	West View					
Edmonds, William A.	Oct 28, 1957	Jeff Co	Tn		76	Ng			Edmonds, Mary Ruth		Lowery, Mrs. Marie-Von - Dixon, Floyd-Julie - Dixon, Harold - Hunnicut, Edwin - Chnestian, Wade	West View					
Edmonds, William Earl	Jan 31, 1991	J.M.H.	Tn	Aug 22, 1923	52	Mc Bee, Venida	Edmonds, Oscar		Celia, Elnora		Edmonds, Venida M.	Piney					
Edmonds, James R.	Mar 2, 1992	Claiborne Co, Tn	Claiborne Co, Tn	Mar 17, 1904	87	W	Edmondson, Robert		Goin, Mary		Keck, Gertrude [Daug]	J.M.G.					
Edmondson, Madge Marie	Jan 3, 1986	J.M.H.	Tn	Oct 5, 1906	81	Edmondson, James R.	Wylie, Edward		Hollingsworth, Viola		Edmondson, James R.	West View					
Edwards, Clyde Jr.	Apr 24, 1964	Knox Co	Tn	Dec 8, 1923	40	Ng					Demonds, Mrs. Clyde	Hillcrest					
Edwards, Ina Marie	Mar 6, 1973	Knoxville, Tn	Tn	Feb 6, 1872	101	W					Edwards, Roy-J.C. - Vanderwort, Fannie - Gaylor, Mrs. E.D. (Ashland, My)	Piedmont					
Edwards, Kyle Cornett	Apr 10, 1950	Ashland, Ky	Tn		3		Edwards, Glenn		Purley, -		Edwards, Glenn C.						
Edwards, Luckie Azelia	Dec 24, 1961	Sevier Co	Tn	Sept 7, 1885	76		Edwards, John		Reneau, Margie Jane		Davis, John - Collins, Mr. - Boyd & Clyde-Ed	Hill Creek - Dandridge					
Edwards, Lula	Oct 4, 1931	Peachmont	Tn	May 19, 1908	23	Edwards, Ray	Densumus, L.	Tn		Unk	Edwards, Ray & Fleet	Peachmont					

NAME	DDATE	DLOCAT	BLOCAT	BDATE	AGE	SPOUSE	FATHER	FELOCAT	MOTHER	MFLOCAT	BY	BURIAL	VET	SON	DAUG	BROTHER	SISTER
Edwards, Maude Wright	Apr 27, 1979	Huntsville, Alabama			88		Higgins F.H. [Fayetteville, Tn]				Higgins F.H. [Fayetteville, Tn]	Jefferson Memorial					
Edwards, Vera	Jun 22, 1989	U.T.H.	Jeff Co	Apr 16, 1917	72	Edwards, Roy	Rimmer, Claude		Cox, Flora		Edwards, Roy	Piedmont					
Ehrlich, Hannah Olivia	Jul 9, 1996	Jeff City	New York, Ny	Dec 18, 1991	4		Hubbard, Martin		Hubbard, Sharon		Kincaid, Charlene [Aunt]	Haven Rest - Grenada, Ms					
Ehrlich, Sharon	Jul 9, 1996	Jeff City	Grenada Co, Ms	Jul 17, 1957	38	Ehrlich, Martin	Hubbard, Bennie Jr.		Steward, Olivia		Kincaid, Charlene [Sister]	Haven Rest - Grenada, Ms					
Eisenhour, Carroll Calvin	Feb 6, 1992	J.M.H.	Greene Co, Tn	Aug 3, 1932	59	Sereiko, Linda	Eisenhour, Wayne O.		Winters, Mary		Wills	Greenlawn Memorial - Greeneville, Tn	unk				
Elder, Beulah M.	Mar 3, 1987	Jeff Co	Tn	Mar 4, 1897	89	W	Mc William, Robert		Wigland, Margaret		Elder, Glenn	Greenlawn Memorial - Greeneville, Tn					
Elder, C.G.	Feb 17, 1929	Jeff Co	Tn			Ng					J.M.G.	J.M.G.					
Elder, Charles	Apr 14, 1931	Sevier Co	Tn	Nov 25, 1854	76	Ng	Elder, John		Mount, Sallie	Tn	Elder, Blaine	Dumplin					
Elder, Fred William	Jun 12, 2000	Dandridge, Tn	Tn	Dec 2, 1923	68	Lowe, Beulah	Mc William, Beulah		Mc William, Beulah		Wills	Dumplin					
Elder, N.C.	May 17, 1937	Tn	Tn	Jul 15, 1867	69	S	Elder, William R.	Tn	Douglass, Mary K.		Elder, N.C.	Dumplin					
Elder, Randie Mae	Apr 15, 1950	Jeff Co		Feb 22, 1890	60	S	Elder, Charles G.		French, Hariah J.		Elder, Clarence & J.P.	Dumplin					
Elder, W.H.	May 7, 1941	Dumplin			52-2-23	Elder, Sarah Emma			French, Emma		Elder, Mrs. Hershel [Wife]	Dumplin					
Eldridge, Ann	May 20, 1935	Jeff Co		May 19, 1935							Greer, Joe - Eldridge, James	Mill Springs					
Eldridge, Carolyn	Dec 17, 1945	Jeff Co			abt 85		Unk	Tn	Unk	Tn	County	Mill Springs					
Eldridge, Dorothy Lucille	Jun 15, 1995	Knoxville, Tn	Grainger Co	May 14, 1941	54	Mc Bee, Thomas			Love, Charles [Son - Newport, Tn]		Love, Charles [Son - Newport, Tn]	Narrow Valley		Love, Ronnie	Love, Dortha - Haynes, Kitty	Leroy-Earn-Jake	Hill, Berth
Eldridge, James Jim	May 6, 1970	Tn	Tn	Jan 7, 1903	67	Ng			Wice, Jill		Eldridge, Julia	Mill Springs					
Eldridge, Bernice	Aug 1, 2000	Jeff City	Pa	Apr 15, 1918	82	Eldridge, Alfred R. [D]	Trechock, Stanley		Mary		Norton, Mary Jane & Bob [Daug]	James & Val [N]					
Elder, Alice	Jan 6, 1941	Talbott	Sullivan Co		74-6-9	W					Pollard, Mrs. Joe [Daug] - Andrew Chattee-Carroll [Sons]	Mt. Pleasant					
Elder, J.P.	May 4, 1935														5 [D]		
Ellis, John William Sr.	May 7, 1983	Jeff City	Tn	Dec 26, 1897	85	Harris, Margaret	Ellis, John P.		Coller, Mollie		Ellis, Mrs. Margaret	Lynhurst					
Ellis, Martha J.	May 14, 1938	Tn	Tn	Sep 22, 1875	60	W	Parrott, Robert	Tn	Hobbert, Barbara	Tn	Ellis, J.T. & Mack & James & C.M.	Shilo					
Ellis, J.P.	Nov 19, 1962	Jeff Co	St. Marys, Mo	Feb 15, 1879	88	W					Ellis, J.W.	Lynnhurst					
Ellis, James Fernando	Jun 6, 1947	Jeff Co	Morristown, Tn	Feb 15, 1879	68-3-21	Ng	Ellis, Samuel H.	Tn	Manning, Matilda C.	Mo	Ellis, Mrs. J.F.	West View					
Ellis, Margaret	Apr 7, 1990	J.M.H.	Tn	Sept 20, 1903	87	W	Harris, John E.		Hayes, Hollie		Ora Mrs. Dorothy	Lynnhurst - Knoxville, Tn					
Ellis, Mary	Aug 25, 1957	Home	Tn	Sept 20, 1874	83	Ellis, J.P.	Cofer, Jackson		Cooper, Mary		Ellis, J.P-W.J. - Scott, G.O.	Lynnhurst					
Ellis, Nancy Angeline	Jul 14, 1927		Tn		85-10-15	Ellis, S.L.	Randle, William		Keene, Narcissa			West View					
Ellis, Nellie	Oct 5, 1989	Jeff Co	Madison Lodge, Kansas	Mar 1, 1897	92	W	Hill, Edd		Tatum, Minnie		Naylor, Mrs. Hildred	Crestwood - Gadsdson, Ala.					
Ellison, Charles Mack	Sep 22, 1974	Tn	Tn	Jul 4, 1916	58	Div	Ellison, Charles L.		Purkey, George W.		Ward, Lucy - Ellison, Katherine	West View	WW 2				
Ellison, Fannie P.	Feb 9, 1964	Tn	Tn	July -, 1896	67	Ellison, Lou [D]			Greene, Katherine		Word, Mrs. Ray - Ellison, J.W.	West View					
Ellison, George James	Dec 29, 1995	Jeff Co	Tn	May 24, 1914	51	Ng			Purkey, Fannie		West View	West View					
Ellison, Georgia Vera	Apr 18, 1976	Hamblen Co	Tn	Jul 25, 1897	78	W	Hammer, Joe		Clevenger, Lucy		Bishop, Wayne - Cornwell, Faye - Marsh, Mrs. Raye - Ellison, Bill & Howard	Lebanon					
Ellison, James Carroll	Dec 21, 1974	Knoxville, Tn	Tn	Mar 9, 1919	55	Miller, Georgia	Ellison, James S.		Hammer, Georgia		Ellison, Mrs. Corum	Lebanon - Hamblen Co	WW 2				
Ellison, James S.	Aug 16, 1944	Jeff Co	Tn	Dec 1, 1896	47	Hammer, Georgia	Ellison, James P.	Tn	Keener, Mary Ann	Tn	Ellison, Mrs. Joe Jr.	Lebanon					
Ellison, Jo Ann	May 31, 1996	Knoxville, Tn	Knox Co	Sep 18, 1931	66		Whitter, Luther Thomas		Franklin, Ina Pauline		Cox, Mrs. Joe Jr.	Lebanon Baptist			Finocheck, Linda Jo		
Ellison, Martha Lou	Dec 1, 1999	New Market	Tn	Aug 31, 1915	44	Ellison, Lou [D]		Tn	Talbott, Mary	Tn	Chappel, Diana [Daug]	Sunderland		Keppes, George [Gla]		Dewey-James	Pruitt, Marime - Barlow, Margie - Ow Curtis, Imogene
Ellison, Mary Alice	Oct 28, 1994	Jeff City	Tn	Jul 10, 1907	87	W	Bradley, J. Shannon		Van Dyke, Nellie		Ellison, Gladys [Sister-In-Law]	West View					
Ellison, Mrs. J.P.	Jan 22, 1994	Jeff City	Tn	Jan 21, 1862	72	Ellison, J.P.	Keener, G.W.		Henderson, E.	Tn	Ellison, J.P.	Lebanon					

NAME	DDATE	DLOCAT	BLOCAT	BDATE	AGE	SPOUSE	FATHER	FBLOCAT	MOTHER	MFBLOCAT	BY	BURIAL	VET	SON	DAUG	BROTHER	SISTER
Ellison, William Cecil	Jun 29, 1994	Morristown,Tn	Jeff Co	Jan 18, 1929	65	Ellison, Jo Ann W.	Ellison, James S.		Hammer, Georgia V.		Wife	Lebanon Baptist	veteran	[Ship] Kappes, George	Willis, Vera Ann [Ship]; Campbell, Diana-Linda	Harold	Minch, Mrs. Tommy - Cornmeal, Mrs. Lowell - Cox, Elizabeth
Ellison, William Larry	Jul 22, 1974	High Point, Nc	Va.	Jul 31, 1953	22	S	Ellison, William C.	Tn	Ellison, Jo Ann		Wife	Lebanon	veteran				
Ellison, Charlie Beverly	Nov 26, 1943	Jeff Co	Tn	Nov 26, 1883	60	W	Ellison, T.S.	Tn	Williamson, Sarah Ann	Tn	Robert & Mary [Children]	New Market					
Elmore, Alice	May 14, 1947	Jeff Co	Jeff Co	Jan 1, 1889	76-4-13	Ng	Witt, William K.	Tn	Anderson, Sidney	Tn	Spoon, Mrs. Frank - Elmore, H.M.	Sunderland					
Elmore, Bobby Jean	May 28, 1942	Jeff Co	Jeff Co	May 24, 1942	2d		Unk		Elmore, Florence	Jeff Co	Elmore, Earl	Dumplin					
Elmore, Earl	Dec 27, 1932	New Market	Tn	Dec 29, 1930	1		Elmore, E.S.	Tn	Cate, Virgia	Tn	Elmore, E.S.	Home [Service]					
Elmore, Earl S.	Jul 4, 1988	Jeff Co	Tn	May 31, 1898	70	Cate, Virgia	Elmore, Samuel		Hubbard, Stacey		Elmore, Virgie & Jack - Harris, Jessie - Burgin, E.J. - Denton, Ross Lee	Cates - Jeff Co	WW 1				
Elmore, Edgar Philip	Jun 8, 1985	Jeff City	Tn	Apr 18, 1907	77	Duncan, Thelia Mae	Elmore, Calvin		Banks, Avie		Elmore, Thalia	Banks, Avie					
Elmore, Elizabeth Fielden	May 13, 1927		Tn	Apr 18, 1907	54-7-11	Elmore, W.W.	Fielden, Richard	Tn	Billinger, Cordelia	Tn		Friends Station					
Elmore, Frank D.	Mar 20, 1998	Strawberry Plains	Tn	Mar 28, 1915	82	Alley, Beulah	Elmore, Calvin		Banks, Angeline		Wife	Pleasant Grove		Frank Jr.			
Elmore, Hattie B.	Dec 16, 1950	Jeff Co	Tn	Apr 3, 1867	73	S	Elmore, William		Brazelton, Harriet		Elmore, Joel [Chattanooga, Tn]	East View Memorial	1944		Prentice, Margaret - Kelsey, Jundia		
Elmore, Johnnie Maude	Feb 19, 1979	Strawberry Plains		Dec 18, 1901	77	Ng	Griffin, Frank		Jones, Della		Elmore, Paul	Piney					
Elmore, Laude Erstt [M]	Nov 16, 1945	Jeff Co	Tn	Jan 6, —		S	Elmore, William B.	Tn	Felder, —		Elmore, Hattie & Joel - Ore, Joel	West View					
Elmore, Leota Gladys	Jul 5, 1940	Anderson Co. Tn	Hawkins Co. Tn	Jul 22, 1910	38	W			Wright	Sarah	Elmore, Nushell & Harris - Hoode, Mrs. Ann	Asbury					
Elmore, Lula Mae	Aug 3, 1946	New Market, Tn	Ohio Co, Ky	Jan 1, 1869	57	Elmore, Fred P. [Age-53]	Wilkison, Joseph Henry	Ohio Co, Ky	Bullock, Dora	Ohio Co, Ky	Elmore, Fred P.	New Market					
Elmore, Paul David	Jul 16, 1979	Knoxville, Tn	Tn	May 13, 1906	73	W	Elmore, Dave		Riley, Nancy		Bailey, Mrs. Vida	Pleasant Grove					
Elmore, Sam Horace	Mar 28, 1958	Jeff Co	Tn	Sep 25, 1976	81	Ng	Elmore, Thad		Russell, Stacey		Elmore, Raymond-Lee-Earl-Howard	Friends Station					
Elmore, Stacey	Jul 15, 1958	Jeff Co	Tn	Jun 25, 1880	78	W	Russell, Will		Payne, Margaret		Elmore, Raymond-Howard-Lee-Earl	French - Jeff Co					
Elmore, Virgie	Apr 12, 1984	J.M.H.	Tn	May 5, 1904	79	W	Cate, Jess		Odum, Martha		Beasley, Florence [Pat] Harris, Jessie-Jack [Children]	Cates - Jeff Co					
Elmore, W.S.	Jan 24, 1933	New Market	Tn	Feb 18, 1864	68	Ng	Elmore, James		Elmore, Abbie		Devette, Rosa Lee - Elmore, Mrs. E.S.	New Market					
Elmore, William B.	Oct 8, 1921	Tn	Tn		89-2-7	W	Elmore, Joel	Tn	Fielden, Nancy	Tn	Elmore, Joe	West View					
Elwood, Margaret Marie	Dec 1, 1998	Jeff City	Frederick, OK	Jul 21, 1921	77		Cannon, Frank		Lawson, Minnie		Elwood, Robert H. Sr. [Son]	Asbury				Frank-Roy Harald	
Ely, Arta E.	Apr 23, 1981		Tn			Ng	Munson, George W.	Tn	Furgerson, Mary	Tn	Ely, Bob [Son - Seeverkie, Tn]	West View					
Ely, Florence Rose	Aug 1, 1931	Knoxville	Tn	Jun 6, 1897	34	Ng	Pratt, Sam L.		Brogan, Frances	Tn	Lynchurst - Knoxville	Lynchurst - Knoxville					
Emert, Bertha Luthenia	Dec 1, 1944	Jeff Co	Knox Co	Oct 24, 1905	39	Ng	Pratt, Sam L.		Gunter, Mrs. B.		Pratt, Amos & Sam - Gunter, Mrs. B.	Trentville					
Emert, Lono Thomas	Oct 15, 1984	J.M.H.	Tn	Nov 10, 1904	80-11-5	W	Thomas, John A.		Chambers, Mattie L.		Thomas, James L. - Wood, Helen	West View					
Emert, Mrs. Shell	Feb 16, 1941	Jeff Co	Sevier Co	May 26, 1906	46	Emert, Shell			Mc Mahan, Elizabeth	Sevier Co	Rhoton, Mrs. J.A. [Dung]						
Emert, Rosie D.	May 9, 1986	Nc		May 9, 1986	81	W	Dillis, William C.		Early, Cordelia		Alley, Virginia E.	New Market					
Emory, John L.	Dec 22, 1965	Jeff City	Sevier Co	Oct 31, 1900	65	Ng	Emory, John M.		Harkness, Ida	Tn	Emory, Mrs. John - Finey, Roegan - Alley, Vincent	New Market	WW 1				
England, Ida	Sep 21, 1948	Jeff Co	Greene Co. Tn	May 8, 1874	74-6-11	W	Russell, Thomas B.	Tn	Dverstows, Sarah	Tn	Harmon, M-S-W.W. [Greeneville, Tn]	New Market					Fordtner, Juanita - Behr, Francis - Mize, Evelina

NAME	DDATE	DLOCAT	BLOCAT	BDATE	AGE	SPOUSE	FATHER	FBLOCAT	MOTHER	MTBLOCAT	BY	BURIAL	VET	SON	DAUG	BROTHER	SISTER
Eslinger, Allie Ellison	Jan 26, 1971	Jeff Co	Tn	Apr 13, 1893	77	Eslinger, G.P.	Ellison, Sherman		Williamson, Ann		Eslinger, G.P.	Memorial Gardens					
Eslinger, Ethel Elnora	Jan 10, 1966	J.M.H.	Tn	Aug 8, 1912	73	W	Kimbrough, Floyd		Smith, Nolia		Kimbrough, Glenna	Jarnigan					
Eslinger, George Pearl	Jun 10, 1974	At Home	Tn	Oct 26, 1893	80	W			Patterson, Violet		Eslinger, Bruce [Son]	Jefferson Memorial					
Eslinger, Harry Bruce	Aug 21, 1999	Knoxville, Tn	Jeff Co	Mar 21, 1920	79	Jones, Ezalee	Ellison, Allie J.				Eslinger, William [Son]	J.M.G.			Stansberry, Janice		
Eslinger, Houston C.	Sep 26, 1957	Knox Co	Tn	Oct 14, 1895	71	S	Eslinger, George P.		Patterson, Violet P		Eslinger, G.P.-J.H.	New Market					
Eslinger, James G.	May 29, 1954	Douglas Lake	Tn	Oct 14, 1886	77	W	Eslinger, Creed		Patterson, Violet		Eslinger, Ralph - Langston, Mrs. Robert	New Market					
Eslinger, William L.	Mar 11, 1962	Ypsilante, Mich.	Tn	1883	79						Eslinger, Hal [Men]	Hills Union					
Ester, Helene A.	Dec 28, 1997	Jeff City	Madison, Wi	Feb 2 1912	85		Link		Link		Ester, Richard [Step-Son]	Cremated					
Ester, Gertrude Elizabeth [Col]	May 14, 1972	Jeff Co	Tn			W	Smith, Walter				Ester, Donald Ellsworth	West View					
Evans, Hannah Cochran	Aug 26, 1958	Greene Co	Tn	Jan 20, 1893	65	W	Milone, Thomas		Murdock, Ella Caroline		Wooldridge, Mrs. Calvin - Milone, Lee & Eugene	Mill Springs					
Evans, Lucille	Jun 9, 1982	Knoxville, Tn	Newport, Tn	Jul 15, 1916	75	Div	Brady, John Wesley Sr.		Smith, Nellie		Solomon, Dorothy A. [Daug]-Hill, Deanna-Loveday, Brenda	J.M.G.					
Evans, Mary E.	Feb 18, 1980	Kingsport, Tn	Tn	Dec 19, 1886	73	W	Treece, Thomas J.		Cooper, Sarah J.		Cress, Katherine [Claude] - Evans, Claude	Macedonia - Hamblen Co					
Evans, Patrick Conway	Jan 20-22, 1984	J.M.H. [Fair Md]	Tn	Jan 6, 1953	31	S	Evans, James		Conway, Mrs.		Durst F.H. [Friedburg, Md]	Friedburg Memorial - Md	70-74				
Evans, Rose Deloris	Dec 14, 1981	Columbus, Ohio	Tn	Dec 3, 1915	76	W	Priestas, Charlie		Toka, Mary		Evans, George W. [Son]	Russian junction - Worthington, Ohio					
Evans, Shannon Dawn	Aug 28, 1974	Jeff City		34-6-15	Ng		Evans, Richard		Milone, Linda		Evans, Richard	Flat Gap					
Evans, Van Roy [Col]	Jun 4, 1927		Tn			Ng	Evans, Calvin	Tn	Mc Cowen, Maudy			Colored					
Everett, Janie Thornton	Jan 11, 1949	Jeff Co	Faison, Nc	Oct 25, 1872	71	W	Thornton, Moore Lee	Nc	Williams, Jane Ellen	Nc	Everett, John D.	West View					
Everett, Lisk	Jan 2, 1943	Jeff Co	Faison, Nc		70	S	Thornton, Moore Lee	Nc	Williams, Jane Ellen	Nc	Everett, J.D.	West View					
Everhart, Betty Jo	Jul 1, 1999	Union Co, Tn	Tn	Jan 22, 1940	51	Everhart, Gerald	Nicely, Horace H.		Mabry, Louise		Dalton, Bonnie R. [Sister]	J.M.G.		Wood, Charles	Moore, Paula		
Everhart, Janice Diane	Jan 29, 1953	Jeff City	Tn	Apr 3, 1951	1	Ng	Everhart, Robert H.		Haworth, Ola Mae		Everhart, Robert	New Market					
Everhart, Pauline	Aug 18, 1961	Jeff City	Tn		43	Ng	Mc Nish, Mack L.		Howard, Minerva		Mc Nish, Eula	Pleasant Grove					
Everhart, Fred	Jun 4, 1927																
Fain, Fred	Apr 5, 1942	Jeff City	Tn	Mar 12, 1875	67	S	Fain, Robert	Tn	Mignott, Clarinda	Tn	Fain, Johnny - Mc Cowen, R.H.					Hall, Barbara	
Fain, Jack Le Roy [Col]	Apr 27, 1957	Jeff City	Tn	Jul 17, 1912	54	S	Patterson, Kid		Fain, Lila		Williams, Mary - Fain, Duke	West View					
Fain, John Richard	Mar 28, 1944	Jeff Co	Jeff Co	Dec 7, 1873	70	S	Fain, Samuel N.	Tn	Fain, Sallie	Tn	Elizabeth	Greenwood					
Fain, Martha Gillispie	Jul 15, 1944	Jeff Co	Jeff Co	Nov 3, 1870	73	S	Fain, Samuel N.	Tn	Fain, Sallie	Tn	Fain, Elizabeth R.	Greenwood - Knox Co					
Fain, Mary	Mar 7, 1952	Jeff City	York, Sc	May 5, 1875	76	W	Clark, Frank		Riddle, Margaret Jane	Tn	Fain, Margaret & Frank	Presby - Dandridge					
Fain, Paul	Apr 11, 1932	Jeff City	Tn	Mar 4, 1911	21	S	Fain, Milligaree	Tn	Howell, Jennie		Fain, Milligaree	Dandridge					
Fain, Samuel Clark Sr.	Oct 30, 1981	U.T.H.	La Grange, Tn	Jul 25, 1902	79	Hunt, Virginia	Fain, Samuel White		Clark, Mary		Fain, W.S.C.	Hopewell					
Fain, Virginia	Jul 11, 1992	J.M.H.	Tn	Jul 3, 1903	89	W	Hunt, John Willis		Turner, Annie		Fain, George A. [Son]	Hopewell					
Farmer, Amanda	Jul 19, 1928	Tn	Tn		86	W	Brabson, John	Tn			Puckett, C.A.	Piedmont					
Farmer, Nettie Nora	Dec 18, 1953	Grainger Co	Tn	May 16, 1893	60	S	Farmer, James W.		Harrell, Mrs. Tina		Butler, Mrs. Charles & Mrs. Johnnie - Carroll, Mrs. L.K.	Mc Ginnis - Grainger Co					
Farmer, Aline Taylor	Feb 24, 1961	Jeff City	Lincoln Co, Tn	May 5, 1900	60	Ng	Taylor, Walter Clayton		Renegar, Clora A.		Farmer, R.E.	West View					
Farmer, Bessil Thurl	Dec 4, 1925		Tn			S	Farmer, Samuel		Spencer, Amanda	Tn	Farmer, Thula	Sunrise					
Farmer, Cleophia	Dec 21, 1925		Tn				Farmer, Willie		Colbrum, May	Tn	Farmer, Willie	Shilo					
Farmer, Cynthia Arie	Jun 7, 1926			69-3-24		Farmer, W.R.						Shilo					
Farmer, Edward Taylor	Sep 24, 1925			0-3-6			Farmer, R.S. Sr.	Tn	Taylor, M. Olive	Tn	Farmer, Ida & Jess	West View					
Farmer, Harry Clay	Jun 8, 1939	Jeff Co	Tn	Nov 1, 1900	38	Div	Farmer, Riley	Tn	Clevenger, Harriet	Tn	Farmer, Riley	Shiloh				Ricky	
Farrar, Roy Everette Sr.	Sept 6, 1984	Jeff Co	Tn	Dec 21, 1896	87	Denton, Ruth	Farrar, William Franklin	Tn	Richards, Mary Emma	Tn	Farrar, James C.	West View					

NAME	DATE	DLOCAT	BLOCAT	BDATE	AGE	SPOUSE	FATHER	FBLOCAT	MOTHER	MFBLOCAT	BY	BURIAL	VET	SON	DAUG	BROTHER	SISTER
Farrar, Ruth D.	Jan 10, 1997	Lithonia, Ga		Aug 1, 1907	89	Choate, Mary	Denton, E.A.		Martin, Barbara C.		Martin, Barbara [Dau]	West View		[Step] Farrar, James~Joe T.- & James~Joe T.- Dorothy~Wilder, Brenda	[Nephews] Scott-Todd~Fred~Bruce		
Farrar, William Roy	Jul 2, 1995	Morristown, Tn	Morristown, Tn	Sep 23, 1957	37		Farrar, James Clayton		Walkins, Agnes Elese		Wife	West View	William Clayton			Britt Clayton [Uncles] R.E.-Jr.-Joe T.- William	
Farris, Della Beatrice	Jan 3, 1994	J.M.H.	Va	Sep 12, 1902	81	S	Farris, John		Wicker, Nancy Jane		Underwood, May	Piedmont					
Farris, Elsie	Oct 21, 1990	Dandridge, Tn	Knoxville, Tn	Sep 6, 1900	90	W	Morris, Marshall		French, Jeanne		Farris, John Wayne	J.M.G.					
Farris, Johnny Orrin	Aug 26, 1988	U.U.H.	Tn	Jan 27, 1923	65	W	Morris, Elsie		Morris, Elsie		Farris, Petit Sue- Johnny Wayne	J.M.G.					
Farris, Johnny Wayne	Dec 9, 1983	J.M.H.	Va	Dec 29, 1900	82	Forerly, Minnie Bell	Farris, George		Wicker, Nancy		Farris, Mrs. Elsie	Jefferson Memorial					
Farrow, Franklin D.	Feb 2, 1990	J.M.H.	Grainger Co	Sep 28, 1905	84	Forerly, Minnie Bell	Farrow, Marion		Lumpkins, Maggie								
Farrow, Minnie Bell	Apr 6, 1991	Dandridge, Tn	Jeff Co	Aug 10, 1907	83	W	Forgety, Will		Underwood, Mettie		Farrow, Earl [Son]	J.M.G.					
Felknor, Agusta Lafayette	Feb 18, 1943	Jeff Co	Jeff Co	1878	65	S	Felknor, John L.	Tn	Shockton, Dorothula	Tn	Felknor, G. Ross	Hopewell					
Felknor, George Ross	Dec 8, 1944	Hamblen Co	Jeff Co	Apr 18, -44	60	S	Felknor, John L.	Tn	Shockton, Dorthula	Tn	Seaborn, Robert	Dandridge					
Felknor, Female	Dec 5, 1963	Jeff Co		Dec 5, 1963			Felknor, James		Howell, James		Howell, Betty	Friends Station					
Fennell, John Newton	Jan 28, 1945	Grainger Co	Grainger Co	May 20, 1866	77	Davis, Mary Elizabeth			Hunsucker, Martha Jane	Tn	Fennell, Mrs. Horace	Indian Ridge					
Fennell, Mary Elizabeth~Catherine	Mar 9, 1947	Grainger Co	Grainger Co								Fennell, Mrs. H.R. - Vinyard, Mrs. Clifford - Moore, Mrs. John - Fennell, Elaine	Indian Ridge					
Ferguson, Margaret L.	Jun 6, 1991	J.M.H.	Bristol, Tn	Sep 20, 1906	84	S	Ferguson, John T.		Moore, Sarah		Powell, William L [Nephew]	A.R.Dykes Memorial - London, Ky					
Ferguson, Sylvester Tillotson [F]	May 17, 1975	Jeff Co	Miss.	Apr 7, 1891	84	W	Tillotson, Robert S.		Mc Nair, Laura E.		Richardson, Mrs. W. Edwin	Jackson, Miss.					
Fielden, Alexander	Oct 5, 1931	New Market	Tn	Dec 12, 1890	80	W	Fieldman, John W.	Tn	Bayot, Susie	Tn	Elmore, Mrs.	Pleasant View					
Fielden, Elnora	Nov 28, 1944	Jeff Co	Tn	Jul 1, 1878	66	W	Howard, J.C.	Tn	Simpkins, Mahathturn	Tn	Vernon & Mrs. Maryatt	Mill Springs					
Fielden, Essie	Oct 3, 1933	New Market	Tn	Jul 5, 1880	53	Ballinger, W	Ballinger, Jackson	Tn	Northen, Archie	Tn	Spira	Pleasant Grove					
Fielden, Horace R.	Jul 3, 1954	Jeff Co	Tn	Feb 23, 1883	71	Ng	Fielden, Richard		Ballinger, Candile		Fielden, Eugene	West View					
Fielden, Ida	May 1, 1953	Grainger Co	Grainger Co	Oct 25, 1886	66	Ng	Fennell, John		Dunn, Mattie		Fielden, H.R.	West View					
Fields, D.C.	March 19, 1935	Massy Creek	Va	May 12, 1855	79	Ng	Fields, L.C.	Va	Fields, L.C. (Knoxville)	Va	Mt. Pleasant						
Fields, Emma Kiersey	Jun 28, 1973	Rogersville, Tn	Tn	Jan 5, 1883	90	Ng	Kiersey, David		Cox, Mary	Va	Kiersey, Ed	White Pine					
Fields, Harvey	Oct 21, 1934	Jeff City	Tn	Jul 8, 1945	88	W						West View					
Fields, J.A.	Mar 25, 1927	Va	Va		64-9-8	Ng				Va		West View					
Fields, Josephine	Mar 23, 1925	Tn	Tn		72	Fields, J.H.	Hickman, Plez		Allison, Beckie	Tn	Fields, J.H.	West Springs					
Fields, Mary Elizabeth	Mar 7, 1986	Care Inn	Tn	Aug 28, 1911	74	W	Mc Cown, R. M. [Sr.]	Tn	Tittsworth, Nellie		Jones, Elizabeth F. [Emporia, Va.]	West View					
Fields, William Hoyle	May 18, 1978	Jeff Co	Va	Apr 29, 1910	66	W	Fields, J.A.		Bettis, Corona		Fields, Mrs. Julia	West View					
Finchum, Addie Rhea	Jul 21, 1986	E.Th. Baptist	Tn	Nov 10, 1906	79	S	Jeffers, Rufus		Jeffers, Nancy		Finchum, Hooper	Beaver Creek					
Finchum, Angel Deneen	Jan 17, 1978	Knoxville, Tn	Tn	Jan 16, 1978	17		Finchum, James		Skeen, Anita		Finchum, James	Beaver Creek					
Finchum, Arlie Lester	Feb 11, 1967	Residence	Tn	May 23, 1967	69-8-17	Payne, Mrs. Mayme	Finchum, Joseph F.		Baker, Molly E.		Finchum, Steve [Son]	West View					
Finchum, Arthur Lindsey	Nov 14, 1983	J.M.H.	Tn	Feb 11, 1900	83	Witt, Grace	Finchum, Rusen		Byrd, Ida		Finchum, Don & Sisters	Beaver Creek					
Finchum, Austin Hooper	Jan 31, 1993	Jeff City	Jeff Co	Feb 23, 1911	81	W	Finchum, Orville		Lewis, Clemmie M.		Finchum, Clyde [Son]	Beaver Creek		[G] Kenneth	[G] Cooper, Donna - Wood, Lisa		
Finchum, Christine	Aug 20, 1971	Knox Co	Tn	Sep 27, 1963	17	S	Finchum, Floyd O.		Jarnigan, Grace		Finchum, Floyd	West View					
Finchum, Edward Lynn	Oct 30, 1982	Knoxville, Tn	Tn	Apr 22, 1963	19	S	Finchum, Donald, Edward		French, Phyllis		Finchum, Don	Beaver Creek					
Finchum, Grace Will	Feb 14, 1985	Jeff Co	Tn	Aug 19, 1906	78	W	Witt, Frank		Branton, Martha		Finchum, Donald	West Creek					
Finchum, J.F.	Sep 30, 1931	Morristown	Tn	May 21, 1856	75	Ng	Finchum, Henry		Belton, Louise	Sc	Children	West View					
Finchum, James M.	Sep 2, 1926	Tn	Tn		82-10-17	Ng	Finchum, Henry	Tn	Belton, Louisa	Sc	Finchum, J.F.	Russellville					
Finchum, Jessie Marie	Jun 24, 1998	New Market, Tn	Claiborne Co, Tn	Nov 11, 1915	82		Greenlee, Jessee		Loop, Merdie		Finchum, James [Son]	Beaver Creek			Emily Sue - Musick, Mary Ellen		

NAME	DATE	B.LOCAT	B.LOCAT	BDATE	AGE	SPOUSE	FATHER	F.B.LOCAT	MOTHER	M.F.B.LOCAT	BY	BURIAL	VET	SON	DAUG	BROTHER	SISTER
Finchum, Mamie	May 26, 1993	Rockwood, Tn	Coppethill, Tn	Apr 24, 1902	91	Payne, Luther		Tn	Heth, Jennie		Coppinger, Jannie [Daug]	West View		Jack-Frank [Ky]-Joe [Ky]-Lee [Ga]-Steve [Fla]		Donald	Deatherage, Mary
Finchum, Mary	Oct 1, 1931	Morristown	Tn	Jul 31, 1858	73	Finchum, J.F.	Baker, G.W.	Tn	Vineyard, Mary		Finchum, Bill	Beaver Creek					
Finchum, Mary Elizabeth	Feb 5, 1942		Jeff Co		1m-5d	S	Finchum, Bill		Finchum, Elizabeth	Jeff Co	Finchum, Bill	Beaver Creek					
Finchum, Myrtle Lexie [F]	Nov 24, 1965	Jeff Co	Tn	Aug 24, 1889	76	W	Louis, James		Fox, Nancy		Finchum, Hooper & Sam	Fox - Seeker Co					
Finchum, Nellie Lou	Jul 6, 1932	Dandridge	Tn	Jun 22, 1884	48	Finchum, J.S.	Mc Spadden, M.M.	Tn	Fox, Ellen	Tn	Finchum, J.S.	Dandridge					
Finchum, Ollie	May 27, 1967	Seeker Co	Tn	Sep 26, 1900	66	W	Folland, Rufus F.		Jeffers, Nancy C.		Finchum, Susan	Hillcrest					
Finchum, R.H.	Jun 28, 1927		Tn		1-9-29		Finchum, Alton		Finchum, Ida	Tn	Finchum, Alton	Fox					
Finchum, Samie H.	Sep 5, 1987	U.T.H.	Tn	Nov 10, 1915	71	Jessee, Jessie G.	Finchum, Silas Arville		Lewis, Canna Myrtle		Finchum, Jessie E.	Beaver Creek	WW2				
Finchum, Virgie Ruby	Feb 1, 1941	Jeff Co	Tn		27-6-11	Finchum, A. Hooper			Finchum, Matilda	Tn	Finchum, A.H.	Piney Grove Baptist					
Finks, Hugh W.	Sept 28, 1934	New Market	Jeff Co	Sep 7, 1934	21d		Finks, Rufus	Tn	Strange, Lillie	Tn	Finks, Rufus	New Market					
Fink, Richard Orville	Apr 5, 2000	Jeff City	Tn	May 1, 1935	64	Div			Griffin, Matilda			New Market	Army				
Finley, Archie F.	May 10, 1945	Jeff Co	Granger Co	Dec 23, 1877	67	Ng	Finley, Will		Williams, Minerva	Tn	Mrs. Ollie	West View					
Finley, Ollie Estelle	Sep 30, 1990	Jeff Co	Tn	May 12, 1900	90	W	Finley, William		Williams, Minerva		Finley, Floyd-Freddie-Franklin, Bonnie [Children]	Sunrise - Granger Co					
Finley, Betty Imogene	May 3, 1996	Rutledge, Tn	Knoxville, Tn	Dec 25, 1935	62	Finley, Harold Wayne	Butler, George R.		Young, Margaret		Nelson, Ruby F.- Finley, Floyd-Freddie-Franklin, Bonnie [Children]	Spring Place Presby.- Knoxville, Tn		Merit	Brooks, Candace		
Finley, Cheryl Lynn	Aug 20, 1956	Hamblen Co	Tn	Aug 18, 1956		Ng	Finley, Donald		Profitt, Carolyn		Hubbard	West View					
Finley, Floyd C.	Nov 23, 1981	J.M.H.	Tn	Sep 5, 1917	64	Jenkins, Gladys	Finley, Archie		Farrow, Maude		Finley, Floyd C.	Jefferson Memorial					
Finley, Ruby Arleen	Oct 4, 1977	Jefferson Memorial Hosp.	Tn	Jul 29, 1926	51	W	Mc Ghee, Tilda		Grove, Bonnie		Kelley, Mrs. Charles - Lawson, Mrs. - Finley, James	West View					
Finley, Ruth	Nov 7, 1967	Tn	Tn	May 26, 1890	77	Finley, Will	Noe, George		Moyes, Alice		Noe, George	Shiloh					
Finley, William A.	May 7, 1959	Granger Co	Granger Co	Sep 5, 1985	73	Ng	Finley, Will		Finley, Minerva		Finley, George R.	Shiloh					
Fish, Sandra Kay	Apr 13, 1996	Talbott, Tn	Talbott, Tn	May 3, 1949	48	Fish, James	Dickau, Roy A.		Cox, Alice		Husband	Cremated		Morgan, Timothy	Towell, Malinda		
Fisher, James Thomas	Jun 14, 1996	Jeff City	Corryton, Tn	Feb 16, 1937	59	Fisher, Billie S.	Fisher, William		Brock, Susie		Wife	Trentville		Jimmy-James	Oliver, Gail [Nc] - Stallings, Sylvia [Sia]	Roy	
Fite, Esther Goldie	Jun 3, 1980	Jeff City	Autenttown, Tn	Jul 1, 1903	76	Fite, D. Harley	Robinson, Robert		Willard, Nettie		Flks, Harley	West View					
Fitzer, Carol Elizabeth	Aug 13, 1980	Jeff City	Jeff City	Jan 29, 1971	9		Fitzer, John W. Jr.		Woodson, Rosie Ann		Fitzer, John W. Jr.	Jefferson Memorial					
Fleming, Charles Edward [Negro]	Jan 28, 1975	Nc		Jul 9, 1926	48	Wright, Ethel	Fleming, Robert		Noble - Kelsey - F.H.		Noble - Kelsey - F.H.	Prosperity - Prosperity, Tn					
Flowers, Carrie	Dec 9, 1997	Cross Co, Ar		Sep 5, 1907	90	Summerlot, Homer	Waggnor, Homer		Vanderhoff, Susan		Thies, Doris Virginia [Daug]	Lebanon Baptist					
Flynn, Zelma Jean	Dec 9, 1976	Morristown, Tn	New Jersey	Oct 31, 1971	5	S	Flynn, Roger		Flynn, Roger		Flynn, Roger [Daug]	Pleasant Grove					Smith, Ruby [Memphis] - Gahr, Mabel [Ar]
Ford, James Edward	Oct 27, 1951	Knox Co	Clay Co, Tn	Nov 28, 1927	23	S	Ford, Edward L.		Napier, Annie		Ford, Edward L. [Celina, Tn]	Celina - Clay Co, Tn					
Ford, Lyle Ferguson	Jun 28, 1983	J.M.H.	J.M.H.	Sep 1, 1912	70	Higdons, Nellie	Cox, Mayme		Ford, Mrs. Nellie		Ford, Mrs. Nellie	Hamblen Memorial					
Forester, Charles Frederick	Feb 1, 1996	Tn	Athens, Tn	Dec 29, 1910	85	Keith, Lillian	Forester, Curn		Morton, Nettie		Wife	Wife		Donald	Dodson, Corjlen - Moore, Sandra		Smith, Betty - Matlock, Mary - Hicks, Wilma - Kern, Peggy
Forester, Lillian	Apr 22, 1998	Knoxville, Tn	Knoxville, Tn	Jan 23, 1914	84	Keith, James T.	Keith, James T.		Francis, Grace		Dodson, Carolyn [Daug]	Greenwood - Knoxville, Tn		Donald	Moore, Sandra	Lawrence-Ralph-Eugene-Dermit-Curtis	[B+Leaf Keith, Jean]

NAME	DATE	BLOCAT	BLOCAT	BDATE	AGE	SPOUSE	FATHER	FBDLOCAT	MOTHER	MFBLOCAT	BY	BURIAL	VET	SON	DAUG	BROTHER	SISTER
Forgaty, Fred Albert	Jan 7, 1959	Jeff Co	Jeff Co	Jan 25, 1909	83	Lapa, Janie	Forgaty, William		Underwood, Mattie		Wife	J.M.G.		Don	Bell, Wanda F. - Bowling, Shirley A. - Tindell, Norma	Joon-Leonard	Gray, Tiley - Carter, Agnes - Forgaty, Emily
Forgaty, John	Apr 13, 1949	Cocke Co	Hawkins Co				Forgaty, James	Tn	Maxwell, Sarah		Forgaty, Telford	West View					
Forgaty, Mable Lee	Oct 5, 1981	Jeff City	Tn	Sep 24, 1890	45	W	Underwood, James	Tn	Lee, Malinda		Forgaty, Will	Bullhow					
Forgaty, Mrs. John	Apr 18, 1933	Jeff City	Tn		42	Forgaty, John	Henson, S.E.	Tn	Henson, Mollie		Forgaty, John	West View					
Forgaty, Richard Edward	Jun 21, 1940	Jeff City	Tn	Oct 21, 1910	29	Ng	Underwood, Mattie E.	Tn	Forgaty, Mrs. Edd		Forgaty, Mrs. Edd						
Forgaty, Telford Earl Sr.	Feb 4, 1987	Rogersville, Tn	Hawkins Co	Sept 20, 1916	70	Phox, Gladys	Forgaty, John	Va	Newman, Ollie		Forgaty, Gladys	Hillcrest	WW 2				
Forgaty, Will	Mar 4, 1947	S.M.H.	Hawkins Co	Feb 29, 1879	68	W	Forgaty, James		Maxwell, Sarah	Tn	Bates, Mrs. Frank	Buffalo Grove	573				
Forney, Elizabeth	May 15, 1994	Jeff City	Williamsburg, Va	Sep 11, 1904	89	Forney, Samuel W. [D]	Langford, Henry		Forney, James W. [Son]		Forney, Richard - Crooke, Miss Ruth	West View		[G] Forney, David	[G] Rhodes, Susan [Pa]	Leonard	
Forrester, Wilma Jean	May 27, 1939	Talbott	Tn	Mar 14, 1938	1		Forrester, Robert	Arkansas	Crooke, Lula	Nc	Forrester, Robert - Crooke, Miss Ruth	Buffalo					
Foster, General Roy	Jul 17, 1994	Jeff City	Jeff Co	Jun 20, 1913	81	Byrd, Beulah	Foster, Frank		Marsh, Sallie		Wife	Blackwell Branch			Carter, Wanda & Allen - Walker, Opral & Eddie [Bi-Law] Foster, Mary Alice		Cameron, Nellie Mae - Williams, Edna - Manning, Irene - James, Ruby
Foster, Hamilton	1925		Hawkins Co								Hodgson, J.R.						
Foster, Mack Sr.	Feb 25, 1970	Jeff Co	Tn	Jan 22, 1910	59	Ng	Foster, J.W.		Largin, Dycie Bell		Foster, Mack Jr. Largin, Dycie Bell	Brethern				Charlie-Otto-Jim	
Foster, Mammie L.	Aug 31, 1956	Jeff Co	Tn	Dec 7, 1881	74	W	Clawson, -		Clawson, -		Hodge, Mrs. Milburn - Northern, Mrs. Edd [Daug] Shaw, Susan R.	Mill Springs					
Foster, Mary Alice	Feb 17, 2000	New Market, Tn	Tn	Dec 29, 1936	63	W	McCarter, James P.		Charlotte		Shaw, Susan R.	J.M.G.					
Foster, Ray Edward	Feb 18, 1994	Jeff City	Granger Co.	Jun 29, 1939	54	McCarter, Mary Alice	Foster, General Roy		Foster, Beulah		Wife	J.M.G.		[Bi-Law] Haynes, Marty	Lee, Teresa & Christel - Carter, Yonda & James - Keister, Susan		Carter, Wanda & Allen - Walker, Opral & Eddie
Foster, Vina	Feb 9, 1984	Jeff Co	Tn	Nov 21, 1888	75	Ng	Wright, Albert		Ballinger, Amanda		Howard, Herbert - Foster, J.S.	Mill Springs					
Foust, Mary E.	Dec 2, 1925	Jeff Co	Tn			Ng	Foust, Wesley	Tn	Jennings, Catherine	Tn	Cox, Mrs. - Seaborn, Urk	New Market					
Foust, Milton Lee	Jan 5, 1955	Jeff City	Tn	Apr 28, 1850	84	W	Foust, Wiley	Tn	Sawyer, Louisa	Tn	Sons	New Market					
Fowley, David Preston	Apr 16, 1983	Knoxville, Tn	Worcester, Ma		69	Bates, Katherine	Preston, Ruth		Preston, Ruth		Wife	J.M.G.		Douglas & Suzanne-Mark	Coppenheavel, Carole & Ralph		
Fox, Alma	Dec 20, 1983	J.M.H.	Tn	Jul 4, 1891	92	W	Swann, Robert		Nichols, Nancy		Hobert, Mrs. Mabie Fox	Hillcrest					
Fox, Alonzo Eli	Jun 6, 1944	Jeff Co	Tn	Oct 18, 1881	62	Ng	Fox, W.C.	Tn	Fox, Mrs. Mabel Blackburn		Fox, Mrs. Mabel Blackburn	Shady Grove					
Fox, Bonnie Janelle	Oct 24, 1996	Knoxville, Tn	Jeff Co	Oct 5, 1922	74	Fox, Robert T.	Layman, Hobart M.		Miller, Nettie		Husband	Hillcrest					[Bi-Law] Holbert, Mable Fox
Fox, Ellen	Oct 4, 1943	Dandridge	Jeff Co	Dec 25, 1855	87	W	Zirkle, William	Va	Gouit, Mary	Tn	Hill, E.F. - Rainwater, Ralph - Rimer, Carl - Gass, F.L. [Daughters]	Shady Grove					
Fox, George Walter	Mar 25, 1956	Mt. Horne	Tn	Dec 9, 1896	59	W	Fox, James E.	Tn	Snapp, Hattie		Fox, J.T.	West View	WW 1				
Fox, James S.	May 23, 1972	Jeff Co	Tn	Nov 18, 1914	58	Simms, Ruby	Fox, J.		Swann, Alma S.		Fox, J.T. - Fox, Ruby	Hillcrest					
Fox, James Taylor	Jan 30, 1959	Jeff Co	Tn	Nov 10, 1890	68	Ng	Fox, J.E.		Snapp, Hattie		Fox, Robert	Hillcrest					
Fox, Lallie Lanette	Apr 7, 1979	Jeff Co	Tn	Mar 30, 1894	85	W	Willis, William E.		Collier, Florence		Cash, Mrs. Clara M.	West View					
Fox, Wilma Lois	Dec 18, 1983	Knoxville, Tn	Jeff Co	Apr 12, 1945	48	Fox, William M.	Carr, Ezra		Rush, Myrtie Louise		Husband - Viola [Step Mother]	Mt. View		Jeff	Loy, Tammy & Rick		Maples, Georgia & Carl
Fraker, Albie Orlando	May 8, 1980	Jeff City	Tn	Sep 8, 1910	69	Hodgson, Dena	Fraker, Thomas M.		Armstrong, Sarah		Fraker, Mrs. Dena & Children	Jefferson Memorial					
Fraker, Carrie Pauline	Jul 19, 1973	Jeff City	Tn	Oct 10, 1897	75	S	Fraker, T.F.M.		Sarah		Fraker, Albie	Jefferson Memorial					
Fraker, Daisy Dena	May 21, 1997	Jeff Co	Jeff Folly	Apr 17, 1912	85	Fraker, Albie [D]	Hodgson, Thomas R.		Mundy, Ellis		Fraker, Tom [Son]	J.M.G.		Bill	Fraker, Kitty - Estes, Deena	Avery-Ellis	
Fraker, Frank Lilburn	Nov 26, 1960	Greenes Co., Tn	Greenes Co., Tn	Jul 27, 1902	58	Ng			Armstrong, Sarah C.		Fraker, Inez	J.M.G.					
Fraker, Inez	Jun 11, 1987	Morristown, Tn	Jeff Co	Mar 7, 1905	82	Fraker, Frank [D]	Carmichael, T.A.		Douglas, Lillie		Carmichael, Ethel - Mrs. C.I.	J.M.G.					Fraker, Frank - Shanks, Millersburen - Green Co., Tn
Fraker, Sarah Katherine	Nov 8, 1951	Greene Co., Tn		Sep 3, 1873	78	W	Armstrong, Michael		Peters, Susie		Fraker, Frank - Shanks, Mrs. C.I.	J.M.G.					

NAME	DDATE	DLOCAT	BLOCAT	BDATE	AGE	SPOUSE	FATHER	FBLOCAT	MOTHER	MFBLOCAT	BY	BURIAL	VET	SON	DAUG	BROTHER	SISTER
Fraker, Thomas Franklin Milburn	Oct 24, 1940	Jeff Co	Tn	Sep 1, 1867	73	Ng	Fraker, Billie	Va	Milburn, Jane	Tn	Frank L.- Nate [Sons]	Milburnton, --					
Fralix, George Grant	Sep 6, 1944	Knox Co	Tn	Nov 18, 1870	73	Ng	Fralix, Grant	Tn	Jones, Mary	Tn	Newlin, Mrs. Grace - Fralix, Rafie	Roseberry					
Frame, Mattie	Oct 2, 1951	Knox Co	Tn	Oct 28, 1866	87-11-4	S	Frame, John H.		Kesler, Malitda		Murphy, Leila	Baptist [S. Swann House]					
France, Melinda Caldonia	Jun 24, 1943	Shaw Plains	Alabama	Apr 12, 1861	82	W	Gregory, Henry	Alabama	Knox, Dauf	Alabama	France, Mavik & George						
France, Mark Brooks	Mar 13, 1967	Jeff Co	Tn	Jul 8, 1894	72	Ng	France, William W.		Gregory, Melinda		France, Charlie Mark- Johnny-George-Bonnie - Humphrey, Christine [Children]	Strawberry Plains					
Franklin, Bessie	Feb 13, 1972	Jeff Co	Tn	Feb 13, 1896	76	Ng	Wilson, Joseph		Rawlings, Isabelle		Leonard, June & Francis [Daugs]	Piedmont					
Franklin, Barbara Jean	Oct 7, 1990	Margartineld, Ky	Birmingham, Ala.	Dec 27, 1940	49	Ng	Holcomb, James E.	Tn	Shelton, Ann		Franklin, Dallas	J.M.G.					
Franklin, Benjamin F.	Mar 10, 1927		Tn		81-5-8	Ng	Franklin, T.P.		Corbett, Emely	Tn	Franklin, Mrs. Jessie	Hebron					
Franklin, Benjamin N.	Dec 6, 1926		Tn		81-5-8	Ng					Franklin, Paul-Howard- Clarence [Sons]	Hebron					
Franklin, Chester Arthur	Jul 9, 1956	Greeneville, Tn	Tn	May 23, 1913	43	Ng	Franklin, Charlie		Shaffer, Dora		Franklin, C.R.R.- Eddie	West View					
Franklin, Ellie B.	Feb 10, 1970	Columbia, Sc	Tn			W					Franklin, Fred [Sc]	Hopewell					
Franklin, Eldora Schaffer	Mar 12, 1957	Knox Co	Mo	Jul 6, 1866		Franklin, Charles [D]					Franklin, C.R.	Piedmont					
Franklin, Elura	Feb 25, 1968	Jeff Co	Tn	Jan 20, 1890	78	Div	Davis, John W.		Hicks, Orpha		Franklin, Ruth	West View					
Franklin, Floyd Eugene	Nov 9, 1933	Jeff City	Tn	Feb 7, ---		Ng	Jarnigan, Martha	Tn	Jarnigan, Martha	Tn	Franklin, Mrs. George	Grants Chapel					
Franklin, George M.	Jan 20, 1935	Dandridge	Tn	May 2, 1870	64	Ng	Franklin, William	Tn	Cline, Mary	Tn	Granklin, Mrs. George	Grants Chapel					
Franklin, Gladyp Ruth	Oct 18, 1973	Cocke Co	Tn	Sep 25, 1912	61	W	Shemot, James H.		Mc Melhan, Birdie		Franklin, Ray-LR - Frank, Eddie - Veal, Kay	West View					
Franklin, Ida Jane	Nov 28, 1959	Jeff Co	Tn	Oct 31, 1871	87	S	Franklin, Thomas P.		Corbett, Sarah Emily		Franklin, Lucy	Hebron					
Franklin, J. Gray	Jul 24, 1963	Milligan Clinic	Tn	Oct 6, 1892	70	Ng	Franklin, William		Whitlock, Francis		Leonard, Une [Daug]	Piedmont					
Franklin, James Andrew	Nov 2, 1951	Jeff Co	Tn	May 25, 1898	63	Div	Franklin, Sam		Miller, Sarah		Denton, Mae	Shady Grove					
Franklin, James Henry	Apr 26, 1982	Knox Co	Tn	Apr 11, 1881	80	W	Franklin, John		Brannom, Margaret		Ruth	Lebanon - Hamblen Co					
Franklin, Jennie	Jun 24, 1950	Jeff Co	Tn	Nov 3, 1890	69	W	Blackburn, William A.		Hall, Mrs. Georgia B.		Cotin, Ray- Turner, Earl	Hebron					
Franklin, Joel Benjamin	May 2, 1958	Jeff Co	Tn		58	S	Corbett, Martha		Corbett, Martha		Colln, Ray- Turner, Earl	Mt. Pleasant					
Franklin, Kenneth Virgil	Aug 30, 1951	Jeff Co	Jeff Co	Oct 19, 1911	39	Ng	Davis, Elma		Davis, Elma		Franklin, Ruth - C.A.	Grants Chapel					
Franklin, Lillie E.	Jan 18, 1956	Knox Co	Tn	Aug -	87	S	Franklin, Benjamin		Mc Marren, -		Franklin, John F- Cal & Howard	Hebron					
Franklin, Lucy Elgin	Jul 28, 1982	Jeff Co	Tn	Sep 28, 1890	72	S	Franklin, Thomas P.		Corbett, Sarah Emily		Franklin, Patrick	Hebron					
Franklin, Mack Calvin	Feb 6, 1982	Jeff Co	Tn	Sep 18, 1880	81	Ng	Franklin, George		Bell, Satie		Franklin, J.B.& Fred G.[Sc] & Hal D. [Tnee]	Hebron					
Franklin, Martha B.	Apr 29, 1957	[Res New Market]	Tn		66	Franklin, James	Jarnigan, Joe		Lacey, Eliza		Jarnigan, Bess - Jim- Frank-Hubert - Woods, Glover	Greenbrier - Hamblen Co					
Franklin, Mrs. Ben	Feb 17, 1929		Tn			W						Hebron					
Franklin, Nelie Ruth	Feb 21, 1979	Knoxville, Tn	Tn	Nov 13, ---	99-3-8	S			Culbert, Mrs. Margaret Cordelia		Culbert, Mrs. Clarence- Carpenter, Margaret	Hebron					
Franklin, Ollie H.	Aug 2, 1943	Jeff Co	Jeff Co	Nov 30, 1944	69	Ng	Franklin, Patrick	Tn	Corbett, Emily		Franklin, Jennie - Hale, Georgia	Hebron					
Franklin, Ora Georgette	Dec 10, 1944	Jeff Co	Tn	Nov 30, 1944	10d	Ng	Franklin, George William	Tn	Blackbon, Harriet	Hamblin Co	Franklin, Mrs. George	Grants Chapel					
Franklin, Pauline [Polly]	Jan 15, 1966	Kox Co	Tn	Sep 12, 1903	62	Franklin, T.P.	Cate, W.J.	Tn	Harrigain, Rachiel		Cole, Mrs. Julia [Daug]	Memorial Gardens					

NAME	DDATE	DLOCAT	BLOCAT	BDATE	AGE	SPOUSE	FATHER	FBELOCAT	MOTHER	MFELOCAT	BY	BURIAL	VET	SON	DAUG	BROTHER	SISTER
Franklin, Robert H.	Oct 15, 1995	Jeff City	Mc Minn Co, Tn	Aug 12, 1922	73		Franklin, Mack		Webb, Annis		Cline, Lucille [Sister]	Oak Ridge Memorial	42-45				
Franklin, Ruby Jean	Oct 30, 1995	Jeff Co		Dec 1, 1934	60	West, Clarence Edgar			Groves, Regina [Daug]			J.M.G.			Franklin, Janice Elaine [G] Gilbert, Jessica - Groves, Jaymee	F.D. [Buddy]-William- J.C.	
Franklin, Sallie Ann	Apr 13, 1949	Tn		May 12, 1859	89	W	Bell, Calvin H.	Tn	Biddix, Eliza	Tn	Franklin, Mark C. Franklin, Charlie Gray, Ruby	Mt. Horeb					
Franklin, Suda Sarah	Jul 13, 1951	Monroe/		Aug 9, 1881	69	Ng	Gareh, Elias		Hale, Jane			Mill Springs					
Franklin, Terrance Lee	Jan 20, 1995	Germany		Dec 17, 1964	30	Franklin, Susan L.	Franklin, Joseph H. Fr.		Dietz, Nancy		Franklin, Joseph H Jr.	Reid Lawn - Radcliffe, Nc					
Franklin, Thomas Patrick	Sep 20, 1994	Jeff City	Jeff Co	May 24, 1934	60	Suntter, Buddie Ruth	Franklin, Thomas S.		Cole, Pauline		Wife			Jim		Mc Leod, Carolyn - Franklin, Nancy - Cole, Julia [D]	
Franklin, Thomas S.	Jul 19, 1975	Jeff City	Tn	Sep 14, 1884	90	Cole, Polly [D]	Franklin, Thomas Patrick		Cole, Mrs. Julia			Jefferson Memorial					
Franklin, William Charles	Jan 30, 1959	Jeff Co	Tn	Jul 30, 1874	81	W	Franklin, James		Sutherland, Dorthula		Franklin, Charles W.	Mt. Springs					
Frazer, Infant	Nov 5, 1933	Jeff City, Tn	Tn	Nov 4, 1933	1d		Frazer, Ernest	Tn	Edmonds, Dorcus	Tn		Piney					
Frazier, Charles Ernest	Apr 1, 1983	Knoxville, Tn	Tn	Mar 3, 1925	70	W	Frazier, Charles W.		James, Lillie E.		Frazier, Charlie [Son]	Piney					
Frazier, Charles W.	Jun 18, 2963	Jeff Co	Tn	Apr 13, 1879	84	W	Frazier, John		Clark, Sarah		Frazier, Kenneth-Willia-Ernest J.C.	Piney					
Frazier, Clarence H.	Apr 19, 1966	Strawberry Plains	Tn	Nov 2, 1910	55	Beard, Flora	Frazier, Fredrick E.		Reed, Sally B.		Frazier, Flora	Holston Memorial - Kno Co					
Frazier, Donald Edward	Aug 28, 1987	Houston, Tx	Tn	Jun 18, 1947	40	Ng	Frazier, James F.	Tn	Bailey, Mildred	Tn	Frazier, James F.	Pleasant Grove		Ralph	Solomon, Bonnie - Covert, Sandy - Finley, Becky		
Frazier, James Fredric	Dec 7, 1997	New Market, Tn	New Market, Tn	May 7, 1922	75	W	Frazier, Fred		Reed, Sallie		Frazier, Ralph [Son]	Pleasant Grove	42-43		Solomon, Bonnie - Covert, Sandy - Finley, Becky	Frazier, Annabelle	
Frazier, James Willis	May 13, 1973	Jeff City	Tn	Nov 19, 1908	64	W	Frazier, Charles W.		James, Lillie		Frazier, Ralph & Sons	Memorial					
Frazier, Jessie	Oct 5, 2000	Jeff City	Tn	Sep 13, 1907	93	W	Hart, O.M.		Carmichael, Orpha J.		Frazier, Roy K.	J.M.G.					
Frazier, Kenneth B.	Feb 4, 1917	Dandridge, Tn	Tn	Jul 6, 1917	73	S	Frazier, Charles W.		James, Lillie E.		Frazier, E. Bruce [Nephew]	Piney	unk				
Frazier, Lillie Estelle	Feb 14, 1952	Jeff Co	Tn	Nov 3, 1879	72	W	James, C.W.		Bais, Estelle		Frazier, C.W.	Piney					
Frazier, Lucille	Jul 21, 1992	S.M.M.C.	Jeff Co	Dec 27, -92	77	S	Frazier, Fred E.		Reed, Sallie		Frazier, Annabelle [Sister]	Pleasant Grove					
Frazier, Mary Milford	Feb 5, 1994	Knoxville, Tn	Jeff Co	Nov 24, 1920	73	Frazier, James F.	Bailey, Claude		Lyle, Beatrice		Husband	Pleasant Grove			Solomon, Bonnie & Lloyd - Covert, Sandy & Bill - Finley, Becky & Ron	[Br-Law] Frazier, Annabelle	
Frazier, Rachael Dorcus	Oct 5, 1942	Jeff Co	Tn		80	Frazier, Ernest	Edwards, George	Tn	Griffin, Tilda	Tn	Frazier, Er???	Piney			Ralph & Miltram		
Frazier, Sallie B.	Nov 28, 1984	Jeff Co	Tn	Feb 14, 1894	90	Frazier, Fred E. [D]	Reed, James J.		Cannon, Corolline		Cannon, Velma - Jim	Piney		Solomon, Ralph Collins, Ralph Jeremy Grant			
Frees, Arthur W.	Dec 25, 1985	J.M.H.	Tn	Dec 26, 1908	76	Div	Shaffer, Fannie		Shaffer, Fannie		Frees, Mrs. Maude- Oliver, Ollie	Hopewell					
Frees, Clifford	Jan 2, 1971	Jeff Co	Tn	Nov 1, 1893	77	Ng	Frees, John		Unk		Frees, Nicholes	Mt. View	WW 1				
Frees, Debra Darlene	Apr 28, 1953	Jeff Co	Tn	Mar 25, 1953			Frees, Nicholes		Glass, Emma Lee		Frees, Nicholes	Oakland					
Frees, Harold Dean	Oct 2, 1980	Knoxville, Tn	Tn				Frees, Harry Dean		Grinser, Peggy		Frees, Harry Dean	Jefferson Memorial					
Frees, Infant Male	Feb 14, 1954		Tn				Frees, Nicholes	Knox Co.	Glass, Emma Lee	Jeff Co	Frees, Nicholes	Oakland					
Frees, Lennis Lyle	Nov 20, 1995	Jeff Co	Jeff Co	Oct 30, 1929	66		Frees, Clifford		Edmonds, Maude Ray		Collins, Dorothy [Sister]	Mt. View		[Nephews] Collins, Ralph Timothy			
Frees, Maude Raye	Apr 18, 1996	Morristown, Tn	Jeff City	Nov 18, 1909	88		Edmonds, Henry		Brown, Susan		Collins, Dorothy [Daug]	Mt. View					
Frees, Fannie	Jan 9, 1953	Knox Co	Tn	Aug 21, 1888	64	W	Edmonds, Nancy		Unk		Frees, Husband	French Broad					
Freels, Jerrilyn Engert	Feb 27, 2000	Jeff City	Tn	Aug 16, 1935	64	Freels, Edward			Armstead, Mattie Lee			West View					
Freeman, Agnes Adair	Nov 12, 1964	Alabama	Alabama	Aug 2, 1912	52	Freeman, B. Worth	Armstead, B.C.		Greeman, B. Worth		Greeman, B.R.	Sheffield, Alabama				Walker, Ellie Mae [Mich.]	
Freeman, Dessie	Jan 14, 1927	J.M.H.	Va		21	Freeman, E.R.	Baltes, James		Freeman, E.R.		Freeman, E.R.	Sunrise					
Freeman, John Mack	Dec 11, 1994	Va		Feb 2, 1947	37	Bolling, Barbara	Freeman, Chester C. Sr.		Popp, Mary		Freeman, Barbara Bolling	Everlasting Life - J.M.G. Veteran				Cannon, Violet - Mc Spadden, Lorene - Hutsell, Gladys	

NAME	DDATE	DLOCAT	BLOCAT	BDATE	AGE	SPOUSE	FATHER	FELOCAT	MOTHER	MFELOCAT	BY	BURIAL	VET	SON	DAUG	BROTHER	SISTER
French, Ada Harriet	Dec 11, 1975	J.M.H.	Tn	Apr 17, 1910	65	French, Troy	Swaggerty, Thomas A.		Petty, Rebecca		French, Troy	Pleasant Grove					
French, C.B.	Dec 21, 1995	Piedmont	Tn	May 31, 1877	98	Ng	French, Moise	Tn	Nelson, Margaret	Tn	French, Mrs. C.B.	Piedmont					
French, Clyde Sam	Apr 16, 1976	Jeff Co	Tn	Dec 23, 1902	73	French, Lillie	French, Bleicher L.		Whitlock, Eva		French, Mrs. Lillie	Jefferson Memorial					
French, Florence	Mar 5, 1982	Morristown, Tn	Tn	Oct 6, 1891	79	French, James A. [D]	Jones, Press Henry		Skeen, Susan		French, Glen Eugene - Kenneth	Piedmont					
French, Infant	Jul 13, 1946	Jeff Co	Jeff Co	July 12, 1946		Ng	Haworth, --	Tn	Haworth, --		French, Sherman	New Market					
French, James Albert	Apr 17, 1952	Jeff Co	Tn	Dec 1, 1874	77	French, Randle			Hodge, Sara		French, Kenneth & Gene	Piedmont					
French, Jessie [F]	Mar 7, 1970	Jeff City		Jan 7, 1903	67	French, Clyde	French, R.M.		Whitlock, Minnie		French, Clyde	Jefferson Memorial Gardens					
French, John Clement	Jul 22, 1939	Nashville, Tn			41						Caldwell, Mrs. Mary F.	Piedmont					
French, Lillie Mae	May 2, 1968	Jeff Cith	Jeff City	Mar 19, 1911	87	Mills, William			Ellison, Julia Ellen		Cass, Ruth [Daug]	Hills Union - Dandridge, Tn			Bakeman, Rhea	Mills, Annie - Mills, Amos	
French, Lottie	Aug 19, 1952	Jeff Co	Tn	Jun 12, 1895	57	S	French, J.P.		Scarlett, Sarah		French, Curtis [Son]	Dumplin					
French, Sara	Feb 17, 1996	Maryville, Tn	Jeff Co	Feb 14, 1911	87		Manley, George D.		Witz, Anna		French, Curtis [Son]	J.M.G.		William T.	Finchum, Phyllis	Clyde, Hugh	
French, Troy Milton	Feb 18, 1978	Morristown, Tn	Tn	Nov 4, 1906	69		French, Buford		Dalton, Carrie		French, Troy A.	Piney					
French, Velma H.	Jul 22, 1935	Jeff Co	Tn	Mar 28, 1903	32	French, W.A.			Payne, Parthenia	Tn	French, W.A.	Thorne Grove					
French, William Taft	Jan 10, 1986	Thorne Grove, Tn	Tn	Mar 26, 1909	76	Manley, Sara	Brogdon, Joe		French, William Austin		French, Mrs. Sara	Jefferson Memorial					
Freshour, Matthew D.	Jan 16, 1998	Albany, Ga	Tn	Jan 8, 1976	22		Freshour, David Eugene		Haworth, Nykia		Teague, Nyokia [Mother] - Teague, Thomas [Step-Father] - Freshour, David [Father] Freshour, J.V. & Bertha [G-Parents]	West View				Freshour, Chris - [Step] Teague, David	Freshour, Rachel
Fritts, Billy Joe	Jun 20, 1960	Jeff Co	Tn	Jun 20, 1960			Fritts, Warren		Shelton, Sallie Blaine		Fritts, Tom	West View					
Fritts, Ellas	Feb 3, 1972	Jeff Co	Tn	May 17, 1894	77	Gitins, Tom	S	Yates, George M.		Hensley, Florence		Fritts, Tom	West View					
Fritts, Infant	Jul 18, 1965	Jeff Co	Tn	Jul 18, 1965			Fritts, Warren		Shelton, Sallie Blaine		Fritts, Warren	West View					
Fritts, Thomas James	May 26, 1973	Jeff Co	Tn	Apr 11, 1896	77	W	Fritts, David		Church, Maggie		Swann, Mrs. John	West View					
Frye, Carl Leavaughn	Dec 18, 1997	White Pine, Tn	Wrashburn, Tn	Dec 19, 1930	66	Mc.Michael, Donna Jean	Frye, M.B.		Beets, Rhoda L.		Wills - Hairston, F.H. [Daug]	Perry Mt. Park	51-52	Ernest & Tammy	Johnston, Medina Ann	Bruce	
Frye, Mollie Josie	Jan 5, 1946	Jeff Co	Tn	Sep 28, 1881	64	Frye, M.B.	Mc.Spaddon, William	Tn	Fox, Ellen	Tn	Frye, M.J.	Shady Grove					
Fulford, Mary Agnes	Sep 26, 1985	J.M.H.	Pa	Mar 6, 1894	91	S	Fulford, Henry B.		Shaw, Fannie		Hallen, Leslie G.	Hillcrest - Clearfield, Pa					
Fulton, George	Feb 2, 1943	Straw Plains	Sevier Co	Apr 5, 1879	63	Ng	Mc.Claine, Frank	Tn	Fulton, Ellen		Fulton, Gertrude	Gillettes					
Fulton, Ruth [Boots] [Black]	May 6, 1986	U.T.H.	New York	Oct 4, 1919	66	Die	Donaldson, Charlie		Rogers, Margie		Washington, Joyce	West View					
Furgonson, Dr. M.W.	Jun 18, 1956	Piedmont	New York	Jul 1, 1856	79		Furgonson, A.J.	New York	Curry, Mehaliis		Kelly, T.B.						
Gagliano, Jessica Ann	Jun 25, 1985	Jeff City	Tn	Jul 1, 1983	1		Gagliano, Roger	Tn	Wohlfarth, Ann	Tn	Gagliano, Roger	Holy Sepulcher - Cudahy, Wis.					
Galbraith, Frank W.	Jun 3, 1928		Tn	Dec 1, 1852	72	Ng	Galbraith, F.W. Sr.		Cobb, Louisa		Galbraith, Mrs. F.W.	West View					
Galbraith, Frank Wanton [Doc]	Jul 23, 1965	Jeff Co	Tn	Dec 7, --	19-9-8	Ng	Honegan, Mammie				Galbraith, Mrs. Lula Mae	West View	WW 1				
Galbraith, John Carl	Dec 24, 1982	Jeff Co	Tn	May 7, --	19-9-17	Ng	Galbraith, John		Watkins, Sallie L.		Galbraith, Mrs. Carl	West View					
Galbraith, Sallie Watkins	Sep 18, 1932	Jeff City	Tn	May 31, 1856	76	W	Watkins, Albert G.	Tn	Brittin, Louisa	Ky	Galbraith, Carl	Galbraith, Carl					
Galbraith, Odessa Trent	May 24, 1947	Jonesville, Va	Hancock Co, Tn	May 13, 1921	26	W	Trent, Claude	Tn	Smith, Lussanna	Tn	Galbraith, T.W. [Jonesville, Va]	Mulberry Gap - Hancock Co					
Gallihan, Abigall Steadlova	Apr 2, 1992	Jeff City	Coffeton Co, Sc	Mar 3, 1910	82	W	Provenzux, Irving		Jones, Louisa		Galloway, John B. [Son]	Dandridge Memorial					
Galloway, Moses Leon	Mar 22, 1983	V.A. - Perry Pt, Md	Miss.	Jul 28, 1896	86						Galloway, Charles M. [Columbus, Ohio]	West View	WW 1				
Galvan, Bonfachio Torres	May 19, 1971	Jeff Co	Mexico	May 14, 1971	37	Maxenina	Torres, Urban		Torres, Jeana	Tn	Galvan, Jose [Baltimore, Md]	Mt. Carmel - Baltimore, Md					
Galvan, Joana [Mex]	May 19, 1971	Jeff Co	Mexico	Jun 24, 1906	64	W	Torres, Urban		Zdraga, Balentina		Galvan, Jose [Baltimore, Md]	Mt. Carmel - Baltimore, Md					

NAME	DATE	DLOCAT	BLOCAT	BDATE	AGE	SPOUSE	FATHER	FRLOCAT	MOTHER	MRFRLOCAT	BY	BURIAL	VET	SON	DAUG	BROTHER	SISTER
Gann, Alfred Tracy	Jan 24, 2000	Jeff City		Mar 7, 1912	87	W	Gann, S.R.		Rhoda		Lynn, Thelma [Daug]	J.M.G.		Gene & Ruby Bettis	[In-Law] Bettis, Patty [Ve]		
Gann, Benjamin Frank	Nov 1 1967	Jeff City	Tn		56-72	Parker, Evelyn	Gann, S.R.				Gann, Lucy - V.A.	Mt. View	unk.				
Gann, Carroll Amos	May 18, 1999	Knoxville, Tn	Dandridge, Tn	Aug 22, 1944	54	Messengill, Annie	Gann, Vollie		Miller, Pauline		Wife	Mt. View		Terry-Johnny Carroll-George	Stanley, Kathy - Marah, Carolyn - Gann, Tammy Sue	Bob-Otis	Feegin-John - Green, Nancy - Gregg, Martha - Boots, Betty - Hall, Frances
Gann, Ethel	Feb 4, 1978	Jeff City	Tn	Mar 31, 1982	75	Walker, David	Denton, Ellen			Gann, Bill-Frank - Purkey, Mrs. Elizabeth - Myrtle		Jefferson Memorial					
Gann, Ethel Smelcer	Apr 28, 1994	Greene Co., Tn		Mar 13, 1911	83	Gann, John Preston [D]	Smelcer, E.S.		Cobble, Nellie		Cox, Lois Stelaire & Robert [Daug]	Mt. View		[G] Stelaire, John Michael	[G] Stelaire, Sandy		
Gann, James Howard	Sep 13, 1949	Jeff Co	Tn	Jun 20, 1920	29	Ng	Gann, Sam		Christopher, Belle		Gann, Mrs. Virginia Co	Millican Cove - Sevier Co	unk				
Gann, Jimmy Amos	Apr 23, 1982	J.M.H.		Apr 23, 1982		Ng	Gann, Carroll		Messengill, Annie M.		Gann, Carroll	Mt. View					
Gann, John	Jul 28, 1978	Jeff City	Tn	Spe 13, 1926	51	Ng	Gann, John H.		Walker, Ethel		Jefferson Memorial		WW 2				
Gann, John H.	Feb 12, 1966	Jeff Co	Tn	Feb 7, 1898	68	Ng	Gann, Anderson		Miller, Sarah		Gann, Mrs. John [Geneva Boatman ?] - Gann, Jim-Billy- Gann, John Elizabeth	Jefferson Memorial					
Gann, John Preston	Sep 13, 1988	Jeff Co	Tn	Oct 13, 1906	81	Smelcer, Ethel	Gann, Samuel		Miller, Rhoda		Gann, Ethel - Stelaire, Lois	Jefferson Memorial					
Gann, Johnny Lee	Nov 29, 1992	Knoxville, Tn	Tn	Nov 2, 1950	42		Gann, John J.		Boatman, Geneva Brinkley		Mother	J.M.G.	69-70				Cannon, Mrs. Danny
Gann, Judd Kay	May 31, 1957	Decatur, Ga	Jeff City		3-10-20		Gann, Vollie		Miller, --		Gann, Vollie	Mt. View					
Gann, Loy Stanley	Oct 25, 1964	Jeff Co	Tn	Feb 3, 1919	45	Phillips, Ruth	Gann, John	Tn	Bird, Martha		Gann, Mrs. Ruth P	Buffalo Grove					
Gann, Paula Darlene	Dec 19, 1968	Knoc Co	Tn	May 1, 1968	20		Gann, Billy		Pruitt, Margaret		Gann, Margaret P.	Jefferson Memorial					
Gann, Pauline	Jul 24, 1979	Knoxville, Tn	Tn	May 30, 1917	62	Gann, Vollie L.	Miller, Amos		Love, Bertie		Gann, Vollie L.	Mt. View					
Gann, Randolf Anthony	Jul 31, 1961	Jeff Co	Tn	Mar 5, 1958	3		Gann, Carl		Shrader, Betty		Gann, Carl & Betty	Jefferson Memorial					
Gann, Una Mae	Jan 5, 1998	Jeff City	Hamblen Co., Tn	Jan 2, 1914	84	Gann, Alfred T.- Bettis, Walter [D]	Carmichael, Jim N.		Miller, Missouri T.		Gann, Thelma Lynn [Daug]	J.M.G.		Bettis, James E. [D] Walter E. [Gene] [G] Bettis, Barry- James D. Jr.	[In-Law] Bettis, Betty Ruby [G] Lamplin, Terri		
Gann, Victoria Rhoda	Jul 27, 1953	Tn	Tn	Nov 22, 1874	78	W	Gann, John		Byrd, Martha		Children	Wesleye Chapel					
Gann, Vollie Lee	Apr 23, 1985	Dandridge, Tn	Tn	Jan 24, 1914	71	W	Gann, John		Holt, Clyda		Gann, Ottis	Mt. View					
Gannon, Imogene Ellison	Jan 17, 1992	J.M.H.	Cocke Co., Tn	Jan 2, 1922	70	Gannon, Lenoy	Ellison, Paul A.		Hubbard		Hubbard	J.M.G.					
Garber, John	Aug 29, 1965	Jeff Co	Tn	Jan 13, 1881	84	Kate	Garber, John		Pointer, Mattie		Kate	Lebanon - Mt. Horeb					
Garber, John M.	Aug 20, 1928		Va		74-7-4	W	Garber, Martin	Va	Wine, E.	Va	Garber, J.R.	Forrest Hill					
Garber, Katherine	Mar 24, 1968	Jeff Co	Tn	May 13, 1886	81	Garber, John [D]	Lyle, John		Newman, Margaret		Miller, Mrs. Lizzie	Lebanon					
Gardner, Vernon Ray	Jul 4, 1967	Jeff Co	Tn	May 12, 1919	48	Ng	Gardner, Joseph Porter		Bell, Jennie		Gardner, Mrs. Willie Newman	Strawberry Plains					
Garland, Frank	Jan 14, 1983	V.A. - Mt. Home	Blount Co, Tn	Jan 8, 1922	61	Mc Neil, Margaret Ruth	Garland, Fonzo A.		Dunlap, Susie		Garland, Mrs. Ruth	Mc Daniel - Grainger Co	WW 2				
Garland, Dale	Sep 4, 1951	Oak Ridge, Tn	Anderson Co, Tn	Sep 1, 1951	3d		Garland, Benson		Lowe, Boodie		Garland, Benson	West View					
Garrett, Eula	Mar 30, 1957	Jeff Co [Pea Ark.]	Arkansas	Jan 18, 1887	80	Garrett, Dr. E.P.	Mayfield, W.E.	Arkansas	Cass, Mary Catherine		Bohner, Mrs. C.J.	Batesville, Arkansas					
Garrett, Eulice Paul	May 29, 2000	Knoxville, Tn	Tn	Jan 26, 1924	76	Roberts, Kathleen	Garrett, British Briscoe		Caldwell, Edith M.		Wife	J.M.G.					
Garrett, Florence B.	Aug 7, 1992	Jeff City	Rockingham Co, Nc	Oct 7, 1992	68	Garrett, Lloyd	Unk		Bladon, Annie		Husband	Buffalo Grove					
Garrett, Hazel Nell	Jul 6, 1986	J.M.H.	Tn	May 30, 1914	72	Garrett, Paul R.	Hill, Walter		Bowen, Nell		Garrett, Paul R.	Buffalo Grove					
Garrett, James Robert	Feb 3, 1999	Jeff City	Jeff Co	Aug 3, 1920	78	Walker, Maxine	Garrett, B.B.		Wife		Wife	J.M.G.			Houpt, Patsy - Swann, Linda	Eugene	Garrett, Pauline
Garrett, John Watson Jr.	May 28, 1997	Strawberry Plains	Little Rock, Ar	Mar 9, 1943	54		Garrett, J.W. Sr.		Bickel, Sherry [Daug]		Cremated					Paul	

NAME	DDATE	DLOCAT	BLOCAT	BDATE	AGE	SPOUSE	FATHER	FBLOCAT	MOTHER	MFBLOCAT	BY	BURIAL	VET	SON	DAUG	BROTHER	SISTER
Garrett, Lloyd Marshall	Feb 9, 1995	Jeff Co.	Jeff Co	Jul 4, 1919	75		Garrett, Edwin		Johnson, Love		Bradley, Brenda & Gary [Daug]	Buffalo Grove	41-45			Fred	Brewer, Sue
Garrett, Lora Love	Jan 22, 1948	Jeff Co	Jeff Co	Apr 6, 1874	73-# 16	W	Unk			Tn	Brewer, Mrs. Freeman	Buffalo Grove					
Garrett, Paul R.	Jan 2, 1997	Knoxville, Tn	Jeff City	Mar 13, 1911	86		Garrett, William Mays		Wyatt, Malvina Jane		Horner, Claude [Cousin]	Buffalo Grove					Wallace
Garrett, Rilla Faye	Jan 23, 1996	Jeff City	Alexandria, Va.	Jan 17, 1945	51		Garrett, John		Paul, Lou		Cremated	Cremated			Bickell, Sherry	Paul Ervin-Melvin	
Garrett, Sgt. Marshall Alan	May 18, 1978	Camp Le Juine, Nc	Tn	Feb 4, 1955		S	Bradley, Ervin A.		Belton, Florence		Husband	Buffalo Grove	U.S.A.F	Michael			
Garrett, William Harrison	May 10, 1983	Tn	Tn		74	S	Garrett, Elias		Hale, Mary Jane		Franklin, Charles - Hudson, K.P.	Rocky Valley					
Garvey, James Thomas Jr.	Jun 30, 1998	Knoxville, Tn	Billings, Montana	Feb 15, 1924	74	Garvey, Jean	Garvey, James T. Sr.	Tn	Johnson, Annie L.		Willie	Shiloh		James Thomas 3 Rd	Brabson, Mary		Francis, Dorothy
Gass, Benice	Sep 27, 1992	Jeff City	Murfreesboro, Tn	Feb 26, 1992	61	W	Gass, James		Carroll, Lydia Mae		Husband	J.M.G.					
Gass, Bryan Keith	Oct 25, 1983	Tn	Tn	Oct 25, 1983		Ng	Gass, Eddie		Messengill, Zelton		Gass, Eddie	Memorial Gardens					
Gass, Callie	Jul 10, 1980	Jeff Co.	Tn	Jan 9, 1894	86	W	Snow, George		Pendergrass, Mary		Gass, E.T. - Bob, Mrs. J.T. - Charles-James-Bob	West View					
Gass, Charles C.	Feb 22, 1928	Tn	Tn		58-0-8	W	Gass, Fred	Tn	Hoyle, Sallie	Tn	Gass, E.L.	Mt. Horeb					
Gass, Ernest L.	Feb 1, 1949	Jeff Co	Tn	Feb 26, 1882	56-11-5	Ng	Gass, Charles C.	Tn	Gass, Nellie	Tn	Gass, Mrs. Collie S???	West View					
Gass, Frank L.	Jan 13, 1996	Jeff Co	Tn	Oct 3, 1903	92	W	Gass, Charlie Kaywood		Bettis, Nelly			Mt. View					
Gass, Frank Leon	Sep 23, 1943	Dandridge	Tn	Apr 1, 1872	71	Ng	Gass, James		Fain, Retta	Tn	Dandridge	Dandridge	WW 2				
Gass, Frank Leon	Nov 14, 1917	Jeff City	Tn	Jan 14, 1917	0	Ng	Gass, Wade		Messengill, Minnie		Gass, Mrs. & Children	West View					
Gass, Helen Elbie	Nov 12, 1992	Knoxville, Tn	Tn	Jul 17, 1925	67	Gass, Paul Snow	Winter, Charles		Wright, Helen Young Gass [Ala.]		Husband	West View	WW 2			Wright, Jack Richard- Finley, Margaret	
Gass, Howard Edwin	Mar 12, 1989	Jeff City	Jeff Co	Sep 27, 1924	64	Marks, Mary Margaret	Messengill, Will		Messengill, Minnie		Husband	Wesleys Chapel	WW 2	Daniel & Barbara			
Gass, Ida	Aug 31, 1933	New Market	Tn	Dec 25, 1872	60	W	Gass, Porter	Tn	Bettis, Lina	Tn	New Market	New Market					
Gass, Infant	Aug 15, 1927	Tn	Tn		0		Gass, Frank	Tn	Collier, Dona	Tn	Gass, Charles	Lebanon					
Gass, Jane	Dec 1, 1957	Jeff City	Morristown, Tn	Jan 7, 1924	73	Gass, John R.	Brock, John Lee		Ault, Gwendolyn		Husband	West View					
Gass, John Raymond	Dec 28, 1999	Jeff City	Jeff City	Jun 24, 1920	79	W	Gass, Samuel Porter		Mc Ghee, Nora		Meeks, Green & Harold [Daug]	Cremated		Meeks, Green G. & Harold Jr.- Smith, Linda G. - Watrington, Susan G. & Charles	Harvey, Susan B. & Charles		Burton, Helen - Smith, Wilma & Charles K. [In-Law] Gass, Charlotte
Gass, Mae	Nov 18, 1996	Jeff City	Tn	Nov 18, 1896	68	Gass, Scott	Carr, Robert		Yoakley, Mary E.		Patterson, Eugene - Gass, Scott & Children	Deep Springs					
Gass, Mary E.	Feb 28, 1995	Jeff Co	Jeff City	May 15, 1929	65	W	Burchfield, C.O.		Stayton, Mattie S.		Mc Carter, Jack [Exe.]	West View					
Gass, Mayma Katherine	Feb 18, 1959	Jeff Co	Tn	Jun 20, 1887	71	W	Messengill, Will	Tn	Gibbons, Jane		Gass, Phillip-George-Howard-Frank - Smith, Mrs. Harvey- Dowery, Nathan	West View					Spock, Virginia - Emerson, Faye
Gass, Mrs. Charlie	Jan 7, 1927	Jeff City	Tn		62-8-18	Gass, Charlie	Bettis, Anderson	Tn	Phillips, Martha	Tn	Gass, Charles	Lebanon					
Gass, Nora Irene	Dec 10, 1960		Tn		60	Gass, Samuel P.	Mc Ghee, Leonard				Gass, Howard	West View					
Gass, Patricia Ann	Mar 28, 1982	Hamilton Co	Tn	Nov 21, 1961		Ng	Gass, Howard		Marks, Mary Margaret		Gass, Mrs. Howard Children	Wesleys Chapel					
Gass, Samuel Porter	Nov 12, 1958	Jeff City	Tn	Sep 14, 1897	61	Ng	Gass, William		Bettis, Lutisia		Gass, Mrs. Nora & Children	West View					

NAME	DDATE	DLOCAT	BLOCAT	BDATE	AGE	SPOUSE	FATHER	FELOCAT	MOTHER	MFBLOCAT	BY	BURIAL	VET	SON	DAUG	BROTHER	SISTER
Gass, Scott Beecher	Sep 11, 1957	Jeff Co	Tn	Jan—	78	W	Gass, William		Betts, Sarah		Patterson, Mrs. Elizabeth - Smith, Mrs. James	Deep Springs					
Gass, Thelia Irene	Dec 17, 1982	Tn	Tn	Jul 7, 1900	82	W	Kariga, Ace		Baer, Lucy Jane		Gass, Edward - Linebarger, Sarah - Smith, Margaret Lucille - Free, Emma Lee	Jarnigan					
Gass, Wade L.	Sep 27, 1953	Jeff Co	Tn	Aug 25, 1887	66	Ng	Gass, William		Betts, Sarah L.		Gass, Mrs. W.L. Stephens, Charles [Lawyer]	Wesleys Chapel					
Gass, William Henry	Jan 4, 1975	Knoxville, Tn	Tn	Mar 9, 1907	47	S	Johnson, Helen		Sherlott, Bessie		Gass, Mrs. Helen	West View					
Gass, Donna	Nov 3, 1956	Jeff City	Va	May 9, 1907			Gass, Frank L.		Ramsey, Cora		Gass, Frank	Mt. View					
Gaston, George W.	Jun 23, 1951	Jeff Co	Ga	May 6, 1886	85	W	Gaston, Daniel		Lewis, Sarah		Harvie, Mrs. J.D.	West View					
Gates, Ola Mae	Feb 10, 1982	J.M.H.	Tn	May 27, 1919	62	Div			Swafford, Ada		Forgety, Bobby J.	Goochester, Alabama					
Gaut, Jessie M.	Oct 9, 1980	Jeff City	Tn	Jul 4, 1919	61	Gaut, William R.			Brooks, Cleveland		Gaut, William R.	Jefferson Memorial					
Gaut, Mrs.	Mar 14, 1935										Gaut, Joe E. - Rudder, Mrs. Joe	Hillcrest					
Gaut, William Alfred	Mar 28, 1983	Germany	Michigan	Jul 23, 1947	35	Doris	Gaut, William R.		Wolfenbarger, Jessie	Husband	Beal, Doris	Hillcrest	army				
Gauthier, Bonnie Sue	Aug 13, 1999	Jeff City	Mooresburg, Tn	Jun 5, 1918	81	W	Carpenter, Felix H.		Parker, Susie		Price, Ruby [Niece]	Carpenter - Mooresburg, Tn					Felix Reece-Calvin Wayne-Alan L.	Carpenter, Madge
Gentry, Aurelia Rae	Apr 26, 1986	Hamblen Co	Tn	Jul 19, 1881	86	W	Rice, John				Gentry, Earl	Lebanon					
Gentry, Eliga W.	Mar 1, 1986	Hamblen Co	Va	Jan 23, 1884	82	Ng					Helia, Mrs. Marvin - Gentry, Earl - Harris, J.H. 7 Pearl - Templin, Charles [Md] - Elmer- Charles [Md] - Ethel- Vance	Lebanon - Greenbrier					
Gerber, Beatrice Pearl	Oct 4, 1994	Jeff City	W. Orange, NJ	Oct 13, 1920	73	Garber, Louie G.			Essig, Henrietta		Craig, Henrietta	Husband		Gerard [NJ]- Richard [Nev.]	Hossler, Mary Ann [Ala.]	Nelson [NM]	Starr, Elise [Cal]- Sterner, Elizabeth [Cal]- Baron, Margie- Bodkine, Loretta [NE]
Gerber, Nelson August	Jan 5, 2000		Illinois	Jun 2, 1919	80	Horton, Vivian	Garber, Frederick A.		Brooks, Florence Mabel	Wife		Brookdale - Elyria, Ohio	U.S.A.F.				
Garlich, Joseph Frank	Nov 6, 1974	Morristown, Tn	Illinois	Jan 11, 1924	42	W	Garlich, Peter		Bowman, Christina		Garlich, Mrs. C.E. Illinois	Greenwood - Galena, Illinois					
Gibbon, Ozelle Elaine	Feb 28, 1966	Jeff Co	Tn	Jan 11, 1924	42	S	Gibbons, Otis H.		Lane, Okha		Gibbons, Mrs. Otha - Orr, H.M.	Mt. Horeb					
Gibbons, Elsie Ilene	May 11, 1971	Hamblen Co	Tn	Mar 6, 1926	45	S	Gibbons, Ott		Love, Okha		Gibbons, Mrs. Otha - Love & Children	Mt. Horeb					
Gibbons, Ernest H.	Feb 28, 1985	Jeff Co	Tn	May 18, 1888	76	W	Gibbons, John A.		Mc Glamory, Adaline		Hill, Mrs. Rudolph	Community Chapel					
Gibbons, Mattie	1936					Ng											
Gibbons, Ola Homan [M]	Sep 24, 1957	Jeff Co	Tn	Aug 12, 1893	64	Ng	Gibbons, Harry H.		Kimbrough, Vina		Gibbons, Mrs. Otha - Cox-Gerald-Ozelle Rudd, Charualde- [Tenn.]	Mt. Horeb					
Gibbons, Otha Stella	May 22, 1972	Hamblen Co	Tn	Nov 4, 1903	68	W	Love, Marshall		Collier, Callie		Gibbons, Mrs. Otha - Rudd, Charualde [Tenn.]	Mt. Horeb					
Gibson, Hebert Lee	Dec 30, 1976	Jeff City	Va	Jan 26, 1932	44	Griffin, Juno	Gibson, Walter		Compton, Enid		Gibson, Mrs. H.L.	Jefferson Memorial					
Gibson, Howard D.	Jul 28, 1953	Jeff Co									Jeff Co. Sheriff	Picns Farm	WW 1 & 2				
Gibson, John William	Jul 14, 1986	J.M.H.	Ky	Jun 24, 1912	74	Ingram, Emma M.	Feinstan, Annie		Smith, Jack - Gibson, Tom		Jefferson Memorial					
Gibson, Martha Ellen	May 27, 1965	Jeff Co	Tn	Nov 7, 1892	72	Ng	Smith, J.M.		Jordan, Josie		Smith, Jack - Gibson, Tom	Beaver Creek					
Gibson, Patricia A.	Dec 6, 1982	Hamblen Co	Alabama	Apr 1, 1943	39	Div	Perkins, James E.		Fogle, Sarah L.		Perkins, James E.	Cremated					
Gibson, Thomas	Feb 14, 1970	Jeff Co	Tn	Dec 24, 1887	82	W			Fain, Jack - Smith, Tom		Fain, Jack & Alfred E.	Beaver Creek					
Gilbert, Charlie E.	Jun 16, 1979	Morristown, Tn	Tn	Jun 7, 1901	78	W	Gilbert, Floyd		Jones, Nannie		Harris, Mrs Christine [Whitesburg, In.]	West View					
Gilbert, Charlie E.	Mar 29, 1943	Jeff Co	Va	Mar 17, 1876	67	W	Gilbert, Ben		Brennam, Melinda	Va	Gilbert, John [Son]	Lebanon Baptist					
Gilbert, Claude	Apr 26, 1988	Hillmen	Tn	Jun 10, 1916	71	S	Gilbert, Floyd		Jones, Nannie		Harris, Christine	Buffalo Grove					

NAME	DDATE	DLOCAT	BLOCAT	BDATE	AGE	SPOUSE	FATHER	FBLOCAT	MOTHER	MFBLOCAT	BY	BURIAL	VET	SON	DAUG	BROTHER	SISTER
Gilbert, David Gale	Nov 2, 1970	Jeff City	Florida	Jan 8, 1908	19-4-12	S	Gilbert, Dale T.		Haigh, Mrs. Isabel		Haigh, John - Gilbert, Charlie	Gulf Port - Florida					
Gilbert, Dora Ann	Jul 7, 1974	Morristown, Tn	Tn		66	S	Baker, Jim		Gaddis, Elizabeth		Hargrus, John - Gilbert, Charlie	New Market					
Gilbert, Floyd	Feb 10, 1955	Jeff Co		Jan 29, 1914	55	Ng	Gilbert, Charlie		James, Elizabeth		Gilbert, Charlie-Roy-Claude-Albert [Johnabula, Ohio]	Buffalo Grove					
Gilbert, Hugh J. Sr.	Jan 11, 1969	Knox Co	Tn			Ng	Gilbert, Charlie		James, Elizabeth		Gilbert, Mrs. Hugh / Gilbert, Hugh - Edwards, Hattie -	Lebanon					
Gilbert, John E.	Apr 25, 1965	Jeff Co		Apr 10, 1901	64	S	Gilbert, Charlie		James, Elizabeth		Gilbert, Mrs. Bill - Richardson, Mrs. William	Lebanon					
Gilbert, Louise	Nov 29, 1941	Jeff City	Jeff Co		24-7-27	Gilbert Charlie Jr.			Hubbard, Bessie	Tn	Hubbard, Bessie						
Gilbert, Mary E.	Mar 19, 1943	Jeff Co	Tn	Apr 18, ----	26-11-0	S	Gilbert, Charles	Va	Jones, Elizabeth	Tn	Adams, Mrs. Frank	Lebanon					
Gilbert, Nannie	Feb 4, 1958	Hamblen Co	Tn	Nov 27, 1880	77	W	Jones, Calloway				Gilbert, Charlie-Albert [Steel - Roy (Mich.)- Claude	Buffalo Grove					
Gilbert, Nellie	Mar 28, 1935		Tn	Jun 22, 1919	16		Gilbert, Hugh		Newman, Cillie	Tn	Gilbert, Hugh	Lebanon - Hamblen Co					
Gilbert, Rebecca Elizabeth	Oct 5, 1942	Jeff Co	Va	Nov 8, 1876	65	Ng	James, Will	Va	Clark, Lina	Va	Gilbert, Charlie	Lebanon					
Gilbert, Roy Lee	Jul 5, 1984	Hamblen Co, Tn	Hawkins Co, Tn	Nov 6, 1909	80	Morton, Ida	Jones, Floyd		Jones, Nannie		Hanks, Mrs. Lucille	Jefferson Memorial					
Gilbert, Sam John	Jan 28, 1990	F.S.H.	F.S.H.		60	W	Gilbert, David Eli		Howard, Maggie		Milline, Hilda	Park Lawn - Commeree, Calif.					
Gilbert, Tincy Emmaline	May 30, 1981	Nc	Nc	Mar 11, 1900	81	Gilbert, Roy Lee	Elrod, Thomas		Jones, Mary N. [Lucille]		Hanks, Mrs. Gene [Lucille]	Jefferson Memorial					
Gilchrist, Nellie Gray	Dec 11, 1996	Newport, Tn	Jeff City	May 10, 1890	106		Dirt. Thomas, C.		Messengill, Mary Elizabeth		Jordan, Ethel E. [Daug] - Keester, Nadine	West View					
Gillett, David	Nov 28, 1980	Jeff City	Tn	Mar 5, 1899	81	Ng	Unk		Billiet, Mrs. Helen		Gillett, Mrs. Helen / Harris	Gillett, Strawberry Plains					
Gillette, Ida	Nov 21, 1988	Knoxville, Tn	Tn	Mar 3, 1894	94	W	Thomas, Eddm		Rice, Carrie		Smith, Agnes	Gillette- Straw Plains, Tn					
Gilliam, James D.	Apr 15, 1989	Jeff City	Wise, Va	Jun 6, 1914	78	Dotson, Belvia	Gilliam, Jerome F.		Beverly, Melissa	Wilse	Gilliam Family - Wilse, Tn			Ronald		
Gilliam, Ralph Hugh	Feb 24, 1994	Johnson City, Tn	Jeff Co	Jun 8, 1922	71	Gilliam, Maggie H.	Gilliam, Joe		Newman, Iva		Wille - Horner, Hannah [Mother-in-Law]	Ebenezer	42-46	Rick		Eugene-J.W.	Franklin, Geraldine - Bradley, Thelma - Wood, Edna - White, Beulah [D]
Gillispie, Kitty	Sept [17], 1931	Johnson City, Tn															
Gilliman, Raymound Newton	Aug 15, 1947	Jeff Co [Res - Conn.]	S. Dakota	Sep 6, 1892	54-11-9	W	Gilliam, George L.	Conn.	Gaines, Emma Oline	Illinois	Gilliam, Mrs. Gladys [New Britain, Conn.]	New Britain, Conn.					
Glass, Della Kate	Aug 28, 1959	Va	Va	Sep 16, 1892	67	W	Owens, W.A.		Taylor, Michelia		Glass, Tipton-Harold-Blanche	West View					
Glass, Eugene	Oct 8, 1933	Johnson City-Vet H	Tn			S					Glass, Mrs. Stella	Shiloh					
Glass, Harold William	Jul 25, 1986	Nashville, Tn	Tn	Dec 1, 1947	38	S	Glass, Harold William Sr.		Vineyard, Martha		Glass, Mrs. John R. & Martha	Shiloh					
Glass, Harold William Sr.	Nov 27, 1983	J.M.H.		Dec 20, 1920	62	W	Glass, John A.		Owens, Della		Glass, Martha V.	Jefferson Memorial	WW 2				
Glass, J.L.B.	Jan 7, 1926	Rutledge, Tn [Va] [D-Granger Co]			68-6-11	W	Glass, Jerome	Va	Roanis, Nancy	Va	Glass, W.J. & J.A.	Shiloh					
Glass, Tipton O.	Feb 3, 1996	Granger Co	Granger Co	Jun 19, 1917	80		Glass, John A.		Owens, Delia		Moore, Tom	West View			[Niece] Snell, Gayle - Sheen, Rebecca		Johnson, Blanche - [b-Law] Glass, Martha
Gleeson, Joseph Francis	Oct 3, 1941	York, Pa	York, Pa	Jan 1, 1889	66-2-2	Ng					Mams, Mrs. Edd [York, Pa] [Daug]	York, Pa					
Glenn, Jim C.	Jul 9, 1945	Jeff City	Jeff Co		76	S	Glenn, John	Sc	Beck, ---	Pa	Glenn, Sam	West View					
Glenn, Mary	Dec 13, 1928				83	W	Hodge, Jim	Nc	Hodge, Mary	Tn	Mc Knight, Grizzie	West View					
Gleopia, Mary E.	Jul 25, 1932	Granger Co		Apr 16, 1918	14	S	Gillespie, J.F.	Tn	Glenn, S.A.	Tn	Gillespie, S.A. / Glenn, J.F.	Shiloh					
Glloosip, Claude											Kelly, Mrs. J.F. - Patrick, Mrs.						

NAME	DDATE	DLOCAT	BLOCAT	BDATE	AGE	SPOUSE	FATHER	FERLOCAT	MOTHER	MIPLOCAT	BY	BURIAL	VET	SON	DAUG	BROTHER	SISTER
Glover, Edward Walton	Jul 16, 1911	Jul City, Tn	Bluff City, Tn	Dec 2, 1912	68	Dyke, Jean	Watson, Lilly		Doyle, Mrs. Jean (Glover		U.T. Medical - Memphis, Tn						
Gmeimeubar, Annie T.	Oct 25, 1970				74		Tripp, Jarvey		Gmelmeiser, C.H.		Mimosa - Lawrence Co., Tn						
Gmelmeiser, Clarence H. (Ned)	Apr 30, 1978	Lawrenceburg, Tn	Tn	Feb 11, 1896	82	Ng	Gmeimeiser, John		Tripp, Anna Lou			West View					
Goan, Seth Andrew	Sep 20, 1993	Morristown, Tn	Morristown, Tn	Jul 21, 1915		S	Goan, Randall Lee		Dunn			White Pine					
Gobble, Hubert	Aug 8, 1928	Tn	Tn		26d		Gobble, H.R.	Tn	Robertson, Mary (Niece)	Tn	Gobble, H.R.	Shilo					
Gobble, Mary	Jul 13, 1928						Gobble, Ross		Patterson, Luella		Gobble, H.R.	Shilo					
Gobble, Kenneth Eugene Sr.	May 28, 1997	Talbott, Tn	Louisville, Ky	Oct 4, 1924	72	Tompkins, Rena E.	Gobble, Walter Marvin		Scheringger, Leona		Wife - Dianne K. (Ramsey, In)	Bethlehem - Ramsey, In		Terry			
Gobble, Althea	Oct 13, 1974	Jeff City	Tn	Oct 7, 1882	82	W	Beals, Hyder		Lewis, Mary Jane		Newman, Mrs. Thelma	West View					
Gobble, Bessie	Dec 11, 1988	J.M.H.	Tn	Sep 21, 1893	95	W	Allen, Reece		Cox, Terry		J.M.G.						
Gobble, Eugene Walter (Chicken)	Nov 28, 1990	Jeff City	Jeff City	Aug 22, 1930	60	Div	Couch, Ivie Marie		Casey, Kim [Daug]		West View			unk			
Godwin, Fred Hamilton Jr.	Sep 5, 1991	Morristown, Tn	Knoxville, Tn	Sep 9, 1991	55	Div	Adams, Greta		Lakins, Leigh Anne [Daug]		West View						
Godwin, Iva M.	Nov 9, 1993	Jeff City	Tn	Mar 14, 1898	95	W	Brown, Elizabeth		Spivey, Patricia [Daug]		West View			Roger			
Godwin, Maggie Reese	Mar 28, 1939	Jeff City	Tn	Jan 18, 1855	84	W	Mc Daniel, Lacey	Tn	Copeland, Orbona	Tn	Wkater & Sisters	West View					
Godwin, Nora Bell	Jan 5, 1935	Jeff City	Tn	Aug 30, 1873	61	Godwin, Oscar E.	Betts, J.O.	Tn	Johnson, Martha	Tn	Godwin, Oscar E. - Robert-Bell, Mrs. Glen; Mrs. C.G. [Children]	Jeff City					
Godwin, Ora Lee	Sep 11, 1963	Knox Co	Tn	Jun 25, 1892	71	Ng	Irwin, James		Cato, Sallie		Godwin, R.H. Jr. - Godwin, Robert H. - Katherine	West View					
Godwin, Oscar E.	Oct 18, 1952	Jeff Co	Tn	Nov 19, 1888	80	W	Gjodwin, Jack				West View						
Godwin, Ralph Keith	Mar 20, 1947	Jeff Co	Jeff Co	Nov 19, 1898	48-4-1	Couch, Iva	Godwin, Oscar	Tn	Sawyers, Elizabeth	Tn	Godwin, Iva	West View	unk				
Godwin, Robert Hood Sr.	Oct 8, 1974	E.S. Hospital	Tn	Aug 1, 1894	80	W	Godwin, Oscar	Tn	Betts, Nora	Tn	Godwin, R.H. Jr.	West View					
Godwin, W.H.	Jan 2, 1936	Jeff City	Tn	Aug 3, 1874	61	S	Godwin, Z.T.		Sawyers, Elizabeth		West View						
Godwin, Walter Cleveland	Jun 10, 1990	Jeff Co	Tn	Dec 21, 1984	75	Ng	Godwin, Reece B.		Mc Daniels, Margaret M.		Godwin, Mrs. Walter (Althea R.)	West View	2495				
Godwin, Z.T.	Nov 2, 1933	Knoxville	Tn	Apr 12, 1885	48	Ng	Godwin, Z.T. Sr.	Tn	Adams, Green	Tn	Godwin, Mrs. Z.T.	West View					
Godwin, Myrtle Hamilton	Jan 5, 1975	Knoxville, Tn	Tn	Apr 27, 1888	86	Godwin, Zack T. [D]	Hamilton, Francis		Miller, Lucy		Fitzgerald, Mrs. Betty Ann - Mc Millan, Mrs. LA	West View					
Goehler, Bobby Ray	Jan 13, 1992	U.T.H. Addyston, Ohio	Mar 6, 1936		55	Goehler, Brenda	Goehler, John		Collins, Esther		Wife	J.M.G.	Navy				
Gogan, Richard C.	Dec 20, 1992	Jeff Co/Ft. Hicksville, Ny	New York	Sep 23, 1934	18	S	Gogan, George		Langston, Leila B.		Wife						
Goin, Audra June	Aug 3, 1996	Talbott, Tn	Knoxville, Tn	Jun 1, 1930	66		Burchell, H.M.		Williamson, Hassie		Elwood, Janet [Daug]	East View Memorial - Knox Co			[Step] Shuler, Shannon - [Step] Elwood, Janet	
Goin, Clarence Edward	Apr 9, 1996	Knoxville, Tn	Knoxville, Tn	May 7, 1929	66	Burchell, Audra J.	Goin, Arve				Wife	East View Memorial - Knox Co				Poynter, Lorraine	
Golden, Joyce Edwards	Jul 30, 1971	Michigan	Tn			Ng			Edwards, Roy			Memorial					
Goldsmith, Margaret Lee	Jan 19, 1994	Eastville, Va	Jan 24, 1913		80		Mears, Lambertine		Roberts, Ella		Brittenghain, Jacqueline & Jerry L. [Daug - So]	Edwards, Roy				[G] Peachey, Christine - Hatcher, Amy	
Gonce, Bertha	Sep 8, 1988	J.M.H.	Tn		96	Gonce, Walter			Shuler, Lula		Gonce, Walter	J.M.G.					
Gooch, Ben Lillie	Dec 4, 1970	Jeff Co	Tn			Gooch, Carlos			Wright, Blanche		Gooch, Carlos	Memorial Gardens					
Gooch, Bobby Don	Apr 18, 1981	Akron, Ohio	Tn	Oct 7, 1932	48	Pacheco, Barbara	Goin, Don Carlos		Eally, Bon		Gooch, Mrs. Barbara - Buffalo Grove, Ill.]	Jefferson Memorial					

NAME	DDATE	BLOCAT	BLOCAT	SDATE	AGE	SPOUSE	FATHER	FRLOCAT	MOTHER	MRLOCAT	BY	BURIAL	VET	SON	DAUG	BROTHER	SISTER
Gooch, Don Carlos	May 15, 1995	Jeff Co		Sep 14, 1905	89		Gooch, William A.		Dyer, Fannie		Noe, Mildred [Ex.]	J.M.G.		[G] Gooch, William	[G] Young, Margaret Ann		[In-Law] Barton, Evelyn
Gooch, Lula Kate	Jul 30, 1947	Hamblen Co	Jeff Co	May 26, 1887	60-2-4	W	Cannon, William T.	Hamblen Co	Newman, Margaret	Jeff Co	Cannon, Ben F. - William-Jon-James	Lebanon					
Gooch, James	Dec 12, 1998	Jeff City		May 16, 1930	68	W	Peerman, Garena		Slick, Oweena		Gooch, Daniel [Son]	J.M.G.					
Good, Garena Kate	Dec 12, 1998	Jeff City	Tn	May 16, 1930	68	W	Peerman, Garena		Slick, Oweena		Good, Garena	J.M.G.		Neal-Joey	Walton, Norma - Hensley, Judy		
Good, Joe Neal	Apr 17, 1976	U.T.H.	Tn	Sep 25, 1963	53		Good, Tom		Richards, Hulda		Peerman, Garena - Cole	Jefferson Memorial			Donald		
Good, Phyllis Jean	Mar 3, 1967	Residence	Tn	Dec 23, 1925	3	Johnson, Faye	Good, Joe N.	Tn	Stubblefield, Sarah	Tn	Good, Joe N.	Jefferson Memorial	WW 2				
Gordon, Dale Lee	Aug 11, 1994	J.M.H.	Burnsville, Nc	Apr 20, 1930	98	Johnson, Faye	Gordon, W.J.		Garland, Martha		Gordon, Mrs. Dale L.	Piedmont					
Gortney, Troy Lee	Jan 5, 1999	Jeff City	Nc	Dec 23, 1925	67	W	Gortney, Carlin		Wallace, Katherine		Shepherd Memorial - Baskerville, Nc						
Gosnell, Bessie Lee	Dec 14, 1989	Jeff Co	Union Co, Tn	Feb 24, 1904	85	W	Wyrick, Bessie		Baker, Eliza		Schubert, Ruby J.	Beech Springs - Kodak, Tn					
Gosnell, Sherman A.	Feb 27, 1976	Jeff Co	Tn	Apr 17, 1904	71	Ng	Gosnell, Robert		Gosnell, Bessie		Earnest	New Market					
Graham, J.R.	Dec 24, 1931	Jeff City	Tn	Apr 2, 1856	75							Beech Springs - Sevier Co					
Graham, James Luke	Jul 16, 1983	Hamblen Co	Hamblen Co	Aug 29, 1914	78	Roy, Mayme	Graham, William Patrick		Dickerson, Norma		Wife	J.M.G.		David C. - [Step] Flanery, Wayne	Ann - Conti, Gienna - [Step] Smith Ann [Mich]		Huk, Helen - Travis, Alma - Headrick, Zula - Hopkins, Polly - Trent, Phyllis
Graham, Joe W.	Jan 5, 1980	Jeff City	Tn	Oct 30, 1936	43	Bailey, Shirley	Graham, Pat		Dickerson, Naomi		Hopkins, Polly - Whitehead, Grace	Lebanon	Korea				
Graham, Naomi	Mar 19, 1969	Jeff Co	Tn	Dec 11, 1886	72	Ng	Dickerson, Henry		Robinson, Sarah		Graham, Pat & Children - Polly	Lebanon					
Graham, William Patterson	Feb 4, 1977	Talbot, Tn	Nc	May 30, 1894	82	W	Graham, Joseph		Caudill, Laura		Higgins, Mrs. Polly	Lebanon					
Grant, John W.	July 29, 1954	Jeff Co	Tn	May 2/4, --	81-2-3	Ng	Grant, James		Unk		Grant, Mrs. Estelle L.	Buffalo Grove					
Grant, Virgil Davis	Oct 7, 1987	Va	Va	Feb 28, 1901	86	Grant, Ulysses S.	Doris, Jefferson B.		Fletcher, Nancy E.		Grant, Ulysses S.	Lebanon [Greenbrier] - Hamblen Co	69				
Graves, Eunice	Jul 18, 1979	Knoxville, Tn	Tn	Jul 27, 1900	78	W	Lusk, Joe		Vineyard, Iva-Andy		Vineyard, Iva-Andy	Trenholm - Knox Co					
Gray, Anna	Feb 16, 1932	Grainger Co	Tn	Nov 3, 1801	68	Ng	Mc Nish, R.	Tn	Brown, Nancy	Tn	Gray, C.W.	Shilo					
Gray, Bessie	Mar 21, 1932	Grainger Co	Tn	Feb 15, 1932	23	Ng	Lamy, Thomas	New York	Bruner, Callie	Ky	Blackwell Branch	Blackwell Branch					
Gray, Blanche	Sep 25, 1998	Grainger Co, Tn	Tn	Jan 24, 1910	58	Gray, Buford	Cockrum, Milford		Travis, Willie		Gray, Buford & Daughters	Oakland					
Gray, Carl Bartley	Dec 30, 1974	Jeff Co	Tn	Mar 18, 1906	68	Div	Gray, George W.		Mc Nish, Anna		Gray, Buford - Machburn, Pearl	Oakland					
Gray, Cora	Nov 6, 1970	Jeff Co	Tn	Jun 1, 1886	84	Gray, J.D. Sr.			Brown, Jo Ann		Gray, J.D. Sr.	Sunderland - Hamblen Co					
Gray, Dorothy Rickey	Dec 15, 1992	Jeff City	Jeff Co	Sep 15, 1920	72	W	Dyer, William Ernest		Smith, Bessie		Sunderland - Hamblen Co		69			Jack	Brotherson, Sarah Dean
Gray, Fannie	Mar 18, 1932	Grainger Co	Tn	May 8, 1909	52	W	Gray, George W.	Tn	Mc Carty, Soence	Tn	Gray, Morgan D. [Son]	J.M.G.		[G] Caleb- Boone			
Gray, George Robert Sr.	Oct 27, 1991	Nashville, Tn	Lenoir City, Tn	Aug 11, 1916	56	Cline, Sue	Gray, George W.		Nelson, Helen		Nelson, Helen	West View					
Gray, George William	Aug 25, 1972	Knoxville, Tn	Tn	Aug 11, 1916	56	Nelson, Helen Marie	Gray, James Robert	Tn	Hodges, Emma		Gray, James R. [Son]	Jefferson Memorial					
Gray, George William	Mar 2, 1946	Jeff Co	Grainger Co	Feb 18, 1872	74	Ng	Gray, James		Noe, Elizabeth	Tn	Noe, Lucy - Morgan, Lucy - James, Bessie - Gray, Buford	Shiloh - Grainger Co					
Gray, James Andrew	Dec 5, 1979	Knoxville, Tn	Tn	Jun 20, 1901	78	W	Gray, George		Kinder, Mary		Houk, Elizabeth	West View					
Gray, James Thomas	Aug 25, 1991	Dandridge, Tn	Hamblen Co	Jan 4, 1922	69	Dyer, Dorothy	Gray, John Dudley		Brown, Nancy		Gray, Dorothy D.	J.M.G.	unk				
Gray, John Dudley Sr.	Apr 4, 1971	Hamblen Co	Tn	Nov 2, 1888	82	W	Gray, Fred		Martha		Gray, Donald [Brother]	Sunderland					
Gray, Leah Anne	Apr 18, 1968	Knox Co		Feb 15, 1916	52	S	Shanks, Cora		Shanks, Cora		Shanks, Cora	Calvary					
Gray, Leo Clinton	Jun 18, 1946	Dowagiac, Mich.	Tn	24-3-0		Ng	Gray, Clinton	Mich.	Hodgson, Alice	Mich.	Gray, Doyle [Son] - Gray, Clinton [Father]	Sunderland					
Gray, Nancy Ruth	Jun 7, 1974	Jeff City	Tn	Jan 12, 1910	64	Ng	Hurst, John		Mc Cheney, Julia		Gray, Eugene [Bro] - Gray, Clinton [Father] - Gray, Pete & George	West View					
Gray, Sarah	Jul 29, 1957	Grainger Co	Tn	Sep 30, 1893	73	Ng	Ogle, William		Whaley, Rebecca		Gray, Henry - Gray, Pete & George	West View					
Gray, William	Aug 28, 1906										Gray, Arthur [New Market] Govt.						
Green, Ada	Jun 2, 1954	Dandridge	Va	Nov 2, 1878	56	Ng	Greenwood, William	Va	Greely, Sarah	Va	Green, J.A. & Sons	Chestnut Grove					

NAME	DDATE	DLOCAT	BLOCAT	BDATE	AGE	SPOUSE	FATHER	FELOCAT	MOTHER	MFELOCAT	BY	BURIAL	VET	SON	DAUG	BROTHER	SISTER
Green, Claude H.	Sep 8, 1993	Jeff City	Jeff Co	Dec 11, 1910	82	Carr, Cora	Green, Jesse Albert		Greenwood, Ada E.		Wife	Mt. View		Jerry [Ky]-Ervin - Roger-Allen	Courtney, Irene	Jesse-Ernest	
Green, Infant	Apr [28], 1955								Green, Mrs. Myrtie			Flat Gap					
Green, Jimmie Dean	Mar 28, 1956		Tn	Mar 28, 1956			Green, Kenneth Dean		Groves, Edna Louise		Green, K.D.	Flat Gap					
Green, Sallie R.	Jun 26, 1963		Tn	Aug 30, 1883	79	W	Humbard, Henry				Green, Jack-Loyd-Charldes-Earl-Carl	Friends					
Greene, Arthur Reiben Sr.	Jan 4, 1962	Jeff City	Alabama	Feb 29, 1882	70	Ng	Greene, Jules W.		Bowers, Lisle Mae		Greene, A.R. Jr.-Edd-	Jefferson Memorial					
Greene, Bill Jack	Jan 27, 1966	New Market, Tn		May 26, 1917	68	Davis, Nancy	Greene, Henry S.		Stapleton, Beulah		Greene, Mrs. Nancy Davis	Jefferson Memorial					
Greene, Dorothy Maxine	May 1, 199?	Jeff City	Jeff Co	Feb 14, 1936	63	Greene, Wayne	Patterson, Hull		Patterson, Martha		Greene, John C. [Son]	Jefferson Memorial					
Greene, Mary Nancy	Apr 2, 1995	Jeff City	Jeff City	Sep 25, 1920	74	Greene, Bill J. [D]	Davis, J. Frederick		Ellison, Mary K.		Greene, Daniel & Ann [Son]	J.M.G.		[In-Law] Greene, Cindy-Millicent	Lane, Carol		
Greene, Ocie	Oct 20, 1981	Jeff City	Alabama	Jun 28, 1897	84	W	Winslow, Katherine O.		Greene, John C. [Son]		[In-Law] Greene, Cindy-Millicent	J.M.G.			Lane, Carol	Stanley-Robert-Jack-James [D]	Byrd, Maxine - Johnson, Lula Davis
Greenlee, Amanda Katherine	Dec 9, 1928	Jeff Co	Tn	Jan 26, 1887	84-0-16	W	Hearn, Mary T.	Tn	Stockbury, Mrs. Evelyn M.	Tn		Jefferson Memorial					
Greenlee, David Bernard [Col]	Mar 9, 1947	Jeff Co	Jeff Co	Jan 9, 1897	50	Ng	Greenlee, Esther		Mitchell, Blanch	Tn		Shilo					
Greenlee, Dora Eliza [Col]	Jul 21, 1953	Jeff Co	Tn	Aug 16, 1899	54-11-4	W	Webb, Joseph		Link			Colored					
Greenlee, Horace M.	Jan 20, 1970	Grainger Co	Tn	Nov 6, 1892	77	Potter, Minnie	West, Kelley		Dinwoody, James C.			West View Colored					
Greenlee, Hubert W. [Col]	Feb 11, 1942	Grainger Co	Tn	Mar 30, 1903	38	Washington, Jenetta [Age 25]	Greenlee, David	Nc	Greenlee, Bernard	Tn	Greenlee, Mrs. Minnie-Dana-Harold-Boyd-Don-Burt - Metcalf, Rosemary	Blackwell Branch					
Greer, Gene Eric	Aug 2, 2000	Morristown, Tn	Ky	Sep 24, 1939	60	Div	Greer, E.W.		Greer, Eric [Son]		Greer, Eric [Son]	J.M.G.					
Greer, Minnie Grace	Jan 15, 1939	Dandridge	Tn	Sep 7, 1894	44	Greer, Joe M. Jr.	Hudson, J.M.	Tn	Greer, Joe M.		White Pine	J.M.G.					
Greeson, Caroline Louise	Jan 7, 1962	Dandridge, Texas	Morristown, Tn	Dec 11, 1952	39	Div	Dobson, Paul		Mason, Ethel Lynn	Tn	Lowe, Brenda [Sister]	J.M.G.					
Gregg, Infant Male	Dec 12, 1950	Jeff Co	Tn	Dec 12, 1950		Ng	Gregg, Charles		Woods, Betty Jean		Gregg, C.H.	Mt. Horeb					
Gregory, Glenn Earl	Oct 30, 1976	Jeff City	Tn	Aug 21, 1913	63	Ng	Gregory, Charles		Allen, Susie		Gregory, Mrs. Laura	Lebanon	WW 2				
Gregory, Randall Lee	Jan 4, 1994	Morristown, Tn	Tn	Jul 30, 1961	22	S	Gregory, Samuel		Gregory, Laura		Gregory, Mrs. Laura	Lebanon					
Gregory, Rhona	Nov 28, 1971	Jeff Co	Tn	July 16, 1893	78	Ng	Gregory, Glenn Randall		Gregory, Mrs. Laura - Randall Lee		Lebanon (Greenbrier)	Lebanon (Greenbrier)					
Gregory, Imogene	Jun 25, 2000	Jeff Co	In	Mar 4, 1913	87	W	Otey, Serena	Tn	Otey, Serena		Jernigan	Jernigan					
Gressley, Paul B.	Dec 12, 1993	Jeff City	In	Sep 5, 1903	90	Mc Curtain, Imogene	Greesley, Elijah		Clem, Martha			J.M.G.		Larry	Hoster, Marcia - Cameron, Doris [Ind] - Wesley, Friend [Pal]	Irvin [Iowa]	Ormiston, Iris [Ind.]
Grey, Clem Cecil	Sep 25, 1954	Lebanon, Indiana	Tn	Dec 31, 1904	45	Gray, John	Robinson, Lydia		Gray, Mrs. Willa Mae		West View	West View					
Griffey, Donald Curtis	Apr 15, 1987	Maryville, Tn	St. Paul, Va	Jan 4, 1939	58	Snyder, Lois	Stiffey, Rufus		Smith, Eva		Wife	J.M.G.					
Griffey, James W.	Mar 22, 1959	Knoxville, Tn	Tn	Sep 6, 1881	77	Ng	Ferver, Martha		Ferver, Martha			East View Memorial - Sevier Co	61-63	Donny-Danny	Underwood, Cathy	4	3
Griffey, Thomas Wilson	Aug 23, 1963	Sevier Co	Tn	Feb 13, 1963	78	Griffey, John	Faxer, Martha V.				Griffing, Boyd-Robert-T.R.Mae - Johnson, Lucille - Garrdel, Nina - Ramsey, Martha - Jackson, Edith	Underwood - Sevier Co	Korea				
Griffin, Annie Maude	Nov 28, 1935	Mossy Creek		Oct 26, 1863	72	S	Griffin, Everett D.		Murph, Novella		Wesford, Mass.	Garden Of Gethsemane - J.M.G.					
Griffin, Johnny Ray [Pete]	Nov 19, 1984	Knoxville, Tn	Tn	May 14, 1930	54	Ng	Rapass, J.C.	Va	Griffin, Bonnie H.		Wife	Pleasant Grove					
Groceclooe, Roda	May 14, 1956		Va	Dec 10, 1856	79	W	Grocecloee, W.M.		Groovecloee, W.M.	Va	West View	West View					
Grogam, Henry Franklin Jr.	Jan 8, 1950	Jeff Co	Jeff Co	Jan 9, 1950	71	Grogam, Henry H.	Grogam, Henry Sr.		Grogam, H.P.		Gregram, H.P.	West View					
Gross, Walter Thornton	May 13, 1999	Knoxville, Tn	Jackson, Tn	Jan 17, 1928		Bewley, Margaret	Richardson, Cordie		Richardson, Cordie		Cremated	Cremated	navy	Walter L.	Lambert, Loretta		
Gross, Willie C.	Jan 24, 1996	Jacksboro, Tn / Morristown, Tn	Jacksboro, Tn	Feb 26, 1920	75	Cartley, Hazel	Gross, Stanley		Richardson, Sarah		Wife	J.M.G.					

NAME	DDATE	DLOCAT	BLOCAT	BDATE	AGE	SPOUSE	FATHER	MOTHER	MFBLOCAT	BY	BURIAL	VET	SON	DAUG	BROTHER	SISTER
Grout, Rosa Etta	Apr 23, 1928	Tn	Tn	Mar 21, 1894	69	Grout, Ernest	Glass, C.C.	Buttis, Hettie	Tn	Glass, Ernest	Mt. Horeb					
Grout, Verdie Estella	Sep 1, 1963	Jeff Co	Tn			W	Lynch, Isaac	Haskell, Mary	Tn	Stratton, Bessie	Buffalo Grove					
Groves, Eula V.	Feb 22, 1950	Knox Co	Tn	Jul 25, 1937	12		Groves, Ferd	Nash, Pearly	Tn	Groves, Ferd	Flat Gap					
Guffey, William Hal	Apr 26, 1986	J.M.H.	Tn	Jul 19, 1921	64	Lowe, Currie	Guffey, Hobart	Quinton, Emma		Guffey, Mrs. Carrie L.	Gethsemane - J.M.G.	WW 2				
Guinn, John Robert	Jan 17, 1944	Jeff Co	Tn	Feb 18, 1940	4		Guinn, Jesse	Wisa, Elsie	Tn	Guinn, Jesse	New Market					
Guinn, Richard Allen	Jan 21, 1957	Jeff Co	tn		1m		Guinn, James W.	Brooks, ---		Guinn, J.W.	New Market					
Guinn, Shirley Lee	Jan 5, 1954	Jeff Co	Tn	Jul 31, 1942	11		Guinn, Frank	Lowery, Melba		Guinn, Melba	New Market					
Guilford, Harley	Jan 26, 1998	Jeff Co	Brooklyn, My	Sep 12, 1919	78	Rysek, Victoria	Guilford, Emil	Johnson, Hilma		Wife	43-46		Gregory & Kathy			
Guilford, Victoria	Nov 26, 1998	Louisville, Ky	Lexington, Missouri	Apr 4, 1921	77	W	Rysek, Joseph	Madenika, Frances		Guilford, Gregory L. & Kathy	J.M.G.					
Gunter, Mattie	Dec 14, 1994	Va		Aug 19, 1989	65	W	Tumbilin, Samuel	Shaver, Kuffie	Nc	Hale, J.D.	West View					
Gup, David Lowell Sr.	Jul 14, 1996	Jeff City	Jeff City	Apr 14 1942	56		Gup, Chas Cecil	Hunter, Willa		Gup, David L. Jr. [Son]	Lebanon Presby.	67-90				
Haag, Blanche	Jan 13, 1983	Jeff City	Jeff Co	Oct 25, 1938	66	W	Knight, Hugh	Satterfield, Bonnie		Barnes, Kathy [Daug]	Mt. Pleasant		Mickey Michael David	Will, Shirley Faye	
Haag, Frank	Mar 24, 1980	Jeff City	Tn	Dec 31, 1889	90	W	Haag, Henry	Breeden, Susan		Haag, Emmett [Son]	Community Chapel					
Haag, Jesse	Nov 25, 1972	Jeff Co	Tn	Jul 8, 1918	54	Knight, Rosie Lee	Haag, Frank	Welch, Oma		Haag, Emmett [Son]	Community Chapel					
Haag, Emmett	Aug 31, 1981	J.M.H.	Tn	May 18, 1921	70	Knight, Blanche	Haag, Frank	Welch, Oma		Mt. Pleasant	unk					
Haag, James Paul	Mar 20, 1987	S.M.H.	Tn	Dec 17, 1953	33	Turner, Brenda	Haag, James C.	Davis, Anna Ruth		Haag, Brenda	Mt. Pleasant					
Haggard, Martha Malinda	Aug 13, 1956	Knox Co	Tn	Sep 4, 1881	74		Day, James	Pollard, Rebecca		Haggard, James M.	Pleasant Grove					
Haggard, Robert Monroe	Aug 8, 1960	Plant City, Fla.	Tn	Dec 16, 1906	73	Haggard, Willie M.	Haggard, Alexander A.	Shackeford, Sarah Ann		Morris [Fla] - Harvey Haggard, Forbert F.H. [Fla]	Pleasant Grove					
Haigh, Joseph Paul	Nov 2, 1970	Jeff Co	Illinois	Feb 24, 1951	19	S	Haigh, Joseph Paul	Haigh, Isabel	Ohio	Haigh, Mrs. Isabel	Memorial Gardens					
Haigh, Paul Joseph	Nov 3, 1970	Jeff City	Ohio	Oct 27, 1927	43	S	Haigh, Joseph	Jones, Nina		Haigh, Mrs. Isabel	Jefferson Memorial					
Harris, Debra	Feb 19, 1994	Jeff City		Jun 12, 1932	1	Hale, Isabel	Harris, Alford	Carnon, Bell	Tn	Mt. Horeb					
Hale, Blanche	Jan 31, 1965	Bristol, Tn	Tn	Mar 13, 1875	89	W	Thomas, Jacob	Mc Clellan, Mary		Kingswell, Mary [Wash D.C.] - Hale, W. Powell	West View					
Hale, Edward Kenneth	Jan 8, 1989	J.M.H.	Va	Feb 8, 1914	74	Haworth, Mildred	Hale, John B.	Hodge, Ida Mae		Hale, Mrs. J.F. Jr.	West View					
Hale, Effie Maude	Dec 24, 1953	Jeff Co	Tn	Dec 14, 1881	72	S	Hale, James	Ferguson, Sarah		Hale, Charles & Virgie	Sunderland					
Hale, Mae	Apr 20, 1960	Jeff Co	Tn	Apr 12, 1879	81	Ng	Hodges, George W.	Lowe, Annie		Shrader, Mrs. James H. [Fannie - Daug]	West View					
Hale, Mary De.	Apr 10, 1981	Jeff City	Tn	Aug 20, 1905	75	W	Hale, James E.			Hale, Kenneth	West View					
Hale, Mildred Aline	Feb 8, 1961	Jeff Co	Tn	Jul 5, 1943	17	S	Hale, Kenneth	Haworth, Mildred		Memorial Gardens						
Hale, Infant	July 7, 1933	New Market		Mar 14, 1852	90	Ng	Hale, J.D.	Moore, Mary	Tn	Hale, Mrs. J.F.	New Market					
Hale, J.F.	Jul 24, 1932									Hale, Mrs. J.F.	New Market					
Hale, Joe Allen Sr.	Jun 14, 1965	Goldsboro, Nc	Va	Nov 30, 1909	55	Grubb, Cleta	Hale, Emmett	Moore, Mary	Tn	Hale, Mrs. Joe A. Sr - Joel-Larry-Reba	New Market					
Hale, John Howard	Feb 23, 1996	Jeff City	Tn	Nov 25, 1910	85	Ng	Hodges, John	Hodges, Mary	Tn	Universal Mines ?	Jefferson Memorial					
Hale, Mrs. S.	May 24, 1936				86-9-9		Breeding, Stephen	Breeding, Blanche		Hale, Mrs. W.E.	Jefferson City					
Hale, William Byron	Aug 6, 1975	Jeff Co	Tn	Jun 17, 1900	75	Div	Hale, W. Powell	Thomas, Blanche		Kingswell, Mrs. [Mary] - W.E.	West View					
Hale, William Powell	Dec 21, 1959	Jeff City	Tn	Nov 22, 1873	86	Ng	Hale, Samuel Stony	Breeding, Abbie E.		Russell, Bryon - Mary & W. Powell Jr.	West View					
Hall, Amy Elizabeth	Sep 18, 1988	J.M.H.		May 3, 1967	21	S				Daniels, James D. [Norton, Va] - Hagy F.H. [Norton, Va]						
Hall, Arthur Carnel	Jan 24, 1949			May 27, 1874	74-8-1	Ng	Hall, William Franklin	Taylor, Mary Catherine		Hall, Floyd - Morgan, Mrs. A.C.	Friends Station					
Hall, Caswell G. (Bus)	Apr 20, 1969	Jeff Co	Tn	May 9, 1914	54	Ng	Hall, Joe	Rymer, Rosa		Hall, Mrs. Cas & Lee	New Market					
Hall, Hugh Donald	Dec 2, 1984	Morristown, Tn	Jeff Co					Mikona, Mattie		Hall, Eddie [Son]	Bethern		Eddie-Hugh Donald-Hardy L.-Dale-Teddy [Colored]/ Me. Clsh, William Don [Colored]	Lowery, Letha		
Hall, Irma Katherine	May 5, 2000	Jeff City	Iowa	Feb 27, 1915	85	S	Edstrom, Unk	Hall, Francis		Hall, Eddie [Son]	Cremated					
Hall, Lillie Amanda	Aug 2, 1990	J.M.H.	Manhattan, Montana	Sep 8, 1912	77	W	Hantal, Adolph	Thing, Lillis S.		Dyer, Bob [Son]	Cremated				Albert	Cantwell, Polly

NAME	DDATE	DLOCAT	BLOCAT	BDATE	AGE	SPOUSE	FATHER	FELOCAT	MOTHER	MFELOCAT	BY	BURIAL	VET	SON	DAUG	BROTHER	SISTER
Hall, Lon Samuel	Jul 4, 1974	Jeff Co.	Tn	Aug 25, 1887	86	Midkins, Mary Ann	Hall, John M.		Johnson, Lillie		Hall, Buster & Otto - Hall, Albert	White Pine					
Hall, Minnie	Nov 3, 1959	Jeff City	Tn	Nov 18, 1907	51	Hall, Buster	Mc Swain, Frank		Guinn, Nancy		Hall, Buster & Otto - Hall, Albert	New Market Presby					
Hall, Mary	Nov 6, 1979	Boat Station, Tn	Tn	Apr 17, 1887	82	Hall, Lon	Midkins, Tom		Hancock, Caroline		Mundock, Mrs Cecile - Hall, Albert	Flat Gap		Mc Clain, William Don - Hall, Teddie-Hardy L.-Eddie-Dale			
Hall, Martin Lou	Dec 28, 1993	Morristown, Tn	Greene Co., Tn	May 2, 1916	77	Hall, Hugh Donald	Mc Lain, William H.		Bullington, Mary M.		Hall, Arnold (Son)	Brethern			Lowery, Leatha	Mc Clain, John	
Hall, Persilee A. Churchman	Aug 11, 1947	Knox Co (Ree.-Okla.)	Grainger Co., Tn	Nov 4, 1870	76-7-7	W	Alexander, James J.	Tn	Einert, Mary Elizabeth	Swier Co.	Goclwin, Mrs. W.M. [Okla.] - Churchman, Cleut	West View					
Hallen, Leslie George Jr.	May 27, 1991	Clearfield, Pa	Pa	Mar 3, 1923	68	Simmons, Jane	Hallen, Leslie George Sr.		Fulford, Nan Elleen		Hallen, Jane Simmons	J.M.G.	unk.				
Hallen, Nan Eileen	Jan 7, 1985	J.M.H.	Pa	Jun 21, 1896	88	W	Fulford, Henry B.		Shaw, Fannie		Hallen, Leslie G.	Hillside - Radyn, Pa					
Hallen, Mary [Dot]	Mar 8, 1951	Knox Co (Ree Hallen, Ky)	Tn	Aug 30, 1895	55	Ng	Hodge, Joseph		Hodge, Florence		Bassett, Leona	West View Colored					
Hambrick, George R.	Nov 8 1928	Nc			22-1-9	Ng	Hambrick, G.C.	Nc	Lancaster, Ella	Sr.	Hambrick, G.C.	Bethel - Nc					
Hamilton, Cornelia Elizabeth	Oct 25, 1982	J.M.H.	Nc	Sept 7, 1886	96	Hamilton, D.S. [0]	Hopson, Abraham, L.		Branson, Susan A.		Jennings, Mrs W.W. - Hamilton, Howard-Ralph-Clifford - Blair, Frank - Clairborne, Nick	West View					
Hamilton, Frank	Jan 3, 1908	Jeff Co	Tn	Aug 3, 1880	76	Ng	Hamilton, Peter		Hickman, Patricia		Jennings, Mrs W.W.	Wolfardtown					
Hamilton, George Lewis	Jan 15, 1995	Knoxville, Tn	Tn	May 8, 1906	78	S	Hamilton, Joe		Hennigan, Trula		Hamilton, Graham	Brooklyn Heights - Cleveland, Ohio			Lee, Norma & Gary	Mallett, Sally	
Hamilton, Howard A.	Jan 28, 2000	Jeff City	Tn	Jun 3, 1963	91	Kerr, Mildred	Hamilton, Adam D.		Kerr, Mildred	Jeff Co.	Hamilton, Howard	Mc Campbells Chapel Wills		[Nephew] Hamilton, Doug & Rhett	Clifford-Ralph		
Hamilton, Infant Female	Jun 17, 1946	Jeff Co	Tn		14		Hamilton, Howard				Hamilton, Howard Privy	Mc Campbells Chapel					
Hamilton, James Monroe	Mar 15, 1995	Knoxville, Tn	Jeff Co	Feb 5, 1922	73		Hamilton, Adam		Campbell, Katie		Hamilton, Mary R. [Sister]	Strawberry Plains					
Hamilton, Kate	Mar 19, 1970	Knox Co	Tn	Oct 8, 1891	78	Hamilton, A.D.	Campbell, George		Shell, Alice		Hamilton, Mary Ruth-Jim-Bill-A.D.Jr. [Children] [Sic]	Strawberry Plains					
Hamilton, Mary Katherine	Feb 27, 1959	Knox Co	Tn	Jan 23, 1884	75	W	Wright, Alex		Mxxay, Mollie		Hamilton, Ralph	Mc Campbells Chapel - Jeff Co.					
Hamilton, William Andrew	Sep 1, 1983	Dr. Jorudans Office	Tn	Jul 4, 1920	63	Wadsworth, Hilda	Hamilton, Adam D.		Campbell, Mary Kate		Hamilton, Mrs.- Hilda W.	Strawberry Plains	WW 2				
Hammer, J.C.	Jun 3, 1931	Oak Grove	Tn	Jun 3, 1931	77-11-14	W	Hammer, Samuel	Tn	Range, Elizabeth	Tn	Seaborn Chapel	Seaborn Chapel					
Hammer, Mary Lucy	July 10, 1955	Jeff Co	Tn	Oct 8, 1879	79	W	Chevegan, Will		Byrd, Nancy		Ellison, Mrs.- Jim - Hammer, Cecil - Ball, Mrs.	Lebanon					
Hammond, Elsie	Mar 27, 1982	Hamilton Co	Jeff Co	Jun 16, 1878	83	W	Tipton, William Henry		Messonghi, Rebecca		O' Dell, Mrs. Carr E.	Sunderland					
Hance, Herbert William	Aug 7, 1996	J.M.H.	Tn	Jun 9, 19--	67-1-28	Sellers, Bonnie	Hance, Walter		Sneap, Ida		Hance, Bonnie	J.M.G.	WW 2				
Hance, Inbert Male	Aug 18, 1980	Morristown, Tn	Tn				Hance, Harry Wayne		Hill, Charlotte Jean		Hance, Harry	Jefferson Memorial					
Hance, Millie Griffin	Mar 1, 1942	Dandridge	Tn	Jun 28, 1859	82	W	Phillips, Jerry	Tn	Edmonds, Annie	Tn	Peneau, Zylphia S./Kathrite, Nic] - Griffin, Sam - Hutcheson, Dorothy [Children]	Ellsmore - Nc					
Hancock, C.E.	Oct 22, 1928	Tn	Tn	Jun 9, 1900	54	W	Hancock, John	Tn	Johnson, Martha	Tn	Strawberry Plains	Strawberry Plains					
Hancock, Charles Edgar	Dec 2, 1976	Jeff City	Tn		76	Stiles, Frances	Hancock, Frank		Smith, Margaret		Jarnigan, Mrs. Harold - Hancock, Mack	Pollards - Sevier Co					
Hancock, Frances Irene	Dec 4, 1976	Knoxville, Tn	Tn	Jun 7, 1906	70	Hancock, Charles Edgar [D]	Stiles, Charles		Bushman, Martha Jane		Jarnigan, Mrs. Harold - Hancock, Mack - Everett	Pollards - Sevier Co					

NAME	DDATE	DLOCAT	BLOCAT	BDATE	AGE	SPOUSE	FATHER	FELOCAT	MOTHER	MFELOCAT	BY	BURIAL	VET	SON	DAUG	BROTHER	SISTER
Hancock, Frank Harrison	Mar 22, 1999	Jeff City	Knoxville, Tn.	Jan 13, 1942	57	Wilson, Betty	Hancock, James Eli		Overton, Opalee		Willis - Eslinger, George & Clara [Father]-Hills Union - Dandridge, In-Law] - Wilson, Ray & Verna [Father-In-Law]	Tn		Wayne-Jon	Yankiewald, Cathy-Thomas, Connie	James-Stephen	
Hancock, John Carroll	Apr 30, 1979	Knoxville, Tn	Jeff Co	Aug 2, 1926	51	Hartley, Maxine	Hancock, John Franklin		Petty, Leona	Jeff Co	Hancock, Mrs. J.C. - V.A.	West View	WW 2: Korea				
Handy, Serah E.	Jan 18, 1941	Jeff Co				Hartley, J.C.	Mc Bribe, Jane				Hanley, Frank [Son]	Economy					
Hankins, Charles Leroy	Jan 10, 1998	Knoxville, Tn	Knox Co	Apr 19, 1931	66	Marshall, Juanita	Hawkins, Robert		Lawson, Stella		Wife	J.M.G.	66-68		Dunlopcoe, Norma - Dunn, Carol - Fleenor, Louise - Pollack, Jennifer	Raymond	Joiner, Oeta
Hannah, Willie Orvilie	Mar 30, 1952	Jeff Co	Tn	Mar 29, 1952			Hannah, Truman		Walker, Willie Mae		Hannah, Truman	Mt. Pleasant					
Hansford, Muriel	Aug 15, 2000	Jeff City	Ky	Apr 15, 1913	87	W	Miller, Matthew		Keith, Ellen		Rimbeck, Ellen [Daug]	Greenwood - Greenwood, Ky					
Harbin, Hubert Elmer	Jan 4, 1980	Hamblen Co	Tn	Sep 7, 1906	73	Green, Dora	Harbin, George		Harbin, Lucy	Granger Co	Harbin, Ida Pearl	Sunderland					
Harbin, Infant	Oct 10, 1965	Jeff Co	Tn	Oct 10, 1965		Dev	Harbin, Helen F.				Harbin	Harbin					
Harbin, Joshua Henry	Sep 22, 1984	Detroit, Mich.		Feb 6, 1941	79		Steele, Liza		Harbin, Ida Pearl		Harbin, Miss Ida	Sunderland					
Harbin, Martha Idora	Sep 25, 1989	Talbott, Tn		Jul 12, 1909	79	W	Green, Isaac		Snider, Anna		Harbin, Ida Pearl [Daug]	Sunderland					
Hardesty, Shelburn William	Oct 18, 1996	Jeff City	Shelbyville, Ky	Jun 13, 1912	84		Hardesty, Thomas				Gilbert, Marshelle [Daug]	Cave Hill - Louisville, Ky					
Hardin, Noah	Jan 25, 1944	Knox Co	Sevier Co	May 24, 1865	58	Ng	Hardin, William	Tn	Underwood, Sarah	Tn	Hardin, Margaret - Hickman, Mrs. W.B. - Hall, Gastonia - Hardin, H.H.	Oak Grove - Sevier Co					
Hardy, Harry L.	Dec 21, 1957	Knoxville, Tn	Ohio	Mar 7, 1892	65	Ng					Hardy, Mrs. Augusta Ann	West View					
Hardy, Joseph D. Jr. (Black)	Oct 1, 1995	Jeff City	Careitts, Wv	Jul 23, 1942	53		Hardy, Joseph D. Sr.		Swain, Geneva		Cole, E.O. [Step-Father]	West View				Cole, Ronnie	Cole, Sharon-Disavie-Oris
Hargis, Zella	Feb 11, 1993	Jeff City	Jeff Co	Apr 11, 1906	84		Talibry, John Calvin		Benatield, Rena		Moyere, Ruth [Sister]	West View				Vernon	
Hargrove, Walter C. (Rev.)	Dec 13, 1946	Jeff Co	Nc	Mar 28, 1874	72-8-15	Ng	Unk		Unk		Hargrove, Lecitia [Wife]	Dandridge					
Hargus, Billy	Jan 19, 1985	E.T. Baptist Hosp.	Nc	May 31, 1938	47	S	Hargus, William L.		Hargus, Miss Mae		Hargus, Miss Mae	Strawberry Plains					
Hargus, Nora	Jan 28, 1984	Knoxville, Tn	No	May 15, 1902	81	W	Unk		Unk		Hargus, Gladys	Strawberry Plains					
Harmon, Albert	Oct 18, 1975	Jeff Co	Mc Cracken Co, Ky	Sep 12, 1915	100	W	Harmon, J.B.		Pierce, Eliza		Harmon, Gladys	West View					
Harmon, Colleen	Apr 24, 1998	Chattanooga, Tn	Lenoir City, Tn	Nov 14, 1921	76	W	Keebler, Charles E.		Ada		Harmon, Tom [Son]	Lenoir City		Harry [Sid - Ralph [Gai- Brad			
Harmon, Minnie Lee	Nov 13, 1989	Jeff Co	Tn		83	Harmon, Albert					Hinton, Mrs. Gladys	Lenoir City - Lenoir City, Tn					
Harmon, Roy Edward	Apr 6, 1989	Knox Co	Tn	Sep 7, 1917	51/5?	Ng	Dixon, Callie				Harmon, Mrs. Colleen	Tn					
Harp, Clinton	Jul 18, 1963	Texas	Tn	Apr 5, 1908	55	S	Harrell, Charlie		Coffey, Thalia		Ellison, Harold	Country Home					
Harrell, Alfred Kenneth	Dec 11, 1996	At Home	Tn	May 1, 1889	90		Harrell, W.P.		Rittar, Katherine		Wife	J.M.G.					
Harrell, Charles Henderson	Feb 11, 1980	J.M.H.	Tn	Sep 14, 1923	62	Harrell, James P.			Brendon, Essie		Harrell, Mrs. C.H.	Jefferson Memorial					
Harrell, Dorothy	Jul 25, 1996	Morristown, Tn	Texas	Nov 10, 1932	67	W	Lloyd, R. Grage		Irene		Acuff, Terry & Gage [Daug]	J.M.G.					
Harrell, Rebehah	Jan 25, 2000								Irene		Harrell - Swan Station, Tn				Harmon, Laura & Ruey		
Harrell, Thalia	May 31, 1985	J.M.H.	Tn	Feb 10, 1896	89	W	Coffey, Alfred		Monk, Cynthia		Harrell, Alfred K.	Jefferson Memorial					
Harrington, Aubrey Elmer	Apr 27, 1985	J.M.H.	Tn	Nov 14, 1898	86	Parker, Thelma	Harrington, W.T.		Harrington, Ollie		Harrington, Mrs. A.E.	West View					
Harrington, Cillie	Sep 22, 1946	Jeff Co	Apr 19, 1876	70		Harrington, W.T.	Browning, G.W.		Whitehead, Vina	Tn	Harrington, W.T.	West View					
Harrington, Thelma B.	Feb 7, 1997	Knoxville, Tn	Cartersport, Ga	Dec 25, 1900	96		Parker, William S.		Brewer, Laura		Clark, Jean & Gary [Daug]	West View		Robert & Allie	Stevens, Lorraine & William	Messengill, Mrs. Paul
Harris, Albert [Col]	Jul 7, 1989	Jeff Co	Tn	Jul 6, 1994	65	Ng	Harris, Boston		Ray, Nettie		Harris, Mabel	West View					
Harris, Beston	Sep 1, 1995	Jeff Co	Tn	Dec 23, 1865	69	Ng	Harris, Glenn		Eckler, Aggie		Harris, Albert	Colored					
Harris, Bob	Sep 1, 1995	Jeff Co															
Harris, Delia [Col]	Dec 1, 1925	Jeff Co	Tn	Feb 24, 1886	164	Ng	Talbott, Jerry		Sharps, Mary		Harris, Robert	Colored					
Harris, Clemmie [Col]	Jun 11, 1947	Jeff Co	Tn		49-5- 17	Ng	Harris, Robert	Tn	Harris, Clemmie	Tn	Harris, Robert	Martha Davis Baptist					

NAME	DDATE	DLOCAT	BLOCAT	BDATE	AGE	SPOUSE	FATHER	FBLOCAT	MOTHER	MFBLOCAT	BY	BURIAL	VET	SON	DAUG	BROTHER	SISTER
Harris, Dicly	Apr 14, 1958	Knox Co	Tn	Jun 24, 1876	81	W	Hayes, James Terrill		Beverly, Sarah		Clark, Mrs. Ness - Hawkey, Mrs. Ben E. [Dgt.] - Ellis, J.W., Harris, Beulah	Jarnigan					
Harris, Frank [Col]	Apr 24, 1927		Tn		25	S		Tn	Mary	Tn	Raper F.H. [Lincoln, Neb.]	Colored					
Harris, Helen Crawford	Apr 20, 1986	Lincoln, Nebraska		Dec 17, 1901	87	Harris, Frank W. [D]					Harris, Corrine-Bob-Byrd, George	West View					
Harris, Infant Female [Col]	Feb 16, 1950	Jeff Co		Feb 16, 1950			Byrd, George		Harris, Corrine	Jeff Co	Harris, Corrine-Bob-Byrd, George	West View Colored					
Harris, Jessie Louise	Jul 12, 1993	Ft. Lauderdale, Fla.		Aug 29, 1920	72	Harris, Melvin		Celts, Virginia M.	Va	Husband	J.M.G.		Pitts, Cecil [Fla]	Jones, Juanita - Redding, Elizabeth	
Harris, Josephine [Col]	Jan 8, 1940	Jeff City	Tn	Feb 20, 1867	72	Harris, Pryor		Shelton, Sallie		Ingram, Anna - Harris, Bob	Colored				Burgin, Florence - Donoho, Ross Lee	
Harris, Mabel Beulah [Black]	Mar 28, 1997	Bristol, Tn	Tn	May 2, 1911	85	W	Donaldson, Samuel		Watkins, George Ann		Taylor, Arthur [Nephew]	West View				Donaldson, Carl B. [Nc]-Eugene [Nc]	
Harris, Mary Ellen [Col]	May 28, 1943	Jeff Co	Tn	Jul 5, 1889	85	W	Watkins, Charles		Jones, Nancy	Tn	Harris, Albert	Colored				[Step] Smith, Lucille	
Harris, Mary Kate	Nov 27, 1956	Inox Co	Tn	Oct 29, 1888	74	Harris, Boston [D]	Tn	Hubbard, Katherine D.		Neff, Mrs. W.B.	West View					
Harris, Porter	Jan 18, 1926		[D. Asheville, Nc]								[On Flywheel]						
Harris, Pryor [Col]	Feb 15, 1929					Ng						Colored					
Harris, Robert [Col]	Feb 22, 1948	Jeff Co	Tn	Mar 18, 1924	23	Ng	Harris, Robert	Tn	Talbot, Clemmie	Tn	Harris, Robert Sr. - Melne E.[Prentances, Va]	Colored	WW 2				
Harris, Robert Henry [Col]	Jan 7, 1959	Jeff Co	Tn	Mar 24, 1892	66	W	Harris, Pryor		Donaldson, Josephine		Fain, Ruth - Price, Reba - Pittard, Pauline - Cole, Myrtel - Harris, Curtis - Rudival, Corine	West View					
Harrison, James	Jun 16, 1973	Jeff Co	Tn	Dec 24, 1884	89	W	Harrison, John		Jordan, Nancy		Fain - Jeff Co						
Harrison, Julia Pollard	Mar 17, 1977	Care Inn	Tn	July 29, 1898	79	W	Wilson, Ella Mae		Hargis, Mrs. Edith - Pollard, P.H.		Piedmont						
Harrold, Elizabeth H.	Jul 4, 1977	Care Inn	Iowa	Jun 23, 1901	76	W	Hotchkwithe, Charles		Marshall, Isabella		Harrold, John C.- [Columbus, Ohio]	Sunset - Columbus, Ohio					
Hart, Joe M.	Jun 22, 1944		Nc	Jul 9, 1851	92	W	Hart, Floyd	Nc	Slaton, Mary Ann	Tn	Thomas, Mrs. J.H.- Hart, Ezil [Fla]	Dandridge					
Hart, Mabel Leona	Aug 22, 1999	Dandridge, In	Indianapolis, In	Jul 9, 1906	91						Coleman, Sherry [K]-[Daug.]- N. Salem, In]- Singleton Mortuary [Indianapolis, In.]	Mt. Pleasant - Green Valley, In					
Hartley, Chple J.	Dec 11, 2000	Knoxville, Tn	Tn	Jun 8, 1928	72	Trent, Dorothy	Hartley, George W.		Green, Elizabeth		Hartley, Elsa [Hd]						
Hartley, Jo Ann	Apr 16, 1977	Jeff Co	Tn	Mar 27, 1977		Hartley, Chple J.					Wife	J.M.G.					
Hartley, Lewis	May 6, 1939	Flat Gap	Tn	Jul 1, 1880	58	W	Gartley, Joe		Michalm, Sarah		Hartley, Joe	Macichiln - Hawkins Co					
Hartness, William Victor	Sep 6, 1990	Cartersville, Ga	Murphy, Nc	Jan 28, 1990	41	W	Moody, John	Tn	Bullinger, Linda		Rankin, Carroll & Wife	Hebron					
Hartness, Dorothy Mia	Dec 8, 1985	J.M.H.	IL.	Jul 13, 1916	69	Div	Harlness, Charles		Gilmore, Mary	Tn	Hartness, Thomas W. [Son]	West View	unk				
Hatcher, Alice George Ann	Jun 15, 1940	Jeff Co	Mar 10, 1880	60	W	Middleswart, J.T.		Ladd, Dorothy Westbrook, Priscilla E.		Clark, William Paul	Everlasting Life - J.M.G.						
Hatcher, Charles C.	Dec 24, 1957	Jeff City	Mo	Jul 18, 1876	81	W	Nicholson, Henry	Tn	Bryan, Nancy	Tn	Wiles, Mrs. E.M. [Knoxville]	Piedmont					
Hatmaker, Beulah Mae	Apr 30, 1960	Tn	Sep 1, 1903	56	Hatmaker, Charles L.	Hatcher, W.G.		Keys, Mary		Hatcher, Harry B.- Bachanc, Stanley	La Code - Mo					
Hatmaker, Charlie Luther	Jun 21, 1982	Jeff Co	Tn	Jul 2, 1900	68	W	Hatmaker, James		Isley, Mary		Nelson, Mrs. Ann - Mc Kee, Zora - Roberson, Tom - Nelson, Ann	Jefferson Memorial					
Hatmaker, Elmer Lester	Sep 23, 1976	Jeff Co	Tn	Nov 9, 1921	54	Finchum, Mary		Prator, John F.		Reed, Buelah		Hatmaker, Elmer & Roy [Sons]	Jefferson Memorial					
Hatmaker, John Dawson	Sep 15, 1991	Campbell Co, Tn	Aug 8, 1928	63	Div	Hatmaker, Charles L. Luther		Prator, Beulah Mae		Hatmaker, Gary & Mark [Sons]	Family Plot - Jeff City, Tn						

NAME	DDATE	DLOCAT	BLOCAT	BDATE	AGE	SPOUSE	FATHER	FBLOCAT	MOTHER	MFBLOCAT	BY	BURIAL	VET	SON	DAUG	BROTHER	SISTER
Hawkins, William Alonzo	Oct 23, 1947	Jeff Co	Tn	Jan 17, 1872	75	W	Messenger, Melissa	Tn	Valentine, Opal [Concord, Tn]			Mt. Zion					
Haun, Bessie Kate	Feb 14, 1955	Knox Co	Greene Co, Tn	Aug 1, 1900	54	Ng					Haun, Sherman	Phillips - Greene Co, Tn					
Haun, Richard E.	May 16, 1998	Jeff City	Anamosa, Iowa	Jan 3, 1941	57	Nelson, Bonnie	Koppenhaver, Ione				Wife - Haun, Doris [Step-Mother]	West View		Richard E. Jr.- Brandon P.	Buchanan, Kristi	[In-Law] Nelson, Clifford, Mary - Wright, Margaret - Miller, Pauline - Bergman, Lois	
Haun, Sherman Earl	Apr 27, 1987	Norcross, Ga	Tn	May 11, 1898	88	W	Haun, Joseph				Pulley, Beulah	Phillips - Greene Co, Tn		Tommy - [G] Clinton- Ryan - Lee, Morgan	Dede, Wanda - [G] Haun, Chris		
Haun, William Ray	Dec 4, 1992	Knoxville, Tn	Morristown, Tn	Jul 31, 1934	58	Coffey, Pearl	Haun, Thomas Lewis		Rhea, Bonnie Gray		Haun, Bobby [Son]	Hamblen Memorial					
Hauser, Bernadine A.	Jan 29, 1994	Morristown, Tn	Hamilton Co, Ohio	Sep 9, 1997	96		Kemp, George		Duecker, Anna		Hauser, Lawrence G. [Son]	Cremated					
Hauser, Marjorie	Jul 19, 1989	S.M.H.	Cleird, Ohio	Jul 19, 1932	57	Hauser, Lawrence G.	Bockelman, Carl		Hammon, Marie		Hauser, Lawrence- L.G. Jr.	Cremated					
Hawley, Earl K. [Jack Combine]	Mar 14, 1982	J.M.H.	Tn	Mar 12, 1904	78	Div	Hawly, James C.		Austin, Sarah L.		Hawly, Robert	Economy					
Hawley, Hazel	Jan 26, 1997	Lumberton, Tx	Jeff City	Aug 6, 1907	89	Div	Kelley, Walter		Martin, Molly		Bradley, Patty & Robert [Daug]	J.M.G.					Walter Jr.
Hawly, Lillian Ethel	Apr 27, 1989	J.M.H.	Jeff Co	Aug 1, 1909	79	Div	Russell, Joseph J.		Stubblefield, Mollie		Hawly, Robert	Coldwell - Hawkins Co, Tn					Jernigan, Bess
Hawly, Robert Howell	Feb 24, 1995	Knoxville, Tn	Jeff City	Aug 29, 1933	61	Cain, Elsie	Hawly, Earl		Russell, Ethel		Wife	J.M.G.		Jason- Tracy	Radcliff, Elaine		
Hawly, William Benton	Mar 14, 1995	J.M.H.	Tn	Jun 21, 1952	82	Ng	Hawly, James		Austin, Sally		Wife	West View				Kenneth- Gordon	
Hawes, Josephine M.	May 18, 1997	Jeff City	Pike Co, Ohio	Aug 22, 1916	80		Frost, Wilber Edwin		Johnson, Eliza Jane		Haldeman, Beverly [Daug - Fredericktown, Ohio] - De Vore F.H. [Sunbury, Ohio]	Cheshire					
Hawkins, Thala	Mar 10, 1958	Hamblen Co	Tn	Feb 21, 1890	68	Hawkins, Robert N.	Hannon, Robert P.		Blais, Sadie		Hicks, Mrs. Paul R.	Sunderland					
Hawkins, William J.	Jan 17, 1965	Jeff Co	Buncombe Co, Nc	May 7/8, 1905 [59-6-9]		Margaret	Hawkins, William A.		Duckett, Ella		Hawkins, Mrs. Margaret - William Jr.-Patsy	Memorial Gardens					
Haun, Bonnie Gay	Apr 29, 1982	Morristown, Tn	Tn	Oct 11, 1905	76	W	Rhea, Charlie		Klis, Martha		Haun, William R.	Catherine-Nanny- Hamblen Co					
Haworth, Clura Watson	Jul 16, 1983	J.M.H.	Tn	Nov 11, 1912	70	S	Haworth, Isaac R.		Thompson, Effie		Hale, Mildred & Kenneth - Miller, Reba	West View	WW 2				
Haworth, Donald L.	Mar 25, 1977	V.A.- M. Home	Tn	Nov 24, 1922	55	Haworth, Ivan	Haworth, Isaac R.		Thompson, Effie		Hale, Mildred - Mrs. Paul-Miller, Kenneth- Miller, Mrs. Paul-Reba- Haworth, Ivan-Claude- Talley, Helen	West View					
Haworth, Edith Inez Walker	Jul 17, 1980	Jeff City	Tn	May 13, 1908	72	Haworth, Ivan	Coe, Joe				Haworth, Ivan-Isaac- R.- Walker, Virgil & Jack - Teague, Nyoka - Sparks, Inez - Mc Daniels, Cna Lee	West View					
Haworth, Ellie Fay	Apr 18, 1982	Jeff Co	Va	Aug 24, 1886	75	Haworth, Isaac R. [D]	Thompson, Robert B.		Reed, Elizabeth		Hale, Mildred & Kenneth- Talley, Mrs.-Ivan	West View					
Haworth, Isaac Richard	Feb 15, 1944	Jeff Co		Jan 25, 1879	65	Ng	Haworth, Isaac Franklin	Tn	Ballinger, Leona	Tn	Sparks, Inez [Daug]	West View					
Haworth, Ivan Richard	Jan 15, 1981	Jeff City	Tn	Jul 7, 1910	70	W	Haworth, Isaac Franklin		Thompson, Ellie Faye		Sparks, Inez [Daug]	West View					
Haworth, James Clarence	Apr 22, 1983	J.M.H.	Tn	Feb 10, 1913	70	Walters, Mossie Lee	Haworth, John F.		Peck, Porter		Haworth, Mossie Lee	Jefferson Memorial					
Haworth, Lura Adaline	Dec 5, 1970	Jeff Co	Va	Aug 19, 1885	85	W	Thompson, Robert B.		Reed, Elizabeth		Hale, Mrs. Kenneth	West View					
Haworth, Maggie E.	Jun 18, 1983	Tn	Tn	Mar 24, 1882	81	Haworth, R. Frank [D]	Pulley, George W.		Green, Mary K.		Haworth, Raymond	West View					
Haworth, Mossie Lee	Feb 6, 2000	Dandridge, Tn	Tn	Aug 14, 1910	89	W	Walters, Oscar N.		Stone, Lillie		Swamy, Jane [Daug]	J.M.G.					

NAME	DDATE	DLOCAT	BLOCAT	BDATE	AGE	SPOUSE	FATHER	FBLOCAT	MOTHER	MFBLOCAT	BY	BURIAL	VET	SON	DAUG	BROTHER	SISTER
Haworth, Olin Sidney [M]	Jun 26, 1957	Jeff Co	Tn	May 12, 1915	42	S	Haworth, Isaac		Thompson, Effie		Hahn, Mrs. Kenneth - Haworth, Mrs. Effie	West View	WW 2				
Haworth, Porter Peck [F]	Apr 22, 1961	Jeff Co	Tn	Nov 18, 1876	84	S	Peck, James M.		Newman, Elizabeth		Haworth, Clarence - Jeff Co	West View					
Haworth, Robert Franklin	Jan 3, 1957	Tn	Tn	Dec 18, 1874	82	M	Haworth, Franklin		Brazelton, --		Haworth, Raymond & Mother	West View					
Haworth, Samuel [Col]	Dec 21, 1960	Jeff City	Tn	Mar 17, 1876	84	W	Unk		Unk		Wilkerson, Flora	West View Colored					
Haworth, Stanley Thompson	Jun 28, 1964	Jeff Co	Tn	Sep 28, 1920	43	S	Haworth, Isaac		Thompson, Effie		Hahn, Mrs. Kenneth - Roger - Miller, Paul	West View					
Haworth, William Reese	Apr 20, 1950	Jeff Co	Tn	Oct 16, 1882	67	Ng	Haworth, L.F.	Tn			Haworth, Mrs. W.R. [Lura T.]	West View					
Hayes, Grace Ethel	Oct 20, 1980	Fort Pierce, Fla	Tn	Sep 24, 1898		Hayes, William C. [D]					Yates F.H. [Fort Pierce, Fla]	Jefferson Memorial					
Hayes, John Edd	Jul 21, 1946	Jeff Co	Tn	Aug 11, ---	66-11-10	W	Newman, Hugh		Smith, Susan	Tn	Williams, Mrs. Edd	Lynchurst - Knoxville					
Hayes, Lois	Dec 11, 1980	Riverside, Ga	Jeff Co	Jul 11, 1918	72	W	Newman, Hugh Campbell		Walkins, Augusta Drucilla		Dickens, Glen [Son]	Mt. Pleasant					
Hayes, William Clarence	May 7, 1954	Jeff Co	Ky	Dec 7, 1885	68	No	Hayes, George F.		Bishop, Mary		Hayes, Mrs. W.C.	Jefferson Memorial					
Haynes, Annie T.	Jun 28, 1964	Jeff City	Bedford Co, Tn	Nov 8, 1899	94		Crowell, Thomas L.		Jennings, Margaret Jane		Haynes, Raymond, A. [Son] - Gowen-Smith Chapel [Shelbyville, Tn]	Unionville					
Haynes, Bobby Don	Jun 29, 1963	Douglas Lake	Tn	Aug 11, 1931	31	S	Haynes, Jennings Don		Shrader, Fannie	Tn	Haynes, Don	Oakland	korea				
Haynes, Charleston Nathaniel	Sep 25, 1990	San Francisco, Ca	Tn	Jan 11, 1945	35	Div	Haynes, John Robert		Spivey, Mary Kate			Jefferson Memorial	vietnam				
Haynes, Ernest Raymond	May 4, 1983	Bedford Co, Tn	Tn	Jul 7, 1902	90	Crowell, Annie T.	Haynes, Thomas		Potts, Minnie		Haynes, Raymond A. [Son]	Unionville - Shelbyville, Tn					
Haynes, Fannie Clarice	Apr 18, 1999	Dandridge, Tn	Jeff Co	Mar 16, 1909	90	Shrader, James H.			Hale, Mary Ann		Haynes, Gladys R. [Daug]	Oakland Methodist					
Haynes, Frances Eva	Aug 16, 1945	Jeff Co	Tn	Feb 16, 1880	65	Div	Williford, Jacob	Tn	Traylor, Mary		Williford, Miss Mary [Daug]	French Broad					
Haynes, Hester Iowa	Aug 25, 1961	Jeff Co	Nc	Sep 8, 1961	83	W	Boling, M.D.I.		Smith, Rhoda J.		Haynes, Don	Oakland					
Haynes, Jackie Doyle [M]	Dec 25, 1973	Community, Calif.	Tn	Nov 8, 1899		S	Haynes, Alfred	Tn	Carson, Anna Belle	Tn	Thomas, Mrs. Hal - V.A.	Mt. Horeb	vietnam				
Haynes, Jennings Don	Nov 23, 1974	New Market, Tn	Tn	Dec 7, 1901	72		Shrader, Fannie		Bolding, Iowa		Haynes, Fannie	Oakland					
Haynes, John Robert Jr.	Dec 27, 1989	F.S.H.	Jeff City	Apr 5, 1943	46	Love, Kitty June	Haynes, John R. Sr.		Spive, Mary Kate		Haynes, Kitty June	J.M.G.		Joseph Wendall			
Haynes, Josie	Sep 21, 1959	Jeff Co	Tn	Mar 5, 1959	96	W	Cox, James		Line, Nancy		Collier, Leiah	Underwood, Sevier Co					
Haynes, Mildred	Aug 22, 1987	Jeff City	Jeff Co	Jun 24, 1916	81		Gann, Marion				Haynes, Donald [Son]	Mt. Horeb					
Haynes, Ora Jane	Apr 27, 1980	[Res St. Petersburg, Fla]	Tn	Dec 4, 1901	78	W	Haynes, John Robert				Johnson, Mrs Ora Lee	New Market		[Step] Haynes, Floyd [Ark.]	Woods, Brenda Kay		
Haynes, Robert Nathaniel	Nov 9, 1982	Jeff Co	Tn	Nov 9, 1982		W	Haynes, John Robert		Tresco, Vivian Elaine		Haynes, Mary Kate	New Market					
Hayworth, Bessie Pearl	Jul 26, 1981	Texas	Tn	Jul 16, 1882	99	Div	Haworth, William Frank		Ballinger, Elizabeth	Tn	Douglas, William H.	West View					
Hayworth, Hugh Grant	Mar 27, 1943	New Market	Tn	Nov 6, 1867	75	W	Haworth, Jonathan		Malcolm, Jane	Tn	Haworth, Swan	New Market Presby					
Hayworth, Jeff	Dec 23, 1940	New Market	Tn		70-5-11	W			Stone, Harriet	Tn	Whitlock, Bess	New Market					
Hayworth, John F.	Feb 9, 1996	Jeff Co	Tn	Nov 9, 1857	75	W	Ballinger, M.	Tn	Foster, Annie	Tn	Hayworth, Ike	West View					
Hayworth, Leanna	Feb 29, 1932																
Hayworth, Mrs.	May [11] 1933																
Hazelwood, Bobby A.	May 4, 1988	Hamblen Co	Tn	Mar 25, 1946	22	S	Hazelwood, Floyd		Walker, Maude		Hazelwood, Floyd	West View					
Hazelwood, Donald Leon	Nov 4, 1982	Greenville, Tn	Tn	Feb 9, 1968	14	S	Hazelwood, Loen		Lamb, Joyce		Hazelwood, S.R.	Jefferson Memorial					
Hazelwood, Irene	Jul 24, 1989	S.M.H.	Jeff Co	May 31, 1916	73	Hazelwood, Sherman R.	Rogers, Robert		Pollard, Genevia		Hazelwood, Sherman	J.M.G.					

NAME	DDATE	DLOCAT	BLOCAT	BDATE	AGE	SPOUSE	FATHER	FBLOCAT	MOTHER	MFBLOCAT	BY	BURIAL	VET	SON	DAUG	BROTHER	SISTER
Hazelwood, La Donna Jean	Feb 4, 1993	Jeff City	Jeff City	Mar 14, 1957	35	Hazelwood, Junior	Shelton, Jack D.		Cox, Shirley Mc Daniel		Mother - Mc Daniels, Charles [Step-Father] - Newman, Becca - Oliman, Edith - Ellison, Bessie [G-Mother]	West View		Collins, Shane	Collins, Beth	Mc Daniels,Michael	
Hazelwood, Lou Gertrude	Feb 17, 1973	Cocke Co	Tn	Feb 28, 1898	74	Ng	Smith, George		Nolan, Margarette		Nolan, Raymond	Jefferson Memorial					
Hazelwood, Peg Pryor	Aug 1, 1998	Jeff City	Jeff Co	Jun 15, 1916	82	Russell, Willie	Smith, Martha		Moore, Barbara [Dang]		Moore, Barbara [Dang]	J.M.G.		[Step] Hurst, Peggy - Rogers, Beatrice	Jack Sherman		
Hazelwood, Rebecca E.	Sep 29, 1928				89-2-21	Hazelwood, R.A.	Sitzer, John	Tn	Morris, Mandy	Tn	Morris, Glenn	Macedonia - Hamblen Co					
Headrick, Linda Gail	Sep 24, 1984	Hamblen Co	Jeff Co	Sep 24, 1984	69	[D]	Headrick, Glenn		Welch, Gladys Alvena		Headrick, Glenn	Macedonia - Hamblen Co					
Heaney, Edna L.	Jan 4, 1974	Maryville, Tn	Mo	May 4, 1884	89	[D]	Carter, Luther		Pollard, Frances		Mallory, Mrs. R.C.	West View					
Heard, Daisy	Jan 4, 1967	Jeff City	Campbell Co, Tn	Jun 17, 1905	91		Chapman, John A.		Skaggs, Nora		Turney, Louise [Cousin]	Cremate - [Ashes] Ft. Sam Houston					
Heatherington, Susie B.	Aug [13], 1973	Knox Co	Tn	Jul 9, 1879	72	Ng	Unk		Heck, Mary Ann		Mallory, F.H.	Mt. Pleasant					
Heck, Marion Walter	Jul 19, 1951	Knox Co	Tn	Jul 8, 1879	58	W	Unk		Churchman, Mary Jane		Heck, Mrs. & Stacy	Piedmont					
Helm, Cleo	Sept 18, 1931	Knoxville	Tn	Sep 14, 1875	58	W	Lett, Dave		Tate, Cleo		Tate, Cleo	Stilo					
Helm, Dorcas	Aug 8, 1927		Tn		20-4-24	S	Tate, Henry B.	Tn	Tate, Cleo	Tn	Tate, Cleo	Stilo					
Helm, Estela	Feb 10, 1925		Tn		25-4-5	Helm, John	Dennis, W.W.	Va	Tate, Tennessee	Tn	Helm, John	Stilo					
Helm, Frances Kathleen	Oct 8, 1965	J.M.H.	Tn	Mar 6, 1918	67	Ng	Mink, Willey S.		Anderson, Celia	Tn	Helm, Dean	West View					
Helm, Hattie Tate	Nov 28, 1959		Jeff Co	Jan 2, 1962	54	Helm, U.V.	Tate, John K.		Churchman, Hulda	Tn	Helm, U.V.	Shiloh					
Helm, John Fritz	Jun 23, 1926		Tn		25-9	W	Helm, Henry B.	Tn	Tate, Cleo	Tn	Tate, J.N.	Shiloh					
Helm, John Fritz	Apr 3, 1931		Tn		19	W	Helm, Henry B.	Tn	Tate, Cleo	Tn	Tate, J.N.	Shiloh					
Helm, Kermit Wane	May 16, 1915	Granger Co	Tn		15	S	Helm, H.B.	Tn	Tate, Cleo	Tn	Helm, Edward [Son]	Stilo					
Helm, Nelson Dean	Sep 16, 1912	Highland, Utah	Tn		73	W	Helm, William		Alexander, Minnie		Helm, Edward / Anderson, T.H.	West View					
Helm, W.S.	Aug 24, 1937		Tn	Apr 29, 1877	60		Helm, U.V.	Switzerland	Baker, Martha		Helm, Paul	Shiloh					
Helm, Amanda	Nov 17, 1969	Jeff Co	Tn		88	Helm, Paul	Taylor, Tivis	Tn	Ng	Tn	Helm, Ruth	Jefferson Memorial					
Helm, John	Sep 23, 1925		Tn	Jun 10, 1904	75-6-6	Mc Daniel, Helen	Helm, Gilbert		Ward, Rhoda		Helm, Paul	Shiloh					
Helm, John G.	Mar 28, 1965	Jeff City	Tn		60	Ng	Ward, John		Howard, Thedis		Helm, Helen	Memorial Gardens					
Helm, Paul	May 1, 1972		Tn	Dec 14, 1895	76	Ng	Ward, John				Helm, Mrs. Maude	Memorial Gardens					
Helm, Rhoda K.	Nov 15, 1934	Granger Co				W	Ward, Glass	Tn	Coleman, Lizzie	Tn	Helm, W.B. - John [Son]	Reeds Chapel					
Helton, Ryan Jay	Sep 12, 2000	Knoxville, Tn	Tn	Sep 12, 2000			Helton, Willard Jay Sr.		Monday, Cara		Father	Wesleys Chapel					
Helton, Roy Edward	Mar 18, 1961	Jeff Co	Tn	Jun 28, 1917	43	Ng	Helton, Sherman		Helton, Mary		Jefferson Memorial	Jefferson Memorial					
Helton, Helen Lucille	Sep 2, 1998	Morristown, Tn	Jeff Co	Nov 23, 1934	63	W	Jordan, Fred	Tn	Adams, Hettie	Tn	Stanley-Leslie-Darrell - Lamb, Jaunita - Jo Ann - Michi, Margie - Canning, Helen	J.M.G.				J.D.-R.B.	Single, Mary Edith
Henderson, G.M.	Oct 11, 1927	Knoxville, Tn	Tn		59-7-17	S	Henderson, James C.	Tn	Thomas, Nancy	Tn	Henderson, Dr. J.D.	Greenwood					
Henderson, Helen Ruth	Feb 20, 1982	Knoxville, Tn	Tn	Nov 9, 1898	83	S	Henderson, Robert A.		Timmons, Helen		Mims, George - Sullivan, Mrs. Jen	West View					
Henderson, Nancy Angeline	Aug 13, 1927				81-9-14	Henderson, J.T.	Thomas, Jeremiah	Tn	Denton, Mary	Tn	Sons	Greenwood					
Henderson, Robert Anderson	Oct 7, 1940	Concord, Tn	Tn	Feb 13, 1860	80	W	Henderson, Benjamin Peck		Hammond/Ives, Margarette	Tn	Henderson, Miss Ruth [Richmond, Va]	West View					
Henderson, Robert Ashly	Mar 26, 1970	Knox Co	Tn			S	Henderson, R.B. Sr.		Mims, -----	Tn	Henderson, Miss Ruth [Richmond, Va]	West View					
Henderson, Susan Denise	Feb 25, 1986	Houston, Tn	Newfoundland, Canada	May 31, 1964	21	S	Henderson, John H. Jr.		Collie, Ruth Irene		Collie, Ruth L. - Henderson, John H. Jr., Beulah	Collie - Jeff Co					
Hendricks, Clarence A.	Dec 17, 1957	Sevierville, Tn	Tn	Nov 28, 1900	65	Ng	Hendricks, Jim		Bogus, Rosie		Hendricks, Joel & Beulah	West View					

NAME	DATE	BLOCAT	BLOCAT	BDATE	AGE	SPOUSE	FATHER	F#LOCAT	MOTHER	M#LOCAT	BY	BURIAL	VET	SON	DAUG	BROTHER	SISTER
Hendricks, Clarence Jr.	Feb 8, 1995	Knoxville, Tn	Knox Co	Apr 8, 1924	70	Ng	Hendricks, Clarence Sr.		Willis, Beulah		Hendricks, Jermaine [Son]	Cremated			Johnson, Carmen - Blair; Renae - Green; Tonya - Hendricks; Monica - Glenn; Christine	4	3
Hendricks, Daniel [Cal]	Jul 20, 1970	Va		Sep 8, 1938		Ng	Hendricks, Clarence		Willis, Beulah		Hendricks, George & Beulah	West View					
Hendrix, Edith	Nov 2, 1998	Jeff City	Claiborne Co, Tn	Jun 29, 1912	86	Ng	Mayes, James Andrew		Moody, Martha Victoria			J.M.G.					
Hendrix, Johnny	May 11, 1974	U.T.H.	Hoboken, Ga.	Jan 15, 1920		Collette, Ruby	Hendrix, Haskel		Altman, Julia		Hendrix, Vance [Son]	West View					
Hendrix, Ray S.	Dec 23, 1966	Jeff Co		Aug 2, 1910	56	Ng	Hendrix, Joel		Brown, Willie		Hendrix, Mrs. Ray-Crawford, Mrs. Vance-Wiseman F.H. (Fayetteville, Tn)	Memorial Gardens					
Hensley, Infant Male	May 6, 1983	Jeff Co		May 6, 1983							Wiseman F.H.						
Henry, Blake Jackson	Jan 21, 1998	Nashville, Tn	Knoxville, Tn	Jan 13, 1998		Ng	Henry, Jack Brockton		Barnett, Kathy Ann		Henry, Brock	J.M.G.					
Henry, Dale Mims	Aug 8, 1952	Jeff Co	Tn	Jun 16, 1893	59	Ng	Henry, Thomas C.B.		Wilmoth, Eliza		Allen, Mrs. Fred	Sunderland					
Henry, Emma Sue	Dec 27, 1959	Knox Co	Tn	Apr 7, 1909	50	Ng	Rimmer, C.B.		Smith, Mattie Emma		Jane-Bobby-Linda	Hillls Union	unk				
Henry, Ema	Dec 24, 1989	J.M.H.	Sevier Co	Mar 25, 1931	58	Henry, Jack	Free, Will		Gledford, Bertha		Henry, Jack	J.M.G.					
Henry, Hal Harrison	Aug 28, 1959	Knox Co	Tn	Sep 18, 1903	55	Ng	Henry, Oliver W.		Layman, Melvin Jane		Henry, Mrs. Linda	Hills Union					
Henry, Nellie H.	Dec 16, 1985	J.M.H.	Tn	Jan 26, 1908	69	Div	Henry, Ralph		Epperson, Sarah		Lay, Mrs. Linda	Jefferson Memorial	WW 2				
Henry, Ida	May 21, 1998	Jeff Co	Tn	Sep 27, 1897	w	Kincaid, Ed	Henry, Jack	Riddle, Mollie	Kincaid, Ida		Henry, Jack	Sunderland					
Henry, Jack Gleason	Aug 16, 1991	F.S.H.	Grainger Co	Oct 28, 1927	63	W	Henry, Dale M.		Kincaid, Louisa		Henry, Edward M. (Rockford)	New Market	unk				
Henry, James B.	Jan 14, 1940	Jeff Co	Tn	Feb 25, 1864	75	Ng	Henry, John		Blackburn, Louisa	Tn	Henry, Brock [Son]	New Market					
Henry, James L.	Jul 28, 1934	Hamblen Co	Tn	Jul 16, 1915	19	S	Henry, W.B.	Tn	Liane, Lucy	Tn	Wright, W.B. (Dandridge)	Swangylvania					
Henry, John Edward	Feb 5, 1986	U.T. Hosp. V.A. - M. Home	W. Va. Yamato, Washington	Jan 12, 1935	51	Johnson, Ovella	Henry, John W.		Smith, Mattie Emma		Wright, W.B. (Randridge)	West View, Tn					
Henry, John Lewis	Aug 28, 1991	Home		Jul 23, 1931	60	Melvin, Grace M.	Henry, Vernon C.		Rock, Bessie E.		Henry, Gregory [Son]	Veterans New Market, Tn	unk				
Henry, John William	Jan 9, 1974		Tn	Mar 18, 1905	68	Ng	Henry, William H.				Henry, Mrs. Mary Lou Yates	West View					
Henry, Nellie H.	Jan 8, 1958	Jeff Co	Tn	Dec 23, 1884	73	S	Henry, W.A.				Bates, Mrs. Charles - Henry, Mrs. Ralph	New Market					
Henry, Ralph Edward	Sep 24, 1949	Jeff Co	Tn	Sep 12, 19427	59-0 12		Henry, W.A.		Ruth, Florence		Henry, Mrs. Ada D.	New Market					
Henry, Robert Hugh	Oct 24, 1980	Nashville, Tn	Tn	Dec 8, 1931	48	Div	Henry, Hal H.		Rimmer, Emma Sue		Moore, Mrs. William (Linda)	Hills Union	korea				
Henry, Robert M. Sr.	Nov 7, 1978	Knoxville, Tn	Tn	Feb 6, 1913	65	Ng	Henry, Vernel		Bates, Mary Jo		Henry, Mrs. Edna Collins	Mc Campbells Chapel					
Henry, William	Nov [18], 1932 June 15-17, 1972										[Tg] Holdren F.H.						
Hensley, ---																	
Hensley, Burton	May 27, 1978	Jeff City	Tn	May 28, 1894	84	Ng	Henry, Laydolle		Corum, Mary M.		Hensley, Casper F.	Little Valley - Grainger Co					
Hensley, Casper Laphayette	Feb 12, 1999	Jeff City	Tn	Sep 20, 1925	73	Ng	Hensley, Burton		Watson, Mamie		Hensley, Casper F.	Little Valley - Grainger Co		Casper [Lenny] David			
Hensley, Ike	Jun 6, 1956	Johnson City	Tn	Mar 27, 1875	81	S	Hensley, Howard		Bayless, Amanda		Wife	J.M.G.					
Hensley, James Garfield	Jul 17, 1985	Knoxville, Tn	Tn	Dec 24, 1894	50	Div	Hensley, Burton		Hensley, Minnie		Hensley, Charles Kenneth	Livston - Washington Co					
Hensley, Mertie Maples	Apr 17, 1989	Blaine, Tn	Grainger Co	Dec 28, 1895	93	W	Watson, Sam		Maples, Darthedy	Tn	Hensley, Casper - Mamie	Little Valley Baptist - Blaine, Tn					
Hensley, Sheryl Janine	Feb 5, 1995	Jeff City	Tn	Feb 3, 1995			Hensley, Garfield		Bates, Barbara		Hensley, Garfield Husband - Hensley, Daniel & Stellia -	Little Valley Baptist - Indian Ridge					
Hensley, Tonia Sue	Sep 5, 1967	Jeff City	Buckley, Wv	Aug 9, 1967	30	Hensley, Todd J.	Hensley, Clarence A.		Goddard, Leola		Hensley, Upyssa & Judy (Parents)- Hensley, Larry-Carl - Yvat, Mrs. Eseth	J.M.G.					
Hensley, William Herbert	Jan 6, 1978	Cara Inn	Va	Jul 3, 1962	75	Div	Hensley, Lloyd		Stamper, Mary			West View				Dohman-Randy-David	

NAME	DDATE	DLOCAT	BLOCAT	BDATE	AGE	SPOUSE	FATHER	FBLOCAT	MOTHER	MFBLOCAT	BY	BURIAL	VET	SON	DAUG	BROTHER	SISTER
Hopper, Zelpha Thelma	Dec 8, 1982	Jeff Memorial Hospital, Tn	Tn	Mar 10, 1925	57	Hopper, F.M.	Jett, John		Colley, Nannie		Stapleton, Dorothy - Hopper, F.M.	Mt. View					
Herendon, Lucy Terrell	Feb 4, 1955	White Pine, Tn (Res Ky)			37						Pender, Mrs. James	Harlan, Ky					
Herron, Hubert Burt	Feb 26, 1983	Jeff Co	Tn	Nov 10, 1886	76	Ng	Herron, Calloway		Bradley, Rebecca Jane		Herron, Earl - & Mrs. H.B.	Memorial Gardens					
Herron, Mary Berry	Oct 10, 1970	New Market, Tn	Tn	Feb 7, 1890	80	W	Berry, Pryor		Lynch, Sadie		Herron, Earl	Jefferson Memorial					
Herron, Paul Joseph	Jun 29, 1985	J.M.H.	Tn	Mar 25, 1921	64	Ng	Herron, Hugh B.		Berry, Mary		Herron, Isabella G.	Jefferson Memorial	WW 2				
Hickey, Ada Elizabeth	Apr 21, 1976	Jeff Co	Tn	Jan 24, 1901	75	Hickey, E.I.	Swafford, Charlie		Owens, Eva		Hickey, E.I.	Jefferson Memorial					
Hickey, Edgar James	Mar 16, 1983	Oak Ridge, Tn	Tn	Aug 21, 1897	85	W	Hickey, Press		Forgety, Bobby Joe		Forgety, Bobby Joe	Jefferson Memorial					
Hickey, Magnolia	Oct 29, 1955	Grainger Co	Tn	Apr 27, 1883	72	Ng	Williams, John		Cooper, Sarah		Hickey, Will	Economy - Hamblen Co					
Hickey, Sandra G.	Jun 7, 1982	Knoxville, Tn	Knoxville, Tn	Dec 17, 1959	32	S	Hickey, J.C.		Whitt, Irene		Mother	Blue Springs - Rutledge, Tn					
Hickman, Burl O.	Nov 9, 1993	Jeff City	Jeff Co	Apr 16, 1920	73	Snyder, Venus	Hickman, William D.		Bailey, Bessie		Willie	Pleasant Grove			Province, Pat & Roy		
Hickman, Charles Freeman	Aug 27, 1980	Knox Co	Tn	Feb 7, 1920	48	Ng	Hickman, William		Hickman, Nettie Lee - Shirley		Hickman, Nettie Lee - Shirley	Piney					
Hickman, Francis La Nette (F)	Sep 22, 1983	Jeff Co	Tn	Feb 18, 1950	13	W	Hickman, Bruce		Wollard, Mary O. (F)		Woolards	Woolards					
Hickman, Mary A.	Jun 30, 1936		Tn	Aug 26, 1863	72	W	Sanders, Dave	Tn	Sockmith, Nancy	Tn	Hickman, Mary O.						
Hickman, Nettie L.	Mar 8, 1999	Jeff City	Sevier Co, Tn	Aug 29, 1915	83	Ng	Payne, Samuel		Pollard, Thania		Newman, Shirley [Daug] - Huffaker, Ira [Aunt]	Pleasant Grove				W.J.-C.E.-Alexander	
Hickman, O.H.	May 23, 1931	New Market	Tn	Nov 17, 1931	51	Ng	Hickman, A.J. Sr.	Tn	Shackelford, Mary E.	Tn	Willie	Concord					
Hickman, Paul Ray	Jan 28, 1992	F.S.H.	Sevier Co	Mar 31, 1925	66	Elmore, Lucille	Hickman, Walter		Wollard, Carrie Lou		Wife	East View - Strawberry Plains	unk				
Hickman, T.L.	Apr 18, 1931	Sevier Co	Tn	Oct 18, 1858	72	Ng	Hickman, William	Tn	Petty, Julia	Tn	Hickman, Mrs. T.L.	Pleasant View					
Hickman, Terry Wayne	Apr 11, 1993	Johnson City, Tn	Tn	Feb 5, 1972	21				Clark, Judy		Father - Clark, Ralph & Alma - Hickman, Ross & Jean [G-Parents]	J.M.G.				Tyler	
Hicks, Blanche	Jul 8, 1957	Cocke Co	Cocke Co	Apr 3, 1878	77		Roberts, John	Tn	Link		Hicks, Ralph [Son]	Buffalo Grove					
Hicks, Clyde I	Jan 12, 1987	Knox Co	Tn		28	S	Hicks, Crockett		Hicks, B.D.		Hicks, B.D.	Sevier Co					
Hicks, Jimmie Raymond	May 24, 1975	Decatur, Ga	Tn	Apr 18, 1908	67	Forgety, Mollie	Hicks, James M.		Denton, Jane	Tn	Hicks, Addie	Buffalo Grove					
Hicks, Louis Lemuel	Aug 4, 1956	Knox Co	Tn	May 25, 1878	78	W	Hicks, James M.		Dunn, Eliza Jane		Hicks, Ralph	Buffalo Grove					
Hicks, Marjorie M.	Jan 12, 1975	Jeff Co		Jan 14, 1889	75	W	Murphy, Joss		Lewis, Leona		Wagner, F.H. [Jefferson, Ind.] - Flaherty, Esther	Oak Hill - Lebanon, Ind.					
Hicks, Mollie Alice	Mar 4, 1987	Jeff City		Jan 22, 1912	75	W	Forgety, William		Underwood, M. Elizabeth		Hicks, James E. [Dau] - McGhee, Jane	Buffalo Grove					
Hicks, Necta	Dec 29, 1941	New Market	Cocke Co		44-1-14	Hicks, William			Nicholson, Mrs. Tom [Sister] - Hicks, William		Nicholson, Mrs. Tom [Sister] - Hicks, William	Hopewell					
Hicks, Ralph Pryor	Feb 23, 1977	Knoxville, Tn	Tn	Nov 13, 1905	71	Ng	Hicks, L.I.	Tn	Rutherford, Lena	Tn	Hicks, Mrs. Ralph	Highland Memorial - Knox Co	WW 2				
Hicks, Samuel Stephens	Oct 23, 1939	Dandridge	Dandridge	Oct 23, 1939	6d	Ng	Hicks, S.B.		Roberts, Blanche		Father	Dandridge					
Higgins, Mary A.	Jan 21, 1959	Tn	Tn		71	Ng	Minton, Morris		Reneau, Gladys		Higgins, William Allen	West View					
Higgins, Roy	Apr 7, 1987	Hamblen Co	Tn	Jan 22, 1912	75	Colley, Rose	Higgins, George W.	Tn	Atkins, Nora		Higgins, Rose	Sunderland					
Higgins, William A. Sr.	Aug 15, 1959	Tifton, Ga	Tn	Jan 30, 1921	69	Crooke, Lillie	Higgins, John A.		McDonald, Hazel		Higgins, Lillie	J.M.G.	WW 2				
Hightower, Dock H.	Nov 24, 1989	Plains	Strawberry	Aug 1 1894	75	Monday, Goldie	Holland, John		Hightower, Betty		Hightower, Goldie	Bookwalter - Knox Co					
Hightower, Eugene	Oct 10, 1932	Jeff City	Tn	Jul 11, 1897	35	Ng	Hightower, John	Tn	Glass, Jennie	Tn	Hull Bros.	Greenbriar					
Hill, A.C.P.	Nov 9, 1932	Jeff City	Tn	Feb 23, 1844	88	Hill, I.A.		Tn	Austell, Nancy	Tn	Hull Family	Bullhow					
Hill, Benjamin David	Nov 3, 1960	Jeff Co	Tn	Apr 3, 1896	92	W	Hill, Alfred		Denton, Susan		Higgins, James F.	Jefferson Memorial					
Hill, Bobby Don	Dec 26, 1950	Jeff Co	Tn	Nov 9, 1950	1m 17d	W	Hill, James		Pitts, Amanda		Greenbriar	Greenbriar					
Hill, Bonnie E.	Nov 18, 1999	Morristown, Tn	Washington College, Tn	Nov 18, 1929	69	Brobeck, Lunsford P.			Brobeck, Ethel		Hill, William R. Jr. [Son]	J.M.G.					
Hill, Buford	Jul 18, 1985	Jeff Co	Tn	Oct 31, 1930	34	Gray, Mary Agnes	Hill, Charlie		Rhinehart, Sue		Mrs. Buford	Oakland	WW 2				
Hill, Cagion B.	Jan 29, 1969	Jeff Co	F.S.H.	Nov 13, 1918	70	Collier, Dorothy	Hill, Walter		Bowers, Nellie		Hill, Dorothy Red	Buffalo Grove	WW 2				

NAME	DDATE	BLOCAT	BLOCAT	BDATE	AGE	SPOUSE	FATHER	FRLOCAT	MOTHER	MFRLOCAT	BY	BURIAL	VET	SON	DAUG	BROTHER	SISTER
Hill, Ellis B.	Jan 19, 1941	Jeff Co			59-6-3/25		Hill, W.E.		Lyles, Linda	Jeff Co	Hill, W.E. - Rudolph & Raymond [Sons]	Mt. Pleasant					
Hill, Elmer	Sep 10, 1925				25	S		Tn	Finchum, J.T.	Tn	Finchum, J.T.	West View		W.T. Fain			
Hill, Eugene	May 18, 2000	Jeff City	Tn	Jun 16, 1910	89	Knowling, Grace	Hill, Willis W.		Finchum, Laura		Lowe, Mrs. Kenneth [Daug]	Lebanon Baptist			Wheeler, Betty - Robbins, Nannie		
Hill, Fine Ben	Jan 25, 1977	Jeff City	Tn	Oct 13, 1901	75	Div	Hill, Dock		Finchum, Laura		Wife	West View					
Hill, Frank Earl	Jan 30, 1994	Sevier Co		Aug 11, 1906	87	Div	Hill, Albert		Allen, Arora		Hodges, Barbara [Daug]	J.M.G.			Stiles, Mary - Mc Daniel, Mildred - Ayers, Jeanette - Pryor, Lydia		
Hill, George W.	Mar 7, 1996	Jeff City		May 16, 1871	64	S	Hill, T.O.P.		Carter, Mary			Buffalo Grove					
Hill, George Walter	Mar 6, 1999	Dandridge, Tn		Jan 24, 1912	87	Bickle, Lillian			Moore, Melinda		Wife	Shady Grove - Jeff Co	army			James	
Hill, Grace A.	Oc 22, 1989	Jeff Co		Sep 27, 1887	82-0-25	S	Hill, A.O.P.		Carter, Mary			Buffalo Grove					
Hill, Hattie A.	Aug 15, 1987	Jeff Co	Tn	Feb 11, 1887	90/95	Ng	Hall, I.W.	Tn	Hudson, Lucy	Tn	Hill, James	Memorial Gardens					
Hill, Infant	Aug 8-4, 1926	Jeff Co			0		Hill, J.W.		Hudson, Lucy			Buffalo Grove					
Hill, J. Walter	Mar 26, 1951	Jeff Co	Tn	Nov 12, 1883	67	Ng	Hill, James B.		Malcolm, Margaret		Hill, Mrs. Lucy H. - Hinchey, Mrs. Clifford	Buffalo Grove					
Hill, James Roe	Nov 13, 1996	Jeff City	Hammond, In	Sep 24, 1942	54	Malone, Martha Ann	Hill, James D.	Tn	Roe, Helen	Tn	Wife	Cremated					
Hill, Laura Puralee	Apr 11, 1948	Jeff City		Dec 13, 1946	71-3-26	W	Finchum, Joseph F.	Tn	Baker, Mollie	Tn	Hill, H.R. & Fine	West View			Parrops, Laura [Cal.] - Micheletti, Alycia - Hill, April [III.]		
Hill, Leonard Seymour	Oct 24, 1944	Jeff Co	Morristown, Tn	Apr 29, 1903	41	W	Finchum, Nathniel T.	Tn	Finchum, Laura	Tn	Hill James L. [Brother-In-Law]	West View	WW 2				
Hill, Lillian	Jan 10, 2000	Jeff Co		Feb 22, 1909	90	W	Hill, Charles		Will, Mary		Hill, James L. & Raymond	Shady Grove					
Hill, Lucy Hudson	May 10, 1972	Jeff Co	Tn	Feb 26, 1889	83	W					Hill, Blair & Margaret	Shady Grove					
Hill, Margarette	Dec 17, 1924	Tn, (L. Lebanon)			89	Hill, William	Know, Dave		Schultz, P.M.	Pa		Lebanon					
Hill, Mary Carter	Apr 25, 1827				76-8-27	Hill, O.P.	Carter, George	Tn	Coleman, Nancy	Tn		Buffalo					
Hill, Mrs. James P.	Jun 17, 1944	Tn		Dec 15, 1852	90	Hill, James P.	Thurman, William	Tn	Shipp, Martha Elizabeth	Tn	Hill, Claude - Swann, Mrs. R.L.	Dandridge					
Hill, Mrs. John	Nov 29, 1940	White Pine	Tn	Apr 28, 1890	73	W	Moore, Samuel W.	Tn	Waterson, Laura	Tn	Hill, R.L.	Shady Grove					
Hill, Nannie Myrtle	Jun 5, 1960	Jeff Co	Tn	Apr 16, 1886	73	W	Trusks, David		Pierce, Nannie		Hill, Eugene & W.H.	Lebanon					
Hill, Ruth	Jan 11, 1987	J.M.H.	Tn	Oct 12, 1895	91	W	Fox, W.C.		Zirkle, Ellen		Hill, Frank	Hillcrest					
Hill, William Harvey Sr.	Mar 10, 1986	S.M.H.	Pa	Sep 16, 1912	73	Ng	Hill, William Carroll		Rea, Stella		Hill, Mrs. Hattie V. - Garden Of Gethsemane - J.M.G.	Garden Of Gethsemane - J.M.G.					
Hill, William Carroll	Dec 25, 1943	Dandridge	Tn	Jul 1, 1873	70	Ng	Hill, James P.	Tn	Thurman, Mollie	Tn	Hill, Mrs. W.C. - Harris	Mt. Pleasant					
Hill, William Ernest	Jan 5, 1956	Tn	Tn	Jun 22, 1872	82	W	Hill, James B.		Carter, --		Hill, Rudolph & Raymond	Mt. Pleasant					
Hill, William R. Sr.	Oct 9, 1996	Jeff City	White Pine, Tn	Jun 10, 1918	78	Brabock, Bonnie E.	Hill, Ben		Raines, Hattie		Wife	J.M.G.	41-45	William R. Jr.			
Hill, Willie Howard	Jan 24, 1995	Hamblen Co		Aug 4, 1916	78	Hopkins, Ethel	Hill, Willie W.		Raines, Myrtie		Wife	Sartain Springs		Buddy Howard - Donald & Debbie	Rudnick, Deborah & Neal - Moore, Marilyn & Jim - Eugene-James B. Sr. [D]		
Hilton, Frankie	Mar 21, 1986	Cana Inn	Va	May 3, 1890	95	S	Hilton, Robert		Brown, Lucy M.		Moore, Martha H.	Sperryville - Sperryville, Va					
Hilton, Robert Gregory	Sep 18, 1978	Va	Tn	Apr 3, 1916	62	Ng	Hilton, Thomas H.		Gregory, Evelyn		Hilton, Mrs. Robert	Strawberry Plains					
Hinchey, Birsha	Sep 18, 1953	Jeff Co	Tn		70-6-24	Ng	Clevenger, Albert		Cate, --		Colburn, Mrs. Kas	Flat Gap					
Hinchey, C.L.	Apr 25, 1931	Newmarket	Tn	Jan 6, 1862	69	Ng	Hinchey, Henry	Tn	Waugh, Ann	Tn	Hinchey, Mrs. C.L. - Hinchey, Mrs. Juanita H.	New Market					
Hinchey, Clifford Frank	Feb 15, 1984	Jeff Co	Tn	Jul 5, 1904	79	Ng	Hinchey, Robert P.		Clevenger, Birsha		Hill, Mrs. T.C. - Hinchey, John & Oscar	West View					
Hinchey, E.L.	Feb 6, 1946	Jeff Co	Tn	Sep 26, 1867	78	Ng	Hinchey, Jim G.		Carter, --	Tn	Hinchey - Gilbert, Mrs. Sarah - Gilbert, Mrs. Oscar	West View					Elizabeth-Lois - Bacon, Virgie - [B-Law] Hill, Aileen - Clara
Hinchey, Carlos Mao	Jul 5, 1948	Knox Co	Tn	Apr 8, 1872	76-2-27	W	Unk		Unk			Woodlawn - Knox Co					

NAME	DDATE	DLOCAT	BLOCAT	BDATE	AGE	SPOUSE	FATHER	FBLOCAT	MOTHER	MFBLOCAT	BY	BURIAL	VET	SON	DAUG	BROTHER	SISTER
Hinchey, J. Will	Jan 30, 1949	Jeff Co	Tn	Oct 1, 1879	70-3-29	Ng	Hinchey, Lee	Tn	Russell, Mary	Tn	Hinchey, Mrs. J.W.	New Market					
Hinchey, John W.	Jan 16, 1948	Jeff Co		Jan 21, 1875	72-11-25	S	Unk				Haskell	West View					
Hinchey, Juanita	Nov 12, 1990	Jeff Co	Jeff Co	Jun 22, 1911	79	W	Hill, Walter		Bowers, Nellie		Hinchey, James R. [Son]	West View					
Hinchey, Melinda	Sep 20, 1941	New Market			73-11-21	W			Elliott, Lucinda	Tn	Miller, Mrs. Frank [Daug]-Hinchey, W.E.						
Hinchey, Mary Gladys	Nov 13, 1955	Jeff City	Jeff Co	Mar 3, 1908	87	Hinchey, Robert T.	Miller, J.J.		Corbett, Ethel Mae		Husband	J.M.G.		Cecil & Milfred	Dodson, Maxine		Mc Gee, Pauline - Colley, Blanche
Hinchey, Nannie	Nov 17, 1965	Knox Co	Tn	Sep 7, 1878	87	W	Breeding, Pryor		Dance, Mrs. 7.E.		J.M.G.	New Market					
Hinchey, Paul Lenord	Mar 28, 1956	Jeff Co	Tn	Sep 15, 1910		W	Hinchey, Robert P.		Clevenger, Elmira		West View	West View					
Hinchey, Robert Patterson	Dec 8, 1945	Jeff Co	Tn	Jun 11, 1873	72	Ng			Pierce, Lucinda			Flat Gap					
Hinchey, Robert Taft	Dec 23 1996	Jeff City	Jef Folly	Sep 16, 1908	88	Ng	Hinchey, Robert P.	Tn	Clevenger, Blanche	Tn	Hinchey, Cecil [Son]	J.M.G.			Dodson, Maxine [Ala.]		
Hinchey, Ruth M.	Mar 27, 1997	Morristown, Tn	U.S.A.	Jun 9, 1913	83		Murray, Charles		Bacon, Ida		Hinchey, Betty Johnson [Daug-in-Law]	West View					Chase, Olivene - Rood, Mary Emma - Holtsinger, Blanche
Hinchey, Stuart Paul	Nov 29, 1994	Houston, Texas	Lake Charles, La	Jul 11, 1959	35		Hinchey, Frank		Orr, Sarah Jane		Father [TX]	West View					[in-Law] Hinchey, Karen [TX]
Hines, Clifford J.	Oct 12, 1983	Jeff Co [Res Mich.]	Michigan	Jan 16, 1918	65	Addison, Rose Marie [D]			Boyd, Mary		Houghton Lake, Mich	Houghton Lake, Mich	WW 2				
Hines, Lee Everett Sr.	Apr 26, 1948	Knox Co	Tn	Dec 27, 1880	68	Ng	Hines, Joseph				Lynnhurst	Lynnhurst					
Hines, Rose Marie	Oct 12, 1983	Jeff Co [Res Mich.]	Michigan	Jun 12, 1918	65	Hines, Clifford [D]	Addison, John		Jarokowsky, Marie		Hines, Ronald Dennis [Son - Fla]; Williams, Brad [Mich]	Houghton Lake, Mich					
Hinkle, Allie Dionne	Feb 2, 1956	Jeff Co	Tn	Jul 18, 1891	64	W	Walker, Marshall		North, Callie E.		Hines, Hanley [Atty] - Ira Maples	Oak Grove					
Hinkle, Bessie W.	Apr 4, 1987	Knoxville, Tn	Tn	Jun 10, 1893	93	Hinkle, Roy [D]	Williams, James		Henry, Nannie		Patterson, Inez - Zollers, Olive	Buffalo Grove					
Hinkle, Grant James	Jun 21, 1974	Jeff City	Ky	Aug 6, 1918	55	W	Hinkle, James Abe	Tn	Hyden, Martha		Hinkle, William & Dennis	Buffalo Grove	WW 2				
Hinkle, Harold Jessie	Aug 30, 1947	Jeff City		Aug 26, 1917	30	Glynn, Mable	Hinkle, James B.		Howard, Mrs. Fred		Jones Hurst - Barbourville, Ky	Barbourville, Ky	WW 2				
Hinkle, Katherine Ruth	Nov 29, 1990	J.M.H.	Jeff City	Jan 8, 1923	67	Hinkle, Hanley R.	Phillips, Arthur		Anderson, Katherine Ruth		Hinkle, Hanley R.	Buffalo Grove					
Hinkle, Roy Branner	Jul 9, 1983	Jeff City	Tn	Aug 30, 1892	90	Williams, Bessie	Hinkle, Arthur		Walker, Lou		Hinkle, Mrs. Bessie	Buffalo Grove					
Hinkle, William Grant	Aug 21, 1980	Jeff City	Tn	Aug 11, 1980	88	Ng	Hinkle, Neil Grant		Kelley, Christina		Hinkle, Neil G. [Son]	West View					
Hinton, Gladys	Mar 25, 2000	Jeff City	Ky	Jan 18, 1902	98	W	Harmon, Albert		Lee, Minnie		Hankins, Juanita [Friend]	West View					
Hipshire, Albert Dana	Jul 19, 1957	Talbott, Tn	Granger, Co	Jan 28, 1927	69	Graham, Mary	Hipshire, Lewis		Lamb, Beulah		Wife	Army	Army			Ronald	
Hixon, Houston Thomas	Jul 30, 1996	Rutledge, Tn	Rutledge, Tn	Feb 12, 1927	71	Hixon, Clirie		Hixon, Lee		Foster, Doris	Wife	Avondale Baptist	45-46		Jinks, Barbara - Sisson, Linda - Blair - Rita - Vittatoe, Gail		Hixon, Mary - Nutt, Lois - Satterfield, Wanda
Hobbs, David Alan	Mar 23, 1996	F.S.H.	Tn	Jan 8, 1959	27	S			King, Betty		Hobbs, Charles C.	Lynnhurst - Knoxville, Tn					
Hodge, Addie	Feb 16, 1929				78-5-23	W						Lebanon					
Hodge, Alford	Jan 8, 1927				81	W						Lebanon					
Hodge, Buford Homer	Aug 24, 1957	Jeff Co	Tn	Aug 3, 1908	49	Ng	Hodge, Luther		Kerr, Julia		Hodge, Roy & Brothers [Son]	West View					Nina Lilly - Knoll, Gale - Kimbrough, Villian - Drake, Faye
Hodge, Colkin Coolidge	Sep 14, 1997	Morristown, Tn	Tn	Sep 4, 1924	73	Hurst, Hilda	Hodge, Ben Harrison		Mynatt, Cora		Wife	West View	WW 2		[Step] Yeary, Linda & James Ashley	B.H.-Lonas-Carroll	
Hodge, Carter (Colf)	Apr 29, 1953	Jeff City	Tn	Apr 4, 1898	55	Ng	Hodge, Pryor				Hodge, Lillie	Blue Springs - Rutledge, Tn	West View Colored				
Hodge, Carter Jr. (Negro)	Feb 6, 1982	Jeff City	Tn	Jul 1, 1925	56	Johnson, Juanita	Hodge, Carter Sr.		Harris, Lillie		Hodge, Mrs. Juanita	Jefferson Memorial					
Hodge, Cynthia J.	May 13, 1988	Hillhaven - Jeff City	Tn	May 12, 1907	81	W	Slagle, James		Reneau, Sara		Slagle, William C.	West View					

NAME	DATE	DLOCAT	BLOCAT	BDATE	AGE	SPOUSE	FATHER	FBLOCAT	MOTHER	MFBLOCAT	BY	BURIAL	VET	SON	DAUG	BROTHER	SISTER
Hodges, Daisy	Jul 13, 1927		Tn	Feb 10, 1951	23	s	Hodges, Jessie		Patterson, Irene		Hodges, Ben	Central Parks					
Hodges, James Harrison	Apr 20, 1952	Jeff Co	Tn	Feb 14, 1965	1		Hodges, Ben H.		Mauley, Margaret		Hodges, Ben	West View					
Hodges, James T.	Nov 25, 1958	Jeff City	Tn	Feb 14, 1965	92	Ng	Hodges, Harry				Hodges, Rufus & Fred	Mill Springs					
Hodges, Jessie	Oct 10, 1928		Tn [D. Grainger Co.]		19-11-10	s	Hodges, Jessie	Tn	Biddle, Emma	Tn							
Hodges, Lela Belle	Mar 31, 1975	Knoxville, Tn	Tn	May 10, 1935	39	s	Hodge, Carter		Cloud, Lilly		Hodge, Steven Clark / Carter, Pryor	Jefferson Memorial					
Hodge, Lillie Mae (Magna)	Jun 26, 1977	Knoxville, Tn	Tn		72	w	Harris, Ernest		Fehn, Bell			Jefferson Memorial					
Hodges, Margaret Annete	Jul 27, 1945	Jeff Co	Grainger Co	Oct 1 1868	76	Ng	Kinder, George		Churchman, Amanda	Tn		Mill Springs					
Hodges, Martha Ruth	Aug 1, 1996	Knoxville, Tn	Hamblen Co	Aug 23, 1917	78		Treece, John		Chestnut, Lydia		Hodges, Fred E. - Brooks, Rosa / Griffin, Jacqueline - Northern, Elmer / Dyer, John - Treece, Rufus (Nephews)	J.M.G.				Charlie	Lucille
Hodges, Mary Emily	Oct 28, 1956	Tn	Tn	Oct 22, 1886	60	s	Hodge, Alford		Hull, Addie		Moody, Mrs. Taylor	Lebanon - Greenbrier - Hamblen Co					
Hodges, Mrs. Rue K.	Apr 9, 1912?	Tn	Tn		31-3-27	Hodge, Rue K.	McClaine, J. Marshall	Tn	Ballinger, Link	Tn	Moody, Mrs. Taylor	West View					
Hodges, Norma Faye	Dec 1, 1967	J.M.H.	Tn	Apr 7, 1967	69	w	Callelin, Frank		Chariton, Mintie Bell		Hodge, R.K.	West View					
Hodges, Reba	Jan 27, 1969	Jeff Co	Tn	Oct 21, -17	51-3-6	Hodge, Charlie	Clevenger, Joel C.		Neal, Judy			Mill Springs					
Hodges, Roy K.	Sep 16, 1967	Jeff Co	Tn	Jan 25, 1891	76	s	Hodge, Alfred		Solomon, Hattie		Hodge, Charlie	J.M.G.					
Hodges, Rue K.	Jul 5, 1970	Jeff Co	Tn	Oct 19, 1895	74	s	Jolley, Addie		Smith, Nettie		Hodge, Cynthia	West View					
Hodges, Rufus Mitchell	Dec 25, 1975	J.M.H.	Tn	Mar 27, 1890	85	s	Hampton, Margaret		Kinder, Margaret		Hodge, Margaret	Jefferson Memorial					
Hodges, Sallie	Oct 30, 1947	Jeff Co	Tn	Aug 14, 1868	79-2-16	s	Hodge, Logan	Tn	McDaniel, Mary Ann	Tn	Cooper, D.H. (Washington D.C.)	West View					Dyer, Lucille
Hodges, Samuel Davis	Dec 8, 1940	Jeff Co	Sullivan Co.	Mar 26, 1925	78-11-26	w	Marshall, Juanita		Chissis, Eliza	Tn	Hodges, Eckel	J.M.G.					
Hodges, Talmadge Rayford	May 4, 1967	J.M.H.	Tn	Feb 8, 1938	62	Ng	Hodge, Jessie		Biddle, Emma Alice	Tn	Hodges, Juanita M.	Hodges					
Hodges, Tommy Joe	Aug 21, 1970	Jeff Co	Tn		32	Ng	Hodge, Charles		Clevenger, Reba	Tn	Hodges, Brenda Joyce	Mill Springs					
Hodges, Annette Brown	Feb 24, 1925		Tn		67-3-9	Hodges, Joe [D]	Smith, W.M.		Bier, Mary Jane	Tn	Hodges, Irene - Smart, Mrs. George H. [Cal.]	West View					
Hodges, Ethel	Dec 15, 1964	Grainger Co	Tn		76	Hodges, J.A. [D]	Seymour, Leroy		Hupson, Matilda		Hayes, Mrs. Clyde - Hodges, James Edgar	West View					
Hodges, Fred Myers	Jun 20, 1947	Knox Co	Jeff Co		46-1-19	s	Hodges, Albert	Tn	Nance, Mollie	Tn	Wilcox, Mrs. Robert L. - Brown, Roy	Straw Plains					
Hodges, Grace Alexander	Aug 27, 1989	Knox Co	Tn	Mar 21, 1886	83	s	Hodges, Calloway		Smith, Margaret	Tn	Smith, Mrs. J.L.	Straw Plains					
Hodges, J.L.	Oct 27, 1934	Straw Plains	Tn	Oct 17, 1859	75	Ng	Hodges, Urik	Tn	Douglas, Mary	Tn	Hodges, Mrs. J.L. / Hodges, Robert	Straw Plains					
Hodges, Kerse Tipton	Nov 6, 1954	Knox Co	Tn	Nov 5, 1954		w	Hodges, Robert		Goble, Virginia		Hodges, Robert	West View					
Hodges, Mary L.	Jan 9, 1990	Knox Co	Tn	Mar 19, 1872	87	w	Hodges, C.B.C.		Smith, Margaret E.		Hodges, Edward (Chattanooga)	Hodges - Jeff Co					
Hodges, Maude Bushong	Dec 14, 1972	Jeff City	Tn	Jun 15, 1970	72-5-29	w	Bushong, Joseph William		Cummins, Grace		Hodges, Mrs. W.A. & W.A.	West View					
Hodges, Randall Ellison	Sep 16, 1952	Jeff City	Tn	Sep 16, 1952			Hodges, Robert		Boggs, Virginia		Hodges, Mrs. Robert	West View		Randall Ellison - Kene Tipton			
Hodges, Robert Ellison	Jan 27, 1986	Grainger Co	Tn	Nov 29, 1919	78	s	Hodges, James A.	Tn	Seymour, Ellen Lora		Haney, Jama S. [Friend]	West View	army	[s] Haney, Robert Brittian		Hodges, Edgar, Edward-Edwin- J.A.	Hayes, Rena / Hodges
Hodges, Robert L.	Jul 7, 1931	Tn	Jeff Co		27	s	Hodges, A.L.		Nance, Mollie	Tn	Hodges Bros.	Hodges					
Hodges, Robert Lemuel	Jan 12, 1991	J.M.H.	Jeff Co	-25, 1932	58	Barbee, Elizabeth	Hodges, Charles		Hodges, Susie		Hodges, Elizabeth B.	J.M.G.	unk				
Hodges, Susie Jane	Mar 17, 1996	New Market, Tn	Tn	May 27, 1903	94	w	Watkins, Samuel		Eldridge, Mary		Hodges, N.M. [Son]	J.M.G.		Martin, Mary - Murph, Tressia [In-Law] / Hodges, Elizabeth			
Hodges, Thelma H.	Mar 10, 1979	Jeff City	Tn	Mar 8, 1902	77	Hodges, Fred M. [D]	Boggs, James A.		Epps, Lone		Shirely, Mrs. John H. [Virginia]	West View					
Hodges, Virginia	Dec 5, 1993	Knoxville, Tn	Tn	May 24, 1922	71	Hodges, Robert E.	Gobble, Tipton		Owens, Stella		Husband	Strawberry Plains					
Hodges, William Albert [Dud]	Jan 12, 1978	Jeff City	Tn	Sep 2, 1924	53	Steven, Katy	Hodges, G.M.		Vance, Willie Kate		Hodges, Mrs. W.A.	West View					
Hodges, William C.	Sep 29, 1996	Tn	Tn	May 21, 1890	46	s	Hodges, Sam D.	Tn	Hailo, Mary		Govt.	West View	WW 2			Cole, Bessie - Hicks, Charlice	[1/2] Keisling, Betty

NAME	DDATE	DLOCAT	BLOCAT	BDATE	AGE	SPOUSE	FATHER	FBLOCAT	MOTHER	MFBLOCAT	BY	BURIAL	VET	SON	DAUG	BROTHER	SISTER
Hodgen, Calloway	Oct 28, 1944	Knox Co.	Jeff Co	May 26, 1868	76	S	Hodgen, C.B.C.	Tn	Smith, Margaret E.	Tn	Hodges	Holly Springs - Randolph Co, Nc					
Hodgin, Ida Mary	Nov 27, 1958	Straw Plains (Rea Nd)	Nc	Jul 15, 1876	82	W	Stout, Caron		Osborne, Sophia		Newman, Okra	West View					
Hodgson, Daisey Ella	Jan 25, 1947	Jeff Co	Tn	Oct 24, 1874	72-9-2	Ng	Monday, J.S.	Tn	Hommel, Kate	Tn	Hodgson, T.R. Sr.	West View					
Hodgson, Elizabeth Viola	Jan 15, 1988	J.M.H.	Tn	Jul 26, 1901	86	Hodgson, Ellis M.	Wilson, Sam		Anderson, Hattie		Hodgson, Ellis M. Sr.	West View					
Hodgson, Ellis Mack	Jun 29, 2000	Dandridge, Tn	Tn	Sep 21, 1907	102	Wilson, Elizabeth [D] - Imogene [D]					Shands, Joyce [Daug]	West View	unk	Hollie-Ellis Jr.	Galey, Jane -		
Hodgson, Hazel Dawn	Sept 24, 1950	Jeff Co	Tn		23-8 15 23-2 17	Ng	Shelby, George		Painter, Austra		Hodgson, Hollie	West View					
Hodgson, Jack Allen	Jan 29, 1941	Jeff City	Knox Co	Oct 4, 1954	24	S	Hodgson, James Gary		Moo???, Daisy	Knox Co	Hodgon, J. Gary	Jefferson Memorial					
Hodgson, Viski	Jan 30, 1979	Hamblen Co	Ga	Oct 4, 1954	24	S	Brimmiler, Charles Mead		Tilley, Esther		Hodgson, J. Gary	Jefferson Memorial					
Hoffer, Lena Bea Lee	Mar 6, 1977	Charleston, Sc	Tn	Nov 21, 1973	33	Hoffer, Glany Paul	Lee, James Robert		Aull, Mc Daniel		Lee, Mrs. Mc Daniel	Gariden Of Gethsemane - Jeff Co		Roland-Larry Rocklick-Randy			
Holbert, Elsie Marie	Mar 22, 1999	Jeff City	Lynch, Ky	Mar 20, 1919	80	W	Bosch, Ignatz		Peter, Mary		Hoffman, William C. Jr. (Son - Co.)	Cremated		William (Graham)			
Holbert, Mable Clora	Jun 6, 1942	Jeff Co	Tn	Jun 18, 1900	41	W	Gass, John	Tn	Gass, Ida Jane	Tn	Gass, Buford	New Market					
Holcomb, James E.	Nov 18, 1996	Morristown, Tn	Tn	Jan 15, 1920	76	Shelton, Ann	Holcomb, James W.		Smith, Mary L.		Willis	J.M.G.	44-45	Finley, Mary Frances & Ralph - Collins, Ann Jeanette & Joe Bates, Nicki & Danny		
Holder, Troy Henry	May 5, 1983	Knoxville, Tn	Redding Camp, Al	Jan 15, 1920	76	Shelton, Ann	Holder, Kyle		Willis		Willis	J.M.G.	51-54	Walsh, Joyce - Wolfe, Connie - Hazelwood, Janet		
Holloway, Curtis R.	Feb 3, 1951	Granger Co	Oct 14, 1931		61	Howard, Daphine			Syramon, Elva		Holloway, Charles Lee	Memorial Gardens					
Holloway, Joseph Lee	Apr 8, 1975	Morristown, Tn	Tn	Apr 8, 1975		Holloway, John R.	Jones, Sherry	Tn	Holloway, Charles Lee	Tn	Willis				Nice, Dorothy	
Holloway, Ruby Jean	Oct 23, 1942	Union Co, Tn	Tn	May 20, 1936	6	Ng	Johnson, Minnie		England, Dottie	Union Co	Holloway, Curtis	Oak Grove - Union Co					
Holloway, Willis Charles	Jul 19, 1996	Jeff City	Tn	May 23, 1920	76	Mcc Bee, Vila	Johnson, Minnie		Willis		Willie	41-46	Charlie-Michael-David & Judy			
Hollifield, Eva Kate	Oct 9, 1975	Talbot, Tn	Tn	May 28, 1906	69	W	Lawson, Pete		Giles, Ethel		Willis	Jefferson Memorial					
Hollifield, James T.	Sep 5, 1983	Talbot, Tn	Tn	Apr 20, 1984	79	Lawson, Kate	Hollifield, John	Tn			Homer, Mrs Bruce - Beverly Gail - Preisston, Mrs. Harry [Daug]	Jefferson Memorial					
Holman, John R. Sr.	Sep 12, 1974	Hammond, Indiana	Tn	Jan 1, 1908	80	W					Holloway, Lee	Taylor - Union Co					
Holsclaw, James Lon	Sep 26, 1988	J.M.H.	Nc	Oct 7, 1909	90	Graham, Margaret	Holsclaw, William		Miller, Elmyra		Holsclaw, Margaret C.	J.M.G.		William (Graham)	Graham, Frank [D]- Ted [D]	Wolfe, Ruth Graham [D]	
Holsclaw, Margaret India	Jul 12, 2000	Jeff City	Tn	Oct 7, 1909	90	Holsclaw, James L. [D]					Welch, Peggy [Daug]	J.M.G.					
Holt, Sam Boyd (Frank)	May 24, 1986	J.M.H.	Tn	Aug 20, 1902	83	Sharp, Bonita	Holt, John		Jolley, Jennie		Holt, Mrs. Bonita	West View					
Holt, Bonita	Apr 29, 1998	Clarksville, Tn	Elizabethton, Tn	May 13, 1905	93	Sharp, Jake H.					Holt, Joe & Frieda [Son]	West View			[In-Law] Icides, Edith - Holt, Jean - Hamm, Betty Ann	
Holt, Ethel Pauline	Jun 2, 1975	U.T.H.	Ga	Jul 9, 1915	59	Holt, Wade H. [D]	Blackburn, Mark W.		Johnson, Allice M.		Holt, Michael	Jefferson Memorial					
Holt, Margaret E.	Mar 5, 1993	Claiborne Co, Tn	Feb 19, 1924		69	Coffey, David D.			Finch, Lydia Mae		Holt Roland [Son]	Granger Memorial		Milton-Floyd-Chester	Winstead, Ester	
Holt, Tennie Carmichael	Oct 27, 1955	Jeff Co	Tn	Apr 26, 1881	74	W	Miller, William		Bettis, Lizzie Jane		Carter - Hamblen Co	Carter - Hamblen Co					
Holt, Wade H. (Phil)	Mar 21, 1969	Grundy, Va	Tn	Apr 3, 1916	52	Blackburn, Ethel	Holt, William W.		Glenn, Mrs. Alfred		Holt, William W.	Jefferson Memorial					
Holtsinger, Arthur	Apr 2, 1954	Knox Co	Tn	Dec 5, 1881	72	Ng	Holtsinger, George W.		Dotson, Loretta Arnold		Hog/Dip, Mrs. Frank	Presby - Dandridge					
Honeycutt, Granville Buford	Jul 28, 1941	New Market	Honeycutt, Carzell Brazelton		26-6-3		Young, Lida		Honeycutt, Carzell - Young, Lad		Honeycutt, Carzell - Young, Lad	Jefferson Memorial					
Hoosier, John Owen	Nov 21, 1976	Knoxville, Tn	Tn	Feb 21, 1898	78	Long, Katharine	Hoosier, William H.		Hunter, Lucy	Jeff Co	Hoosier, Mrs. John	Jefferson Memorial					

NAME	DDATE	DLOCAT	BLOCAT	BDATE	AGE	SPOUSE	FATHER	FBLOCAT	MOTHER	MFBLOCAT	BY	BURIAL	VET	SON	DAUG	BROTHER	SISTER
Hoosier, Margaret Katherine	Jan 10, 1996	Hamblen Co.		Jun 20, 1904	91		Long, W.H.		Wright, Maggie		Hoosier, Margie [Daug-In-Law]	J.M.G.					Fields, Ruth - Shipley, Agnes - [In-Law] Long, Josie
Hopkins, Bobbie Jane	Sep 8, 1996	Jeff City	Jeff Co	Mar 26, 1941	57	W	Hopkins, William		Knowling, Pearl		Hill, Ethel [Sister]	Sertain Springs					Mullins, Bernice - Kenner, Bobbie - Posey, Charlene
Hopkins, Henry Hugh	Nov 25, 1985	J.M.H.	Tn	Feb 14, 1906	79	W	Hopkins, W.A.		Mc Cubbin, Lizzie		Hopkins, Lewis	Ebenezer					
Hopkins, Leona Viola	Nov 9, 1985	Jeff Co	Tn	Mar 9, 1908	55	W	Smith, William		Hopkins, Laura Ann		Hopkins, Henry	Ebenezer					
Hopkins, Mary Belle	Apr 23, 1957	Jeff Co	Tn	May 17, 1884	72	W	Stamps, William T.		Campbell, Virginia E.		Morgan, Mrs. Earl - Thomas, Lee	J.O.O.F. - Piedville, Ky					
Hopkins, Mary Pearl	Feb 15, 1973	Jeff Co	Tn	Jul 21, 1905	67	W			Cannon, Minnie		Hopkins, J.I. [Child]	Sertain Springs - Jeff Co					
Hopkins, William Marshall	Jan 12, 1972	Jeff Co	Tn	Feb 5, 1905	66	Ng	Hopkins, William M.		Mc Clanahan, Elizabeth		Hopkins, Mrs.	Sertain Springs - Jeff Co					
Hopper, Nell Davis	Jan 13, 1927	Jeff Co	Tn		28-3-11	Ng	Davis, John	Tn	Maples, Sarah	Tn	Hopper, H.G.	West View					
Hoppes, Frances Mc Neer	Jan 23, 1997	Pigeon Forge, Tn	Bristol, Tn	Nov 13, 1911	85	W	Hopper, William Southwick [D]		Springer, Mae	Tn	Johnson, Jackie [Daug]	Oak Dale - Marysville, Ohio		William S. Jr [Delaware, Oh]	Gordon, Louise [Marysville, Oh]		
Hopson, Earl William	Jan 22, 1998	Talbott, Tn	Claiborne Co, Tn	Feb 18, 1938	60	Manning, Estel	Hopson, George		Coffey, Alice		Wills	J.M.G.		Danny-Mark	Cox, Sherry	Ernest	
Horace, Elizabeth Jane (Belle)	Jan 22, 1988	J.M.H.	Madison, Wis.	Feb 24, 1902	86	W	Marvin, Frank		Lambert, Mary		Gerber, Vivian M. - Curtis F.H. [Elyria, OH]	Ridge Lawn - Elyria, Oh					
Horace, Harold Mc Sr.	Sep 13, 1979	Jeff City [Res Ohio]	Ohio	Jan 13, 1902	77	Monroe, Elizabeth	Horace, Edward L.		Dutton, Dora		Horace, Harold M. Jr [Elyria, OH]	Ridgetown - Elyria, Oh					
Horace, Adam	Oct 23, 1984	Jeff City	Tn	Apr -, ---	7-1-5 / 29	Dennis, Dorothy	Horace, Edward		Welch, Maude Z.		Horace, Mrs. Dorothy [Mother]	Garden Of Gethsame - J.M.G.	WW 2				
Horner, Annie May	Jul 30, 1993	Tn	Tn		5-11-25	W	Horace, Ollie	Tn	Turner, Ollie	Tn	Horner & Turner	Pleasant View					
Horner, Bobby Ray	Feb 19, 1973	Jeff Co	Tn	Feb 19, 1973			Horner, Haskell H.		Lawson, Helen Louise		Horner, Haskell H.	Pleasant View					
Horner, Charlie Francis	Mar 1, 1984	Hamblen Co	Tn	May 27, 1906	55	Bates, Hattie	Horace, William		Whitehead, Mary Alice		Horner, Mrs. Hattie- Mateer & Jackie - Keith, La???	Pleasant View					
Horner, Dewey Esco	Mar 19, 1973	Talbott, Tn	Tn	Jan 14, 1899	74	Ng			Turner, Ollie		Horner, Ollie-Mrs. Dewey-Hal	Pleasant View - Hamblen Co.					
Horner, Dorothy Dee	Jan 25, 1994	Jeff Co	Tn	Dec 22, 1928	65		Dennis, Mack		Kinder, Mary		Trull, Don [Daug]	J.M.G.		Mark - [In-Law] Trull, Stacy - Tate, Jimmy	Graves, Gwen - Mabona, Pat - Shrader, Kathryn - Underwood, Marilyn	William E. Roger	
Horner, Edna Lois	Oct 30, 1992	Dandridge, Tn	Jeff Co	Feb 27, 1910	82		Bethi, Ed		Wiggins, Reba		Cross, Dwight [Son]	West View		Cross, Steve		Curtis	Evans, Mary
Horner, Frank	Dec 24, 1926			74-2-6		S						Economy					
Horner, Gladys Quarles	Aug 15, 2000	Talbott, Tn	Tn	Aug 8, 1909	91	Horner, James E.	Lawson, Helen				Sterling, Jean [Daug]	J.M.G.					
Horner, Haskell Hobart	Apr 8, 1979	Tn	Tn	Sep 26, 1942	36	Lawson, Helen	Horner, Pleas		Turner, Carrie		Horner, Helen	Pleasant View - Hamblen Co.					
Horner, Helen	Oct 5, 1947	Hamblen Co	Tn	Apr 23, 1923	23	Horner, James A.	Hill, Frank	Tn	Hux, Annie	Tn	Horner, James A.	Pleasant View - Lebanon					
Horner, Herman Esco	Dec 6, 1995	Knoxville, Tn	Hamblen Co	Aug 27, 1937	58		Horner, Raisie Roscoe		Welch, Maude Z. [Ex-Wife]		Horner, Anne H. [Ex-Wife]	West View	WW 2	Kelley [Step] Trent, Jeff	Trent, Amy		
Horner, Houston Kirk	Dec 2, 1987	F.S.H.	Sc.	Apr 24, 1930	57	Tate, Sarah	Horner, Edward		Rainwater, Jean		Horner, Sarah T.	West View					
Horner, Infant Male	Mar 1, 1956	Knox Co.	Tn	Mar 1, 1956			Horner, Bobby Joe		Horner, Wilma		Horner, Bobby	Westview Chapel					
Horner, Infant Twins	Jun 16, 1994	Morristown, Tn	Morristown, Tn	Jun 16, 1994		Ng			Horner, Elizabeth		Mother - Horner, Claude [G-Father]	J.M.G.					[Uncles] Horner, Alton-Randy
Horner, J.D.	May 23, 1977	Knoxville, Tn	Tn	Nov 8, 1915	61	Ng	Horner, Dee W.		Henson, Maggie		Horner, Mrs. J.D. & Children	Jefferson Memorial					
Horner, James A.	Jun 27, 1989	J.M.H.	Hamblen Co	Feb 24, 1919	70	Div	Horner, Dewey E.		Turner, Ollie K.		Miller, Shirley	Lebanon [Greenbrier]					
Horner, James Harold	Aug 7, 1950	Jeff Co	Tn	Jun 5, 1942	8		Horner, James Archie		Hill, Helen		Horner, James	Lebanon					
Horner, James Samuel	Jan 2, 1946	Hamblen Co	Hamblen Co	Nov 25, 1890	55	Ng	Horner, Will	Tn	Whitehead, Alice	Tn	Horner, Mrs. Sam [Mae]- Knott, G.C.	Lebanon					

NAME	DDATE	DLOCAT	BLOCAT	BDATE	AGE	SPOUSE	FATHER	FRLOCAT	MOTHER	MFRLOCAT	BY	BURIAL	VET	SON	DAUG	BROTHER	SISTER
Horner, James Scott	Jan 31, 1959	Jeff Co	Tn	Aug 15, 1959	29-5-16	Ng	Horner, Roy		Kimbrough, Hannah		Horner, Mrs. James - Proffitt, Haron [Indiana]	Ebenezer	WW 2				
Horner, Joseph Raymond	Jan 15, 1999	Jeff Co	Tn	Sep 30, 1910	88	Ng	Horner, D.W.		Henson, Magnolia		Horner, Bobby J. - [Nephew]	Ebenezer					
Horner, Joseph Walker	Aug 17, 1994	Knoxville, Tn	Jeff Co	Sep 9, 1931	62	Horner, Jennie	Horner, William Roy		Hannah		Wife			Jason	Prater, Cindi & Jeff	Mack-Dewitt-Ray	Mills, Ann - Gilliam, Maggie - Kinder, Flora - Barboe, Edna
Horner, Nellie Mae	Aug 24, 1989	J.M.H.	Hamblen Co.	May 8, 1898	91	W	Bishop, Obus		Milligan, Eva		Moore, Fannie - Miller, Shirley - Horner, Hall B.	Lebanon Baptist					
Horner, Ollie Katherine	May 21, 1984	J.M.H.	Tn	Aug 5, 1901	82	Horner, Dewey [D]	Turner, W.P.		Cox, Harriet		Pleasant View	Pleasant View					
Horner, Pearl Daniel	Aug 13, 1984	Knoxville, Tn	Tn	Sep 13, 1915	68	Eslinger, Pauline	Horner, John		Maples, Bertie Whitehead, Mary Alice		Horner, Mrs. Pearl D.	Jefferson Memorial					
Horner, Ras Roscoe	Apr 7, 1965	Hamblen Co	Tn		62	Ng	Horner, William				Horner, Cory-James-Raymond	Pleasant View					
Horner, Sarah Jane	Nov 15, 1996	Jeff City	Granger Co. Tn	Aug 11, 1922	76		Tate, Dave E.		Davis, Mae		Watson, Doris [Sister]	West View					Dodd E. [Popeye]
Horner, Shirley Marie	Jan 28, 1940	Jeff Co	Jeff Co	Jan 4, 1940			Horner, Archie	Tn	Hill, Helen	Tn	Horner, Archie	Lebanon - Hamblen Co					
Horner, W.L.	Jul 22, 1950	Knox Co			80	W					Horner, Charlie-Dewey-Ras-Bonnie-Wiley [Children]	Pleasant View					
Horner, Wanda Louise	Sep 22, 1990	Jeff Co	Jeff Co	Apr 4, 1927	63	Horner, Claude	Harris, Louis		Garnett, Blanche		Horner, Claude	J.M.G.					
Horner, William Coy	Dec 16, 1984	Morristown, Tn	Tn	Sep 14, 1927	57	Hill, Nellie	Horner, Ras		Turner, Carrie		Horner, Mrs. Nellie	Pleasant View - Hamblen Co					
Horner, William Roy	Jan 1, 1969	Jeff Co	Tn	Nov 21, 1892	76	Ng	Horner, Dewitt		Henson, Maggie		Horner, Mrs. Hannah B. - Horner, Roy F. - Hackett-Stanley - Barboe, Edna -Gilliam, Ralph - V.A.	Ebenezer	unk				
Horton, Buenda Loretta [Col]	Aug 20, 1954	Knox Co	Tn	Apr 15, 1944	10		Horton, Franklin		Long, Vaultine		Horton, Franklin	West View Colored					
Horton, Franklin Lazell [Black]	Dec 15, 1989	J.M.H.	Tn	Apr 18, 1924	65	Long, Vanillene	Horton, James		Greenlee, Margaret		Horton, Vanillene	West View					
Horton, James H. Jr. [Black]	Jun [29], 1989	Atlanta, Ga	Tn		26	S	Horton, J.H. Sr.		Wilson, Dorothy		Horton, J.H. Sr.	West View					
Horton, James Harold Sr. [Black]	Oct 31, 1991	Boone, Nc		Mar 7, 1991	69	Wilson, Doris	Horton, James		Greenlee, Margaret		Horton, Diana [Diaug]	West View	WW 2-Kor				
Horton, Mabel Mae	Jan 31, 2000	Riverdale, Ga		Dec 14, 1904	95	W					Bales, William Gordon [Son-In-Law] - Kennamer, Karen	Ebenezer					
Horton, Michael Darryl	Jan 22, 1986	Johnson City, Tn	Tn	Nov 6, 1960	25	Hodges, Jennifer	Horton, Harry		Whaley, Verl		Horton, Jennifer H.	Hillcrest					
Horton, Terrell Wayne	Oct 21, 1986	U.T.H.	Tn	Oct 21, 1986		Ng	Horton, Willard W.		Brown, Vickie		Horton, Willard W.	West View					
Horton, Terry Wade	Oct 21, 1986	U.T.H.	Tn	Oct 21, 1986		Ng	Horton, Willard W.		Brown, Vickie		Horton, Willard W.	West View					
Horton, Virginia	Jan 14, 1999	Dandridge, Tn	Big Stone Gap, Va	Jun 29, 1917	81	Ng	Bush, John B.		Allen, Zelma [Daug]		Horton Family - Big Stone Gap, Va	West View				Elmo	
Horville, Wiley	Jun 18, 1954	Knox Co	Tn	Jun 9, 1909	55	Ng	Horville, George		Melliconte, Mary		Carnihon, Ester - Denton, Dwight	Ebenezer					
Houk, Claude Ernest	Apr 2, 1991	Sevier Co	Sevier Co	Sep 7, 1913	77	Love, Lucille	Houk, William Beecher		Houk, Lee		Houk, Lucille L.	J.M.G.					
Houser, Mary Lee [Black]	Jun 13, 1992	Jeff City	Jeff Co	Apr 5, 1940		W	Owens, Flowers		Evans, Lillie Mae		Housewl, Leslie R.[Diaug]	Belmont					
Housewright, Clora Jane	Sep 9, 1950	Jeff Co	Indiana	Sep 12, 1882	67	Ng	Robinson, James		Beck, Amunda		Talley, Mrs. Paul	Mill Springs					
Housewright, James Henry	Aug 19, 1953	Jeff Co	Tn	Jun 26, 1877	76	Div					Talley, Mrs. Paul	Mill Springs					
Housler, W.H.	Nov 13, 1928				63-3-11	Ng	Housier, John	Tn	Martin, Nancy Jane	Tn	Housier, Lydia	West View					
Housley, Effie Elnora	Mar 13, 1954	Talbott, Tn	Tn	Feb 11, 1890	64	S	Housley, Ephraim Willie		Housley, Mrs. Herman -Miriconit-Mrs. Pearl		Housley, Mrs. Herman -Miriconit-Mrs. Pearl	Jernigan - Morristown					Turley, Margaret - Ferrar, Kathleen - Kirkwood, Wanda
Housley, Herman B.	Jan 6, 1957	Jeff Co	Tn	May 8, 1892	64	Bible, Pearl	Housley, Ephriam W.	Tn	Underwood, Minerva E.	Tn	Housley, Pearl	Jernigan					

NAME	DDATE	BLOCAT	BLOCAT	BDATE	AGE	SPOUSE	FATHER	FBLOCAT	MOTHER	MFBLOCAT	BY	BURIAL	VET	SON	DAUG	BROTHER	SISTER
Housley, Mitchel William	Dec 11, 1991	J.M.H.	Morristown, Tn	Oct 3, 1907	84	S	Housley, H.B.		Underwood, Minerva		Kinnick, Roy E. [Cousin]	Jarnigan	unk				
Housley, Pearl	Oct 6, 1984	Care Inn	Tn	Jun 6, 1902	82		Blite, Patrick L.		Kinnick, Ross		Kinnick, Roy C.	Jarnigan					
Howard, Alfonso H.	Jan 7, 1996	New Market, Tn	Jeff Co	Mar 16, 1902	93	Housley, Herman [D]					Dugger, Virgie [Daug]	Pleasant Grove		J.E. Martin-Frank-Herbert			
Howard, Charles Edward	Jan 22, 1940	New Market Tn	Tn	Jan 21, 1940	1d	Howard, Raymond	Tn		Starling, Pansy	Tn	Howard, Raymond	Pleasant Grove		Harry, Hazel - Holder, Daphine - Shelby, Virginia			
Howard, Charles H.	Jul 28, 1979	Jeff City [Res Ky]	Ky	Sep 3, 1916	62	Rago, Tilda			Moore, Flora		Howard, Tilda Rago	Roseblam - Middlesboro, Ky		Taylor			Vineyard, Pauline
Howard, Edna Belle	Apr 6, 1998	Jeff City	Jeff Co	Sep 26, 1912	85		Betts, Myrtle				Scott, Earl [Nephew]	Elkhoazer					
Howard, Elmer Wayne	Jun 11, 1994	J.M.H.	Tn	Sep 30, 1912	71	Mc Daniel, Vendy M.	Howard, Rod R.		Betts, Alice		Howard, Mrs. Verdyh	Jefferson Memorial					
Howard, Grace Ellen	Aug 27, 1952	Jeff Co	Tn	Mar 8, 1866	82	W			Hodge, Nancy		Millard, Minnie	Piedmont					
Howard, Hannah	Aug 14, 1923	New Market	Tn	Jun 25, 1894	67	Howard, Sam			Lewis, Mandy		Howard, Sam	Pleasant Grove					
Howard, Herbert	Jan 8, 1959	Jeff Co	Tn	Jun 25, 1894	64	Miller, Rosie	Howard, John	Tn	Simpson, Mattie		Caraoke, Richard	Mill Springs					
Howard, John Lilburn [Lind]	Apr 11, 1966	Knox Co	Tn	Feb 13, 1886	80	Ng	Howard, J.C.		Simpson, Methuhda		Howard, Margaret [Mrs. J.R.]	Memorial Gardens		John L. Sr.		Frank	
Howard, Margaret M.	Oct 3, 1982	Jeff Co	Tn	Dec 7, -97	94	W	Davis, Luetta		Howard, Pat [Dugar]			J.M.G.					Lee, Arlence
Howard, Martha Elizabeth	Mar 18, 1990	J.M.H.	Knox Co, Tn	Sep 17, 1906	83	Howard, A.H.			Bates, Minerva		Dugger, Virgie	Pleasant Grove					
Howard, Mary Jane	May 22, 1972	Knox Co	Tn	Sep 2, 1895	87	W	Northern, William L.		Hawkins, Elzaro			Pleasant Grove					
Howard, Mrs. Josie	Jan 12, 1927		Tn			Ng	Betzinger, L.	Tn	Butterworth, Martha	Tn	Howard, W.T.	Wheat Grove					
Howard, R.T.	Oct 13, 1959	Jeff Co	Tn	Oct 8, 1878	81	W	Howard, John		Children			Mill Springs					
Howard, Rod R.	Mar 27, 1960	Jeff Co	Tn	Mar 15, 1879	81	W	Howard, Wesley		Dinwiddie, Henrietta		Howard, J.E. & Elmer	Wesleye Chapel					
Howard, Rosa	May 24, 1959	Hamblen Co	Tn	Apr 25, 18585	73	Howard, Bert [D]	Miller, George		Bledsoe, Bertie			Mill Springs					
Howard, Ruby Ayers	Jan 31, 1959	Jeff Co	Indiana	May 25, 1884	74						Howard, Herbert	Mill Springs					
Howard, Thelma Jean	Jan 25, 1998	New Market, Tn	Knoxville, Tn	Mar 6, 1923	68	Howard, Jessie Eugene	Floyd, Ollie		Bailey, Edna E.		Hubbard	Pleasant Grove		David & Alice	Howard, Carol [Dr.] - Marshall, Diane & Randy		Bil+Lowl Holden, Elaine
Howard, Walter	Sep 27, 1994	Knoxville	Tn	Sep 4, 1879	55	Ng					Howard, Mrs.	Pleasant Grove					
Howard, Wesley Charles	Feb 4, 1999	Knoxville, Tn	Jeff Co	Sep 29, 1932	66	Hux, Joanna	Howard, Samuel F.		Wife			East View Memorial	Air Force	Tony & Beth			
Howard, Alen Blaine [Coll]	Jan 29, 1940		Tn	Mar 3, 1939	9m		Howell, J.W. [D]	Tn	Howell, Ivo D.	Tn	Wife	Colored					
Howell, Betty	Nov 6, 1992	Hot Springs, Nc	Tn	Apr 10, 1925	67	Howell, William Y. [D]	Unk		Cureton, Molly		Bishop, Deborah	J.M.G.		William Steven			Hostetler, Wallene
Howell, Clarence Calvin	Aug 23, 1951	Jeff Co	Tn	Jan 24, 1883	68	Ng	Howell, William		Morgan, Adline		Howell, Mrs. Elizabeth	Friends Station	WW 1				
Howell, Esta Mae [Coll]	Aug 11, 1953	Jeff Co	Va	Jan 20, 1928	25	Ng	Taylor, James		Donaldson, Clora		Howell, Leon	West View Colored					
Howell, Florence	Aug 6, 1990	J.M.H.	Ga	Mar 2, 1906	84	W	Corn, C.J.		Mutt, Corble N.		Howell, Betty J. [Dang-In-Law]	West View					
Howell, Gertrude Fain	Jan 10, 1979	Jeff City	Tn	Aug 11, 1895	83	W	Fain, Sam		Snagg, Lillia		Williams, Mary N. - Kyle, Sadie	West View					
Howell, Mike [Coll]	Nov 15, 1931	Jeff City	Tn									Jeff City Colored					
Howell, William [Coll]	Oct 17, 1926	Tn		0-7-19		Woods, Betty	Woods, William	Tn	Woods, Carrie	Tn	Woods, Will	Colored					
Howell, William Y.	Nov 2, 1992	Knoxville, Tn	Copperhill, Tn	Nov 5, 1922	69	Justice, Betty	Howell, Fred T.	Tn	Corn, Florence	Tn	Wife	Colored		William Steven	Bishop, Deborah		Loudermilk, Kathleen
Hubbard, Everett	Jun 12, 1939	Grainger Co		Jun 12, 1939			Hubbard, Charlie	Tn	Parks, Annie	Tn	Hubbard, Charlie Smith, Mrs. Ralph [Lucille]	Beaver Creek					
Hubbard, Flora N.	Jul 16, 1957	Knox Co	Tn	Jun 9, 1899	68	Hubbard, J.W. [D]	Northern, James Riley		Davis, Arlena			Beaver Creek					
Hubbard, Fred Allen	Nov 22, 1998	Knox Co	Tn	Oct 28, 1940	28	Ng	Northern, Hubert		Northern, Edith		Hubbard, Mrs. Stella	Holston View - Knox Co					
Hubbard, Lucy	April [29], 1933	Knox Co		Mar 12, 1882	73	Ng	Gilbert, Ben		Brannam, Linda		Hubbard, Samuel	New Market					
Hubbard, Ollie Jane	Oct 22, 1955	Lee Co, Va		Mar 12, 1913	41	Ng	Morgan, Richard		Watson, Minnie		Hubbard, Rev. Sam	Nance's Grove					
Hubbard, Pauline	Oct 17, 1954	Knox Co	Tn			W					Hubbard, Paul - William	West View					
Hubbard, Samuel H.	Apr 24, 1957	Jeff Co	Tn	May 15, 1969	97	W			Miller, Mrs. Hattie-Paul - Hubbard, Paul-William			New Market					
Hubbard, Thomas P.	Jan 17, 1966	Jeff Co	Tn	Sep 3, 1901	64	Ng	Hubbard, James S.		Maples, Alice		Hubbard, Mrs. Tom	Beaver Creek					Vineyard, Pauline

NAME	DDATE	DLOCAT	BLOCAT	BDATE	AGE	SPOUSE	FATHER	FBLOCAT	MOTHER	MFBLOCAT	BY	BURIAL	VET	SON	DAUG	BROTHER	SISTER
Hodgens, Tommy D. [SRSgt.]	Jun 18, 1986	Tegucigalpa, Honduras	Tn	Mar 8, 1958	28	Norton, Lisa Ann	Hodgens, James D.	Tn	Miller, Ethel		Hodgens, Lisa Ann (Fayetteville, Nc)	Everlasting Life - J.M.G.	unk				
Hudson, Carl L.	Jan 27, 1949	Jeff Co	Tn			W						West View					
Hudson, Emma Lee	Aug 13, 1945	Knox Co	Jeff Co	Jan 24, 1868	77	Ng	Rankin, John F.	Tn	Williams, Martha J.	Tn	Hudson, Paul & Claude	West View					
Hudson, J.M.	Mar 13, 1939	Dandridge	Tn	Jan 20, 1856	82	W	Hudson, Sterling	Tn	Haynes, Link	Tn	Hudson, C.L. & Sons	Willsie Pine					
Hudson, Kerry Peak	Nov 25, 1980	Jeff City	Tn			Ng			Otey, Sherenee		Hudson, Floyd-John - Walker, Dorothy - Kinnick, Beth [Children]	West View					
Hudson, Anna Bell	Oct 20, 1964	Jeff City	Tn	Jan 20, 1881	77	Hull, J.B.					Hudson, Floyd-John - Walker, Dorothy - Kinnick, Beth [Children]	West View					
Hudson, Marjorie Nell	May 19, 1995	Jeff City	Newport, Tn	Feb 11, 1918	78	Hudson, John W. Sr.			Burke, Lola		Husband	West View		John W. Jr. & Charlotte	Julia Ann-Lillian	Don-Walter-Hayne	
Hudson, Paul M.	Oct 9, 1969	Jeff Co	Tn	Oct 8, 1871	78	Hudson, K.P.	Shanley, John D.	Tn	Martin, Cora		Hudson, K.P.	West View					
Hudson, William A.	Mar 5, 1946	Florida	Tn		74	D	Hudson, Carl		Rankin, Emma Lee		Tettie	West View					
Hull, Amy	Apr 16, 1940	Jeff City	Tn	Jan 26, 1881	59	Ng			Sawyers, Elizabeth	Tn	Hudson, K.P.	West View					
Huffaker, Anna Bell	Oct 20, 1964	Tn		Mar 24, 1887	77	Huffaker, S.N.			Arwood, Elizabeth		Norton, Siola & Pauline - Huffaker, S.N.-J.C.- Charlie	Oak Grove - Sevier Co					
Huffaker, Infant Female	May 26, 1970	Knox Co	Knox Co	May 26, 1970			Huffaker, Bobby	Tn	Wilson, Jeannette	Tn	Huffaker, Bobby	Jefferson Memorial					
Huffaker, Infant Male	Sep 8, 1942	Jeff Co	Knox Co	Sep 8, 1942			Huffaker, Clarged Irene				Huffaker, C.I.	Jefferson Memorial					
Huffaker, John C.	Sep 22, 1970	Jeff Co	Tn	Oct 26, 1910	59		Huffaker, S.M.		Griffey, Anna Belle		Huffaker, Mr S J.C.	Beech Springs					
Huffaker, John Cleophas Jr.	Aug 2, 1989	Hawkins Co, Tn	Tn	May 5, 1957	18		Huffaker, John C. Sr.	Tn	Cook, Lucille		Huffaker, John C. Sr.	Jefferson Memorial					
Huffaker, John Edward	Jul 5, 1985	Knox Co	Tn	Aug 12, 1942	22	Huffaker, Linda	Huffaker, Charlie		Aukman, Mary		Huffaker, Mrs. Charlie - Belle, Mrs. Sallie & Charlie	Jefferson Memorial Gardens					
Huffaker, Samuel N.	Dec 19, 1908	Jeff Co	Tn	Jan 10, 1886	82	Ng	Huffaker, Rufus		Atchley, Elizabeth		Underwood, Sevier Co	Jefferson Memorial					
Huggins, James Dorman	Feb 5, 1978	Knoxville, Tn	Tn	Nov 29, 1905	72	Div	Huggins, J.I.		Dorman, Virginia Lee		Huggins, Andrew & Brothers	Oak Grove - Sevier Co					
Huggins, James Swann	Jan 14, 1989	Jeff City	Tn	Feb 25, 1903	85	S	Huggins, J.I.		Mc Corkle, Virginia		Cremated - French Broad Baptist	French Broad - Dandridge					
Huggins, Alleene	Oct 23, 1992	Jeff Co	Ky	Nov 29, 1873	78	Ng	Adams, David M.		Adams, Nannie		Hughes, B.W., Frankfort, Ky	Cremated - French Broad					
Hughes, Alice Margaret	Oct 1, 1949	Jeff Co	Tn	May 11, 1876	73	Ng	Prince, George		Morgan, Lisa		Hughes, C.H.- Faulkner, J.A.	Raseberry					
Hughes, Edward Jack	Sep 2, 1990	J.M.H.	Tn	Oct 6, 1936	53	Ng					Nie-F.H. [Murphy, Nc]	Old Martin Creek - Murphy, Nc					
Hughes, Georgia C.	Dec 1, 1982	Dandridge, Tn	Tn	Sep 17, 1899	93	Schultz, Isabelle	Combs, John		Tucker, Terry [Alt.]		Hughes, Mrs. Georgia C. - Govt.		unk				
Hughes, John J.	Oct 16, 1950	Grainger Co	Tn	Oct 13, 1891	59	Ng	Hughes, Andrew				Hutton, Mrs. Gladys	Shiloh					
Hutton, Halgas Eldon [M]	Jul 30, 1985	Jeff Co	Ky		76	Ng			Austin, Sara		Luna, Jane H.	Shiloh	WW 1				
Hull, Alice Josephine	Jun 18, 1998	Jeff Co	Tn	Nov 30, 1925	82	W	Hendly, James C.				Hendly, Mrs. H.L.	J.M.G.					
Hull, Amanda	Nov 25, 1934	Hamblen Co		Jul 2, 1810		Ng					Hull, Hugh & H.L.- Bradley, Mrs. J.S.- Hightower, Ethel - Smith [Children]	Lebanon					
Hull, Clarence G.	Sep 10, 1996	Jeff Co	Tn	Jul 2, 1810	56	Hull, Grace	Hull, W.A.		Erwin, Laura		Hull, Grace	Memorial Gardens	WW 2				
Hull, Elizabeth Shipley	Apr 17, 2000	Kingsport, Tn	Tn	Mar 20, 1911	89	W	Hull, William A.		Erwin, Lena J.		Hull, Erwin Patrick (Son)	West View					
Hull, Erwin, L.	May 17, 1988	J.M.H.	Tn	Jan 25, 1908	80	Shipley, Elizabeth	Hull, William A.		Erwin, Lena J.		Hull, Elizabeth (Wife)	West View	WW 2				
Hull, Frank Daniel	Aug 3, 1989	J.M.H.	Jeff Co	Apr 1, 1925	64	Div	Hull, Gen D.		Hendly, Josephine		Hull, Fred F.	J.M.G.	WW 2				
Hull, Fred Farrell	Mar 8, 2000	Knoxville, Tn	Tn	Apr 23, 1934	65	Cate, Esther					Wife	J.M.G.					
Hull, Grace Frances	Feb 13, 1996	Callaway Co, Mo	Tn	Feb 18, 1916	79		Hull, Henry		Harshbarger, Katie Irene		Sellers, Linda & David [David]	J.M.G.			Kooch, Earlene		
Hull, Hugh	Oct 4, 1974	Jeff City	Tn	Sep 1, 1880	84	W	Hull, Henry		Lacy, Amanda		Mc Murray, Mrs. Martha Lebanon - [Greenbrier]	Lebanon - Hamblen Co					[In-Law] Dyer, Janie - Hull, Elizabeth
Hull, Hurd Lonas Sr.	Oct 13, 1975	Tn	Tn	May 30, 1899	76	Ng	Hull, Henry		Lacy, Amanda		Wilson, Roy	Lebanon (Greenbrier)					Myrtl, Dene - Deskins, Joanne

NAME	DDATE	DLOCAT	BLOCAT	BDATE	AGE	SPOUSE	FATHER	FBLOCAT	MOTHER	MFBLOCAT	BY	BURIAL	VET	SON	DAUG	BROTHER	SISTER
Hull, Isaac Lafette	Jun 24, 1956	Hamblen Co		Jan 15, 1885	71	Ng	Hull, Henry		Lacy, Amanda F.		Hull, Hazel - Hull, Mrs. Goldie Arnine	Lebanon					
Hull, James Michael	May 17, 1952	Jeff Co		May 17, 1952			Hull, James Henry	Jeff Co	Hooper, Lorena	Granger Co	Hull, James H.	West View					
Hull, Keith Enastus	Feb 12, 1970	Neppanca, Indiana	Tn		41		Hull, Earl				Wright & Yoder						
Hull, Laura	May 5, 1945	Jeff Co	Greene Co	Oct 10, 1882	62	Hull, W.A.	Erwin, Joseph		Campbell, Martha	Tn	Hull, W.A.	West View					
Hull, Lucy Belle	Aug 14, 1995	Talbott, Tn	Mt. Airy, Nc	Jul 2, 1901	94		Graham, Joseph		Caudill, Laura Anice		Wilson, Elvira [Daug]	Lebanon Baptist		Lonas & Clara [In-Law] Wilson, Roy	Lindsey, Edna Earle & Fred		
Hull, Lucy Ellison	Oct 31, 1965	Jeff Co	Tn	Nov 15, 1969	88	Hull, Hugh	Ellison, James		Keener, Mary Ann		Hull, Hugh	Lebanon					
Hull, William A.	Mar 22, 1958	Jeff Co	Tn		88	W	Hull, Isaac B.		Edwards, Margaret		Hull, Agnes	West View					
Hull, William Stephen	Feb 14, 1954	Knox Co	Jeff Co	Mar 3, 1947	6		Hull, Erwin	Jeff Co	Shipley, Elizabeth		Hull, Erwin	West View					
Hull, Willie Agnes	Sep 18, 1984	Jeff Co	Tn			S	Hull, William S.				Hull, Erwin	West View					
Humbard, Charles B.	Aug 17, 1942	Shell Emert Farm	Tn	Feb 13, 1885	61	Ng	Humbard, Henry	Tn	Tittle, Phoeba Jane	Tn	Green, Mrs. Sallie	Woalens Chapel					
Humbard, Lillie	May 4, 1954	Friends Station	Tn	Jan 16, 1879	74	W	Elmore, W. Thad		Day, Katherine		Green, Mrs. Ada & Ralph	Friends					
Humbard, Samuel Robert	Nov 3, 1951	Jeff Co	Tn	Jun 3, 1877	74	Ng	Humbard, William				Humbard, Allison - Majoria, Mrs. Helen - Ralph-Henry-Fairy-Floyd-Lawrence- Hensley, Dorothy	Friends Station					
Humbard, Thomas Monroe	Jun 29, 1953	Jeff Co	Tn	Oct 17, 1878	74	Tittle, Phoebe Jane	Humbard, Henry				Twin, Mrs. [Chattanooga]-Alley, Mrs.-Webb, Mrs.-Badenheimer, Mrs.-Herbert [Children]	Loy					
Humphrey, Robert J.	Feb 20B, 1949	Jeff City			79	W					Humphrey, R.J.	West View					
Humphreys, Anna Mae	Feb 10, 1925		Tn				Humphreys, Robert	Tn	Humphreys, Maggie	Tn	Humphreys, Robert J.	West View					
Humphreys, James Brownlow	Apr 11, 1896	J.M.H.		Sep 4, 1900	85	Gilbert, Hazel	Humphreys, William B.		Barnes, Ellen		Humphreys, Hazel G.	Garden Of Love - J.M.G.					
Humphreys, Margaret Heister	Nov 9, 1943	Jeff Co	Monroe Co, Tn	Jun 24, 1876	67	Humphreys, Robert J.	Peak, William	Tn	Maugis, Mary Jane	Tn	Humphreys, R.J.	West View					
Humley, James	Jan 25, 1979	Granger Co		Mar 4, 1913	83						Breach F.H. [Middeston, Ky]						
Hunter, Margie Elizabeth	Feb 19, 2000	Jeff City	Tn	Dec 19, 1929	70	Div					Hunter, Ernie [Son] - Madison F.H. [Marshall, Nc]						
Hunter, Mrs. Gene	Aug 11, 1937	Knoxville, Tn	Tn	Jan 11, 1871	66	Hunter, Gene [0]	Blake, Frank	Tn	Newman, Martha	Tn	Hunter - Marshall, Nc	Sunderland					
Hurney, Myron James	Dec 30, 1996	Cincinnati, Ohio		Oct 10, 1916	80	Vernon, Jean	Hurney, Myron L.		Sodler, Ernestine		Wile	Cremated					
Hursh, John A.	Mar 9, 1926	Jeff City	Tn		53-6-	Ng	Hursh, John	Va	Morgan, Nancy	Tn	Hurst, Mrs. John & Greene Co	Mitchell Springs - Greene Co		Dolan, Kitty & Edwin [Va]			
Hurst, Chilnecssie [Chad]	Feb 11, 1990	J.M.H.	Jeff Co	Dec 21, 1910	79	W	Ellison, Charlie B.		Van Dyke, Nellie Ann		Hurst, Jimmy	West View					
Hurst, Harley	Mar 18, 1965	J.M.H.	Tn	Oct 13, 1898	66	W	Hurst, John		Mc Elhaney, Julia		Hurst, Roy-Hollis - Wilson, Mrs. Jane A.	West View					
Hurst, Helen Mae	Nov 16, 1945	Jeff Co	Tn	Nov 30, 1929	24	W	Hurst, Claude	Tn	Jones, Fannie	Tn	Hurst, Harley-Raymond & Hazel	West View					
Hurst, Hollis	Aug 9, 1982	V.A.- Mt. Home	Jeff Co	Sep 26, 1931	50	Blankey, Mamie	Hurst, Harley		Jones, Jessie		Hurst, Mrs. Mamie B.	Jefferson Memorial	unk.				
Hurst, James Alvin Jr.	Dec 28, 1981	Knoxville, Tn	Ky	Jul 4, 1957	24	Div	Hurst, James A. Sr.		Shatton, Hilda		Hurst, Mrs. Hilda	Lebanon [Greenbrier]					
Hurst, James Alvin Sr.	Jan 10, 1976	Talbott, Tn	Tn	Apr 18, 1912	63	Shatton, Hilda	Hurst, Marion		Ryder, Eliza		Hurst, Mrs. Hilda	Hamblen Memorial					
Hurst, Jessie Pearl	Apr 7, 1944	Green Co	Jeff Co	Dec 16, 1911	32	Ng					Hurst, Harley	West View					
Hurst, Julia Cordelia	Dec 7, 1957	Jeff City	Tn	Jan 6, 1879	78	W	Allen, John		Mc Henkley, Emma		Gray, Mrs. James A. - Bishop, Mrs. - Hurst, Harley	West View					
Hurst, Roy	Apr 21, 1980	J.M.H.	Tn	Jan 9, 1919	61	Hurst, Faye	Hurst, John		Mehana, Julia		Hurst, Faye	West View	WW 2				
Hurst, Vickie Lee	Sep 27, 1952	Jeff Co	Tn	Sep 27, 1952			Hurst, Rella		Shrader, Lydia		Hurst, Rella	Swanns Chapel					

NAME	DATE	DLOCAT	BLOCAT	BDATE	AGE	SPOUSE	FATHER	FBLOCAT	MOTHER	MFBLOCAT	BY	BURIAL	VET	SON	DAUG	BROTHER	SISTER
Hurst, William Horace	Apr 13, 1963	Jeff Co	Tn	May 20, 1900	62	Ng	Hurst, John		Mc Elhaney, Julia		Hurst, Mrs. Chelnessie	West View					
Husley, Aaron Drake	Aug 3, 1995	Knoxville, Tn	Knoxville, Tn	Oct 22, 1988	6		Unk		Husley, Stacie		Mother - Hodge, Roger [Step-Father] - Lowsley, Jerry & Arnetta - Husley, Ed-Brenda-Pearl [Grandparents]	Oak Grove				Hodge, Jared	Hodge, Sarah
Husley, Elmer C.	Jul 15, 1973	VA - Mt Home	Tn	Mar 25, 1900	73	Combs, Velma	Husley, Noah	Tn	Mc Neece, Minnie	Alabama	Husley, Velma - V.A.	West View	WW 1				
Husley, Isic L.	Oct 19, 1981	Jeff City	Tn	Apr 1, 1925	6	S	Husley, Isic L.		Clifton, Ann		Husley, Isic L.	Weides Creek					
Husley, Katherine	Jun 8, 1979	Greeneville, Tn	Tn	May 29, 1919	60	S	Husley, William		Brdson, Ada		Husley, Mrs. Daisy	Waldens Creek - Sevier Co					
Husted, Marjorie Alvina	Nov 25, 1987	Jeff City	Wis.	Oct 24, 1928	59	W	Christopherson, William		Stenburg, Clara		Husted, Perry A.	J.M.G.					
Husted, Philip Emory	Dec 25, 1985	J.M.H.	Wisconsin	Jan 26, 1923	62	W	Husted, Martin		Hansen, Anna		Husted, Mrs. Marjorie A.	Everlasting Life - J.M.G.	WW 2				
Husted, Dorothy Sue	Apr 18, 1983	Jeff City	Tn	Oct 10, 1913	79	Husted, Ralph W.	Harris, Kate		Harris, Kate		Hubbard	J.M.G.		Jimmy E.		Hubert-James	
Hustell, James Dennis	Jun 5, 1987	Jeff Co	Tn	Jul 7, 1918	68	Ng	Hustell, Lee		Lockhart, Ethel		Hustell, Ruth Kenley	J.M.G.	WW 2				
Hustell, Lee Roy	Sep 30, 1949	Jeff Co / Blount Co	Tn	Dec 5, 1892	56	Ng	Hustell, Jeff		Carpenter, Martha		Hustell, Mrs. Lee	Lebanon					
Hustell, Paul Leroy	Apr 18, 1986	J.M.H.	Tn	Aug 7, 1923	62	Pary, Bonnie	Hustell, Leroy		Lockhart, Sarah E.		Hustell, Mrs. Bonnie R.	Lebanon - Mt. Horeb	WW 2				
Hustell, Ralph Waldo	Jun 19, 1996	Jeff City	Mc Minn Co, Tn	Dec 8, 1911	86		Hustell, Eugene		Sharr, Belle		Shannon, Anita G. [Grand-Daug]	J.M.G.		Jimmy E.	Smicker, Diana & Wayland		Hustell, Clyde - Hustell, Helen - Dobson, Frances
Hustell, Ray P.	Jul 23, 1993	Morristown, Tn	Tn	Oct 18, 1925	67		Hustell, Lee		Lockhart, Ethel		Hustell, Joe & Bertha [Son & mother]	J.M.G.		Jimmy E.	Jack-Earl		
Hustell, Sarah Ethel	Jul 30, 1979	Jeff City	Tn	Aug 19, 1983	85	W	Lockhart, Rankin		Mooreland, Sarah		Hustell, Jack	Lebanon					
Hutson, James Landon	Oct 19, 1989	Jeff City	Forrest Hill, Md	Mar 30, 1944	49	W	Hutson, Charles		Hanson, Doris		Cox, Karen L. [Daug]	William Walkers - Coopstown, Md	army	Jim	Husley, Christine	Larry	
Hutton, Carl Kendrick	Oct 30, 1980	Jeff City	Va	Dec 9, 1909	70	Ng	Hutton, Thomas C.	Ky	Beousci, Maori		Hutton, Mrs Agnes S.	West View	WW 2				Mc Elwain, Linda
Hutton, Maori Boisseau	Jan 2, 1980	Jeff City	Frankfort, Ky	Jan 30, 1891	68	Ng	Boisseau, Leo	Ky			Hutton, C.K. - Hicks, Mrs. L.R.	J.M.G.					
Hutton, Mary Elizabeth	Aug 29, 1995	Jeff Co	Ga	Jan 27, 1919	16	S	Hutton, Dr. T.C. [II]		Bicklidan, Maori	Ky	Hutton, T.C.	West View					
Hutton, Thomas Carlyle	Jun 29, 1947	Honaker, Va		Jan 28, 1883	64	B., Maori	Hutton, Alson	Wachington, Va	Kendrick, Margaret	Honaker, Va	Hutton, Carl K.	West View		Robert & Jewell			
Hux, Cleda Mae	May 3, 1967	Hamblen Co	Tn	Mun 15, 1883	65	Ng	Hux, Alexander		Hammonds, Sophia		Howard, Jeanne & Wesley [Daug]	East View Memorial - Knox Co				Horner, Hattie	
Hux, Robert Lee	May 3, 1949	Hamblen Co	Tn	Aug 2, 1910	65	Ng	Hux, Robert Lee		Workman, Sallie		Hux, Mrs. Roy E.	Pleasant View					
Hux, Roy Elmer	Sep 1, 1980	Knoxville, Tn	Tn	Feb 9, 1916	70	Bates, Cabella / Chambers, Jeanette	Hux, Robert Lee		Suttie, Della M.		Hux, Mrs. Matie / English, Lura [Marshall, Nd] - Hylemon, Mrs. J.M	E. Highland Memorial - Ben-A-Venture - Haywood Co, Nc					
Hyatt, Charles Russell	Jun 30, 1984	Jeff City	Heywood Co, Nc	Feb 9, 1916	78	Hyatt, Edna	Hyatt, James R.				Hyatt, Douglas [Son] - Suttle, Mrs. Jettie - Greenwood, Sd]	Haywood Co, Nc					
Hylemon, Edith Rhea	Jun 28, 1953	Ky	Tn	Jun 19, 1931	22	S	Hylemon, James		Wilson, Charlotte		White Pine	White Pine					
Hyles, Jeanette	Jun 7, 1989	J.M.H.	Winfield, La	Jun 7, 1943	46	Div	Jolly, Henry S. Sr.		Johnston, Gladys		Gulcoar F.H.] Jerseyville, Ill.]						
Hylewer, Ethel	Nov 3, 1976	Morristown, Tn	Tn	Jun 29, 1894	82	W	Huff, Henry		Lacy, Amanda		Swann, Calvin	Lebanon					
Idol, Laura Mae	Nov 22, 1966	Jeff City	Tn	Feb 14, 1889	77	W	Jackson, Peter		Frazier, Laverna		Idol, William S.	Kitts - Grainger Co					
Idsins, James Franklin	May 1, 1985	J.M.H.	Tn	May 22, 1911	73	Holt, Edna	Idsins, Joseph Franklin		Chandler, Lucy		Idol, Edna H.	West View					
Idsins, Lucy	Jan 4, 1989	Knox Co	Tn	Dec 21, 1878	90	W	Chandler, Richard		Taylor, Amanda M.		Magnolia - Maryville, Tn	Magnolia - Maryville, Tn					
Idsins, Mary Sizer	May 25, 1974	Hallmark Home	Tn	Jan 29, 1907	67	W	Mooer, John		Sizer, Helen		Idsins, James F.	West View					
Idsins, Mildred Lucille	Mar 24, 1988	Jeff City	Tn	Sep 14, 1915	72	S	Idsins, Joseph Franklin		Chandler, Lucy		Idsins, Mae	Magnolia - Maryville, Tn	WW 2		[G] Drinnon, Anita Gail		
Idsins, Susie Mae	Mar 19, 1989	Knoxville, Tn	Knoxville, Tn	May 5, 1905	83	S	Idsins, Joseph Franklin		Chandler, Lucy		Jolley, Helen L.	Magnolia - Maryville, Tn					

NAME	DDATE	BLOCAT	BLOCAT	DDATE	AGE	SPOUSE	FATHER	FELOCAT	MOTHER	MFELOCAT	BY	BURIAL	VET	SON	DAUG	BROTHER	SISTER
Ingram, Anna Clifford [Col]	Apr 11, 1965	Jeff Co					Harris, Pryor		Donaldson, Josephine		Wife	West View Colored					
Ingram, Benjamin Kenneth	Dec 25, 1957	Jeff City	Marianna, Fl	Oct 18, 1946	51	Mc Donald, Kathy	Ingram, John William		Lee, Lula Flora		Cremated			Stone, Benjamin K.- William G. [Step] Lee, Thomas A.	[Step] Meyers, Dana		
Ingram, Floyd Young	Mar 15, 1973	Jeff Co	Tn	Apr 16, 1889	84	Wukens, Lucy	Ingram, John		Livesey, Mrs. Kermit [Daug]		Wife	Mt. Pleasant					
Ingram, Hardon Arthur	Sep 28, 1972	Talbott, Tn	Tn	Jun 6, 1895	77	Ng	Ingram, Bud		Ingram, Mrs. H.A.		Wife	Community Chapel					
Ingram, Hessie Cornelia	Aug 8, 1985	Morristown, Tn	Tn	Feb 5, 1902	83	Ingram, Hardin [b]		Moore, Mollie		Knowling, Mrs. Hazel	Community Chapel					
Ingram, Howard Roy	Apr 9, 2000	Jeff City	Tn	Apr 6, 1916	84	Ely, Edith Franklin	Ingram, James Locke		Jennie		Wife						
Ingram, James Louie [White]	May 17, 1948	Jeff Co	Hamblen Co	Oct 23, 1881	66-6-14		Ingram, James	Tn			Ingram, Mrs. Jennie-Howard	Colored					
Ingram, James Robert	Nov 28, 1983	V.A. Resp.	Tn	Jun 3, 1924	59	Ng	Ingram, Hardin		Collett, Cornelia		Ingram, Mrs. Gladys L.	Community Chapel	WW 2				
Ingram, Jennie	Jan 1, 1874	Jeff Co	New York	Apr 18, 1885	88	W	Husband, Joseph				Ingram, Howard & Sisters	West View					
Ingram, Nannie Lucretia	Oct 29, 1979	Jeff City	Tn	Jan 19, 1897	82	W	Walkitis, Isaac		Carter, Nannie		Livesey, Kermit	Mt. Pleasant					
Ingram, Roy [Col]	Feb 26, 1927	Jeff Co	Tn		44-3-25	Ng	Ingram, James L.	Nc	Ingram, Anna	Tn	Ingram, Anna	Colored					
Ingram, Sylvia [Col]	Jan 23, 1959	Tn	Greene Co, Tn	Nov 19, 1877	81	S	Ingram, James R.		West Lucy		West View Colored						
Ingram, Tommy Lee	May 30, 1980	Knox Co	Tn	May 25, 1980	5d		Ingram, Johnny		Walker, Barbra		Ingram, Johnny	Hills Union					
Ingram, William C.	Oct 28, 1997	Jeff City	Jeff Co	Dec 5, 1926	70	W	Ingram, Greed		Genoe, Kate		New Blackwell Branch-Grainger Co						
Heidberger, Carrie Mc Nah	May 1, 1973	Knoxville, Tn	Tn	Apr 16, 1899	74	W	Mc Nah, James		Robertson, Betty [Daug]		Robinson, Ruby	Pleasant Grove					
Innes, Andrew John Jr.	Apr 15, 1973	Detroit, Mich.	Tn	Apr 15, 1928	69	W	Innes, Andrew J. Sr.		Wraugh, Angelsin		Wife	Cremated	navy				
Ireland, James Floyd	Jan 4, 1984	Jeff City	Birmingham, Ala.	Jul 28, 1895	88	Ashworth, Willis	Ireland, John H.		Toers, Ann		Elmwood -Birmingham, Ala.						
Irving, Donald Louis	Dec 4, 1972	Maryland	Jllard	Dec 6, 1926	45	Ng	Erving, William O.		Gray, Julia M.		Erving, Donald [dad] Mc Crman, Howell K. [bd]	Colesburg Memorial -Abington, Md	WW 2	Larry & Phillip- Jerry Rae [D]	Stoney, June & Howard		
Isley, Flossie Mae	Nov 19, 1978	Lake Shore M.H.	Tn	Apr 2, 1916	62	Ng	Rinhehart, Molly				New Blackwell Branch-Puckett, Linda	Mc Bee, Kathleen-Puckett, Linda [Md]					
Israf, Rachel	Apr 27, 1929	Nc			18		Unk	Nc		Nc	Israf, C.O.	Grant Chapel					
Issler, Bessie R.	May 6, 1992	Bradford Co, Pa	Oct 6, 1918	73	W	Marshall, George E.		Birisk, Coral E.		Robinson, Verna	National - Phoenix, Az	45-46					
Ivee, Alice Dunbar	Mar 1, 1929	Maine			72	W	Dunbar, E.R.	Maine	Spencer, Sallie	Nc	Israf, C.O.	No					
Ivey, Infant	Jan 23, 1957	Jeff Co					Ivey, Steve Arnold		Frye, Sharon Ann Lee	Tn	Ivey, Steve	Liberty Hill - Grainger					
Ivy, Gene Ebert	Apr 17, 1956	Tn		Oct 2, 1935	20	Ng	Ivy, Mingus J.		Linkous, Mary Lou		Ivy, M.J.	No					
Jackson, Claude Hayes	Aug 17, 1998	Granger Co. Indianapolis, In	May 5, 1919	79	W	Jackson, Benjamin		Jimmey, Melba		Sunderland	Sunderland	korea					
Jackson, Thurman Salter Jr.	Apr 3, 1996	Indianapolis, In	Feb 16, 1946	50	Brewer, Carolyn	Jackson, T.S. Sr.		Lewis, Myrtle		Wife	J.M.G.	64-67	Gary	Delons, Shannon Young, Myrtle [Mau.] Stewart, Karen [Flu.]	Coffey, Ole	Kathy-Jean-Patsy
Jacobs, Elaine Ann	Dec 31, 1996	Jeff City			Feb 12, 1949	49				Karpas, Irene		Mother - Rees F.H. [Hobart, In]					
James, Jessie Earl	Oct 20, 1950	Jeff Co	Tn	Mar 31, 1941	19	S	Franklin, James		Finchum, Dorothy		Lowe, Dorothy - Lame, Wm. [Hobart, In]	Jefferson Memorial					
James, Bascomb	Aug 17, 1955	Tn	Tn	Sep 7, 1951	83	W	James, Collin		Brek, Nancy		James, Mrs. Kenneth James, Lee C.	Piney					
James, Charles C.	Jan 5, 1987	Hawkins Co, Tn	Jan 8, 1880	69	Ng	James, Stansull	Tn	Reid, Lizzie	Tn	James, Mrs. Robert [Nei]	Sunderland					
James, Helen Ann Bennett	Jan 5, 1987	Jeff Co	Jul 25, 1911	James, Robert V.	Bennett, W.E.		Hollingsworth, Edith		Musick, Mrs. Larry	J.M.G.						
James, Infant	Aug 30, 1942	Jeff Co		Aug 30, 1942	75		James, John	Tn	Spencer, Sue Ellis	Tn	James, John	Nance's Grove					
James, Katherine	Jul 18, 1934	Jeff City		Mar 21, 1933	1-3-15		James, F.N.	Va	James, Lillie	Va	James, F.M.	Lebanon					

NAME	DDATE	DLOCAT	BLOCAT	BDATE	AGE	SPOUSE	FATHER	FBLOCAT	MOTHER	MFBLOCAT	BY	BURIAL	VET	SON	DAUG	BROTHER	SISTER
James, Lee Calvin	Nov 18, 1957	Knox Co.	Tn	Apr 21, 1897	60	Wilson, Lola	James, Bascomb		Nichols, Elizabeth		James, Lola - Acuff, V.I - Vinyard, Halliwell	Pleasant Grove	WW 1				
James, Lina E.	Mar 5, 1926		Va		79-3-5	W	Harris, Rebeca	Va	Harris, Rebeca	Ky	James, J.E. & Frank	Shilo					
James, Nellie	Feb 2, 1984	Jeff Co	Tn	Mar 7, 1890	83	James, Charles [D]	Duncan, James		Betts, Martha		James, Mrs. Robert V. & Nell	Sunderland					
James, Robert Thomas	Dec 21, 1958	Jeff Co	Tn	Mar 19, 1882	76	W	James, Samuel		Reed, Elizabeth		James, Mrs. Robert	Sunderland					
James, Robert V.	Jul 22, 2000	Jeff Co	Tn	Jun 19, 1908	92	W	James, Robert Taylor		Duncan, Velley Eva [Daug]		Masick, Mary Evelyn [Daug]	J.M.G.	unk				
James, Sarah Adalade	Nov 4, 1958	Jeff Co	Tn	Sep 9, 187-	81	S	James, Sam		Reed, Elizabeth		James, R.V.	Sunderland					
James, Shelby Jean	Aug 10, 1995	Talbott, Tn	Cooke Co. Tn	Jun 18, 1954	41	James, Mark	Holt, Cloyd		Cureton, Doris		Husband	Reedhaven - Newport, Tn		[Step] James, Justin-Steven		Holt, Billy & Carlotta	Holt, Janice - Caldwell, Joyce & Denny
James, Virginia Lou	Dec 28, 1958	Jeff Co	Tn	Jan 27, 1879	77	W	Cockrum, David		Cockrum, Virginia		Husband	Sunderland					
James, Walter E.	Jan 20, 1972	Jeff Co	Tn	Jun 2, 1911	60	Jones, Laverne Fanly	James, Jim		Cockrum, Virginia		James, Laverne [W]	Sunderland	unk				
James, William Frank	Mar 2, 1973	Jeff Co	Tn	Jun 21, 1916	54	Div	James, Jim		Cockrum, Virginia		Sunderland	Sunderland	WW 2				
Jamison, Houston Lynn	Feb 14, 1995	Jeff City	Cash, Arkansas	May 3, 1920	74		Jamison, Hubert Lesley		Mc Alister, Emma		Lane, Faye J. [Sister] - Emerson F.H. [Jonesboro, Arkansas]	Oaktown					
Janeway, Nancy Emily	Sep 28, 1944	Jeff Co	Tn	Mar 19, 1855	89	S	Janeway, Benjamin	Tn	Talley, Katherine	Tn	Watson, J.D. - Janeway, James Benjamin	Strawberry Plains					
Jarnigan, Bessie Louise	Aug 25, 1997	Jeff City	Tn	Oct 6, 1909	87		Kelley, Walter		Martin, Mollie		Moody, Gerald [Son]	J.M.G.					
Jarnigan, Edgar Grover Cleveland	May 14, 1956	Jeff Co	Tn	Nov 25, 1891	72-11-4	Ng	Berthel, Thena	Tn	Wall, Mrs. Guy	Tn	Wall, Mrs. Guy	West View					
Jarnigan, Eliza	May 3, 1982	Jeff City	Tn	Nov 25, 1891	90	W	Lindy, John		Jarnigan, Roy		Jarnigan, Roy	West View					
Jarnigan, Frank W.	Nov 18, 1968	Jeff Co	Tn	Oct 14, 1879	89	Ng	Jarnigan, Milton P. Sr.		Watkins, Agnes V.		Jarnigan, Mrs. Frank Sr.	West View					
Jarnigan, Helen Faye (Black)	Oct 4, 1993	Jeff City	Tn	Jan 9, 1932	61	W	Lauderback, Dana		Donaldson, Wilma		Peck, Marsha [Daug]	West View	Marvin-Milford	Goodson, Michele		Johnson, Justine - Simmons, Charlotte
Jarnigan, Howard	Feb 25, 1975	U.T. Hospital	Tn	Apr 18, 1910	64	Kelley, Bessie	Hux, Walter		Jarnigan, Martha		Jarnigan, Mrs. Bessie	Jefferson Memorial					
Jarnigan, Howard L.	Jul 6, 2000	Rutledge, Tn	Tn	Sep 19, 1913	86	W	Jarnigan, Jerry Nelson		James, Tina		Boling, Nancy [Daug]	West View					
Jarnigan, Jamie Harold	Jan 6, 1998	Jeff City	Rogersville, Tn	Aug 16, 1979	18		Jarnigan, Johnny		Hannah, Penny Lee		Mother - Crittenden, Bert & Eris - Hannah, Nancy [G-Parents] - Hannah, Clifford C. [Step-Father] - Roach, Mrs. Dedrick [Sister]	Bidens Chapel - Greene Co, Tn				Jarnigan, Chris - Hannah, Herman-Scott	Jarnigan, Shannon - Bell, Hope
Jarnigan, Katherine Elizabeth	Dec 12, 1941	Jeff City	Granger Co			W			Noe, Sarah	Granger Co							
Jarnigan, Lillie	May 25, 1983	J.M.H.	Tn	Feb 10, 1889	86	W	Phillips, Reba		Carter, Mary		Wife	West View					
Jarnigan, Lloyd E.	Apr 26, 1996	Jeff City	Jeff Co	Nov 5, 1909	86	W	Jarnigan, Edward		Collier, Lillie		Wife	J.M.G.			Pega A.		Dixon-Raymond-Tom-Dick
Jarnigan, Marion [F]	Mar 26, 1998	Knoxville, Tn	Tn	Jun 16, 1962	85	W	Franklin, James		Hux, Betsy		Jarnigan, James H.	Lebanon Baptist					Weil, Fannie - Litz, Daisy - Hodges, Dean - Kitts, Carol
Jarnigan, Mary	Aug 26, 1987	Nashville, Tn	Virginia	Dec 9, 1896	100	W	Mc Pheeters, William		Morrison, Emma G.		Bradley, Mary & Chigwel	West View					
Jarnigan, Mrs. Jerry	Jan 19, 1941	Granger Co	Granger Co			W			Hargrove ?, Mary	Granger Co	Jarnigan, Jerry						
Jarnigan, Mrs. Kate	Dec 30, 1924		Tn [D. Knoxville]		73	Jarnigan, J.S.	Howard ?, H.H.	Mrs.			Nott, Mrs. Ebel J.	Jefferson City					

NAME	DDATE	DLOCAT	BLOCAT	BDATE	AGE	SPOUSE	FATHER	FBELOCAT	MOTHER	MFBLOCAT	BURIAL	BY	VET	SON	DAUG	BROTHER	SISTER
Jarnigan, Myrtle A.	Sep 13, 1994	Morristown, Tn	Tn	Jun 2, 1906	88		Chuck, Richard		Richard, Fiona		Cross, Billie A. - Greene, Naomi - Hutton, Agnes - Scott, Ruth (Nieces) - Surprise, Harold (Nephew)	Buffalo Grove Church					
Jarnigan, Nannie	Nov 21, 1961	Hamblen Co.	Tn	May 29, 1915	46	Jarnigan, Robert	Clevenger, Minnie		Jarnigan, Robert - Jarnigan, Harold - Fannie-Deleny		Jefferson Memorial					
Jarnigan, Ola Grace	Jan 4, 1955	Jeff City	Tn	Jan 24, 1932	22	Nig	Tittle, Cecil		Roach, Thelma		Jarnigan, Harold - Fannie-Deleny	Lar - Jeff Co.					
Jarnigan, Oral [Dick]	Aug 16, 1992	Jeff Co	Tn	Sep 25, 1919	72	Campbell, Blanche	Jarnigan, Edd		Collier, Lillie		Wife	J.M.G.					
Jarnigan, Robert William	May 25, 1996	J.M.H.	Tn	Mar 22, 1916	68	Mc Daniel, Edna	Jarnigan, Lee		Church, Claudia		Jarnigan, Mrs. Erna - Meyers, Sam	Everlasting Life - J.M.G.					
Jarnigan, Roy	Jul 25, 1956	New Market	Tn	Jan 26, 1882	64	Div	Jarnigan, Joe		Lacy, Eliza		Lebanon	Lebanon					
Jarnigan, William Robert	May 21, 1970	Knox Co	Tn	Mar 3, 1908	68	Nig	Jarnigan, Sam		Burchfiel, Carrie		Lebanon - Greestahn	Lebanon - Greestahn					
Jarnigan, William Mc Phesters Sr.	Dec 22, 1990	Plainfield, NJ	Jul 4, 1923	67		Donnelly, Margaret	Jarnigan, Frank W.		Mc Phesters, Mary		Jarnigan, Margaret D.	West View					
Jarnigan, William Raymond [M]	Nov 13, 1978	Knoxville, Tn	Tn	Dec 15, 1907	68	Forrester, Allce	Jarnigan, Edd		Collier, Lillie		Jarnigan, Mrs. Allce - Jaynes, William & Mrs.	Jefferson Memorial					
Jaynes, Cleo Duncan [M]	Aug 10, 1982	Jeff Co	Tn	Mar 4, 1923	59	Nig	Jaynes, Paul T.		Williams, Anna Lee		Jenkins, Gerald - F.H.	Jefferson Memorial					
Jenkins, Edna Martha	Jul 13, 1988	F.S.H.	Ohio	May 15, 1901	87	W	Bickel, Joseph		Heenes, -		Ridge Hill Memorial - Loraine, Oh	J.M.G.					
Jenkins, Gerald Martin	Sep 14, 1984	Lorain, Ohio	Tn	Apr 19, 1930	54	Martin, Donna	Jenkins, Lewis D.		Bickel, Edna		Wife	J.M.G.					
Jenkins, Zula	Jan 5, 1931	Tabost, Tn	Tn	Aug 1, 1867	33	Nig	Gray, J.F.	Tn	Underwood, Martha	Tn	Wife	Blackwell Branch					
Jennings, Edward B.	Jul 26, 1968	Jeff Co	Wisconsin	Oct 17, 1896	71	Griffith, Virginia	Jennings, Edward Payson		Fitzgerald, Ida		Jennings, Virginia	Memorial Gardens	WW 1				
Jennings, Hazelle	Feb 16, 1966	Grainger Co	Mar 12, 1910	55		W	Hamilton, Daniel Scott		Blanc, Cornelia		West View	West View		William W.		Daniel Scott [Vel]	
Jennings, Ida Fitzgerald	Oct 16, 1963	New York	Lake Pt., Utah	Aug 7, 1963	91-2-7?	W	Jennings, Charles		Hall, Mary		Blanc, Sylvia [Daug]	Memorial Gardens					
Jennings, Virginia	Jan 13, 1997	Jeff Co	Lake Pt., Utah	Mar 12, 1907	69	Hamilton, Hazelle	Griffin, Charles		Jennings, Edward & Linda [Son]		Jennings, Edward & Linda [Son]	J.M.G.			Howard, Joan & Tom	Burnestor, Maureen [Ut]
Jennings, William Wesley	Dec 2, 1989	Jeff Co	Tn	Oct 24, 1911	78	Hamilton, Hazelle	Jennings, Jacob M.		Enoch, Martha E.		Jennings, Hazelle	West View	WW 2				
Jessee, James Atkins	Jul 26, 1959	Jeff Co	Tn	Sep 7, 1882	76	Loop, Martie	Jessee, John D.		Kelley, Louisa		Jessee, Mrs. Martie - Finchum, Mrs. Stan	Beaver Creek					
Jessee, Martha	Apr 7, 1987	Jeff Co	W		72	W	Loop, Bellard		Ousley, Verda Jane		Finchum, Sam	Beaver Creek					
Jett, Alma Pauline	Jun 6, 1988	Jeff City	Tn	Apr 12, 1917	71	Jett, Willey C.	Fines, Walter		Swann, Florence		Jett Willey C.	West View					
Jett, Carl L.	Jun 7, 1990	Jeff Co	W	Apr 12, 1910	79	Underwood, Leora	Jett, Horace		Hall, Mary		Loveday, Wilma - Jett, Lenora	West View	WW 2				
Jett, Charles H.	Jan 18, 1996	Jeff City	Jeff Co	Dec 21, 1928	69	Smith, Bobbie	Jett, Harvey A.		Mc Murray, Cora M.		Wife	J.M.G.		Devin	Kennel, Brenda	Austin, Janie - Handley, Agnes
Jett, Grace	Jan 8, 1992	J.M.H.	Jeff Co	Oct 5, 1995	86	W	Colley, Holiday		Ramsey, Cora		Wife	J.M.G.					
Jett, Harvey A.	Nov 24, 1996	Jeff City	Va	Oct 1, 1900	66	Colley, Grace	Jett, Charlie		Barbon, Martha Ellen		Austin, Janie [Daug]	Mt. View					
Jett, James	Dec 24, 1996	Camden, Tn	Jeff City	Aug 7, 1956	42	Garren, Evonne	Jett, James Mayford		Paschall, Margaret		Jett, Charles Jr.	Mt. View					
Jett, Nannie	Feb 2, 1971	Jeff Co	Tn	Apr 9, 1903	67	W	Colley, Holiday		Ramsey, Cora		Wife	Memorial Gardens					
Jett, John J.	Feb 2, 1972	Jeff Co	Tn	Oct 7, 1896	69	W	Jett, Charlie		Barbon, Ellen		Stapleton, Lula - Mayford	Memorial Gardens					
Johnson, Albert Sidney	Jan 16, 1966	Ga.	Ga.	Aug 30, 1900	30	Nig	Johnson, William K.	Ala.	Lyle, Fannie	Ga.	Jett, John	West View	WW 1				
Johnson, Annie Belle	May 25, 1931	Knox Co.	Ga.	Jan 1, 1916	75	S	Johnson, W.K.		Lyle, Fannie		Johnson, Mrs. Mitchel	West View					
Johnson, Beulah Blanche [Robbie]	Jul 12, 1991	J.M.H.	Birmingham, Ala.	Jan 3, 1916	75	W	Johnson, Collen J.		Minor, Beulah Caroline		Johnson, Roy Daniel Jr. [Son]	J.M.G.					
Johnson, Blanche	Jul 29, 1998	Jeff City	Grainger Co., Tn	Dec 5, 1914	83		Glass, John A.		Owens, Della		Moore, Tommy [Nephew] - Scott, Gaye Shawn, Rebecca [Niece]	West View			Kennel, Brenda		[In-Law] Glass, Martha
Johnson, Cordie	Dec 22, 1933	Dandridge	Tn	Feb 8, 1864	69	W	Black, Jim		Brandon, Nancy		Sons - Hines, Elmer - Haynes, Mrs. Anna - Johnson, Oscar	Deep Springs					
Johnson, Dora	Nov 16, 1931	Peadmont	Tn	Jun 8, 1890	31		Murphy, M.		Davis, Carwithia	Nc	Johnson, J.H.	Deep Springs					
Johnson, Elbert Jay	Dec 26, 1985	Knoxville, Tn	Tn	Sep 26, 1927	58	Turner, Ethel	Johnson, George O.	Tn	Swatts, Ida	No	Johnson, Mrs. Ethel T.	French Broad - Dandridge	WW 2				

NAME	DDATE	DLOCAT	BLOCAT	BDATE	AGE	SPOUSE	FATHER	FBLOCAT	MOTHER	MFBLOCAT	BY	BURIAL	VET	SON	DAUG	BROTHER	SISTER
Johnson, Eliza Jane	Jan 25, 1993	Jeff Co	Jeff Co		93	Coleman, Gus Taylor	Francis, Martha Jane		Quarles, Dorothy J. [Daisy]		Chestnut Hill			[G] Quarles, Larry-Gary-Mark-Rodney	[G] Craig, Brenda		
Johnson, Elmer Lee	Aug 10, 1997	Knoxville, Tn	Hancock Co, Tn	Feb 14, 1946	51	Mc Anally, Barbara	Johnson, Ralph		Kinsler, Myrtle		Wife	J.M.G.		Jerry	Hall, Jodi - Johnson, Leanne	Eddie-Gary	
Johnson, Elnora [Coll]	Feb 10, 1950	Jeff Co	Cocke Co	Jun 4, 1882		Ng	Williss, T.		Davis, Ellen		Carter, Carrie E. - Johnson, Sam [Husband]	New Market					
Johnson, Emma Lena	Oct 15, 1985	New Market, Tn	Tn	Aug 3, 1896	89	W	Jett, Texanna		Jett, Texanna		Gordon, Faye	Piedmont					
Johnson, Everett J.	Aug 17, 1975	Jeff Co	Indiana	May 3, 1917	58	Div.	Johnson, J.C.		Merick, Anna		Johnson, Ronnie	West View					
Johnson, George H.	Dec 8, 1966	Jeff Co	Tn	Feb 9, 1884	82	Ng	Johnson, Thomas		Lyle, Fannie		Johnson, Mrs. Tilda -	Memorial					
Johnson, Hattie Gaby	Mar 1, 1982	Tn	Tn	Sep 12, 1883	98	W	Gaby, John Need		Morrison, Polly Ann		Johnson, Blanche G.	West View					
Johnson, Joe E. Jr.	Apr -, 1980	Hohenwald, Tn	Greenville, Tn	Nov 12, 1915/18	44-5-9	Ng	Mc Lain, Hattie		Mc Lain, Hattie		Johnson, Mrs. Joe	West View	WW 2				
Johnson, John Emil	Jun 2, 1958	Finland		Jun 6, 1877	80	Ng	Johnson, John Abel		Gustoffson, Amanda		Johnson, Mrs. J.E. - Melton, Mrs. Quentin, Mrs. Ray Husband	West View	WW 2				
Johnson, Justine L. [Black]	Sep 21, 1995	Jeff Co	Jeff Co	May 5, 1925	70	W	Lauterbach, Daniel		Donaldson, Wilma			J.M.G.		Eugene Jr.	Phipps, Beverly		
Johnson, Leonard C.	Apr 19, 1990	J.M.H. [Res Pal]	New Jersey	May 8, 1910	79	W	Unk		Unk			Cremated					
Johnson, Letha B.	Oct 26, 1996	Jeff Co	New York	Nov 3, 1899	76	Johnson, Maurice	Green, William		Madison, Sallie		Townsley, Charles [Oklahoma City, Ok] Pardue, Mrs. Gene	Memorial Gardens					
Johnson, Mack W.	Oct 12, 1971	Jeff Co	Tn	Oct 6, 1894	77	Johnson, Maurice	Dance, Lena		Johnson, James		Johnson, Lena	Piedmont	WW 1				
Johnson, Matilda E.	Jul 1, 1972	Jeff Co	Tn	Apr 15, 1886	86	Johnson, George [D]	Purkey, George N.		Green, Nancy C.		Miller, Mrs. Leon	Jefferson Memorial					
Johnson, Maude Zella	Apr 28, 1981	Tn	Tn	Mar 14, 1894	87	W	Webb, Harve		Brooks, Sidney		Harner, Adam & J.K.	West View					
Johnson, Maurice V.	Aug 14, 1972	Knox Co			85-2 16	W	Johnson, Edward		Sprague, Mary H.		Pardue, Marie & Gene	Jefferson Memorial					
Johnson, Morgan Nichols	Mar 14, 1977	Tn	Tn	Dec 1, 1906	70	Bryant, Evelyn	Johnson, Bedford		Boyd, Otis		Johnson, Evelyn	Jefferson Memorial					
Johnson, Oscar Andrew	Apr 21, 1999	Jeff City	Mt. City, Tn	Jul 21, 1916	82	Conner, Pauline			Johnson, Mrs. Wife			J.M.G.					
Johnson, Robert Elton Sr.	Feb 4, 1983	Jeff City	Alabama	Aug 26, 1903	79	Jackson, Elizabeth	Johnson, Eagle		Nance, Etta		Johnson, Mrs. Elizabeth Jackson	U.T. Medical					
Johnson, Ray Daniel Sr.	Dec 19, 1990	Knoxville, Tn	Indiana	Aug 27, 1910	70	Johnson, Beulah Blanche	Johnson, J.E.		Merrick, Anna		Johnson, Mrs. Ray Sr.	Jefferson Memorial					
Johnson, Roy E.	Dec 18, 1961	Knox Co	Tn	Sep 12, 1910	51	S	Jernigan, Thenia		Green, Nancy C.		Goss, William & Helen Lona	National - Knox Co	WW 2				
Johnson, Sam Wilbert	Jan 27, 1987	S.M.H.	Tn	Sep 27, 1930	56	Div.	Williss, Elnora		Merrick, Anna		Johnson, Elizabeth - Bryant, Nora J.	West View					
Johnson, Samuel Franklin [Coll]	Jan 27, 1965	Jeff Co	Va.	Sep 4, 1886	93	W	Jackson, Elizabeth		Patin, Amanda		Johnson, Onella & Jaunita	Zion - Jeff Co					
Johnson, Samuel Paris	Oct 21, 1979	Care Inn - Jeff City, Tn	Va.		93	W	Johnson, Goldie Ethel		Speers, Lillie		Dickerson, Lucille - Lebanon F.H. - Lebanon, Ga]	Sabras Chapel - Castlewood, Va					
Johnson, Thuria	Apr 1, 1941	Knoxville		Sep 4, 1896	59	Johnson, W.F.			Lacey, Eliza	Granger Co	Johnson, W.F.	Lebanon					
Johnson, Wanda [Black]	Jan 7, 1993	Kansas City, Kansas	Granger Co	Jan 12, 1934	58	Williamson, Bucket T.			Hayworth, Flora		Husband	J.M.G.		William Jr.- Michael-David	Jones, Adina - Boatright, Minnie - Talley, Frances	Donald-Robert	
Johnston, Dorothy	May 23, 1964	Mo		Dec 5, 1905	58	W	Dierling, William		Herbath, Treda		Homer, Mrs. Ray [Dorothy], Johnston, William - Homer, Bill & Rosemary	Queen City, Mo					
Jolley, Bernice Aileen	Oct 14, 1985	Jeff Co	Tn	Sep 26, 1908	77	Jolley, James A.	Burnett, T.C.		Carter, Myrtle		Jolley, James A.	Mt. Pleasant					
Jolley, Bertha	Oct 9, 1987	Knoxville, Tn	Tn	Jan 13, 1894	93	S	Jolley, J.A.		Collett, Martha		Mt. Pleasant - Talbott, Tn	Mt. Pleasant - Talbott, Tn					
Jolley, James A.	Jul 31, 1990	F.S.H.	Tn	Apr 30, 1906	84	W	Jolley, Joseph A.		Collette, Martha		Jolley, Dwayne	Mt. Pleasant					
Jolley, Joseph Abner	Jan 11, 1946	Jeff Co	Tn	Apr 10, 1865	80	W	Jolley, Bertha		Ricks, Mary	Tn	Jolley, Bertha	Mt. Pleasant - Jeff Co					
Jones, C.I.	Sep 13, 1953	Jeff Co	Carthage, Miss.	Oct 24, 1908	43	W	Jones, Bruce A.		Whitney, Elizabeth	Tn	Willis F.H. - Carthage, Miss.	Carthage, Miss.					
Jones, Danny Curtis	Jan 21, 1954	Jeff Co	Tn	Jan 19, 1954	2d	Ng	Jones, Curtis J.		Kerr, Mary Jean		Jones, C.I.	Piedmont					

NAME	DDATE	DLOCAT	BLOCAT	BDATE	AGE	SPOUSE	FATHER	FBLOCAT	MOTHER	MBRLOCAT	BY	BURIAL	VET	SON	DAUG	BROTHER	SISTER
Jones, Alvin Hawkins	Feb 25, 1954	Jeff Co	Tn	May 22, 1885	68	Ng	Jones, Zack		Link		Jones, Bobby Joe	Pleasant View					
Jones, Anice	Sept 17, 1993	Jeff City		57		Ng	Jones, Zack		Watts, Elizabeth	Tn	Jones, Mrs Anice	Shilo					
Jones, Anna	Jan 1, 1947	Cloresburg Va	Jeff Co	Apr 28, 1891	56-1-9	W	Glass, John	Tn	Rich, Anna	Tn	Jones, George	Shady Grove					
Jones, Betty Lou	May 2, 1943	Tn		May 21, 1929	13	S	Link		Rush, Georgia	Tn	Franklin, Mrs. C.T.	Shiloh - Grainger Co					
Jones, Buford	Feb 13, 1977	J.M.H.	Tn	Apr 25, 1909	67	S	Jones, Charlie E.		Lykes, Julia		Jones, Laura	West View					
Jones, Carrie Wilson	Jun 19, 1972	Jeff Co	Tn	Feb 22, 1912	60	Bettis, Bertha			Howard, Nancy E.	Tn	Bassett, Elizabeth & Buford	Memorial Gardens	WW 2				
Jones, Charles Edward [Col]	Feb 3, 1947	Knox Co	Va	Oct 7, 1965	81-3-26	Ng	Jones, Henry	Va	Lanue, Ellen	Tn	Jones, Mrs. Ida M.	Colored					
Jones, Charles Monroe	Oct 19, 1948		Va	Nov 28, 1870	77-10-21	Ng	Jones, Lee				Jones, Mrs. Ida M.	West View					
Jones, Curtis James	Oct 27, 1997	Knoxville, Tn	Jeff Co	Aug 3, 1927	70	Kerr, Jean	Jones, Hal C.	Tn	Frye, Leora	Tn	Wife	J.M.G.					
Jones, David	Mar 29, 1928		Hawkins Co. Tn	Oct 23, 1870	8d	Ng	Jones, James		Hicks, Martha	Tn	Horner, Mrs. Ella - Jones, Lou-Troy-D.J. Jr.	Sevier Co					
Jones, Dedrick Theodore	Jan 16, 1949	Jeff Co	New Market, Tn	Oct 23, 1870	88-2-23	Ng	Hayes, Harmon		Capo, Veda		Jones, Clint & Daug	Pleasant View					
Jones, Dora	Jul 10, 1973	New Market, Tn	Tn	May 15, 1899	84	Jones, Clint					Jones, Clint & Daug	Mill Springs					
Jones, Ellen [Col]	Jan 23, 1933	Jeff City	Tn	Jan 17, 1871	79	S	Jones, John C.				Jones, Charley Neubill, Mrs. Emily Jones						
Jones, Emily	Feb 27, 1950	Jeff Co	Tn	Jan 17, 1871	79	S	Jones, John C.				Brooks, Fannie - Jones	Jones					
Jones, Eula Florence	Nov 3, 1950	Jeff Co	Tn	Dec 14, 1911	48	W	Mc Campbell, Jessie		Bell, Rebecca A.		Brown, Fannie - Woolanbown	Woolanbown					
Jones, Eula Mae	Nov 20, 1981	Jeff Co	Tn	Nov 14, 1913	48	Jones, Bill	Brown, Bill		Lunsford, Hattie		Brown, Mary - Jones, W.H. [Bill] - Allison, Mrs. Charlie	Mt. View					
Jones, George Eugene	Feb 15, 1941	Jeff City	Tn		8-5-20	S	Jones, George		Hill, Louise	Jeff Co	Jones, George	Shady Grove					
Jones, Henry Lee	Jun 5, 1961	Jeff Co	Tn	Jan 27, 1876	85	W	Jones, Calloway		Jones, Artie		Ramlree, Pink & Opal Jones, Mrs. Mary	Mill Springs					
Jones, Herman A.	Aug 9, 1963	Jeff Co	Tn	Oct 3, 1898	64	Ng	Jones, Adam		Van Dyke, Ida		Jones, Mrs. Ben - Cannon, Mrs. Ben - Lyon, Mrs. J.W. - Glenn, Mary T. -	Hillcrest					
Jones, Ida	Aug 21, 1946	Knox Co	Tn	Nov 23, 1873	72	W	Carpenter, Elias A.	Tn	Reed, Sarah	Tn	West View	West View					
Jones, Ida M.	Oct 16, 1965	Jeff Co	Tn	Dec 11, 1896	69	W			Finchum, Laura P.		Hill, Fina B.	West View					
Jones, Infant Daug	Feb 15, 1942	Piedmont	Tn	Jan 13, 1942			Jones, Jake	Tn	Lee, Fannis		Jones, Jake	Piedmont					
Jones, Infant Female	Feb 20, 1949	Jeff Co	Jeff Co	Feb 20, 1949			Jones, Jack	Sevier Co	Anderson, Patricia	Knox Co	Jones, Jack	Wofford					
Jones, Infant Female	Aug 26, 1949	Jeff Co		Aug 26, 1949			Jones, William V.	Tn	Esslinger, Edna	Tn	New Market	New Market					
Jones, J.P.	Nov 26, 1932	Jeff City	Tn	Jan 11, 1872	69	Ng	Jones, Sam	England	Witt, Adine	Tn	Jones, Mrs. J.P.	West View					
Jones, John Wresley	Aug 9, 1925		Tn		70	S	Link	England		England	Franklin, S.H.	Cleveland, Ohio					
Jones, Johnnie Marie	Apr 7, 1990	J.M.H.	Tn	Sep 30, 1912	77	W	Hamilton, Tilman		Mephenbidge, Neal		Bailey, Rosemary-Georgia R.-Juanita-Jones, G.W.	Strawberry Plains					
Jones, Julia Josephine [Col]	Dec 8, 1956	Jeff Co	Tn	Dec 10, 1873	82	W			Lykes, Laura		Jones, Laura & Buford	West View Colored					
Jones, Kenneth Curtis	Jan 17, 2000	Knoxville, Tn	Tn	Jan 26, 1935	65	Mary C.	Jones, Charles		Kc Kiddy, Love		Wife	Pleasant Grove					
Jones, Laura Etta	Oct 13, 1982	J.M.H.	Tn	Apr 13, 1904	78	S	Jones, C.E.		Lykes, Julia		Pine, Mrs Eola M. [New York]	West View					
Jones, Lawrene	Dec 28, 1955	Jeff City		Dec 14, 1913	22	S	Jones, Mrs. Sidney	Ga			C.C.C.	Georgia					
Jones, Lee Archer	May 7, 1925																
Jones, Lizzie	Feb 6, 1980	Alabama	Jun 8, 1890		89	W	Taylor, Oscar		Reynolds, Elizabeth		Jones, Claudie- Sapp, Mattie	West View					
Jones, Lucy Ann	Jun 11, 1947	Jeff Co	Tn	Jan 18, 1863	84-4-23	W	Riley, George	Tn	Van Dyke, Jonessia	Tn	Van Dyke, T.H.	New Market					
Jones, Martha	Oct 30, 1950	Jeff Co	Tn	Oct 1, 1882	68	W	Pendergrass, Walter		Hensel, Harriet		Cameron, Mrs. Joe T.- Jones, J.R.- Cox, Adrian	Lebanon					
Jones, Mary A.	Feb 5, 1935	Jeff City	Tn	May 4, 1874	60	Jones, J.R.	Cox, W.K.	Tn	Ferguson, Clarrissa	Tn	Jones, J.R.- Cox, Adrian	West View					
Jones, Mary Jane	Dec 20, 1985	J.M.H.	Tn	Apr 25, 1902	83	W	Galyean, William		Hicks, Isabelle		Jones, Mrs. Gartha	Hillcrest					
Jones, Maude H.	Dec 16, 1954	Jeff Co	Tn	Dec 2, 1876	76	W	Hill, James D.		Malcolm, Margaret		Ryder, Mrs. Mary M.	Buffalo Grove					
Jones, Raymond Bruce	Apr 26, 1976	Jeff Co	Tn	May 30, 1909	66	Hamilton, Johnnie M.			Bailey, Sallie		Jones, Mrs. R.B.	Straw Plains					Hobert, Virginia - Merle, Ethel - Durklin, Thelma
Jones, Reese C.	Aug 21, 1931	Jeff Co	Tn	Jan 25, 1883	48	Ng	Jones, Nelson	Tn	Clevenger, Celia	Tn	Jones, Mrs. Reece	Lebanon					Virgil-Robert-Clyde-Frank-Conrad

NAME	DDATE	DLOCAT	BLOCAT	BDATE	AGE	SPOUSE	FATHER	FELOCAT	MOTHER	MBLOCAT	BY	BURIAL	VET	SON	DAUG	BROTHER	SISTER
Jones, Richard Dale	Dec 28, 1997	Rutledge, Tn	Morristown, Tn	Mar 7, 1962	35	Jones, Robert H. [Age 72]	Jones, Bobby		Bull, Doris	Tn	Jones, Robert H. (Call)	Catholic - Escoudito, Calif.				Randy	Sherry
Jones, Rita	Apr 11, 1964	Jeff Co [Pee Calif]	California	Aug 6, 1877	76		Orosco, Jesus	El, Murdo			Jones, Imogene W.- Leland	Eastview Memorial - Knoxville, Tn					
Jones, Robert Maurice	Mar 30, 1989	J.M.H.		Aug 20, 1916	72	Wilson, Imogene	Jones, William		Bailey, Sallie		Clevenger, Jackie Jones	Pleasant Ridge					
Jones, Rose Marie	May 28, 1995	J.M.H.		Nov 24, 1932	53	Div	Dennis, Ohl T.		Lawless, Pauline		Jones, Leland	Pleasant Ridge					
Jones, Sallie B.	Aug 15, 1961	Knox Co	Tn	Aug 10, 1961	70	Div	Bailey, Porter		Hibbs, Amanda			Strawberry Plains					
Jones, Samuel Thurlon	May 17, 1946	Jeff Co		Jul 24, 1871	74	Ng	Jones, David	Tn	Brimmer, Barbara	Tn	Jones, George - Peck, Mrs. - Mary Ruth Harley	Shady Grove					
Jones, Tip	Nov 29, 1942	Jeff Co	Va	Feb 22, 1936	70	Ng	Jones, Lee	Va	Baker, Mary	Va	Jones, Walter - Hurst, Hanley	West View					
Jones, Tommie Crain (Black)	Sep 26, 1987	J.M.H.	Ala.	Jun 18, 1872	51	S	Unk		Unk		Jones, Claudie Lee	West View		Billy	Scott, Deloris		
Jones, William A.	Oct 16, 1993	Nashville, Tn	Tn	Feb 25, 1943	50	Glenn, Sharon	McCormick, Myrtle P.		Sepp, Mattie K.			Cremated			Natalie-Yvette - Wooten, Joni		
Jones, William Cline	Jan 25, 1985	J.M.H.	Tn	Sep 7, 1884	100	W	Jones, Calloway		Jones, Artis		Franklin, Ada - Bunch, Bonnie	Mill Springs					
Jordan, Hallie Jane	Nov 17, 1994	Dandridge, Tn	Claiborne Co, Tn	Jan 29, 1906	88	S	Adams, Archie		Cox, Mary A.	Tn	Staple, Mary J. [Daug]	J.M.G.		J.D.-Roscoe Buttle	Staple, Anna Mae - Helton, Lucille		
Jordan, Pearl	Dec 25, 1925	Jeff Co	Tn		5-3-0	S	Jordan, W.F.		Laugh, Susan	Tn	Spencer, C.C.- Jordan, Hattie - Cropie, Walter	Pleasant Grove			[In-Law] Adams, Anna Lee		
Jordan, Hubert	Jul 11, 1971	Jeff Co	Tn		59	S	Jordan, James		Griffin, Mary		Griffin, Mary	Sandy Ridge					
Joslin, Clarence Webster	Jan 24, 1941	Cambridge City, Indiana	N.Y.		85-6 16	W	Whitaker, J.J. (Cousin) Howard, Clifford [Cambridge City, Ind.]				Joyce, Bobby [G-Son - Lebanon, Ohio]	Cambridge City					
Joyce, Robert Carl	Mar 31, 1997	Jeff City	Grainger Co	Oct 6, 1918	78	W	Joyce, Robert T.		Maples, Della		Joyce, Bobby - Lebanon, Ohio	Hills Union		[In-Law] Joyce, Louise		Paul	Irene
Justice, Columbus Albert	Jun 26, 1979	Jeff City	Ky	Jun 24, 1913	65	Blackburn, Martha	Justice, Green F.		Justice, F.H. - Justice, Martha		Anna O. Yoank - Shelbornia, Ky	Anna O. Yoank - Shelbornia, Ky	WW 2				
Justice, Joe F. Jr.	Nov 4, 1976	Washington, Nc	Nc	May 25, 1918	58	W	Justice, Joe F. Sr.		Norville, Ella Jane		Justice, Mrs. Ruth	West View	WW2				
Justice, Ruth Lee	Dec 19, 1987	Jeff City	Tn	Jul 17, 1923	64	W	Jackson, William G.		Hawley, Ora Lee		Justice, Joe F. 3rd	West View					
Katten, Leonard T.	Oct 10, 1987	Jeff City	Chicago, Ill.	Aug 27, 1917	80	West, Barbara	Katten, Theodore	Tn	Katten, Sallie		Wife	J.M.G.	44-45	Dennis [Ill.]-Thomas [Minn.]-Michael [Nevada]			
Kaiser, Coralyn Ruth	Feb 17, 2049	Jeff Co	Feb 6, 1949			Kaiser, James	Kaiser, James		Dobek, Sallie		Wife	Piney					
Kanipe, Infant Male	Jul 22, 1948	Jeff Co		Jul 22, 1948			Denton, James C.	Tn	Denton, Rebecca	Tn	Denton, James C.	Brazelton					
Kanipe, Twila Jane	May 9, 1971	Tn	Tn	Nov 5, 1918	52	W	Vesser, Warrie		Miller, Belle		Kanipe, Twila Vesser	Memorial Gardens					
Kanipe, Univee	Apr 19, 2000	Nashville, Nc	Tn	Jul 21, 1941	58	W	Ausmus, William Hobert		Yeary, Lillie		Lee, Karen [Daug]	J.M.G.			Thomas, Linda - Lee, Karen & Missouri	Charles-Pete-Lowell-John	
Kanipe, William Roger	Jun 2, 1996	Knoxville, Tn	Jeff Co	Sep 27, 1937	60	W	Kanipe, Vincent		Griffin, Zula		Wife	J.M.G.			Thomas, Linda - Lee, Karen		
Karnes, Bessie Jane	Dec 18, 1999	Jeff City	Tn	Mar 29, 1914	85	Div	Ausmus, Univee		Hammer, Rebecca [Daug]		Hammer, Rebecca [Daug]	Pink Ridge - Metcalf Co, Ky					Whittemore, Zella - Wilson, Brenda - Moxley, Debbie - Southerland, Bonnie - Foulden, Jean
Kautz, James Richard Jr.	Apr 12, 1991	Jeff City	Lancaster, Pa	Jun 28, 1915	76	Div	Kautz, James R. Sr.		Myers, Iva		Kautz, Juanita P.	West View	unk				
Kowalsaki, Edward	Apr 19, 1983	Jeff Co	Poland	Jun 22, 1913	48-11-27	Spiller, Ursula	Kowalsaki, Joseph	Poland	Rines, Louisa	Poland	Kowalsaki, Mrs. Ursula	West View					
Kearney, John C.	Apr 16, 1949	Jeff Co	Tn	Mar 27, 1905	84	W	Kearney, Isaac		Spraie, Emmaline		Kearney, H.C. & Truda	Rocky Valley - Jeff Co					
Kea, Ida Elaine	Dec 11, 1957	Knox Co	Tn	Aug 8, 1886		W	Collins, Elishie	Tn	Stalsworth, -	Tn	Donaldson, Mrs. Zora	Mill Springs					

NAME	DATE	BLOCAT	BLOCAT	BDATE	AGE	SPOUSE	FATHER	FELOCAT	MOTHER	MPSLOCAT	BY	BURIAL	VET	SON	DAUG	BROTHER	SISTER
Kee, Jordan Herbert	Mar 2, 1983	Jeff Co.	Tn	May 26, 1886	74	Ng	Kee, Buford		Bateman, Mary E.		Donaldson, Richard & Zora - Kee, Mrs. Jordan	Mill Springs					
Keebler, Ada Belle	Mar 10, 1999	Chattanooga, Tn	Blount Co., Tn	Feb 4, 1903	96		Malones, Agnes				Harmon, Henry D. (G-Son)	Lenoir City, Tn		[G] Harmon, Brad-Ralph-Tom	[In-Law] Keebler, Donna - [G] Duckbridge, Angela		
Keeney, Alice Mae	Dec 8, 1996	Knoxville, Tn	Tn	Aug 2, 1919	77		Noe, Maggie				Hensley, Peulette Sue [Dau]	Shiloh					
Keeney, Charles James	Jan 18, 1975	Jeff Co.	New York	Dec 27, 1927	47	Ng	Keeney, Noble		Bacon, Ella		Avery, William E. [Bros, NY]	North Lansing, Ny	navy				
Keeney, Ramona	Feb 18, 1975	Jeff Co.	New York	Aug 27, 1928	46	Keeney, Robert	Ballinger, Ramona				Avery, William E. [Bros, NY]	North Lansing, Ny					
Keeney, Robert Bacon	Feb 18, 1975	Knoxville, Tn	New York	Dec 18, 1975	52-3-0	Ballinger, Ramona	Keeney, Noble		Bacon, Ella		Avery, William E.	Mill Springs					
Keirsey, Nannie	Dec 30, 1991	Jeff Co	Hamblen Co	May 25, 1912	79	Keirsey, E.F.	Crockett, King		Morn, Luorella		Kelver, Dennis [Son]	White Pine					
Kelley, Nellie Pearl	Mar 12, 1965	Jeff City	Hamblen Co	Jan 28, 1914	50	Trisela, Henry Ard	Homer, Emma		Husband			Pleasant View		Bobby			
Kelley, Benjamin E.	Aug 28, 1992	J.M.H.	Granger Co	Jan 18, 1900	92	W	Kelley, Walter		Martin, Mollie		J.M.G.	J.M.G.	unk				
Kelley, Charles Edward	Nov 4, 1983	Morristown, Tn	Mascot, Tn	Aug 20, 1918	75	Williams, Mary Jane	Kelley, Isaac Franklin		Fralix, Grace		Wife	West View	army	Jarmee-Frank-Charles R.-Jerry E.			
Kelley, Elsie	Jul 5, 1986	Tn	Tn	Oct 7, 1905	80	Kelley, Ben E.	Spoon, Clay	Tn	Cameron, Naomi		Jefferson Memorial	Jefferson Memorial					
Kelley, Eugene	Nov 27, 1944	Jeff Co.	Tn	Mar 7, 1944		Neal, Helen	Kelley, Isaac F.		Tinkley, Ruth		Kelley, Mrs. Fred [Father] & Children	West View					
Kelley, Fred	Nov 21, 1978	At Home	Tn	Sep 15, 1914	64	Kelley, Isaac F.	Kelley, Isaac F.		Fralix, Grace		Kelley, Billie Jean	Roseberry - Knox Co					
Kelley, Helen Marie	Mar 15, 1991	J.M.H.	Hamblen Co	Nov 25, 1911	79	Neal, Herbert	Neal, Herbert		Collins, Sara		Layman, Billie Jean [Dau]	Roseberry					
Kelley, Ila Belle (Coil)	Feb 4, 1957	New Market	Tn	Jun 16, —	82	W	Dardis, Dane		Thompson, Eliza		Cunningham, Rosa	Youngs - New Market					
Kelley, Jennie	Sep 5, 1942	Granger Co	Tn	Feb 24, 1873	69	W	Noe, Johnson	Tn	Cameron, Mary	Tn	Eppa, Mrs. Jdack -	West View					
Kelley, John Jenkins	May 10, 1966	Jeff City	Tn	Mar 10, 1885	81	W			Webb, James Richard		Jernigan, Howard-Rosa - Kelley, Ben-J.-Walter-Beulah-Hazel-Frank	West View					
Kelley, Mary	Dec 13, 1964	Mascot, Tn	Tn	Feb 12, 1882	82	W	Martin, David		Watson, Susan		Shiloh	Shiloh					
Kelley, Mary K.	Apr 9, 1982	Jeff Co.	Tn	Jan 13, 1925	7	Kelley, Charles	Kelley, Ben	Tn	Spoons, Ebony	Tn	Kelley, Ben	Reeds Chapel					
Kelley, Mary Ruth	Jun 13, 1977	Granger Co	Tn	Nov 4, 1918	58	Kelley, J.J.	Finley, Don		Davis, Ohio		Kelley, Charles	West View					
Kelley, Nettie Gilcrisp	Jan 18, 1964	Union Co, Tn	Union Co, Tn	Oct 20, 1883	80	Ng	Gloosip, John		Waymire, Nancy		Kelley, J.J.	Shilo					
Kelley, W.P.	Sep 9, 1928	Jeff Co	Tn		59-8-5	Ng	Kelley, A.G.	Tn			Kelley, W.P & Daughter	Daughter					
Kelley, Walter Thomas	Jul 19, 1990	Rutledge, Tn	Tn	Oct 10, 1957	22	Lee, Margaret	Kelley, Walter Jr.		Pruitt, Francis		Kelley, W.A.Jr.	Mill Springs					
Kelly, Lois	May 8, 2000	Jeff City	Ohio	Dec 14, 1920	79	W	Smith, William B.		Teague, Sadie		Seale, Margaret [Doug] Argo - Paul F.H. [Germantown, Ohio]	City - Germantown, Ohio					
Kelly, Walter A.	Jul 13, 1941	Knox Co	Tn		68-3-14	Kelley, Mollie	Pruitt, Rhuths	Tn	Pruitt, Frances A.	Tn	Kelley, Mollie						
Kenney, Paul F.	Jan 25, 1987	Rutledge, Tn	Tn	Feb 8, 1915	51	Roach, Maggie	Keeney, Edward		Fralker, Rhaths		Maggie	Shiloh					
Kerns, Egon William (German)	Aug 5, 1997	Riga, Latvia	Lawrence Co, Ohio	Nov 13, 1920	76	Kerns, Anna P.	Link				Wife	Cremated					
Kerns, H.T.	Oct 5, 1950	Jeff Co [Rke Ashland, Ky]	Ohio		82-10-18	Ng	Kerns, George		Sturgill, Belle		Kerns, Kenneth [Shelby, Ky]	Ashland - Ky					
Kerr, Amy Louise	Mar 16, 1997	Asheville, Nc	Tn	Sep 24, 1941	55	Kerr, Ronald, R.	Noland, Eugene R.		Shillings, Texas Arizona		Husband	Community Chapel			White, Sean		
Kerr, Chris Clark	Sep 9, 1983	J.M.H.	Tn	Nov 6, 1901	81	W	Taylor, Zachary		Clark, Sarah R.			Jefferson Memorial			Bones, Angela		
Kerr, Daniel Mack	Feb 1, 1944	Granger Co	Tn	Jan 30, 1873	71	Neg	Kerr, Henry C.				Kerr, Arthur - Bowling, Pearl - Hickman, Martha - Shoemaker, Myrtle [Va]	New Market					
Kerr, Diana Estelle	Apr 25, 1970	Jeff Co	Tn		23	Kerr, Kenneth	Byrd, James	Tn	Phillips, Hattie		Kerr, Kenneth Sr.	Shiloh - Granger Co					
Kerr, Dwight Gleason	Aug 24, 1954	Hamblen Co	Tn	Dec 16, 1930		Div	Kerr, Raymond Alonzo		Vineyard, Hazel		Kerr, Mrs. Lori [Clover, Sc]	New Market		[In-Law] Smith, Robert L.		Hill, Patricia - Brewer, Linda - Whitehead, Joyce	

NAME	DDATE	DLOCAT	BLOCAT	BDATE	AGE	SPOUSE	FATHER	FRLOCAT	MOTHER	MPRLOCAT	BY	BURIAL	VET	SON	DAUG	BROTHER	SISTER
Kerr, Edith Georgia	Sep 26, 1998	Jeff City	New Market, Tn	Oct 23 1926	71		Kerr, Thomas Jackson		Lawrence, Juanita		Kerr John [Brother] - Jones, Jean	J.M.G.				Tommy & Martha- Rogers, Mildred- [Br-Law] Johnny & Jackie - [Br-Law] Jones, Curtis	Moody, Elizabeth - Rogers, Mildred - Kerr, Jane-Jill - Gordon, Peggy & Carolyn
Kerr, Ella Mae	Jun 2, 1958	Jeff Co.	Tn	Jul 31, 1880	77	Kerr, Hugh	Wilson, Joe		Rawlings, Isabella		Kerr, Mrs. Lou - Bateman, Mrs. J.D. - Hodge, John	Piedmont					
Kerr, Eunice	Apr 18, 1978	Jeff City	Nc	Mar 20, 1928	50	Kerr, Beulas	Street, Joseph R Sr.		Hughes, Lillie Belle		Hughes, John	Jefferson Memorial					
Kerr, Gladys	May 18, 1982	J.M.H.	Tn	Jun 4, 1910	71	Kerr, J. Clarence	Whittaker, Lum		Diist, Sally		Kerr, J. Clarence	Jefferson Memorial					
Kerr, Hazkell H.	Jul 5, 1971	Jeff Co.	Tn	Oct 12, 1900	70	Ng	Kerr, Hugh		Wilson, Ella		Kerr, J. Clarence & Children	Jefferson Memorial					
Kerr, Hugh C.	Apr 28, 1963	Jeff Co	Tn	Jun 15, 1875	94	W	Kerr, Jack		Lowery, Harriet		Kerr, L.C.-H.H.- Slatsworth, Jack- Bateman, Dud - Bush, Vida - Hodge, John - Brown, Julia - Lon & Courtney, Wanda - Roach, Linda	Piedmont					
Kerr, J. Clarence	Nov 19, 1989	J.M.H.	Jeff Co	Jan 24, 1912	77	Whittaker, Gladys [D]	Kerr, John W.	Tn	Hurst, Tennie	Tn	Kerr, Mrs. Robert - Kerr, James - Maury, Mrs. Fred - Oates, Hazel	J.M.G.					
Kerr, J.W.	Apr 2, 1936	Jeff Co	Tn	Aug 18, 1880	55	Ng	Kerr, D.W.	Tn	Finchum, Delona	Tn	Kerr, Edith	Piney					
Kerr, Juanita	Sep 14, 1982	Jeff Co	Tn	Apr 5, 1905	57	Kerr, Tom J.	Carmichael, Kinnie K.		Kerr, Edith		Kerr, Edith	Piedmont					
Kerr, John C.	Apr 13, 1949	Jeff Co	Tn	Dec 13, 191-	35-4-1	Ng	Lawrence, James H.	Tn	Jordan Ada Lou		Kerr, Margaret	West View					
Kerr, Kenneth Sr.	Oct 13, 1983	Jeff City	Tn	Feb 4, 1924	59	W	Kerr, Tom		Lawrence, Juanita		Kerr, Kenneth Jr -Larry Stallings, Dianne	Shiloh	WW 2				
Kerr, Leona Virginia	Apr 25, 1960	Jeff Co	Va	Mar 8, 1884	76	W	Quisenberry, Amos		Campbell, Nancy		Shiloh	Shiloh					
Kerr, Margaret Jane	May 12, 1946	Jeff Co	Tn	Jul 22, 1931	14	S	Kerr, Tom J.	Tn	Lawrence, Juanita	Tn	Kerr, T.J.- Edith & Kenneth	Piedmont					
Kerr, Paul L.	May 21, 1984	Knoxville, Tn	Tn	Apr 7, 1909	74	Patterson, Leoda	Kerr, John		Hurst, Tennie		Kerr, Mrs. Leoda	Jefferson Memorial					
Kerr, Raymond Alonzo	May 16, 1970	Knox Co	Tn	Mar 30, 1909	60	Vineyard, Hazel	Kerr, Hugh		Wilson, Ella Mae		Kerr, Mrs. Imogene	New Market					
Kerr, Robert Willie (Buck)	May 23, 1969	Jeff Co	Tn	Jan 26, 1922	47	Ng	Kerr, Andy		Quisenberry, Leona		Kerr, Mrs. Imogene Cox	Jefferson Memorial	WW 2				
Kerr, Spurgeon D.	Apr 12, 1946	Hamblen Co	Tn	May 1, 1896	49	S	Kerr, A.A. Sr.	Nc	Etchison, Elizabeth J.	Nc	Kerr, Louise	West View					
Kerr, Tennie H.	Apr 2, 1957	Rocky Valley	Tn	May 20, 1882	74	?	Hurst, Zeled		Weans, Dinah		Hamilton, Mildred - Kerr, Clarence & Paul Moody, Mrs. Carl - Kerr, Beatrice	Piney					
Kerr, Thomas J.	Dec 3, 1970	Knoxville, Tn	Tn	Apr 21, 1899	71	Ng	Kerr, Andrew		Sellers, Lethia		Kerr, Wayen [Son]	Piedmont					
Kerr, Willie Leoda	Dec 3, 1990	J.M.H.	Tn	May 5, 1914	76	W	Patterson, Callie		Palmer, Sally		Kerr, Mrs. Joe A.- Wells, Mrs. Joe A - Burchfield, C.O. & Barton Spartenburg, Scl	J.M.G.					
Ketner, Bessie	Sep 3, 1955	Sevier Co	Tn	May 20, 1888	67	Ketner, Mitchell	Burchfield, Russ		Brimmer, Edia		Fox - Sevier Co	Fox - Sevier Co					
Key, John C.	Oct 24, 1991	J.M.H.	Friendsville, Tn	Sep 24, 1991	75	Lambert, Pearl	Key, Wesley		Purkey, Jennie		Willie	Big Springs - Blount Co. Tn	unk				
Key, Mary Pearl	Jun 20, 1998	Jeff City	Maryville, Tn	Feb 18, 1923	75	Lambert, Pearl	Lambert, Fred C.		Keller, Oxie M.		Key, Gene [Son]	Big Springs, Maryville, Tn		Key, Cynthia- John Ronald	Whitie, Beverly		
Kidd, Gladys	Jun 23, 1974	Jeff City	Ky	Apr 22, 1895	79	W	Gilliam, Will		Heller, Maggie		Puryear, Homer	Oak Grove - Paducah, Ky					
Kidwell, Jessie	Oct 4, 1995	Jeff City	Jeff Co	Mar 20, 1901	94	W	Mc Nish, William H.		Campbell, Sallie		Hancock, Maxine [Niece]	West View				Howard	[In-Law] Mc Nish, Catherine- Elizabeth
Kidwell, Raymond Louis Sr.	May 17, 1986	Humana Hosp.	Maryland	Jan 9, 1905	81	Fortney, Anna E.	Kidwell, Silas B.		Horseman, Bertie		Kidwell, Mrs. Anna E. - Garrett, Mrs. Fred - Kilbourne, Miss Annie B.	Garetwmare - J.M.G.					
Kilbourne, Grover C.	Apr 18, 1954	Jeff Co	Washington Co, Va	Jan 30, 1892	62	W	Kilbourne, Jefferson Davis		Barber, Veeta		Garrett, Mrs. Fred - Kilbourne, Miss Annie B.	Community					Brown, Irena - Lingfelter, Kathryn

NAME	DATE	BLOCAT	BLOCAT	BDATE	AGE	SPOUSE	FATHER	FBLOCAT	MOTHER	MFBLOCAT	BY	BURIAL	VET	SON	DAUG	BROTHER	SISTER
Kilgore, William H.	Feb 7, 1997	Knoxville, Tn	Whitesburg, Tn	Feb 2, 1922	75	King, Brenda	Kilgore, Arthur		Durham, Lucy		Wife - Mattie, Fred & Ruby (Parents Of Brenda King)	Community		Rector, Scott - Kilgore,	Patterson, Lisa & Bryan	George	[In-Law] Koral, Gwen [OH] Kilgore, Selma - Marion
Kilbourne, Reba Leona	Feb 5, 1953	Jeff Co	Tn	Feb 13, 1905	47	Ng	Messengill, George		Carter, Roe		Kilbourne, G.I.C.	Jefferson Memorial					
Killion, Ella	May 16, 1983	Knoxville, Tn	Tn	Jul 17, 1900	82	Killion, Artie	Wickman, J.W.		Cochran, Angie		May, Mrs. Henry	Buffalo Grove					
Killion, Joel Lemon	Apr 2, 1955	Jeff Co	Tn	Oct 7, 1869	85	Ng	Killion, William		Swedera, Matissia		Mc Kinley (War??'s Father-In-Law) [Bible]						
Killion, Mrs. J.L.	Nov (17), 1932	J.M.H.				w					Buckner, Mrs. Robert	J.M.G.					
Killion, William Arlie	Feb 23, 1987	J.M.H.	Tn	Jun 23, 1897	89	w	Lawson, Joel	Tn	Rhienhart, Rhoda			West View					
Kilpatrick, Charles	Apr 12, 1925	Pa			77-11-20	Ng	Kilpatrick, Thomas	Pa	Richardson, Rebecca	Pa	Kilpatrick, Mrs. Charles	West View					
Kilpatrick, John T.	Sep 2, 1972	Greensboro, Nc				Owens, Katherine					Kilpatrick, Katherine	West View					
Kilpatrick, Katherine Hinds	Jan [18], 1987				91						Haines F.H. [Greensboro, Nc] Pitt, Sherry Bands [Daug]	West View				John Brad-Tate	
Kimbrough, Daniel Porter	Dec 5, 1982	Waitesvere, Tn	Tn	Jan 8, 1918	74	w	Kimbrough, John L.		White, Rosa		Kimbrough, Paul & Lloyd	West View	[Gr] Pitt, Benjamin				
Kimbrough, Dora S.	Dec 6, 1982	Jeff Co	Tn	Oct 30, 1880	82	w	Anderson, George		Stames, Sallie		Kimbrough, Porter	West View					
Kimbrough, Evelen	May 11, 1980	Knoxville, Tn	Tn	Jan 9, 1919	61	Kimbrough, Porter	Kimbrough, Marlon		Hasims, Beatrice		Jarrigan	Jarrigan					
Kimbrough, Floyd S.	Sep 3, 1957	Jeff Co	Tn	Dec 2, 1883	73	Nola S.	Stallsworth, Douglas R.		Dixon, Pearl M.		Nels & Children	Jarrigan					
Kimbrough, Georgia	Jul 3, 1983	Knoxville, Tn	Tn	Jul 6, 1921	61	Kimbrough, Theart	Kimbrough, Floyd		Kimbrough, Theart		Kimbrough, Theart	Indian Ridge - Grainger Co					
Kimbrough, Gertha Dora	Jul 31, 1965	Jeff Co	Tn	Jun 21, 1914	51	S	Kimbrough, Floyd		Smith, Magnolia		Lunce, Mrs. Hubert	Jarrigan					
Kimbrough, H.H.	Feb 11, 1935	Jeff Co	Tn	Nov 27, 1874	60	Ng	Kimbrough, R.	Tn	Henson, Jane	Tn	Kimbrough, R.	West View					
Kimbrough, Magnolia	Jun 10, 1960	Jeff Co	Tn	Dec 1, 1889	70	w	Smith, William		Henson, Laura		Harris-Gennee-Ethel-Anna-Gertrude [Children]	Jarrigan					
Kimbrough, Paul Hall	Sep 6, 1980	Jeff City	Tn	Sep 3, 1907	73	Ng	Kimbrough, Henson		Anderson, Dora		Kimbrough, Hazel Kelley	Jarrigan					
Kimbrough, Theart Samuel	Jun 25, 1998	Mascot, Tn	Tn	Nov 19, 1920	68	w	Kimbrough, Floyd		Smith, Nola		Kimbrough, Mickey	Indian Ridge - Rutledge, Tn	WW 2				
Kimbrough,Charlie Lemuel	Sep 17, 1942	Hamblen Co	Hamblen Co	Aug 18, 1942			Kimbrough, Lemuel	Tn	Pierce, Edith	Tn	Kimbrough, Lemuel & Johnnie - Pierce, Frank	Pleasant View					
Kimorly, Charlotte Ruth	Jun 12, 1991	Jeff City		Dec 18, 1944	46	Div	Pitts, Hubert		Elmore, Jessie		Smarty, Elisa A. [Daug]						
Kimorly, Augusta H.	Dec 18, 1957	Jeff City	Tn	Aug 28, 1880	77	w	Moody, Woolson T.		Gray, Mary		Doyle, Mrs. Ray - Dennis, Mack - Kinder, J.F.	Shiloh - Grainger Co					
Kinder, David H.	Nov 29, 1936	Tn	Tn	Nov 26, 1936	78	w	Kinder, J.F.	Tn	Williams, May		Shaver, Myrtle	J.M.G.					
Kinder, Elizabeth Mae	Dec 5, 1984	J.M.H.	Tn	Apr 24, 1906	78	Byrd, Hazel	Williams, Joel		Farr, Maggie		Kinder, Hollis-Don-Harold	Jefferson Memorial					
Kinder, Hollis Edward	Jul 2, 1974	Knoxville, Tn	Tn	Aug 18, 1914	59	Ng	Kinder, Edward		Moody, Augusta		Shaver, Mrs. Myrtle - Kinder, Robert	Jefferson Memorial					
Kinder, James Franklin	Jul 27, 1981	Jeff Co	Tn	Jul 5, 1906	75	Ng	Kinder, Edward		Moody, Augusta		Kinder, W.H.	Jefferson Memorial					
Kinder, Lala Beatrice	Apr 28, 1952	Davidson Co, Tn	Tn	Nov 4, 1896	55	Ng	Helm, W.S.		Alexander, Minnie		Kinder, W.H.	West View					
Kinder, Ned	Mar 3, 1955																
Kinder, W.H. [Dr.]	Mar 16, 1970	Jeff City		1896	73-9-17	w	Helm, Martha		Hilton, Martha		Taspcot Lodge - Kimbrough, Porter & Evelyn - Klingler, Helen [Call]	West View					
Kinford, Rachel	Mar 24, 1997	Knoxville, Tn	Knoxville, Tn	Mar 24, 1997			Kinford, Robert Allan		Brown, Miriam Elaine		Father	West View					
Kinett, James Lewis	May 15, 1947	Loudon Co	Union Co, Tn	Jan 9, 1923	23	S	Kinett, H.C.	Union Co	Capps, Dessie M.		Kinett, H.C. & Loyd	New Market					
King, Ann	Jul 13, 1947	Jeff Co				King, W.F. [D]		Knox Co		Grainger Co	King, Don	West View					
King, Bessie	Mar 18, 1990	J.M.H.		Nov 16, 1915	74	S	Huffaker, Marshall A.		Campbell, Mary Jane	Tn	King, Jerry C. - Mayford - Reba Sue	West View					
King, Clark	Apr 1, 1987	Humana Hosp.	Sevier Co	Feb 6, 1903	83	King, Mayford	Trentham James W.		Williams, Susie		King, Sam	City - Tracy City, Tn		King, Frank Sr.	Pearson, Nancy Jane		

NAME	DDATE	DLOCAT	BLOCAT	BDATE	AGE	SPOUSE	FATHER	FBLOCAT	MOTHER	MBLOCAT	BY	BURIAL	VET	SON	DAUG	BROTHER	SISTER
King, Cornelia	Mar 9, 1963	Jeff Co.	Tn	Jun 11, 1873	89	King, Furus, G. [2]	Minton, John		Lynch, Evelyn		Kind, Edward & Ebert	West View					
King, Edward Telford	Dec 24, 1975	J.M.H.	Tn	Jan 5, 1912	63	Cosby, Maggie	Minton, Cornelia		Minton, Cornelia		King, Mrs. Edward	West View					
King, Elbert	Mar 16, 1978	Knoxville, Tn	Tn	Mar 11, 1904	74	W	King, Rufus B.		Minton, Cornelia		King, Mrs. Edward - V.A.	West View	WW 2				
King, Gladys	Jul 10, 1979	Knoxville, Tn	Va	Feb 12, 1910	65	King, Wade	Carmichael, Minnie	Tn	Moreland, Ed	Tn	Moreland, Sally	West View					
King, J. Floyd	Aug 31, 1936		Va	May 15, 1826	80		Bull, Reed Sr.	Va	King, H.C.			West View					
King, Jo Ann Acuff	Mar 12, 1999	Atlanta, Ga	Jeff Co	May 4, 1936	62	King, Donald	Bull, Reed Sr.		Gaddis, Maggie		Acuff, Kathye [Daug]	Greenwood			Calbert, Rebecca		
King, Kay Moe	Apr 22, 1974	Jeff Memorial	Tn	Sep 17, 1906	67	King, Elbert	Pitton, William		Yeary, Nancy		King, Elbert	West View					
King, Leander A.	Jan 28, 1983	Jeff City	Knox Co, Tn	Jan 24, 1916	77	King, J.F.	Baird, Samuel		Lackey, Eliza		Shands, Mary R. [Sister]	Thorngrove - Knox Co, Tn	42-45	Acuff, Dan- Robert			
King, Mrs. J.F.	Jan 30, 1931	Jeff City	Pa	Mar 4, 1858	72	King, J.F.			Baird, Samuel	Pa	King, J.F.	West View					
King, Ruby	Oct 15, 1969	S.M.M.C.	Tn	Nov 23, 1909	78	W	Edgar, William		Kyle, Ellen		Murphy, Eula (John A.)	West View					
King, Rufus Benton	Sep 9, 1944	Jeff Co.	Claiborne Co.	Jan 8, 1870	74	Ng	King, Hiram	Tn	Bales, Emma	Tn	Hurst, Mrs. - Elbert & Edward	West View					
King, Teresa Ann	Dec 27, 1980	Mascot, Tn		Dec 27, 1980		Ng	King, Joe Willis		Shipley, Fern Delsie		King, J.W.	Roseberry - Knox Co.					
King, Teresa Dianne	Mar 8, 1981	Milligan Clinic	Tn			Ng					King, Paul E.	Roseberry - Knox Co.					
King, Unk	Dec 27, 1931		Tn			Ng					King, Luther	J.M.G.					
King, W.F.	May 28, 1931	Jeff Co (Plea Dayton, OH)	Tn	Mar 8, 1882	69	Ng	Martin, Margaret	Ky	Gardner, Mr. E.E.			West View					
King, Wade H.	Aug 15, 1970	Jeff Co (Plea Dayton, OH)	Tn	Feb 8, 1911	59		King, —		King, Gladys (Dayton, OH)	Ky		West View					
Kingston, Charles William	Apr 28, 1995	Talbott, Tn	Mascot, Tn	Oct 7, 1932	63	Lindsey, Jo Ann	Kingston, Curtis Hayden Sr.		Chenouth, Georgia Janette		Wife	Scott-Robert		Coley, Shady- Leonard, Patti		John	Yoakum, Margaret Fosher; Ruth - Lea, Betty
Kingswell, William Edward	Aug 11, 1972		Isle Of Wright	Feb 27, 1882	80	Hale, Mary			Mary Alice		Kingswell, Mary Hale	West View					
Kinney, George Pike	Dec 10, 1970	Ingles, Fla	New York	Nov 6, 1901	75	W	Eldridge, Lena		Mayers, Mrs. Richard (Sue)		Kinney, George P.	J.M.G.					
Kinney, Lesa Katy	Apr 3, 1973	Jeff Co	Tn	Jul 21, 1915	57	Ng	Fannon, Maggie		Hooper, Della		Kinney, George P.	Jefferson Memorial					
Kinnick, Charlie Elmer	Jul 25, 1988	J.M.H.	Tn	Apr 7, 1904	84	Ng	Eldridge, James V.		Hooper, Della		Kinnick, Eloy E.	White Pine					
Kinnick, Phoebe	Aug 13, 2000	Tn	Tn	Sep 17, 1913	86	Ng	Underwood, Marshall		Langston, Ida		Keans, Ann [Daug]	J.M.G.					
Kirby, Sarah E.	Oct 12, 1950	Knox Co	Tn	Mar 12, 1871	79	W	Miles, R.H.		Harper, Emmaline		Mascot - Knox Co.	Mascot - Knox Co					
Kirk, Benny	Sep 11, 1989	U.T.H.	Jeff Co	May 16, 1952	37	Div	Kirk, Joseph Elvis		Cochran, Barbara Kirk		Cumberland Presby.- Mt. Horeb	Cumberland Presby.- Mt. Horeb					
Kirk, Bonnie	Feb 18, 1976	Greene Co., Tn	Greene Co., Tn	Mar 1, 1921	54	W	Gardner, Joseph		Taylor, Kate		Rankin, Mrs. Barbara	Bible Chapel - Greene Co., Tn					
Kirk, Cecil J.	Feb 25, 1981	Knoxville, Tn	Tn	Apr 1, 1921	59	Burgin, Mary	Allen, Emma Jean		Kirk, Omsilla		Rankin, Mrs. (Cecil J.)	Jefferson Memorial					
Kirk, Emma Gaye	Jan 1, 1993	Jeff City		Dec 17, 1907	85	Ng	Kirk, Omsilla		Me William, Deneah		Kirk, Franklin (Son)	Lynxhurst					
Kirk, Joseph Elvis	Sep 20, 1976	At Home	Tn	Feb 7, 1912	64	W	Kirk, Frank		Courtney, Dannah		Rankin, Mrs. Barbara	Bible Chapel				Robert-Albert	
Kirkpatrick, Myrtle Hanks	Dec 15, 1947	J.M.H.	Hawkins Co., Tn	Feb 7, 1886	28	W	Rogers, Thurman		Mollie		Hanks, Gene	Jarnigan					
Kitts, William Horace	Nov 6, 1987	New Market, Tn	Greneger Co	Apr 3, 1919	84	W	Kitts, George W.		Hopson, Margaret		Kitts, Mrs. Velma	Asbury - Knox Co					
Kivett, Dessie Mae	Dec 15, 1947	Knox Co	Tn	May 30, 1903	84	Seets, Velva	Capps, Jim B.		Hopson, Margaret		Asbury, Ruby - Kivett, Lloyd G.	New Market					
Kivett, Wanda Sue	Oct 17, 1953	Jeff Co	Tn	May 11, 1942	11	W	Kivett, Elbert W.		Beeler, Rachel		Kivett, Dorothy	New Market					
Klasemer, John Albert	Oct 20, 1982	Talbott, Tn	Monroe, Mich.	Jul 17, 1927	55	Deaton, Inez	Klasemer, John K.		Klasemer, Mrs. Inez	Tn	Klasemer, Mrs. Inez	Jefferson Memorial					
Klepper, Thomas Kurtz	Dec 13, 1966	Knox Co	Tn	Feb 20, 1890	80	S	Klepper, Mannas P.		Mundlow, Selrah		Allen, Rosie	Buffalo Grove					
Klepper, James P.	Jul 6, 1926	Tn	Tn	Jul 6, 1926	80	S	Klepper, Barney		Mallory, Nancy	Tn	Klepper, J.K.	Buffalo					
Klepper, M. Trennie	Apr 11, 1940	Tn	Tn	Mar 5, 1878	62	S	Klepper, James P.	Tn	Mallory, Nancy	Tn	Klepper, Tom & Sibs	Buffalo Grove					
Knedia, Robert William	Mar 30, 1996	Knoxville, Tn	St. Joseph, Missouri	Apr 23, 1935	62	Swisher, Jacqueline	Knedel, William Clifford		Wesen, Myrtis Ione		Wife	Cremated		Chapman, Frank	Stone, Brenda [Ark.] - Wynner, Robin - Jasper, Jeanie		
Knight, Betty Olita	Aug 22, 1998	Chattanooga, Tn		Apr 14, 1952	46	Jones, Edward			Knight, Natasha Renee [Daug]		Wife	Community- Morristown, Tn					
Knight, Carl Hubert	Jan 5, 1980	Knoxville, Tn	Tn	Sep 25, 1925	57	Barry, Phyllis	Carmichael, Maude		Knowling, Hannah		Knight, Mrs. Phyllis	Jefferson Memorial	WW 1				
Knight, Elihue H.	Apr 13, 1976	Talbott, Tn	Tn	Jul 24, 1897	78	Carmichael, Maude	Knowling, Hannah		Carmichael, Maude		Knight, Carl [Son]	Sunderland	WW 1				
Knight, Haynes Thomas	Nov 29, 1973	Jeff Co	Tn	Jun 30, 1894	79	Cannon, Rowena	Knight, Sam		Knowling, Hannah		Knight, Roy	Mt. Pleasant					

NAME	DDATE	DLOCAT	BLOCAT	BDATE	AGE	SPOUSE	FATHER	FRLOCAT	MOTHER	MRLOCAT	BY	BURIAL	VET	SON	DAUG	BROTHER	SISTER
Knight, Hugh Edward	Jan 17, 1987	Jeff City	Tn	Jan 8, 1904	83		Knight, John		Solomon, Lou	Tn	Knight, Ray (James/Sons)	Mt Pleasant					
Knight, Josie	May 23, 1950	Jeff Co	Tn		47	Ng	Brooks, John		Lynch, Linda		Whte, Glenn	Mt Horeb					
Knight, Louise	Jan 4, 1926	Jeff Co	Tn		46	Ng					Hunter, Unit	Mt Pleasant					
Knight, Manuel	Mar 2, 1986	J.M.H.	Tn	Dec 25, 1904	81	W	Knight, Joe		Shaver, Mary		Knight, Tommy (Son)	Sunderland					
Knight, Meade	Jan 20, 1991	J.M.H.	Tn	Sep 16, 1902	88	W	Campbell, William Thomas		Campbell, Nancy Jane		Knight, Cecil G. (Son)	Mt Pleasant	WW 2				
Knight, Rowena Cannon	Aug 3, 1981	Talbott, Tn	Tn			W					Knight, Roy	Mt Pleasant					
Knowles, Thomas Jeffrey	Apr 25, 1999	Sevierville, Tn	Dayton, Ohio	Oct 1, 1941	57		Knowles, Arthur		Knowles, Margaret		Stallings, Robert (Not Related)	Pleasant Grove					
Knowling, Elmer William	Jan 6, 1999	Jeff City	Jeff Co	Oct 23, 1907	91	Hopkins, Julia	Knowling, T.H.		Cannon, Minnie		Hopkins, Dale (Nephew)	J.M.G.					Horace (Marchioes)
Knowling, Minnie	Mar 9, 1961	Jeff Co	Tn	Sep 5, 1878	82	W	Cannon, Woods		Hickey, Mary		Hill, Eugene	Mt Pleasant					Hill, Grace
Knowling, Thomas H.	Jun 24, 1955	Jeff Co	Tn	Dec 2, 1875	79	Ng	Knowling, Porter		Givens, Amanda		Knowling, Elmer - Eugene	Mt Pleasant					
Knox, Basil Phillip	Apr 27, 1942	Cherokee Lake	Marion Co	Nov 24, 1925	16	S	Knox, Basil Erastus	Tn	Westmoreland, Kathryn	Tn	Pelletris	Victoria, Tn					
Koontz, Amos Leon Jr.	May 24, 1982	U.T.H.	Tn	Jul 29, 1917	64	W	Kantz, Amos L. Sr.		Caton, Amanda		Brady, Mrs. Edith - Seaborn, Leon	Flat Gap					
Koontz, Daisy Moore	Oct 17, 1982	Jeff Co	Tn		55	Koontz, Amos					Koontz, Amos	Hills Union					
Koontz, J.A.	Dec 15, 1932	New Market	Tn	Jul 7, 1863	69	Ng	Koontz, Gus	Tn	Hutchenson, Sallie	Tn	Mc Cobbins, Jessie - Smith, R.H.	Friends Station					
Koontz, William N.	Jul 11, 1949	Jeff Co	Tn	Jan 19, 1876	73	Ng	Koontz, John		Cate, Rachael		Stallings, Mrs. Mack - Sharpe, Mrs.	Straw Plains					
Koontze, Ella Estelle	May 23, 1965	Knox Co	Tn	Aug 26, 1891	73	S	Koontze, James		Smith, Mattie		Mc Cobbins, Jessie	Friends Station					
Kowalski, Joe E.	Mar 6, 1987	J.M.H.	Michigan	Jan 28, 1918	69	Toth, Martha	Kramer, Phillip		Fanning F.H. (Welch, W. Va.)			Bluewell, W. Va.	WW 2			Philip & Alvira [Fla]	
Kramer, Rudolph Adolph	Jan 28, 1994	J.M.H.	Austria	Sep 9, 1899	94		Kramer, Phillip		Zintel, Elizabeth		Haigh, Joyce S(Dag)	Cremated		Ronald	Semanchuk, Alice [Nc]		
Krisik, Harry Eric Sr.	Aug 19, 1979	Morristown, Tn	Pa	Mar 25, 1914	65	Krailk, Kathryn	Krailk, Paul H.		Marchbl, Leopoldine		Krailk, Mrs. Katherine	Florida					
Kouskop, Jack Fillmore	Feb 25, 1991	J.M.H.	Logan Co, Ohio	Jun 10, 1930	60	Hurley, Elaine	Kouskop, Emmett		Williams, Nellie		Kouskop, Elaine	Cremated	unk				
Kuhn, Benjamin A.	Aug 31, 1991	J.M.H.	Williamsburg, Pa	Jun 18, 1948	43	S	Kuhn, Frederick		Johnson, Kathleen		Kuhn, Kathleen	unk	unk				
Kuhn, Frederick A. Sr.	Dec 23, 1996	Knoxville, Tn	Pittsburg, Pa	Nov 7, 1915	81	Kuhn, Kathleen	Andrew, Spencer		Bogel, Bertha		Wife	J.M.G.		Michelle P. & Jean [Neice] - Fred Jr. - Michael P.		Kuch, Virginia	
Kuhn, Mabel Kathleen	Jan 4, 1989	Knoxville, Tn	Hancock Co, Tn	Sep 2, 1915	63	Johnson, James	Hoover, James		Roberts, Mary Lou (Niece)		Roberts Mary Lou (Niece)	J.M.G.					
Kuhn, Jack Calvin	Dec 6, 1976	Jeff City	Tn	Jul 31, 1905	71	Ng	Kyle, John				West View	West View					
Kyle, Margaret Jane [Coll]	Sep 24, 1983	Jeff Co	Tn	Aug 9, 1896	67	S	Kyle, John		Kyle, Mary Alice		Donaldson, Louise - Williams, Mrs. Nola	West View Colored					
Kyle, Marvin Carroll	Feb 16, 1998	J.M.H.	Texas	Jun 21, 1922	65	Mancum, Meryel	Mancum, Walter		Mancum, Minnie		Cline, Patsy & Mexgail	West View	WW 2	Danielle, James R. & Dorothy	Wright, Dorothy		
Kyle, Meryel Hallican [F]	May 29, 1998	Jeff City	Smithville, TX	Nov 20, 1901	96		Mancum, Walter		Clark, Bertha		Williams, Patricia Ann & Larry (Daeg)	West View					
Kyle, Ronald Joseph	Jun 7, 1982	Greeneville, Tn	Tn	Nov 14, 1956	25	S	Kyle, Robert		Mills, Alfreda		Southhalt, Algnsda M.	West View					
Kyle, Roy Arvilin	Apr 28, 1988	J.M.H.	Texas	Aug 22, 1918	69	Div	Kyle, Roy Leslie		James, Ruby Jo		Newton, Darlene (Daeg)	West View					Andis, Mildred & Carl
Kyle, Russell D. (Negro)	Oct 15, 1977	Nashville, Tn			17	Ng					Southhalt, Mrs. Fracia - Kyle Sr. (Nashville, Tn)	West View					
Kyle, Alice Lucile	Jan 2, 1971	Jeff Co	Tn	Jul 8, 1895	75	Granville [D]	Jenkins, Andrew		Butler, Ellen		Kyle, Conard - Wilma - Mary J. - Howard - Wayne - Carroll - Mullins, Ruby	Piedmont					
Kyle, Granville A.	Jul 18, 1966	Jeff Co	Tn		83	Ng	Kyle, Tom		Morris, Eveline		Piedmont	Piedmont					

NAME	DDATE	DLOCAT	BLOCAT	BDATE	AGE	SPOUSE	FATHER	FRLOCAT	MOTHER	MFRLOCAT	BY	BURIAL	VET	SON	DAUG	BROTHER	SISTER
Kyle, James A.	Feb 20, 1945	Jeff Co	Jeff Co	Jul 12, 1875	69	Ng	Meris, Evaline	Tn	Meris, Evaline		Billy Lee-C.E & Jewell [Children]	Piedmont					
Kyle, Minnie	Aug 9, 1936	New Market		Jan 28, 1872		Ng	Whitlock, William	Tn	French, Emmaley	Tn	Kyle, Billy Lee	Piedmont					
Kyle, Ralph Hazen	Dec 14, 1942	Jeff Co	Tn	Oct 15, 1918	24	Ng	Kyle, James A.	Tn	Wilson, Mary E.	Tn	Kyle, James A. - French, Clyde	Piedmont					
Kyle, Rufus Milton	Sep 17, 1949	New Market	Tn	Dec 8, 1867	81	W	Kyle, William		Meris, Evelyn		French, Clyde	Piedmont					
Lacy, Mattie Josephine	Apr 12, 1944	Hamblen Co.	Hamblen Co.	Feb 7, 1867	77	W	Prince, Robert	Tn	Hodge, Margaret	Tn	Carmichael, Miss - Lacy, Walter /Akron, Ohio/ - Pierce, Joe	Lebanon					
Lahay, Hazel	Aug 17, 1972	Asbury	Mo	Jul 7, 1890	82		Carter, Luther		Pollard, Frances		Mallory, Margaret - Lahay, Linda Sue -	West View					
Lahre, James Tony	Jan 28, 1963	Jeff City	Tn	Jan 26, 1963							Lahre, James Tony	West View					
Lamb, Cassie Lee	Mar 25, 1965	J.M.H.	Tn	Aug 2, 1901	83		Kirk, Frank		Courtney, Donna		Lamb, Rex - Minnis	Jefferson Memorial					
Lamb, Roy Minnis	May 29, 1995	Knoxville, Tn	Greene Co. Tn	Aug 19, 1905	87	Harper, Hazel	Lamb, Rufus		Renner, Edda		Lamb, Hugh [Son]	J.M.G.		Paul-Bill-Ralph-Harold	[Step] Pace, Sonda		
Lamdin, Iva Carback	Nov 10, 1983	J.M.H.		Apr 14, 1893	90	Lamdin, J. Carl [D]	Carback, Oscar		Wineyard, Mary Ellen		Rinsenthaler, Miss Jean - Beckman, Mrs. Dorothy L. [Fla]	West View					Ramsey, Lillie
Lambert, Helen	Feb 13, 1974	Jeff City	Tn	Nov 9, 1921	52	W	Miller, G.C.		Carter, Ruth		Miller, G.C. & Meris	Piedmont					
Lamberton, Phillip H.	Jul 20, 1986	Cabot, Vermont		Jan 26, 1922	74	McDougal, Ruth	Lambertson, Raymond W.		Nardini, Victoria		Wife	J.M.G.	42-47	Eric- [Step] Cox, Tony		Curt	
Lancaster, Clarence T.	Aug 22, 1973	Jeff Co	Tn	Jan 31, 1896	76	W	Lancaster, James	Tn	Henson, Mollie		Sellars, Mrs. Nell	Mt. View					
Lamb, Rappie	Aug 17, 1928	Jeff Co	Tn	Jan 28, 1919	63	W	Caldwell, James		Gout, Ng	Tn	Peck, Wiley	Bearden					
Lamb, Frank Lee Jr.	Jan 19, 1959	Jeff Co	Tn	Jan 19, 1959	98	W	Lamb, Frank Sr.		Miller, Anna V.		Lamb, Frank Sr.	Mt. View					
Lane, Ida Belle	Oct 16, 1972	Jeff Co	Tn	May 26, 1874	98	W	Monroe, M.S.		Unk		Barnes, R.O. - Stapleton, Leslie	Mt. View					
Lane, Jonathan Tracey	Dec 1, 1984	Knox Co	Tn	Jan 19, 1959	1-3-0		Lane, George B.		Miller, Barbara		Lane, Ruth & Howard	Mt. View					
Lane, Margaret J.	Jun 15, 1971	Hamblen Co	Tn	Jul 30, 1917	53	W			Riggs, Laura		Miller, Nancy Ruth - Lyons, Helen [Mich.]	Mt. View					
Lane, Samantha Nicole	Feb 3, 1994	Knoxville, Tn	Morristown, Tn	Jan 30, 1994			Lane, Robert M.		Denton, Tasha		Father - Denton, Danny & Kathy - Lindsey, Gary & Marlene - Lane, Sharon Barbee [G-Parents]	Mt. View					
Lane, Tony Douglas	May 19, 1990	Jeff Co	Tn	Aug 10, 1946	43	Laney, Lonnie	Lane, Robert M.		Faulrbrth, Pauline		Lane, Sharon B.	J.M.G.	Vietnam				
Laney, Avis Lydia	Dec 30, 2000	Knoxville, Tn	Ky	Oct 19, 1927	73	Barker, Sharon	Keeton, William		Nardini, Victoria		Husband	J.M.G.		Michael-Jack	Hamrick, Karen		
Langston, Hollis Lee [Col]	Dec 23, 1957	Jeff City	Tn	Jan 28, 1919	38	Ng	Langston, Marshall		Smith, Mattie		Wife	West View Colored					
Langston, Howard Clarence	Jan 12, 1980	Strawberry Plains	Tn	Feb 9, 1906	74	Ng	Langston, Marshall		Hickman, Julia		Langston, Mrs. Vola K.	Pleasant Grove [Piney]					
Langston, Margaret [Col]	Aug 15, 1969	Knox Co	Tn	Apr 19, 1920	49	W	Donaldson, Ralph		Tate, Nellie		Langston, William - Harve Dene	West View					
Langston, Mattie [Col]	Aug 31, 1983	Jeff Co	Tn	Dec 24, 1891	71	W	Smith, Jim		Mary		Langston, Mary Lee - Johnson, Helen	West View Colored					
Langston, Stanley Owens [Col]	Mar 17, 1949	Jeff City	Tn			Ng	Langston, Hollis		Mills, Elizabeth	Tn	Mills, John & Hollis	West View Colored					
Langston, Will [Col]	Dec 20, 1926	Gis		Dec 27, 1948	55	Ng	Langston, Paris	Gis	Mc Cowan, R.M.		Smith, Fay	Mt. View					
Langston, William Harold [Col]	May 27, 1982	Jeff Co	Tn	Aug 16, 1916	35	Ng	Langston, Will		Smith, Mattie		Langston, Margaret	West View Colored					
Langston, Willie Thelma [Col]	May 7, 1982	Jeff Co	Tn	May 4, 1914	48	D	Langston, Will	Tn	Massengill, Lou		Langston, Mary Lee & Sisters	Colored					
Large, Bessie	Jun 3, 1970	Jeff City	Tn	Jun 8, 1902	76	W	Baker, Charlie		Smith, Mattie	Tn	Large, Lillian [Daug]	Lebanon					
Large, Charles	Nov 5, 1936	Jeff City	Tn	Oct 23, 1936		S	Large, F.L.		Baker, Bessie		Large, Lester	Mt. Horeb					
Large, Dorothy Jean	Jul 10, 1951	Jeff Co	Tn	Apr 12, 1951	24	S	Large, Lester	Tn	Baker, Bessie		Large, Lester	Mt. Horeb					
Large, Gerald York Jr.	Sep 13, 1975	Medina, Ohio	Knoxville, Tn	Aug 15, 1954	21	S	Large, Gerald York Sr.		Gay, Wanda		Large, Gerald Sr.	Lebanon - Mt. Horeb					
Large, Ivel	Sep 4, 1953	Tn	Tn	Oct 8, 1898		Ng	Large, Frank		Hinchey, Lillie Mae		Large, Mrs. Adneh	Lebanon					
Large, Janie	Jun 20, 1968	Jeff Co	Tn	Sep 5, 1902	65	Ng	Alley, Henry		Carey, Mary		Large, Walter & Children - Ingram,	Memorial					
Large, Jessie Neil	Oct 3, 1956	Hamblen Co	Tn	May 4, 1933	23	S	Large, Lester F.		Baker, Bessie		Large, Lester - Glorie	Lebanon - Mt. Horeb					
Large, Lester Frank	Jan 1, 1967	Knox Co	Tn	Apr 11, 1900	66	W	Large, Frank		Hinchey, Lillian		Large, Lester	Lebanon					
Large, Lillie Mae	May 1, 1958	Knox Co	Tn	Aug 12, 1870	87	W	Hinchey, Henry		Pierce, Lucinda		Large, H.L.	Lebanon					

NAME	DDATE	BLDCAT	BLLOCAT	BDATE	AGE	SPOUSE	FATHER	FBLLOCAT	MOTHER	MBLLOCAT	BY	BURIAL	VET	SON	DAUG	BROTHER	SISTER
Large, Robert Baker Sr.	Jan [13], 1992	J.M.H.	Jeff Co	Nov 20, 1941	50	Tate, Dortha	Large, Lester F.		Baker, Bessie		Wife	J.M.G.					
Large, Shirley	Dec 27, 1946	Jeff Co	Tn	Dec 17, 1946	10d		Unk		Baker, Bessie	Tn	Large, Mrs. Lester	Mt. Horeb					
Large, Thomas La Rue	Jan 1, 1980	U.T.H.	Tn	Jan 24, 1943	36	S	Large, Lester F.				Large, Lillian & Sisters [Daug]	Mt. Horeb					
Large, Walter Ray	Sep 15, 1994	Morristown, Tn	Sevier Co	Nov 6, 1991	92		Huff, Mary		Howerton, Wilma [Daug]		Large, Lillian [Daug]	J.M.G.			Milia, Edith - Ingram, Gladys	Large, Grace - McGehe, Connie
Large, William Franklin	Jul 18, 1981	Tn	Tn	Jun 16, 1925	56	S	Large, Lester F.		Larmer, Mrs. Conard		Large, Mrs. Conard	Lebanon Presby.	WW 2				
Larmer, John Edward	Nov 12, 1963	Jeff Co	Tn	Oct 24, 1963			Large, Conard		Bailey, Dorothy		Bailey, Faye - Larmer, Oscar	Piney					
Larmore, Cleo Elnor	Jun 24, 1987	U.T.H.	Tn	Mar 15, 1918	69	Larmore, Oscar	Williard, Earl		Wilson, Frankie		Larmore, Oscar	J.M.G.					
Larmore, Mrs. J.A.	Sep 12, 1942	New Market	Oct 15, 1873	69	w		Carmicheal, P.C.	Tn			Children	Piedmont					
Larmore, Richard Tyler	Jan 28, 1988	S.M.M.C.	Knoxville, Tn	Jan 28, 1988	w		Larmore, Richard Raymond		Underwood, Teressa		Larmore, Teressa	J.M.G.					
Larson, Harriet	Oct 13, 1977	Knoxville, Tn	Tn	Dec 30, 1901	75	Larson, Herman G.	Tilley, Thomas G.		Mc Elroy, Nora		Larson, Herman G.	Jefferson Memorial					
Larson, Herman Gregory	Apr 6, 1992	Jeff City	Russia	May 14, 1901	90	Ng	Larson, Max M.		Cogan, Nunia		Grosack, Theodore [Cousin]	J.M.G.					
Lauderback, Olie W.	Dec 30, 1965	Jeff Co	Russia	Aug 1, 1901	88	W	Williams, Alexander		Haskins, Sallie		Dana-Crayton-Beulah- [Daug]	West View					
Lauderback, Carl James [Col]	Nov 6, 1955	Jeff Co	Tn	Feb 6, 1920	35	S	Lauderback, Earl		Williams, Ollie		Lauderback, Dana-Kenneth-Crayton-Beulah	West View Colored	WW 2				
Lauderback, Clayton A. [Negro]	Mar 22, 1982	Pittsburg, Pa	Tn	Mar 23, 1915	66	Houston, Dorothy	Lauderback, Earl		Williams, Ollie		Lauderback, Mrs. Dorothy	West View					
Lauderback, Dana [Negro]	Jan 27, 1976	Jeff Co	Tn	Apr 23, 1902	73	Ng	Lauderback, Earl		Williams, Ollie		Lauderback, Mrs. Wilma & Children	West View					
Lauderback, Early	May 10, 1937		Jeff Co		24					Jeff Co	Lauderback, Dana [Fr'd]	Lauderback Davis Baptist					
Lauderback, Melvin [Col]	Jun 20, 1941								Williams, Ollie		Jarnigan, Helen - Simmons, Charlotte [Mr] - Justine Bebo, Tom	West View					
Lauderback, Wilma [Black]	Aug 21, 1983	J.M.H.	Tn	Sep 2, 1899	83	W	Donaldson, John W.		Geer, Willie B.		Martha Davis Baptist	West View					
Laudrum, Sam R.	Dec 6, 1940		Jeff Co		66	W			McGuire, Elizabeth	Tn							
Lawless, Leatha Aline	Jun 11, 1994	Jeff City	Tn	Feb 19, 1911	83		Knight, Adline		Hayes, Elizabeth		Messengill, Doris [D-Daug]	Mt. Horeb Presby.			Miller, Louise	White, Nancy
Lawless, Andy Arville	Jan 4, 1954	Knox Co	Tn	Feb 4, 1902	51	Ng	Hayes, Isaac		Hayes, Elizabeth		Lawless, Mrs. A.A. [his W.]	Mt. Horeb				Arlie	
Lawless, Bessie M.	Jul 12, 1957	Pa		Jan 15, 1880	67	W					Lawless, Mrs. Paul / Peters, Mrs. Paul	Mt. Horeb					
Lawless, Robert Lawrence	May 23, 1983	Knoxville, Tn	Ky	Jun 12, 1911	71	Cox, Allene	Cox, George		Hayes, Elizabeth		Lawless, Mrs. Robert L & Children	Mt. Horeb					
Lawless, Una Vee	Dec 15, 1980	Jeff City	Tn	Oct 31, 1900	80	W	Holt, Talbert		Buckner, Julia		Lamb, Mrs. Ruby & David - Lawless, Virgil	Mt. Horeb					
Lawless, Virgil B.	Oct 1, 1999	Jacksonville, Nc	Tn	Oct 6, 1928	70	Brown, Edith	Holt, Unavee		Holt, Unavee		Wife	J.M.G.					
Lawrence, Allice Magaline [Jew]	Sep 13, 2000	Jeff City	Tn	May 2, 1939	61	Brown, Edith	Brown, Richard Cantrell		Jarrett, Bonnie Lou		Husband	Woodlawn - Knoxville, Tn					
Lawrence, Andrew Porter [Jew]	Apr 17, 1974	Newmarket, Tn	Tn	Feb 14, 1914	60	W	Alley, Ruby		Carmichael, Connie		Lawrence, Ruby	Jefferson Memorial					
Lawrence, Hosley [F]	Jul 10, 1946	Strawberry Plains	Jeff Co		59	Lawrence, Monroe	Smith, Abe		Housewright, Sarah	Jeff Co	Lawrence, Monroe	Beaver Creek					
Lawrence, James Bryson Jr.	Aug 6, 1999	Jeff City	Long Island, Ny	Jun 9, 1935	64	W	Smith, Abe		Carlson, Margaret		Winmeier, Susan	Cremated	61-62				
Lawrence, Laura B.	May 11, 1996	New York		Apr 4, 1900	96	W	Rich, Fredrick		Underhill, Frances		Durland, George [Cousin]	Green Hill - Waynesville, Nc					
Laws, Sarah D.	Jul 9, 1945	Blount Co		Feb 29, 1857	77	W	Bird, J.M.		Bird, Nan - Moore, Mrs. George		West View						
Lawson, Bridge	Oct 31, 1954	Tn		Mar 6, 1871	83	W	Duignam, Mike	Tn	Stipes, Ann	Tn	Duignam, George - Lawson, D.O.	Straw Plains					
Lawson, Georgia Mae	Jun 28, 1995	Morristown, Tn	Hancock Co, Tn	Jun 15, 1930	65	W	Johnson, Andy		Kissler, Anna		Masick, Mary [Daug]	Chestnut Chapel - Shooksville, Tn		Charles-Don-Leonard	Garland, Lula - Bell, Judy - Ambarose, Doris	

NAME	DDATE	BLOCAT	BLOCAT	BDATE	AGE	SPOUSE	FATHER	FBELOCAT	MOTHER	MFRLOCAT	BY	BURIAL	VET	SON	DAUG	BROTHER	SISTER
Lawson, Mary Ann	Sep 17, 1991	San Diego, Calif.	Cape May, NJ	Mar 1, 1953	38	Lawson, Gary R.	Gordon, James		Galbreath, Ann		Lawson, Gary R.	West View					
Lawson, Milvina	Mar 13, 1964	Strawberry Plains	Tn	Nov 14, 1897	66	Lawson, Jonace [D]	Cook, J.O.		Cook, Lissie		Lawson, Carl-Frobel- Harold-Bill-Clarence- Ralph-Russell - Webb, Ann Lou-Gardner, Gladys-Breeden, Jan	Strawberry Plains					
Lawson, Robert	Dec 6, 1948	Jeff Co	Tazewell, Va	Mar 13, 1869	79-8- 23	Ng			Diskin, Mary	Va	Cochran, Mrs. Lucy - Boling, Mrs. - Edmon, Mrs. Stapleton, J.S. - Collins, Steve - Finchum, Bill - Hopkins, Mildred - Lowdey, Charlie	Piney Grove					
Layman, Algar Blaine	Apr 17, 1989	Hillhaven	Tn	Apr 8, 1903	86	S	Layman, James		Moore, Nancy		Layman, Mrs. Paul T.	Beaver Creek					
Layman, Christopher	Apr 5, 1949	Knox Co	Knox Co		0-7-29				Merlin —		Layman, Mrs. Paul T.	New Market					
Layman, D.F.	Mar 13, 1939	Jeff City	Tn	Nov 6, 1872	66	W	Layman, O.W.	Tn	Durkin, Mary	Tn	D.F., Jr. & Goddard, Paul	New Market					
Layman, Daniel Frank Sr.	Dec 17, 1986	Roanoke, Va	New Orleans, La	Jan 18, 1910	86		Layman, Daniel Frank		Betts, Florence		Upside F.H. [Bedford, Va]	New Market		Daniel Frank [Va]-Robert Eugene [Va]	Layman, Nancy M. [Tx]		
Layman, Dora Mae	Aug 11, 1978	Jeff Co	Tn	Jul 27, 1895	81	Layman, Hobart	White, Luther		Erwin, Cordia		Collins, Mrs. Fred Jr. - Layman, Gerald - Breeden, Mrs. Tom - Hopkins, Mildred	Piedmont					
Layman, Eugene Miller	Oct 11, 1948	Knox Co	Knox Co	Oct 4, 1948	8d		Layman, D.Frank	La	Miller, Elsie	Nc	Layman, D. Frank	Winston-Salem, Nc					
Layman, Herbert Mc Kinley	May 16, 1995	New Market, Tn	New Market, Tn	Jan 22, 1933	62	Kelley, Billie Jean	Layman, Hobart		White, Dora		Wife	53-55	53-55	David & Cindi	Terri	Gerald	
Layman, Hobart Mc Kinley	Feb 7, 1985	VA.- Mt. Home	Tn	Nov 15, 1896	88	W	Layman, James		Moore, Nancy		Piedmont	WW 1	WW 1				
Layman, Hobert Mc Kinley	Mar 9, 1947	Knox Co	Jeff Co	Oct 18, 1896	50-4- 21	Ng	Layman, W.L.	Tn	Denton, Ada	Tn	Layman, Mrs. Hobart - Fox, Robert T.	Hillcrest					
Layman, Infant Female	Jul 2, 1954	Maryville, Tn	Tn	Jun 30, 1954	25		Layman, D. Frank	Tn	Mills, Elsie	Nc	Layman, D.F.	Winston Salem, Nc					
Layman, Infant Male	Aug 23, 1950	Knox Co	Knox Co	Aug 23, 1950	57		Layman, D. Frank	Tn	Miller, Elsie	Nc	Layman, Frank - Fox, Mrs. Robert -	New Market					
Layman, Nell	Dec 5, 1986	Knox Co	Tn	Nv 13, 1896	72	Layman, Hobart [D]	Miller, Benjamine		Renolas, Barbara		Layman, Mrs. Bonnie Fox	Hillcrest					
Lea, Marvin W. Jr.	Mar 11, 1987	Jeff City	Tn	Jan 22, 1917	70	Lea, Marilon W. Jr.	Mc Knight, Lucia		Lea, Lucille		Lea, Lucille	WW 2	WW 2				
Ledi, Ted Jeffrey	Oct 26, 1978	Knoxville, Tn	Tn	Oct 26, 1978		Ledi, Ted Jeffrey Sr.	Ohio		Stallings, Cynthia Darlene	Tn	Stallings, Mrs. Carl	Strawberry Plains					
Lee, Andrew Johnson	Oct 3, 1949	Jeff Co	Tn	Feb 8, 1850	99-7- 25	W	Lee, Tom		Calhoun, Jennie		Lee, Mrs. Dick	Carter - Hamblen Co					
Lee, Andrew Victor [abel]	Sep 7, 1985	Jeff City	Tn	Jun 23, 1928	57	Williams, Mary	Lee, Andrew [Dick]		Mc Clenn, Katherine		Lee, Mrs. Mary W.	Dandridge Memorial					
Lee, Annie Katheryn	Feb 2, 1996	Jeff City	Greene Co., Tn	Oct 25, 1906	89		Mc Lain, Walter		Garin, Alberta I [Daug]		Garin, Alberta I [Daug]	Hillcrest		Albert [D]- Victor [D]	Sellers, Ann - Boatman, Frances - Mary Ellen - [In-Law] Mary E- Jaunita		Lockhart, Naomi
Lee, Louise	Apr 27, 1999	Holt Springs, Nc	Tn	Oct 25, 1929	69	Lee, Clyde	Evans, Unk		Unk		Husband - Franklin, M.	West View		2 [Diff. Marriage]	6 [Diff. Marriage]		
Lee, Mc Daniel [F]	Feb 10, 1983	J.M.G.	Tn	Nov 10, 1919	63	Div	Auld, Horace B.		Mc Daniel, Elma		Clark, Mrs. Judy - Lee, Jim	Jefferson Memorial					
Lee, Robert Edward	May 6, 1989	Talbott, Tn	Hamblen Co.	Oct 4, 1908	84	Miller, Arlenice			Petty, Amanda Novella		Wife	West View					Crosby, Ella Mae - Gregory, Esta Lee - Green, Vivian & Ted R.
Leedy, Evelyn Louise	Nov 3, 1992	Knoxville, Tn	Jeff Co	Feb 7, 1911	81		Lee, Pierce D.		Zikde, Virginia		J.M.G.	J.M.G.		Self, Frank [In- Law]			
Leedy, Victor Zack	Mar 23, 1974	Jeff City	Tn	Nov 3, 1971	72	Rankin, Evelyn	Rankin, Trappan		Perkey, Alpha		Self, Dorutha [Daug] Self, Dorotha - Lord, Mrs. York	Jefferson Memorial		Self, Frank [In- Law]			

NAME	DDATE	DLOCAT	BLOCAT	BDATE	AGE	SPOUSE	FATHER	FELLOCAT	MOTHER	MPSLOCAT	BY	BURIAL	VET	SON	DAUG	BROTHER	SISTER
Leeper, Robert John	Oct 9, 1995	Jeff City	Hamilton Co.	May 4, 1916	79	Couch, Mary	Leeper, Robert Jernigan		Zirkle, Cremora		Wife	French Broad Baptist		Terry	Williams, Lisa & Gregory		Lively, Aileen - Drinnon, Edith
Lefevers, Walter	Sep 22, 1971	Jeff Co	Ky	May 31, 1918	53	Codie, June	Elliott, Hannah		Lefevers, Noah			Jefferson Memorial Gardens					
Lemons, Melinda Jane	May 10, 1949	Jeff Co	Wythe Co, Va	Mar 12, 1872	77	Ng	Woods, James C.		Woods, Jessie		Lemons, W.R.	Lebanon					
Lemons, William Robert	Mar 29, 1958	Jeff City	Tn	Aug 1, 1871	76	W					Brinkley, Ernest	Lebanon					
Lenard, Eugene	Aug 8, 1935	Jeff City	Tn	Feb 6, 1869	4m		Lenard, W.B.	Tn	Merriwett, Martha	Tn	Lenard, W.B.	Oakland					
Leonard, Maude Louisa	May 25, 1951	Jeff City	Tn	Jan 15, 1914	88	W					Hensley, Jean (Doug)	Grants Chapel					
Lester, Edith Pearl	Feb 3, 2000	Jeff City	Tn	Dec 11, 1911	88	W	Lester, Della		Lester, Della		Hensley, Jean (Doug)	J.M.G.					
Lester, Guy Noe	Oct 13, 1990	J.M.H.	Tn	Jan 15, 1914	76	Kimbrough, Edith	Ink				Combs, Mrs. Ollie - Merriwette, Della	J.M.G.					
Lester, Johnston A.	Nov 7, 1943	Jeff Co	Floyd Co, Va	Nov 4, 1851	92	W		Va		Va	Combs, Mrs. Ollie - Merriwette, Della	West View					
Lethco, Frank Armstrong	Aug 26, 1996	Talbott, Tn	Jeff City	Apr 1, 1906	92		Lethco, Jim		Lethco, Rachel		Homer, Jennie [Step-Daug]	J.M.G.				Corbett, Frankie Jane - Trent - Saldana - Rhoder - [Bye] - Smith, Nancy - Sandifman, Billie	
Lethco, Mary	Apr 23, 1997	Morristown, Tn	Talbott, Tn	Nov 14, 1911	85	Lethco, Frank	Miller, Roy		Shultz, Lula		Husband	Nance's Grove			Smith, Nancy - Sandifman, Billie - Homer, Jennie - [Bye] - Corbett, Jane - Trent, Barbara - Rucker, Ruby	
Lewis, Attra J.	Jun 7, 1967	Jeff Co	Tn	Apr 27, 1890	77	W	Staple, William		Griffin, Ludicia		Stripland, Mrs. Tom - Elmore, Mrs. Raymond	Nance's Grove					
Lewis, James T.	Apr 22, 1962	Jeff Co	Tn	Jan 16, 1882	90	S	Lewis, John		Hackney, Rebecca		Lewis, Mrs. P.T. [Ruby]	Nance's Grove					
Lewis, Mary [Cull]	Apr 17, 1955	Jeff City	Tn	Mar 14, 1883	62		Cunningham, William		Johnson, Harietta		Cunningham, Ross - Lewis, Bobby	A.M.E. Zion - Jeff Co					
Lewis, Perry	Jun 7, 1992											Nance's Grove					
Lewis, Pleasant Franklin	Jan 16, 1945	Jeff Co	Jeff Co	Jul 21, 1866	78	Ng	Hackney, John	Tn	Hackney, Rebecca	Tn	Lewis, Ruth - Elmore, Mrs. Raymond	Nance's Grove					
Lewis, Robert Lee	Dec 7, 1944	Jeff Co	Tn	Feb 27, 1883	61	W	Lewis, John	Nc	Snead, Matilda	Nc	Lewis, Elhu - Malone, Mrs. Reuben	Shady Grove					
Lewis, Earl B.	Apr 15, 1965	Jeff Co	Tn	Jul 27, 1924	40	S	Lewis, Eugene				Lewis, Eugene B.	Hillcrest					
Libhowl, Joseph	Dec 28, 1992	J.M.H.	Belgium	Jul 10, 1899	83	W					Henson, Lucille - Latour, Amanda Marie	A.M.E. Zion - Jeff Co					
Libhowl, Laura Agnes	Jul 2, 1973	Jeff City	Virginia	Dec 19, 1900	72	Libhowl, Joseph	Hinchie, John Lye		May, Lou Ella		Mc Cormick, Ed	Jefferson Memorial					
Lickes, Orville W.	Sep 30, 1965	Galena, Illinois	Tn	Dec 14, 1911	53	Ng	Lickes, John		Conley, Caroline		Lickes, Mrs. Carmen Greenwood - Galena, Illinois	Greenwood - Galena, Illinois					
Lillard, Wallace Lee	Oct 10, 1988	Jeff City	Tn	Oct 29, 1905	82	Gilbert, Adeline	Lillard, John M.		Love, Elizabeth		Lillard, Adeline G.	J.M.G.					
Lindswood, Charles	May 11, 1947	Hancock Co, Indiana	Sep 18, 1883	S3-7-23		Ng	Lindswood, James	Indiana	Jessup, Cora T.	Indiana	Lindswood, Charles H. [Greenfield, Indiana]	Greenfield, Indiana					
Lindsay, Gertrude B.	Nov 15, 1934	Dandridge	Tn	Nov 17, 1907	26	Lindsay, Algie	French, Perry	Tn	Elder, Sarah	Tn	Lindsay, Algie - Wappooner, Luther	Dumplin					
Lindsay, Infant	Jun 7, 1946																
Lindsay, Isaac Floyd	Oct 16, 1959	V.A. Hospital	Tn	Jan 1, 1897	62	Ng	Lindsay, P.W.		Riggs, Rebecca		Lindsay, Mattie-Fred-Elizabeth	Shady Grove					
Lindsay, Jack Franklin	Jan 30, 1996	Jeff Co	Tn	Apr 24, 1941	55	Young, Loritta	Lindsay, Carl		Henderson, Helen J.		Wife	J.M.G.			Nancy [G] Kathryn-Karen		
Lindsay, John Seldon	Jul 13, 1995	Jeff City	Tn	Dec 13, 1911	83	Stallings, Reva	Lindsay, Horace Milburn		Lindsay, Rebecca		Wife	West View		Kenneth & Joan			
Lindsay, Leona	Sep 19, 1983	J.M.H.	Ohio	Apr 1, 1906	77	W	Mc Clane, James Marshall		Ballinger, Delia		Blair, Mrs. Kieba	West View					
Lindsay, Mack	May 20, 1946	Knox Co	Sevier Co	Mar 21, 1918	28	Varnell, Maude	Lindsay, Jesse Medium	Sevier Co	Sizemore, Ida	Carter Co	Sindoey, Maude	Flat Gap					
Lindsay, Mattie W.	Jul 25, 1992	Hilltown	Jeff Co	Feb 7, 1901	91	W	Williamson, Oscar		Chambers, Farley		Moreland Helen L. [Doug]	Shady Grove - Jeff Co					
Lindsay, Nannie Belle	Mar 21, 1968	Tn	Jul 30, 1918	49	W	Wright, John W.		Beckner, Willie		Lindsay, Donald	Rocky Valley						
Line, Addie	Mar 2, 1991	Kingsport, Tn	Jeff Co	Oct 9, 1900	90	Line, Clifford C.	Mills, George W.		Reeves, Laura		Line, Johnnie M. [Son]	J.M.G.					

NAME	DDATE	DLOCAT	BLOCAT	BDATE	AGE	SPOUSE	FATHER	FBLOCAT	MOTHER	MFBLOCAT	BY	BURIAL	VET	SON	DAUG	BROTHER	SISTER
Line, Barbara Ruth	Jun 11, 1960	Jeff City, Tn	Tn	Aug 21, 1936	24	S	Line, J. Earl		Chiles, Inez		Line, J. Earl	Jefferson Memorial					
Line, Bernard R.	Aug 31, 1976	Talbott, Tn	Tn	Dec 26, 1907	68	Horner, Cornelia	Line, John Albert		Quarles, Jemima		Line, Mrs. Bernard	Jefferson Memorial					
Line, Clarence Farley	Feb 26, 1982	Jeff Co		Apr 8, 1899	82	Crouch, Janet	Line, John Albert		Quarles, Mary Jemima		Wife	Sunderland					
Line, Cornelia	Dec 27, 1985	Knoxville, Tn	White Pine, Tn	Mar 11, 1911	82	Line, Bernard [R]	Horner, James M.		Hall, Maggie		Newton, Mary [Sister]	J.M.G.					
Line, Edna	May 15, 1987	J.M.H.	Tn	Aug 30, 1901	85	Ng	Sharbs, William N.		Brown, Jo Ann		Line, James F.	J.M.G.					
Line, Grace P.	Jul 15, 1954	Knox Co	Tn	Jul 30, 1903	90	Ng	Newman, Frank		Owen, Sue		Line, Clarence F.	Sunderland					
Line, Inez	Sep 3, 1981	J.M.H.	White Pine, Tn	Oct 23, 1913	77	W	Chiles, David P. Sr.		Betts, Viola M.		Julian, Patsy L. [Daug]	Sunderland					
Line, James Ray	Mar 23, 1990	Jeff Co	Tn	Apr 25, 1895	94	W	Line, John A.		Quarrels, Mary J.		Line, James F.	J.M.G.					
Line, John Albert	Jan 30, 1951	Jeff Co	Tn	Jul 4, 1864	86	W	Line, James H.		Line, Charity E.		Line, Ernest	Mt. Pleasant					
Line, John Earl	Feb 7, 1989	J.M.H.	Jeff Co	Jul 6, 1894	94	Chiles, Inez	Line, John Albert		Quarles, Mary G.		Line, Inez C.	J.M.G.					
Line, Mayme	Oct 9, 1951	Hamblen Co	Tn	Jun 29, 1878	73	Line, Sherman	Macomb, W.B.		Hall, Mrs. Horace - Virginia		Line, J.A.	Mt. Pleasant					
Line, Nelson Horner	Jun 222, 1954	Jeff Co	Tn	Aug 12, 1874	79	W	Line, Andrew		Quarles, Catherine		Mrs. Horner - Virginia, Mrs. Sallie & Zane	Mt. View					
Line, Sally P.	Sep 21, 1995	Jeff Co	Tn	Mar 12, 1908	87	Line, N.H.			Williams, Marjorie [Cousin]		Rogers, James H. [Cousin]	Mt. View					
Line, William Sherman	Sep 30, 1949	Talbott, Tn	Tn	Jan 1, 1876	73	Ng	Line, James		Williams, Charity		Line, Mrs. Marilyn	Mt. Pleasant					
Line, Zanie Franklin (Jack)	Aug 20, 1966	Jeff Co	Tn	Jul 4, 1906	60	S	Line, Nelson, H.				Line, Sallie - Rogers, Mrs. Frank - Bladen, ?	Mt. Pleasant					
Liner, Mary Jane	Jan 17, 1931	Talbott	Tn	Dec 25, 1870	60	Line, J.A.			Williams, Marjorie A.	Tn	Sunderland, Martha	Mt. Pleasant					
Link, B.D.	Jan 31, 1940				73		Quarles, C.T.	Tn			Line, J.A. [Parisburg, Va] - Link, R.E. [Johnson City]	New Market					
Lindford, Mary Ethel	May 11, 1927	Tn			42.5 10	Lunsford, M.R.	Morgan, Alex		Baxter, Hanna	Tn	Mertha, Sharmila [Friend - N.J.]	New Market					
Link, William R Jr.	Jun 11, 1997	Daytona Beach, Fl	Lynch, Ky	Mar 4, 1923	74							West View					
Link, Mary May	Jun 20, 1991	Birmingham, Ala.	Tn	Jun 19, 1919	72	Little, Lewis Lee	May, John A. Sr.		Quarles, Nora		Ashworth, Sally [Niece]	Sunderland					
Little, William G.	Apr 11, 1985	Tn	Tn	Sep 12, 1895	49	Ng	Little, Sam		Walker, Alice	Tn		Rossberry					
Litton, Marshall Terry	Jul 11, 1994	Houston, Texas	Tn	Dec 28, 1912	81	Catlett, Mattie Belle	Litton, Dick		Terry, Edna		Wife	West View		Ted C. [T4] - Richard H. [T4]			
Livesay, Charles Woodrow	Jul 19, 1978	Park-West Hosp.	Oneida, Tn	Jun 19, 1934	44	Pugh, Evelyn	Kinney, Dwight		Cox, Ada Mae		Hickory Valley - Loudon Co	West View	Korea				
Livesay, Elmer	May 16, 1954	Hancock Co, Tn	Tn	Jul 7, 1907	46	Ng	Livesay, George		Courtney, Nealy		Livesay, Mrs. Charles & Children, Mrs. William T. & Kenneth	Livesay					
Lopez, John David	Nov 26, 1997	Philadelphia, Pa	Hancock Co, Tn	Nov 17, 1915	82	Ng	Lopez, John L.		Stimson, Ella Frances		Wife	Cremated		[Step] Sandusky, Larry [Ma]	Conway, Carol [Pa] - Smith, Natalie [Pa]		
Lloyd, Parter	Sep 1, 1933	Jeff City	Philadelphia, Pa	Jun 21, 1935	28	Ng	Lloyd, J.M.	Tn	Enton, Henry		New Market						
Lloyd, R. Gage	Aug 12, 1996	Rutledge, Tn	Baltimore, Tx	Dec 5, 1906	91	Felicitana	Lloyd, John Filerson		Rudish, Myrtle		Harrell, Rebecca L. [Daug]	Trinity Memorial - Big Springs, Tx					
Logon, Zosimo	May 13, 1998	Jeff City	Phillippines	Dec 26, 1917	80	Felicitana	Logon, Atanasid		Cole, Roberralis		Wife - Mc Carty Mortuary [Knoxville, Tn]				Logon, Zosita		
Locke, Alice Anita	Jun 17, 1999	New Market, Tn	Mc Minnville, Tn	Sep 26, 1907	91	Ng	Smart, Thomas Dibrell		Jennings, Margaret		Moore, Mary Ellen [Daug]	Cremated					
Lockhart, Anna Bailey	Jul 7, 1936	Tn	Tn	Sep 30, 1881	54	Ng	Bailey, John	Tn	Miller, Jane	Sc	Lockhart, Mrs. Callie - M.H-Cecil-B.P.- Caldwell, T.E. - Barnes, C.H. - Calvert, E.E.	West View					
Lockhart, Benjamin Martin	Jan 7, 1954	Jeff Co	Tn	Jul 4, 1890	93	Ng	Lockhart, Jessie		Elliott, Lucinda		Barnes, Mrs. C.H.[Jessie] - Clark, Hazel - Lockhart, Cecil - Morris, Bonnie	Flat Gap					
Lockhart, Callie G.	Jul 4, 1970	Knox Co	Tn	May 17, 1880	90	W	Edwards, W.D.		Bettis, Sarah		Barnes, Mrs. C.H.[Jessie] - Clark, Hazel - Lockhart, Cecil - Morris, Bonnie	Flat Gap				Jim	Jean

NAME	DDATE	DLOCAT	BLOCAT	BDATE	AGE	SPOUSE	FATHER	FRLOCAT	MOTHER	MRLOCAT	BY	BURIAL	VET	SON	DAUG	BROTHER	SISTER
Lockhart, Grace	Jul 27, 1976	Jeff Co	Tn	May 24, 1892	84	Lockhart, Melvin H.	Miller, John H.		Cox, Sarah J.		Cox, Mrs. Joe F-Dale-Vesser, Jim - Lockhart, Melvin H.	Jefferson Memorial					
Lockhart, J.A.	Sep 7, 1999	Jeff Co	Tn	Aug 24, 1871	98	Ng	Elliott, Lucinda		Lockhart, Mrs. Clara		Jefferson Memorial	Mill Springs					
Lockhart, James Thomas	May 24, 1986	Oak Ridge Medical	Tn	Mar 2, 1943	43	Rogers, Lorene	Mr. Chase, Naomi		Lockhart, Lorene		Lockhart, Mrs. Clara	Flat Gap					
Lockhart, Lawrence Wayne	Mar 7, 1965	V.A. Hospital - Mt. Home	Tn	Jun 6, 1915	49	Div	Miller, Met H.	Tn	Miller, Grace	Tn	Jefferson Memorial	Jefferson Memorial	WW 2				
Lockhart, Mattie B.	Jan 4, 1969	Knox Co	Tn	Nov 18, 1881	87	S	Hinchey, George		Hinchey, Rebecca		Lockhart, Joe	Flat Gap					
Lockhart, William Harrison	Jan 20, 1979	Jeff City	Tn	Apr 3, 1888	90	W	Lockhart, Benjamin		Lockhart, Rebecca		Lockhart, Mrs. Mildred Cox	Jefferson Memorial					
Lockhart, Mrs. V.T.	Sep 7, 1928		Tn			W						Mt. Horeb					
Lockhart, Theodore C.	May 2, 1949	Jeff Co	Tn	Mar 24, 1892	57-1-8	Ng	Lockhart, Ben		Hinchey, Rebecca		Lockhart, Mrs. Henrita Dean	Piedmont					
Long, Addie Louise	Jul 6, 1996	Jeff City	Jeff City	Jul 8, 1906	89	D	Long, Jeff		Ople, Annie		Russell, Susan - Lyle, Betty Long [Nieces], Long, Ron - Russell, Jeff [Nephews]	J.M.G.					
Long, Connie C.	Jan 21, 1971	Knox Co	Tn	Feb 7, 1904	66	D	Long, Frank	Tn	Long, Alldzo - Vineyard, ___ V.A.	Tn	West View	WW 2				
Long, D.B.	Jan 1, 1934	Jeff City	Tn	Nov 15, 1855	78	Ng	Long, Harvey		Stubblefield, Martha		Long, Jeff	Sunderland					
Long, David B.	Nov 5, 1982	Morristown, Tn	Tn	May 7, 1957	35	Cannon, Rena		Long, Kyle		Sams, Ann		Wife	Lebanon Baptist					
Long, Jeff	Mar 3, 1954	Beverly Hills, Knox Co	Tn	Jan 7, 1882	72	W	Long, Dan		Brooks, Eliza		Sunderland	Sean-Dagon				Miller, Rena
Long, Katherine Rosalee	Feb 12, 1978	Jeff City	Tn	Dec 10, 1910	67	S	Long, Jeff		Ople, Annie		Long, Miss Addie Russell, Mrs. Penny	Jefferson Memorial					
Long, Mrs. Lemmie	Dec 23, 1924	Tn (D, Knoxville, Tn)	Tn (D, Knoxville, Tn)		40	Long, L.M.	Burger, John	Granger Co	Burger, Susie	Granger Co	Jefferson City					
Long, R.E.	Apr 28, 1933	New Market	Tn	Oct 1, 1888	45	Ng	Long, G.W.	Nc	Mathews, Susie	Nc	Long, Mrs. R.E.	New Market M.E.					
Long, Rhoda	Feb 18, 1927		Tn		83-5-13	W	Douglas, Alexander	Tn	Ruth, Rhoda	Tn	Newman, Mrs.	West View					
Longmire, Arkie Snell	Mar 17, 1982	Talbot, Tn	Tn	Sep 28, 1904	77	Longmire, Carl [D]	Livesay, John		Batty, Molly		Harrison, Mrs Jank [Anne]	Seal - Sneedville, Tn					
Longmire, Casnock Austin	Apr 2, 1982	J.M.H.	Tn	Jul 24, 1895	86	W	Longmire, William Henderson		Corwin, Mrs. Joan L.		West View	West View					
Longmire, Georgia	Sep 2, 1979	Jeff City	Tn	Apr 30, 1899	80	Longmire, C.A.	Longmire, Marion Austin		Longmire, Georgia		Longmire, C.A.	West View					
Longmire, Slothia Ruth	Apr 10, 1996	Knoxville, Tn	Tn	Jan 5, 1935	51	S	Longmire, Condia		Clark, Estella		Longmire, William M.	West View					
Loomis, Ives Eugene	Apr 14, 1978	New York	Tn	Jan 22, 1910	68	Ng	Loomis, Henry Ives	Tn	Eller, Bonnie	Tn	Loomis, Mrs. I.E.	Mt. Pleasant					
Looney, Infant Male	Apr 20, 1949	Jeff Co	Jeff Co	Apr 19, 1949			Looney, Chyde				Barbee, Mrs. Robert						
Lord, Gladys	Nov 3, 1999	Knoxville, Tn	Dandridge, Tn	Mar 10, 1906	93		Graham, James Rufus		Manley, Mary Caroline		Lord, John E. [Son]	Lynnhurst		[G] Lord, Stephen [Japan]-Timothy [TN] - Gastrock, Barry Jr.[OH]-Kurt C. [MI]		
Loudermilk, Lake Worth [M]	Jan 13, 1999	Rutledge, Tn	Tn	Jan 12, 1924	75		Loudermilk, Lee Washington		Finks, Ocie Lee		Loudermilk, Lake F. [Son]	Copper Ridge - Blue Ridge, Ga					
Love, Collie	Mar 28, 1958	Jeff City	Tn	Feb 17, 1881	77	Love, H.M. [D]	Collier, William L.		Carter, Mary		Warren, Mrs. Dallas - Bettis, Nina - Palmer & Boodie	Mt. Horeb					
Love, Charlie	Jan 9, 1999	Jeff City	Jeff Co	May 14, 1913	85	Ng	Homer, Dwett		Henson, Maggie		Love, Jack [Son]	J.M.G.					
Love, Estil Claude	Jul 28, 1983	V.A. - Mt. Home	Tn	Jun 24, 1910	73	Ng	Love, Harrison		Elledge, Maggie		Winstead, Mrs. Velma	Jefferson Memorial	WW 2			John-Raymond	
Love, Franklin Lee	Oct 13, 1998	Jeff Co	Tn	Mar 7, 1937	31	Ng	Lane, Hubert A.		Hedrick, Margaret		Lane, Mrs. Annie V.	Mt. View	unk				
Love, Fred Bettis	Oct 10, 1961	Jeff Co	Tn		47	Ng	Love, John		Hayes, Nannie E.		Lane, Wilburn & Mrs. Ruth - John, Lewis, Sallie - Mr. Murray, Mrs. John	Mt. View					
Love, Henry Marshall	Jan 1, 1946	Jeff Co	Jeff Co	Aug 7, 1878	67	Ng	Love, Sam	Tn	Barbee, Lou	Tn	Love, Mary Lou [Daug]	Mt. Horeb					

NAME	DDATE	DLOCAT	BLOCAT	BDATE	AGE	SPOUSE	FATHER	MOTHER	PBLOCAT	BY	BURIAL	VET	SON	DAUG	BROTHER	SISTER
Love, John	Dec 2, 1940	Jeff City	Tn	Aug 9, 1939	1	W	Love, Palmer	Homer, Clarcie	Tn	Love, Palmer	West View					
Love, John	Jan 21, 1937	Jeff Co	Tn	Nov 27, 1936	7		Love, Billin	Holt, Elizabeth	Tn	Love, Artie	Mt. Horeb					
Love, Lola Ruth	Mar 21, 1956	J.M.H.	Virginia	Sept 11, 1898	52	W	Love, Frank	Brooks, Esther		Love, Artie	Bethel - Jeff Co					
Love, Mack Lee	Dec 28, 1954	J.M.H.	Tn	Jul 17, 1890	64	Ng	Martin, Jim	Beard, Lettie		Love, Wilburt	Branham					
Love, Marshall H.	Oct 21, 1983	Jeff Co	Tn	Nov 23, 1896	67	W	Love, John	Lane, Jim		Love, Mrs. Mack	Beech Springs - Sevier Co					
Love, Palmer O.	May 27, 1974	Jeff Co	Tn	Jul 25, 1909	64	Hufflaker, Jamie	Homer, Clarice	Hayes, Nannie		Love, Mrs. Palmer	Jefferson Memorial					
Lowdey, Crabe Grayton	Jul 28, 2000	Jeff City	Tn	Feb 16, 1914	86	Geraldine [2 Nd] - Reno, Mary Margaret [D]	Lowdey, Luther Jesse	Glenn, Cora		Wife	Hills Union - Dandridge, Tn	WW 1	James & Dockie	Donahoo, Mrs. Richard Cotton - Galyon, Lorene & Kenneth - Jerry - Banks, Georgia - [Step] Perry/Bobel, Kentucky	Jessie [D]	Banks, Marie [D]
Lowdey, Frances	Jan 19, 1982	Jeff City	Tn	Mar 19, 1919	63	W	Baysinger, Earnest E.	Werner, Julie		Smith, Sara - Baysinger, Joe-Bill- Ernest-Viola	Penrig Hollow - Grainger Co					
Lowdey, Race	Nov 21, 1977	Jeff Co	Tn	Dec 17, 1907	69	S	Lowdey, Green	Hurst, Bethena		Denton, Mrs. Bertha	Sexson Chapel					
Lowdey, Robert Lee	May 5, 1983	Knoxville, Tn	Tn	Aug 19, 1929	53	Ng	Lowdey, Jesse	Wise, Rosa		Lowdey, Mrs. Jesse	Jefferson Memorial	Korea				
Lovegrove, Fred David	Sep 14, 1951	Jeff Co	Washington Co, Tn	Apr 23, 1898	53	Ng	Lovegrove, Albert	Cinyal, Callie		Longmore, Mrs. Maggie	Jarnigan					
Lowdein, James Carl	Apr 27, 1957	Jeff City	Tn	Sept 25, 1880	76	Ng	Lowdein, James	Young, Dorothy		Lowbdin, Mrs. Ina C.- Beckman, Mrs. A. Farrington, Mrs. John	West View	WW 1				
Lowe, Anne	Jan 12, 1986	J.M.H.	Tn	Sep 25, 1911	76	S	Thorpen, Martin	Brandt, Mary E.		Woods [Daug] - Rizenfalter	J.M.G.					
Lowe, Bertha Ann Jarnigan [Ca]	May 11, 1948	Grainger Co	Utah	Jan 20, 1884	64+/21	Lowe, Montgomery [D]	Unk	Peck, Ophelia		Lowe, R.H.	Colored					
Lowe, Cleo	Sep 2, 1927	Jeff City	Grainger Co		33+/14	Lowe, R.H.	Murph, W.T.	Jarnigan, Lizzie	Tn	Lowe, G.R.	Shiloh					
Lowe, Gladys Marie	Feb 28, 1983	J.M.H.	Pa	Sep 10, 1930	82	S	Lowe, Paul W.	Goldsle, Lizzie	Tn	Lowe, David-Walter	Jefferson Memorial					
Lowe, Grover Rauben	Apr 27, 1962	Jeff Co	Tn	Sept 11, 1886	75	Ng	Lowe, Newton	Taylor, Sarah Ann		Lowe, Eletha	Drumplin					
Lowe, Infant	May 4, 1940	Sevier Co	Sevier Co	Dec 30, 1939	54		Lowe, J.N.	Payton, Maudie	Tn	Lowe, Paul	Lebanon - Mt. Horeb					
Lowe, Jack Fain	Feb 29, 1944	Jeff Co	Sevier Co	Nov 15, 1937	6	S	Lowe, Paul	Taylor, Sarah	Tn	Lowe, Paul	Lebanon - Mt. Horeb					
Lowe, Jackie William [M]	Oct 1, 1957	Hamblen Co	Tn	Nov 10, 1943	14	S	Lowe, J. William	Bacon, Gladys	Tn	Lowe, William	Pleasant View					
Lowe, Jerry Daryl	Sep 3, 1964	Hamblen Co	Tn	Aug 17, 1964	7		Lowe, Tommy	Ladd, Mary Ellen	Tn	Lowe, Tommy	Jefferson Memorial					
Lowe, Jessie Floyd	Feb 25, 1981	Newmarket, Tn.	Newmarket, Tn.	May 27, 1950		Riddle, Leota	Lowe, Jessie Nathan	Lowe, Aaron W.	Tn	Lowe, Aaron W. [Son]	Piney					
Lowe, Leota	Sep 11, 1991	Jeff Co	Jeff Co	Aug 24, 1904	87	W	Childress, Cordelia	Murph, Cleo	Tn	Lowe, G.R.	Shiloh					
Lowe, Little Cleo	Nov 11, 1927	Tn	Tn		0-3-6	S	Lowe, G.R.	Lowe, G.R.	Tn	Lowe, G.R.	Lebanon					
Lowe, Paul W. Jr.	Nov 2, 1936	J.M.H.	Tn	Jan 11, 1908	75	W	Lowe, Daniel Harlen	Morgan, Aggie		Lowe, Paul	Shiloh					
Lowe, Paul Wesley	Jul 4, 1983	Ne	Ohio	Oct 1, 107	93	W	Morgan, Edward	Morgan, Aggie		Lowe, Paul	Jefferson Memorial					
Lowe, Richard Harold	Oct 1, 2000	Jeff City	Jeff City	Jan 16, 1909	72	W	Taylor, Boden	Murphy, Margaret		Lowe, Bruce [Son]	J.M.G.					
Lowe, Samantha Rachael	Aug 8, 1942	Grainger Co	Grainger Co	May 8, 1889	80	W	Morgan, Edward	Morgan, Aggie	Tn	Morgan, Grover & Ray	Shiloh					
Lowe, Sarah Ann	Jan 17, 1981	Jeff City	Nc	Jan 16, 1909	72	Lowe, Paul W.	Taylor, Boden	Murphy, Margaret		Lowe, Kenneth-T.E.-W.I.	Jefferson Memorial					
Lowe, Stella	Feb 23, 1981	Jeff Co	Va	Sep 14, 1889	91	W	Owens, W.A.	Hodges, Mrs. Robert		Hodges, Mrs. Robert	Shiloh					
Lowe, W.E.	Apr 20-22, 1928	J.M.H.	Tn	Dec 21, 1948	78	W	Lowe, Kenneth	Lowe, Donald		Lowe, Donald	J.M.G.					
Lowe, William Jack	Jan 11, 1987	J.M.H.	Tn	Dec 6, 1912	38	Winstead, Betty	Reece, Ella Vee	Lowe, Betty W.		Lowe, Betty W.	West View	vietnam				
Lowery, Cora Winnifred	Jan 2, 1995	J.M.H.	Tn	Jul 20, 1905	80	Lowery, Omer	Peck, Georgia	Miles, James		Lowery, Run [Buck]	West View					
Lowery, Delmar Ray	May 7, 1975	Strawberry Plains	Tn	Dec 6, 1912	62	Ng	Lowery, David	Bolden, Frances		Lowery, Mrs. Delmar	Thorn Grove - Knox Co					
Lowery, Ernest Elbert	Jun 22, 1982	Jeff City	Tn	Feb 2, 1900	62	Ng	Lowery, John	Lowery, Charlie-Harold James W. [Son]		Lowery, Charlie-Harold James W. [Son]	West View					
Lowery, Francis [F]	Aug 31, 1925	Henderson, Ky	Tn	Aug 26, 1904	49	Lowery, Dave	Buddens, William	Lowery, Sarah	Tn	Lowery, N.M.	Weslays Chapel					
Lowery, Gene J.	Apr 24, 1979	Knoxville, Tn	Tn	May 13, 1920	54	Irene	Miles, Winifred	Lowery, Omer		Lowery, Paul-Elburt & Sisters	West View					
Lowery, Harold William	Feb 22, 1982	Tn	Tn		61	Div	Trilley, Katherine	Lowery, Ernest		Lowery, Jim	West View	WW 2				
Lowery, James Edward	May 27, 1952	Alabama	Alabama	Dec 26, 1908	43	Ng	Lowery, John	Dixon, Sallie C.		Lowery, Mrs. Lucille - Hutchinson, Christie [Ala]	Valley Helly - Beesemer, Ala.					

NAME	DDATE	BLOCAT	BLOCAT	BDATE	AGE	SPOUSE	FATHER	FBLOCAT	MOTHER	MBFLOCAT	BY	BURIAL	VET	SON	DAUG	BROTHER	SISTER
Lowery, John	Jul 6, 1941	Mascot	Knox Co		68-9-28	W					Lowery, Oner [Son]	Mascot M.E.					
Lowery, Katherine	Mar 16, 1990	J.M.H.	Tn	Jul 31, 1901	88	W	Talley, John		Benefield, Rena		Lowery, Charles W. [Tunnell Hill, Ga]	West View					
Lowery, Oner E.	May 29, 1967	Jeff Co.	Tn		65	Ng			Brooks, Nola		Lowery, Mrs. Winifred M.	West View					
Lowery, Mary	Apr 6, 1937	Knox Co	Tn	Dec 30, 1873	63	Lowery, John [B]	Lowery, John	Tn	Lowery, Nerida	Tn	Lowery, Oner	New Market					
Loy, Ada Maude	Apr 21, 1974	Tn	Tn	Nov 16, 1883	90 ?	Loy, John C.	Odem, Gideon	Tn	Miller, Nancy	Tn	Loy, Elwood [Son]						
Loy, Bessie	Mar 19, 1961	Piedmont	Union Co, Tn	Dec 14, 1886	74	Loy, Scott	Snodderly, Rice		Petree, Mary L.		Snodderly, Gaines	Piedmont					
Loy, Frank	Jan 23, 1923	Cleveland, Fla	Tn		62	S	Loy, George B.		Hodge, Ellen		Loy, George - Annie R.	Wooden Chapel					
Loy, Hodge	Feb 8, 1954	Knox Co	Tn	Jan 12, 1892	62	S	Loy, George P.		Hodge, Ellen		Hodge, Ellen						
Loy, J. Harvey	Apr 10, 1934	Knoxville, Tn	Tn	Dec 18, 1871	62	Ng	Loy, George	Tn	Hodge, Ellen, Tn	Tn	Loy, Mrs. J. Harvey & Miss Grace	Friends Station					
Loy, John W.	Oct 25, 1962	Jeff Co	Tn	Oct 28, 1878	86	Div	Loy, George		Martin, Matilda		Loy, C. Woden	Friends Station					
Loy, Martha	May 27, 1953	Jeff Co	Tn		78	W	Miller, Alfred		Hodge, Ellen		Loy - Jeff Co. Wooden						
Loy, Mary Grace	Dec 5, 1982	Knox Co	Tn	Jun 4, 1874	79	S	Loy, George B.		Hodge, Ellen		Loy, C.W.	Wooden					
Loy, Mattie	Dec 31, 1950	Jeff Co	Tn	Jan 13, 1886	64	Div	Cole, I.M.		Mauley, Mrs. R.W. - Cabbel, Ben S.		Mauley, Mrs. R.W. - Cabbel, Ben S.	West View					
Loy, Ralph Mc Bee	Apr 1, 1999	J.M.H.	Tn	Oct 2, 1906	80	Randles, Lorene	Thomas		Thomas, Millie		Hopkins, Margaret Overbry, Mrs. Betty	Friends Station					
Loy, Rabrd Brown	Aug 1, 1959	Knox Co	Tn		80	S	Jeff City		Cole, Mollie		Overbry, Mrs. Betty	Friends Station	WW 1				
Loy, Scott W.	Feb 18, 1962	Jeff Co	Union Co, Tn	May 2, 1876	83	W	Loy, William		Langims, Phoebe		Loy, Edward & Emert	Piedmont					
Lucas, Frank	May 15, 1986	J.M.H.	Poland	Jan 12, 1916	70	Spivia, Pauline	Unk		Kidwell, Pauline Spivia		Kidwell, Pauline Spivia	West View					
Lucas, Margaret	Sep 28, 1927		Poland		64-4-28	Lucas, Dr.	White, Albert	Tn	Unk	Tn	White, Margaret P. Mc Farland, Mary Ruth	West View					
Lucas, Novella Jane	Apr 18, 1946	Hawkins Co, Tn	New Market, Tn	Nov 8, 1886	59	S	Lucas, S.T.		Malone, Pop		Haynes, Mary Kate [Sister]	West View					
Lucas, Pauline	Oct 18, 1984	Jeff City	New Market, Tn	Nov 14, 1928	65		Spia, Samuel		White, Margaret P. Mc Farland, Mary Ruth		White, Margaret Kate [Sister]	Van-Clarence					
Luengen, Verna Alice	Mar 5, 1999	Wyoming, Ny		Dec 19, 1921	77		Strathearn, John		King, Mary E.		Luengen, Dale & Laura Wolfersfield Spring, Ny	Union Park- Wolfersfield Spring, Ny					
Lunce, Anna Belle	Mar 31, 1999	Morristown, Tn	Jeff Foo	May 3, 1916	82	Lunce, Hubert [B]	Kimbrough, Floyd		Ramsey, Sharon [Niece]		Ramsey, Sharon [Niece]	Jarrigan					Gertha Christine- Oka, Mary
Lunce, Ellen	Oct 1, 1956	Jeff Co	Tn	Feb 8, 1907	51	Ng	Lunce, Ray		Barboe, Irene		Lunce, Ray	Mt. Horeb					
Lunce, Fred Elmore	Mar 22, 1995	Oak Ridge, Tn	Jeff Co	Jun 3, 1905	89		Edmonds, Jacob		Edmonds, Margaret		Edmonds, Margaret [Son]	Mt. Horeb		Carroll [Tn]			
Lunce, Hubert Woodrow	Jan 4, 1985	J.M.H.	Tn	Feb 18, 1913	71	Kimbrough, Anna Belle						Jarrigan					
Lunce, Jacob L.	Jan 28, 1956	Sullivan Co, Tn	Tn	Jun 28, 1879	76	Ng	Unk		Lunce, Anna Belle		Baker, Mrs. Mary	Jarrigan					Marshall, Inez
Lunce, Jake		1931															
Lunce, Jake Leonard Jr.	Feb 21, 1976	V.A.- Mt. Home	Tn	May 21, 1918	57	Smith, Ida Merton	Lunce, Jake L. Sr.				Lunce, Mrs. Ida	Mt. View	WW 2				
Lunce, Mamie Assmus	Feb 17, 1980	At Home	Tn	Nov 16, 1912	67	Lunce, Fred		Assmus, John D.	Edmonds, Margaret	Elllson, Sarah	Lunce, Fred	Mt. View					
Lunce, Margaret E.	Feb 8, 1957	Tn	Tn	Oct 26, 1881	75	W			Woods, Tennessee		Baker, Mary [Daug]	Mt. View					
Lunce, Ruby	Mar 21, 1995	Jeff City	Jeff Co	Jan 19, 1914	81	Lunce, Stanley [B]	Mc Munry, C. Johomy		Moore, Sarah Emily		Mc Spadden, Norma & Ralph [Daug]	J.M.G.		[G] Mc Spadden, Rex			
Lunce, Stanley	Mar 22, 1970	Tn	Tn	Jan 12, 1912	59	Mc Munry, Ruth	Lunce, J.L.		Edmonds, Margaret E.		Lunce, Ruby & Norma	Memorial Gardens					
Lunce, Stella	Nov 5, 1992	Jeff Co	Tn	Oct 14, 1912	64	Lunce, Fred	Stellers, Fred		Breeden, Ellen	Tn	Lunce, Fred	Mt. Horeb					
Lunce, William Ray	Nov 27, 1957	Jeff Co	Tn		20	Lunce, Fred	Lunce, Fred		Breeden, Ellen		Lunce, Mrs. Eva Grubbs	Mt. Horeb					
Lunceford, Mary Jane	Feb 27, 1945	Johnson Co, Tn	Tn	Nov 25, 1871	73	W			Lunceford, Amanda		Edwards, Margaret	Mt. View					
Lunceford, Marion Lee [M]	May 18, 1957	Tn	Tn	Jan 19, 1876	79	W	Unk			Nc	Lunceford, Ross [Washington D.C.]	West View					
Lunsford, Rose Lynn	Jun 12, 1973	Washington D.C.	Tn	Sep 24, 1902	70	W					Lunceford, Ross [Washington D.C.] Lunsford, Charles [Md]	West View					
Lundford, Wallice D.	Jun 11, 1935	Tampa, Fla.									Lundford, M.L.	Jeff City					

NAME	DDATE	DLOCAT	BLOCAT	BDATE	AGE	SPOUSE	FATHER	FBLOCAT	MOTHER	MFBLOCAT	BY	BURIAL	VET	SON	DAUG	BROTHER	SISTER
Lusk, Catherine	Aug 13, 1999	Jeff Co	Jeff Co	Mar 20, 1934	65	Lusk, J.W.	Besson, Luther		Woods, Frances Gladdn			Strawberry Plains		Steve & Libby-Keith & Opal	Mc Call, Karen & Rick		
Luttrell, Howard Vasco	May 15, 1952	Knox Co		Oct 24, 1936	15	S			Cook, Dona			Roseberry					
Luttrell, Terry Wayne	Nov 26, 1968	Knox Co	Tn	Nov 26, 1968		S			Hodges, Evelyn		Luttrell, Raymond	Holston View - Knox Co					
Lutz, Victor Robert	May 26, 1973	White Pine, Tn	Washington, D.C.	Aug 6, 1953	19	S	Lutz, Robert Oliver		Holland, Edna E.		Hodges, Mrs. Evelyn & John F. Arlington F.H. (Arlington, Va)	Falls Church, Va					
Lyle, Annie Elizabeth	Mar 17, 1958	Jeff City Tn	Tn	Dec 17, 1896	61	Lyle, Mack [D]			Brown, Martha		Lyle, Merlie & Albert Colie, Rose - Atchley, Mrs.	Mt. View					
Lyle, Ben J.	Sep 26, 1957	E. S. Hospital	Tn	Oct 26, 1977	79	W	Lyle, David		Brown, Martha			Pleasant Grove					
Lyle, Bessie Faye	May 26, 1985	J.M.H.	Tn	Mar 3, 1928	57	Lyle, Franklin	Brendon, Harrison		Lowday, ---	Tn	Lyle, Franklin	Everlasting Life - J.M.G.					
Lyle, Carrie	Jul 17, 1984	New Market	Tn	Nov 14, 1875	48	Ng	Ewiss, John	Tn	Mc Milliin, Eliza	Tn	Lyle, Ben	Pleasant Grove					
Lyle, Chelsie L.	Dec 14, 2000	Jeff City	Tn	Aug 11, 1923	77	W	Stapleton, Robert		Green, Birdie		Lyle, Robert L [Son]	Mt. View					
Lyle, Crockett C. [Col]	Jul 7, 1955	White Pine, Tn	Tn	Jun 14, 1887		W					Millis, Agnes	Salem Baptist (Service)					
Lyle, Della B.	Dec 5, 1984	Knox Co	Tn	Oct 22, 1900	65	W	Bell, Sam		Norton, Molly								
Lyle, Ella Cutts	Apr 6, 1976	Roanoke, Va				W					Lee, Marjorie Lyle [Gal] Lyle, Tony-Frank-Bessie- Perkins, Anna (John T.- Willington, Delaware)- Rankin, Rose [Va]						
Lyle, Frank M.	Jan 31, 1973	Morristown, Tn	Tn	Mar 25, 1891	81	W			Bradshaw, Margaret		Worthington, Carl & Mary	Mt. View					
Lyle, Franklin L.	Sep 21, 1993	New Market, Tn	Jeff Co	Jun 9, 1923	70	Lyle, W.E.	Lyle, Elbert		Wife		Wife	J.M.G.	43-45	Ronnie-Frank-Terry-Bill- (GT) Whittlie, James C.-Harry	Hance, Regina		Perkins, Amam Mae - Reece, Mary R.
Lyle, J.C.	Aug 30, 1928				6-7-25		Lyle, Frank	Tn	Lundford, Minnie	Tn	Lyle, F.						
Lyle, J.R.	Oct 1, 1926																
Lyle, Lou	Feb 19, 1939	Mt. Horeb		Apr 22, 1864	74	Lyle, J.R. [D]	Bettis, P.J.	Tn	Edgar, Martha J.	Tn	Lyle, George & Harry	Lebanon					
Lyle, M.D.	Jan 6, 1950	Jeff Co	Tn	Sep 9, 1875	75	Ng	Lyles, David		Mount, Martha		Lyle, Mrs. Mattie Riggs	Piney Grove					
Lyle, Mary Alice	Nov 8, 1942		Tn	Sep 3, 1882	60	Lyle, W.E.	Hughs, Cyrus	Tn	Davis, Martha E.	Nc	Wife	Loy					
Lyle, Mary Louis	May 27, 1994	Jeff City	Jeff City	May 25, 1934	60	Barker, Thomas Clint			Hughes, Esta Mae		Lyle, Steve & Vivili [Son]	J.M.G.		Gary & Debbie-Thomas & Becky [Ken]	T.G.-Daniel		Roberts, Hazel - Armitage, Dorothy - Barker, Wilma
Lyle, Mattie Elizabeth	Apr 3, 1957	Rock Valley	Jeff City	Jun 29, 1879	79	W			Bailey, Claude			Piney					
Lyle, Minnie Lunsford	Dec 21, 1959	Ky	Ky	Aug 2, 1898	61	W	Lunsford, Mary Jane		Lyle, Margaret-Frank			Mt. View					
Lyle, Mrs. Harry	Oct 31, 1940	Mt. Horeb	Tn			Lyle, Harry	Link		Lyle, Harry			Hebron					
Lyle, Nina [Col]	Mar 1, 1954	Jeff Co	Tn	Apr 8, 1894	59	Ng	Watkins, Nathaniel		Stewart, Carrie		Millis, Agnes - Lyle, C.C.	Community					
Lyle, Troy Harding	Jun 10, 1980	Jeff City	Tn	May 13, 1921	59	Ng	Lyle, Elbert Franklin		Bell, Della		Lyle, Mary Louise	Jefferson Memorial					
Lyle, William Albert Sr. [Raymond]	Sep 29, 1984	Jeff City	Tn	May 14, 1921	63	Lyle, Mack [D]	Lyle, Elbert Franklin		Lunsford, Annie		Lyle, Mrs. Chelsie	Mt. View	WW 2				
Lyle, N.E.	Oct [30], 1934																
Lynn, J.P.	Nov 5, 1928		Tn		76-5-22	W	Lynn, K.M.	Nc			Lynn, Sid	Lebanon					
Lynn, Kathleen Smith	Apr 28, 2000	Knoxville, Tn	Tn	Oct 10, 1921	78	W			Brown, Cordelia		Lynn, Gary [Son] Walker, John	Sunderland					Smith, Joyce - Lawson, Agnes - Langston, Mary
Lynn, Nancy Stower	Feb 3, 1977	J.M.H.	Tn	Mar 3, 1892	84	W	Stower, William				Walker, John	West View					
Lynn, Roberta Augusta	Nov 23, 1997	Hamblen Co	Tn	Aug 4, ---	75-3-19	W	Morgan, Houston		Byrd, Alvy		Brown, Cordelia	Jefferson Memorial					
Lynn, Sidney E.	Jan 29, 1998	Jeff Co	Tn	May 31, 1891	75	Stower, Nancy			Walker, John & Mrs. Lynn		Holt, Gene - Smith, Carl - Lynn, Bertha	West View					
Lynn, T.E.	Jun 26, 1935	Jeff Co	Tn	Apr 17, 1876	59	Ng	Lynn, James L.		Stewart, Katherine Pleasant, Regina Joyce	Va	Lynn, Sid [Son]	Narrow Valley					
Mabe, Ernie Darrell	Jan 11, 1959	Jeff Co	Tn	Jan 11, 1988			Mabe, Paul Manuel		Lynn, Sid [Son]	Va	Mabe, Paul	West View					
Madden, Gertrude M. [Nonnie]	Feb 5, 1982	Knoxville, Tn	Pa	Oct 20, 1902	79	Div	Brink, Rhue		Eddy, Sarah		Rennelsen, Niel A.	Jefferson Memorial					

NAME	DDATE	DLOCAT	BLOCAT	BDATE	AGE	SPOUSE	FATHER	FBLOCAT	MOTHER	MFBLOCAT	BY	BURIAL	VET	SON	DAUG	BROTHER	SISTER
Maggard, Mary Lewis	Dec 1, 1996	Jeff City	Cuatin, Ky	Feb 9, 1909	87	W	Lewis, John L.		Pennington, Betty		Maggard, Warren [Son]	Lewis		Osteen	Williams, Evelyn - Shepard, Vernie Dean		
Malihos, Thelma	Jan 30, 1990	J.M.H.	Fulton, La	Jul 21, 1915	74	W	Misic, Indis ?				Malihos, Larry E.	Hampton Memorial - Elizabeth, La					
Malicoln, Edward Emmit	Apr 3, 1976	Knoxville, Tn (Res Ohio)	Tn	Jan 9, 1903	72	W	Finley, Esther Pauline		Wheeler, Nancy		Malicoln, Mrs. Pauline	Collinsville, Ohio					
Malicoln, Emmit E.	May 4, 1959	Jeff Co	Tn	May 14, 1870	89	Ng	Malicoln, Blair		Balsie, Julia		Malicoln, Virginia & Edward	Mt. Pleasant					
Malicoln, Nannie	Jul 24, 1961	Jeff Co	Va	Jun 16, 1870	91	Malicoln, E.E. [D]	Wheeler, William Raleigh		Lindsey, Mary		Malicoln, Virginia - Hale, Mrs. Horace	Mt. Pleasant - Jeff Co					
Malicoln, William Blair	Sep 24, 1946	Murfeesboro, Tn	Jeff Co	Nov 7, 1905	40	Stepp, Leona	Malicoln, E.E. [D]	Tn	Nannie C.		Malicoln, Mrs. Pauline - Sprancer, Mrs Nancy Lee [Ohio]	Mt. Pleasant	unk				
Malicoln, Virginia Vasell	Nov 26, 1981	Jeff Co	Tn	May 5, 1898	83	S	Malicoln, E.E.		Nannie C.		Malicoln, Virginia	Mt. Pleasant					
Mallory, Margaret Marion	Jan 8, 2000	Jeff City		Dec 18, 1905	94	W	Heaney, Edward		Cater, Edna		Hull, Margaret M. [Dug]	J.M.G.					
Mallory, Russell Channing	Nov 1, 1975	Hannibal, Missouri		Dec 22, 1903	71	Heaney, Margaret	Mallory, Everett		Seeley, May		Mallory, Mrs. R.C.	Jefferson Memorial					
Mallory, Albert	Nov 27, 1977	Jeff Co	Tn	Jul 2, 1905	72	S	Mallory, Thomas		Murdock, Ella		Cox, Mrs. Alice - James - Ruben	Flat Gap					
Mallory, Caroline Ellis	Dec 8, 1965	Jeff Co	Tn	Sep 30, 1872	93	W	Murdock, W.R.		Ellis, C. Caroline		Mallory, Reuben - Lee - Jam - Cox, Alice	Flat Gap					
Mallory, Howard William	Apr 13, 1979	Morristown, Tn	Tn	Dec 29, 1926	52	Berry, Audeo	Mallory, James F.		Vollas, Flossie		Mallory, Mrs. Howard - VA.	Jefferson Memorial	WW 2				
Mallory, Infant	Jul 17, 1937	J.M.H.		Dec 17, 1937			Mallory, J.F.	Tn	Murdock, Caroline Etta		Mallory, Dana	Flat Gap					
Mallory, James Francis	Apr 2, 1988	J.M.H.		Dec 17, 1900	87	Vollas, Minnie [D]	Malone, Thomas			Tn	Mallory, J.F.	Flat Gap - New Market, Tn					
Malone, Janice Ruth	Apr 14, 1987	Knoxville, Tn	Jeff City	Nov 15, 1957	39	Malone, Jerry	Abriss, Wallace		Trresit, Ruth		Husband - Malone, Tom & Betty [Parents Of Jerry]	Flat Gap		Tyler		Ronnie [In-Law] Malcomb's-Bible Donald	Sevia, Connie - Wells, Nancy - Robbfoss, Tricia - [In-Law] Bible, Cindy
Malone, Jessie Burie	Dec 4, 1969	Knoxville, Tn	Jeff City	Sep 5, 1894	65	Lacy, Bonnie	Lewis, Rueben Stanford		Lewis, Myrtle	Wife	Lewis	Flat Gap	army				
Malone, John F.	Aug 2, 1973	Knoxville, Tn	Tn	Nov 1, 1903	69	S	Malone, T.D.		Murdock, Caroline		Malone, Rueben	Flat Gap					
Malone, Minnie (Flossie)	Aug 18, 1981	Jeff City	Tn	Nov 28, 1903	77	Malone, James F.	Vollas, George A.	Jeff Co	Wallace, Lucile		Malone, James F.	Flat Gap					
Malone, Mona Margaret	Dec 29, 1942	Jeff City	Tn	Apr 12, 1938	4		Malone, Rueben Stanford		Malone, Myrtle	Jeff Co	Malone, R.S.	Flat Gap					
Malone, Myrtle Lucille	Feb 16, 1998	Jeff City	Jeff City	Oct 7, 1911	86	Lewis, Robert Lee	Walker, Elizabeth		Malone, Tommy [Son]		Malone, Tommy [Son]	Flat Gap		Jessie Burie- Jack Stanford	Tommy Dale & Betty Wright-Jack Stanford		
Malone, Richard Dale	Nov 14, 1997	Knoxville, Tn	Jeff City	Oct 16, 1908	88	Ng	Malone, Tommy D.		Wright, Betty M.		Father	Flat Gap					
Malone, Ruben Sanford	May 22, 1981	Jeff Folly	Jeff City	Apr 18, 1909	72	Ng	Malone, Thomas D.		Murdock, Ella		Malone, Mrs. Myrtle L.	Flat Gap				Jerry	Bible, Cindy
Malone, Steve Allen	Jun 27, 1978	Knoxville, Tn	Tn	May 1, 1951	25	Div	Malone, George Lee		Murdock, Martha		Malone, George L.	Cross Anchors - Green Co					
Malone, Clyde Leon	Nov 19, 1990	Morristown, Tn	Knoxville, Tn	May 1, 1912	78	Div	Malone, Joseph A.		Malone, Bertha		Malone, Charles K. [Bricher]	Lynnhurst					
Malony, Paul Donald	Aug 17, 1982	Morristown, Tn	Tn	Nov 25, 1902	79	Feth, Catharine	Malony, Andy		Fine, Sarah		Malony, Mrs. Paul D.	Fort Steubenv- Steubenville, Ohio					
Menard, John N.	Mar 5, 1948	Jeff Co				Ng	Menard, M. Shadrick	Tn	Menard, Harriet		Nicholson, George T. - Melin [Old] J. Frank [Melin] - Mrs. Mary James - Margaret	Shady Grove			Dalton, Mona Adair & Blanor Eugene - Rabins, Kristie Marie & Gregory Allen		
Menck, Betty Jean	Apr 28, 1941	Athens, Ga	Jeff Co	1d		S	Menck, Clarence L.		Thomas -		Menck, Marshall Neal & Pollo	West View					
Menley, Effie	May 2, 1968	Jeff City	Tn	90		S	Collin, Marshall		Manley, Annie Ruth	Jeff Co	Manley, Clarence L.						
Menley, Ethel	Apr 27, 1971	Jeff City	Tn	86-8-4		Manley, R.W. [D]	Mullins, W.H.		Mannon, Miranda		Manley, Kathleen	Jarrigan					
Manley, Kathleen Sender	May 24, 1987	Jeff City	Tn	Jul 29, 1906	80	S	Manley, P.M.		Mullins, Ethel	Jeff Co	Spotts, Mrs. Billye	Jarrigan					
Manley, Lucy S.	Nov 24, 1933	Knoxville	Tn	Sep 28, 1884	49	Cleverger, D.P.	Young, Virginia	Tn	Manley, Miss Elva	Tn		Shilo- Granger Co					

NAME	DDATE	DLOCAT	BLOCAT	BDATE	AGE	SPOUSE	FATHER	FBLOCAT	MOTHER	MFBLOCAT	BY	BURIAL	VET	SON	DAUG	BROTHER	SISTER
Manley, Mary Cate	Jul 4, 1927				25-10-15	S		Tn		Tn	Manley, R.W.	West View					
Manley, Rufis R.	Mar 16, 1997	Jeff City	Mio, la	Jun 19, 1904	92	Homer, Shirley	Manley, W.		Cato, Effie		Manley, R.W.	West View				Neil & Gladys	
Manley, Shirley Joe	Jan 29, 1996	Morristown, Tn	New Market, Tn	Oct 28, 1917	80	Nance, Evelyn	Manley, George Henry		Wilk, Anna		Wife	West View		Gale & Val	Kuykendall, Juanita - Irwin, Judy (Step) Willis, Nancy Dawn, Alice	Manley, Hugh	
Mann, Lillian Pearl	May 29, 1978	Hamblen Co	Tn	Jun 1, 1905	72	Mann, Charlie	Mann, John D.	Tn	Pardon, Lilly		Mann, Charlie	Flat Gap					
Manning, Aline Arbelia	Jun 6, 1948	Hamblen Co	Jeff Co	Dec 26, 1920	27	W	Collins, J.D.		Clark, Emma Lou	Tn	Bradey, Mrs. Mary - Collins, Fred-Carroll & J.D.	West View	43-46	Mr. Way, Kenneth Sm. (Step) Peck, Carl Larry			
Manning, Callie Mae	Dec 14, 1999	Knoxville, Tn	Knoxville, Tn	Mar 8, 1922	77	Div	Taylor, Linley		Webb, Ethel		Manning, Garry D. Sr. (Son)	Manning Garry D. Sr.		James D. (Mich.)	Riley, Carolyn Faye - Belcher, Betty Jo		
Manns, Lawrence L. Cortez (Black)	Feb 22, 1994	Morristown, Tn	Morristown, Tn	Feb 22, 1994			Manns, Lawrence		Maxwell, Michelle		Father - Maxwell, Cortez & Betty Ann-Manns, Drucilla (G-Parents)	J.M.G.					
Maples, Anna	June 3, 1934	Jeff City	Tn	Jul 19, 1859	75	W	Hall, William G.		Elkins, Elizabeth	Tn	Maples, Walter P.	West View					
Maples, John Lewis	May 9, 1945	Hamblen Co	Tn	Aug 31, 1871	73	Ng	Maples, Cyrus		Davis, Elizabeth	Nc	Maples, Mrs. & Dorothy	Woodmes Chapel					
Maples, Karen Carlene	Feb 24, 1980	Jeff Co	Tn	Feb 22, 1980	abt 78	W	Maples, Carl T.		Carr, Georgia C.		Maples, Carl	Mt. View					
Maples, Samuel	Dec 8, 1945	Grainger Co	Unk		S				Unk		County	Poor Farm - Grainger Co					
Maples, Walter P.	Feb 28, 1949	Jeff Co	Sevier Co	Aug 5, 1882	66-6-15	Ng	Maples, John		Hall, Anna	Tn	Maples, Mrs. Jewel T.	West View					
Marks, Calvin Roosevelt	Jan 12, 1971	Jeff Co	Tn	Jun 2, 1916		Gann, Martha	Marks, J.H.		Brother, Tennis L.		Martha	Jefferson Memorial	WW 2				
Marks, Clarence Albert	Nov 5, 1955	Jeff City	Tn	Jul 15, 1915	40	Ng	Marks, Joseph H.		Brannon, Tennel		Marks, Mrs. C.A.	Jefferson Memorial	WW 2				
Marks, Emma Alice Fralic	Nov 17, 1994	J.M.H.	Tn	May 7, 1899	85	Div	Grant, George		Williams, Beatrice		Fralic, Burl	Rosaberry - Knox Co					
Marks, J.N.	Nov 27, 1952	Jeff City	Tn	Feb 7, 1852	80	W			Unk		Frank - Bradley, Mrs.	Peadmont					
Marks, Patsy Alice	Mar 22, 1998	J.M.H.	Tn	May 6, 1904	83	W	Underwood, Elisha		Combs, Gillie		Marks, John L.	J.M.G.					
Marks, Tennis Louise	Dec 23, 1958	Jeff Co	Jeff Co	Jun 15, 1886	72	Ng	Brannon, Bud		Frank, Tabitha		Marks, Joe H. Calvin - Williams, Mrs. Fred	Oakland - Jeff Co					
Marks, William Edward Sr.	May 28, 1980	Jeff City	Tn	Dec 2, 1894	85	Ng	Marks, Jasper Newton		Laws, Sarah		Marks, Mrs. Patsy	Jefferson Memorial					
Marshall, Burl	Apr 25, 1974	New Market	Hawkins Co, Tn	Sep 7, 1910	31	Ng		Tn	Pratt, Kelpa	Tn	Marshall, Gaius	Pleasant View					
Marshall, Gaines L.	Oct 16, 1948	Hamblen Co	Hawkins Co, Tn	Feb 1, 1879	69-8-5	Ng	Unk		Marshall, Sarah	Hawkins Co	Marshall, Mrs. Gaines	Pleasant View - Hamblen Co					
Marshall, James A.	Jun 8, 1959	Hamblen Co	Tn	Jul 30, 1892	66	Pratt, Nettie	Marshall, Houston		Coats, Mary		Marshall, Mrs. Duncan, Lattie - Bragg, Hazel	Pleasant View - Hamblen Co					
Marshall, John H.	Jan 28, 1974	Jeff City	Tn	Apr 3, 1901	72	W	Elliott, Sarah		Elliott, Sarah		Dalton, Christine - Mc-Gee, Mrs. Gladys	West View					
Marshall, Kelpa	Feb 18, 1983	J.M.H.	Tn	Jun 28, 1888	94	Marshall, Grimes	Pratt, George W.		Jones, Cordelia			Pleasant View					
Marshall, Nancy Faye	Mar 5, 1943	Hamblen Co	Tn	Feb 4, 1943		W	Unk		Marshall, Lattie Grimes	Tn	Marshall, Lattie						
Marshall, Nettie Mae	Jun 4, 1982	Morristown, Tn	Tn	May 19, 1893	89	Marshall, James A. (D)	Pratt, George W.		Jones, Cordelia		Hodge, Mrs. Juanita	Pleasant View					
Marshall, Preaux Earl	Nov 4, 1991	Newcomb, Tn	J.M.H.	Feb 23, 1922	69	Lsirce, Inez	Marshall, John Earl		Lockaday, Sara Mary		Willie - Roberts, Mrs. Wayne	Mt. View		unk			
Marshall, Sarah Jane [Col]	Apr 17, 1946	Jeff Co	Tn	Dec 9, 1871	74	Ng	Seaborn, Peter	Tn	Seaborn, Mary	Tn	Bragg, Mrs. Hazel John-Maudie	Martha Davis Colored					
Marshall, William [Col]	Oct 28, 1956	Jeff Co	Tn	Jan 20, 1871	85	W	Marshall, William J.		Unk		Bragg, Mrs. Hazel	West View Colored					
Martin, Alice	May 28, 1978	Jeff City	Tn	May 27, 1903	74	W	Miller, George W.		Swann, Docy		McGinnis, Mrs. Willey-Martin, T.-Mrs. Turpin, Mrs. Slay	West View					
Martin, Cecil Wayne	Sep 9, 1999		Tn						Brooks, Esther		Martin, Winfred Doug (Brother) - Carr, Jeanette (Aunt)	Temple Hill, Castlewood, Va					
Martin, Charles R.	Jul 2, 1986	Dickerson Co, Va		Jul 24, 1928	71		Martin, James D.				Dunbar F.H. [Columbia, Sq]	Dunbar F.H. [Columbia, Sq]	army				

NAME	DDATE	DLOCAT	BLOCAT	BDATE	AGE	SPOUSE	FATHER	FBLOCAT	MOTHER	MBLOCAT	BY	BURIAL	VET	SON	DAUG	BROTHER	SISTER
Martin, Esther	Aug 11, 1995	Jeff City	Dickenson Co, Va	Jul 28, 1901	94		Brooks, William		Colley, Emma		Martin, W.D. (Son)	Temple Hill - St. Paul, Va		Cecil W.			
Martin, Eugene Benjamin	Sep 6, 1985	Strawberry Plains		Oct 2, 1914	70	Wilson, Irene			Colbach, Sally		Martin, Mrs. Irene	Pleasant Grove					
Martin, Gladys O.	Apr 9, 1992	Dandridge, Tn	Sevier Co	Jul 22, 1908	83	W	Denton, William E.				Olsen, Nancy M. [Daug]	J.M.G.					
Martin, Hal	Jan 14, 1960	Jeff City	Tn	Sep 22, 1882	67	Ng	Martin, Arch		Brimer, Rhoda		Martin, Mrs. Alice - [Daug]	West View					
Martin, Hollis L.	May 22, 1968	Jeff City	Tn	Feb 12, 1915	53	Ng	Martin, Fritzrell W.		Rimmer, Thalia		Martin, Mrs. James / Turpin, James	Rockerfield - Bluefield, W. Va					
Martin, Josie Ethel	May 17, 1952	Cumberland Co		Sep 15, 1879	72	Martin, L.B. [P]	Cannon, Joel		Graham, Minnie		Martin, Thalia	Presby - Dandridge					
Martin, Minnie Mae	Dec 11, 1999	Jeff City	Tn	Oct 15, 1906	93	W	Tiller, Sue E.		Myriatt, Gertrude (Niece)		Thurman, Eleanor (Niece)	Oak View - Big Stone Gap, Va					
Martin, Noah Raymond	Jan 31, 1984	Tn	Tn			Denton, Gladys			Newman, Edith Nancy		Martin, Mrs. Gladys	Jefferson Memorial	WW 2				
Martin, Richard F.	Apr 12, 1953	J.M.H.	Tn	Dec 25, 1872	80	W	Denton, Ike N.		White, Mrs. Sam - Taft & French		Martin, Mrs. Robert A. - Henry-Milton-Frank - Dalton, Mrs. J.H. - Fox, Mrs. D.E.	Piedmont					
Martin, Robert A.	Jul 12, 1949	Knox Co	Grainger County	Feb 8, 1880	69	Ng	Martin, Thomas		Wyatt, Mary		Martin, David	Blackwell Branch - Grainger Co					
Martinez, Julian Anglar [Ney]	May 19, 1971	Jeff Co	Mexico	Jan 7, 1921		Gonzer, Akonas	Martinez, Bictoreino		Palperon, Margaretta [Texas]		Palperon, Mauricio [Texas]	Piedrias - Mexico		[G] Julian, Alan, Brad - Hilliard, Michael	Julian, Anne - [G] Minton, Deidre - Rutledge, Karen - Long, Jeanne		Suggs, Anna Kate
Mason, Alice Odessa	May 27, 1994	Dandridge, Tn	Cooke Co	Apr 18, 1904	90	Fox, Alton			Mc Andrew, Louisa Anna		Mc Dougal, Barbara [Daug]	Memorial Gardens Green Co					
Mason, Homer Ray	Aug 9, 1972	Knoxville, Tn	Knoxville, Tn	Dec 13, 1902	69	Ng	Mason, Linton		Mentcoth, Cora		Mason, Mrs. H.R.	Green Co					
Mason, Joe [Col]	Apr 10, 1927								Mason, James B.		Mason, James B.	Lebanon					
Mason, William Frank	Aug 11, 1957	Milligan Clinic	Tn	Aug 7, 1957	77,11-7	Ng			Guinn, Hazel R.	Tn	Mason, James B.	Lebanon					
Massengill, Emily Artissa	Dec 6, 1927	Tn	Tn			W	Jernigan, Paschal	Tn	Norton, Mary	Tn	Norton, Mary	Family					
Massengill, Eulice B.	Sep 2, 1971	Hamblen Co Care Inn	Tn	Apr 15, 1907	64	Wigut, Pearl	Byrd, Perslee		Byrd, Perslee		Byrd, Perslee	Pleasant View					
Massengill, Hattie	Apr 13, 19085	Care Inn	Tn	Jan 12, 1883	102	W	Massengill, James		Couch, Mrs. Jamie M.		Couch, Mrs. Jamie M.	Jefferson Memorial					
Massengill, Ira Eber	Aug 8, 1978	Morristown, Tn	Knox Co, Tn	May 20, 1915	63	W	Massengill, James H.		Gass, Mrs. Edd		Gass, Mrs. Edd	Flat Gap	WW 2				
Massengill, J.W. [Tdee]	Aug 18, 1981	Jeff Co	Tn	Apr 28, 1902	59	Disney, Pauline	Henson, Samuel		Henson, Polly & Jamie		Jefferson Memorial	Jefferson Memorial					
Massengill, James Dwight	Sep 3, 1969	Jeff Co	Maryland	Sep 29, 1940	28	Matthews, Fred Caroline	Galyon, Ruth		Massengill, Jamie		Massengill, Polly & Jamie	Flat Gap					
Massengill, Joseph M.	Aug 13, 1956	Jeff Co	Tn	Nov 18, 1885	70	Ng	Gibbons, Mary J.		Massengill, Mrs. Freda		Massengill, Mrs. Freda	West View					
Massengill, Mercy	May 29, 1928	Jeff Co	Tn		83	W		Tn		Tn	Massengill, Mrs. Vada	Macedonia					
Massengill, Otis T.	Feb 26, 1997	Jeff City	Jeff City	May 29, 1924	72	Allen, Ruby	Massengill, Joseph M.		White, Lilly L.		Wife	J.M.G.		Terry & Carldreo Snowden, Kim & Eddie Jr. - Roop, Tammy	Dale, Judy & Glenn - Snowden, Kim & Eddie Jr. - Roop, Tammy	Lawrence	Clark, Clara
Massengill, Pauline	Apr 23, 1987	J.M.H. Morristown, Tn	Tn	Oct 21, 1904	82	W	Disney, Andrew J.		Couch, Jami [Daug]		Couch, Jami [Daug]	J.M.G.					
Massengill, Pearl	Jul 30, 1990	Dandridge, Tn	Dandridge, Tn	Sep 28, 1911	78	W	Wright, Oscar		Henry, Molly		Wright, Rose	Pleasant View					
Massengill, Porter C.	Jul 17, 1970	Jeff Co		Sep 16, 1890	79	Watts, Hester	Gibbons, Jane		Gibbons, Jane		Massengill, Hester	Community					
Massengill, Ray William	Jul 12, 1985	Knoxville, Tn	Kansas	Mar 7, 1915	70	S	Massengill, William		White, Vada		Massengill, Bill	West View	WW 2				
Massengill, Robert Coy	May 5, 1975	V.A. Hosp. [Res Ind]	Tn	Mar 2, 1925	50	Div	Massengill, Robert		Reba		Massengill, Lawrence	West View	WW 2				
Massengill, Roe Hale [F]	Jan 28, 1967	Jeff City	Tn	Jun 8, 1878	89	W	Carter, Alfred		Malcolm, Kate		Massengill, W.C. - Massengill, Helen - Walker, Kate - Burchfiel, Yvonne	Mt. Pleasant					
Massengill, Ruth Mae	Jan 5, 1956	Jeff Co	Grainger Co	Feb 26, 1918	37	Ng	Gaylon, James		Moody, Bessie		Messengill, E.H. - Gass, Eddie	Flat Gap					Barbee, Vachey - Riley, Evelyn - Holcomb, Beulah - Carr, Jenette

NAME	DATE	BLOCAT	BLOCAT	BDATE	BDATE	AGE	SPOUSE	FATHER	FRLOCAT	MOTHER	MTRLOCAT	BY	BURIAL	VET	SON	DAUG	BROTHER	SISTER
Messengill, Samuel Simpson	Jan 25, 1982	Jeff City	Ky	Dec 22, 1--		80-1-4	Ng	Messengill, William		Greve, Mary Jane		Couch, Robert & Janie - Messengill, Mrs. Pauline	Jefferson Memorial					
Messengill, Tony Shelton	Aug 27, 1975	Jeff Co	Tn	Jun 24, 1975				Varner, Larry		Messengill, Larry-Addie Mae		Messengill, Larry-Addie Mae Father	Workman - Madison, W. Va					
Mathis, Infant		Jeff Co	Tn	Mar 9, 1959									Workman - Sunderland					
Matijevich, Ell	Apr 5, 1995	Jeff City	Duquesene, Pa	Aug 1, 1922		72		Matijevich, Andrew		Sipich, Emma		Matijevich, Ell N. & Karen [Son]	St. Nicholas Orthodox - Weirton, W. Va			[G] Ms. Karris, Johnna ,Kezlie	Miko-Adam	Loscher, Sally - Madi, Mary - Kicheak, Mildred
Matlock, Joseph Thomas	Jul 10, 1982	Morristown, Tn	Tn	Jul 4, 1913		69	Hill, Millicent	Matlock, Joe Jefferson		Stegar, Flora Lee		Matlock, Joe L.	Jefferson Memorial					
Matousek, Joseph E. [Black]	Aug 1, 2000	Morristown, Tn	Il	Dec 26, 1916		83	W	Roberts, Carol M.				Roberts, Carol M.	Cremated, Glen Oak- Chicago, Ill.	unk				
Matthews, James Burnell [Black]	Oct 14, 1978	Hillcrest Beverly	Ga	May 18, 1902		76	Div	Matthews, Tom		Raines, Josephine		Mc Ghee, George - Evers - Josephine C.M. Jr.	St. Nicholas Orthodox - Weirton, W. Va					
Mattis, Evelyn B.	May 20, 1997	Swisers, Pa	Talbott, Tn	Aug 21, 1929		67		Eller, Andrew		Quarles, Nell		Mattsville, Brenda K. [Dad]	Mt. Pleasant - Talbott, Tn		Bufry, Albert-Mike	Rogers, Andrea B.		Clark, Dorothy
Mattison, Bascom Carlisle [Col]	Sep 3, 1943	Jeff Co		Jan 7, 1917		26	S	Mattison, Charles	Anderson, No.	Morris, Myrtle	Jeff Co	Mattison, C.C.	M.E.					
Mattison, Charles Columbus [Col]	Apr 12, 1947	Hamblen Co	Sc	Apr 1, 1877		70	W	Mattison, Charles	Sc	Latimer, Mary	Sc	Mattison, C.C.	West View Colored					
Mattison, Charles Jr. [Col]	Oct 26, 1983	Xenia, Ohio		Oct 6, 1912		41	Ng			Myrtle		Winty, Lewis [Xenia, OH] ,Mattison, Mrs. C.M.Jr.	West View Colored					
Mattison, Joseph Gordon	Oct 18, 1971	Frankfort, Ky	Tn	May 7, 1925		56		Mattison, Charles		Morris, Myrtle		Mattison, Claudelle	West View	WW 2				
Mattison, Myrtle [Col]	Apr 2, 1983	Jeff Co	Tn	Feb 28, 1890			Mattison, C.C. [D]	Morris, --		Mills, Charlotte		West View Colored - Clarisa	West View Colored					
Mattison, William Dewayne	Jan 11, 1974	Jeff City	Tn	Jan 10, 1974			Mattison, Gilbert		Delaney, Brenda	Morristown ,Tn	Mattison, Gilbert	Rock Of Ages - Hamblen Co.					
Mattock, Flora Starnes	Mar 17, 1978	Care Inn		Oct 18, 1889		88	W			Shanklin, Maude		Mattock, J.T.	Mattock, J.T.					
Mattock, George E.	May 5, 1974	Morristown, Tn		Aug 27, 1897		76	Johnson, Reable	Mattox, Samuel W.				Mattox, Rosalie	Jefferson Memorial					
Mattox, Paula Rose	May 24, 1961		Indiana	Apr 12, 1954		7		Cram, Richard B.		Mattox, Lorena		Cram, Lorena - Mattox, George	Memorial Gardens					
Mauley, James A.	May 9, 1928		Tn				[Mauley, David]		Hudson, Katherine	Tn	Mauley, Kate & Willie	Shiloh					
Mauley, Reed W.	Jun 17, 1958	Jeff Co	Tn	Feb 27, 1879		77	Ng	Mauley, Robert D.		Loy, Mary		Mauley, Bettie C.	West View					
Mauley, Marvin J.	Oct 4, 1963	Jeff Co	Sc	Mar 20, 1907			Ng	Mauley, Reeder H.		Burton, Nettie E.		Mauley, Mrs. Evelyn G.	Memorial Gardens					
Mauley, Jefferson Charles	Jun 16, 1990	Knoxville, Tn	J.M.H.	Aug 13, 1922		67	Homer, Reba			Mauley, Isaac W.		Mauley, Reba H.	Hamblen Memorial	WW 2				
Mauey, Reba	Mar 19, 1994	Knoxville, Tn	Hamblen Co	Oct 3, 1928		65		Homer, Dewey E.		Turner, Ollie K.		Drinnon, Rita & Hershel [Daug]	Hamblen Memorial		Hal- William		Wells, Lucille - Harris, Edith - Miller, Shirley - Trend, Cora Elmore, Ann
May, Robert Judson	Aug 28, 1983	Jeff City	Tn	Feb 12, 1887		96	W	May, James T.		Brooks, Margaret		Harrell, Mrs. Dorothy M. - May, J.T.	Jefferson Memorial					
May, Essie Zelma	Sep 4, 1994	Milligan Clinic F.S.H.	Tn	Sep 23, 1898		95	May, R.J.	Rice, Virginia		Rice, Virginia		May, R.J. J.M.G.	Jefferson Memorial					
May, Hazel Inez	Sep 15, 1991	Memphis, Tn	Tn	Sep 1, 1911		80	May, Roy	Crothett, Horace C.		Martin, Alice D.		May, Roy	Buffalo Grove					
May, Henry Lee	Sep 3, 1970	Jeff Co	Tn	Oct 24, 1894		75	Ng	Brooks, James T.		May, Mrs. Marcie		May, Mrs. Marcie Kellon	Buffalo Grove					
May, John A.	Feb 5, 1990	Jeff Co		Jan 15, 1906		44	Ng	May, James T.	Tn	Brooks, Margaret A.		May, Mrs. Nora	Sunderland					
May, Lloyd E.	Jan 19, 1996	Maxy Creek	Tn	Dec 1, 1982		86	May, Lloyd E. [D]	May, Lloyd E.		Cagle, Dorothy		May, Bernice	Sunderland					
May, Minnie	Jun 28, 1979	Hamblen Co	Tn				May, Hubert Sr. [D]	Mc Daniel, Samuel		Rhinehart, Rhoda		May, Bernice	Buffalo Grove					
Mayes, Grace Beatrice	Jun 11, 1977	Hamblen Co	Tn	Jun 27, 1911		65		Mc Daniel, Samuel		Turner, Mattie		Homer, Mrs. Beulah - Heiner, Estelle [Daug]	Jefferson Memorial					
Maynard, Carrie Lee	Jan 4, 1982	Jeff Co	Tn	Nov 11, 1898		73	Ng	Farmer, Mary Jane		Turner, Mattie		Maynard, R.B.	West View					
Maynard, Maude Elvira	Mar 20, 1992	Memphis, Tn	Jeff Co	Sep 1, 1902		89	W	Burchfield, Mattie		Burchfield, Mattie		Johnson, Thelma [Christine [Daug]]	West View					
Maynard, Robert Bruce	Dec 31, 1974	Jeff Co	Tn	Feb 12, 1886		88	W	Maynard, Shadrick		Nelson, Belle		Maynard, Turner M.	West View					
Maynard, Turner M.	Mar 14, 1988	S.M.H.	Tn	Feb 14, 1911		77		Maynard, Robert B.		Irwin, Carrie L.		Maynard, Maude R.	Sunderland					
Mays, Infant Male	Jul 16, 1954	Jeff Co	Tn	Jul 16, 1954			Runimeo, Maude			Hill, --		Mays, James	West View					

NAME	DDATE	DLOCAT	BLOCAT	BDATE	AGE	SPOUSE	FATHER	FRLOCAT	MRFRLOCAT	BY	BURIAL	VET	SON	DAUG	BROTHER	SISTER
Maye, Margaret A.	Apr 21, 1925		Tn		63-7-8	Maye, J.T.	Brooks, Alex	Tn	Tn		Buffalo Grove					
Maye, Margaret Adaline	Jan 12, 1947	Knox Co.	Grainger Co.	March 5, 1869	77-10-7	Maye, J.W. [D]	Long,--	Grainger Co	Grainger Co	Maye, Hubert-Carl-Jack-Amos - Morgan, Eb-Jack A. - Byrd, George-Satterfield, J.F.	Whitside - Grainger Co					
Mc Anally, Emma Nola	Dec 27, 1978	Morristown, Tn	Tn	Jul 21, 1905	73	W	Beets, Ulyses			Johnson, Mrs. Barbara - Ranson, U.A.	Lebanon					
Mc Anally, William Newton	May 12, 1959	Hamblen Co	Tn	Jun 22, 1894	64	Ng	Mc Anally, James	Tn		Mc Anally, Mrs. Nola	Lebanon - Greenbrier					
Mc Bee, Della	Oct 13, 1955	New Market	Tn	Jan 23, 1883	72	W	Mitchell, J.	Tn		Nance, Sallie	Mc Bee					
Mc Bee, Clova	Feb 6, 1983	J.M.H.	Tn	Aug 2, 1897	85	Mc Bee, Henry Sexton [D]	Cook, Isaac			Holiway, Mrs. Lee (Vila)	Jefferson Memorial					
Mc Bee, Frank [Dot]	Sep 3, 1939	Jeff Co	Tn	Sep 1, 1900	82	Mc Bee, Andy		Asti, Mela		Bales, Link - County	New Market					
Mc Bee, Julia	Sep 2, 1983	Knoxville, Tn	Ga			Mc Bee, Pat	Raines, Josephine			Mc Bee, George	Gillette - Straw Plains					
Mc Bee, Nell	April 7, 1982										Gillette - Straw Plains					
Mc Bee, Pat [M]	Mar 20, 1988	J.M.H.	Tn	Apr 5, 1907	90	W	Williamson, Sallie			Mc Bee, George A.	Gillette - Straw Plains, Tn	WW 1				
Mc Bride, Henry Floyd	May 9, 1982	Jeff Co.	Tn	Sep 12, 1879	74	Ng	Mc Bride, Benzrel			Mc Bride, Mrs. Floyd	Lynchurst					
Mc Bride, Willie Kate	Sep 21, 1988	Oak Ridge, Tn	Tn	Nov 10, 1893	94	W	Vance, William T.			Kennedy, Margaret	Lynchurst					
Mc Call, Barkley D.	Aug 25, 1998	Knoxville, Tn	Knox Co	Jan 8, 1965	33		Mc Call, Wayne			Rilpp, Brenda	Pleasant Grove					
Mc Call, Hattie Lee	Mar 2, 1982	Jeff Co.	Tn	Apr 1910, 1891	70	D	Snyder, Henry			Damon, Edd-Charlie-William B. -John C. - Dudrick-Frank-Sherman-Kelly-Dorothy Frances [Children	Underwood - Sevier Co					
Mc Campbell, C.C.	Oct 20, 1986		Tn		54		Mc Campbell, John	Tn	Tn	Mc Campbell, Ray Mc Campbell, Mrs. J.F.-Jack-Mc Chandler-Mary Alice	Mc Campbells Chapel					
Mc Carter, James Perry	Mar 28, 1978	Jeff City	Tn	Feb 20, 1910	68	Ng	Mc Carter, T.Z.			Proffitt, Martha	Flat Gap					
Mc Carter, Martha	Mar 15, 1986									Mc Carter, Mrs. LZ.						
Mc Carter, Mary Charlotte	Sep 2, 1983	J.M.H.	Tn	Mar 6, 1914	69	Mc Carter, J.P. [D]	Anderson, James T.			Mc Carter, James T.						
Mc Carter, Mary Elizabeth	Feb 21, 1989	Hamblen Co	Tn	Mar 7, 1904	84	W	Hayter, John			Armstrong, Sarah Marlor, -	New Gray-Knox Co					
Mc Carter, Minnie Marler	Jul 29, 1941	Asthville, Nc		Jun 29, 1884	59	Ng				Willford, Margaret [Daug]	Alder Branch - Sevier Co					
Mc Carter, Nancy Jo	Jan 8, 1985	Sevier Co	Tn	Aug 8, 1908	68	Mc Carter, S.M.	Lee, Mary			Mc Carter, Mrs. Nancy C.	Alder Branch - Sevier Co					
Mc Carter, Noah Albert	Dec 14, 1983	Care Inn	Tn	May 16, 1911	72	Ng	Blalock, Alice			Mc Carter, Lloyd	Alder Branch - Sevier Co			Andrews, Ann Ruth		
Mc Carter, S.M. (Rev.)	Jan 28, 1948	Jeff Co	Ga	Jun 17, 1909	78-7-11	Ng	Mc Carter, Aaron	Tn	Tn	Mc Carter, Mariah	New Gray-Knox Co					
Mc Claine, Dora Mae	Mar 23, 1928		Tn		42-2-10	Mc Claine, S.R.	Hodge, H.H.	Nc	Tn	Manley, Margaret	Mills Springs					
Mc Clanahan, Robert Leon	May 15, 2000	Jeff City	Nc	Oct 9, 1921	78	Div	Mc Clanahan, Joseph Andrew			Jones, Mary Louise	Cremated					
Mc Clere, Della	Jul 29, 1981	Jeff City	Tn	May 1, 1877	84		Ballinger,--			Northern, Arcena	West View					
Mc Clere, Howard S.	Jul 23, 1991	Jeff Co	Tn	Mar 26, 1916	75	Murph, Sallie	Mc Clere, Samuel R.			Bibbs, Lyman - Hoyle, Mrs.	West View	unk.				
Mc Clere, J. Marshall	Aug 5, 1939	Jeff City	Tn	Jun 21, 1873	66	Ng	Mc Clere, James Houston		Knox Co	Ledgerwood, Eliza Jane	West View					
Mc Clere, Samuel Roger	Jan 5, 1972	Jeff City	Tn	Dec 25, 1882	89	W	Mc Clere, James H.	Jeff Co		Children	Mill Springs					
Mc Cleary, Audrey Garrett [M]	Sep 21, 1991	J.M.H.	Blandville, Ill.	Sep 30, 1929	62	Ginn, Ruth	Mc Cleary, Clarence		Tn	Mc Cleary, Dennis [Son] Mc Clere, James & Howard	Cremated					
										Garrett, Helen	Mc Cleary, Ruth S.					

NAME	DDATE	DLOCAT	BLOCAT	BDATE	AGE	SPOUSE	FATHER	FBLOCAT	MOTHER	MFBLOCAT	BY	BURIAL	VET	SON	DAUG	BROTHER	SISTER
McClennen, Paul Douglas	Jan 15, 1972	Jeff Co	Mo	Jul 31, 1955	16	s	McClennen, V. Eugene		Coleman, Beverly		McClellen, V. Eugene	Sunset Hills - Mo					
McCloud, Johnny Robert	Sep 22, 1998	Jeff City	Logan, W. Va	Sep 27, 1949	48	s	McCloud, John L.		Hicks, Helen		Blankenship, Helen Hicks [Mother]	Forest Lawn - Pocahontil, W. Va					
McClure, William Henry	Sep 9, 1988	J.M.H.	Tn	Apr 1, 1918	70	s	McClure, William F.		Crawford, Emma F.		McClure, Alfred	Jarnagin	WW 2	McPheters Bevd - Hawkins Co			
McCorkle, Gertrude	Oct 2, 1988	Jeff City	Tn	Jul 19, 1908	80	W	Huggins, J.I.		Dorman, Virginia Lee		McCorkle, Virginia [Daug]	Jarnagin					
McCosh, Rhonda Gail	Dec 28, 1992	Morristown, Tn	Nashville, Tn	Mar 21, 1954	38	McCosh, Devon C.	Brown, James C.	Tn	Dead, Nannie L.	Tn	McCosh, Dr. Earl [Father-In-Law]	Springhill - Nashville, Tn		Phillip Andrew		Larry K, James C, Jr.	Douglas, Susan - Wheeler, Shirley
McCowen, Martha [Cord]	Mar 17, 1925	Tn			85	W			Lenningen, Sarah		McCoy, Kathryn [Mother]	Colored					
McCoy, Hester Caroline	Oct 1, 1991	White Pine, Tn	Tn	Jun 27, 1963	28	s	McCoy, Alton Ray		Stensbaugh, Kathryn		McCoy, Kathryn [Mother]	Cremated					
McCoy, Marie	May 23, 1993	Morristown, Tn	Nc	Mar 25, 1932	61	McCoy, Bernard [W.Va.]				Meadows F.H. [Hinton, W. Va]	Hillcrest					
McCoy, William Gordon	Oct 14, 1979	Rutledge, Tn	Nc	Jun 2, 1894	85	W	McCoy, W.R.	Tn	Durand, Henrietta		Leavitt, Mrs. Joyce [Statsboro, Ga]	Woolram	WW 1				
McCubbins, Infant Female	Jul 15, 1956	Knox Co	Knox Co	Jul 15, 1956			McCubbins, James		Best, Jane		McCubbins, James [Father]	Woolram					
McCubbins, Infant Male	Aug 7, 1955	Jeff Co	Jeff Co	Aug 7, 1955			McCubbins, James B.		Best, Jane		McCubbins, James Purdie [Peoria, Illinois]	Woolram					
McCubbins, Jessie Leona	Aug 3, 1952	Jeff Co	Tn	Dec 26, 1888	63	W	Koontz, James		Smith, Martha		Brown, Leona - Willson, Woodran - Whiteman - Howard - Mr. Cubbins, Bruce - Askew, Martha	Friends Station					
McCubbins, Roy Sherman	Aug 21, 1996	Jeff City	Feb 17, 1907	Feb 17, 1907	89		McCubbins, George		Oller, Francis E.		Castro, Reama [Daug -]	Cremated	army				
McCurry, Betty Ann	Jul 31, 1935	Murfordsville, Ky	Tn	Apr 21, 1935	3d		McCurry, Paul L.	Tn	Holt, Queenie	Tn	McCurry, P.L.	Flat Gap					
McCurry, Vera Elizabeth	Jun 16, 1995	Jeff City	Gary Mt. Nc	Apr 19, 1918	77	McCurry, Jim		Randolph, Biscomb		Sparks, Sarah		Husband	East View Memorial - Knox Co		James E.			
McCurtain, Olive A.	Aug 12, 1999	Jeff City		Apr 18, 1905	94		McCurtain, John Alexander		Price, Eva Louise		Hostler, Marcia K. [Niece]	J.M.G.					
McDaniel, Aaron S.	Jan 26, 1997	J.M.H.	Tn	Jul 2, 1899	97	Willings, Pansy	McDaniel, Edward K.		Turner, Celia Ann		McDaniel, Lawrence	J.M.G.					
McDaniel, Britt T.	Jul 5, 1971	Michigan			86						Hurst, Mrs. Oby [Michigan]	Woodran - Whiteman - Aaron - Oba, Mrs. Tom					
McDaniel, Celia Ann	May 25, 1961	Jeff City	Tn	Feb 26, 1870	91	McDaniel, E.K.	Turner, Spence		Hayes, Katherine		Howard, Helen	Blackwell Branch - Grainger Co					
McDaniel, Eli	Feb 17, 1950	Grainger Co	Tn		83		McDaniel, Sam					Shiloh					
McDaniel, George T. [JReese]	Aug 11, 1981	Jeff Co	Tn	Oct 10, 1906	74	Ng	McDaniel, Sam		Turner, Mattie		McDaniel, Mrs. Ellie L.	Jefferson Memorial					
McDaniel, George William	Aug 15, 1964	Jeff Co	Tn	Aug 30, 1899	64	Bates, Beulah	McDaniel, Eli		Byrd, Nancy		McDaniel, Beulah & Verlin-James - Houn, Estelle - Kitts, Mrs. Curtis [Children]	Mitchell Springs - Grainger Co					
McDaniel, Georgia Inez	Mar 31, 2000	Jeff City	Tn	Feb 17, 1913	87	W	Smith, Robert H.		Koontz, Sarah E.		McDaniel, Doyle [Son]	Strawberry Plains					
McDaniel, Hascal	Dec 31, 1933	Jeff Co		Oct 23, 1910	23	s	McDaniel, Britt	Tn	Dotson, Lizzie	Tn	McDaniel, Britt	Mt. View					
McDaniel, Helen Louise	Jul 15, 1997	Knoxville, Tn	Knox Co	Oct 26, 1923	73	McDaniel, Glenn	Elmum, Edgar		Shively, Nell		Husband	West View		Jerry & Faye	Chapman, Glenda & Rick	Henson, Vanda Ruth	
McDaniel, Infant Female	Nov 1, 1941	Jeff Co	Jeff Co				McDaniel, Glenn		Lennum, Helen Stalsworth, Verelita Dianna	Jeff Co	McDaniel, Glenn	West View					
McDaniel, Joshua Trever	Jul 16, 1982	J.M.H.	Tn	July 16, 1982		McDaniel, Brit		McDaniel, Michele E.			McDaniel, Charlie & Michael	Mt. View					
McDaniel, Lizzie	Mar 22, 1961	Michigan	Tn			s	McDaniel, Edward K.		Turner, Celia Ann		McDaniel, Ray [Michigan]	New Blackwell Branch - Grainger Co					
McDaniel, Lora Jane	Sep 7, 1975	Jeff Co	Tn	Oct 15, 1895	79	s			Byrd, Nancy		Howard, Verelyn - Helms, Johnny - Roach, Mae - McDaniel, Arthur & Bill	Mitchell Springs - Grainger Co				J.D.	
McDaniel, Mary Katherine	Aug 16, 1958	Grainger Co	Tn	Jul 14, 1901	57	s	McDaniel, Eli				Daniel, [Mrs. Katherine Cronk] - McDaniel, Harriet [Mrs. Katherine George	Grainger Co					
McDaniel, Mattie Maughie	Jan 6, 1971	Jeff Co				W	Turner, Robert		Purphton, Harriet ?								

NAME	DDATE	DLOCAT	BLOCAT	BDATE	AGE	SPOUSE	FATHER	F/B LOCAT	MOTHER	MFBLOCAT	BY	BURIAL	VET	SON	DAUG	BROTHER	SISTER
Mc Daniel, Michael Ray	Sep 15, 1957	Knox Co	Tn	Aug 23, 1954	3		Mc Daniel, Glenn S.		Elmore, Helen		Mc Daniel, Glenn	West View					
Mc Daniel, Nellie	Jun 17, 1955										Mc Daniel, Anson	West View					
Mc Daniel, Otis Abraham (Mack)	Jan 14, 1985	Knoxville, Tn	Tn	Feb 7, 1907	77	Smith, Inez			Sherlin, Amanda		Mc Daniel, Inez	Strawberry Plains					
Mc Daniel, Stella	Dec 19, 1971	Jeff Co	Tn	May 16, 1898	73	Ng	Morgan, Houston A.		Byrd, Aircy		Mc Daniel, Aaron & Children	Jefferson Memorial					
Mc Donald, Linda Jeanette	Feb 23, 1975	Jeff Co	Michigan	Sep 9, 1953	21	S	Mc Donald, Willis E.		Faulk, Dorath		Mc Donald, Gary E. - Idey/J.H. [Rackxl, Ark.]	Woodland Heights, Ark.					
Mc Dougal, S.A.	Feb 18, 1992	Jeff City	Tn	Oct 22, 1879	52	Ng	Mc Dougal, B.	Ga	Edward, Bell	Ga	Mc Dougal, Mrs. & Son	West Union					
Mc Dougal, Isaac Edward	Jan 19, 1992	Jeff City	Ga	Jul 8, 1901	60	Ng	Mc Dougal, Samuel H.		Cox, Ruth [Night] - Mc Dougal, Sam [Son]			Jefferson Memorial					
Mc Dougal, Rebecca	Aug 27, 1953	Ga	Ga	May 20, 1883	70	W	Kincald, Caleb		Laird, Persilee		Mc Dougal, Isaac	West View					
Mc Dougal, B.A.	Jul 23, 1936	Jeff Co									Mc Dougal, W.O.	West View					
Mc Dow, Eldon Roy Jr.	Jan 4, 1974	Jeff City	Tn	Mar 5, 1972	1		Mc Dow, Eldon Roy Sr.		Bryant, Brenda		Mc Dow, Eldon Roy Sr.	Liberty - Sublicee, Okla.					
Mc Elwen, Annette	Sep 16, 1964	Knox Co	Tn	Jul 3, 1909	55	S	Mc Elwen, Hugh R.		Sunderland, Mima		Dublin, Mrs. James [Schattnooga, Tn]	West View					
Mc Elwen, Hugh R.	Aug 3, 1933	Knox Co	Tn	Oct 23, 1879	73	W	Mc Elwen, R.D.		Peck, Elizabeth		Mc Elwen, Annette & Morgan	West View					
Mc Elwen, Mima	May 19, 1939	Mascot	Tn	Jul 7, 1883	56	Mc Elwen, Hugh	Sunderland, William W.	Tn	Carter, Harriet N.	Tn	Mc Elwen, Hugh	West View					
Mc Elwen, Pryor M.	Oct 27, 1951	Cumberland Co	Jeff Co	Nov 5, 1883	67	S			Peck, E.	Tn	Mc Elwen, Lee	West View					
Mc Elwen, Robert Lee	Jan 9, 1953	Jeff Co	Tn	Nov 27, 1886	64	S	Mc Elwen, R.D.		Peck, Elizabeth		Mc Elwen, Hugh	West View	unk				
Mc Farland, Dallas [Col]	May 24, 1934	Jeff City	Tn	Mar 22, 1930	4	S	Mc Farland, Roy	Tn	Cunningham, Emma	Tn	Mc Farland, Roy	Jeff City					
Mc Farland, Earl	Jul 19, 1946	Washington D.C.	Tn		26	S			Emory, Mrs. John - Dilis, Sam			New Market					
Mc Farland, Emma Lee [Col]	Feb 29, 1972	Jeff Co	Tn	Dec 1, —	60	Mc Farland, Leroy [B]	Cunningham, William		Tate, Mellie		Galoer, Carolyn	West View					
Mc Farland, Florence	Jun 10, 1989	Abingdon, Va	Tn	Dec 5, 1874	84	W					Mc Farland, William S.-Frank-Leroy	West View					
Mc Farland, Katherine	Jan 26, 1925		Tn		9		Mc Farland, Will	Jeff Co	Sunderland, Mima	Jeff Co	Mc Farland, William S.-Frank-Leroy	Jefferson City					
Mc Farland, Le Roy	Feb 13, 1971	New Market	Tn	Apr 19, 1909	61	Cunningham, Emma	Mc Farland, William Simpson		Williams, Florence		Mc Farland, Emma	West View					
Mc Gee, Gertie	Jan 11, 1939		Tn			W	Mc Nish, Simpson	Tn	Martin, Mary	Tn	Mc Gee, Leonard	Pleasant Grove					
Mc Ghee, Alexander	Jan 16, 1957		Tn	Jan 30, 1859	77	W	Mc Ghee, Henry	Tn	Morgan, Martha	Tn	Mc Gee, Leonard	Nance's Grove					
Mc Ghee, Anthony Dewayne	Sep 26, 1988	Jeff City	Jeff City	Sep 23, 1986	32	Bensay, Karen	Mc Ghee, Wayne D.		Petty, Carolyn		Petty, Carolyn	Petty	Craig Anthony-Chase Daniel				
Mc Ghee, Cora Marie	Sep 10, 1961	Jeff Co	Tn	Sep 17, 1911	49	Mc Ghee, Robert W.	Blackburn, M.W.		Frody, Lola May		Mc Ghee, Mrs. Earl	Memorial Gardens			Holt, Wade - Clibbs, Betty - Wedlock, Buddy Jewell, Issie - Mc Ghee, John & Hazel - Petty, Wilma [G-Parents]		
Mc Ghee, Earl	May 26, 1973	Cherokee Lake	Tn	Jan 1, 1936	37	Jett, Bernice	Mc Ghee, Earl Sr.		Marshall, Gladys		Mc Ghee, Mrs. Earl	Jefferson Memorial					
Mc Ghee, Earl W. Sr.	Jan 15, 1954	New Market, Tn	Tn	Apr 10, 1908	85	Marshall, Gladys	Mc Ghee, Joseph		Jones, Lizzie		Wife	Beaver Creek		Frank-L.H.-Roger [T/4-Buddy [D]	Hicks, Betty - Dalton, Christine - Curze, Earlene - Strong, Shirley [Ns]	Buford-James	Mary Elizabeth [D] - Morris, Ruth - Martin, Polly - Luttrull, Louise - Howard, Nina Bea
Mc Ghee, Floyd H.	Apr 23, 1954	Jeff Co	Tn	Jan 26, 1903	60	Ng	Mc Ghee, Leonard		Marshall, Gladys		Mc Ghee, Mrs. Floyd & Children	Jefferson Memorial					
Mc Ghee, Infant Female	Apr 12, 1948	Jeff Co	Tn	Apr 12, 1948		Ng	Mc Ghee, Earl	Tn	Mc Ghee, Earl	Tn	Mc Ghee, Earl	Beaver Creek					

NAME	DDATE	DLOCAT	BLOCAT	BDATE	AGE	SPOUSE	FATHER	FELOCAT	MOTHER	MFELOCAT	BY	BURIAL	VET	SON	DAUG	BROTHER	SISTER
Mc Ghee, James	Sep 9, 1964	Jeff Co.		Oct 18, 1879	84	W	Mc Ghee, John		Bratcher, Nancy		Haskins, Mrs. Joe - Petiofaux, Edith - Dandrins, Bessie - Allsup, Geneva	Pleasant Grove					
Mc Ghee, Leonard W.	Apr 22, 1940	New Market	Tn	Oct 18, 1877	62	W	Mc Ghee, John	Tn	Bradshaw, Nancy Mitchell, Varlia Mae	Tn	Children	Pleasant Grove					
Mc Ghee, Stella Mae	Jan 22, 1975	Decatur, Ga	Tn	May 20, 1907	67	W	Williams, Harlan		Mitchell, Varlia Mae		Mc Ghee, Vaughn	Jefferson Memorial					
Mc Ginnis, John Coleman	Feb 14, 1965	Jeff Co	Tn	Mar 26, 1925	39	Katherine	Mc Ginnis, George M.		Williams, Nellie		Mc Ginnis, Mrs. J.C.	Memorial Gardens					
Mc Ginnis, John C.	Jul 17, 1968	Jeff Co		May 31, 1903	65	Ng	Mc Ginnis, William		Collins, Sarah L.		Mc Ginnis, Mrs. Laura Scott	Strawberry Plains					
Mc Ginnis, LuVurra Zeal	Nov 19, 1968	Strawberry Plains, Tn	Tn	Nov 30, 1890	77	Mc Ginnis, John C. [D]	Scott, Solomon D.		Ekert, Sarah J.		Mc Ginnis, Mrs. Jerry	Holden View - Knox Co					
Mc Glamery, Anna Delena	Aug 18, 1931	Jeff Co	Tn	Dec 28, 1873	58	W	Hatcher, W.A.	Tn	Hatcher, Nancy	Tn	Mc Glamery, J.A.	Friends Station					
Mc Glamery, John A.	Sep 28, 1956	Jeff Co	Tn	Sep 23, 1956	78-9-5	W	Mc Glamery, Jacob		Mc Workman, Eliza		Bates, Mrs. L.H.	Friends					
Mc Goldrick, Marion Ruth	May 5, 1998	Jeff City	Anderson Co, Tn	Sep 30, 1912	85		Hamblin, Abner		Dagley, Josephine		Mc Goldrick, George [Son]	J.M.G.			Moore, Bipdelia	Hublert & Katherine Catlett	Hamblin, Louise & Hublert - Catlett, Coppock, Toledo - Simmons, Virginia
Mc Goldrick, Rudolph George	Nov 8, 1993	Knoxville, Tn	Morgan Co, Tn	Feb 20, 1908	85	Hamblin, Ruth	Mc Goldrick, G.W.		Mehlhorn, Mary		Mc Goldrick, George & Linda [Son]	J.M.G.			Moore, Bobbie		
Mc Guire, David	Mar 10, 1929	Tn	Tn	Sep 1, 1958	17-8-29	S	Mc Guire, George	Tn	Smith, Bell	Tn	Mc Guire, Will & George	Dandridge					
Mc Inelna, Laura Lyn	Jun 15, 1987	Knox Co	Tn	Sep 1, 1958	8		Duggan, Layette		Duggan, Layette		Mc High, Joe	West View					
Mc Inelna, Eugene Thomas Jr.	Apr 11, 1988	New York, Ny	Jacksonville, Fla.	Sep 3, 1915	73	Mc Inelna, Jean	Mc High, Joe		Edmundson, Nena		Mc High, Joe [Ny]	West View					
Mc Kay, Gladys	Feb 3, 1970	Jeff Co		May 1, 1903	79	Mc Kay, Gordon R.	Mc Inelna, Eugene T. Sr.		Henderson, Nancy		Mc Cay, Mr. W.G.	Hillcrest					
Mc Kee, Cecil Edward	Jul 9, 1973	Asheville, Nc		Oct 22, 1887	46		Mc Kay, Garden		Sufis		Jefferson Memorial					
Mc Keaney, Howard	Dec 15, 1977	Blaine, Tn		Jan 9, 1931	46	Div	Mc Kee, S.E.		Brock, Armogia		Mc Kinney, Clarence A.	Hillcrest	Korea				
Mc Kinney, Andy	Apr 8, 1979	Jeff City		May 17, 1883	95	W	Mc Kinney, John		Merihorn, Mrs. Joe.		Mc Kinney, Clarence - Wilson, Mrs. Charles - Henderson, Mrs. Marie	Hillcrest					
Mc Kinney, Beulah Harrell	Jan 14, 1987	Knoxville, Tn	Tn	Aug 2, 1899	87	W	Parkey, Cecil V.		Sumpter, Ollie		Harrell, Henry W.	Lynnhurst					
Mc Kinney, Mahalia	Feb 17, 1935	Jeff City	Tn	Dec 6, 1856	78	W	Denton, David L.	Tn	Perman, Jane	Tn	Mc Kinney, G.W.	Mt. Pleasant					
Mc Kinzie, Oma	Apr 21, 1989	Dandridge, Tn	Jeff Co	Apr 16, 1905	94		Winstead, George		Winstead, Sally		Hickman, Ross [Nephew] - Widener, Russel [Niece]	J.M.G.				Jess [Mss.]	
Mc Lain, Mary Ellen	Nov 9, 1982	Jeff Co		Oct 7, 1873	89 9m-12d	Mc Lain, W.	Gaby, John N.		Morrison, Polly Ann		Mc Lain, Clarence [Jack] - Lockhart, Mrs. - John	Jarrigan					
Mc Lain, Ruxie Lee	Nov 28, 1924	Jeff Co					Mc Clave, S.R.	Tn	Hodge, Dora Anne	Tn	Mc Clave, S.R.	Mills Springs					
Mc Lain, Walter V.	Jun 18, 1961	Jeff Co		Sep 29, 1884	76	Ng	Mc Lain, William		Doud, Mary		Mc Lain, Calvin [Jack] - Lockhart, Mrs. - John W.	Jarrigan					
Mc Lain, Wilma Eulella	Feb 8, 1984	Tn		Mar 21, 1910	73	S	Mc Clain, Walter Vicker		Gaby, Mary Ellen		Seale, Sally	Jarrigan					
Mc Laughlin, Joe Neal	Jun 22, 1982	Jeff Co [Ples Texas]	New Mexico	Apr 13, 1926	56	S	Mc Laughlin, Joseph L.		Hollis, Nona Mae		Chaffin, Mrs. H.T. L.	Llano - Patter Co, Texas	WW 2				
Mc Laun, Bandora Hoffman	Nov 21, 1982	Morristown, Tn	Fla	May 4, 1903	79	Mc Laun, George R.	Hoffman, William Fredrick		May, Minnie Mae		Mc Inelna, Mrs. Thomas [Jean]	West View					
Mc Laun, George Robert	Jul 25, 1978	Jeff Co	Mass.	Oct 22, 1887	90	Ng	Mc Laun, Ellias Hiram		Schwedie, Anna Jane		Mc Laun, Mrs. G.R.	West View					
Mc Mahan, Nan	Feb 17, 1923	Jeff City	Tn	Aug 23, 1867	74	W	Henderson, W.Y.	Tn	Runion, Mary	Tn	Servise Baptist Church [Bershul]	Servise Baptist Church					
Mc Michael, Charles Ernest	Jun 20, 1995	Dandridge, Tn	Illinois	Jul 24, 1918	76		Mc Michael, Ernest		Russell, Isabelle		Frye, Donna [Daug]	Perry Mount Park - Portliac, Mich.					
Mc Millian, Jonnie Mae	Jul 17, 1970	Knox Co	Tn	Nov -, 1910	59	Ng	Atchley, Press		Charles, Becky		Mc Millian, Walter	Holden View - Knox Co					
Mc Millian, Zola [Black]	Apr 6, 1984	Care Inn	Tn			Ng	Brown, Tom		Mc Bee, Mollie		Mc Millian, Mrs. John R.	Holly Hills - Knoxville, Tn					

NAME	DDATE	DLOCAT	BLOCAT	BDATE	AGE	SPOUSE	FATHER	FBLOCAT	MOTHER	MFBLOCAT	BY	BURIAL	VET	SON	DAUG	BROTHER	SISTER
Mc Murray, Anne Belle	Apr 5, 1958	Jeff Co	Tn	Mar 18, 1975	83	S	Mc Murray, James M.		Rankin, Almyra M.		Crawford, Mrs Tommy John-Ben-Elda	Mt. Horeb					
Mc Murray, Ben W.	Apr 28, 1966		Tn	Jun 6, 1982	83	W	Mc Murray, James		Rankin, Almena		Fallhour, Edward - Blackburn, Don - Rankin, Ralph & Mildred [Children]	Mt. Horeb					
Mc Murray, Elda Mae	Jun 30, 1992	Dandridge, Tn	Jeff Co	Mar 7, 1888	104	S	Mc Murray, James		Rankin, Almyra		Crawford, Mary Ruth [Niece]	Mt. Horeb					
Mc Murray, Eva	Nov 10, 1959	Jeff Co	Tn	Jun 5, 1886	72	W	Mc Murray, William W.		Miller, Harriet R.		Mc Murray, Ben & Daughter	Mt. Horeb					
Mc Murray, James Garnett	Apr 8, 1996	Jeff City	Grainger Co	Jul 4, 1917	78	Hayes, Martha	Mc Murray, Ben W.		Evans, Mildred		Wife	J.M.G.					
Mc Murray, John Mc Campbell	Sep 2, 1968	Jeff Co	Tn	Nov 18, 1879	88	Ng	Mc Murray, Joe		Rankin, Almyrla ?		Mc Murray, Mrs. John Peck, Mrs. Charles	Mt. Horeb					
Mc Murray, Louella	Aug 10, 1974	Knoxville, Tn	Tn	Mar 10, 1892	82	W	Caldwell, James W.		Hattie Isabelle		Crawford, Mary Ruth-Peck, Mrs. Charles	Mt. Horeb					
Mc Nish, Annie B.	Dec 8, 1939	Jeff Co	Tn		82	Mc Nish, Clifford	Lindsey, Joe	Tn	Chambers, Martha	Tn	Mc Nish, Clifford	Mt. Horeb					
Mc Nish, Charlie	Jan 16, 1984	Knox Co	Tn	Sep 17, 188-	75-3-19	W	Mc Nish, Simpson		Morgan, Mary		Mc Nish, Don [Illinois]	Pleasant Grove					
Mc Nish, Clifford Oscar	Oct 18, 1978	Jeff City	Tn	May 16, 1902	74	W	Mc Nish, John		Woods, Mrs. Lucille		Mc Nish, Don [Illinois]	West View					
Mc Nish, Elizabeth L.	Jan 7, 1969	Jeff Co	Tn	Feb 12, —	52-10-25	Mc Nish, Clifford [Sally]	Mc Nish, John		Walker, Elizabeth		Mc Nish, Clifford	West View					
Mc Nish, Eula Elizabeth	Aug 14, 1975	U.T.H.	Tn	Jan 16, 1916	59	S	Mc Nish, M.L.		Howard, Minerva		Miller, Donald - Mc Nish, M.L. Jr.	Pleasant Grove					
Mc Nish, Howard E.	Feb 7, 1987	Jeff City	Jeff Co	Feb 25, 1912	84	Elizabeth E.	Mc Nish, William		Campbell, Sarah E.		Wife	J.M.G.			Holloway, Elizabeth & Charles		
Mc Nish, Infant	Jun 8, 1926	J.M.H.	Tn	Feb 2, 1906	0		Mc Nish, Clifford		Lindsey, Annie	Tn	Lindsey, Annie Satterfield, Della	West View					
Mc Nish, Jennie	Apr 27, 1982	Jeff City	Tn	Jul 2, 1906	76	S	Mc Nish, Rufus M.		Satterfield, Della		Mc Nish, Frank	West View					
Mc Nish, John Wayne	Apr 24, 1954	Hamblen Co	Tn	Oct 4, 1953	0		Mc Nish, James		Loveday, Mary Ruth		Mc Nish, James	West View					
Mc Nish, Mack Leonard Jr.	Nov 28, 1987	Talbott, Tn	Tn	Jul 3, 1921	66	S	Mc Nish, Mack Leonard Sr.		Miller, Kelly [Sister]		Pleasant Grove [Toad Hop]	Pleasant Grove					
Mc Nish, Mack Leonard Sr.	Jul 1, 1959	Jeff City	Tn	May 10, 1882	76	W	Mc Nish, John A.		Howard, Minerva		Mc Nish, Eula E. & Children	Pleasant Grove					
Mc Nish, Minerva	Jan 28, 1981	Jeff City	Tn		78	Ng	Mc Nish, Mack L. [D]		Howard, Unk		Mc Nish, Eula-Patty-H.H. Jr.-Billy-Katy	Pleasant Grove		David A. & Rhonda			
Mc Nish, Oscar E.	Apr 29, 1994	Metairie, La	Jeff City	Jul 11, 1928	65	Edmonds, Peggy	Mc Nish, Clifford		Lindsey, Anna B.		Wife	Pleasant Grove					Wood, Lucille
Mc Nish, Roscoe Raymond	Nov 28, 1983	Jeff City	Tn	May 6, 1903	60	Div	Mc Nish, James F.		Spencer, Sallie		Inkleburger, Mrs. Carrie	Pleasant Grove					
Mc Nish, Rufus G.	Mar 7, 1981	Grainger Co, Tn	Tn	Aug 28, 1909	71	S	Mc Nish, Rufus M.		Satterfield, Della		French, Mrs. Does [Katherine] Mc Nish, Jennie	Pleasant Grove	WW 2				
Mc Nish, Rufus M.	Sep 10, 1965	Jeff Co	Tn	Feb 14, 1874	91	W	Mc Nish, Simpson		Martin, Mary		Mc Nish, Jennie-Rufus Jr.-Earl - French, Katherine	Mill Springs					
Mc Nish, Sarah Elizabeth	Nov 5, 1987	Jeff City	Tn	Mar 12, 1870/80	87-7-23	Mc Nish, Robert [D]			Mc Nish, Howard-Jim-George		Mc Nish, Howard-Jim-George	West View					
Mc Nish, Smith	Feb 14, 1957	Jeff City	Illinois	Aug 31, 1914	42	S	Mc Nish, Rufus Sr.		Satterfield, Deddy	Tn	Mc Nish, Rufus Sr.	Mill Springs					
Mc Nish, William Ray	Sep 20, 1995	Knox Co	Jeff Co	Apr 29, 1875	90	Sallie C.	Mc Nish, Will		Bashett, Mary		Mc Nish, Jamie-Howard-Jim-George	West View					
Mc Spadden, Stephen Doyle	Aug 8, 1942	Jeff Co	Tn	Jul 20, 1942	20d	Mc Spadden, Spencer	Mc Spadden, Milton	Tn	Franklin, Lorene	Tn	Mc Spadden, Milton	Shady Grove					
Mc Spadden, Vera	Jun 8, 1981	Knox Co	Tn	Feb 5, 1918	42	Mc Spadden, Spencer	Rainwater, Floyd		Perrott, Arlie		Mc Spadden, Spencer	Hillcrest					
Mc Swain, Frank	Oct 9, 1953	New Market	Tn	Jul 10, 1888	65	Ng	Mc Swain, France		Gray, Eliza		Hall, Mrs Mannie - Ralph	New Market					
Mc Swain, Jess Lee	Nov 10, 1966	Jeff City	Tn	Jan 6, 1895	71	Ng	Mc Swain, Will		Tittis, Nancy		Mc Swain, Mrs. Jess Hall, Mrs. Caswell	New Market					
Mc Swain, Nancy	Apr 21, 1954	Jeff Co	Tn	Jan 27, 1870	84	W	Guinn, Isaac				Meads, Robert W. [Son] Hall, Robert W.F. [Son] Gla.] Cook F.H. [St. Paul, Va]	New Market					
Meads, Robert Jerry	Aug 9, 1980	Va	Va	Mar 16, 1942	38	Meads, Ann Ruth	Meads, Robert R.		Edwards, Thelma			Pleasant View					
Meadows, J.J.	Aug 13, 1932	Talbott	Grafton, W. Va	Jul 19, 1870	62	W	Meadows, Albert		Whitehead, Vicry	Tn		Bluemont - Grafton, W. Va					
Merriman, Orlena June	Nov 20, 1998	Koville, Tn	Grafton, W. Va	Apr 5, 1943	55	Merriman, Richard	Kissmem, Claude Rutherford		Barrett, Cora Irene	Tn	Husband	Pleasant View - Grafton, W. Va					

NAME	DDATE	DLOCAT	BLOCAT	BDATE	AGE	SPOUSE	FATHER	FBLOCAT	MOTHER	MBLOCAT	BY	BURIAL	VET	SON	DAUG	BROTHER	SISTER
Merritt, George Hayden	Oct 26, 1999	Jeff City	Pensacol, Fl	Aug 29, 1935	64	King, Virginia	Merritt, Ernest Sr.		Rhodes, Willa Pearl		Wife - King, Maggie [Mother-in-Law]	West View		Jesse 3rd - Christopher - David - George Allen	Fodia, Teresa - Merritt, Linda		
Messer, David S.	Jun 27, 1970	Jeff Co	Tn	Mar 12, 1909	61	Ng	Messer, John		Whaley, Lucy		Ingram, Berry Jean	Pleasant Ridge					
Messer, Edith	Dec 1, 1993	Sevier Co	Sevier Co	Mar 3, 1913	80		Price, Willie		Carthell, Isabella		Messer, Ralph [Son]	Pleasant Ridge		Robert Lee	Ingram, Betty M.	Glen-Avery	Haddock, Lena - Myles, Lula - Mc Carter, Vernie - Ollis, Alma Ruth
Messer, Ellen Cecil	Nov 27, 1992	Talbott, Tn	Tn	Jan 29, 1953	29	Hammons, Rebecca	Messer, Robert Lee		Messer, Robert Lee		Messer, Robert Lee						
Messer, Grover C.	Feb 9, 1939	Knoxville	No Sneedville, Tn	Feb 17, 1894	45	S	Messer, John T.	Nc	Hannah, Willa	Nc	Messer, Crawford	Jarnigan					
Messer, Mary Ruth	Dec 27, 1997	Jeff City	Tn	Nov 29, 1931	66	Messer, Robert Lee	Nichols, Henry		Weston, Nevia		Husband	Pleasant Ridge		Johnny-Bobby			
Messer, Millie Hannah	Oct 23, 1943	Jeff Co	Nc	Sep 6, 1891	51	W	Hannah, John	Nc	Simmons, Julia	Nc	Messer, W.C. & J.T.	Jarnigan					
Messer, Martie	Jul 1, 1943	Hamblen Co	Granger Co	Sep 6, 1891		Messer, W.C.	Wexter, P.N.	Tn	Payne, Julia	Tn	Messer, W.C.	Jarnigan					
Metcalf, Infant	Sep 10, 1931	Granger Co		Sep 10, 1934			Spooks, Richie	Tn	Metcalf, Lida	Tn	Carrier Point						
Metcalf, Zula Susan	Aug 21, 1993	Jeff City	Sevier Co	Apr 23, 1913	80		Burns, George Andy		Ogle, Minnie		Metcalf, Roy [Son]	J.M.G.		Paul	Parley, Phyllis - Williard, Nellie [D]		
Metzler, Infant	Sep 9, 1941	Shipe Addition				S	Metzler, Clyde R.		Shovel, Cecila Eilene		Metzler, C.R.	West View					
Michaels, Joel Leonard	Jul 3, 1995	Jeff City	Cheyenne, Wyoming	Nov 15, 1972	22		Michaels, Gordon		Clark, Johnnie	Tn	Calhoun	Calhoun				Ricky-Jerry	[In-Law] Michaels, Jennifer
Michel, R.T.	Sep 25, 1933	Grainger Co	Tn	Nov 7, 1897	35	S	Michel, W. W.		Unk		Michel, Mrs. W. W. Clark, Mrs. Paul -	Indian Ridge					
Middlesworth, Estelle	Apr 14, 1974	Jeff City	Tn	Jun 6, 1888	85	W	Westbrook, Stephen D.		Unk		Harnett, Mrs. Dorothy Tillman, Charlene [Daug]	Greenlawn - Cohra, Ill.					
McNutt, Charles W. Sr.	Sep 25, 1991	Ivanhoe, Va.	Jul 5, 1902	89	W	McNutt, Walter Preston		Johnson, Julia Cleaves			J.M.G.					
McNutt, Margaret Collins	Jun 11, 1991	J.M.H.	Jeff City	Aug 29, 1914	76	McNutt, Charles W.	Collins, Fred		Turner, Martha		Bissell, Nancy [Daug]	J.M.G.					
Milam, Carl Smith	May 13, 1983	Morristown, Tn	Nc	Sep 21, 1913	69	Bamhart, Dorothy	Milam, Lester		Foster, Naomi		Milam, Mrs. Dorothy - Milar, Sonja	Hamblen Memorial	WW 2				
Miller, Elbert Edwin [Al]	Jun 3, 1984	Sevier Co	Tn	Apr 5, 1924	60	Emory, Flossie	Miller, Willie K.		Layman, Frances		Miller, Flossie	Oak Grove - Kodak, Tn					
Miles, Alfred Edward	Nov 25, 1989	Tell City, Indiana	Tn	Jul 29, 1919	70	Jones, Eva	Hinton, Birdie		Miller, Eva - V.A.			WW 2				
Miles, Cecil	Jul 1,1 1968	F.S.H.	Jeff Co	1907	61	Ng	Peck, Georgia		Miller, Bruce	West View						
Miles, Dorothy	Nov 6, 1974	Jeff City	Washington	Jul 11, 1918	63	Ng	Anderson, Mattie		Wilson, Dr. Hubert J. - King, Arthur E. [Moth]	Jefferson Memorial					
Miles, Ella Mae	Oct 7, 1988	Jeff City	Nc	Jun 9, 1907	61	W	Miles, Cecil		Wilson, Gussie								
Miles, Georgia	Mar 6, 1982	Tn	Nov 27, 1883	78	W	Peck, Joseph		Caldwell, Mary		Lowery, Mrs.Cher - Warwd, Mrs. James - Joe-Bruce-Haskell- Walker, Mrs. James-Cecil [Children]	West View					
Miles, James Monroe	Dec 16, 1961	Knox Co	Tn	Jul 27, 1883	78	Ng	Willard, Pauline		Father								
Miles, Lorena K.	Dec 20, 1965	Jeff Co	Tn	Jul 7, 1919	41	Miles, J. Haskell	Lucas, Clara		Walker, Lloyd Miles, Haskell	Memorial Gardens						
Miles, Thomas Alfred	May 31, 2000	Pierce Mt. , Indiana	Apr 9, 1950	50	Div	Morte, Robert		Jones, Eva L.		Mother	J.M.G.					
Miller, Alfredo	Jul 13,1994	Pembroke Pines, Fla.	Mar 6, 1907	87		Roach, Wesley		Lee, Allance [Sister]		West View					
Miller, Alice	Mar 24, 1959	Little Rock, Ark.	Tn	Mar 6, 1907	59	W	Roach, Thea		Roach, Susie		Roach, Theo	West View					
Miller, Bessie Allie	Dec 29, 1949	Hamblen Co	Tn		39	W	Reneau, W.O.		Mt. View							
Miller, Bessie Pauline	Jun 30, 1976	Greeneville, Tn	Apr 1, 1884	92	W	Goddard, Hugh		Kibby, --		Stone, Mrs. J.E.	West View					
Miller, Boyd James	Apr 20, 2948	Corna, Va	Jun 6, 1898	49	S	Miller, James B.	Va	Lachs, Margaret Elizabeth	Va	Miller, Everett	Sunderland					
Miller, C. Eugene	May 19, 1982	Knox Co	Tn	Jan 12, 1894	88	Frank, Elizabeth	Miller, William A.		Howell, Michael		Miller, Mrs. G.E. - Baker - Ballew	Jefferson Memorial					
Miller, Carrie Lou	Apr 6, 1956	Jeff Co	Tn	May 28, 1955		Miller, James		Miller, Bertha J.		Miller, Mrs. C.E. - Baker - Ballew	Mt. View					
Miller, Carroll H.	Feb 4, 1989	S.M.M.C.	Jeff City	Apr 23, 1919	69	Campbell, Jessie	Miller, Jessie Robert		Mertin, Grace Leota		Miller, Jessie C. - V.A.	J.M.G.	WW 2				

NAME	DDATE	BLOCAT	ELLOCAT	BDATE	AGE	SPOUSE	FATHER	FELOCAT	MOTHER	MFELOCAT	BY	BURIAL	VET	SON	DAUG	BROTHER	SISTER
Miller, Cecil V. [Twrely]	Sep 9, 1991	J.M.H.	Jeff City	Sep 12 1924	66	Div	Miller, Hobert		Martin, Grace		Johnson, Blanche Fried	J.M.G.					
Miller, Chandler Vernon Jr.	Nov 2, 1985	Jeff Co	Tn	Dec 13, 1913	51	S	Miller, C.V. Sr.		Goddard, Bessie		Miller, Mrs. C.V. Sr - Stone, Mrs - Richardson, Mrs - Franklin, C.R.	West View					
Miller, Charles Edward	Sep 9, 1983	Tn	Tn	Aug 14, 1983	25 d		Miller, Edna				Miller, Edna (married Bobby) Henry, Dorothy	Mt. View					
Miller, Charles Otis	Aug 8, 1990	Hilltown	Tn	Aug 10, 1898	92	Wlow, Veda	Miller, William		Howell, Mollie		Miller, Mrs. Veda	J.M.G.					
Miller, Charlie Gaylon	Aug 5, 1976	Jeff Co	Tn	Jan 12, 1890	86	Brown, Minnie	Miller, Will		Smith, Mary		Miller, Mrs. Minnie	Hillcrest					
Miller, Chloe	Feb 25, 1959	New Market	Tn	Mar 17, 1901	57	Ng	Hinchey, Hal H.		Lockard, Martha M.		Miller, W.H. & Frank	Piedmont					
Miller, Coris Melinda	Feb 2, 1984	Hamblen Co	Tn	Feb 2, 1984			Miller, James		Pellam, Patricia Diana		Miller, Edna (married Bobby)	Jefferson Memorial					
Miller, Coris C. [Granny]	Mar 17, 1982		New Market, Tn	Jun 8, 1901	90	W	Hubbard, Samuel		Magers, Minnie		Davis, Mary [Daug]	New Market					
Miller, Dave A.	Nov 24, 1957	Jeff City	Jeff Co	Nov 11, 1886	71	White, Maude	Miller, A.W.		Cox, Martha		Miller, Ethel Relph-Joe-Earl-Kate-Raelle-Bobbie	Mt. Horeb					
Miller, Dixie Jane	Aug 9, 1950	Jeff Co		Jun 12, 1883	67	Ng	Swann, William		Ellison, Melinda		Martin, Mrs. Hal - Frank	West View					
Miller, Donald Wayne	Jan 28, 1995	Knoxville, Tn	Jeff City	May 26, 1928	66	Mc. Nish, Kelly	Miller, Charles Otis			Wife	Miller, Veda	J.M.G.				Mix	Mc. Claire, Bonnie - Jean - Prince, Virginia
Miller, Elizabeth Frank	Nov 5, 1973	Jeff Co	Tn	Aug 21, 1893	80	Miller, Eugene [D]	Frank, William		Woods, Ida		Miller, Clifford [Son]	Memorial Grdens					
Miller, Ella	Feb 21, 1985	Jeff Co	Tn	Apr 1, 1894	90	Miller, Floyd [D]	White, Rea		Colter, Florence		Miller, Fred	Memmorial Gardens					
Miller, Everett Leonard	Jan 11, 1982	Jeff City	Va	Feb 6, 1909	43	Miller, Mary	Miller, James B.		Stones, Margaret Elizabeth	Va	Miller, Mrs. Mary	Sunderland					
Miller, Floyd L.	Mar 20, 1984	Jeff City	Tn	Feb 21, 1894	90	Ng	Miller, W.A.		Howell, Mollie		Miller, Fred-Leon-Ruth-Louise	Memorial Gardens					
Miller, Frances Elizabeth	Dec 28, 1995	Jeff City	Tn	Jan 26, 1911	85	Johnson, George		Purkey, Matilda		Meyers, Jill [D-Daug] Miller, John Frank & Son - Martin, Mrs. Hal	J.M.G.					
Miller, Frank L.	Jan 15, 1985	Jeff Co	Tn	Sep 2, 1912	52	Ng	Miller, George		Swann, Dicy		Miller, Mrs. Frank	Buffalo Grove					
Miller, George	Nov 29, 1956	Jeff Co	Tn	May 7, 1918	38	S	Miller, G.W.		Swann, Dicy		Miller, Frank	West View					
Miller, George [Bud]	Nov 30, 1950	Jeff Co	Tn	Sep 24, 1880	70	W	Miller, Ben		Reneska, Barbara		Miller, Mrs. Hal	West View					
Miller, Gertrude	Oct 24, 1983	Jeff City		Dec 5, 1905	67		Underwood, Bill		Hickman, Belle		Miller, Hazel [Daug]	J.M.G.		[G] Miller, Randy	[In-Law] Miller, Dorothy S. - [G] Fleming, Judy		
Miller, Grace	Jul 22, 1977	Knoxville, Tn	Tn	May 3, 1900	77	W			Martin, Lem		Miller, Cecil-Carroll - Seaman, Anna Rhea	Jefferson Memorial					
Miller, Hall Harris	Feb 16, 1977	Knoxville, Tn	Tn	Sept 3 1909	67	Carter, Odessa	Miller, George		Swann, Dicy		Miller, Mrs. Hal	Jefferson Memorial					
Miller, Hattie Alone	Nov 4, 1980	Jeff Co	Jeff Co	Sep 26, 1907	86		Hubbard, Sam		Gilbert, Ollie Mae		Combs, Ethel [Daug]	New Market		James-Jerry-Dee-Harold	Spires, Katherine - Spires, Margaret	Paul	
Miller, Helen	Oct 8, 1995	Knoxville, Tn	Jeff Co	May 16, 1893	102		Tarr, James A.		Lones, Mary		Miller, Jill [Daug] Middlebrook, Mary [Daug]	West View		James Edgar			
Miller, Howard W.	Sep 10, 1996	Jeff City	Chicago, Illinois	Jun 17, 1913	83	Axtell, Dorothy	Miller, William Albert		Moody, Illinois	Wife		J.M.G.		William & Barbara	Thompson, Jean & Gerald	Mummery, Helen Jane & Sam	
Miller, Infant Female	Sep 1, 1948	Jeff City	Tn	Sep 1, 1948			Miller, James William	Jeff Co	Messengill, Lorraine	Jeff Co	Miller, J.W.						
Miller, Infant Female	Jul 30, 1949	Jeff City	Tn	Jul 30, 1949			Miller, James William	Tn			Miller, J.W.	West View					
Miller, Interdemelle	Feb 5, 1946	Jeff Co	Tn				Miller, Will		Riley, Nannie	Tn	Miller, Will	Bech					
Miller, Ira Leon	Feb 10, 1977	J.M.H.	Tn	Oct 22, 1904	72	Johnson, Elizabeth	Miller, Floyd		White, Ellen		Miller, Mrs. Elizabeth	Jefferson Memorial					
Miller, Irene S.	Dec 19, 1981	Williamsport, Pa	Tn				Miller, Floyd				Miller, Jimmie L.	Jefferson Memorial					
Miller, J. Hobert	Jul 12, 1966	Jeff Co	Tn	Apr 11, 1887	71	Ng	Howell, Mollie		Martin, Matilda		Miller, Mrs. Grace & Carroll [Son]	Memorial Gardens					
Miller, Jack G.	Jul 15, 1952	Jeff Co	Jun 14, 1880		72	Ng	Miller, Alfred				Miller, Mrs. Vera Davis	New Market					
Miller, James Burns	Jul 8, 1941	Jeff Co	Va		[89-1-6]	W			Calmon, Katheryn	Va	Miller, H.C.-H.D. & Edd [Knox-Jeff-Knox] - Sons				Kinsley, Beverly & John - Fowler, Kay & Ronnie			

NAME	DDATE	DLOCAT	BLOCAT	BDATE	AGE	SPOUSE	FATHER	FRLOCAT	MOTHER	MTRLOCAT	BY	BURIAL	VET	SON	DAUG	BROTHER	SISTER
Miller, Jewel	Sep 13, 1988	Knoxville, Tn	Tn	Sep 22, 1922	65	Comton, Charles Wesley	Lester, Minnie O.				Miller, R.L.- Warren, Jo Ann	Shiloh					
Miller, Joe Ben	Feb 13, 1958	Jeff Co.	Tn	Sep 21, 1918	39	Div	Miller, Dave A.		White, Maude		Miller, Everett-Ralph-Curt - Davis, Mrs. Johnny-Shaver, Mrs. Joe - Ida	Mt. Horeb	WW 2				
Miller, Letitia	Feb 27, 1953	Jeff Co.	Tn	Aug 25, 1862	80	Ng	Davis, Lee		Davis, Elsie Jane		Howard, Mrs. J.L. - Miller, T.N.	West View					
Miller, Luxella	Jan 27, 1984	Morristown, Tn	Tn	Feb 9, 1919	64	W	Cameron, Lee		Cameron, Rosie		Mc Bee, Johnny - Saul, Margaret - Cameron, Robert - Langm, Dee-Paul-Marlo - Nice, Mrs. - Cotter, Jessie - Frank - Collins, Frances	Mt. Pleasant					
Miller, Lula S.	Apr 7, 1971		Tn	Mar 19, 1884	87	Miller, Roy	Shultz, William B.		Cockrum, Julia		Breedon, Bertha - Letson, Mary	Sunderland					
Miller, Madison Russell	Mar 3, 1989	Hillhaven	Knox Co	Apr 12, 1924	64	S	Miller, C. Vernon	Knoxville, Tn	Goddard, Bessie		Stone, Philomene [Mrs. John E.]	West View					
Miller, Margret [Lizzie]	Nov 13, 1935	Talbott	Va	Sep 21, 1867	68	Ng	Sivers, Henry	Va	Baker, Emma	Va	Miller, H.D.	Sunderland					
Miller, Martha Elizabeth	Nov 23, 1959	Tucson, Az	Jeff Co	Apr 4, 1916	79		Mc Cubbins, Charlie		Knoozt, Jessie		Hodges, William R. - Son	J.M.G.					Brown, Leona
Miller, Mary Lizzie	Sep 14, 1978	Newport, Tn	Tn	Dec 1, 1898	89	W	Lyle, John		Newman, Margaret Jane		Miller, Mrs Genova	Jefferson Memorial					
Miller, Mary Pearl	Oct 8, 1977	Talbott, Tn	Tn	Sep 9, 1896	81	Miller, George [D]	Cameron, W. E.		Knowling, Elizabeth		Cotter, Mrs. Roy [Lela]	Mt. Horeb					
Miller, Michael Shawn	Jul 1, 1977	Morristown, Tn		Jul 1, 1977			Miller, Paul	Tn	Lamb, Shelia	Tn	Miller, Michael Ray	Hamblen Memorial					
Miller, Mildred Geneva	Oct 20, 1941	Jeff Co.			44-3	S	Brown, Charles G.		Hubbard, Cora	Jeff Co	Miller, Paul	Hillcrest					
Miller, Minnie Brown	Aug 14, 1983	Knoxville, Tn	Tn	Jun 14, 1896	87	Ng	Brown, John N.		Jordan, Nancy		Miller, John J.	Little Lot - Hickman Co [Nashville ?]					
Miller, Myke Rhodes	Aug [10], 1991	J.M.H.	Huntington, W. Va	Feb 5, 1955	36	Ng	Harvill, Mary Jane		Sheets, Betty Ann		Miller, Mary J.	Piedmont					
Miller, Nancy Ruth	Feb 5, 1996	New Market, Tn	Tn	Mar 20, 1896	99	W	Miller, George C.		Miss Marna			Piedmont					
Miller, Nora	Oct 23, 1948	Jeff Co	Tn	Nov 25, 1872	75-10-26	Miller, G.A. [Age 76]	Carter, Alfred	Tn	Newman, Sarah	Tn	Miller, G.A.	Nance's Grove					
Miller, Paul Franklin Sr.	Aug 27, 1977	Jeff Co	Tn	Nov 28, 1903	73	Hubbard, Cora	Miller, William		Smith, Mary		Miller, Mrs. Paul F. Sr.	New Market					
Miller, Ralph Barton	Nov 1, 1972	Cocke Co	Tn	May 2, 1886	86	Ng	Miller, John		Hubbard, Cora		Miller, Mrs. Genova	Jefferson Memorial					
Miller, Ralph James	Feb 4, 1979	Jeff City	Tn	May 13, 1913	65	Ng	Miller, Dave A.		White, Maude		Miller, Mrs. Ralph A.	Mt. Horeb					
Miller, Ralph S.	Mar 25, 1967	Knx Co	Tn	May 4, 1900	66	Miller, Gertrude Underwood	Miller, William		Howell, Mollie		Miller, Gertrude-Hazell & Wallace	Memorial					
Miller, Ray Curtis	Jan 1, 1997	Knoxville, Tn	Tn	Mar 28, 1937	59	Lane, Ruth	Miller, Robert		Reneau, Allie		Wife	Mt. View		Robert-Ray-William	Smith, Sissy		
Miller, Rhea Faye	Dec 6, 1989	F.S.H.	Jeff City	Feb 10, 1925	64	Ng	Hepworth, Isaac R.		Thompson, Effie		Miller, Danny Paul	West View					
Miller, Robert Clifford	Oct 27, 1987	F.S.H.	Tn	Oct 12, 1917	70	Ng	Miller, Clifford E.		Frank, Elizabeth		Miller, Gladys	J.M.G.	WW 2				
Miller, Robert Henry Thomas	Feb 28, 1947	Jeff Co	Jeff Co	Sep 7, 1909	38-5-21	Ng	Miller, J.K.	Tn	Barbor, Irene	Va	Lance, Mrs. Ray	Mt. View					
Miller, Robert Lyle	Jun 12, 1969	Knox Co	Jeff Co	Aug 17, 1914	54	Ng	Miller, Robert		Lyle, Lizzie		Miller, Mrs. Genova	Memorial Gardens	WW 2				
Miller, Robert Marlon	Nov 1, 1986	Lakeside, Calif.	Tn	Nov 9, 1925	60		Winstead, Pauline				Harrill, Psaline - Willis, J. Jackson (Coronado, Calif.)	J.M.G.	navy				
Miller, Roy E.	Dec 1, 1952	Talbott, Tn	Tn		72		Miller, J.W.		Carson, Mary E.		Breedon, Mrs. C.M. & Mary	Sunderland					
Miller, Samuel Henry	Jan 1, 1977	Knoxville, Tn	Tn	99-5-27		Ng	Miller, Samuel Jackson				Miller, Mrs. Dalcie	Friends Station					
Miller, Samuel Tinsley	Jan 5, 1976	Jeff City	Tn	Sep 24, 1915	60	S	Miller, George		Swann, Dicey Jane		Miller, Mrs. Nora	West View					
Miller, Shirley Elaine	Aug 12, 1972	Jeff City	Tn	Aug 2, 1909	63	S	Miller, C.V. Sr.		Goddard, Bessie		Stone, Philomene - Miller, Bessie	West View					
Miller, Sicdie	May 25, 1954	Piedmont	W	Feb 10, 1855	79		Marvo, Alford	Tn	Hagard, Fannie		Marvo, John	Piedmont					
Miller, Stella	Jul 22, 1948	Knoxville	Tn			Miller, Sam H. [Age 62]	Miller, Unk		Unk	Tn	Miller, S.H.	Friends Station					

NAME	DDATE	DLOCAT	BLOCAT	BDATE	AGE	SPOUSE	FATHER	FELOCAT	MOTHER	MFLOCAT	BY	BURIAL	VET	SON	DAUG	BROTHER	SISTER
Miller, Willie T.	Jun 11, 1970	Atlanta, Ga	Tn	Aug 1, 1900	69	S	Miller, T.N.	Tn	Flemmer, Rosa	Tn	Liles, Alrence [R.E.]	West View					
Miller, William A.	Aug 2, 1951	Jeff Co	Tn	Feb 11, 1882	69	Ng	Miller, H.M.		White, Ella		Wife	J.M.G.					
Miller, William Fred	Sep 27, 1995	Jeff Co	Tn	Jun 2, 1913	83	Cook, Sierra	Miller, Floyd				Wife	J.M.G.					
Miller, William Hubert	Jul 27, 1953	Jeff Co	Tn	1900	53	Ng	Miller, William		Smith, --		New Market	New Market	43-45				
Milligan, Frank Leslie [Dr.]	Sep 11, 1995	Jeff City	Jeff Co	Mar 23, 1903	92	Osborne, Mildred	Milligan, Leslie N.		Bates, Sarah Jane		Milligan, Leslie W. [Son]	J.M.G.			Rankin, Sarah J.		
Milligan, Hubert Martin	Aug 15, 1981	Jeff Co	Tn	May 24, 1981	98-2-22	W					Milligan, Virginia S.	West View					
Milligan, Irene	Jul 13, 1982	Knoxville, Tn	Tn	Mar 29, 1927	65	Milligan, Wayne P.	Harrell, Will S.		Parkey, Beulah E.		Harrell, Harry [Brother]	Lynnhurst					
Milligan, John L.	Jan 5, 1937	New Market				Ng		Tn			Highlower, Ethel - Milligan, Virgie						
Milligan, L.N.	Mar 10, 1929		Tn		72-3-23	W			Hall, Evaline		Children	West View					
Milligan, Sara Jane	Jul 1, 1941	Sevier Co			80-6-26	W			Henderson, --	Sevier Co							
Milligan, Thomas Braden	Nov 10, 1974	Jeff City	Tn	Sep 15, 1909	65	De Vault, Dorothy	Milligan, James R.		Braden, Dixie		Milligan, Mrs. Thomas	Buffalo Ridge - Gray Station, Tn					
Mills, Agnes [Col]	Jun 28, 1959	White Pine	Jeff Co	Dec 13, 1914	44	Ng	Mills, Crockett		Watkins, Nina		Mills, Emest	West View Colored					
Mills, Alice [Col]	Sep 27, 1955	Jeff Co	Tn	Feb 12, 1884	71	Ng	Tate, John		Moore, Jane		Mills, Rev. Cecil & Alice	West View Colored					
Mills, Blanche Edna [Black]	Aug 22, 1985	J.M.H.	Ky	May 11, 1925	60	W	Narron, Raymond		Dirl, Nellie		Mills, Sherry	Jefferson Memorial					
Mills, Burns	Nov 28, 1957	Jeff City	Tn	Oct 26, 1904	62	W	Mills, Ava		Tate, Alice		Wells, Nora	West View					
Mills, Carl Haskell [Col]	Nov 24, 1961	Dayton, Ohio	Tn	Oct 10, 1915	43	Ng	Mills, Ava		Tate, Alice		Mills, Katherine	West View Colored					
Mills, Daniel King Jr. [Black]	May 6, 1990	Humana Hosp.	Jeff City	Oct 27, 1922		Coleman, Irene	Mills, Daniel K. Sr.		Hodge, Josie		Mills, Hanson Roger Jr. - Porter, Rhoda - Moore, Nannie - Goins, Gertrude	West View	WW 2				
Mills, Daniel King Sr.	Mar 8, 1975	Morristown, Tn	Tn	Jul 23, 1891	83	Div	Mills, Louis		Whitney, Susie		Mills, Horace	West View					
Mills, Floyd M.	Oct 5, 1982	Jeff Co	Tn	Sep 13, 1886	74	W	Mills, Mace		Mills, Nancy		Mills, Fred Eugene - Francis	West View					
Mills, George A. [Col]	Apr 28, 1940	Cocke Co	Tn	Aug 18, 1916	23	Ng	Mills, W.A.		Tate, Alice	Tn	Mills, Ava & John	West View					
Mills, Gertrude R. [Black]	Nov 4, 1985	Greenbush, New York	Tn	Mar 4, 1911	74	W	Mills, James F.		Chestnut, Linda		Mills, James P. Jr.	West View					
Mills, Hubert [Bugg - Col]	Jun 25, 1966	Jeff Co	Tn	Nov 20, 1900	65	Div	Mills, Louis F.		Whitney, Susan		Mills, Jennie - Deering, Ellie	West View Colored					
Mills, Infant Twins [Col]	Feb 9, 1954	Jeff City	Tn	Feb 9, 1954			Mills, Louis Franklin		Williams, Loretta		Mills, Louis	West View Colored					
Mills, James Paris [Col]	Sep 5, 1966	Jeff Co	Tn	Jul 4, 1924	62	W					Gertrude	West View					
Mills, Jennie [Col]	Sep 17, 1970	Jeff Co	Tn	Mar		S	Mills, Luis		Whitney, Susie		Ellis, John W. - Mills, Liscon - D.K. & Ellie	West View Colored					
Mills, John Lilburn [Col]	Jan 29, 1981	Jeff Co	Tn	Jun 14, 1903	57	Ng	Mills, Aksie		Tate, Alice		Ellis, John W. - Mills, Liscon - D.K. & Ellie Deing	Martha Davis Baptist [Service]					
Mills, Katherine Shaver	Jul 7, 1976	Knoxville, Tn	Carter Co, Tn	Jul 31, 1913	62	Mills, John L. [D]	Stoner, William		Gibbs, Kelizabeth		Cunningham, Mrs. Willis [Dote]	West View					
Mills, Lewis	Jul 28, 1932	Jeff City	No	Aug 13, 1859	72	Ng	Mills, Dennis	Nc	Hodge, Josie		Mills, Katherine	West View					
Mills, Lewis Franklin [Col]	Oct 18, 1906	Knox Co	Nc	Jan 15, 1827	39	Ng	Mills, D.K.		Whitney, Susie		Mills, Susie	West View					
Mills, Luscious Lewis	Jan 6, 1977	Mt. Home, Tn	Narron, Blanche	Dec 25, 1995	61	Narron, Blanche	Mills, Lewis		Whitney, Sadie		Mills, Marcella	West View	Army				
Mills, Peter Nathaniel [Black]	Sep 5, 1993	Knoxville, Tn	Jeff City	Aug 11, 1952	41		Mills, William Ernest		Lyle, Agnes C.		Mills, William A. [Brother]	West View	WW 2	Tarell-Chris [Dayton, Ohio]			
Mills, Sina [Col]	Dec 7, 1952	Jeff City	Tn	Mar 30, 1887	65	Ng	Sheppe, Wesley		Whitney, Nancy		Kids, Mrs. Ray	Dandridge					
Mills, Stella	Nov 14, 1957	Jeff City	Tn	Sep 6, 1892	65	Ng	Parrott, Isaac		Whitney, --		Talbert, Mrs. Reece	West View					
Mills, Susie [Col]	Dec 28, 1949	Sc		1880		W					Deering, Effie - Lucsar Bug	West View Colored					
Mills, Walter Deering [Black - Alex, Field]	Mar 17, 1984	Knoxville, Tn	Tn	Jun 14, 1929	54	Div	Mills, Daniel K. Sr.		Hodge, Josie		Mills, Mess Teresa E.	Jefferson Memorial	Korea				
Mills, William Anderson [Col]	Aug 21, 1996	Jeff City	Tn	Jan 12, 1873	83	W	Mills, Henry		Howell, Fannie		Mills, John	West View Colored					
Mills, William Ernest [Negro]	Oct 8, 1975	Jeff Co	Tn	Dec 10, 1912	62	W	Mills, William Anca		Tate, Alice		Bradford, Mary - Wall, Alma-Peter - Langston, Hollis-Freddie-Eddie	West View Colored					
Mills, William Henry	Feb 2, 1969	Tn	Tn	Nov 5, 1974	94	W	Mills, Joseph		Henderson, Mrs. Lillie			Hills Union					

NAME	DDATE	DLOCAT	BLOCAT	BDATE	AGE	SPOUSE	FATHER	FBLOCAT	MOTHER	MBLOCAT	BY	BURIAL	VET	SON	DAUG	BROTHER	SISTER
Mims, Elna	May 7, 1992	Newport, Tn	Newport, Tn	Feb 23, 1897	95	W	Talley, Robert L.	Tn	Huff, Mary		Bowen, Mrs. Gayle [Niece]	Union - Newport, Tn					
Mims, Emma A.	Oct 6, 1947	Jeff Co	Jeff Co	Dec 8, 1882	64	W	Timmons, George S.		Timmons, Emma	Tn	Timmons, Forest	Crestview					
Mims, George A.	Jul 20, 1964	At Home	Tn	Jul 1, 1912	72	S			Rhodin, Martha W		Bivens, Mrs. Max [Mary Ann]	West View [New Part]					
Minkler, Marshall Dean Jr.	Dec 29, 1994	Rutledge, Tn	Virgie, Ky	May 27, 1951	43	W	Minkler, M.D. Sr.		Adkins, Theda		Wife	Granger Memorial		M.D. 3rd	Tillbury-Holly-Rosanne-Oden, Farrah	Curtis-Dana	Haley, Ernestine-Durham, Gloria-Jean
Minshew, Alexander Pierce Jr.	May 17, 1990	Knoxville, Tn	S. Hampton Co, Va	Feb 20, 1920	70	Chastian, Janelle	Minshew, Alexander Sr.		Griffin, Emma		Minshew, Janelle-Thomasville, Ga	Laurel Hills - Thomasville, Ga					
Miser, Daisy	Mar 9, 1974	Jeff Co	Ga	Oct 25, 1926	47	Miser, J.T.	Spivey, Clarence		Carr, Laura		Miser, J.T. - Bivens, Sam-Charles	Jefferson Memorial					
Miser, Lewis George	Oct 29, 1953	Jeff Co	Tn	Jun 10, 1911	42	Ng	Miser, Robert		Palsy Belle		Miser, Mrs. Lewis	West View					
Miser, Robert J.	Mar 9, 1958	Jeff Co	Tn	Mar 15, 1888	69	W	Miser, Jim		Gibson, Venta		Hubbard, Mrs. Carl [Mary]	West View					
Miser, Robert Jr.	Jul 22, 1946	Jeff Co	Hancock Co	Dec 23, 1927	18	S	Miser, Bruce	Tn	Gibson, Hattie		Miser - Hancock Co	West View					
Mitchell, Cordelia	Jun 9, 1985	Blaine, Tn	Tn	Nov 17, 1897	87	W	Mc Nish, Edward		Mc Nish, Rhan	Tn	Staines, Mrs. Lou Ella	Pleasant Grove					
Mitchell, Douglas Juanita [F]	Dec 28, 1991	Jeff Co	Jeff Co	Sep 28, 1921	70	Mitchell, James P.	Hickman, Lonzo		Winston, Ethel		Pinkston, Kay [Daug]	J.M.G.					
Mitchell, James Robert	Jun 11, 1997	Jeff City	Mo	Feb 11, 1907	90	S	Mitchell, Joshua J.	Tn	Williams, Virginia V.		Pinkston, Kay & Dennis [Daug]		42-45	Lorain & Teressa	Mc Pherson, Viola & Dockey - [O] Finchum, Kayla		
Mitchell, Lydia	Nov 23, 1936	New Market	Tn	Unk	90	S	Green, Alf	Tn	Mitchell, Alice		Mitchell, J.H.	Nance's Grove					
Mitchell, Martha [Coll]	Sep 6, 1925		Sc		75	W	Thompson, Leon	Sc			Mitchell, Tom M.						
Mitchell, Martha Margaret Melissa [Coll]	Sep 25, 1996	Jeff Co		Apr 23, 1924	72	Mitchell, William [D]	Groetken, David		Dyer, Maggie		Mitchell, James & Franklin - Mitchell, W.E. [Columbus, Oh]	West View					
Mitchell, William Spencer	Feb 19, 1953	Granger Co	Granger Co	Jan 5, 1880	73	Ng	Mitchell, P.L.		Davis, Mary C.		Mitchell, Mrs. Melissa [Wife]	Mitchell - Granger Co					
Moncier, Louis Mauldien	Jun 15, 1980	Jeff Co		Dec 26, 1907	52	Bell, Mildred	Moncier, James Oliver		Webb, Mattie		Moncier, Mrs. Marlene-Dorothy-Larry	Memorial Gardens					
Monday, Charles Edwin	Sep 20, 1999	Chattanooga, Tn	Chattanooga, Tn	Mar 2, 1934	65	Cate, Bonnie	Monday, Robert Edward		Wilson, Ruby		Wife	Cate - Jeff Co		Michael	[Step] Unk	Arnold	
Monday, Naomi	Jul 7, 1980	Kronville, Tn	Tn	Apr 5, 1923	57	W	Russell, Henry Clay		Newman, Ada		Nash, Mrs. Raymond - Barnard, John H.	Hebron					
Monday, Aletha Hartland	Nov 8, 1982	J.M.H.	Tn	Aug 10, 1905	77	S	Pierce, Napoleon		Pierce, Bessie		Mondy, Ralph	Shiloh					
Moody, Alma Lorene	Apr 1, 1998	Dandridge, Tn	Rutledge, Tn	Jan 9, 1919	79		Noe, David Wilson		Harbin, Minnie B.		Moody, Douglas R. [Son]	Shiloh		Rick	Thurman		
Moody, Alma Louise	Apr 13, 1996	Jeff City	Granger Co	Aug 30, 1907	88		Moody, Napoleon		Pierce, Bessie		Moody, Ralph & Lorene [Brother]	Shiloh					
Moody, Amanda H.	Nov 28, 1936	Jeff City	Tn	May 12, 1859	77	W	Moody, Jesse		Gilmore, Presdila	Tn	Cunningham, Mrs. J.A.	West View					
Moody, Bessie Lee	Oct 31, 1958	Knox Co	Tn	Jan 3, 1880	78	W	Pierce, Robert		Hodge, Teresa		Shiloh - Granger Co	Shiloh - Granger Co					
Moody, Carl O.	Nov 18, 1996	Jeff City	Granger Co	Aug 5, 1908	88		Mc Daniel, Jossie		Mc Daniel, Jossie		Moody, Gerald [Son]	Shiloh	1945		[S] France, Carla-Moody, Krissi-Morgan, Kim-Lewis, Teressa-O'Hewer, Vickie-Seelvard, Sonja-Green, Kathy		
Moody, Elizabeth Kerr	Oct 19, 1979	Jeff City	Jun 19, 1922	Jun 19, 1922	57	Moody, Carl O.	Kerr, Thomas J.		Lawrence, Juanita		Moody, Carl - Ford, Mrs. Patsy	Piedmont					
Moody, Fain O.	Apr 25, 1965	Grainger Co	Tn	Oct 2, 1917	47	Ng	Moody, N.O.		Moody, Mrs. Fain		Moody, Mrs. Fain	Shiloh	WW 2				
Moody, Georgia Gertrude	Dec 5, 1963	Jeff Co	Tn	Nov 5, 1888	75	W	Gilmore, Noah		Kelsay, ---		Moody, Joe & Noah	Shiloh - Grainger Co					
Moody, Homer Tipton	Dec 14, 1970	Jeff Co	Tn	Sep 5, 1970	90	W	Moody, Samuel		Gray, Jemaitha		Moody, Carl	Shiloh					
Moody, Jack Overton	Aug 14, 1991	Atlanta, Ga	Jefferson City, Tn	Feb 19, 1935	46	Clark, Helen	Moody, Carl O.		Kellog, Reba		Moody, Mrs. Helen C.	Jefferson Memorial	Korea				
Moody, James Dedrick	Jan 27, 1982	Jeff Co	Tn	1882	79-11-15	Ng	Moody, James		Moody, Jessie		Moody, Joe	Shiloh					
Moody, Jessie H.	Dec 10, 1944	Jeff Co	Grainger City, Tn	May 14, 1863	81	Ng	Moody, Jessie	Tn	Gilmore, ---		Harrison, Mrs. J.W.	Dumplin					
Moody, Linda	Aug 5, 1992	J.M.H.	Jeff Co	Sep 28, 1954	37	Moody, James C.	Purkey, John Jake		Murray, Dorothy		Hubbard	J.M.G.					

NAME	DDATE	DLOCAT	BLOCAT	BDATE	AGE	SPOUSE	FATHER	FELOCAT	MOTHER	MFRLOCAT	BY	BURIAL	VET	SON	DAUG	BROTHER	SISTER
Moody, Mary Ann	Mar 8, 1932	Grainger Co		Apr 27, 1850	81	W	Gray, J.S.	Tn	Garnett, Priscilla	Tn	Moody, No.C.O & Brothers	Shilo					
Moody, Napoleon Overton	Nov 10, 1941	Grainger Co	Grainger Co		69-8-29	Ng			Gray, Mary Ann	Granger Co	Moody, Ralph-Alema-Alma-Fern [Children]	Shilo					
Moody, Ralph Pierce	Feb 16, 1998	Jeff City	Rutledge, Tn	Aug 2, 1911	86	Now, Alma	Moody, Napoleon Overton		Pierce, Bessie		Moody, Rick [Son]	Shiloh	Doug				
Moody, Rixe	Apr 16, 1947	Jeff Co	Grainger Co	Mar 31, 1947	35	Ng	Moody, Lewis	Tn	Marry, Mollie	Tn	Moody, Carl	Shiloh					
Moody, Roy	Sep 8, 1943	Jeff Co	Grainger Co	Jun 1, 1884	59	Ng	Kelley, Walker	Tn	Morgan, Lawrina	Tn	Moody, Mrs. Ray	Grainger Co					
Moody, Syphia	Jan 18, 1984	Morristown, Tn	Tn		86	Moody, Taylor [D]	Jolley, Addie		Jolley, Addie		Moody, Donald H.- Thompson, Estel V.	Lebanon					
Moody, Susan	Jan 28, 1966	Jeff City	Tn	Jul 3, 1895	70	Ng	Hull, Alfred		Moody, Carl - H.T.		Moody, Carl - H.T.	Shiloh					
Mooney, Nella Evelyn Witt	Jun 28, 1985	Lexington, Ky	Tn	Apr 4, 1915	70	Div	Nos, George		Meyers, Alice		Yishul, Sandra [Lexington, Ky]	Jefferson Memorial					
Moody, Albert Evans	Mar 20, 1951	Hamblen Co	Tn	Jan 13, 1897	60	Bessie K.	Moody, Ephraim L.		Eshley, Margaret		Moody, Mrs. John Bessie	West View					
Moore, Amanda [Col]	Oct 15, 1960	New Market	Tn	Apr 17, 1885		W	Moore, John		Talls, Lou		Methodist - New Market	West View					
Moore, Bessie K.	Jan 17, 1966	Fort Sanders Hosp.	Tn	Sep 16, 1910	75	W	Kinder, Bob		Glossip, Elizabeth		Moore, George E. [Son]	Methodist - New Market					
Moore, Cora Alberta	Feb 13, 1946	Madrid, Mo	Tn	Sep 8, 1882	63	S	Moore, John W.	Tn	Me Caul, Nora	Tn	Moore, Mrs. John H.[Overio, Illinois]- Knox, Pearl [Detroit, Mich.]	West View					
Moore, Daisy	Apr 7, 1984	J.M.H.	Tn	Apr 12, 1902	81	Moore, Eugene	Simms, John		Barbee, Sallie		Snodderly, Mrs. James	Hillcrest					
Moore, George P.	Aug 22, 1983	Knox Co	Tn	Apr 27, 1878	85	Byrd, Jane	Byrd, J.R.		Cato, Sarah		Trotter, Geneva - Perdue, Marjorie	West View					
Moore, Georgia Maddie	Jun 15, 1961	Cocke Co	Tn	Jul 9, 1903	57	S	Moore, Albert H.		Reneau, Louvenia		Patterson, Ralph - Pat- Sam-Grace	Hillcrest					
Moore, Henry Hal	Dec 13, 1954	Knox Co	Grainger Co	Jul 17, 1898	58	Ng	Moore, Charles		Long, Rosa		Mane's Grove	Piedmont					
Moore, Hollis	Nov 11, 1961	E.S. Hospital	Tn		66	Ng	Carmichael, --		Moore, S.B.		Moore, S.B.	Piedmont					
Moore, Hollis Burl	Dec 7, 2000	Mt. Clemons, M	Tn	Mar 1, 1908	92	W	Moore, Robert		Lewis, Willia		Moore, Harold [Son]	Sunderland					
Moore, Infant Female	Jul 19, 1969	Jeff Co	Jeff Co	Jul 19, 1969			Moore, Bobby		Homer, Norley Louise		Moore, Bobby	Pleasant View					
Moore, James Nicholas	Mar 28, 1970	Hamblen Co	Tn	May 23, 1970							Moore, James H. Sr.	Forest View - Jeff Co					
Moore, James Preston	Sep 28, 1982	E.T.B.H.	Tn	May 16, 1898	84	Lyle, Ruth	Moore, James Preston		Bonds, Mrs Charlotte		Bonds, Mrs Charlotte	Dandridge Memorial					
Moore, James Preston	Mar 3, 1959	Jeff Co	Tn	Feb 1, 1871	88	W	Moore, Anderson		Fox, Mahnita		Moore, Dexter	Hills Union					
Moore, Jane	Jun 20, 1960	E.T. Baptist Hospital	Tn	Aug 19, 1880	79	Moore, George P.	Moore, Lee A.		Moore, Lou - Pardon, Major		Moore, Lou - Pardon, Major	West View					
Moore, Jennie Gray	Oct 11, 1987	J.M.H.	Tn	Oct 18, 1917	69	W	Byrd, J.M.		Lowery, Pearl		Dennis, Lillian	New Market					
Moore, Jessie	Feb 1, 1959	Washington Co	Tn	Sep 26, 1893	64	W	Mc Swain, Jess		Messengill, Lou		Large, Mrs. Lester	Mt. Horeb					
Moore, John H. [Col]	Aug 11, 1953	Jeff Co	Tn				Baker, William		Moore, Mrs. Amanda		Moore, Mrs. Amanda	Mt. Horeb					
Moore, John Wallace	Dec 2, 1999	Jeff City	Ks	Jul 5, 1915	84	Taylor, Emily T.	Moore, Walker F.		Bettis, Vera B.		Willis	West View Colored	James [Vej- Edward]	Mary Jane			
Moore, Johny	Apr 5, 1984	J.M.H.	Tn	Oct 29, 1912	71	Mc Swain, Jennie	Moore, Runy		Reed, Lillie		Moore, Mrs. Jennie P.	West View					
Moore, Lee Artis	Dec 13, 1975	Jeff Co	Tn	Mar 23, 1913	62	Rickerd, Ellen	Moore, Robert A.		Lewis, Willie		Moore, Mrs. Lee A.	Sunderland	WW 2				
Moore, Leon	Dec 7, 1982	J.M.H.	Tn	Mar 10, 1936	46	Johnson, Betty	Moore, Lee A.		Richard, Ellen		Moore, Betty J.	Sarfin Springs - Jeff Co					
Moore, Mable Ruth	Oct 9, 1982	Knoxville, Tn	Tn	Mar 30, 1905	77	Moore, James P. [D]	Lyle, William C.		Clabough, Julia		Bonds, Charlotte M.- Moore, Harold	Dandridge Memorial					
Moore, Martha	Nov 24, 1982	Kingsport, Tn	Tn	Mar 28, 1898	84	Moore, Wesley	Linco, Jacob L.		Edmonds, Margaret		Walker, Mrs. Mildred	Mt Horeb					
Moore, Martha Elizabeth	Apr 18, 1958	Mascot, Tn	Tn	Jul 19, 1877	80	Moore, W.A.	Miller, Mode		Hughes, Sadie		Brooks, Mrs. Coy - Miller, Stella - Johnson, Mollie - Roy-John-Clifford	Piedmont					
Moore, Mary [Col]	Feb 19, 1940	Jeff City	Tn	Jan 25, 1870	70	Moore, W.A.	Unk		Unk		Willis	Colored					
Moore, Mary F.	Aug 7, 1990	F.S.H.	Tn	Dec 5, 1942	47	Div	Moore, Albert E.		Kinder, Bessie		Moore, George [Brother]	West View					
Moore, Mattie A.	Jan 13, 1989	Brownsville, Tn	Brownsville, Tn	Jun 24, 1891	87	S	Moore, Henry Hal		Hood, Martha Rebecca		Wilson, Martha B.	Woodlawn - Nashville, Tn					

NAME	DDATE	DLOCAT	BLOCAT	BDATE	AGE	SPOUSE	FATHER	FELOCAT	MOTHER	MFELOCAT	BY	BURIAL	VET	SON	DAUG	BROTHER	SISTER
Moore, Myrta Ruth	Mar 9, 2000	Jeff City	Tn Sturgis, Miss.	Jul 11, 1911	88	Moore, Hollis	Mc Ghee, Joe		Jones, Lizzie		Husband	Harold [Mich]		Harold [Mich]		Buford	
Moore, Nobie Hannah	Aug 26, 1982	Jeff City	Tn	Nov 18, 1896	95	W	Henrah, Ralph E.		Livingston, Francis H.		Husband	Forrest Hills - Memphis, Tn					
Moore, Oscar Leslie [Col]	Jun 14/15, 1990	Jeff City	Tn	Apr 20, 1900	60	W	Moore, Will		Brown, Mattie - Hardy, Pauline			Sunderland West View Colored					
Moore, Pearl Vesser	Sep 4, 1941	Jeff City	Tn		29-3-14	Moore, John A.	Vesser, Walker	Va	Jones, Hattie	Va	Vesser, Walter - Vesser, Jimmie - Moore, John A. - Norita, Virgi	Hills Union					
Moore, Sallie	Sep 5, 1954	Jeff Co.	Tn	Feb 24, 1871	83	Ng			Denton, Delia		Moore, Chester	Piedmont					
Moore, Samuel B.	Jan 10, 1971	Knox Co	Tn	Jan 30, 1888	83	W	Moore, Sam		Fennessa, Mattie		Carmichael, H.M.	Piedmont					
Moore, Samuel Russell	Nov 13, 1944	Jeff Co	Tn		77-5-28	Ng	Moore, James	Va	Dickey, Mary	Tn	Moore, George S.	Ebenezer					
Moore, Vellie May	Jun 4, 1985	J.M.H.	Tn	Apr 18, 1911	74	W	Pollard, Joe E.		Elder, Cordelia		Moore, J.B. Cochran F.H.	Sunderland					
Moore, William Frank	Apr 7, 1985								[Alwessee, Georgia] Morgan, J.E. [Talbott]			Lakewood					
Moore, Vestal Clark	May 8, 1936	Jeff Co	Tn	Dec 5, 1935	56	W	Morgan, J.E.	Tn	Bishop, Elizabeth	Tn	Morgan, J.E. [Talbott]	Lebanon					
Moree, John Cox	Mar 31, 1945	Dandridge	Jeff Co	Aug 17, 1866	78	W	Moree, Alfred	Tn	Haggard, Fannie	Tn	Moree, Harley - Patterson, Mrs.	Mt. Zion					
Moree, Lloyd	Aug 21, 1982	Knox Co	Tn	Feb 15, 1908	54	S	Moree, Marshall		French, Joann		Ferris, Mrs. O.W.	Piedmont					
Moree, Martha B.	Feb 6, 1941	Dandridge	Tn		71-2-1	Moree, J.C.		Tn		Tn	Moree, J. Harvey [Son] - Patterson, George	Mt. Zion					
Moreland, Fred E.	Jul 25, 1939	Jeff City	Tn	Oct 18, 1915	23	S	Moreland, Edd E.		Carmichael, Minnie	Tn	Minchew, Janice M. [Dau]	West View					
Moreland, Helen	Dec 10, 2000	Jeff City	Tn	May 17, 1921	79	W	Lindsey, Floyd		Wilkerson, Mattie		Moreland, Sally & Gladys-Harold-Robert-Lee - Pruden, Mrs. Frank [Children]	West View					
Moreland, Minnie	Aug 22, 1964	Jeff Co	Tn	Jun 14, 1884	80	W	Moreland, Edd [B]		Carmichael, William		Houser, Sallie	West View					
Moreland, Robert Porter	Jul 13, 1983	Jefferson Memorial Hosp.	Tn	Jun 11, 1917	66	Lindsey, Helen	Moreland, Ed		Moreland, Mrs. Helen			West View	WW 2				
Moreland, Sally Lou	Mar 5, 1994	Jeff City	Tn	May 15, 1907	86	Cogburn, Allen Sr.	Carmichael, Minnie		Rhodon, Frank [Brother In-Law]		West View					
Morelock, Wanda Anna Lee	Mar 4, 1983	Knoxville, Tn	Tn	Nov 21, 1939	43	Morelock, William W.	Jones, Agnes Ruth		Morelock, William W. In-Law		Nance's Grove					
Morgan, Albert	Jun 16, 1952	Jeff Co	Tn	Oct 8, 1885	66	W	Morgan, William		Morgan, Winnie		Watson, Mrs. Frank Beam, Frederick [Friend] - Brown - Dawson F.H.	Nance's Grove					
Morgan, Alexander	May 9, 1992	Des Moines, Iowa	Tn	Jun 1, 1969	22	S	Little, Charles		Nelson, Arlene	Hamilton, Ohio	Cremated						
Morgan, Billy	Feb 17, 1944	Sevier Co	Sevier Co	Feb 16, 1944	69		Morgan, Lee		Reilly, Frances		Morgan, Billy - Meyers, Mary B.	Fain - Jeff Co					
Morgan, Charles A.	Apr 8, 1987	Rutledge, Tn	Tn	Apr 8, 1918	69	Gass, Betty T.	Morgan, James A.	Tn	Mc Daniel, Louisa	Tn	Morgan, Betty J. Morgan, Lee	Shiloh - Jeff Co	WW 2				
Morgan, Eli	Aug 6, 1952	Jeff Co	Tn	Aug 3, 1895	57	Ng	Morgan, Allen		Satterfield, Thursa		Morgan, Mrs. Eli	New Market					
Morgan, Ellis Inez	May 13, 1997	Knoxville, Tn	Tn	Mar 2, 1941	56	Mc Anally, M			Staley, Nola		Husband	Blackwell Branch		[Step]Morgan, Jerry	Bradley, Barbara - Noe, Kathy - [Step] Morgan, Sherry	Milton-Kenneth	[In-Law] - Moreland, Helen-Christine - Forguity, Bess
Morgan, Fred N.	Feb 27, 1997	Knoxville, Tn	Tn	Aug 6, 1934	62	Palmer, Charlotte	Morgan, Fred		Smith, Mary		Morgan, Jeffery E. [Son]	Strawberry Plains		[Step]Morgan, Jerry	Bradley, Barbara - Noe, Kathy - [Step] Morgan, Sherry		
Morgan, Infant Female	Jul 26, 1954	Jeff Co	Jeff Co	Jul 26, 1954			Morgan, Buddy		Collins, Leona		Morgan, Buddy [Son]	West View					
Morgan, James Howard	Sep 6, 1995	Rutledge, Tn	Jeff Co	Aug 6, 1923	72		Morgan, Joe Henry		Satterfield, Thursa		Morgan, Charles M. & Michelle [Son]	New Blackwell Church				Walker, Mossie	
Morgan, Jimmy James	Nov 7, 1999	Jeff Co	Jeff Co	Mar 12, 1916	83		Morgan, Rich		Watson, Minnie		Bradley, Helen [Sister] Nance's Grove - New Market, Tn						
Morgan, Joe Henry	Sep 15, 1958	Granger Co	Tn	Mar 20, 1886	72	Ng	Morgan, John		Mc Cann, Susie		Morgan, Thurson S.- Joe-J.H.-Henry [Children]	Blackwell Branch - Granger Co					

NAME	DDATE	BLOCAT	BLOCAT	DDATE	AGE	SPOUSE	FATHER	FRLOCAT	MOTHER	MFLOCAT	BY	BURIAL	VET	SON	DAUG	BROTHER	SISTER
Morgan, Lora	Aug 26, 1968	Dayton, Ohio			70	W	Smith, Sherman		Maddox, Florence			West View					
Morgan, Louis Edward	Apr 22, 1990	J.M.H.	Granger Co. Tn	Mar 22, 1933	57	Walker, Doris	Morgan, Herbert	Tn	Dunlap, Ollie	Tn	Morgan, Ellis	Buffalo Grove	U.S.A.F				
Morgan, Margaret	Dec 3, 1995	New Market		Jun 22, 1931	4		Morgan, Ellis		Gray, Lucy		Morgan, Ellis	Shilo					
Morgan, Mary Lennie	Jan 16, 1982	Knoxville, Tn		Aug 20, 1913	68	Div	Smith, Anter		Owens, Lourenia		Campbell, Mrs. Mabel - Morgan, Fred -Bill	Strawberry Falls					
Morgan, Naree Elizabeth	Sep 26, 1990	J.M.H.	No		91	W			Almy, Mrs. Gertrude		Almy, Mrs. Gertrude	Sumber- Grainger Co					
Morgan, Palla Pedk	Jan 11, 1955	Knoxville, Tn			73	S						West View					
Morgan, Thalbert John	Aug 5, 1997	Inconite, Tn	Tn	Jan 19, 1914	83	Holloway, Bonnie	Morgan, Eli		Mayo, Gertrude		Wife	J.M.G.		James E. & Jo Anne	Allen, Pauline & Carl	Lewis-Buford [Ind.]- Tony	Barkhart, Pearl- O' Dell, Florence
Morgan, Thurma Anna	Apr 11, 1974	Grainger Co	Tn	Jul 25, 1885	88	Morgan, Joe [Jr]	Sutterfield, Alex		Cameron, Susie		Morgan, H.E. -Jamie-Henry -J.R. - Walker, Morgan	Blackwell Branch- Grainger Co					
Morgan, Anna Ruth	Mar 26, 1993	Tn		Jan 25, 1885	86	W	Jeffers, John		Morris, Jackie L. [Son]		J.M.G.	J.M.G.					
Morris, Artie Solomon	Mar 24, 1993	Rutledge, Tn	Jeff Co	Feb 13, 1913	80	W	Jeffers, John		Morris, Jackie L. [Son]		J.M.G.	Shady Grove		[G] Leroy George		Theodore	
Morris, Clara	Nov 21, 1972	Fredericksburg, VA	Frederickburg g. Va	Sep 19, 1893	79	W	Lucas, Spencer		White, Margaret		Morris, Bud	Shady Grove					
Morris, Clarence Leon	Feb 20, 1973	Jeff Co	Tn	Jul 30, 1890	83	Div	Morris, R.C.		Lucas, Clara		Morris, Clarence & Sellers	West View					
Morris, Cordia	Feb 14, 1988	J.M.H.	Tn	Oct 12, 1915	72	Jeffers, Anna Ruth	Morris, John	Tn	Parks, Martha	Tn	Morris, Anna J.	J.M.G.					
Morris, George Melvin	Feb 4, 1946	Jeff Co	Tn	Jul 26, 1874	71	Ng	Morris, John		Scarlett, Mary		Parks, Mrs. C.M. - Morris, Frank & Earl - Parks, Mrs.	Flat Gap					
Morris, Lockie Lee	Dec 21, 1953	Jeff Co	Tn	Aug 25, 1869	84	W	Morris, Isaac		Scarlett, Mary		Morris, Mrs. Earl - Parks, Mrs.	Flat Gap					
Morris, Robert C.	Aug 26, 1993	Jeff Co	Tn		65	Morris, Earl	Morris, William		Carden, Cornelia		Morris, Earl	Flat Gap					
Morris, John Richard	Oct 18, 1950	Powell Station	Tn	Dec 18, 1891	58	Div	Morris, I.A.		Carden, Dorthais		Morris, Clarence - Pumles, W.R. - Essie	Shady Grove					
Morris, Charles Mc Kay	Sep 5, 1944	J.M.H.	New Hampshire	Nov 18, 1937	46	Div	Morris, Joseph		Patten, Arkenen		Vincent, Michael G. [N.H.]	South Road - Belmont, N.H.	WW 2				
Morrisett, Della Mae	Dec 23, 1997	Jeff City	Abilene, TX	Jan 3, 1929	68	Drinsley, Janet	Morris, A.B.		Mc Kay, Rebecca		Wife	Crenalled					
Morrisett, Katie Kathlene	Feb 15, 1988	Hill Haven N. Home	Virginia	Aug 10, 1895	92	W	Lester, Johnson, A.		Boyd, Virginia		Lester, Guy	West View					
Morrisett, Lillie Mae	Oct 7, 1944	Jeff Co	Tn		75-6-8	S	Morrisett, Enoch	Tn	Helton, Lucinda	Tn	Jost, Lillie - Morrisett, Dave	Lebanon - Mt. Horeb					
Morrisett, Tom Jack	Jul 24, 1991	Hawkins Co., Tn	Tn	Jan 20, 1905	86	Underwood, Lillie Mae	Morrisett, John		Combs, Gilley		Morrisett, W.R. [Son]	J.M.G.					
Morrison, Infard	May 7, 1967	New Market, Tn	Tn	Sep 14, 1903	63	Underwood, Lillie Mae	Morrison, Jack Leonard		Kim, Rebecca		Daniels, Mrs. J.B.	Jefferson Memorial					
Morrison, Patricia Ann	Nov 14, 1957	Jeff Co	Tn	Nov 14, 1957		W			Miles, Sarah Darlene		Miles, Bruce	Oakland					
Morrisette, Michael Wayne	Apr 6, 1951	Jeff Co	Tn	Apr 6, 1951		W			Morrison, Louise		Manning, Mrs. Ernell	West View					
Mort, Mary	Feb 26, 1995	Knoxville, Tn	Concordia, Ks	Oct 19, 1946	49	Aguilera, Mercedes	Morrisette, Mayo		Heisit, Avis		Wife	Cremated					
Moser, Charles Henry	Oct 18, 1955	Jeff Co	Tn	Jan 20, 1-		W	Fryn, John		Zirkle, Susan		Mort, Bess - Frances & Reba	Shady Grove					
Moser, Helen	Oct 19, 1966	Jeff Co	Tn	Jan 6, 1908	58	Ng	Moser, Hugh J. Sr.		Newmann, Beryl		Moser, Mrs. Mary H. - Cullen, Mrs.	West View					
Moser, Hugh Jarnigan Sr.	Feb 23, 1944	Jeff Co	Tn	Sept 1, 1873	90	Moser, John R.	Sizer, William S.		Wods, Burnett		Kidna, Mrs. - James - Powers, Mrs. - Dick - Moser, Hugh Jr-	West View					
Moser, John R. Sr.	Aug 26, 1956	Jeff Co	Tn	April 13, 1869	87	W	Moser, William A.		Haworth, Adilna		Moser, Hugh Jr- Charles- Virginia Powers J- Moser, M.M. & J.R. Jr.	West View					
Moser, Marvin Mc Fanin	May 13, 1941	Jeff City	Tn	Feb 20, 1891	74	Sizer, Helen	Moser, John R.		Sizer, Josephine		Moser, Mrs. Roberts H.						
Moser, Roberts Henry	Dec 20, 1975	J.M.H.	Tn	Dec 10, 1895	79	W	Henry, Robert Lee		Myers, Luetina Pearl		Jodey, Nelson L.	West View					
Mosier, Mrs. Hugh	Nov 24, 1965	Jeff City	No		48	W						West View					
Mosier, Mrs. Hugh	Oct 8, 1932	Jeff City	Tn	Jul 24, 1884	48	W	Mosier, Hugh	Tn	Newmann, J.E.	Tn	Hollemeister, Francis	Mosier, Hugh					

NAME	DDATE	DLOCAT	BLOCAT	BDATE	AGE	SPOUSE	FATHER	FBLOCAT	MOTHER	MFBLOCAT	BY	BURIAL	VET	SON	DAUG	BROTHER	SISTER
Motta, Charles Alton	Dec 29, 1998	Maryville, Tn	Birmingham, Ala.	Jun 21, 1938	60	Lucy H.	Motta, Talmadge		Baxter, Alma		Wills	J.M.G.		Steven	Huffman, Patricia		Sloan, Irene - Wenner, Eulala - Bennette, Vizella
Moulden, Catherine Cubberson	May 16, 2000	Johnson City, Tn		Oct 24, 1915	84	W					Walker, Cathy [Doug]	J.M.G.					
Moulden, Johnny Pearl [F]	Mar 26, 1966	Jeff Co	Strawberry Plains	Mar 28, 1901	65	Moulden, Madison	Mc Bee, Aaron		Williamson, Sally		Moulden, Imogene [Sister] Leroy [Columbus, Ohio]	Gillette - Jeff Co					
Moulden, Madison	Feb 19, 1970	Tn		Jan 19, 1897	73	W	Moulden, Simon		Mc Bee, Johnny Pearl		Moulden, O. Leroy	National - Knox Co	unk				
Moulden, William Earnest	Mar 26, 1987	F.S.H.	Tn	Jan 28, 1915	72	Cubberson, Catherine	Moulden, George E.		Thomas, Hattie		Moulden, Catherine	J.M.G.	WW 2				
Mountain, Bobby D.	Apr 7, 2000	Knoxville, Tn	Tn	Nov 14, 1913	86	Div	Mountain, Joseph P.		Wylie, Mary Ann		Oxford, Cleo [Sister]	Cremated					
Mowbray, Munsey	Oct 1, 1989	Jeff Co	Jeff Co	Oct 29, 1902	86	Mowbray, R.G. [D]	Titsworth, B.M.		Mc Spadden, Eva		Wiley, Frances [Mrs. E.E.]	West View					
Mowry, William Winton	Dec 21, 1945	Jeff Co	Tn	Nov 3, 1905	40	Div	Mowry, W. S.	Tn	French, Virginia	Tn	Shores, Pauline	Piedmont					
Mowry, Carrel G.	Sep 5, 1981	V.A. Hosp-E. Chicago	Tn	Mar 15, 1917	64	Ng	Mowry, William Sidney		French, Virgie N.		Mowry, Mrs. Willis D.	Jefferson Memorial	WW 2				
Mowry, Virgie Nellie	Aug 16, 1994	J.M.H.	Tn	Dec 28, 1897	96	W	Mott, Mary Ann		Mott, Mary Ann		Mowry, Robert	Piedmont					
Mowry, William Sidney	Mar 16, 1968	New Market, Tn	Tn	Aug 8, 1882	85	French, Virginia	Simpkins, Sarah		Simpkins, Sarah		Mowry, Robert-Burl-Hossed-Cline, Phillip-Shores, Pauline	Piedmont					
Moyers, Everett D.	Jan 17, 1990	J.M.H.	Grainger Co	May 7, 1911	78	Talley, Ruth	Moyers, Sam P.		Owens, Ona		Moyers, Ruth T.	West View					
Moyers, Flora	Mar 11, 1972	Knox Co	Tn	Feb 26, 1889	83	W	Mody, Woodson Taylor		Gray, Mary Ann		Shiloh	Shiloh					
Moyers, Erlk Paul	Jun 26, 1975	Knoxville, Tn	Tn	Dec 10, 1914	60	Allen, Mildred	Moyers, Sam		Owens, Ona		Moyers, Mrs. Frank	Jefferson Memorial	WW 2				
Moyers, Harold Wiane	Jul 17, 1932	Jeff City	Tn	Feb 27, 1932	4m		Moyers, Carl	Tn	Lance, Verna	Tn	Moyers, Carl	Mt. View					
Moyers, Lillian	Jun 12, 1965	Miami, Fla	Tn		82	W					Moyers, Dewey [Ohio] Agranoe, Benjamin [Fla]	White Pine					
Moyers, Mildred Roeana	Oct 9, 1996	Jeff City	Tn	Jun 28, 1915	81		Allen, John Clifford		Godson, Bessie		Moyers, Sam [Son]	Bill-Jim			Flynn, Jannie - Leftwich, Sandra	Edgar	
Moyers, Mrs. Carl	Jun 24, 1932	Knoxville, Tn	Tn	Feb 24, ---	23	Moyers, Carl	Lance, Jake		Edmonds, Margaret	Tn	Moyers, Carl - Lance, J.L.	Mt. View					
Moyers, Ona	Oct 27, 1945	Jeff Co	Grainger Co	Mar 23, 1893	50	Ng	Owens, George	Tn	Brunston, Annie	Tn	Moyers, Sam P.	Shiloh					
Moyers, Ruth T.	Mar 10, 1997	Jeff City	Hamblen Co	Jan 19, 1911	86	W	Talley, John C.		Benefield, Rena		Lowery, Charles [Nephew]	West View					
Moyers, Sam P.	Apr 8, 1950	Jeff Co	Tn	Aug 17, 1873	76	W					Moyers, Everett	Shiloh					
Moyers, William T.	Jun 28, 1958	Straw Plains	Tn	Apr 25, 1890	78	Ng	Moyers, George		Gray, Louisa		Moyers, Herbert	Shiloh					
Mulvany, Archie Lee	Jan 8, 1981	Jeff City	Jeff City	Jun 28, 1888	92	W	Mulvany, Clayton		Walker, Rosa		Allen, Mrs. Eva E.	Shiloh - Grainger Co					
Munn, Robert Bruce	Jul 17, 1976	Jackson, Tn	Apr 29, 1948		28	Evans, Hope	Munn, John Ker		Vogel, Johanna		Munn, R. B.	Jefferson Memorial					
Munsey, Edna Louise	Apr 12, 1996	Union Co, Tn	Apr 16, 1933		62		Belt, Morgan Telt		Masney, Minnie Ellen		Tucker, Roberta [Doug]	Hancock - Washburn, Tn		Munsey, Carl Bailey, Ellis Joe - Hyssett, Mrs. Ahmad	Tucker, Roberta - Smith, Wanda - Campbell, Dorothy - Mc Connell, Ruby
Murph, Isan Lewis	Nov 12, 1982	Jeff City	Grainger Co, Tn	May 21, 1892	70	Rigg, Susan	Murph, Thomas		Gobble, Lewis		Murph, Susan	Memorial Garden					
Murph, Louise	Nov 2, 1996	Grainger Co	Tn	Jan 26, 1887	68	Murph, W.T.	Gobble, Lewis	Tn	Emert, Virginia	Tn		Shiloh					
Murph, Pauline	Nov 8, 1966	Tn	Tn	Aug 29, 1907	61	Murph, W.C. [D]	Northern, Dudley		Talley, Nanette		Mc Clara, Mrs. Howard	Shiloh					
Murph, Thomas D.	Jul 17, 1954	Pell City, Alabama	Grainger Co		22	S	Murph, William T.		Northern, Pauline		Murph, Pauline	Shiloh	Army				
Murph, W.T	Mar 23, 1941	Grainger Co	79-11- 8			W			Lacey, Rebecca		Williams, Mrs. Sarah ? [Daug] - Williams, Lt.H.	Shiloh					
Murph, William Coy	Jun 16, 1943	Jeff Co	Grainger Co	Jun 5, 1898	45	Ng	Murph, Tom		Gobble, Eliza A.		Murph, Mrs.	Shiloh					
Murphey, John D.	Apr 20, 1928	Va			65-10- 0	Ng	Murphey, Preston	Va	Ballard, Nancy	Link	Murphy, John	West View					
Murphy, Agnes	May 1, 1987	J.M.H.	Tn	Sep 18, 1899	87	S	Murphy, John D.		Franns, Mary		Murphy, Georgia [Mrs. John F.]	West View					

NAME	DDATE	DLOCAT	BLOCAT	BDATE	AGE	SPOUSE	FATHER	FRLOCAT	MOTHER	MRSLOCAT	BY	BURIAL	VET	SON	DAUG	BROTHER	SISTER
Murphy, Elsie Edgar	Jun 9, 1999	Jeff City		Jun 19, 1907	92	Ng	Edgar, William		Edgar, Ellen		Murphy, Georgia (Daug-In-Law)	West View					
Murphy, John Waugh	Jul 4, 1955	Jeff Co	Tn	Jun 10, 1901	54	Ng	Murphy, J.D.		Franes, Mary E.		Murphy, Agnes	West View					
Murphy, Luther	Jul 22, 1982	J.M.H.	Tn	Nov 28, 1900	81	S	Murphy, J.D.		Franes, Mary E.		Murphy, Agnes	West View					
Murphy, Mary Elizabeth	Nov 14, 1945	Jeff Co	Sevier Co	Nov 26, 1982	82	W	Franes, John H.	Tn	Keeler, Matilda		Murphy, Agnes	West View					
Murphy, Raymond Mc Giffin	Apr 27, 1948	Knox Co		Sep 27, 1903	45	W	Murphy, J. Dudley		Franes, Mary E.	Tn	Murphy, Bob & Agnes	West View					
Murphy, Theodore M. [Bob]	Jul 2, 1972	Jeff Co	Tn	Jun 25, 1905	67	S	Murphy, J.D.		Franes, Mary		Murphy, Agnes Lelia	New Market					
Marr, John Wesley	May 28, 1956	New Market, Tn	Tn	May 17, 1882	74	Ng	Murphy, J.D.		Welch, Mary		Marr, Mr. Bonnie D.-Russell, Mary	New Market					
Marry, David [Col]	Mar 14, 1948	Jeff Co	Tn		alt 75	S	Marry, Edwin		Black, Charlotte	Tn	Nance, Beulah	Colored					
Marrin, Augustus Lafayette	Jun 8, 1975	Greene Co, Tn		Oct 28, 1882	92	W	Marrin, William M.		Holt, Margaret		Bivens, William J. Father - Malinda, Larry & Mary Swejan	New Market					
Musick, Katherine Suzanne	Sep 27, 1999	Blount Co	Tupelo, Ms	Aug 18, 1999	1m		Musick, Matthew L.		Musick, Susan Gail		Robeson, Gale & Laura (G-Parents) / Mother - Diana, Charlie (Step-Father) - Elmore, Nellie (G-Mother)	J.M.G.		[Nephew] Musiek, Travis			
Musser, Bobby Allen	Jun 12, 1999	Morristown, Tn	Morristown, Tn	Oct 18, 1975	23	Hatfield, Irma	Musser, Edwin Fehn Sr.		Dickenson, Gladys		Purcell, Iva	J.M.G.		[Step] Annis, Tommy Lee	[Step] Sears, Connie	Edwin & Deana	
Musser, Lewis	Apr 4, 1998	Knoxville, Tn	Believue, Ohio	Feb 27, 1923	75	Ng	Musser, Lloyd		Purcell, Iva		Wife	J.M.G.					
Myers, B.C.	Feb 22, 1935		Tn														
Myers, Carl	Feb 13, 1939	Straw Plains	Tn		In	Ng	Unk	Unk	Unk		Myers, Mrs. Carl	Straw Plains					
Myers, Gertrude	Apr 26, 1990	Hilltown	Talbott, Tn	Sep 24, 1899	100	W	Line, John Albert		Quarrels, Mary Jahnine		Myers, Albert L.	West View					
Myers, Jackie Joe	Apr 5, 1986	F.S.H.		Aug 27, 1941	44	Div	Myers, Leon		Hickman, Douglas		Mitchell, Dosutan H.-Mrs. Douglas H.C.	West View					
Myers, John Knight	Mar 13, 1997	Jeff City	Ida, Tn	Jan 24, 1919	78	Ng	Myers, Tandy		Steadman, Gertrude		Cline, Julia [Dana]	Highland Memorial - J.M.G.		John K. Jr.			
Myers, Lena	Oct 28, 1981	Jeff Co	Tn	Dec 17, 1895	78	W	Wood, Powell		Thornhill, Annie		Wood, Clarence - Myers, Francis	West View					
Myers, Nannie Lois	Feb 7, 1987	Washington Co, Tn		Feb 16, 1915	81	W	Hughes, Samuel		Kilburn, Maxine		Myers, James F. & Nan	Mt. Pleasant				Charles & Dorothy	
Myers, Ray	Apr 27, 1959	Jeff Co	Tn	Mar 20, 1891	78	Ng	Myers, James M.		Shelton, Sallie		Myers, Mrs. Ray	West View					
Myeatt, Belling Lindsey	Sept 1, 1959	Dandridge	Tn			Ng					Myers, Mrs. Ray	Lynnhurst					
Myeatt, Samuel King	Apr 21, 1963	Jeff Co	Tn	Dec 12, 1907	55	Ng	Myeatt, Lee K.		Myre, Ersa		Myeatt, Mrs. Alberta Moore	Memorial Gardens					
Myeatt, William Lee	Apr 13, 1978	Jeff City	Tn	Aug 13, 1913	64	Ng	Myeatt, Robert Lee		Moore, Ercie		Myeatt, Mrs. W.L.	West View					
Myrick, Infant Female	Dec 29, 1970	Sevier Co.		Dec 29, 1970			Myrick, Robert F. 3rd		Cline, Sarah Jo		Myrick, Robert	West View					
Nance, Albert	Jan 20, 1958			Sep 25, 1876	81	W	Nance, Newton		Vineyard, Sarah		Nance's Grove						
Nance, Alice B. [Col]	Jan 30, 1951	Jeff Co	Tn	Mar 13, 1872	79	W	Boyls, Jim		Mitchell, Emily		Abrams, Mrs. Ben - Abrams, Bertha - Bonds, Will [Bro-Strange, Val]	Mt. Pleasant					
Nance, Ceasar Augusta [Col]	Nov 11, 1982	Hamblen Co	Tn	Mar 20, 1940	22	S	Nance, Raymond		Donaldson, Pauline		Nance, Luther	West View Colored	Korea				
Nance, Beulah B. [Col]	May 20, 1982	Jeff Co	Tn			W	Boyls, Jim		Mitchell, Emily		Nance, Pauline	West View Colored					
Nance, Hamilton [Col]	Jul 16, 1926	Hamblen Co	Jeff Co		90	S			Phillis	Jeff Co	Nance, G.L. & Rick	Colored					
Nance, Hugh Stanley [Col]	Apr 8, 1941	New Market		14-5-9		S	Brownlow, Beulah	Jeff Co			Nance, Luther	Woodens					
Nance, Mary Alice	Mar 11, 1956	Hamblen Co	Tn	Nov 23, 1882	73	W	Loy, Travis W.		Mr. Eve, Eva		Peck, Mrs. W.T. - Nance, Douglas W.C.	Nance's Grove					
Nance, Minnie	Jan 1, 1957	Grainger Co		Aug 15, 1877	79	W	Colbert, Jasper		Mitchell, Eliza		Nance, William C.	Colored					
Nance, Nettie C. [Col]	Jun 12, 1942	Jeff City	Tn	Sep 21, 1941		Ng	Nancy, Raymond	Tn	Donaldson, ---	Hamblen Co	Nance, Albert	Colored					
Nance, Richard H. [Col]	Mar 11, 1943	Jeff Co	Tn	Jun 10, 1894	49	W	Nance, Hamilton	Tn	Grant, Sarah Lee	Tn	Nance, Raymond	Colored					
Nance, Ronald Franklin [Col]	Feb 18, 1945	Jeff Co	Tn		5m		Unk		Nance, Blanche Ehra	Jeff Co	Nance, Nellie & Luther / Nance, Nellie & Blanche	Colored					
Nance, Sara Lee Grant [Col]	Jan 22, 1925	Grainger Co	Tn	Feb 15, 1862	62		Galilahee, Unk	Tn	Nance, Blanche Ehra	Jeff Co	Nance, Rich & Lewis	Jefferson City Colored					
Nance, William Carl	Feb 9, 1945	Jeff Co	Tn		75		Nance, Alice	Tn	Nance, G.B.	Tn	Nance, Mrs.	Woodens Chapel					

NAME	DDATE	DLOCAT	BLOCAT	BDATE	AGE	SPOUSE	FATHER	FRLOCAT	MOTHER	MERLOCAT	BY	BURIAL	VET	SON	DAUG	BROTHER	SISTER
Nancy, J.P.	May 15, 1932	Jeff City									Washburn, Mrs - Carpenter, Mrs - Manning, W.M.- Greer, John	West View					
Nash, Melisia Jane	May 10, 1925		Tn		85	W	Renfro, Cox	Tn	Mc Kinney, -	Tn	Renfro, Mrs. Jim	Rutledge					
Nash, James Jessie	Aug 7, 1990	F.S.H.	Jeff City	Sep 14, 1920	69	Baradik, Catherine	Nash, Bustin		Cockrum, Nettie		Nash, Catherine B.	West View	unk				
Nash, John O.	Mar 6, 1950		Tn	July 5, 1865	84	W					Nash, Shirley	Flat Gap					
Nash, Stanley Vettie	Feb 2, 1967	Jeff City	Tn	Aug 22, 1896	70	Ng	Nash, John		Johnson, Lillie		Nash, Mrs. Cora R. & Sons	West View					
Naylor, Gerard Wayne	Dec 5, 1996	Knoxville, Tn	Keener, Al	Feb 15, 1922	74	Ellis, Mildred	Naylor, Clem		Whitt, Zettie		Wills	Crestwood - E. Gatlxden, Al	42-45				
Neal, Ellie Lou	Jun 6, 1994	Knoxville, Tn	Tn	Jun 12, 1909	84	W	Neal, Herbert		Collins, Sarah Ann		Layman, Billie Jean (Niece)	Roseberry				Johnny	
Neal, Henry Leslie	Jul 10, 1966	Jeff City	Tn	Sep 24, 1916	49	S	Neal, Herbert		Collins, Sara		Neal, Ellie - Ke??Toy, Mrs. Helen	Roseberry - Knox Co					
Neal, Isaac William	Aug 29, 1978	At Home	Tn	Sep 5, 1901	74	S	Neal, James C.	Tn	Dunnsin, Minnie ?	Tn	Neal, Mrs. L.W.	Jefferson Memorial					
Neal, Jessie	May 17, 1961	Knoxville, Tn	Ga	Jun 16, 1910	70	W	Ballew, Jessie / Neal, Isaac W. (D)	Tn	Burns, Elizabeth	Tn	Neal, William L.	Jefferson Memorial					
Neal, Johnny Charles	Feb 12, 1999	Jeff City	Grainger Co	May 26, 1921	77		Neal, Herbert A.		Collins, Sarah		Layman, Billie Jean - Dockins, Denise (Niece) - Kelley, Wayne - Whitaker, Edward (Nephews)	Roseberry					
Neal, Maxine	Nx 28, 1947	Dayton, Ohio		Nov 19, 1929	18	S	Neal, James	Tn	Ellison, Lola M.	Tn	Neal, James	West View					
Neal, Sarah Ann	Apr 14, 1948	Jeff Co	Tn	Aug 2, 1883	64-8-12	W	Collins, Reubin	Tn	Powers, Betty	Tn	Neal, Ellie-Henry - Chadwick, Mrs. (Children)	Roseberry - Knox Co					
Neal, Shelby Jean	Nov 8, 1947	Jeff Co	Tn	Nov 8, 1947	2-19		Neal, James	Tn	Ellison, Lola Mae	Tn	Neal, James	West View					
Neal, Sylvia Juanita	Jul 11, 1927	Jeff Co	Tn		79		Neal, J.W.	Tn	Ballew, Jessie	Tn	Neal, J.W.	Benjamin - Carryton					
Neal, Will	Oct 13, 1947	Jeff Co			2-19						Neal, L.W.	Narcos Grove					
Neal, William Lee	Jun 5, 1994	Knoxville, Tn	Jeff City	Jun 11, 1929	64		Neal, Isaac William		Ballew, Jessie F.		Neal, Richard L. [Son]	J.M.G.	50-52	Neal, Sylvia - Lewis, Linda - [G] Dring, Crystal - Lewis, Jessie	Carr	Hood, Frankie	
Needham, Lawrence Wayne	Jan 30, 1982	J.M.H.	Tn	Jun 30, 1915	66	Shaver, Margaret	Needham, A.M.		Wollenbarger, Lida		Needham, Mrs. L.W.	Jefferson Memorial					
Needham, Margarie Jane	Jul 29, 1987	Memphis, Tn		Mar 25, 1919	78	Shaver, Johnston			Corum, Edna Elizabeth		Petts, Jane [Daug]	J.M.G.		Don	Garrison, Kay		
Needham, Olive Rose	Apr 18, 1993	Columbus, Ohio	Needham, Henry	Jun 15, 1912	80	Needham, Henry	Turnbull, Leslie		Faulk, Elizabeth		Husband	J.M.G.		[Steps] Needham, James-Leonard	Daughtry, Nancy	Leslie Jr.	
Nelson, Clokin Grant [Col]	Jul 3, 1944	Jeff Co		Jan 4, ---		Ng	Nelson, Calvin	Tn	Mc Farland, Liza	Tn	Nelson, Floyd & Lillie	Colored					
Nelson, Charles Edward	Jul 14, 1945	Jeff Co	Tn	July 28, 1945		Ng	Nelson, W. C.	Tn	Newman, Margaret		Nelson, W.C.	West View					
Nelson, David Otis	Mar 20, 1968	Jeff City	Tn	Aug 20, 1884	83	W	Nelson, Ira	Tn	Saults, Eliza		Roush, Theo	West View Colored					
Nelson, David Otis Jr.	Oct 29, 1988	J.M.H.	Tn	Apr 14, 1915	73	W	Nelson, David Otis Sr.		Huff, Minerva		Nelson, William David-Carolyn Sue	J.M.G.					
Nelson, Edward Eugene	Nov 13, 1987	Morristown, Tn		May 28, 1930	57	Bates, Meredith	Nelson, Grover		Elza, Blanche		Nelson, Meredith Bates	Lebanon Baptist	WW 2				
Nelson, Ernest Keith	Dec 14, 1970	Jeff Co	Multanville, Kansas	Aug 31, 1970			Nelson, Grover		Langston, Dianne		Nelson, Grover	Piney					
Nelson, Francis D.	Oct 13, 1973	Jeff City	Tn	Oct 24, 1886	86	W	Nelson, Ira		Saults, Eliza		Nelson, Edward E. & Robert	West View					
Nelson, Francis Glenn	Mar 10, 1995	Newport, Tn	Jeff City	Jan 14, 1937	58	Whitt, Allison	Nelson, George Francis		Carter, Verna Mae		Wills - Whitt, Mary [Mother]	West View			Trull, Connie - Mehagigry, Brenda	Ronald	
Nelson, Hugh Henry	Jun 10, 1960	Jeff Co	Tn	Oct 9, 1878	81	Ng					Howard, Mrs. Herbert [Gladys]	Mill Springs					
Nelson, Inez Marsh	May 30, 1943	Hawkins Co	Tn	Mar 22, 1887	56	Nelson, Jerry	Shorter, William	Tn	Mc Anally, Cordia	Tn	Nelson, Jerry	Mill Springs					
Nelson, J.M.D.	Sep 22, 1995	Tn	Tn	Jan 9, 1904		Ng	Nelson, Grant		Harris, Lillie		Nelson, Mrs.	West View Colored					
Nelson, James F. [Col]	Mar 23, 1958	Jeff Co	Tn	Mar 23, 1881	66-23-	Ng	Nelson, William				Nelson, Mrs. Addie	Mill Springs					
Nelson, James Perry	May 28, 1947	Jeff Co	Tn		5	S	Nelson, Roy		Newmann, Katherine	Tn	Nelson, Roy	Jefferson Memorial					
Nelson, Kenneth Mack	Dec 10, 1965	Jeff Co	Tn	Dec 20, 1944	20	S	Nelson, Roy		Bell, Margie	Tn	Nelson, Roy	Jefferson Memorial					Haun, Bonnie Br- Lane] Douglas, Doris

NAME	DDATE	DLOCAT	BLOCAT	BDATE	AGE	SPOUSE	FATHER	FBLOCAT	MOTHER	MFBLOCAT	BY	BURIAL	VET	SON	DAUG	BROTHER	SISTER
Nelson, Leonard Monroe	May 16, 1958	Jeff Co	Tn	Feb 28, 1918	40	Ng	Shorter, Inez		Shorter, Inez		Nelson, Mrs. Ruby & Jerry	West View					
Nelson, Lillie [Col]	Dec 9, 1948	Jeff Co	Tn		66	Ng	Harris, Nathan	Tn	Timmons, Mary	Tn	Nelson, Floyd & Grant	Colored					
Nelson, Louise Carothers	Jul 8, 1960	Jeff City	Tn	Jul 15, 1894	65	W	Melton, Tom		Murdock, Ella		Nelson, T.D.	Flat Gap					
Nelson, Lula Beatrice	Jun 24, 1971	Jeff Co	Tn	Jun 24, 1971	62	S	Nelson, Ott Sr.		Huff, Josephine		Bell, Gertrude Nelson- Gooch, Ora	West View					
Nelson, Minerva Josephine	Mar 15, 1958	Greene Co, Tn	Tn	Apr 25, 1881	76	W	Huff, Marshall		Harrison, Cynthia		Otis Sr. & Children	West View					
Nelson, Mrs. Francis		New Market	Tn	Jul 8, 1888	45	W	Miller, Jim	Tn	Miller, Mary	Tn	Nelson, A.N.	Beech Springs					
Nelson, Nina	Jun 15, 1954	Knoxville, Tn	Tn	Apr 25, 1917	63	Nelson, David Otis Jr.	Talley, William A.		Ballinger, Minnie		Nelson, Ott Jr.	Jefferson Memorial					
Nelson, Robert [Col]	May 10, 1937	Tn	Tn	Nov 11, 1912	24	Ng	Nelson, Grant	Tn	Harris, Lillie		Nelson, Lillie	West View Colored					
Nelson, Roy Mack	Jul 29, 1986	F.T.H.	Tn	Jun 11, 1911	75	Bell, Marjorie	Nelson, Alexander		Miller, Frances		Nelson, Marjorie	J.M.G.					
Nelson, Verna	Jan 30, 1998	Jeff City	Jeff Co	Apr 20, 1917	80		Carter, William Spurgeon		Hearn, Bonnie [Daug]		Hearn, Bonnie [Daug]	West View		Ronald L. [Ne]			
Nelson, Wilbur M.	Jun 17, 1933	Jeff City	Nc	Mar 28, 1886	47	Ng	Wilson, T.J.		Adams, Paralee	Nc	Wilson, Mrs.	Knoxville					
Netherland, James	Jul 12, 1965	Knox Co	Tn	Apr 5, 1880	85	W	Netherland, John		Lawrence, Maggie		Lawrence, Mrs. Flora	Gillette - Jeff Co					
Newman, Alice Florence	Aug 16, 1947	Jeff Co	Tn	Jan 23, 1881	66-6-	W	Long, John	Tn	Douglas, Rhoda Caroline	Tn	Newman, C.H.	West View					
Newman, Amanda Paralee	Jul 17, 1950	Asheville, Nc	Tn	Jul 13, 1888	23	W	May, James T.		Brooks, Margaret		Newman, C.H.	West View					
Newman, Arthur A.	Oct 6, 1948	Jeff Co	Jeff Co		92						Daughter - Will, L.F.	Mt. Pleasant					
Newman, Augusta W.	Jun 23, 1957	Knox Co	Tn	Dec 5, 1883	63	Newman, H. Cam	Watkins, Isaac G.		Carter, Nancy		Newman, H.C.- Shields, Lois	Mt. Pleasant					
Newman, Bell	Aug 13, 1928	Tn	Tn		70	W			Fielder, Ng		Newman, H.E.	Branner					
Newman, Blanche	Dec 25, 1967	Jeff Co	Tn	Apr 12, 1892	75	W	Talbot, W.O.		Collier, Nola		Og.E.Mrs. Ira - Newman, Loyd	Sunderland					
Newman, Carroll Dewey	Sep 22, 1979	Jeff City	Tn	Jul 12, 1901	78	Cloc, Blanche Corinda	Newman, George		Gilliland, Mary Elizabeth		Newman, Mrs. Blanche	West View					
Newman, Carter Helm	Apr 17, 1987	Knox Co	Tn	Sep 13, 1909	78	W	Newman, Jacob		Long, Alice		McCoy, Mrs. J.H. [Niece]	West View					
Newman, Dr. C.N.	Apr 17, 1925				70	Ng						Mt. Horeb					
Newman, Earl	Feb 18, 1928	Tn	Tn		6-1-28	S	Nelson, Mary		Nelson, Mary			Mt. Horeb					
Newman, Etha	Nov 9, 1925		Tn		41-9-4	S	Newman, Ben		Long, Alice			West View					
Newman, Ethel	Mar 3, 1984	J.M.H.	Tn	Dec 6, 1883	100	Div	Brooks, Jack					West View					
Newman, Fred William	May 12, 1946	Jeff Co	Tn	Apr 1, 1928	18	S	Newman, James O.	Tn	Haynes, Mattie	Tn	Newman, J.O.	Dandridge					
Newman, George E.	May 5, 1954	Jeff Co	Tn	May 16, 1867	86	Ng	Newman, George Sr.		O'Dell, Amaney		Flowers, Mrs. Ned - Carroll-Ralph-Lucy- Bertha & Lillie	West View					
Newman, George Samuel	Jun 26, 1939	Jeff Co	Tn	May 15, 1918	21	S	Newman, George W.	Tn	Dennison, Beatrice	Tn	Newman, George Pratt, Cathy - Cliff, Nancy (Nieces)/ Dickens, Glenn [Nephew]	Mt. Pleasant					
Newman, Hugh Cam Jr.	Feb 28, 1983	Knoxville, Tn	Tn	May 4, 1922	70		Newman, H.C. Sr.		Watkins, Gussie		Watkins, Gussie	Mt. Pleasant					
Newman, James G.	Oct 24, 1992	Jeff City	Tn	Oct 18, 1901	91		Newman, James F.		Allen, Eva		White, Mary H. [Daug]	West View		Leonard			Roberts, Mary
Newman, Jessie Agnes Anderson	Jul 28, 1986			Sep 10, 1929							Greene, Arthur Jr. - Newman, D.H.	J.M.G.					
Newman, Jewell Marie	May 21, 1996	Jeff City	Davidson, Co., Tn	Aug 4, 1920	75	Ng	Dixon, E.P.		Price, Elizabeth		Owen, Nadine & Ronald [Daug]	J.M.G.					
Newman, Joe Champion	May 15, 1954	Jeff Co	Tn	Feb 3, 1921	33	Ng	Dixon, A.O.		Terry, Lena		Newman, W.A. & Mrs. Ruby	Hills Union	WW 2				
Newman, John A.	May 1, 1960	Jeff Co	Tn	Nov 24, 1875	84	W	Unk		Newman, Katherine		Shaffer, Mrs. Price [Okla.] - Newman, Murrell [Okla.]	Wesleys Chapel					
Newman, John Rhea	Nov 10, 1984	Knoxville, Tn	Jeff City, Tn	Nov 28, 1934	59	Thurman, Elnora	Newman, Aaron	Tn	Brooks, Ethel		Newman, Mrs. Elnora	West View	WW 2				
Newman, John W.	Apr 4, 1944	Jeff Co	Tn	Feb 25, 1865	79	W	Newman, J.T.		Newman, S.G. Sr.		Newman, Mrs. Sam [Son]	New Market					
Newman, Lu R.	Oct 8, 1956	Jeff City	Tn	May 6, 1894	42	Ng	Newman, J.T.	Tn	Reynolds, Elizabeth	Tn	Govt.	West View					

NAME	DDATE	DLOCAT	BLOCAT	BDATE	AGE	SPOUSE	FATHER	FBLOCAT	MOTHER	MBFLOCAT	BY	BURIAL	VET	SON	DAUG	BROTHER	SISTER
Newman, Laura Kathleen	Oct 2, 1925	Tn	Tn		30-1-27	S	Newman, Mark A.	Tn	Douglas, Mary E.	Tn	Newman, M.	Lebanon					
Newman, Lucy Cleo	Jul 10, 1985	Knoxville, Tn	Tn	Jul 4, 1893	92	W	Ellis, James		Ward, --		Gardner, Mrs. Willis N.	Strawberry Plains					
Newman, Lucile	Dec 12, 1956	Jeff Co.	Miss.	Feb 19, 1882	84	Ng	Carter, Jessie		Park, Rosa		Newman, Carter	West View					
Newman, Margaret E.	May 27, 1944	Dandridge	Jeff Co	Jun 29, 1880	83	W	Miller, George		Know, Dicil		Daniel, Mattie	Dandridge					
Newman, Mary	Feb 17, 1987	Morristown, Tn	Tn	Feb 14, 1908	79	Newman, James G.	Roach, Austin J.	Tn	Cowan, Lilly		Newman, James G.						
Newman, Mary Elizabeth	Jul 25, 1957	Jeff City	Tn	Sep 22, 1872	84	W	Gilhulen, John E.		Carmichael, Maggie	Tn	Newman, C.D. [Child] Headrick, Mrs. S.C.	West View					
Newman, Mattie Lee	Oct 5, 1941	Tn	Tn			S			Bradshaw, Oshnurda		[Sister] - Headrick, Sam	Mt. Hands					
Newman, Mettie	Mar 12, 1927	Tn	Tn		99	W	Fulton, Magruity	Tn				Branner					
Newman, Neil R.	Mar 24, 1965	Hamblen Co	Tn			S	Newman, S.J.		Rankin, Mary Ann		Newman, Sam G. Jr.	Mt. Hands					
Newman, Ona	Aug 3, 1966	Knoxville, Tn	Tn		87	W	Newman, J.F.		Brunton, Martha		Harrell, Hazel	Strawberry Plains					
Newman, Oleonas S.	May 27, 1990	J.M.H.	Sc	Nov 11, 1904	85	Newman, James Otha	Hodgin, Edwin N.		Stout, Ida		Newman, Allen G.	Eastview - Straw Plains					
Newman, Ralph Erwin	Aug 18, 1989	V.A. - Mt Home	Jeff Co	Nov 15, 1910	78	Hawkins, Alice	Newman, George E.		Gibbons, Mary		Newman, Alice H.- Ralph E. Jr.	West View	WW 2				
Newman, Robert Blair	May 12, 1975	Talbott, Tn	Tn	Mar 17, 1919	54	S	Newman, Rufus Blair		May, Amanda Persiee		Newman, Jack-Mrs. R.B.	Mt. Pleasant					
Newman, Rufus Blair	Jun 3, 1948	Jeff Co	Tn	Jan 21, 1886	60-4-12	Ng	Newman, Rufus A.	Tn	Sawyers, Maggie	Tn	Portey, Mrs. Eugene	Mt. Pleasant					
Newman, Samuel G.	May 20, 1968	Jeff Co	Tn	Mar 3, 1877	91	Div	Newman, Gideon		Rankin, Mary Ann		Newman, S.G. Jr.	Buffalo Grove					
Newman, Sue	Oct 16, 1955	Talbott	Tn	Jul 2, 1874	61	Ng	Owen, J.P.		McDade, Mary Elizabeth	Tn	Elizabeth	Sunderland					
Newman, Thelos Lynn	Feb 13, 1981	Knoxville, Tn	Tn	Jun 19, 1917	73	Godwin, Elsie	Newman, Thomas L.		Cole, Joella		Newman, Elsie G. Ogle, Mrs. Carl - Newman, Thelos	West View	unk				
Newman, Thomas Lloyd	Oct 9, 1975	Talbott, Tn	Tn	Nov 25, 1882	82	W	Newman, Tobe		Green, Melissa			Sunderland					
Newman, William Alfred	Jul 11, 1989	J.M.H.	Sevierville, Tn	Jul 16, 1919	69	Dixon, Jewell	Newman, Arno		Terry, Lena		Newman, Mrs. Jewell	J.M.G.	WW 2				
Newman, William Henry	Oct 21, 1977	Jeff Co	Tn	Aug 1, 1892	85	Ellis, Lucy Cleo	Newman, A. Nip		Battis, Katherine		Gardner, Mrs. Willis N. - Newman, William H- A.G. - Glass, Freda	Strawberry Plains					
Nicely, Horace Henry	Mar 7, 1982	J.M.H.	Tn	Sep 29, 1912	69	Ng	Niceley, Mitchell		Moseley, Tildy		Dalton, Mrs. Bonnie	Jefferson Memorial					
Nichols, Albert Houston	Feb 3, 1954	Strawberry Plains	Tn	Dec 31, 1907	46	Ng	Nichols, Andy		Rogers, Loudica		Nichols, Mrs. A.H.	Beaver Creek					
Newman, Amanda	Mar 5, 1974	Newport, Tn	Tn	Nov 23, 1896	77	W	Turner, Ruben		Ward, Julia		Nelson, Mrs. Roy	White Pine					
Nichols, Chester R.	Jul 13, 1975	Columbus, Ga.	Dandridge, Tn	Jan 1, 1898	76	Dev	Nichols, Frank		Corbett, Cora S.		Kilgore F.H. [Columbus, Ga] - Sandschuck, Richard	Jefferson Memorial					
Nichols, Cora	Dec 15, 1933	New Market	Tn	Dec 15, 1933	52-4-4	Nichols, F.W.	Corbett, Porter	Tn	Betts, Mary Ann	Tn	Nichols, F.W.	New Market					
Nichols, Frank W.	Oct 31, 1948	Jeff Co	Jeff Co	Oct 14, 1978	70	Ng	Cox, Frank		Cox, Martha	Tn	Nichols, Juanita Swann	New Market					
Nichols, Harley L.	Jun 13, 1975	Tn	Tn	Apr 22, 1901	74	Shrader, Reba	Nichols, Frank		Corbett, Cora		Nichols, Reba	Jefferson Memorial					
Nichols, Infant	Mar 26, 1948	Jeff Co	Jeff Co	Mar 24, 1948		Ng	Nichols, F.W.	Tn	Swann, Juanita	Tn	Nichols, F.W. - Nichols, Mrs. Marie Purdue	New Market					
Nichols, James Robert	Mar 11, 1973	Knoxville, Tn	Tn	Jul 19, 1903	69	Nichols, Frank		Corbett, Cora		Greenville, Texas	Forrest Park - Greenville, Texas					
Nichols, Kathryn Melinda	Jan 18, 1940	Oak Grove	Tn	May 7, 1871	68	W	Hill, Maston		Elledge, Sarah		Jones, Mrs. - Thornton & Jones [White Pine- Knoxville & Dandridge]	Pleasant Hill					
Nichols, Mitchell	Dec 7, 1931																
Nichols, Reba	Oct 14, 1986	Morristown, Tn	Tn	Sep 25, 1901	85	W	Shrader, James		Helm, Mary Ann		Nichols, Hood	J.M.G.					
Nichols, Spencer Finley [Col]	Mar 14, 1954	J.M.H.	Tn	Oct 12, 1861	72	Martin, Katherine	Nichols, George		Dunwoody, Amanda		Nichols, George-John- Frank-James A.	Flat Woods					
Nicholson, Bert C.	Feb 4, 1993	Jeff City	Knox Co	Jul 15, 1910	82	W	Nicholson, Ward		Elder, Sally Mae		Nicholson, Sam C. [Son]	J.M.G.		Walker H.	Garrison, Phyllis		Hodgson, Anna Lynn - Colley, Ruby

NAME	DDATE	DLLOCAT	BDATE	AGE	SPOUSE	FATHER	FBLLOCAT	MOTHER	MFBLOCAT	BY	BURIAL	VET	SON	DAUG	BROTHER	SISTER
Nicholson, Helen Marie	Oct 18, 1999	Claiborne Co, Tn	Oct 28, 1941	57	Nicholson, Walter	Purley, Everit	Nc	Royston, Veda		Husband	J.M.G.		Mike-John			
Nicholson, Katharine	Sep 27, 1995	Jeff Co	May 22, 1907	88	Nc	Martin, Sam		Miller, Lela	Tn	Nicholson, Sam & Nancy [Son]	J.M.G.		Walter & Helen	Garrison, Phyllis & Charles		
Nicholson, M.W.	Sep 30, 1992	Jeff City	Mar 18, 1978	54	Ng	Bryan, Nancy	Nc	Nicholson, Mrs. M.W. Lynn [Aerry] Hodgson, Mrs. Ann			Mt. Horeb					
Nicholson, Robert Soy	Jan 27, 1984	Knoxville, Tn	Sep 27, 1915	54	W	Nicholson, Henry		Elder, Sally M.	Tn	Nicholson, Ward	Jefferson Memorial					
Nicholson, Roy A.	Aug 2, 1997	Jeff City	Jul 6, 1896	101		Nicholson, Abraham Lincoln		Graff, Alma		Nicholson, Truman L. [Son]	J.M.G.	Roger				
Nickerson, Margaret Rhea [Peggy]	Apr 13, 1979	Golden, Colorado	Jul 25, 1923	55	Nickerson, E.I.	Sunderland, Carl R.		Galbreath, Elsie		Nickerson, E.I.	Sunderland					
Nickle, Renewal Mann	Feb 13, 1980	Knoxville, Tn	Dec 23, 1928	51	Nickle, George E.	Mann, John		Lambert, Ada	Tn	Nickle, George E.	Mt. View					
Nichols, Elijah [Cot]	Sep 7, 1934	New Market	Jul 30, 1889	45	Ng	Nicols, George	Tn	Ellis, Mandy		Nichols, Mrs. Floyd - Nelson, Roy	Pleasant View					
Nicnols, William Floyd	Feb 9, 1956	Knox Co	Dec 24, —	82	Ng	Nichols, Henry				Nichols, Mrs. Floyd - Nelson, Roy	White Pine					
Nos. Bessie Foster	Feb 23, 1929	Tn	34-7-10		Tn	Foster, James	Tn	Martin, Lewis	Tn	Nos, R.H.	Shilo					
Nos. Clifford Franklin [Jack]	Oct 21, 1980	Winston-Salem, Nc	Dec 23, 1923		Farrow, Dorothy	Nos, Ernest		Jones, Louise		Nos, Mrs. Clyde	Jefferson Memorial					
Nos. Clyde Alexander	Jun 9, 1940	Granger Co	Sep 17, 1884	55	Ng	Nos, James	Tn	Churchman, Mary Jane	Tn	Nos, Mrs. Clyde	West View					
Nos. Earnest Frank	Dec 8, 1986	J.M.H.	Oct 5, 1898	88		Nos, Frank		Roach, Theria		Hutchins, James	J.M.G.					
Nos. George	Apr 30, 1941	Granger Co		70-6-10	Nos, Allice			Rich, Sarah		Nos, Calvin [Son] - Will - Nos, Calvin	Shiloh					
Nos. Gwendolyn	Mar 13, 1985	J.M.H.	Jan 1, 1907	78	Nos, Jack T.			Miller, —		Nos, Jack T.	Shiloh					
Nos. Hubert E.	Jan 23, 1954	Tn	Sep 21, 1882	71	S	Nos, James P.B.		Russell, Thurman - Costner		Nos, Mrs. Calvin W - Nos, Calvin	Everlasting Life - J.M.G.					
Nos. J.D.	Dec 15, 1929	Tn (D. Granger Co)		90-6-8	W	Nos, N.	Tn	Costman, Katharine		Nos, R.H.	Shilo					
Nos. Jack Tate	Apr 7, 1994	Jeff City	Aug 30, 1901	92		Nos, S.O.		Tate, Comfort		Nos, Mrs. Mildred	Shilo					
Nos. James P	Aug 19, 1931	Granger Co	Sep 24, 1864	66	Ng	Nos, Joe A.	Tn	Kinder, Keefy	Tn	Nos, Mrs. Julia	Shilo					Stinnett, Mary N.
Nos. Julia N.	Feb 15, 1940	Granger Co	Jan 15, 1867	73	Ng	Alexander, James J.	Tn	Emert, Polly A.	Tn	Nos, Hubert	Shilo					
Nos. Katie Lou	Apr 28, 1984	Knox Co [Res Cookeville]	May 13, 1895	68	Nos, Clyde [D]	Chandler, Thomas F.		Powers, Ross F.		Nos, James & Ronald	West View					
Nos. Louise	May 14, 1996	Mosheim, Tn	Apr 7, 1905	91	Jones, Alex	Knight, Bertie		Knight, Bertie		Comer, La Donna [G-Daug]	J.M.G.		[B+Leaf] Nos, Dorothy		Gilliam, Fiona - Poe-Spike	
Nos. Mary Viola Mc Curry	Mar -, 1983	Jeff Co			W	Nos, James	Tn			Nos, Clyde	Shilo					
Nos. R.H.	Nov 6, 1931	Knoxville	Aug 22, 1888	43	W	Nos, Samuel O.		Glass, Jane * John R. [Daug]			Sunderland			[G] Meeks, Gwen R. - Smith, Linda G. - Wellington, Susan G.		
Nos. Sanford T.	Mar 18, 1967	Hamblen Co	Sep 15, 1908	58	Ng	Jarnigan, John S.				Nos, Mrs. Mildred	West View					
Nuff, Estelle	Feb 8, 1982	Jeff Co	Dec 22, 1953	41	Nuff, M.W. Blair	Hubbell, Katharine		Helo, J.D. -		Helo, J.D. -	West View					
Nolen, Larry Charles	Apr 25, 1954	Jeff Co	Dec 22, 1953			Nolen, Bradley		Woods, Kathleen		Nos, Mrs. Glenn	Mt. Horeb					
Nolen, Glenn Orville	Jul 4, 1982	Knox Co	May 22, 1921	41		Nolen, Bradley		Ellison, Lucy		Nos, Mrs. Kathleen W	Jefferson Memorial					
Nolen, Jo Anne		J.M.H.	Nov 17, 1952	31	Nolen, Bill	Wallen, Cecil		Coffey, Ruby		Nolen, Bill	Jefferson Memorial					
Nolen, Mack Edward	Sep 28, 1970	Hamblen Co				Nolen, Eddie		Rogers, Rebecca		Nolen, Eddie	Mt. View					
Nolen, Michael Dianne	Oct 1, 1970	Hamblen Co	Feb 12, 1971	1		Nolen, Eddie		Rogers, Rebecca		Nolen, Eddie	Mt. View					
Nolla, Daudra Diennis	Dec 7, 1972	Knoxville, Tn	Dec 16, 1890	62		Norris, William E.		Langston, Lorena		Nevill, W. E.	Pleasant Grove					
Norman, Henry	Dec 28, 1952	Hamblen Co		5mr-14d	S			Norman, Erba		Norman, Erba	West View					
Norris, Jimmie Franklin	Jun 20, 1941	Jeff Co				Norris, Utah D.		Vosser, Mary Linda	Jeff Co	Norris, U.D.	Jefferson Memorial					
Norris, Linda Marie	Jul 25, 1971	Jeff Co	July 19, 1971	6d		Norris, David D.		Martin, Jeannette		Norris, David	Jefferson Memorial					
Norris, Fred	Apr 7, 1933	Tn	Aug 17, 1866	65		Glass, Fred	Tn	Hayes, Stellna	Tn	Bettis, Nellie	West View					
Northern, Ada	Jun 21, 1931	Jeff City			W	Vanvell, Sarah R.	Tn	Northern, William N.	Tn	Northern, William N.	Piedmont				Northern, Bruce Henry	
Northern, Bruce Henry	Dec 24, 1947	Jeff Co	Dec 22, 1947	2d										Louis Evert Jr -Oto- [B+Leaf] Nicholson, Stan	Robeson, Laura - [B+Leaf] Garrison, Phyllis	

NAME	DDATE	DLOCAT	BLOCAT	BDATE	AGE	SPOUSE	FATHER	FRLOCAT	MOTHER	MFRLOCAT	BY	BURIAL	VET	SON	DAUG	BROTHER	SISTER
Northern, C. Elmer	Aug 5, 1976		Indiana		86	Cox, Reba	Northern, William Lenny		Hankins, Marilda		Combs, Mrs. H.C.	Mill Springs					
Northern, Dudley Armstrong	Sep 5, 1944	Jeff Co	Tn	Dec 9, 1867	76	Ng	Northern, William		Ballinger, Louisa		Northern, Mrs. Reba	Shiloh					
Northern, Emma	May 27, 1971	Chattanooga, Tn	Tn	Oct 1, 1882	88	Northern, John W. [D]	Haygarth, Thomas	Tn	Dinwiddie, Cordelia	Tn	Northern, Earl & John Jr.	West View					
Northern, Helen Beatrice	Oct 13, 2000	Jeff Co	Tn	Jan 10, 1907	93	W	Deatheridge, William C.		Yarberry, Catherine E.		Northern, Earl & John	West View					
Northern, Helen Lodene	Aug 17, 1947	Jeff Co	Tn	Aug 16, 1947	1d	W	Northern, Stanley	Tn	Clevenger, Lorena	Tn	Northern, Stanley	West View					
Northern, James Stanley	Aug 15, 1993	Jeff City	Jeff Co	Jun 1, 1914	79		Northern, Charles E.		Hodge, Myrtle		Northern, Charles J. & Angela (Son - Bruce, NY) - Reba (Step-Mother)	West View	42-46				Weiss, Nadine
Northern, John E.	Dec 30, 1069	Jeff Co	Tn	Mar 1, 1882	87	W	Northern, W.L.		Morilla, Helhea		Northern, Sarah Jane	West View					
Northern, John W. Sr.	Jan 4, 1961	Jeff Co	Tn	Sep 13, 1890	80	Ng	Northern, Allen R.		Hickman, Mollie		Northern, Mrs. J.W.	West View	WW 2				
Northern, Lorena Clevenger	May 29, 1978		Tn	Jan 7, 1914	62	Northern, J. Stanley	Clevenger, Jos C.		Solomon, Hattie		Northern, Sam R.	West View					
Northern, Mable W.	Aug 6, 1943	Jeff Co	Tn	Jul 23, 1923		Northern, George	Whitaker, Bert	Tn	Rowe, Ella	Tn	Northern, George	Asbury					
Northern, Mae Cullen Glass	May 7, 1966	Jeff City	Tn			Ng					Northern, John E.- Janis R.	West View					
Northern, Marietta Talley	Apr 21, 1949	Jeff City	Tn	Mar 25, 1879	70	Ng	Talley, William	Tn	Ballinger, Sarah	Tn	Cowles, Mrs. A. & Wayne	Shiloh					
Northern, Oliver Wayne	Apr 2, 1956	Lakewood, Ohio	Jeff Co	Mar 29, 1912	44	Evans, Mollie	Northern, Dudley		Talley, Mary Etta		Northern, Mable E.	Shiloh	WW 2				
Northern, Raymond Phurie	Oct 8, 1968	Detroit, Mich.	Tn	Dec 5, 1913	54	Div	Northern, John W.		Hisman, Emma		Northern, Earl	West View					
Northern, Thomas	Aug 11, 1944	Knox Co	Jeff Co		33	S	Northern, Sam L.	Tn	Haworth, Emma	Tn	Northern, Sam R. - Pleasant Grove	Pleasant Grove					
Northern, William H.	Dec 27, 1964	Jeff Co	Tn	Nov 5, 1907	57	Ng	Northern, Henry		Dye, Myrtle		Northern, Mrs. O.C. - Puckett, Mrs. H. & Kenneth	Piedmont					
Northern, William Henry	Oct 14, 1996	Knoxville, Tn	Jeff Co	Mar 3, 1929	67		Northern, Henry M.		Deatheridge, Helen		Mother	West View	army				
Norton, James Waylon	Mar 25, 1998	Jeff City	Sevierville, Tn	Oct 21, 1915	82		Northern, John F.		Mc Mahan, Mary E.		Manley, Emmett S. [Not Related]	Hopewell					James T.
Norton, Marvin Compton [Boots]	Feb 15, 1985	Strawberry Plains	Tn	Mar 18, 1914	70	Div	Northern, Rufus		Wagner, Emma		Strawberry Plains	Strawberry Plains					
Norton, Seba R.	Jun 9, 1990	Jeff City	Union Co. Tn	May 12, 1912	78	Huffaker, Pauline	Norton, John		Norton, Pauline H.		Norton, Pauline H.	J.M.G.					
Norton, Sheridan R.	Sep 24, 1958	Jeff Co [Pike Indiana]	Tn	June 6, 1904	54	S	Norton, John W.		Ellison, Margaret A.		Ellison, Margaret Ann	Friends Station					
Norton, Shirley	Nov 3, 1998	Knoxville, Tn	Jeff Co	Feb 15, 1941	57	Norton, William R.	Stallings, Ernest A.		Brock, Mary		Norton, Seba (Half)- Elaine - Clay (Half) Hazbend]	East View Memorial					
Nowlin, Angelo Marvin	Dec 23, 1981	Chattanooga, Tn	Alabama	Oct 26, 1901	75	W	Nowlin, Marvin		Smith, Cora		Nowlin, Angela M.	Jefferson Memorial					
Nowlin, Georgia Grace	Aug 19, 1974	Chattanooga, Tn	Tn	Dec 13, 1896	77	Nowlin, A.M.	Fralix, George		Williams, Beatrice		Nowlin, A.M. [Chattanooga]	Jefferson Memorial					
Noyes, Michael Vincent	Jul 20, 1993	Jeff City	Brenton, Mass.	May 29, 1951	42		Noyes, Irving		Johnston, Kathryn [She]		Father	Cremated		Bejune, Sarah [Cal.]		Christopher [Texas] Gregory D. [Japan]
Nyalka, Stephen Albert	Oct 8, 1989	Jeff City	Pittsburg, Pa	Dec 13, 1925	63	S	Nyalka, Michael		Toth, Elizabeth		Nyalka, Joseph [Canfield, Ohio]	Calvary - Pittsburg, Pa	WW 2				
O' Dell, Frances Louise	Dec 3, 1991	Atlanta, Ga	Tn	Jul 12, 1924	67	W	O'Dell, Fred E.		Bishop, Daisy		Largo, Lisa [Dang]	Resthaven - Cocke Co. Tn					
Oakes, Delphia	Jul 3, 1999	Clinton, Tn	Tn	Mar 4, 1995	94	Hatfield, Delphia	Hatfield, John		Hill, Lucy		Boyd, Jodell & Hugh [Dang]	West View		Styer, Janis & Boyd			
Oakes, Ezra Payne	Jul 3, 1993	Loydston, Tn	Tn	Aug 1, 1908	84	Hatfield, Delphia	Oakes, Howard		Hill, Phoebe		Boyd, Jodell & Hugh [Dang]	West View		Styer, Janis & Boyd		Hurst, Mattie - Lennox, Gladys
Oakley, Harvey	Dec 27, 1949	Davidson Co	Ada, Okla.	Jan 24, 1931	18	S	Oakes, Ezra P.		Hatfield, Delphia		Oakes, E.P.	West View					
Oakley, Wesley F.	Dec 28, 1939	Jeff Co	Tn	Dec 28, 1939	30m		Oakley, Ezra P.		Watson, Eva	Tn	Oakley, Nichols [Father]	Mt. Pleasant					
Oakley, Hazel Nell	Sep 11, 1971	Jeff Co	Tn	Apr 3, 1971	52-5-8	Div	Kerr, Andrew		Quisenberry, Leona		Oakie, Shirley-J.O. - James - Elmer - Jackie	Jefferson Memorial					
Oaten, Emory [L.V.]	Jan 27, 1972	Jeff Co	Tn	Oct 20, 1908	63	Ng	Oaten, William		Carson, Martha		Oaten, Mrs. L.V.	Memorial Gardens					
Oaten, Fannie Mae	Apr 10, 1940	Jeff City	Va	Jul 18, 1895	44-8-2	W	Jones, John Tip	Va	Gilbert, Elizabeth	Va	Oaten, Walter & Daughter [Janet, Raymond]	West View					

NAME	DDATE	BLOCAT	BLOCAT	DDATE	AGE	SPOUSE	FATHER	FBLOCAT	MOTHER	MFLOCAT	BY	BURIAL	VET	SON	DAUG	BROTHER	SISTER
Oaten, George Otis	Oct 26, 1941	Tn			45-11-3	Oaten, Beatrice B. 11/23/1965			Green Co		Oaten, Beatrice B. Oaten, L.V.	Buffalo Grove	WW 1				
Oaten, Luna Belle	May 29, 1995	Jeff City	Talbott, Tn	Mar 20, 1913	82							J.M.G.				Carl	
Oaten, Martha Frances	May 13, 1948	Jeff Co	Grainger Co	May 27, 1871	77-1-16	Ng	Eason, George W.	Ga	Helton, Elizabeth	Tn	Oaten, J.G. (Brother)	Buffalo Grove					Day, Lorene - Wade, Dorothy
Oaten, Shelby Jean	Dec 3, 1939	Jeff Co	Tn	Feb 21, 1938	1	Ng	Unk		Oaten, Frankie	Tn	Oaten, Mrs. Daughters - Father - Sons	West View					
Oaten, William	Dec 11, 1935	New Market	Tn	Oct 13, 1930	5		Oaten, Bert	Tn	Satenfield, Bel	Tn	Bollinger, Robert - Oaten, L.V. Father	Buffalo					
Oaten, William M.	Jan 9, 1952	Jeff Co	Tn	May 1, 1889	82	W	Oaten, Jess		Winkle, Julia		Bollinger, Robert - Oaten, L.V.	Buffalo Grove					
Oster, Charles Rollin Lurstin	Feb 18, 1972	V.A. Hosp - Mt. Home	Poschontas, Va	May 1, 1887	74	W	Oster, Walter W.		Winge, Cora		Oster, Mrs. Nell	West View	WW 1				
Oster, Neil Branham	Apr 17, 1996	Apollo, Pa	Wallace, W. Va	Aug 25, 1900	95	S	Branham, Edward	Poschontas, Va	Temple, Queenie		Oster, Reilen (Son - Pa)	West View					
Oster, Temple Wingo	Aug 19, 1939	Jeff Co	Champaign, Illinois	Feb 27, 1930	9	S	Onealey, John F.		Branham, Nell	W. Va	Oster, Charles	West View					
Onealey, Maggie	Jun 3, 1939	Ky		Feb	81-3-24	S	Onealey, John F.		Rochester, Susan		Norton, Mrs. Wayne (Maryville, Tn)	Stanford - Ky					
Osburn, Carrie Beth	Oct 8, 1980	Knoxville, Tn	Tn	Sep 30, 1980	9		Osburn, Earl Faye		Felts, Claudia Diane		Osburn, Earl F.	Jefferson Memorial					
Osburn, Christy Marie	Oct 5, 1980	Knoxville, Tn	Tn	Sep 30, 1980	9		Osburn, Earl Faye		Felts, Claudia Diane		Osburn, Earl	Jefferson Memorial					
Ogle, Carl Robert Sr.	Aug 15, 2000	Knoxville, Tn	Tn	Oct 25, 1923	76	Mary	Ogle, John		Unk		Wife	J.M.G.	unk				
Ogle, Eva	Dec 18, 1992	Dandridge, Tn	Sevier Co	Oct 15, 1892	100		Mc Carter, Zachary		Unk			J.M.G.	unk				
Ogle, Henry Robert	Jan 30, 1984	J.M.H.	Tn	Dec 22, 1898	95	Mc Carter, Eva	Ogle, Elisha		Lime, Sarah		Lime, Audrey [Daug]	Jefferson Memorial		Newman, Beulah - Lewis, Ruth			Profitt, Laura
Ogle, William Edward	Jun 17, 1996	Jeff City	Tn	Jul 10, 1923	72		Ogle, Cable		Sutton, Unk		Ogle, Earnest S. [Brother - Gundersime, AL]	Cremated	Army				
Oglesby, August Henry	Mar 28, 1996	J.M.H.	Ohio	Jun 22, 1906	77	Commineux, Mary	Oglesby, Nathan E.		Green, Clara		Oglesby, Mary C.	Woodside - Middletown, Oh					
Oliver, D.J.	Jun 5, 1933	Jeff Co	Tn	Dec 11, 1928	24	S	Oliver, Robert S.		Shipley, Nettie		Oliver, E. Ralph & Carroll - Fazadi, Mrs. Clarence	Lebanon - Greenbrier - Hamblen Co					
Orr, Eva	Dec 31, 1983	Knox Co	Tn	Aug 13, 1893	83	Orr, W.J. [D]	Hall, Henry		Lacey, Amanda		Orr, Jeanita	Movelock - Hamblen Co. korean					
Orr, Ella Mae	Nov 23, 1954	Rock Dale, Texas	Murry Co, Ga	Jun 30, 1885	69	W	Brewer, Samuel L.		Frazier, Elizabeth		One, Jaunita	Oak Grove - Blount Co					
Orr, William Albert	Jan 28, 1954	Jeff City	Tn	Aug 29, 1945	48		Orr, Lamar		Ellis, Dorothy		Byrd, Essie	Cremated					
Orszulak, Stanley Albert	Feb 16, 1977	Indiana		Aug 25, 1917	59	Ng	Orszulak, Joseph		Gebas, Frances		Mother	Pine Lake - La Porte, Ind.					
Osborn, Jeffery Allen	Oct 30, 1993	Jeff City	Granite City, Ill.	Mar 28, 1968	25				Orszulak, Clow Jo		Orszulak, Mrs. Stanley	Chapman - Mt. Olive, Ill. Father					
Osborne, Diana	Jul 25, 1989	Jeff City	Pennington Gap, Va	May 19, 1956	42	Osborne, James Wesley Sr.	Osborn, Albert		Ely, Emma		Rogers Virginia Lynn [Daug] - Bishop, Wanda [Step-Mother] - Bishop, Maggie [Mother]	J.M.G.		James Wesley Jr.			
Osen, Charles	Jan 28, 1937	Jeff Co	Tn	Sep 5, 1890	46	Ng	Osen, William		Shipley, Nellie		Osen, Mrs. Charles	Jeff City					
Obey, J.M.	Dec 3, 1932	Jeff Co	Va	Feb 2, 1947	85	Ng	Obey, F.M.	Va	Liner, Syrena	Va	Greenwood, Knoxville, Tn	J.M.G.					
Owen, Ronal Joe	Mar 19, 1997	Kingsport, Tn	Tn	Jan 24, 1933	64	Owen, Nadine	Owen, John Carroll		Lise, Inez	Va	Wife	J.M.G.			Loftis, Trzoey O. & Ed		Bingham, Virginia & Edgar - Caldwell, Hope & Harold
Owens, Bruce Lee	Dec 2, 1975	U.T.H.	Tn	Oct 1, 1940	35	Cox, Ann	Owens, William Lloyd		Weeks, Frankie Leona		Owens, Mrs. B.L.	Marble Hill - Blount Co					
Owens, Charles B.	May 25, 1954	Jeff City	Texas	Aug 28, 1877	85	Hyods, Florence ?	Owens, John		Laychister, Katharine		Owens, Mrs. Florence	Hillcrest					
Owens, Crystal Dawn	Jan 15, 1973	Jeff Co	Tn	Jan 15, 1973		Ng	Owens, Bruce		Cox, Ann			Marble Hill - Blount Co					
Owens, Florence	Oct 5, 1969	Knox Co	Tn	Nov 29, 1900	68	Owens, Charles [D]	Hyods, Alex		Duncan, Ann	Va	Marble Hill, Mrs. Carl	Hillcrest					
Owens, W.A.	Feb 23, 1933	Va	Tn	Mar 15, 1864	68	Ng	Owens, Solomon		Mc Lamin, Mrs. Carl	Va	Gobble, Stella	Shilo					
Owens, William A.	Jan 24, 1929	Grainger Co	Va	Mar 15, 1864	42+14	Ng	Owens, W.A.	Va	Taylor, Mahala	Va	Gobble, Stella	Shilo					

NAME	DDATE	DLOCAT	BLOCAT	BDATE	AGE	SPOUSE	FATHER	FBLOCAT	MOTHER	MFBLOCAT	BY	BURIAL	VET	SON	DAUG	BROTHER	SISTER
Oxentine, Steven	Oct 20, 1993	Jeff City	Alexander Co, Nc	Aug 24, 1970	23		Oxentine, Sam		Martha		Father	City - Taylorsville, Nc					
Oxford, Carl Emlas	Jul 30, 1989	J.M.H.	Claiborne Co, Tn	Oct 26, 1908	80	Mountain, Cleo	Jones, Margaret				Oxford, Mrs. Cleo	J.M.G.		Arnold			
Padlaik, Raymond	Apr 26, 1996	Jeff City	Chicago, Ill.	Dec 1, 1923	72	Ehresman, Josephine	Padlaik, Cyril		Wizingszewski, Anna		Padlaik, Sue [Daug]	St. Nicholas - Chicago, Ill.					
Palik, Salvatore	Sep 26, 1992	Jeff Co [Res NY]	New York								New York	New York					
Painter, Chester Earl	Apr 24, 1989	J.M.H.	Jeff Co	Nov 1, 1916	72	Bond, Helen	Painter, Wrigton		Van Dyke, Stella		Painter, Mrs. Helen	J.M.G.					
Painter, Jennie	Oct 21, 1954	Dandridge	Tn	Jan 20, 1885	69	W	Brown, Jim	Tn	White, Margaret		Painter, J.H.	Grantis Chapel					
Painter, Margaret Lee	Jan 25, 1952	Jeff Co	Texas	Dec 11, 1901	50	Ng	Lothon, James		Eslinger, Rachaal		Hobert + Henry, Mrs. Floyd	Hillcrest					
Painter, Thelma Lenoir	Jan 6, 1994	Jeff City	Ash Co, Nc	Feb 25, 1900	93		Critcher, Gaither		Mc Guire, Josie		Painter, Helen [Daug]			Bond, Vance	Shumlit, Dora [Nc] - Springtown, Vivian [Fla.]	Critcher, Paul-Glenn	Cook, Lena
Palmer, Ida Mae	Jan 5, 1981	Jeff Co	Tn	Apr 3, 1887		W	Palmer, James H.		Palmer, Milford		Palmer, Milford [Son]	Piney					
Palmer, James Harvey	Sep 14, 1958	Jeff Co	Tn		71	Ng	Palmer, John T.		Armstrong, S.E.		Palmer, Milford [Son]	Piney					
Palmer, Robert H. Sr.	Apr 21, 1991	J.M.H.	Cherokee, Nc	Jul 26, 1910	80	Parker, Sally	Palmer, John F.		Lockgood, Margaret		Palmer, Sally P.	J.M.G.					
Pardue, Franklin Eugene	Aug 3, 1971	Tn	Tn	Feb 5, 1907	64	Ng	Pardue, T.T.		Thomas, Ethel L.		Pardue, Marie - Conley, Mrs. Charles	Jefferson Memorial					
Pardue, Franklin Thurman	Aug 4, 1980	Hamblen Co	Tn	Sep 17, 1872	87	W	Pardue, William H.C.		Peeler, Vone E.		Pardue, Eugene - Conley, Mrs. Charles	West View					
Park, Clara	Mar 6, 1989	J.M.H.	Ga	Aug 20, 1912	76	W	Holloway, James N.		Holloway, Clara		Park, Lynn [Temps. Ad]	West View					
Park, Eugene Franklin	Oct 28, 1978	Jeff City	Nc	Jul 9, 1909	69	Holloway, Clara	Park, James Frank		Harrison, Pauline		Park, Mrs. Clara-Kenneth	West View	WW 2				
Park, J. Frank	May 19, 1937	Nc	Nc			W					Wife	West View					
Park, Kenneth Harrison	Apr 13, 2000	Knoxville, Tn	Nc	Jul 21, 1914	85	W	Park, J. Frank		Harrison, Pauline		Wife	West View	WW 2				
Park, Pauline	Oct 9, 1955	Jeff City	Nc	Jan 28, 1889	66	W	Harrison, Thomas Rowell		Jordin, Mary Trewis		Williams, Mrs. Marion [Centerville, Va] - Kenneth-Mary Frances	West View					
Parker, Mary Elizabeth	Nov 26, 1941	Straw Plains	Hawkins Co	Nov 28, 1889	82-3 13	W	Adams, Mary	Va	Miller, Grances		Parker, James [Son] - Smith, Mrs. C.H.	Beaver Creek					
Parks, Hazel Virginia	Jun 12, 1975	Jeff Co	Tn	Oct 2, 1975	57	Parks, Charles	Nelson, Alex				Parks, Charles	Jefferson Memorial					
Parks, Lee A. [Bill]	Oct 21, 1995	Jeff Co	Tn	Mar 5, 1911	54	Clevenger, Wanda	Palmer, Robert		Palmer, Viola Jane		Palmer, Viola Jane - Clevenger, Wanda	Jefferson Memorial					
Parks, Leoda Honeycutt [Coll]	May 2, 1966	New Market	Tn				Young, Thomas		Link		Link	New Market					
Parks, Taylor	Dec 12, 1980	Putnam	Tn	Mar 14, 1913	47	Ng	Parks, Albert		Palmer, Viola		Parks, Mrs. Lula Gentry	West View					
Parrish, Vernon Scott	Jan 31, 1998	Jeff City	Georgetown, Ky	Oct 13, 1931	66	Southerland, Zola	Parrish, Ellen		Rumines, Sally Glenn		Wife	Neafle Chapel - Rutledge, Tn		Darron-Robert		Billy Ray	
Parrott, Amy H.	Apr [18], 1934	Jeff City		Jan [30], ---	77-4 17	W					Parrott, Charles W. [Benton Harbor, Mich.]	West View					
Parrott, James R.	Jun 17, 1944	Jeff Co	Tn			W	Parrott, Jobe	Tn	Denton, Barbara	Tn	Ellison, Mrs. Lillie	Shady Grove					
Parrott, Nan	Mar 3, 1952	Jeff Co		Mar 6, 1861	80	W	Lindsey, John		Patlinson, Lucian		Mill, Mrs. Floyd	Shady Grove					
Parrott, Sarah E.	Aug 19, 1944	Jeff Co	Tn	Feb 23, 1914	22	S	Pascal, Tom		Moore, Mrs. J.W.		Highland Memorial - Rogersville	Rogersville					
Paschal, Cordelia	Oct 21, 1925		Tn			W	Staley, William		Staley, Cordia		Paschal, S.R.	Lebanon					
Paschal, Delia	May 10, 1935		Tn			S	Pascal, Tom	Tn	Shorter, Sarah	Tn	Paschal, S.R.	Lebanon					
Paschal, Elsie	Sep 18, 1986	J.M.H.	Tn	Aug 26, 1904	82	W	Collins, John D.		Clark, Emma		Paschal, Doris	J.M.G.					
Paschal, Herbert Joseph	Jan 21-27, 1927		Tn	Mar 27, 1904	63	Ng	Paschal, Thomas		Staley, Cordelia		Paschal, Samuel B.	Jefferson Memorial					
Paschal, Samuel Roscoe	Nov 25, 1987	Jeff Co	Tn			Ng	Paschal, Grant L.		Shannon, Hattie		New Market Colored	New Market Colored					
Pate, Carl Steely [Col]	Sept 16, 1955	New Market, Tn	Tn	Oct 21, 1900	54	Ng	Pate, Grant L.		Shelby, Cordelia		Shelby, Cordelia	Jefferson Memorial					
Pate, Frank Clifford [Col]	Feb 18, 1955	Lexington, Ky	Tn			S	Pate, Jim		Pate, Jim - Carter, Ethel - Morgan, Earl		Pate, Mrs. Roberta - Morgan, Earl	West Market Colored				Barron, Ellie Anne - Towles, Helen	

NAME	DDATE	DLOCAT	BLOCAT	BDATE	AGE	SPOUSE	FATHER	FRLOCAT	MOTHER	MRFLOCAT	BY	BURIAL	VET	SON	DAUG	BROTHER	SISTER
Pels, James N. [Col]	Feb 25, 1982	Jeff Co	Tn	Feb 7, 1962	61-0-18	W	Pittis, Res		Carter, Carrie		Pels, Kenneth E.	West View Colored					
Pels, Mary Katherine [Negro]	Dec 30, 1974	U.T.H.	W. Va		78	Ng	Wilson, Edward		Calhoun, Starlie		Carter, Ethnel B.	Jefferson Memorial					
Patrick, Henry Larkin	Mar 2, 1950	Knox Co	Nc	Sep 21, 1871	78	Margaret	Patrick, Silas		Kuan, Durth ?		Patrick, Breaulard (Mich.)-Galpin, Carrie Mae [incl.]-Easterday, C.C.-Partich, C.G. (Mich)	West View					
Patrick, Mrs.	Jun 13, 1928		Nc		48-6-6	Patrick, Charles	Kilin, Ng				Patrick					
Patterson, Vest	Jan 27, 1982	J.H.H.	Tn	Mar 26, 1908	73	W	Dalton, Ruben		Darling, Viola		Hodge, Irene - Patterson Children	West View					
Patterson, Clyde Milburn	Jun 18, 1968	Jeff Cc	Tn	Nov 2, 1892	75	Ng	Patterson, Columbus		Williams, Mertha		Patterson, Mrs. Vesta-John R.-Hodge, Irene-Jones, Reuben-Bishop, Kathleen-Colley, Samuel-	West View					
Patterson, Eliza	Feb 14, 1937		Tn	Nov 20, ---	81	Ng	Fentro, James	Tn	Mitchell, Nancy	Tn	Fentro, Earl	Patterson - Granger Co					
Patterson, Henry Hull	May 7, 1984	Hamblen Co		Sep 17 1916	67	Huk, Stelestla	Patterson, T.R.		Hull, Sophia		Ballinger, Mrs. Jean	Lebanon - Hamblen Co	WW 2				
Patterson, James Arlie	Nov 25, 1968	Jeff Co	Tn	Feb 8, 1900	68	Ng	Patterson, George		Hughes, Elletha		Patterson, Mrs. Pearl & Eugene	West View					
Patterson, James P.	Sep 27, 1939					W			Mitchell, Oma	Indiana	Patterson - Jas J.R.	Patterson - Granger Co					
Patterson, James Ray Sr.	Jan 18, 1998	Knoxville, Tn	Jeff Co	Jun 8, 1938	59	Keating, Georgena	Patterson, Ralph		Brooks, Gladys		Wilie - Bognar F.H. (Ridgeville, Ohio)	West Park	57-61	Barnes, Jean Jr. [Oh]	Barnes, Jean [Lakewood, Oh]		
Patterson, Jessie E. [M]	Jan 18, 1969	Jeff Co	Tn	Apr 14, 1914	54	Ng	Patterson, Ernest		Hurst, Barbara		Patterson, Mrs. Earl??-Lee - Jett, Katherine-Barnes, George	Hills Union					
Patterson, Kenneth Cecil	Oct 31, 1957	Jeff City	Tn	Aug 24, 1939	18	Ng	Patterson, Lefford		Lindsey, Frances		Patterson, Lefford-Young, J.	Shady Grove					
Patterson, Leonard Laneda	May 14, 1944	Dandridge	Jeff Co	Jun 6, 1886	57	Johnson, Josephine	Patterson, W.C.	Tn	Newman, Cumilie	Tn	Patterson, Mrs. L.L.	Dandridge					
Patterson, Stredla W.	Aug 31, 1967	Morristown, Tn	Hamblen Co	Jun 15, 1918	79	Patterson, Henry Hull [D]	Huk, Robert		Workman, Sally		Ballinger, Jean [Daug]-Norman - Lafollette, Mrs. Elger	Lebanon Baptist					
Patterson, Zelma Leta	Dec 18, 1963	Hamblen Co	Tn	Aug 12, 1963	72	Shiver, James L	Patterson, Okra		Denton, Nola		Patterson, Clora & Norman - Lafollette, Mrs. Elger	Hills Union					
Patti, Yolanda Forzanni	Sep 27, 1992	Jeff Co [Res NM]	Tn	Jun 19, 1923	29	Patti, Salvatore	Patti, Anthony		Forzanni, Margarite		Forzanni, Anthony	New York					
Patton, William Charles	Jan 2, 1928	Tn	New York		69-11-20	Ng	Patton, S.K.N.	Tn	Walt, Jane	Tn	Patton, Mrs. W.C.	West View					
Payne, William Mye Sr.	Jul 5, 1985	Alabama	Tn	Feb 24, 1909	76	Ng	Payne, Edgar T.		Wellborn, Easter		Payne, Mrs. William - Payne Sr.	Gatlinamate - J.M.G.					
Peak, Melissa [Col]	Sep 14, 1927		Tn	Mar 4, 1853	56	S	Rawson, Henry	Tn				Colored					
Peak, Mrs. C.I.	Oct 31, 1931	Knoxville	Tn	Jun 21, 1899	78	W	Mc Pherson, E.	Tn	Marten, Margaret Simmons, Hannah Elizabeth	Tn	Marten, Mrs. C.- Luttrell, Mrs. Ralph	Greenwood - Knoxville Tn. Valley Memorial - Powell, Tn	unk				
Pearon, Ralph James	Jun 14, 1968	Hamblen Co	Pa	Feb 26, 1920	38	Ng	Pearon, Fred		Lyle, Louise		Pearon, Mrs. Ralph						
Peck, Alice Helen [Black]	Mar 15, 1985	J.M.H.	Tn	Mar 14, 1920	65	Peck, John R.	Donaldson, Charles Frank		Simmons, Hannah Elizabeth		Peck, John R.	West View					
Peck, Della Cordelia	Jul 15, 1948	Jeff Co	Tn	Sep 29, 1881	65	W	Fox, George		Thurman, Didie	Tn	Wilson, Mrs. Lester & J.H.	West View					
Peck, Edgar H.	Mar 25, 1929	Jeff Co	Tn	Sep 29, 1881	66-9-16	S	Peck, M.H.	Tn	Hepworth, Julia	Tn	Peck, Mae & Ella	West View					
Peck, Ellis S.	Apr 21, 1946	Hamblen Co	Tn	Jul 5, 1875	70	S	Peck, Madison H	Jeff Co	Hepworth, Julia	Jeff Co	Peck, John R.	West View					
Peck, George Sr. [Black]	Feb 8, 1985	Tn	Tn	Jun 21, 1899	85	W	Peck, Robert		Byrd, Anna		Peck, John R.	West View					
Peck, Henry [Black]	Aug 17, 1988	J.M.H.	Tn	Feb 1, 1901	87	S	Peck, Robert		Byrd, Anna		Peck, John R.	J.M.G.					
Peck, Henry Gilbert	May 27, 1985	J.M.H.	Tn	Mar 23, 1905	80	W	Peck, Joe H.		Peck, Mary		Peck, Marcy L.	West View					
Peck, Isabella Elizabeth	Jul 3, 1925	Tn	Tn	Feb 8, 1861	79-2-1	Ng	Newman, James N.	Va	Rankin, Unk		Peck, John	Mt. Horeb					
Peck, J.H.	Apr 8, 1931	Jeff City	Tn	Feb 8, 1861	70	Ng	Peck, A.S.	Tn	Mynett, Lydia	Tn		West View					

NAME	DDATE	BLOCAT	BLOCAT	BDATE	AGE	SPOUSE	FATHER	FRLOCAT	MOTHER	MFRLOCAT	BY	BURIAL	VET	SON	DAUG	BROTHER	SISTER
Peck, James Frank	Nov 23, 1966	New Market, Tn		Jan 1, 1911	55	Div	Peck, William T. Sr.		Lawrence, Stella		Peck, W.T. Jr.- M.M.- Cole, Sandra	West View			Peck, Alicia		
Peck, John Carrol Calvin	Sep 16, 1943	Jeff Co		Oct 25, 1884	59	S	Peck, John C.	Jeff Co	Newnham, Isabella Elizabeth	Jeff Co	Peck, Harry E. Jr.	Mt. Horeb					
Peck, John R. (Black)	Mar 9, 1957	Jeff City	Jeff City	Apr 7, 1932	74		Peck, George		Moore, Willie		Meriweather, Marlene [Daug - Chicago, Ill]	West View	42-45		Peck, Alicia	Peck, George Jr.- Henry C.- [In-Law] Nelson, Grant	Nelson, Mary Katherine - Donaldson, Phyllis & Walter
Peck, Lydia Mynatt	Jan 30, 1988	J.M.H.	Tn	Apr 8, 1912	75	S	Peck, Joseph Henry	Tn	Peck, Mary	Tn	Peck, Mae Ruth- Peck, Ella	West Valley					
Peck, Mae	Dec 18, 1931	Jeff City	Tn	Sep 8, 1871	60	S	Peck, M.H.		Hepworth, Julia		Hodges, Mrs. Susan- Peck, Ella	West View					
Peck, Minnie [Col]	Jan 20, 1935	New Market	Tn	Feb 23, 1881	53	W	Hodges, Bright	Tn	Stallinger, Susan	Tn	Hodges, Mrs. Bright [Mother]	New Market					
Peck, Myrtle Alta	May 7, 1955	Jeff Co.	Tn	April 7, 1894	61	Ng	Jones, S.R.		Frye, Alice		Miller, Mrs. Richard - Peck, H.L.	West View					
Peck, Norman C. [Col]	Jan 22, 1951	Oak Ridge, Tn	Tn	Oct 27, 1923	27	Ng	Peck, George C.		Brown, Willie B.		Peck, George	West View Colored					
Peck, Rachel [Col]	Dec 5, 1936	Jeff City		April 13, 1865	71	W	Peck, Joseph				Peck, Irene - Carlton, Ralph [Benham, M]	West City					
Peck, Ruth	Mar 30, 1987	Knoxville, Tn	Jeff Co	Aug 25, 1907	89		Peck, James Henry		Peck, Mary		Peck, James H.-Edwin [Nephews] - Pegues, Mary Jane - Huber, Belle - Wiggin, Mary - Torgenson, Amy - Woodward, Ann	West View					[In-Law] Peck, Nancy L.
Peck, Stella Lee	Jul 28, 1950	Tn	Tn	Jan 6, 1883	67	W	Lawrence, James	Tn	Fudge, Mary C. [Mother]	Tn	Peck, Charles	West View					
Peck, William Leslie [Col]	Sep 25, 1942	Knox Co	Jeff Co	May 12, 1925	17	S	Peck, George		Moore, Willie B.		Peck, George	Colored					
Peck, William Tate	Sep 1, 1947	Jeff Co	Grainger Co	Feb 4, 1881	66	W	Peck, Gilbert	Tn	Graham, Elizabeth P.	Tn	Peck, Mrs. Will & Charles	West View					
Peck, William Tate Jr.	Apr 11, 1969	Jeff Co	Tn	Mar 26, 1915	54	Ng	Nipora, Evelyn		Lawrence, Stella		Peck, Larry & Evelyn	Jefferson Memorial					
Peck, Willie B. [Col]	Feb 7, 1972	Jeff Co	Tn		71		Peck, W.T. Sr.				Peck, George	Martha Dared (Service)					
Peck, Willie Ophelia	Nov 22, 1998			Apr 4, 1914	84		Lowe, Montgomery		Jernigan, Bertha Ann		Husband			Joseph Michael Stephen	Barbara Dean		
Pedigo, Pauline	Aug 9, 1999	Jeff City	Raleigh, Nc	Feb 1, 1924	75		Holland, Charles		Hillary, Alice B.		Pedigo, Chuck [Son] - Bruce	West View					
Pelfers, Ila Lena	Jul 6, 1943	Knox Co	Alexandria, Ohio	Feb 27, 1885	58	W	Beauvent, John C.	Ohio	Patterson, Kezia	Ohio	Pelfers, Will - Williams, Mrs. Joe N.- Sweet, Mrs. Ilea H.- Harper, Mrs.	U.T. Medical (Memphis)					
Pelfers, Will	Feb 28, 1952	Knoc Co	Ohio	Apr 20, 1867	84	W	Pelfers, Elisha		Unk			Pleasant Grove					
Pemberton, Vina Melisisa	Jun 24, 1925	Tn	Tn		50-6 11		Dalton, Colby	Tn	Greenlee, Victoria	Tn	Pemberton, E.L.	Shilo					
Pennywell, David	Dec 31, 1940	Jeff City			61-7- 17				Neff, Amanda E.	Va	Clure, Mrs. D.P. [Wife]						
Perfett, Maria Anne	Jul 6, 1994	New York, Ny		Mar 9, 1923	71		D'Vanzo, Carmine James		Caterelli, Margaret		Perfetti, Arthur [Son]	J.M.G.			Baxter, Maria		Clark, Sophia
Perrin, Charlie P.	May 8, 1983	Hamblen Co	Tn	Apr 7, 1878	85	Ng	Perrin, James H.		Hall, Nancy H.		Watson, John- Coffey, Jaime- Perrin, Mrs. Castle F.H.- Bluff City, Trith	Shiloh - Grainger Co					
Perrin, Jennie E.	Feb [17], 1965		Indiana		56-9 13	Ng	Perrin, Thomas	Indiana	Woody, Sybal	Indiana	Perrin, Mrs. Theo	Shiloh					
Perrin, Theo	Oct 11, 1925		Tn	Jun 12, 1927	56	Ng	Perrin, Thomas		Beck, Ellis		Perrin, Mrs. Theo	West View					
Perry, Lucy Alderman	Feb 25, 1984	Hamblen Co	Tn	Aug 26, 1914	96	W	Murray, Buford		Campbell, Ettie		Horne, Mrs. Evelyn	Rocky Valley - Jeff Co					
Personger, Florence Marie	Dec 28, 2000	Jeff City	Ohio		86	W	Musick, William		Dunham, Eliza Ann		Kirsch, Virginia	Greenfield - Greenfield, Ohio					
Petrey, Ollie Varner	Oct 15, 1963	Jeff Co	Tn	Jun 10, 1887	66	W	Varner, Sam				Varner, Sam - Petrey, Alvis	West View					
Petrey, William E.	May 24, 1959	Jeff Co	Ky	Apr 8, 1877	75	Ng	Petrey, Adam		Rhoter, Daisey Jane		Goode, Mrs. Cecil [W.- Val] - Pitney, Alvis [Ky]	Forge Ridge - Claiborne Co, Tn					
Pelip, Infant Female	Jul 24, 1974	Knoxville, Tn		Jul 24, 1974		Ng	Pedip, William B.		Douglas, Betty		Pedip, William B.	Sunset - Mcdonville, Tn					

NAME	DDATE	BLOCAT	BLOCAT	DDATE	AGE	SPOUSE	FATHER	FBLOCAT	MOTHER	MFBLOCAT	BY	BURIAL	VET	SON	DAUG	BROTHER	SISTER
Petty, Marcia Elizabeth	Aug 20, 1991	Chattanooga, Tn	Edenolla, Ill.	Sep 12, 1912	78	W	Trout, Clement N.		Tison, Lula		Petty, William R. Jr. (Son); Carpenter, Opal - Roger; Green, Opal - Richard; Vera - Phagan, Clarence	Fairlawn - Decatur, Ill.					
Phagan, Fred Howard	Oct 24, 1976	Jeff City	Tn	Oct 20, 1917	59	Div	Phagan, F.H.		Gibbons, Thala A.		Community Chapel	Community Chapel					
Phagan, Ruth Caroline	Nov 21, 1954	Oklahoma		Feb 18, 1877	77	W	Miller, John		Smith, Mary		Stine, Luke & Ruth - Carpenter, Walter & Carl [Calif]	Mill Springs					
Phelps, Margaret Katherine	Jan 3, 1970	Dayton, Oh	Tn			Div	Spencer, Lib		Morgan, Nancy		Spencer, Fred - Eldridge, Julia	Mill Springs					
Phillips, Elizabeth Corbett	Apr 24, 1979	Jeff City	Tn	Jun 20, 1891	87	W	Bettis, Cas		Chaney, Amanda		Breeden, Mrs. Lewis - J.M.G.	Hebron					
Phillips, Lucille	Jul 11, 1999	Jeff City	Tn	Oct 26, 1928	60	Phillips, Dana	Brevett, S.		Terry, Mertie		Phillips, Dana	J.M.G.					
Phillip, William Luther	Mar 16, 1996	J.M.H.	Knox Co	Apr 11, 1902	83	S	Phillips, William Rufus		Diel, Rosa		Frazier, Jewell	Lynchard - Knoxville, Tn					
Phillips, Arvil	Jun 19, 1994	Jeff City	Scott Co, Tn	Dec 10, 1915	78	W	Phillips, Benjamin H.		Byrd, Burnette		Phillips, Arvil [Son]	White Chapel - Troy, Mich.	41-45			Dana-Walter	
Phillips, Bertie Mae	Feb 27, 2000	Knoxville, Tn	Tn	Jun 7, 1925	64	Phillips, Eunice J.	Adkins, Sherman		Lawson, Bertha		Husband	J.M.G.					
Phillips, Burnette	Jul 7, 1983	Jeff City	Nonna, Tn	Oct 27, 1896	96	W	Byrd, Oliver Perry		Hatfield, Manervia Elizabeth		Phillips, Arvil [Son]	J.M.G.		Walter-Dana-Eunice-John			Tellitha - Jernigan, Reba - Pollard, Janice
Phillips, Joseph Arthur	Deec 24, 1982	Jeff City	Tn	Nov 11, 1913	69	Ng	Owens, Orha				Phillips, Jean-Mrs. Grady	Jefferson Memorial					
Phillips, Ephraim	Oct 4, 1980	Rutledge, Tn	Tn	Oct 5, 1908	71	W	Phillips, Mount		Roach, Eliza		Phillips, Jean-Mrs. Grady	Jefferson Memorial					
Phillips, Grady		J.M.H.	Michigan	Oct 5, 1906		Clark, Jean	Phillips, W.E.										
Phillips, Gregory Vincent	Oct 16, 1987	J.M.H.	Michigan	Aug 28, 1944	43	Klug, Barbara J.	Phillips, Edmond		Rigrie, Helen		Phillips, Barbara - S.K.Schafer F.H. [E. Detroit, Mich.] - Whitehead, Mrs. Carroll [Dana]	White Chapel - Troy, Mich. veteran	veteran				
Phillips, Hazel Ada	Apr 6, 1986	Knox Co	Tn	Sept 21, 1915	70	W	Burchell, John		Mc Gill, Josie		Phillips, Mrs. Charles	French Broad					
Phillips, Jack D.	Oct 11, 1983	Jeff City	Tn	Oct 11, 1903		W	Phillips, Jack D.		Cates, Iva Mae	Tn	Phillips, John	Oakland					
Phillips, Jean Clark	Apr 18, 1995	Granger Co	Granger Co	Jul 29, 1910	84		Clark, Tom C.										
Phillips, Johnnie [F]	Jul 5, 1871	Cleveland St. Hospital	Tn	Sept 17, 1894	96	W			Mellicost, Mable		White, Georgia [Sister]	Jefferson Memorial Gardens				John Miller [In-Law] Phillips, John-Sim	
Phillips, Joseph Arthur	Apr 10, 1955	Jeff Co	Tn	Jun 9, 1890	64	Ng	Phillips, Aaron		Conway, Frances L.		Allen, Mary Nell [N. Royalton, OH] Phillips, Bobby Joe	Buffalo Grove					
Phillips, Pauline	Sep 1, 1965	Jeff Co	Tn	Jun 14, 1913	57	Henkle, Pauline	Williams, Roy B.		Williams, Bessie		Phillips, Bobby Joe	Buffalo Grove					
Phillips, Vernie Lou	May 27, 1953	Jeff Co	Tn	Sep 16, 1880	72	Ng	Williford, James				Phillips, Mrs. Charles	French Broad					
Phillips, Von Henry	Jan 25, 1952	Jeff Co	Tn	Dec 19, 1933	18	S	Phillips, John				Phillips, John	Tn					
Phillips, William Bruce	Jan 4, 1925	Granger Col, Tn [D]		9-9-9		Tn	Lacy, Eliza	Tn			Phillips, W.E.	Shilo					
Phillips, William Edgar	Feb 17, 1985	U.T.H.	Tn	Dec 27, 1886	98	Dev	Morgan, John		Morgan, Alice		Phillips, Sam	Shiloh - Granger Co					
Phillips, William John	Oct 12, 1955	Granger Co	Tn	Sep 18, 1928	27	Ng	Phillips, John		Cochram, Georgia		Phillips, Mrs. Francis Jones	Oakland - Granger Co					
Phipps, Lois Madeline	Jan 29, 2000	Dandridge, Tn	Ky	Jul 8, 1914	85	W	Phipps, John		Phipps, Melvin [Son]		Bethwoods - Morristown, Tn	Bethwoods - Morristown, Tn					
Pierce, Betty Sue	Jul 16, 1999	Talbott	Tn	May 18, 1938	61	W	Pierce, Frank	Tn	Pierce, Dora	Tn	Pierce, Frank	Pleasant View					
Pierce, Dora	Aug 26, 1970	Jeff Co	Tn	Oct 8, 1897	72	Pierce, Frank	Pratt, George W.		Jones, Cordelia		Pierce, Frank	Pleasant View - Hamblen Co.					
Pierce, Frank	May 10, 1974	Jeff Co	Tn	Jul 28, 1885	88	W	Pratt, James F.		Meadow, Nancy		Jernigan, Mrs. Glate	Pleasant View - Hamblen Co.					
Pierce, James	May 22, 1981	Jeff Co									Memphis F.H. [Memphis, Tn]						
Pierce, Thomas Jefferson	Dec 30, 1924	Tn			78-6-14	W					Senters, John M.	Pleasant View					
Pierce, Wiley Hampton	Nov 7, 1972	Jeff Co		Sep 13, 1928	44	Hampton, Lorena	Pierce, Patrick		Pratt, Dora		Pierce, Lorena - Williford, Frank	Newton - Granger Co					
Piles, Robert Lee	May 23, 2000	Knoxville, Tn	Tn	Sep 8, 1923	76	Browning, Laura					Phipps, Lora-na - Williford, Frank Wills	Asbury - Knoxville, Tn	unk				
Pilgrim, Raymond Richard Jr.	Oct 24, 1981	Knoxville, Tn	Tn	Nov 15, 1943	37	Owens, Joyce	Pilgrim, Raymond R. Sr.		Welch, Nola		Pilgrim, Mrs. Joyce Owens	Jefferson Memorial				Jernigan, Reba & Lloyd - Phillips, Tellitha - Pollard, Janice	

NAME	DDATE	DLOCAT	BLOCAT	BDATE	AGE	SPOUSE	FATHER	FELOCAT	MOTHER	MFELOCAT	BY	BURIAL	VET	SON	DAUG	BROTHER	SISTER
Pinkston, Harvey Marell	Oct 1, 1982	E.T.B.H.	Tn	Feb 10, 1925	57	Pinkston, Harvey M.	Pinkston, Cleveland		Lawson, Kate		Pinkston, Harvey M.	Jefferson Memorial					
Piper, Marie Babson	Dec 29, 1993	Knoxville, Tn	Bulls Gap, Tn	Oct 15, 1924	69		Obendorfer, Marianne		Brixton, Alice		Wills	Jefferson Memorial		Dennis-Larry [Step-Children] 6	Miller, Diane		
Piper, John T.	Jun 15, 1980	Jeff City Hodges Switch	Tn	Sep 20, 1927	52	W	Piper, Charles		Green, Ruby		Piper, Charles	J.M.G.					Hurley, Beulah - Beck, Pauline
Pirkey, John T.	May 14, 1940	Tn	Tn	Dec 25, 1856			Pirkey, Jacob	Tn	Lawless, Rebecca		Jefferson	Piedmont				Grover-Bill-Harold	
Pirkey, Ralf Edward	Feb 21, 1925	Tn		0-0-9			Pirkey, Robert	Tn	Pirkey, Enis	Tn	Pirkey, Robert						
Pitts, William Carl (Black)	May 20, 1983	B.C., Canada	Tn	Nov 28, 1941	41	W	Pitts, William Mc Kinley		Nance, Mary Ellis		Pitts, Mary Ella	Jefferson Memorial					
Poe, John A.	Nov 16, 1976	Pembroke Pines, Fla	Tn	Nov 10, 1976	65	Walters, Emma Louise	Poe, John E.		Erhart, Sarah		Poe, Mrs. John A.	Jefferson Memorial					
Pollard, Jessie	Sep 6, 1998	Talbott, Tn	Pa	Mar 29, 1916	82	Pollard, William Samuel [D]	Pollard, Bruce		Lewis, Willie G.		Metcalf, Sue [Daug]	Sunderland		Charles & Gertrude	Lehman, Shirley - Metcalf, Flora Sue & Roy	Smith, Lucy - Underwood, Flora - Dukes, Jean
Pollard, Phillip Houston	Feb [28], 1992	J.M.H.			67	Phillips, Janice	Pollard, Bruce		Kerr, Julia		Wills	Pleasant Ridge - Jeff Co	unk				
Pollard, Toye E. [F]	May 22, 1970	Jeff Co	Tn	Sep 1, 1879	90	W	Pollard, Hardin		Brixton, Mary Jane		Woods, Juanita	J.M.G.					
Pollard, William Henry	Apr 24, 1989	Knox Co	Tn	Apr 17, 1913		Ng	Pollard, William B.		Kerr, Julia		Pollard, Mrs. Rubye M.	Memorial Gardens					
Poore, Charlotte Ann	Jul 24, 1951	Jeff Co	Tn	Mar 24, 1951		W	Poore, Raymond Thomas		Brixton, Edith		Poore, R.F.	Friends					
Poore, Frances Caroline	Jun 30, 1984	E.T. Baptist	Tn	Sep 4, 1912	71	Poore, William G.	Shubert, Sarah		Shubert, Sarah		Stallings, Louise	Pollards - Sevier Co					
Poore, George Washington	Aug 11, 1982	Claiborne Co, Tn	Tn	Dec 8, 1915	66	Blalock, Mary	Poore, Frank		Lynch, Mary		Poore, Mrs. Mary - Tri-City F.H. (Benham, Ky)						
Poore, Hazel	Dec 31, 1975	J.M.H. [Res Sq]	Sc	Feb 16, 1910	65	Poore, Robert W.	Stayton, Lula		Stayton, Lula		Porter, Mrs. Walter	Fair Forest Baptist - Sc					
Poore, Hugh	Aug 17, 1931	Ky	Ky		73						Vesser, Will	West View					
Poore, Infant Male	June 15, 1955	Jeff Co	Jeff Co	Jun 15, 1955			Poore, Raymond		Brixton, Edith		Poore, Raymond	Friends Station					
Poore, Infant Male	Jun 20, 1946	Hamblen Co	Jeff Co	Jun 20, 1946			Poore, James Bruce	Tn	Roderick, Mary	Tn	Poore, J.B.	Paw Paw Hollow - Sevier Co					
Poore, Mary Ella	Mar 4, 1950	Jeff Co	Tn	Aug 31, 1909	40	Poore, James F.	Roderick, Fred J.		Poore, Cordia		Poore, James	Pollard - Kodak, Tn					
Poore, William Gray	Dec 18, 1989	J.M.H.	Jeff Co	May 26, 1903		W	Poore, Daniel L.		Bailey, Anna		Stallings, Louise	Memorial Gardens					
Porter, Alice Pearl	Nov 12, 1982	Cincinnati, Ohio	Nc		77	Ng	Porter, William		Davis, ---		Porter, I.M.	Memorial Gardens					
Porter, Mildred Florence [Negro]	Aug 28, 1974	Dayton, Ohio	Tn	May 12, 1949	25	Div	Hodge, Carter Sr.		Harris, Lydia Mae		Hodge, Lilia	Jefferson Memorial					
Posey, Gracie	May 17, 1983	Jeff Co	Ky	Sep 1, 1926	36	Ng	Riley, Roscoe		Minton, Bessie		Posey, Brower C.	New Bethel - Claiborne Co					
Potter, Addie C.	Mar 14, 1974	Jeff City	Tn	Jul 4, 1899	74	W	Hargus, Robert		Davis, Mary		Carson, Mrs. Lon	Jefferson Memorial					
Potts, Katherine	Jun 14, 1980	Va	Va		75-9-1	W	Richardson, Larry Langdon		Posey, Mary Elizabeth		Potts, Langdon-Richard	Greenwood - Knoxville, Tn	829				
Potts, Langdon R.	Jan 19, 1987	Jeff Co	Tn	Feb 28, 1938	58	Needham, Rebecca J.	Potts, Richard P.		Richardson, Margaret [Mother-in-Law]		Wills - Needham, (Mother-in-Law)			Langdon R, 3rd Michelle W - Richard Allen	Cameron, Janie	Richard Allen	
Poynter, Mary	Aug 4, 1977	Jeff Co	Va	Dec 12, 1977	68	Div	Richardson, L.L.		Potts, Mrs. R.P.		Barbourville City, Ky	J.M.G.					
Prater, Bonnie	May 5, 1988	J.M.H.	Tn		74-4-22	W	Phillips, Mary		Phillips, Mary		Potts, Mrs. R.P.	Barbourville City, Ky					
Prater, Carl Cosby	Dec 15, 1991	Akron, Ohio	Oct 24, 1963		28	Div	Prater, Henry Thomas		Adkins, Anna Mae		Prater, Henry T. [Father]	J.M.G.					
Prater, John Franklin	May 2, 1988	Jeff Co	Tn	Aug 14, 1878	89	W	Prater, Henry		Hatmaker, Elizabeth		Prater, Mrs. U.E.	West View					
Prater, Ulyss Everett	Nov 1, 1975	Jeff City	Tn	Oct 18, 1909	66	W	Prater, John F.		Reed, Cordelia		Prater, Mrs. U.E.	Jefferson Memorial					
Prater, Edith Mary	Jan 31, 1925				21-6-3	Prater, Lee W.	Helms, Henry B.	Tn	Tatts, Cleo	Tn	Prater, Lee W.	Shiloh					
Pratt, Hulbert Wade	Jan 14, 1991	Hamblen Co	Feb 26, 1910			Div	Pratt, George W.		Bates, Cordia		Collins, Marie [Daug]	Pleasant View					
Pratt, Martha	May 5, 1980	Knox Co	Tn	Aug 19, 1911		W	Bailey, Noah		Gilbert, Eliza		Pratt, Richard & John	Pleasant Grove					
Pratt, Mary Louise	Sep 10, 1980	Nc	Tn	Dec 2, 1921	58	Pratt, Joe	Huggins, Maggie		Huggins, Maggie		Oak Ridge - St. Paul, Nc						
Pratt, Maude	Jan 23, 1971	Tn	Tn				Horner, Neal		Whitehead, Alice		Humbard, Edna - Pratt, Joe	Friends Station					
Pratt, Richard Earl	Oct 30, 1989	Jeff Co		Mar 6, 1907	82	Berkman, James					Humbard, Mary Haggard - Pratt, Mrs. Mae	Piney					
Pratt, Willey [D]						Horner, Maude					Horner, Maude						

NAME	DATE	DLOCAT	DLOCAT	BDATE	AGE	SPOUSE	FATHER	FBLOCAT	MOTHER	MBLOCAT	BY	BURIAL	VET	SON	DAUG	BROTHER	SISTER
Pruitt, Roscoe	Mar 3, 1981	Ill.		May 16, 1900	80	Firello, Alma	Pruitt, George W.		Jones, Cordia		Pruitt, Bobby-Mrs.	Pleasant View					
Pruitt, Walter Sam	Nov 11, 1958	Jeff Co	Tn								Pruitt, Mrs. Hattie	Lyle - Jeff Co	WW 2				
Pruitt, Wiley B.	Jun 4, 1964	Jeff Co.	Tn	Jan 23, 1886	78	Lane, Hattie	Pruitt, Wiley B.		Homer, Maude		Pruitt, Mrs. Hattie	Friends Station					
Prescott, Marjorie Lee	Dec 9, 1976	Knoxville, Tn		Jan 19, 1974	1	S	Homer, Maude		Wanderholt, Susan		Pruitt, Maude Homer	Pleasant Grove					
Prescott, Victor Sr.	Dec 31, 1995	Jeff City		Nov 11, 1918	77		Prescott, Vincenzo		Gallo, Gaetano		Prescott, Victor Joseph Tn Veterans - Knoxville, Tn (Son - Fla.)		unk.	Eugene - Victor Jr.			
Prescott, Minnie Lorena	Mar 12, 1998	Jeff City		Feb 7, 1999	99		Datk, Albert Lee		Cannon, Ida Von		Pethel, Martha [Daug]	Floral Gardens - High Point, Nc		Gibbs M.-R.W. Jr.	Nees, Nancy		
Prescott, Robert Ward	Oct 11, 1980	Jackson Creek, Nc	Nc	Feb 7, 1899	89	Datk, Minnie	Prescott, Andrew Wesley		Harris, Nancy L.		Prescott, Minnie	Floral Gardens - High Pt, Nc					
Prescott, Agnes Helen	Jan 25, 1996	Jeff Co, Ky		Dec 5, 1977	78		Unk		Unk		Grech F.H. (Middlesboro, Ky)						
Price, Byrd	Oct 8, 1985	Hancock Co	Dec 20, 1902	92		No	Carpenter, Felix H.		Parker, Susie		Price, Ruby [Daug]	Hawkins Co, Tn					
Price, George Clinton	Jan 25, 1953	Jeff Co	Tn	Oct 4, 1889	63		Price, Hiram		Brooks, Alice		Price, L.W.	J.M.G.					
Price, Joyce Marie	Nov 18, 1997	Dandridge, Tn	Wv	Nov 6, 1927	70	Mc Dougal, Isaac Edward		Lowe, Edith Louise		Hustord	Cremated				Sam	
Price, Lillian Russell	Jan 16, 1983	Talbott, Tn	Indiana	Apr 2, 1901	82	W	Woodford, George		Harbaugh, Annie		Jefferson Memorial						
Price, Marvin Jackson Sr.	Jul 3, 1987	Sevier Co	Tn	Aug 9, 1896	86	Carpenter, Byrd		Morris, Martha		Price, Ruby [Daug]	J.M.G.					
Price, Ola	Aug 20, 1979	Knoxville, Tn	Mc Cracken Co, Ky	Apr 2, 1901	81	Price, William Lee		Brannan, Harrison		Lindsay, Margaret		Price, Clyde [Son]	Hillcrest				
Price, Paul M.	Mar 2, 1996	Jeff City		Feb 27, 1925	71	Elrod, Mary E.		Price, Paul M. Sr.		Wife	J.M.G.					
Price, Paul Minor Sr.	Jul 29, 1982	Knoxville, Tn	Co, Ky	Jan 17, 1894	88	Woodford, Lillian		Price, Benjamin		Bryant, Nellie		Wife	Jefferson Memorial		Lloyd Wayne-Michael L.		
Price, William Lee	Jul 19, 1958	Anderson Co	Sevier Co	Sep 9, 1896	61	Price, Ola		Price, Robert		Pector, Maggie		Price, Clyde	Hillcrest				
Pridgen, Jasper Lee	May 1, 1991	V.A. - Asheville, Nc	Nash Co, Nc	Oct 21, 1939	51	Ford, Barbara		Pridgen, William Henry		Braswell, Lonnie		Pridgen, Barbara	Hamblen Memorial				
Price, Dolly M.	Apr 7, 1998	Jeff City		Nov 21, 1913	84		Lewis, Thomas		Sawyer, Cora			Wallie-Hatcher - Egeria, W. Va	[In-Law] Smoothy, Charles				
Prince, George Ronald	Jan 5, 1953	Jeff City	Tn	Nov 23, 1953			Prince, George C. Jr.		Young, Barbara Jean		Prince, G.C. Jr.	West View					
Prince, Margaret Jane	Jun 2, 1991	Jeff City	Nc	Sep 7, 1947	64	Prince, E.A.		Harbaugh, Annie		Snyder, Nancy		Kerr, Tom	New Market				
Prince, Susan E.	May 24, 1957	Jeff Co	Nc	Jul 3, 1873	83	No	Craig, Elaine		Dobbins, Katherine		Prince, George & J.W.	West View					
Pritchard, Othelio Sidney (Bezk)	May 12, 1983	Knoxville, Tn	Ga	Jan 2, 1911	72	Pryor, Helen		Pritchard, John S. Sr.				Pritchard, Helen P.	Cremated				
Proffitt, Caleb Dominique	Nov 8, 1997	Jeff City	Morristown, Tn	Sep 9, 1997	1m		Blanchard, Chris		Proffitt, Jennie Lynn		Mother - Proffitt, James & Christine - Chamberlain, Rick & Kathy (G-Parents) - Proffitt, Robbie & Sonja [Uncle & Aunt]	Bexter				2592	
Proffitt, Charles Clifford	Feb 24, 1984	U.T.H.	Tn	Apr 8, 1911	72	Horner, Lillian		Proffitt, Samuel		Strange, Sarah		Proffitt, Mrs. Lillian-Eddy - Watson, Joyce	Lebanon [Greenbrier]					
Proffitt, James H.	Feb 15, 1992	Knoxville, Tn	Jeff Co	May 17, 1906	85	Silver, Bonnie		Proffitt, Samuel		Strange, Sara		Wife	J.M.G.					
Proffitt, John Wesley	Jan 31, 2000	Strawberry Plains	Tn	Jul 3, 1935	64	Kirkwood, Ive Sue		Proffitt, James Henderson		Silver, Bonnie		Wife	J.M.G.	unk	Johnson, Angela & Norman - Moore, Bucky & Doug		
Proffitt, Laura Catherine	Jul 31, 1983	Jeff Co	Tn	Aug 19, 1994	58	S	Proffitt, S.E.		Smallwood, Sarah		Proffitt, Jennie Clifford - Cecil - Hinchey, Mrs. [Children]	Proffitt - Jeff Co					
Proffitt, Samuel W.	Dec 15, 1957	Jeff Co	Tn	Sep 15, 1881	86	W	Proffitt, James		Smallwood, Sarah		Proffitt, Jim - Hinchey, Mrs. Marshall	Proffitt - Jeff Co					
Proffitt, Sarah S.	Feb 3, 1955	Jeff Co	Tn	Oct 18, 1883	71	Proffitt, S.W.		Strange, W.S.		Edmonds, Edith		Proffitt, Cecil & Clifford	Proffitt - Jeff Co					
Province, Race Cecil	May 11, 2000	White Pine, Tn	Tn	Mar 15, 1926	74	Lane, Mary		Province, Robert Ray		Edmonds, Edith		Province, Roy [Brother]	Trentville - Strawberry Plains, Tn					
Puckett, Barbara Lou	Dec 6, 1944	Jeff Co	Tn	Apr 12, 1944			Puckett, G. Clifford		Coles, Mary Louise		Puckett, G.C.	Piedmont		[Step] Jennigan, Doug	Skidavick, Rose [Delaware] Frsselia, Mae [NJ]	5	Lamberton, Ruth - Mc Carter, Mary

NAME	DDATE	DLOCAT	BLOCAT	BDATE	AGE	SPOUSE	FATHER	F/B LOCAT	MOTHER	M/F LOCAT	BY	BURIAL	VET	SON	DAUG	BROTHER	SISTER
Puckett, Della Mae	Feb 19, 1998	Morristown, Tn	New Market, Tn	May 4, 1910	87	Northern, Henry	Dial, Myrtle				Kilwell, Frances [Daug]	Piedmont		Charles-Wynona Jim-Gene [Mch]	Purkey, Evelyn		
Puckett, Ella Ruth	Apr 12, 1996	Jeff City	Tn	Oct 11, 1931	54	Puckett, William A. [Chuck]	Narron, Mack		Spoone, Martha		Puckett, William A.	Everlasting Life - J.M.G.					
Puckett, Gordon Clifford	Nov 6, 1971	Hamblen Co	Tn	Oct 10, 1903	68	Northern, Della	Uckett, Arthur		Betts, Minnie	Tn	Puckett, Mrs. G.C.	Piedmont					
Puckett, Infant Female	Feb 21, 1948	Jeff Co		Feb 21, 1948			Puckett, G. Clifford	Tn	Northern, Della	Tn	Puckett, Rev. G.C.	Piedmont					
Puckett, Patricia Sue	Oct 12, 1944	Jeff Co		Apr 12, 1944			Puckett, G. Clifford	Tn	Northern, Della	Tn	Puckett, G.C.	Piedmont					
Purdue, James Orville	Feb 8, 1984	Illinois	Illinois	Feb 3, 1884	97	Hay, Vera [D]	Purdue, Joseph		Myers, Martha		Koonon, Virginia & Ray Purdue, William J.	County Line - Keil, Ind.					
Purkey, Vera	Feb 9, 1966	Jeff Co	Illinois	Jan 11, 1889	76	Ng	Hay, W.W.		Pursuit, Amanda		Koonon, Ray - Purdue, J.O.	County Line - Illinois					
Purkey, Adam Jr.	Sep 8, 1967	N	Tn	Jan 28, 1928	39	Ng	Purkey, Robert		Palmer, Eva		Purkey, Elizabeth	West View					
Purkey, Allin	Aug 26, 1989	Knoxville, Tn	Lee Co, Va	Mar 22, 1911	78		Gann, Elizabeth		Brooks, Elizabeth		Ballard, Coleen-Tom	J.M.G.					
Purkey, Amanda West	Sep 18, 1948	New Market	Jeff Co	Jan 9, 1886	62-8-8	Ng	Cato, Jessie	Tn	Odom, Martha	Tn		Cato - Jeff Co					
Purkey, Amon	May 7, 1991	J.M.H.	Tn	Sep 26, 1911	79	W	Purkey, Sam		Purkey, Dora	Tn	Ballard, Colleen [Daug]	J.M.G.					
Purkey, Belle L.	Mar 20, 1938		Hancock Co		100-1-1-	W						Swans Creek Baptist					
Purkey, Betty E.	Feb 16, 1941	Bean Station				W			Ledger, Sallie	Tn	Purkey, John [Son]						
Purkey, Charles Clyde	Feb 1, 1854	Hamblen Co	Tn	Jan 30, 1980	64	Ng	Purkey, John F.		Shorter, Alice		Purkey, Brown-Eugene-E.C.[Children]	Sunderland					
Purkey, Charles William	Jul 3, 1973	Tn	Tn	Jul 28, 1916	57	Ng			Walker, Ethel		Purkey, Mrs. Ruby L. Childress, Sharon [Daug]	West View	WW2				
Purkey, Ellen Elizabeth	Oct 8, 1999	Jeff City	Jeff City	Nov 8, 1932	66	W	Gann, John		Mc Carter, Susan		Stout, Mrs. Myrtle [Daug]	West View		Richard-John			
Purkey, Ena	Jan 30, 1978	Jeff Co	Tn	Jul 11, 1887	90	W	Palmer, Benjamin					West View					
Purkey, George William	Jun 11, 1976	Jeff Co	Tn	Apr 28, 1903	73	Varner, Hazel			Quisenberry		Quisenberry, Margaret Rachel	Jefferson Memorial					
Purkey, Hazel	Apr 9, 1980	Jeff City	Tn	Apr 10, 1914	65	Purkey, George W. [D]	Varner, Lum		Denham, Edith		Carmichael, Ethel	Jefferson Memorial					
Purkey, Ida Mae	Nov 2, 1989	Hamblen Co	Va	Dec 12, 1899	79	W	Musser, Walter		Quiten, Emma		Purkey, E.C.-R.E.Cog A.W.B.	Sunderland					
Purkey, James Edward	Aug 1, 1948	Jeff Co	Va	Aug 1, 1948		W	Purkey, Robert	Tn	Barbee, Katherine	Tn	Purkey, Robert	Sunderland					
Purkey, John Jake	Mar 31, 1961	J.M.H.	Jeff Co	Dec 31, 1910	60	Murray, Dorothy			Palmer, Ennis Elizabeth		Purkey, Dorothy	Mill Springs					
Purkey, Kathleen	May 18, 1981	Jeff City	Tn	Jul 18, 1913	17	S	Preley, R.J.	Tn	Palmer, Emily	Tn	Purkey, R.J.	West View					
Purkey, Larry Richard	Aug 24, 1966	Jeff Co	Tn	Aug 13, 1948	17	S	Purkey, Everett Sr.		Royston, Viola		Purkey, Everett	Sunderland		Frank-Jim-Bud-Bill [Al]			Smith, Mary Evelyn
Purkey, Margaret Rachel	Feb 3, 1984	Jeff Co	Va	Nov 4, 1884	79	W	Quisenberry, -				Carmichael, Mrs. Harry Hurst, Raymond- Taylor, Anna Lee- Cowan, Margaret- Purkey, Frank-Charlie- Robert	West View					
Purkey, Mattie Lee	May 29, 1934	Straw Plains	Tn	Jul 26, 1923	11	W	Purkey, Sam				Purkey, Sam	West View					
Purkey, Opal	Oct 19, 1948	Jeff City	Tn	May 14, 1922	26	Purkey, Bill	Lowery, Omer	Tn		Tn	Lowery, Winifred & Bill	West View					
Purkey, Robert Jackson	Dec 31, 1951	Tn	Tn	Jan 18, 1889	62	Ng	Purkey, George		Greene, Nancy C.		Anderson, Pearl - Jallie- Bill	West View					
Purkey, William A.	Dec 22, 1959	Jeff City	Tn	Aug 25, 1923	87	W	Purkey, George W.		Greene, Nancy		Barnes, Laura	West View					
Pursuit, Iris Orlena	Jul 11, 1989	Knoxville, Tn	Tn	Mar 29, 1918	71	Godwin, Walter C.			Beals, Alpha		Pursuit, John W.	West View					
Pursuit, John Wilbur	Jul 7, 2000	Knoxville, Tn	Tn	May 4, 1913	86	W	Pursuit, John Wilbur [Rev.] Shell, Patricia				Wills	West View					
Quarles, Billy John [M]	Aug 9, 1983	J.M.H.	Tn	Jul 16, 1936	47	Charles, Rachel			Solomon, Lettie		Quarles, Keith	Jefferson Memorial					
Quarles, Cora	Mar 6, 1974	Knoxville, Tn	Tn	Jun 13, 1899	74	Cato, Rachel Camellia Charles, James C. Sr.	Walker, Thomas		Lines, Nancy		Quarles, Rachel C.	Jefferson Memorial					
Quarles, Foye Leonard	Feb 26, 1999	Knoxville, Tn	Talbott, Tn	Apr 6, 1917	81		Quarles, Frank		Hamilton, Anna		Quarles, Doug & Maxine [Son]	J.M.G.			Quarles, Evelyn	Gerald	Myers, Georgia & Bill - Ellis, Carolyn & John - Hall??, Wylene & Maurice

NAME	DATE	DLOCAT	BLOCAT	BDATE	AGE	SPOUSE	FATHER	FBLOCAT	MOTHER	MFBLOCAT	BY	BURIAL	VET	SON	DAUG	BROTHER	SISTER
Quarles, Ida Irene	Feb 3, 1942	Talbott	Claiborne Co.	Jul 21, 1871	70+ 12	W	Brown, Alford		Lindywood, Ellen	Va	Quarles, Brown [Son]	Talbott					
Quarles, James Crawford	Mar 22, 1974	Jeff City	Tn	Oct 1, 1895	78	W	Quarles, William A.		Brown, Ida Irene		Quarles, Keith [Son]	Jefferson Memorial	WW 1				Fells, Ruth - [In-Law] Patterson, Beulah
Quarles, James Crawford 3rd	Dec 26, 2000	Mt. Horne, Tn		Mar 8, 1949	51	Div	Quarles, James C. 2nd		Long, Mary M.		Father	J.M.G.	unk				
Quarles, James Glenn	Nov 5, 1977	Jeff Co	Tn	Sep 15, 1925	52	Div	Quarles, Frank		Hamilton, Anna		Quarles, Johnathan	Jefferson Memorial					
Quarles, Jonathan Frank	Jan 3, 1979	Knoxville, Tn	Tn	Jul 25, 1955	23	S	Quarles, Glenn		Blackburn, Barbara		Quarles, Barbara	Jefferson Memorial					
Quarles, Jonathan Wesley	Oct 8, 1949	Jeff Co	Jeff Co	Jun 25, 1877	72	Ng	Quarles, Wesley T.		Sunderland, Martha		James, Mrs. C.T. - Burnett, Mrs., Mrs.	Sunderland					
Quarles, Lettie Myrtle	Mar 18, 1984	J.M.H.	Tn	Nov 29, 1896	87	Quarles, Ralph H. [D] Ng	Sickmon, John Wesley		Harrison, Rhoda R.		Quarles, Chell	Mt. Pleasant					
Quarles, Martha L.	Jan 27, 1927		Tn			Ng	Sunderland, Unk				Father	Sunderland					
Quarles, Ralph H.	Aug 31, 1983	Jeff Co	Tn	Oct 26, 1903	59	Solomon, Lettie	Quarles, Silby		Brown, Ida		Quarles, Lettie - Hannister, Mrs. - Hal	Mt. Pleasant					
Quarles, Trophia W.	Oct 19, 1983	Jeff Co	Tn	Oct 6, 1982	81	W	Watkins, Isaac		Carter, Nancy		Quarles, Watkins	Mt. Pleasant					
Quarles, W.J.	Jul 6, 1939	Talbott	Tn	Jul 31, 1866	72	Ng	Quarles, W.J.	Tn	Line 7, Margaret	Tn	Frank-Dock-Ralph-Floyd-Ellis & ?? [Sons]	Mt. Pleasant					
Quarles, William Alfred	Aug 21, 1984	J.M.H.	Tn	Mar 5, 1918	66	Patterson, Willie Katz	Quarles, William		Brown, Ida		Quarles, Mrs. Willie K.	Jefferson Memorial	WW 2				
Quarles, Willie Kate	Mar 10, 1987	Knoxville, Tn	Sevier Co	Nov 7, 1920	78	Ng	Patterson, Leonard		Johnson, Josephine		Smith, Jay & Rick [Daug]	J.M.G.			Woods, Gay & Ron		
Quarles, Willie Mae	Aug 2, 1987	Jeff Co	Tn	Apr 13, 1914	73	Quarles, Foye			Henry, Adis		Quarles, Foye & Doug	J.M.G.					
Quillen, Walton W.	Dec 2, 1969	Jeff Co	Tn	Mar 25, 1904	65	Ng	Quillen, P.R.		Harmon, Nola		Quillen, Virginia Moser	West View					
Quillams, Jimmy Maria [M]	Apr 22, 1981	Johnson City, Tn	Tn	Nov 12, 1949	31	Etherton, Nancy					Quillams, Nancy (Wife) Don (Brother)	Straw Plains					
Quinton, Helen Katherine	Feb 11, 1955	Knox Co	Tn	Jul 5, 1917	37	Ng	Helm, William S.		Alexander, Minnie M.		Quinton, Paul	West View					
Quinton, Crather E. [M]	Oct 26, 1983	Jeff Co	Tn	Jan 19, 1904	59	W	Quinton, John		Byrd, Laura		Quinton, Mrs. Emma - Harris, Mrs. Eva - Quinton, R.E.	Economy					
Quisenberry, George	Jun 12, 1936	Jeff City	Tn	Sep 16, 1886	45	Ng		Tn	Parsons, Fannie	Tn	Quisenberry, Annice	West View					
Quisenberry, Addie	Apr 14, 1932	Morristown, Tn									Ely, Lillian L. [W]	West View					
Rackard, Albert	May 16, 1999	Knoxville, Tn	Tn	Nov 2, 1916	82	Ng	Rackard, James		Henry, Laura		Phillips, Kin (Friend)	West View					
Rackard, Lucille	Aug 15, 1987	Harriman, Tn	Tn	Sep 1, 1917	69	W	Frese, Archie		Shaffer, Fannie		Lawson, Ann	Belch					
Rackard, Robert Elmer	Feb 23, 1979	Knoxville, Tn	Tn	Dec 27, 1915	63	Frese, Lucille	Rackard, Allen		Cox, Mae		Frese, Lucille - Rackard, Donald-Robert E.	Belch					
Radcliff, Joseph Glenn	Apr 8, 1987	Lynchburg, Va	St. Charles, Missouri	Nov 5, 1956	30	Hewely, Sarah Elaine	Radcliff, William		Iola		Radcliff, Elaine ? [Lynchburg, Va]	J.M.G.					
Rader, Nancy Dianne	Oct 6, 1952	Jeff Co	Tn			Ng	Rader, John	Tn	Moore, ---	Tn	Rader, John	Hebron					
Rader, T.D.	Feb 11, 1932	New Market	Tn	Jun 19, 1879	53	Ng	Crouch, A.		Wilson, Mary		New Market	New Market					
Raeffer, Charles Wilson	Jul 29, 1998	Jeff C	Texas	Jun 1, 1935	63	Allen, Ruby J.	Raeffer, Haworth		Simmons, Mary		Raeffer, Ruby	Wesleys Chapel					
Raines, Ben L.	Nov 21, 1966	J.M.H.	Tn	Jan 1, 1903	63	S	Raines, Larkin				Raines, LH-George-Earl	Pleasant View					
Raines, James Horace	Dec 22, 1984	Jeff Co	Tn	Feb 25, 1912	72	Shultz, Mattie Kate	Raines, William		Buchanan, Florence		Raines, Mrs. James H.	Garden Of Gethsemane - J.M.G.					
Raines, William Monroe	Feb 28, 1945	Jeff Co	Jeff Co	Feb 28, 1945			Raines, William	Tn	Raines, Florence		Raines, J.H.	Pleasant View					
Rains, John Jackson	Sep 23, 1993	Knoxville, Tn	Fentress Co., Tn	Feb 9, 1930	63	Whitlow, Joan	Rains, James G.		York, Lucy		Wife	Wells River - Jamestown, Tn	48-52		Muncy, Denise - Myers, Jacquelyn - Rains, Darlene	William-Perry	Maxine - Williams, Christine - Holt, Colene - Hinds, Jewelene - Kelley, Arlene
Rainwater, Ann	May 22, 1991	F.S.H.	Tn	Aug 6, 1936	64	Rainwater, Charles O. Sr.	Barker, Henry		Dykes, Lucille		Rainwater, Charles O. Sr.	J.M.G.					
Rainwater, Ann	Mar 25, 1960	Michigan		Mar 20, 1898	63	Rainwater, Floyd	Perrott, George		Denton, Iona								
Rainwater, Arlie Pencilla			Tn								Hurst - Smith - Barbee Mayo - Stevens	Presley - Dandridge					

NAME	DDATE	BLOCAT	BLOCAT	BDATE	AGE	SPOUSE	FATHER	FRLOCAT	MOTHER	MFRLOCAT	BY	BURIAL	VET	SON	DAUG	BROTHER	SISTER
Rainwater, Charles O. Sr.	Dec 2, 1998	Dandridge, Tn	Dandridge, Tn	Sep 30, 1920	78	Maples, Esther Ruth	Rainwater, Chester S. Sr.		Hoskins, Sarah		Wife	J.M.G.	42-45	Charles O. Jr.	Hayes (Lou)ann	Chester S.Jr	
Raney, Willa Drinnen	Sep 21, 1987	Tn	Tn	Dec 23, 1929	57	Lawrence, Martha	Buncher, Sarah		Buncher, Sarah		Wife	J.M.G.	51-57				
Raney, Lester W. [M]	Sep 19, 1992	Petersburg, Ky	Petersburg, Ky	Jan 14, 1927		W	Brady, Vincent L.		Sutton, Thelma		Norton - Grainger Co	unk					
Ramsey, Betty Ann	Dec 1, 1995	Knoxville, Tn	Cocke Co	Sep 3, 1942	53	Johnson, Jimmy	Allison, William D.		Allison, Charles		Husband	Indian Ridge					Lindsey, Carolyn - Rice, Linda - Johnson, Sandra - Allison, Cora Ann
Ramsey, Beverly J. Sr [M]	Oct 18, 1973	Jefferson	Tn	Jan 20, 1892	81	Leedy, Magdie Ramsey, Beverley J. Sr. [D]	Wells, Rhoda		Hudson, Charlie		Indian Ridge	Jefferson Memorial			Whitred-Clarence-William Dennis	
Ramsey, Magdie	Oct 18, 1973	Jeff City	Tn	Sep 1, 1887	76		Leedy, Beverley J. Sr. [D]		Ramsey, James C.		Ramsey, B.J. Jr.	Jefferson Memorial					
Rankin, Ada	Mar 19, 1992	Tn	Tn		76-0 15	S	Portsey, Alpha		Portsey, Alpha		Ramsey, B.J. Jr.	Lebanon					
Rankin, Anna Pearl	May 30, 1976	Maryville, Tn	Tn	Dec 22, 1891	84	S	Rankin, Lon		Armstrong, Phebi		Newman, Nell	Hebron					
Rankin, Arthur Tappin	Jan 11, 1947	Jeff Co	Jeff Co	Oct 22, 1889	77-7-19	W	Rankin, John Gass	Tn	Looney, Josephine		Rankin, R.W.	Lebanon - Mt. Horeb					
Rankin, Benjamin C.	Apr 21, 1928	Jeff Co			87-4-2	Ng	Rankin, Patrick	Tn	Lyle, Adrah	Tn	Lebanon - Mt. Horeb	Mt. Horeb					
Rankin, Courtland T.	May 5, 1956	Knox Co	Tn	May 25, 1871	84	Div			Lockard, Eliza Jane	Tn	Rankin, H.A.	Mt. Horeb					
Rankin, Edward Carroll	Jan 15, 1993	Jeff City	Tn	Feb 7, 1897	95		Daniels, Hubert				Rankin, J.R & C.T. Jr.	West View			[Nieces] Beck, Kathryn - Murphy, Betty - Carpenter, Mary - Bales, Sara	
Rankin, Edwin Mack	Sep 24, 1985	V.A. - Mt. Home	Tn	Feb 7, 1897	88	W			Looney, Josephine		Sawyer, Thomas [Nephew]	Hebron					
Rankin, Elizabeth G. (Dixie)	Aug 11, 1986	J.M.H.	Tn	Jul 18, 1902	84	W			Cox, Dale		Jefferson Memorial	Jefferson Memorial	WW 1				
Rankin, Elnora	Jul 23, 1982	Knoxville, Tn	Knox Co	Feb 21, 1904	68	Daniels, Hubert	Lytle, Herbie		Miller, Willie Mae		Lebanon Presby.	Cremated					
Rankin, Emma Carroll	Jan 1, 1948	Jeff City	Tn	Jun 5, 1863	84	Newman, Andrew		Tn	Lytle, Herbie	Tn	Husband	Mt. Horeb					
Rankin, Ethel Pearl	Apr 18, 1976	Jeff Co	Tn	Jun 18, 1902	73	Rankin, Carroll	Brackhian, Kathryn Emma		Rankin, H.A.		Rankin, H.A.	Mt. Horeb					
Rankin, Ethle Mae	Jul 7, 1998	Knoxville, Tn	Jeff City	Dec 12, 1928	69	Rankin, C.T. Sr.	Dyer, E.		Rankin, Carroll		Rankin, Carroll	Hebron					
Rankin, Fannie Davis	Apr 16, 1947	Jeff Co	Jeff Co	Oct 17, 1871	75-6	Rankin, Lee W.	Dixon, James		Beeler, (Jan [Niece]		Hebron	West View					
Rankin, Florence C.	Feb 6, 1931	Delaque, Cal.	Tn	Jul 31, 1859	29	W	Coldwell, Anderson		Rankin, Martha Jane	Tn	Rankin, Lee W. - Brackhian, Kathryn	Hebron					
Rankin, Grace Ward	Apr 16, 1981	Jeff City	Tn	Feb 18, 1891	90	W	Unk				Thomas, Mrs. Wanda R.	Lebanon					
Rankin, Isaac Lafayette	Feb 21, 1983	Jeff Co	Tn	Nov 18, 1906	76	Ng	Perrott, Myra Jane		Ward, Zenia		Rankin, Mrs. J.B.	Jefferson Memorial					
Rankin, J.A.	Jun 10, 1934	Jeff Co	Tn	Mar 18, 1852	82	W	Rankin, James	Tn	Perrott, Myra Jane	Tn	Rankin, Mrs. J.J.	Mt. Horeb					
Rankin, Katherine	Mar 21, 1930	Jeff Co	Tn	May 12, 1838	92	W	Rankin, James	Tn	Newman, Julia	Tn	Rankin, L.S.	Mt. Horeb					
Rankin, Lea Wilson	Mar 27, 1953	Jeff Co	Tn	Jul 20, 1880	72	W	Rankin, Joseph A.		Perrott, Myra Jane		Rankin, J.R. - Trentham, S.O. (Abilene, Tx)	Hebron					
Rankin, Lon Smith	Apr 4, 1942	Jeff Co	Tn		80-7-8	W	Rankin, John Mack	Tn	Rankin, Rachiel C.	Tn	Rankin, Carroll & Mack	Hebron					
Rankin, Lula Bell	Apr 4, 1980	Jeff City	Tn	Oct 16, 1891	88	Rankin, C.T. [D]	Young, Wesley		Cheverger, Elizabeth		Rankin, Dan-Ethelman	West View					
Rankin, Mabel	Oct 10, 1935	Tn	Tn	Aug 18, 1877	58	Rankin, John	Garber, John	Tn	Painter, Martha		Rankin, John	Mt. Horeb					
Rankin, Mark Roy	Jun 2, 1948	Jeff Co	Tn	Sep 1, 1875	72-9-1	Ng	Rankin, John F.	Tn	Williams, Martha Jane	Tn	Rankin, Mrs. Roy	Hebron					
Rankin, Martha J.	Feb 27, 1925		Tn		77-5 26	W	Williams, Alexander		Rhed, Sarah	Tn	Rankin, L022	Hebron					
Rankin, Mary Catherine	Feb 15, 1946	Granger Co	Tn	Jan 5, 1867	78	Rankin, William Edgar (Age-79)	Nice, David	Tn	Hooker, Eliza	Tn	Parker, Elsie - Hine, George	Shiloh					
Rankin, Matilda Josephine	Jan 31, 1940	Jeff Co	Tn	Dec 31, 1860	79	Ng	Looney, Carroll	Tn	Looney, Rachel	Tn	Children & Mack	Hebron					
Rankin, Nellie	Jan 31, 1971	Jeff Co	Tn	Jun 16, 1877	93	W	Blackburn, William W.		Miller, Harriet R.		Blackburn, Harriet	Hebron					
Rankin, Nora Maples	Dec 5, 1925		Tn		47-1-22	Div	Maples, D.C.	Tn	Brown, Martha	Tn	Butler, D.L.	West View					

NAME	DDATE	DLOCAT	BLOCAT	BDATE	AGE	SPOUSE	FATHER	F/B LOCAT	MOTHER	M/F LOCAT	BY	BURIAL	VET	SON	DAUG	BROTHER	SISTER
Rankin, Pearl	Jan 2, 1979	At Home	Tn	Jun 22, 1900	78	Temple, Frank	Williams, Jesse		Carroll, Emma		Rankin, Mack [Jeff City]	Jefferson Memorial					
Rankin, Ruby Killiah	Oct 3 1941	Jeff Co	Tn	Nov 27, 1876	57	S Rankin, A.T.			Wisdom, Florence	Jeff Co	Rankin, H.A. [Brother]	Mt. Horeb					
Rankin, Virginia ZiAde	Apr 25 1934	Mt. Horeb	Tn								Rankin, H.A. [Brother] Rankin, A.T.	Mt. Horeb					
Rankin, Walter Edgar	Dec 29, 1947	Grainger Co	Jeff Co	Sep 15, 1866	W	Rankin, J.D.		Tn	Kinder, --	Tn	Smith, Mrs. A.P. Cruson(berry, D. [G-Child]	Shiloh					
Rann, Georgia James Rush [F]	Mar 28, 1972	Knoxville, Tn	Iowa	Sep 29, 1915	56	W	James, Jesse		Rush, Mattie		Cross, Katherine - Shaffer, Daisy	Shiloh					
Rauch, Alice	Feb 13, 1969	Knox Co	Tn	Dec 10, 1891	W	Rauch, Sam P. [B]	Gass, William		Betts, Sara Luticia		Northern, Jane Ruth	West View					
Rauch, Joan J.	Jul 10, 2000	Morristown, Tn	Ny	Feb 17, 1931	69	Rauch, George	Johannsen, George O.				Husband	Cremated					
Ray, John	Nov 14, 1931	Grainger Co	Tn	May 13, 1887	44	Ng	Ray, W.M.		Winkel, Barbara	Ky	Ray, Delbert & James	Indian Ridge					
Ray, Ounie Kathleen	Nov 29, 1944	Knox Co	Grainger Co	Jun 11, 1917	27	Ng	Moyers, Sam P.	Tn	Phipe, Rachel	Tn	Moyers, Everett & Ruth	Shiloh - Grainger Co					
Reagan, Bessie	Aug 1, 1952	Jeff Co	Tn	Jun 14, 1923	29	Ng	Huskey, William		Owens, Ova		Reagan, Earl	Flat Gap					
Reagan, Danny Ray	Nov 19, 1975	Knoxville, Tn	Tn	Jan 4, 1957	18	S	Reagan, Carl C.		Bolden, Ada		Taylor, Mrs. John - Reagan, Carl C.	Shiloh - Grainger Co					
Reagan, Lucille	Dec 7, 1983	U.T.H.	Tn	Jan 8, 1919	64	Reagan, Richard M.	Idol, Henry		Williams, Faye		Reagan, Richard M.	Hamblen Memorial			Rauch, Mary - Jefferson, Mary - Gilliam, Hazel		
Reagan, Virginia Katherine	Feb 23, 1986	Knoxville, Tn	Sevier Co. Tn	May 3, 1923	72		Heston, William		McCrillis, Lou		Jones, Evelyn [Daug]	Wesleys Chapel					
Reagan, Oliver Christeen	Apr 25, 1979	Knoxville, Tn	Sevier Co. Tn	Sep 11, 1950	27	Jones, Carolyn	Heston, Katherine		Reagan, Katherine		Reagan, K.W.	Carter					
Rickard, Willie Robert	Aug 13, 1925	Knoxville, Tn	Tn	Sep 11, 1950	99-5	Ng	Rickard, John	Sc	Pollard, Tom	Tn	Carter	West View					
Rector, Ellis	Apr 6 1947	Sevier Co	Tn	Aug 11, 1890	56-7-25	Ng	Shrader, Elizabeth	Tn	Rector, J.R.			West View					
Rector, James Robert	Aug 1, 1950	Greene Co. Tn	Tn	Sep 28, 1883	66	W	Kaiser, Dolly		Myers, Mrs. Osa		Rector, J.R.	West View					
Rector, Mattie Blanchaine	Nov 6, 1925	Tn	Tn			S	Rector, J.R.	Tn	Fox, Ella	Tn	West View						
Redding, Elizabeth Ann	Mar 22, 1999	Knoxville, Tn	Jeff Co	Sep 16, 1938	60	S	Elmore, Jessie		Whitehead, Gary Lynn [Son]		Redding, Elizabeth - [Son]	J.M.G.		Whitehead, Steve-Darryll	Whitehead, Angella	Cecil	Jones, Juanita
Redding, John Lewis	Jan 9, 1989	Jeff City	Versailles, Ky	Jul 23, 1902	86	Redding, Gwelyn	Baker, Matilda		V.A. - Warner, Angela		J.M.G.					
Reece, Clarence Gwendolyn	Jul 8, 1980	Jeff City	Tn	May 20, 1926	54	Lyle, Mary Ruth	Reece, John C.		Kerr, Vola	Tn	Reece, Mary Ruth	Jefferson Memorial	WW 2				
Reed, Alfred [Col]	Feb 6, 1940	New Market	Tn	Jun 26, 1883	S	Reed, Powell	Va	Mills, Ellen	Tn	Branchton, Mary [New Market] - Govt.	New Market	WW 2				
Reed, Joseph Alexandra	Dec 16, 1954	Greenville, Tn	Tn	Mar 17, 1869	75	W	Reed, Daniel		Harman, Sarah		Fairmont - Denver, Kirby, Dorothy Colo.	Fairmont - Denver, Colo.					
Reed, Samuel Dick	Dec 2, 1967	Jeff Co	Tn	Dec 23, 1900	66	S	Reed, Charlie		Swann, Jessie		West, Mrs. C.G. - Trasiarty, Mrs.	West View Colored					
Reedy, Kate	Jan 20, 1926	Tn	Tn		41-10-22	Reedy, Ng	Randolph, Isham	Tn	Beatty, J.J.		Evergreen - Rutherford Co						
Reed, Sarah Evelyn	Nov 29, 1984	Jeff Co	Tn	Nov 27, 1904	80	S	Reed, Ralph		Conant, Sarah		Reed, Ralph	Highland Memorial - Hawkins Co					
Reese, J. Paul	Dec 4, 1952	Jeff Co	Nc	Aug. 16, --	44	Div					Thornton, Mrs. John - Reed, Dor - Collins, Harned	Jarnigan					
Reese, John Clarence	Aug 17, 1989	Tn	May 25, 1904	65	Stranger, Jo Ann [Div]	Reese, John		Chambers, Cora		Rogers, Mrs. Frances Reese	New Market						
Reese, Jollis Louise	Jan 21, 1945	Jeff Co	Tn		S	Reese, James Hugh	Tn	Gass, Francis	Tn	Reece, Ben J.	Jarnigan						
Reese, Lou Ella Hunter	Jan 17, 1942	Hamblen Co	Mar 16, 1882	60	Reece, Ben J.	Sloan, Joe	Tn	Carter, Katheryn	Tn	Reece, Ben J.	Hills Union						
Reese, Walter	Jul 17, 1957	Jeff Co	Tn	Jul 23, 1883	73	Ng	Reese, Randall		Kelner, Matilda		Reese, Mae & Children	West Market					
Reese, Tinie Smith	Jan 22, 1948	Greene Co. Tn	Ng	Nov 20, 1882	55-2-2	Ng	Reese, J.S.		Burgner, Lucia M.	Tn	Reese, T.S. Jr.	Pleasant Hill					
Reese, Max Bell	Oct 5, 1939	Morristown, Tn	W	May 14, 1923	66		Oliver, Thomas		Shipley, Nellie		Colton, Patricia [Daug]	Cremated					
Reichard, Ernest Louis	Feb 7, 1993	Jeff City	Philadelphia, Pa	May 13, 1923	69		Reichard, George Phillip		Kurtz, Emily Sophie		Winch, Marty [Step-Daug] [Ohio]	Buffalo Grove		[Step] 4	[Step] 3	George	

NAME	DDATE	DLOCAT	BLOCAT	BDATE	AGE	SPOUSE	FATHER	FBLOCAT	MOTHER	MFBLOCAT	BY	BURIAL	VET	SON	DAUG	BROTHER	SISTER
Reichardt, Helen	May 25, 1990	U.T.H.	Jeff City	Jan 21, 1921	69	Reichardt, Ernest	Hill, Johnny		Reichardt, Ernest		Reichardt, David	Buffalo Grove					
Relier, Julia M.	Nov 16, 1956	[Rea N.J.]	Ireland	Aug 8, 1882	94	W	Lebon, Judith		Kendall, David			Cremated - N.J.					
Relford, Mose Samuel Sr.	Jul 25, 1991	J.M.H.	Birmingham, Ala.	May 4, 1916	75	Ingram, Gladys	Relford, Mose		Wadley, Emma		Relford, Gladys L.	West View	unk				
Reneau, Bertie	Apr 21, 1945	Dandridge	Cocke Co	Apr 10, 1890	55	Ng	Sutton, Samuel	Tn	Mc Gehia, Jane	Tn	Reneau, John (Ohio) - Reneau, Seldon - Hicks, Gladys	Sandy Ridge					
Reneau, Debra Jane	Jan 8, 1967	Blount Co	Tn	Oct 17, 1902	64	S			Brannon, Mary		Burns, Phillip - Ruster, Hicks, Gladys						
Reneau, Mack C.	Jan 24, 1962	Jeff City	Tn	Nov 30, 1861	90-1-24						Brooks, Roy - Burns, Jessie	West View					
Reneau, Mary E.	Oct 12, 1953	Jeff Co.			84						Brooks, Mrs. Roy	West View					
Reneau, Mary Phoebe	May 29, 1941	Greene Co			48-11-6	Reneau, Will					Reneau, Will	West View					
Reneau, Seldon Robert	Dec 27, 1953	Jeff Co	Jeff Co	Feb 7, 1878	75	W			Unk		Hicks, Mrs. Ben	Hills Union					
Reneau, William Lawiter	Dec 3, 1955	Knox Co	Tn	Oct 19, 1886	69	Ng	Reneau, Jackson		Smith, Maggie		Reneau, Mrs. Adele - Brewer, Mrs. Lois	West View	WW 1				
Renfro, J.R.	Mar 8, 1936											West View					
Renfro, Julian Earl	Mar 3, 1973	Jeff Co	Tn	Jul 14, 1990	65	Cabot, Julia	Renfro, Jones R.	Va	Nance, Minnie	Va	Renfro, Mrs. Julia	West View	WW 2				
Repass, James W.	Mar 31, 1928		Va		79-11-2	W	Repass, John		Creagor, Annie		Repass, Ng - Taylor, P.	New Market					
Rhea, Lucille	Sep 16, 1956	Knox Co	Tn	Jul 1, 1913	43	Ng			Walters, Augusta		Shields, Mrs. Lois N. - Rhea, Oran	Mt. Pleasant					
Rhea, Oren Neal	Sep 20, 1965	Knox Co	Tn	Mar 22, 1905	60	W	Rhea, N.J.		Toppers, Minnie		Clift, Nancy - Rhea, Cathy	Strawberry Plains					
Rhinehart, Emma	Dec 27, 1964	Jeff Co	Tn	Feb 20, 1890	74	Rhinehart, George	Lane, James		Beard, Lottie		Rhinehart, George - Gorman, Willie Mae (John) - Dukes, Pat - Wright, Mrs. Frank	Swanylvania					
Rhinehart, George Jr.	Nov 6, 1963	Jeff Co	Tn	Mar 4, 1889	74	Lane, Emma	Rhinehart, Richard		Hance, Martha		Rhinehart, Emma - Dukes, Pat - Wright, Frank	Swanylvania					
Rhinehart, George	May 14, 1987	Jeff City	Tn	Aug 3, 1928	66	Case, Mary	Rhinehart, George Sr.		Lane, Emma		Wife	West View	46-47	Steve-David			
Rhinehart, Glenn	May 30, 1957	[Rea Detroit, Mich.]	Tn	Jul 9, 1917	39	Ng	Rhinehart, George		Lane, Emma	Tn	Mc Ghee, Mrs. Keith - Rhinehart, Ruth	Swanylvania	WW 2				
Rhinehart, Mollie Malinda	Nov 27, 1962	Jeff City	Tn	Apr 15, 1895	67	S	Rhinehart, Richard		Hance, Martha		Isley, Randell	Blackwell Branch					
Rhodes, Billie J.	Oct 18, 1933	New Market			1-5-26		Thoodes, J.R.	Tn	Patterson, Edith	Tn	Rhoades, J.R.	Piney					
Rhodes, Eulie M.	May 17, 1989	F.S.H.	Tn	Apr 24, 1915	74	Ng	Rhodes, Joe Fred		Brown, Ellen	Va	Rhodes, Margaret - J.M.G.	J.M.G.					
Rhodes, George Williams	Apr 6, 1944	Jeff Co	Knox Co	Jun 26, 1882	61	Ng		Va	Ayers, Agnes	Va	Rhodes, Eulie & Agnes - Property George	Property George					
Rhodes, Elizabeth	Sep 15, 1987	J.M.H.	Tn	Sep 27, 1922	64	W	Rhodes, Frank E.		Carmichael, Minnie		Rhodes, Frank E. - J.M.G.	J.M.G.					
Rhoton, Geneva	Sep 30, 1978	Greenwood, Sc.	Tn	Nov 28, 1910	67	Rhoton, Jacob A. [Di]	Emert, Shell H.		Mc Mehan, Roy		Wife	West View					
Rhoton, Walter Albert	Mar 4, 1945	Jeff Co.	Tn	Aug 27, 1871	74	Ng	Rhoton, Jacob P.	Tn	Redding, Mary	Alabama	Rhoton, Mrs. Edna	West View					
Rice, Joe Douglas	Oct 14, 1990	J.M.H.	Huntington, Indiana	Oct 6, 1924	66	Ng	Rice, Clarence O.		Williams, Hazel		Rice, Zelven L.	Cremated	unk				
Rice, Anna Belle	Dec 29, 1957	Jeff City	Tn	Oct 27, 1897	58	Ng	Bruton, Jessie H.		Henderson, Zilpha		Duff, Mrs. Rosa - Richards, Edd	Sundierland					
Richards, Edward William	Jan 6, 1994	Jeff City	Knox Co, Tn	Nov 10, 1935	58	Kirby, Charles			Richards, Truia		Richards, Hazel [Aunt]	Cremated					
Richards, Rhoda L.	Sep 14, 1959	Jeff Co	Tn	Oct 15, 1898	60	W	Rhoda				Rhoda & Clery	Sunderland					
Richards, Elizabeth F.	Oct 22, 1975	Jeff Co	Tn	Sep 4, 1906	69	W	Beets, Myless		Beeler, Tennessee		Isey, Mrs. Anna Lee - Frye, Mrs. Carl L. [Pontiac, Mich.]	Liberty Hill - Grainger Co					
Richardson, Elizabeth F.	Mar 3, 1986	Bowling Green, Ky	Miss.	Sep 2, 1908	77	W	Ferguson, Thomas E.		Thompson, June		Thompson, June	Sunderland					
Richardson, Raymond E.	Jan 2, 1998	Jeff Ety	Florence, Al	Mar 17, 1912	85	Wylie, Delores	Richardson, Daniel Edward		Hamm, Lillie		Wife	Jackson, Miss.		Ronnie	Melanzano, Bonnie	Bill	Tatum, Lila Mae
Richardson, Victoria Leigh	Dec 21, 1988	Jeff City	Ky	Mar 28, 1946	42	Peatowitz, Edward J.	Richardson, William L.		Richardson, William L.		Richardson, William L.	Lebanon Baptist				[1/2] Lynch, Artie	

NAME	DATE	DLOCAT	BLOCAT	BDATE	AGE	SPOUSE	FATHER	FLOCAT	MOTHER	MFBLOCAT	BY	BURIAL	VET	SON	DAUG	BROTHER	SISTER
Richardson, William Edwin	Sep 1, 1971	Knoxville, Tn	Miss.	Dec 17, 1970	70-8 14	Ferguson, Elizabeth	Richardson, William N.		Dawson, Benelia	Nc	Richardson, Mrs. Elizabeth	Pleasant Ridge - Jeff Co					
Richard, Curt Roosevelt	Mar 9, 1971	Jeff Co	Tn	Dec 1, 1903	67		Richard, Gideon		Pollard, Mary		Richard, Mammie	Hillcrest					
Richard, Homer Ellis	Jul 21, 1996	Jeff City	Jeff Co	Sep 24, 1915	80	Daylene, Ellis	Richard, Edgar		Phegan, Naoma		Moore, Louise [Daug]	Pleasant Ridge					Woods, Helen - Konjes, Hazel
Richard, Minnie Elizabeth	Apr 20, 1996	Talbott, Tn	Jeff Co	Sep 13, 1905	90	Smith, Mamie	Smith, Billy		Collins, Hattie		Knight, Inez [Daug]					James	
Richard, Mc Kinley	Aug 4, 1954	J.M.H.	Tn	Dec 29, 1901	82	Mansfield, Hazel	Richard, William		Bird, Mattie		Richard, Mrs. Hazel	Pleasant Ridge		Earl			
Richard, Verna Hazel	Dec 27, 1993	Fort Worth, Texas	Abington, Va	Sep 3, 1918	75		Mansfield, Isaac		Mansfield, Molly		Parton, Michael [G-son]	J.M.G.			Morgan, Mary Ellen - Valdez, Evelyn		Smith, Ethel
Richard, Wade	Apr 27, 1986	J.M.H.	Tn	Apr 2, 1907	79	Div	Richard, Porter		Rimer, Mary		Moore, Mrs. Ellen [Law]	Carter - Hamblen Co			Alley, Betty		
Ricker, Florence	Feb 20, 1931	New Market	Tn	Jun 10, 1901	29	Ng	Collins, Andrew	Tn	Johnson, Mary	Tn	Collins, Charles	Paint Rock, Nc					
Riddle, Harold Clayton	Sep 27, 2000	Strawberry Plains, Tn	Tn	Sep 13, 1938	62	Snowden, Martha Jo	Riddle, Robert E.		South, Hulla Vean	Nc	Wife	Pleasant Grove					
Riddle, Infant	Sep 24, 1940	Jeff Co	Tn	Sep 24, 1940	9hrs		Riddle, Coy A.	Tn	Cella, Nora		Riddle, C.A.	Patton? - Johnson Co					
Riley, Alice	Jul 4, 1988	J.M.H.	Tn	Oct 2, 1985	69	W	Jett, Charles A.		Barbee, Ellen		Stapleton, Mrs. Late - Jett, Maxford	Mt. Horeb					
Riley, Arthur R.	Oct 3, 1939	Piedmont	Tn	Mar 28, 1898	40	Ng	Riley, Alex	Tn	Merry, Mollis	Tn	Riley, Mrs. Ella &	Piedmont					
Riley, Clarence A.	Jul 19, 1931	Jeff City	Tn	Mar 18, 1912	19	S	Riley, Charles	Tn	Glenn, Nora		Riley, Charles	Piedmont					
Riley, Frank H.	Jan 15, 1977	Jeff Co	Tn	Apr 9, 1905	71	S	Riley, Joe		Sellers, Susie		Bolin, Clive B.	Pleasant Grove					
Riley, Gennes Cele	Dec 3, 1986	New Market, Tn	Jeff Co	Sep 25, 1915	71	Ng	Hickman, James A.		Cella, Nora		Riley, Jim	Pleasant Grove					
Riley, Richard Wilson	Dec 9, 1953	Jeff Co	Tn	May 6, 1876	77		Riley, Wilson Richard		Glenn, Margaret		Riley, Mrs. R.W.	Mt. Horeb					
Rimmer, Floyd Warren	Jun [21] 1979	Jeff City	Tn	Oct 11, 1889	91	Rimmer, Floyd Warren [D]	Rimmer, William		Hart, Mary	Tn	Rimmer, Glenn	Hebron					
Rimmer, Frank Tallmadge	Oct 4, 1944	Dandridge	Tn	Aug 30, 1885	59	Ng	Rimmer, John	Nc	Rimmer, Susan	Tn	Rimmer, Mrs & Children	Presby - Dandridge					
Rimmer, Jessie	Sep 14, 1982	J.M.H.	Tn	Aug 25, 1887	85	W	Bolden, H.G.	Tn	Newman, Emma	Tn	Rimmer, Paul Glenn	Shady Grove					
Rimmer, Leslie	May 24, 1945	Jeff Co	Jeff Co	Aug 7, 1876	68	Rimmer, Frank	Denton, John	Tn	Zirkle, Minalia	Tn	Rimmer, Carl S.	Shady Grove					
Rimmer, Lillie	Sep 21, 1945	Jeff Co	Tn	Dec 2, 1889	55		Thornburn, Whitsell	Va	Bowen, Tilda		Rimmer, Cecil	Dandridge					
Rines, Alice	Jul 18, 1973	Talbott, Tn	Tn	Aug 8, 1894	78	W	Bishop, George		Hill, Lucy		Rines, Annie	Lebanon - Hamblen Co					
Rines, Charlie E.	Dec 11, 1966	Jeff Co	Tn	Apr 23, 1894	No	Ng	Patton, Thomas		Patton, Josephine		Rines, Mrs. Grace	Lebanon					
Rines, Dorothy Evelyn	May 2, 1958	Grainger Co	Sc	Aug 4, 1935	22	Rines, J.R.	Morgan, J.W.		Turner, Ethel		Morgan, Mrs. J.W.	Shiloh					
Rines, Dorothy Jean	Aug 18, 1953	Hawkins Co	Sc	Aug 1, 1924	29	Ng	Davis, Benjamin J.		Powell, Mrs. Emma		Waterberger, Mrs. Joe - Rines, George	Lebanon					
Rines, Ethel Pearl	Jan 19, 1967	Jeff Co	Tn	Feb 8, 1893	73	W	Jett, Charles S.		Barbee, Ellen		Rader, Leona [Daug]	Mt. Horeb					
Rines, Grace W.	Sep 9, 1996	Morristown, Tn	Tn	Jul 16, 1906	90	Workman, J.A.	Cockrum, Angie		Bishop, Alice		Rader, Leona [Daug]	Lebanon Baptist		Robert [D]		King [D]	
Rines, Ida	Oct 9, 1932	Hamblen Co	Tn	Nov 18, 1871	61	Rines, T.E.	Unk		Patten, Mary E.		Rines, T.E.	Sunderland	unk				
Rines, Infant Female	Sep 12, 1946	Jeff Co	Jeff Co	Sep 12, 1946	2m		Workman, Charles Edward	Jeff Co	Workman, Leona	Jeff Co	Rines, Charles E.	Sunderland					
Rines, James Riley	May 13, 1988	J.M.H.	Tn	Mar 28, 1932	5m	Gray, Bertie	Rines, Tom	Tn	Rines, Tom	Tn	Rines, Bertie	Mt. View	unk				
Rines, Jean Elizabeth	Feb 28, 1943	Hamblen Co	Hamblen Co	Aug 31, 1942	5m	Ng	Rines, Charles E.	Tn	Workman, Grace	Tn	Rines, Charles E.	Lebanon					
Rines, John S.	Jan 8, 1954	Hawkins Co	Tn	Jan 25, 1894	59		Rines, Tom		Gregory, Mrs. Glenn		Rines, Mrs. Glenn	Lebanon					
Rines, Justin Lee	Nov 26, 1931	Jeff Co	Tn	Sep 11, 1931	2m	Rines, T.E.	Rines, Charles E.	Tn	Workman, Grace		Rines, Charles E.	Sunderland					
Rines, Marshall Tate	May 7, 2000	Morristown, Tn	Tn	Mar 20, 1926	74	Graff, Virginia	Rines, George		Bishops		Rines, Raymond &	Lebanon Baptist					
Rines, Mary Edith	Jan 12, 1968	Jeff Co	Tn	Jan 6, 1906	52	W	Pollard, William	Tn	Lunsford, Minnie	Tn	Rines, W.R.	Mt. View					
Rines, Mrs. W.R.	Feb 3, 1933	Straw Plains	Sc	Apr 7, 1870	52	Rines, W.R.	Pollard, William		Cameron, Melvina	Tn	Pleasant Ridge	Pleasant Ridge					
Rines, Robert Dennis	Sep 19, 1976	Morristown, Tn	Sc	Mar 30, 1952	24	Ng	Rines, Marshall T.		Davis, Dorothy		Rines, Mrs. W.R. - Diane Clark	Lebanon					
Rines, Rondia Clifford [M]	Apr 15, 1980	Knoxville, Tn	Tn	Feb 5, 1896	84	W	Rines, Tom		Green, Ida Josephine		Tanner, Ruth	West View					
Rines, Shirley Jean	Aug 7, 1977	Valentine Clinic	Tn	Jun 26, 1977		Ng	Rines, Eugene		Green, Shirley Ann		Rines, Eugene	Mt. Pleasant					
Rines, Thomas P.	Feb 27, 1947	Jeff Co	Jeff Co	Jun 16, 1891	55-8 11	Ng	Rines, George	Tn	Patton, Mary E.	Tn	Rines, George W. - Hubbard, Mrs.	Sunderland					Rogers, Lottie [D] - Annie - Gregory, Laura - Shaver, Mary [Va]

NAME	DDATE	DLOCAT	BLOCAT	BDATE	AGE	SPOUSE	FATHER	FBLOCAT	MOTHER	MFBLOCAT	BY	BURIAL	VET	SON	DAUG	BROTHER	SISTER
Rines, Walter King	Aug 5, 1986	Highland, Ind.	Tn	Aug 29, 1928	57	Ng	Rines, John S.		Bishop, Alice		Rines, Michael [Griffith, Ind]	Lebanon - Hamblen Co	korea				
Rinner, Amanda	Jan 19, 1948	Knox Co	Jeff Co	Feb 20, ----	75-3-29	S	Line, Elizabeth	Tn	Barh, Mrs. S.B.		Barth, Mrs. S.B.	Bech					
Rivers, Oscar L.	Nov 29, 1972	Jeff City	Tn	Oct 22, 1896	76	Farrow, Beatrice	River, James F.		Oliver, Kate		River, Mrs. O.L.	Lewisburg - Lewisburg, Ky					
Rivers, Willie Andrew	Feb 17, 1995	Morristown, Tn	Hawkins Co, Tn	Sep 23, 1908	86		Unk		Unk		Boster, Michelle [Eve.] - Carr, George & Frances [Friends]	J.M.G.	43-45			[12] Johnson, Rudell	
Rives, Beatrice	Feb 15, 1999	Jeff City	Covington, Tn	Aug 10, 1902	96		Farrow, William R.		Garrison, Sarah E.		Rives, James [Son]	Liberty Church - Union City, Tn			Cox, Josephine - Brooke, Sarah - Katharine	
Rives, Anna May	Jul 5, 1981	Clmn, Wisconsin	Tn	Mar 4, 1910	71	W	Swann, J.P.		Alley, Bertie		Roach, Stephen - Shennauer F.H. [Wenfield, Wis.]	Hills Union					
Roach, Carl W.	Oct 25, 1955	Texas	Tn	1906		Roach, William M.	Bates, Calonie		Roach, E.F.		Shiloh - Grainger Co					
Roach, Cora Lee	Sep 24, 1939	Grainger Co	Tn	Jul 24, 1883	58	Roach, Leonard	Moyer, George Franklin	Tn	Norton, Isabelle	Tn	Roach, Leonard & Children	Young					
Roach, Edith Susan	Aug 5, 1995	Knoxville, Tn	Tn	Apr 24, 1910	85	Div	Parks, Albert		Palmer, Viola Jane		Underwood, Betty [Dau]	J.M.G.		Franklin	Kiggans, Virginia		
Roach, Franklin T.	Mar 23, 2000	Jeff City	Tn	Sep 3, 1928	71	S	Gooch, Dedrick		Byrd, Rachael		Roach, Michael [Son]	J.M.G.					
Roach, Georgia Pearl	Nov 2, 1950	Jeff City	Tn	Aug 13, 1912	38	S	Roach, James		Hodge, Collie		Roach Dedrick	Shiloh					
Roach, Horace	Dec 2, 1964	Jeff City	Tn	Sep 10, 1884	80	Lola	Roach, T.H.	Tn	Parks, Edith		Lola & Children	West View					
Roach, Infant	Apr 30, 1925		Tn		0		Roach, Neal R.		Blalock, Evelyn	Sevier Co	Roach, Neal R.	West View					
Roach, Infant	Aug 28, 1941	New Market	Hamblen Co		14		Roach, Joseph Golden Sr.	Tn	Jarnigan, Rosie	Tn	Roach, J.G. Sr. - Shadden, Joe	Mt. View					
Roach, Joseph Golden	Mar 11, 1944	Jeff Co	Hamblen Co	Mar 11, 1944													
Roach, Lola	Apr 21, 1980	Vale View	Tn	April 10, 1907	73	W	Byrd, John Joe		Newman, Leona		Valentine, Mrs. Ella Mae - White, Mrs. Barbara - Roach, Dean	West View					
Roach, Lottie Kelley	Dec 25, 1949	Grainger Co	Tn	Nov 17, 1890	59	Roach, Frank		Kelley, William P.			Roach, Frank	Shiloh					
Roach, Luther	Sept 7, 1933																
Roach, Maggie	Jan 26, 1952	Jeff Co	Grainger Co	Jan 15, 1867	85	Ng	Davis, John W.		Noe, Jamie		Roach, S.P.	West View					
Roach, Mary Catherine Vester	Jul 13, 1981	Jeff Co	Tn	Apr 30, 1900	81	W	Poore, Hugh		Brown, Mrs. Mae		Brown, Mrs. Mae	West View					
Roach, Minnie	Aug 21, 1962	Jeff Co	Tn	Jul 11, 1883	79	W	Clevenger, William		Byrd, Nancy		Roach, Raymond - Thomas, Vivian	Oakland - Grainger Co	26/78				
Roach, Minnie J.	Feb 28, 1966	Ridgeview N. Home	Tn	May 14, 1903	82	W	Jenkins, Sam		Alley, Debbie		Cox, Jim, Bill [Esta Mae]	Mt. View					
Roach, Rachael Adaline	Dec 3, 1949	Grainger Co	Tn	Dec 30, 1875	73	Ng	Byrd, Abraham		Noe, Sarah C.		Roach, Dedrick	Shiloh					
Roach, Raymond Arthur	Nov 21, 1984	V.A. - Richmond, Va	Tn	Jan 17, 1912	72		Clevenger, Minnie				Thomas, Vivian J.	Oakland - Grainger Co	WW 2				
Roach, Richard Alex Jackson	May 6, 1973	Jeff Co	Tn	May 6, 1973			Clevenger, Minnie				Roach, Lonnie-Mrs. Minnie	Mt. View	WW 1				
Roach, Robert Arnold	May 6, 1956	Jeff Co	Tn	Aug 26, 1929	26	S	Roach, James		Jones, Percolla		Blackwell Branch - Grainger Co.	WW 2					
Roach, Sam P.	Oct 9, 1967	Jeff Co	Tn	Feb 23, 1879	88	Gass, Alice	Roach, John		Carbeck, Addie		Roach, Mrs. Mabel - West View	West View					
Roach, Theo	Sep 2, 1980	Penna, Ohio	Tn	Jul 18, 1908	64	Ng	Roach, Wesley		Roach, Susie		Roach, Mrs. Theo Memorial Gardens	Sandy Ridge - Jeff Co					
Roach, Theodore R	Nov 22, 1958	Jeff Co	Tn	Feb 25, 1894		Ng	Roach, LM.	Tn	Farley, Maggie		Roach, Mrs. W.K. [Lee Springs]	Indian Ridge					
Roach, W.K.	Apr 12, 1936	Mossy Creek	Tn	Jun 4, 1909	44	Div	Roach, Allen Oscar		Clevenger, Minnie		Roach, Mrs. W.K. [Lee Springs]	Oakland - Grainger Co	WW 2				
Roach, William W.	Nov 16, 1953	Mt. Home, Tn	Grainger Co		86	W	Roach, William Oscar				Roach, N.R. - Gamble, Maine	West View					
Roberts, Belle	Jul 24, 1933	Jeff City	Tn			W	Roberts, William Oscar		Kitts, Maude		Wife	West View					
Roberts, Charles	Feb 23, 1994	White Pine, Tn	Jeff Co	May 11, 1936	57		Roberts, D.N.		Dyel, Elizabeth		Roberts, Juanita	Pleasant Ridge			Martin, Brenda - Scott, Linda	Singleton, Grace - Monstock, Ethel
Roberts, Daniel Newton Jr.	Jan 31, 1982	Knoxville, Tn	Jeff Co	Mar 20, 1933	48	Cannon, Juanita	Roberts, Mr. Cready, Christopher	Oury, Rhoda	Va	Roberts, Mrs. Juanita	Pleasant Grove				Oscar-Jim	
Roberts, Eliza	Oct 26, 1944	Smith Co, Va	Nov 25, 1864	79	W	Lline, James	Miller, Charity	Va	Bower, Mrs. W.A.	West View						
Roberts, Elizabeth	Oct 8, 1952	Hamblen Co	Tn	Sep 5, 1869	83	Ng					Sundwllard	J.M.G.					
Roberts, James Morris	Jul 19, 1987	Newport, Tn	Tn	Apr 25, 1899	88	W	Lline, James		Lline, Elizabeth		Roberts, Wayne	J.M.G.					

NAME	DDATE	DLOCAT	BLOCAT	BDATE	AGE	SPOUSE	FATHER	FELOCAT	MOTHER	MFBLOCAT	BY	BURIAL	VET	SON	DAUG	BROTHER	SISTER
Roberts, Jo Ann	Sep 30, 1951	Hamblen Co	Hamblen Co	Feb 13, 1951	8-2-13		Roberts, Melton		Snelson, Dorothy		Fines, Mrs. Williams						
Roberts, Leander	Mar 4, 1942	Dandridge	Sevier Co	Feb 6, 1883	59	Ng	Roberts, L.A.		Claybough, Susanna	Tn	Roberts, Ray & Blanche [Children]	Dandridge					
Roberts, Lewis Bert	Aug 21, 1996	Morristown, Tn	Lee Co, Va	Feb 22, 1922	74	Ellie Cleo	Roberts, George		Mattie		Wife	Granger Memorial	45-46		Morgan, Ruth - Heather, Darlene	Morris	Peters, Little - Maples, Evelyn - Duff, Pas - Livesay, Martha Kate
Roberts, Minnie Myrtle	Aug 7, 1944	Rockford, Tn	Sevier Co	Jul 27, 1909	68	W	Wynn, T.D.		Settom, Mary	Sevier Co	Perkins, Earl - Roberts, Ray	Presby.- Dandridge					
Roberts, Ruby	Feb 21, 1985	J.M.H.	Tn	Jul 27, 1909	75	W	Jernigan, William R.		Lambdin, Lula		Roberts, Wayne	Jefferson Memorial					
Roberts, Terry Ken	Oct 26, 1993	Knoxville, Tn	Greeneville, Tn	Sep 14, 1962	31	Harmon, Betty Jean	Roberts, Curtis		Tollock, Betty		Roberts, Curtis & Father - Mc Kenny, Ester - Sereski, Brooks, Mildred			T.K.			
Roberts, Thomas L.	Oct 11, 1960	Jeff Co	Tn	May 30, 1893	67	Kills, Myrtle	Roberts, Alfred		Warden, Laura		Trenholte- Knox Co				Timothy-Larry Chris		Bunch, Tena
Roberts, Joyce	Dec 22, 1978	Jeff City	Ohio	Apr 1, 1932	46	Robertson, G.	Shutto, Elmer, L.		Horsley, Marcia		Robertson, William G.	Arlington Memorial - Cincinnati, Ohio					
Roberson, Edward Jesse	May 8, 1984	Talbott, Tn	Tn	Feb 2, 1898	86	Ng	Roberson, Hugh P.	Tn	Patterson, Lula		Roberson, Mrs. Ed	Sunderland - Hamblen Co					
Roberson, Nettie Pearl	Jun 17, 1972	Jeff Co	Tn	Mar 27, 1903	69	Roberson, Robert H.	Murph, Thomas		Goble, Louisa		Roberson, Robert H.	Shiloh					
Roberson, Robert H.	Jan 5, 1990	J.M.H.	Tn	Dec 15, 101	88	W	Roberson, Hugh		Patterson, Luella		Roberson, Tom	Shiloh - Grainger Co					
Robinson, Bernice	Jan 13, 1926		[D. Cleveland, Ohio]								[On Flyleaf]						
Robinson, Billie [F]	Jul 13, 1984	Dandridge, Tn		May 4, 1911	83	Bailey, William P.			French, Minnie B.		Snodsberry, Mildred - Copeland, Viola - Cruze, Maude [Sisters]	Piedmont					
Robinson, John Roland Jr.	Aug 27, 1973	Knoxville, Tn	Alabama	Aug 15, 1927	46	Anderson, Louise	Robinson, John R.		Dozier, Jane		Robinson, Mrs. Louise - Copeland, Mrs. Annie V.A.	Oak Ridge - Pell City, Ala	unk				
Robinson, Walter Edward	May 21, 1986	J.M.H.	Tn	Apr 19, 1900	86	Hoyle, Annie Mc Claire	Robinson, Joseph V.		Watkins, Margaret		Robinson, Mrs. Artie Woodlawn - Knoxville, Tn	Woodlawn - Knoxville, Tn					
Robinson, William	Feb 11, 1987	Jeff City	Lincoln Co, Wv	Dec 8, 1906	80	W	Robinson, Ben		Flakes, Mersir		Maples, Addie [G-Daug]	Forest Lawn - Logan, Wv					
Robinson, Artie [F]	Dec 10, 2000	Jeff City	Tn	Jun 23, 1903	97	W	Mc Claire, Marshall		Ballinger, Della		Bible, Kleta [Sister] & Children	Lynnhurst					
Roderick, Arthur M.	Jun 7, 1971	Knoxville, Tn	Tn	Nov 1, 1886	84	Ng	Roderick, John		Copeland, Sythia		Roderick, Mrs. Nannie & Children	Piney					
Roderick, Bernard R.	Feb 19, 1946	Oltan, Nc	Tn	Feb 2, 1921	25	Ng			Unk		Roderick, Mrs. Edgar	Piney Grove	Army sign air				
Roderick, Daniel A.	May 14, 1986	Mt. Home	Tn	Oct 31, 1881	65	Ng	Roderick, John		Unk		Roderick, D.A. Jr.	Hillcrest					
Roderick, Infant Male	Jul 22, 1944	Jeff Co		Jul 22, 1944		Ng	Roderick, Alvin	Tn	Wollard, Hazel Elizabeth	Tn	Roderick, Alvin	Wollard					
Roderick, James	Aug 28, 1948	Knox Co	Tn	May 10, 1876	72-3-19	Ng	Roderick, John	Tn	Copeland, Sythia	Tn	Roderick, Mrs. James	Piney					
Roderick, Jennie Victoria	Feb 24, 1973	Jeff Co	Tn	Mar 10, 1885	87	Roderick, Dan S. Sr. [D]	Bradley, Ephriam		Swann, Louella		Roderick, D.A., Dr. & Sisters	Hillcrest - Dandridge					
Roderick, John	Sep 19, 1945	Jeff Co	Ky	Dec 10, 1917		S	Roderick, J.A.	Tn	Roberts, Fannie	Welss	Roderick, J.A.	Piney					
Roderick, Mitchell	Nov 9, 1957	Jeff Co	Tn	Dec 20, 1926	30	S	Roderick, J.W.		Day, Minnie		Roderick, C.I.B. - Elmore, Paul	Piney					
Roderick, Ruth	Dec 21, 1979	Jeff Co	Tn	Apr 16, 1917	62	W	Griffin, Benjamin F.		Jones, Della		Bailey, Mrs. Mack	Pleasant Grove					
Roderick, William	Jun 13, 1947	Jeff Co		Dec 23, 1879	67-5-20	W	Roderick, John		Copeland, Sythia	Tn	Roderick, D.A.	Piney					
Rodgers, Alice Charlotte	Nov 10, 1994	Talbott, Tn	Hamblen Co	Dec 9, 1915	78		Riles, John S.		Bishop, Alice		Rodgers, Mrs. [Daug]	Lebanon Baptist	43-45	David George [Nc]		4	3
Rodgers, Elbert	Jul 29, 1978	N.C. Baptist Hosp.	Tn	Mar 3, 1913	65	Ng	Rodgers, William Thomas		Hendenlight, Mildred Gertrude		Rodgers, Mrs. Charlotte [Halftown, Nc]	Lebanon - Hamblen Co	WW 2				
Rodrick, Keneth Eugene	Mar 31, 1931	New Market		Jun 15, 1933		Ng	Rodrick, A.M.		Copeland, Sythia	Tn	Roderick, A.M.						
Rogers, April Dawn	Nov 28, 1995	Knoxville, Tn	Knoxville, Tn	Apr 17, 1971	24		Rogers, Troy		Hidock, Merilyn		Hidock, Merilyn	Rogers			Da'Zae?, Jane & Ernest - Cher?, Mary Ruth & Tim	Maurice	Williford, Lisa

NAME	DDATE	DLOCAT	BLOCAT	BDATE	AGE	SPOUSE	FATHER	F/RLOCAT	MOTHER	M/FLOCAT	BY	BURIAL	VET	SON	DAUG	BROTHER	SISTER
Rogers, Cleo	Sep 29, 1991	J.M.H.	Union Co, Tn	Dec 5, 1910	80	Johnson, Minnie	Rogers, Marshall		Rios, Louis		Rogers, Sillas [Son]	Johnson - Union Co, Tn					
Rogers, Fannie Blow	Jan 28, 1979	Knoxville, Tn	Tn	Oct 14, 1892	86	W	Witt, B.W.		Branner, Sophia		Moffett, Mrs. Dorothy W.	West View					
Rogers, Frances Louise	Jan 30, 1988	J.M.H.	Tn	Feb 26, 1925	62	W	Galss, Frank L. Sr.		Colley, Donna		Soals, Mrs. Rebecca R., Rogers, Donny - Linda	Mt. View					
Rogers, Frank	Mar 24, 1979	J.M.H.	Tn	Oct 18, 1898	80	Ng	Rogers, J.J.		Hanson, Caroline		Rogers, Mrs. Frank	Jefferson Memorial					
Rogers, Frank Lester	Jul 22, 1986	Knoxville, Tn	Jeff Co	Dec 13, 1922	73		Rogers, Frank		Linn, Opal		Brown, Roy [End]						
Rogers, Opal	Jan 7, 1984	Knoxville, Tn	Jeff Co	Dec 24, 1904	89	Rogers, Frank Lester	Smith, George E.		Williams, Marjorie		Rogers, James H. Jr. [nephew]			Frank Lester			Linn, Sally - [In-Law] Brown, Georgia M [Aunt] Burchfield, Mabel Mabelle
Rogers, Patricia S.	May 6, 1988	S.M.H.	Va	Mar 13, 1929	58	Rogers, Frank Lester	Meisinger, Marie M.		Hope, Mabel		Rogers, Frank Lester	J.M.G.					
Rogers, Ray	Jan 26, 1969	Jeff Co	Tn	Mar 13, 1929	58	S	Rogers, Will		Hope, Marjie		Rogers, Mrs. Henry Ralph	West View					
Rogers, Ray Lester [Doc]	Mar 24, 1986	J.M.H.	Tn	Mar 26, 1916	67	S	Rogers, James		Price, Alice		Rogers, Mrs. Roy G.	Mt. View					
Rogers, Tom Nelson	Jun 28, 1979	Knoxville, Tn	Tn	Mar 3, 1907	72	S	Rogers, James D.		Price, Alice		Rogers, Mrs. Roy	Mt. View					
Roland, David Lafayette	Aug 10, 1967	Jeff Co	Nc	Dec 12, 1882	84	W	Roland, George		Clark, Micah		Roland, Luther & Mrs. - Howard, Lilly	Wesleys Chapel					
Roland, Bonnie Faye	Apr 9, 1978	Jeff City	Tn	Jul 30, 1937	40	Rolen, Willie	Ellison, Garfield		Gann, Bertha		Rolen, Willie - Rolen - Sevier Co	Rolen - Sevier Co					
Rolen, Dosia O.	May 1, 1970	Sevier Co	Sevier Co	Oct 17, 1917	52	Ng	Hurst, Tate		Breeden, Bertie		Rolen, Willie - Oddly, Bessie	Bethany - Sevier Co					
Romine, Elbert Pink	Jun 24, 1976	Jeff Co	Tn	Jan 27, 1884	92	Ng	Romine, Bill		Thomas, Zubbie		Romine, James Elbert - Finley, Kila	West View					
Romine, Eugene	Nov 29, 1955	Jeff City	Tn	Nov 10, 1933	2	Ng	Romine, Claude	Tn	Cochran, Margret	Tn	Romine, Claude - Finley, Kila	West View					
Romines, Claude Henry	Oct 2, 1985	Jeff City	Tn	Jan 21, 1914	41	Ng	Romines, E.P.		Denton, Bertie		Miller, Mrs. Ben - Romine, Lois	West View					
Romines, Emma Guffey	Oct 21, 1985	Jeff City	Tn	May 2, 1900	85	W	Quinton, John		Byrd, Laura		Howard, Lilly	Jefferson Memorial					
Romines, Florence	May 27, 1981	Jeff Co	Tn	May 25, 1896	84-1-0	S	Romines, William		Thomas, Jubie		Wisconover, J. Brice - Johnson, Ciny	Shady Grove					
Romines, James Elbert	Oct 3, 1982	At Home	Tn	Aug 10, 1935	47	Hodge, Chery	Romines, Elbert Pink		Jones, Opal M.		Romines, Mrs. Cheryl - Wisconover H.	Pleasant View - Hamblen Co					
Romines, James L.	Nov 18, 1951	Jeff City	Tn		79-4-9	Ng	Romines, William		Jones, Opal M.		Goffy, Mrs. Emma - Clyde & Joe	Shady Grove					
Romines, Opal Marie	Mar 12, 1997	Jeff City	Lee Co, Va	May 8, 1912	84	Ng	Jones, Henry L.		Bush, Amanda V.		Gann, Frank [G-Son]	Shady Grove			Moore, Treva Fleenor [Tx]		
Roper, Florence Margurite	Feb 25, 1941	New Market	Jeff Co		50-11-26	Roper, F.L.	Jennings, Belle		Roper, F.L.		Roper, F.L. - Darnell, Pauline	Piedmont					
Roper, Lois Hankins [Coll]	Feb 19, 1941	New Market	Jeff Co		40	Roper, John	Hodge, Flora		Roper, John		Roper, John	Jefferson Memorial					
Roper, Frank	Aug 22, 1955	Loy Kpte.	Violet, Nc	Jul 14, 1914	40	Ng	Roper, William		Linderman, Teresa	Knox Co	Cassels, Mrs. Mary Earl - Roper, Frank Max & Egbert	Zion Hill - Polk Co, Tn					
Ross, Amelia Fain	Aug 20, 1957	Jeff City	Tn	Oct 23, 1880	76	S	Ross, John F.		Clark, Elizabeth		Titsworth, Mrs. Robby & Mrs. Henry - Medge	West View					
Ross, Audrey Lee	Dec 25, 1987	Blount Co.	W. Va	Jan 26, 1934	53	Ross, Joseph	Unk		Alberty, Elizabeth G.	Jeff Co	Ross, James E.I Louisville, KY, Ross, Arnold [Sister] Johnson	J.M.G.					
Ross, Blanche Katherine	Dec 4, 1956	Jeff City	Tn	Jan 29, 1874	81	S	Ross, John T.				Fennell, John [Powell, Cal]	West View					
Ross, John Clark	Mar 12, 1985	J.M.H.	Tn	Mar 24, 1889	95	S	Ross, John Fain		Clark, Elizabeth		Clark, Elizabeth [Powell, Cal]	West View	WW 1				

NAME	DDATE	BLOCAT	BLOCAT	BDATE	AGE	SPOUSE	FATHER	FRLOCAT	MOTHER	MTR LOCAT	BY	BURIAL	VET	SON	DAUG	BROTHER	SISTER
Ross, Joseph	Feb 19, 1957	Leesburg, Fl	Morivegon, Wv	Dec. 1, 1923	73	Nutt, Bettye	Ross, Frank		Belrora, Margarerua		Wills	J.M.G.	army	Franklie-Anthony-Jonathon [Step] Williams, Ronald Jr. - Glen, Michael - Tony	Susan Connelle - [Step] Alan, Pamela	James Vincent [On]	McCoy, Mary Ann [Ve]
Ross, Lisa Marie	Dec 25, 1987	U.T.H.	Ohio	Sep 23, 1963	24	S	Ross, Joseph		Law, Aubrey			J.M.G.					
Ross, Margaret	Jan 26, 1976	Jeff City	Tn	Jan 29, 1879	97	S	Clark, John Fain		Clark, Lizzie		Ross, John Clark - Tilsworth, Henry	West View					
Rosser, Charlie Faith	Sep 10, 1973	Jeff City	Tn	Aug 28, 1973		S	Rosser, Stephen		Brody, Julie A.		Rosser, Stephen	Memorial Gardens					
Rubin, Prister Mora	Nov 27, 1933	Jeff Co.	Knox Co	Dec 13, 1926	26	S	Rubin, A.L.		Moore, Nina		Rubin, Nina	Greenwood					
Rubin, Zora Nina	Feb 9, 1989	Hilltown	Memphis, Tn	Dec 10, 1899	89	W	Moore, John		Harris, Zora		Seabron, James R.	Greenwood - Knoxville, Tn					
Ruche, Austin Jerome	Oct 7, 1989	Knox Co	Ohio	Oct 1, 1875	93	Ng	Ruche, Rudolph		Kempf, Katherine		Newman, James [Mary]	Belvidere- Winchester, Tn					
Ruckett, Ray	Feb 1, 1931	Knox Co	Tn	Oct 18, 1909	21	Ng	Puckett, Arthur	Tn	Bettis, Minnie	Tn	Maury, W.S. [Sdmn]	Peabhoelf					
Ruddel, Sally Isabelle	Sep 14, 1978	Knoxville, Tn	Tn	Jun 26, 1887	79	W	Ruddel, 73rd		Norton, Mary Ruth		White, Mrs. W.L.	Pleasant Grove					
Rudy, Michelle Lynn	Nov 15, 1972	Hamblen Co		Nov 15, 1972		S	Rudy, Charles M.	W. Va.	Brock, Dorothy Berrice	Ky	Rudy, Charles M.	Jefferson Memorial					
Ruffin, James Pryor [Col]	Aug 23, 1954	Jeff Co	Tn	Feb 26, —	79-5 25	W	Ruffin, James		Unk		Ruffin, Milton	Flat Woods					
Rugel, Earl	Apr 27, 1989	Jeff Co	Jeff Co	Aug 22, 1914	76	Robeson, Pauline		Rugel, Willis Vernon		Franklin, Julia		Rugel, Keith & Patricia [Son] Rugel, Keith D. & Patricia [Son] - Anroia [Step Mother]	J.M.G.				Cadet, Betty & Charles	
Rugel, Pauline R.	Jul 27, 1993	Jeff City	Tn	Jul 9, 1915	78	W	Robeson, Edward		Rice, Cele		Rugel, Earl - Carter, Mrs.	J.M.G.			R.E. Roger Gale	
Rugel, W.B.	Mar 3, 1985	Jeff Co	Tn	82-5 10		W	Rugel, Adelphus		Horner, Jennie			Mt. Pleasant					
Rule, Henry Timberlake	Sep 24, 1974	Talbott, Tn	W. Va	Jul 13, 1903	71	Gillespie, Ruby		Rule, Sidney Wootson		Clayton, Hortense		Rule, Mrs. Ruby	Armistad, W. Va	unk			Cadet, Carrie Lise - Calhoun, Vivian - Smith, June	
Runion, Burton Marshall	Feb 17, 1947	Wythe, Va	Tn	Sep 11, 1879	69	Ng	Runion, J.L.	Nc	Runion, Emma	Va	Runion, R.P. [Pulaski, Va]	New Market					
Rupe, Diana M.	Oct 23, 1999	Jeff City	Cook Co. Il	Nov 30, 1942	56	Rupe, William H.		Nolan, Edgar R.		Husband		Mc Intyre - Wagnelio Co., Iowa					
Rusak, Mabel Edna	Dec 1, 1989	Richmond, Va	Jeff City	Jul 16, 1919	70	Rusak, Matthew J.		Bishop, George D.		Rusak, Matthew J.		Lebanon Church	WW 2				
Rusak, Matthew James	Oct 21, 1990	Plains, Pa	Tn	Nov 18, 1916	83	W	Rusak, John		Niedzwiecka, Bertha		Rusak, Jock B. [Son]	Lebanon Baptist	unk				
Rush, Virginia G.	Aug 29, 1931	Jeff City Morristown, Tn	W. Va	Mar 17, 1854	77	S	Rush, William B.	Va	Hill, Elizabeth	Tn	Long, Mrs.	New Market					
Russell, Adele Emma	Apr 7, 1973	Morristown, Tn	Tn	Sep 14, 1906	66	Russell, Henry		Park, Sarah		Warren, Hoyt	Underwood - Sevier Co					
Russell, Bibby Lynn	May 10, 1963	Jeff Co	ChiChumming a, Ga	May 10, 1963		Russell, Justin		Driven, —		Husband		Lebanon Church					
Russell, Bobbie Hood	Sep 8, 1995	Jeff City	Tn	Aug 20, 1917	78	Russell, Clyde W. Sr.		Cromer, Jessie		Russell, Clyde W. Jr. & Linda [Son]	West View					
Russell, Claiborne Lee	Jul 1, 1944	Hamblen Co	Alabama	Sep 14, 1889	54	Ng	Russell, Elijah B.	Alabama	Long, Mattie		Russell, Mrs. Frances [Penny]	Jarnigan					
Russell, Claiborne Louis	Sep 30, 1983	Jeff City	Tn	Jul 15, 1918	45	Long, Penny ?		Hadlow, Sue		Russell, Mrs. Frances [Penny]	Memorial Gardens					
Russell, Clyde Whitter Sr.	Dec 18, 1998	Appalachia, Va	Tn	Feb 26, 1911	87	W	Russell, William		Firetis, Cordelia		Russell, Clyde W. Jr. [Son]	West View					
Russell, Frances [Penny]	Dec 1, 1981	Knoxville, Tn	Tn	Feb 19, 1923	58	W	Long, Jeff		Ogle, Annie		Russell, Jeff-Seven Epperson, Mrs. Hoyt	Jefferson Memorial					
Russell, Hazel	Feb 28, 1975	Jeff Co	Tn	Sep 10, 1905	70	W	Bundren, James H.		Peck, Margaret		Hawdy, Mrs. Ethel - Fain, Mack - Russell,	Greenwood - Knox Co					
Russell, James Woodrow	Mar 17, 1976	Greeneville, Hospital	Tn	Sept 15, 1913	62	S	Russell, Joseph J.		Stubblefield, Mary Jane		Colchwell - Hawkins Co						
Russell, Kenneth Harold	May 29, 1964	Hamblen Co	Tn	Jan 15, 1909	55	Whitehead, Lucy		Russell, Thomas W.		Catshaw, Mollie J.		Lucy & Children	Bethel - Hamblen Co					
Russell, Mack	Nov 21, 1947	Jeff Co	Tn	Jan 15, 1909	66	W	Russell, James		Laymon, Mollie Duncan	Tn	Laymon, Paul	New Market					
Russell, Mamie E.	Dec 23, 1932	Granger Co	Tn	Oct 12, 1861	43	W	Comba, John W.	Tn	Shultz, Unk	Tn	Russell, T.T.	Shilo					
Russell, Mary Gladys	Nov 4, 1943	Jeff Co	Knox Co	Apr 7, 1915		Russell, Odell		Sharpe, William	Tn	Branson, Mary	Tn	Russell, Odell	Wodieodtown					

NAME	DDATE	DLOCAT	BLOCAT	BDATE	AGE	SPOUSE	FATHER	FBLOCAT	MOTHER	MFBLOCAT	BY	BURIAL	VET	SON	DAUG	BROTHER	SISTER
Russell, Mary June	Mar 27, 1965	Hamblen Co	Tn	Aug 29, 1884	80	W	Stubblefield, James F.		Dodson, Emma		Hanely, Ethel - Russell, Hugh P. - Fain, Mack	Dry Field - Hamblen Co					
Russell, Mollie	Apr 12, 1933	Jeff City	Tn	Sep 7, 1849	83	W	Dunkin, John H.	Tn	Bradford, Elizabeth	Tn	Laymour, Frank	New Market					
Russell, Robert M.	Jul 30, 1931	New Market	Tn	Nov 1 1880	50	S	Russell, A.J	Tn	Branch, Ellen	Tn		Jarnigan					
Russell, Sue Haslewe	Jan 9, 1968	Bedford Co	Tn	Nov 11, 1893	74	W	Haslewe, Sam		Buholk, Ellen			New Market					
Russell, William H.	Mar 10, 1960	New Market	Tn	Oct 19, 1904	55	S	Russell, James Alex	Tn	Bunch, Ellen		Petro, Mrs. P.R. - Heine, Russell - New York City	New Market					
Rutherford, George Williams	Apr 15, 1943	Jeff Co	Tn	Jan 2, 1886	57	W	Rutherford, Joseph	Tn	Click, Mary	Tn	Renessi, Mrs. Jessie - New York City	Sandy Ridge					
Rutherford, James Carl	Jun 12, 1986	Rutledge, Tn	Ky	Jan 19, 1924	62	W	Rutherford, Emmett		Mullins, Theresa		Rutherford, Mrs. Lois H.	Oakland - Grainger Co	WW 2				
Rutledge, Wiley Excel	Apr 12, 1949	Jeff Co	Tn	Oct 1, 1949	56-6-11	Ng	Rutledge, L.D.		James, Nancy Jane	Tn		West View					
Ryder, Mary Margaret	Jul 29, 1987	J.M.H.	Tn	Feb 14, 1913	74	Div	Jones, John		Hill, Maude		Ryder, John H. [Durham, Ne]	Buffalo Grove					
Rymer, Margaret Gertrude	Jun 7, 1994	Mt. City, Tn		Dec 26, 1903	90		Wagner, L.L.		Hawkins, Elizabeth		Rymer, Mrs. Gertrude	West View					
Rymer, Samuel E.	Apr 3, 1949	Knox Co	Tn	Oct 12, 1920	63	Ng	Rymer, David		Hughes, Mary		Evans, Mrs. M.E.	Macedonia - Harriston					
Sagor, Ruth	Sep 26, 1953	Tn	Tn	Oct 12, 1920	32	Ng	Evans, David N.		Treece, Mary E.		Phillips - Bakersville, Nc	West View					
Saltz, Charles Samuel	Aug 25, 1985	J.M.H.	Nc	Jun 14, 1895	43	Div	Saltz, Frank Sr.		Yelton, Orsad		Saltz, Frank Jr. - Hamline-Hughes F.H. [Bakersville, Nc]	West View					
Samples, Anna Lou	Jan 7, 1978	Jeff Co	Tn	Jul 23, 1892	85	W	Anderson, Sam		Snodgrass, Vida		Hutton, Mrs. Carl K.	West View					
Samples, Arthur	Jan 11, 1971	Jeff City	Tn	Nov 5, 1885	85	Ng	Samples, William		Alley, Laura		Hutton, Agnes - Samples, Anna Lou	West View					
Samples, Charles G.	Sep 15, 1995	Jeff City	Jeff Co	Nov 12, 1920	74	W	Samples, Charles O.		Denton, Mahelia		Wife	J.M.G.		Eddie		J.P.-Freeman	
Samples, Tommi Leah	Aug 13, 1992	Morristown, Tn	Morristown, Tn	Aug 14, 1989	3	Lane, Margaret Kathleen	Link		Samples, Martha		Wife	Mt. View					Reneesa, Ethel
Sampson, Ruby Mae	Dec 21, 1996	Knoxville, Tn	Sevier Co	Jun 29, 1912	84	W	Petty, Mary E.		Bates, Mattie		Jones, Viera Webster - Kells & Earl [Dandr]	East View Memorial					
Sampson, Dorothy Crooke	Jun 18, 1979	Wagnersville, Ohio	Indiana	Oct 23, 1897	81	W	Crooke, Frank A.		Crafton, Lillie		Melton, Mrs. Margaret	West View					
Sanders, Edith Mc Cracken Bryant	Jun 25, 1982	Knoxville, Tn	Tn	Aug 29, 1887	94	W			Myrott, Rachel		Childrens, Mrs. Max	West View					
Sanders, James L.	Mar 22, 1984	Knox Co	Tn	Aug 29, 1886	77	Ng	Sanders, Dido		Flamingas, Emily		Flamingas, Mrs. Edith B.	West View					
Sanders, Sarah	Dec 30, 1996	Merrorsborne, Ky		Jan 3, 1930	66	W	Alexander, William Lochman		Price, Georgia		Sanders, Martha [Doug]	City - Merrorsborne, Ky		John-George	Childress, Betsy	James Lochman	Daisy B. - Rounds, Betsy
Sandifer, Otis O.	Dec 17, 1988	J.M.H.	Tn	Feb 6, 1917	71	W	Dobson, Lorene		Rice, Margaret		Sandifer, Lorene	Mt. View					
Sands, Jason Daniel Mowry	Nov 12, 1994	Hamblen Co	Tn	Nov 2, 1976	18		Smith, Mark		Smith, Glenda Gail		Mother	Wesleys Chapel				Mowry, Larry - Sands, Curtis	Sands, Jessica Marie
Sane, Cicero	Nov 25, 1997	Jeff City	Cocke Co	Aug 1, 1931	66	Collins, Betty	Sane, William		Blaine, Myrtle		Wife - Collins, Jennie Vee [Mother-In-Law]			Ricke Jerome	Ness, Cindy & Tim - [Step] Lowe, Belinda Lenora		
Sanin, Roy William	Aug 27, 1995	Jeff Co	Tn	Jul 19, 1952	3	S	Sanin, Robert		Atkins, --		Sanin, Robert	White Pine					
Satterfield, Blanche Della	Sep 6, 2000	Rutledge, Tn	Tn	Oct 30, 1910	89	S			Campbell, Ellen		Greenlee, Hilda [Doug]	Buffalo Grove					
Satterfield, Flossie Seymour	Jan 22, 1987	J.M.H.	Tn	Feb 2, 1902	85	W	Seymour, Leroy		Hopson, Matilda		Satterfield, Donald	Mill Springs					
Satterfield, Henry Clark	Dec 25, 1965	Jeff Co	Tn	Mar 7, 1906	59	Ng	Satterfield, T.R.		Harrell, Susan		Satterfield, Donald	Mill Springs					
Satterfield, James Donald	Dec 31, 2000	Knoxville, Tn	Tn	Jun 29, 1933	67	Smith, Kathryn	Satterfield, Henry Clark		Seymour, Flossie		Wife	Mill Springs				James Clark	
Satterfield, Neil Bacon	May 15, 1946	Knoxville	Tn			D					Walker, Rev. J.S.	Mt. Pleasant					
Satterfield, Ralph Lafayette	May 3, 1990	F.S.H.	Union Co, Tn	Aug 9, 1910	79	Carmen, Catherine	Satterfield, William L.		Johnson, Mary Ann		Satterfield, Catherine - V.A.	Strawberry Plains	WW 2				

NAME	DDATE	BLOCAT	BLOCAT	BDATE	AGE	SPOUSE	FATHER	FRLOCAT	MOTHER	MRLOCAT	BY	BURIAL	VET	SON	DAUG	BROTHER	SISTER
Satterfield, Susan	Dec 1, 1955	Jeff Co.	Tn	Nov 12, 1877	78	W	Harrell, William P.		Ritter, Mary C.		Cochran, Mrs. Heiskell - Satterfield, H.C.	Mill Springs					
Sawyer, Sallie	Mar 2, 1931	Granger Co.		Mar 27, 1867	63	Ng	Combs, Jim	Tn	Combs, Martha	Tn	Dates, L.L.	Stilo					
Sawyer, Andy	Sep 6, 1926	Va			81+	Ng	Sawyers, Martin	Va	Sawyers, Mrs. A.J.	Va	Sawyers, Mrs. A.J.	Stilo					
Sayers, Charles Hobson	Apr 3, 1925	Washington Co, Tn	Nc		15	S	Webster, Nancy	Va	Sayers, Mrs. A.J.	Nc	Sayers, Mrs. A.J.	Stilo					
Saylor, Velma	Oct 16, 1989	Park W. Hosp., Co, Tn		Feb 13, 1919	48	Div	Arnold, O.C.		Young, Helen		Day, Regina S.	J.M.G.					
Scarlett, Charlene	Nov 8, 1993	Jeff City	Tn	Nov 3, 1951	42	W	Smith, Eugene		Talley, Jean		Smith, Teressa [Sister - Sc]	J.M.G.					
Scarlett, Charlie Monroe	Jan 6, 1977	Knoxville, Tn	Tn	Feb 11, 1888	88	W	Scarlett, John		Dixon, Nancy		Scarlett, Neal	New Market		Tommy	Hickle, Faye - Brenda		
Scarlett, Edra Maude	Jun 25, 1979	Knoxville, Tn		Jan 8, 1891	88	W	Trusta, Mick		Martin, Carrie		Richards, Mrs. Pauline	Shiloh					
Scarlett, J.P. Jr.	May 5, 1939	Jeff Co.		May 5, 1939			Scarlett, J.P.		Kerr, Bonnie	Tn	Scarlett, James P. & Father						
Scarlett, John Robert	Aug 29, 1947	Jeff Co	Tn	Dec 27, 1897	50	Ng	Scarlett, Phillip A.	Tn	Mc Farland, Lydia	Tn	Scarlett, Mrs. Maude [Wife]	Piney					
Scarlett, Lula Belle	Jun 26, 1958	Tn		May 2, 1891	67	W	French, J.P.		Elder, Sarah		Scarlett, Neal S.J.P. & Inslburtkart	New Market					
Scarlett, Neal Alger	May 16, 1985	J.M.H.	Tn	Jan 19, 1910	75	W	Scarlett, C.M.		French, Lula		Scarlett, Sam	New Market					
Scarlett, Ollie Frances	Jul 26, 1903	Knox Co	Tn		91	Griffin, Ollie Frances	Griffin, Samuel B.		Catlin, Maggie		Scarlett, Sam & Bobbie	New Market			Cunningham, Frances & Joe		
Schean, Floyd Sidney	Jun 15, 1975	Jeff Co	Tn	Jan 31, 1907	68	W	Schean, Dennis James		Mc Neal, Maude		Schean, Forrest	New Market					Chumley, Margaret
Schechter, Walter Edwin Sr.	Dec 17, 1988	J.M.H.	N. Dakota	Dec 8, 1907	81	Rhyalis, Mary Belle	Schechter, Emanuel E.		Neverenchwander, Mary		Schechter, Mary - Howard F.H. [Palm Beach, Fla.]	Grace Chapel, Concord, Tn	WW 2				
Schechter, Carrie Leeanne	Jun 18, 1991	J.M.H.	Morristown, Tn	Oct 28, 1962	28	Schechter, Tim	Godwin, Eugene W.		Dupre, Ruth		Casey, Kim Godwin [Sister]	Woodlawn - W. Palm Beach, Fla.					
Schrader, Eugene Benson	Apr 10, 1943	Jeff Co.	Tn	Feb 24, 1897	46	Schrader, Pauline	Schrader, Samuel		Kinsamon, Mary	Tn	Schrader, Pauline	Mt. Zion					
Schrader, George Hale	Oct 6, 1979	Jeff City	Tn	Aug 8, 1904	75	Sherrod, Blanche	Schrader, James H.		Hallis, Mary		Schrader, Mrs. Blanche	Hopewell - Dandridge	WW 1				
Schirmacher, Marie	Apr 16, 1974	Chicago, Ill.	Tn	Dec 13, 1927	46	Div	Hammaker, George W.		Phillips, Mary		Pfister, Bonnie - Rous, ?Ariel [Chicago, Ill.]	Jefferson Memorial					
Schnoor, Patrick William	Sep 4, 1982	J.M.H.	Ohio	Jun 24, 1952	30	S	Schnoor, William		Boyer, Ellen		Schnoor, Mrs. Ellen B. - Kemp, Nick Hogan	St. Michaels - Ft. Loramie, Ohio					
Schubert, Ruby Jane	Dec 20, 2000	Jeff City	Tn	Aug 26, 1938	62	Schubert, Leon	Goarelt, Sherman		Wrarck, Bessie		Schubert, Dorothy R. [Daug]	Beech Springs - Kodak, Tn					
Schultz, Edwin Leo	Apr 1, 1987	Morristown, Tn	S. Dakota	Apr 2, 1901	85	Cresnor, Lenore	Schultz, Carl		Rhober, Mary		Schultz, Mrs. Maxine A. - Husband	Cremated					
Schultz, Lenore Ellen	Jan 14, 1988	Knox Co.	S. Dakota	Sep 21, 1903	84	W	Cresgon, Josh		Thomas, Martha		Currie, Mrs. Maxine	Cremated					
Scott, Bonnie Roe	Feb 5, 1983	Knox Co.	Tn	Jan 8, 1896	87	Scott, Henry	Sivan, Melvin F.		Bettis, Cora M.		Scott, Henry [Florida]	Elsberzer					
Scott, Dollie Conner	Jan 15, 1993	Jeff City	Dothan, Alabama	Feb 4, 1908	85	Conner, John			Singletany, Elizabeth		Memory Hill - Dothan, Alabama			Glover, Sarah & Sonny		
Scott, Gwendolyn	Apr 10, 1971	Jeff Co	Arkansas	Feb 26, 1911	60	Scott, Hobert O.	Stephenson, Amanda		Scott, H.O.		G.A.R. - Miami, Oklahoma					
Scott, Jeff D.	Nov 14, 1980	Jeff City	Tn	Dec 12, 1891	88	W	Scott, Sam B.		Gilbert, Stella Mae		Scott, Stella Mae	Shiloh					
Scott, Walter Bruce	Sep 7, 1948	Jeff Co	Tn	Mar 1, ---	abt 75	S	Scott, Sam B.		Riley, Ellen	Tn	Dotson, Mrs. Willie	Walland					
Scroggins, Roxas Lee	Sep 9, 1993	Angelina Co, Texas	Tn	Apr 30, 1914	79		Steele, James Richard		Forrest, Celestine		Scroggins, James Richard & Connie [Son]	West View		[G] Gavin		Chester	Traswick, Georgia - Stephens, Sarah Jane
Seaborn, Anne	Aug 2, 1958	Tn	Tn	Apr 1, 1877	81	Seaborn, John W.	Franklin, Benjamine		Mc Murray, M. Cordelia		Seaborn, Ben & John F. [Illinois]/Stephen [Ga] - Carpenter, Margaret - Culbert, H.J.	Seaborn Chapel					
Seaborn, Annie P.	Apr 20, 1957	Dandridge	Tn	Feb 15, 1871	66	W	Smith, Peyor		Stephenson, Hugh		Seaborn, Hugh [Son]	Seaborn Chapel					
Seaborn, Dorcus	Oct 4, 1927	Tn	Tn		14	Seaborn, Ponder	Hayes, James	Tn	Moore, Dorcus	Tn	Fox, Lon	Widland					
Seaborn, Frank Hodge	Dec 16, 1978	Jeff City	Tn	Sep 4, 1904	74	Allen, Louise	Seaborn, William R.		Steffin, Annie		Seaborn, Mrs Frank	Seaborn Chapel					Wrachial, Dorthea [TN] - Roberts, Alice [TN]

NAME	DDATE	DLOCAT	BLOCAT	BDATE	AGE	SPOUSE	FATHER	F/B/LOCAT	MOTHER	M/F/LOCAT	BY	BURIAL	VET	SON	DAUG	BROTHER	SISTER
Seaborn, Harry Walter	Jan 7, 1980	Jeff City	Tn	Jan 19, 1896	83	Ng	Seaborn, William R.		Sartain, Annie		Seaborn, Mrs. Walter-Leon	West View					
Seaborn, John	Nov 23, 1962	Jeff Co	Tn	Jul 27, 1879	83	W	Seaborn, John Ponder		Hayes, Dorcas		Seaborn, Ben-Stephen [Step-John F. (III.)-Cole, Clarence-Culbert, H.J.-Carpenter, Margaret	Seaborn Chapel					
Seaborn, Mary	Jul 12, 1981	Morristown, Tn	Tn	Jun 10, 1898	83	Seaborn, H. Walter [D]	Cox, Beecher M.		Foust, Edna E.		Seaborn, Leon	West View					
Seaborn, Mary E.	Apr 20, 1925	Dandridge	Tn	Mar 11, 1854	79	Ng	Seaborn, J.P.	Tn	Birchfield, Daisey	Tn	Birchfield, J.C.	Oak Grove					
Seaborn, W.R.	May 21, 1933	Dandridge	Tn		Infant	Ng	Seaborn, John	Tn	Love, Jane	Tn	Sons	Seaborn					
Seal, Douglas Trent	Mar 13, 1989	S.M.M.C.	Tn	Mar 20, 1942	46	Hopkins, Esther	Seal, Lou	Tn	Trent, Jane		Seal, Esther H.	Blue Springs - Strawberry Plains, Tn					
Seal, Marion Wright	Nov 2, 1970	Knox Co	Tn	Sep 25, 1896	84	Purkey, Bertha	Seal, Oliver		Smiley, Rheuma		Smith, Mrs. Ed	Beaver Creek					
Seale, Bertha	Jan 2, 1982	Strawberry Plains	Tn	Nov 1, 1891	90	W	Purkey, Jess		Hatfield, Betty		Smith, Mrs. Ed	Beaver Creek Baptist					
Seals, Jack	Apr 24, 1993	Mt. Home, Tn	Jeff Co	Dec 26, 1936	56		Seals, Alfred Sr.		Hinchey, Ollie Kate		Seals, Rocky [Son]	Flat Gap	55-59	Roger Delmar	Linda - Bozeman, Debbie	Robert-Bart-Alfred-George	Ballinger, Bevy Jean - Daniels, Mary Lou - Minton, Margaret
Seaton, George Willard	Mar 15, 1976	Jeff Co	Tn	Jan 20, 1916	60	S	Seaton, John H.		Cox, Maude		Thompson, Mrs. Willie	West View	WW 2				
Seaton, James A.	Sep 25, 1931	Jeff City	Tn	Feb 2, 1876	55	Ng	Seaton, William B.	Tn	Houser, Catherine	Tn	Seaton, Willard	Shilo - Grainger Co					
Seaton, John Franklin	May 5, 1974	Jeff Co	Tn	May 6, 1913	60	S	Seaton, John H.		Cox, Maude		Seaton, Willard	West View					
Seaton, John Harrison	Oct 23, 1952	Jeff Co	Tn	Jul 6, 1887	65	Ng	Seaton, W.B.		Houser, Kathryn		Seaton, Mrs. Maude [Wife]	West View					
Seaton, Maude	Apr 21, 1959	Tn	Tn	Sep 27, 1884	74	W	Cox, George		Gass, Florida		Henderson, Mrs. T.W. Sons	West View					
Seaton, W.B.	Sept 1, 1933	Jeff City	Tn	May 4, 1849	84	W	Seaton, Alford	Tn			Seaton, Allen	Shilo					
Seay, Dorcas	Aug 28, 1955	Tn	Tn	Jan 29, 1895	60	W	Brannen, Harrison		Fowler, Charity		Seay, Allen	Shilo					
Self, Dorathe L.	Mar 15, 1997	Knoxville, Tn	Bean Station, Tn	Sep 16, 1933	63	Self, Frank	Leedy, Victor York		Rankin, Evelyn		Hubbard	Beth Carr - White Pine, Tn				[In-Law] Self, Carl [Ca]	[In-Law] Neibel, Sylvia [Ca]
Selfridge, Martha	Jun 23, 1990	Mc Donough, Ga		Sep 11, 1911	78	W	White, W.A.		Hammonds, Hattie		Selfridge, Louie D.	City - Mc Donough, Ga			Northern, Vickie & Dan - Roberts, Laura & Teri		
Sellars, Annie Eloulse	Dec 9, 1997	Dandridge, Tn	Jeff Co	Oct 21, 1925	72	S	Lies, Andrew		Hutsell, Bertha [Daug]	Tn		Mt. View					
Sellars, James Louis	Jan 30, 1990	F.S.H.	Tn	Jun 15, 1916	73	Ann E.	Sellars, Charlie A.		Dotson, Bertha		Sellars, Ann E.	Mt. View					
Sellers, E.E.	March [13], 1931																
Sellers, Nancy	Aug 3, 1937	Chestnut Grove	Tn	Jul 10, —	81	W	Hart, Floyd	Nc	Sisson, Mary Ann	Nc	Sellers, Fred	Anabel					
Senter, James Horace [Buddy]	Jul 15, 1958	Knox Co	Hamblen Co	Dec 20, 1910	47	Hale, Virginia	Senter, J.N.	Tn	Turner, Minnie	Tn	Senter, Mrs. J.H.	Sunderland					
Senter, John William	Oct 2, 1972	Knoxville, Tn	Tn	Sep 22, 1912	60	S	Senter, John M.		Senter, Charlie & Hugh		Senter, Charlie & Hugh	Lebanon - Hamblen Co					
Senter, Minnie	Feb 18, 1974	Talbott, Tn	Tn	Jul 19, 1887	86	W	Senter, William P.		Cox, Harriett		Lebanon - Hamblen Co	Lebanon					
Senter, Robert V.	Oct 8, 1936	Tn	Tn	Oct 2, 1918	18		Senter, John	Tn	Turner, Minnie Lee	Tn	Senter, Horace [Father]	Lebanon					
Serilla, William D.	Aug 22, 1984	J.M.H.	Pa	Jul 25, 1924	60	Roth, Bette	Serilla, Michael		Roth, Anna		Roth, Bette - Paradise F.H. [Phoenix, Az]	V.A. - Phoenix, Az	WW 2				
Seuter, John Nelson	Oct 12, 1952	Hamblen Co	Tn	Nov 28, 1872	79	Ng	Seuter, John		Parsley, Mary Jane		Seuter, James H. [Buddy]	Lebanon [Greenbrier] - Hamblen Co					
Seuter, Pleasant F.	Sep 14, 1968	Hamblen Co	Tn	Jan 24, 1915	53	Ng	Seuter, John N.		Turner, Minie		Seuter, Mrs. Dorfina [Texas] - Charles-Hugh	Lebanon					
Seymour, Lou Annie	Dec 7, 1964	Knox Co	Tn	Sep 22, 1893	71	S	Seymour, Lacey		Hopson, Matilda		Satterfield, Mrs. Clark	Mill Springs					
Shackleford, Herman Halbert	Dec 3, 1941	Piedmont	Knox Co		45-2-6	Shackleford, Ellen			Thornton, Florence	Tn	Shackleford, Samuel & Carolyn	Piney	WW 1				
Shackleford, Albert Le Roy	Mar 28, 1973	Tn	Tn	Jun 15, 1894	78	W	Shackleford, James		Thornton, Florence		Stallings, Samuel & Carolyn	J.eesnut Grove	WW 1				
Sheldon, Thomas T.	Dec 22, 1969	Jeff Co	Tn	Sep 6, 1885	84	Cate, Lois	Sheldon, Joseph W.		Dunwoody, Tennessee		Sheldon, Mrs. Lois		WW 1				

NAME	DDATE	DLOCAT	BLOCAT	BDATE	AGE	SPOUSE	FATHER	FRLOCAT	MOTHER	MERLOCAL	BY	BURIAL	VET	SON	DAUG	BROTHER	SISTER
Shedden, Willa [F]	May 6, 1933	Dandridge		Nov 14, 1881	52	S	Shedden, George M.	Tn	Shelborn, Hanna	Tn	Shedden, Joe	Dandridge					
Shetter, David	Oct 13, 1972	Jeff Co							Howard, Pauline		Shetter, Ray	Flat Gap					
Shetter, George Earl	Jul 10, 1955	Jeff Co	Tn		16				Lane, Mae		Shetter, Ben	Brethern					
Shetter, Infant	Jul -, 1954																
Shands, Arlie D.	Mar 30, 1970	Jeff City	Tn	Jan 7, 1906	64	Willis, Opal	Shands, John S.		Baker, Ross		Shands, Mrs. A.D.	Jefferson Memorial					
Shands, Rufus Opal	Mar 27, 1996	Harlan Co, Tn		Aug 22, 1911	84	Shands, Arlie D. [D]	Willis, John Erwin		Herms, Maude Virginia		Shands, Bobby [Son]	J.M.G.		Bill-Jackie-Jerry-Ronnie-Daniel	Denton, Jolene	Linnie	Johnson, Mabel
Sharp, Ernest P.	Nov 15, 1996	Jeff Co	Tn	Jul 27, 1907	59	Ng	Sharp, Milford		Birchfield, Sally		Sharp, Nina Hott, Mrs. S.B.	Jefferson Memorial					
Sharp, Jacob H.	Apr 15, 1956	E. T. State	Tn	Feb 11, 1874	82	W	Sharp, Boyd		Ruts, Mary		Underwood, Mrs. N.V.	West View					
Sharp, Nina Mae	Sep 14, 1987	Jeff Cjo	Tn	Jul 24, 1909	78	W	Stallings, Robert		Hickman, Wallis Mae		Sharp, Bob	J.M.G.					
Sharp, Robert William	Aug 20, 1998	Jeff City	Jamestown, N. Dakota	May 8, 1920	78	Steen, Lucy Kathleen	Sharp, William E.		Riley, Ethel L.		Wills	J.M.G.		John & Jane [Sci-Sam & Ginger-Geri & Lynette [incl.]	Cooper, Karen - Flower, Gwen	Marshall & Betty [incl.]	
Sharpe, Van Alton	May 5, 1986	Jeff City	Leslieville, Nc.	Feb 29, 1932	63	Ng	Sharp, S.A.		Joyce, Lillian O.		Wills	Rutledge Methodist	54-56	Bryan & Michelle	Cherry, Mary Jo & Todd	Steve	Shelts, Lynn & Charlie
Sharer, James William	Aug 25, 1942	Jeff Co	Tn	Aug 21, 1877	65	Ng	Sharer, Charles	Tn	Keith, Margaret	Tn	Sharer, Mrs. James	Sunderland					
Sharer, Joseph E.	Oct 21, 1975	Adrian, Mich.	Tn		52	Treels, Mary			Sharer, Mrs. Joseph E.		Sharer, Mrs. Joseph E.	Sunderland					
Sharer, L.V.	Dec 9, 1987	Morristown, Tn.	Tn	Aug 17, 1917	70	Rines, Mary	Sharer, James W.		Arnett, Mary Isabelle		Sharer, Mrs. Joseph E.	Sunderland - Hamblen Co	WW 2				
Shaver, Mary Capeola	Aug 10, 1996	Trenton, Mich.	Knoxville, Tn	Aug 10, 1919	77	Treels, Henry Orville			Horner, Emma		Sauls, Brenda [Daug]	Sunderland			Cooper, Karen - Flower, Gwen		Cox, Hazel
Sheaffer, Mattie Murray	Aug 5, 1944	New Market	Jeff Co	Nov 29, 1916	51	Sheaffer, Jess	Murray, Mark	Jeff Co	Cross, Nancy	Jeff Co	Sheaffer, Jess - Murray, Luther & O.L.	Flat Gap					
Shedden, Alton Edward	Oct 23, 1949	Va	Va	Oct 28, 1981	29	S	Shedden, Wiley		Wheatley, Ova		Shedden, W.E.	Mt. Horeb	WW 2				
Shedden, Hugh	Apr 6, 1958	Memphis V.A. Hospital	Tn	Oct 26, 1981	66	Ng			Durwoody, Tennessee		Shedden, Mrs. Hugh	Mt. Horeb	WW 1				
Shedden, Joe	Aug 25, 1961	Jeff Co	Tn	Dec 31, 1887	63	Ng	Shedden, Joseph W.		Durwoody, Abshannon, Emmaline		Shedden, Joe & Glen	Mt. Horeb					
Shedden, John A.	May 31, 1937	Dandridge	Tn	Jun 17, 1860	76	W	Shedden, Cooper	Tn		Tn	Chittim, Luke	West View					
Shedden, John Joe	Apr 24, 1986	Rutledge, Tn	Jeff City	Feb 1, 1936	82	W	Shedden, Joe		Zirkle, Elise		Shedden, Glenn-Joe-Amanda [Nephew]	West View					
Shedden, Lois	Apr 28, 1971	Jeff Co	Tn	Sep 4, 1895	75	W					Shedden, Glenn-Joe-Amanda [Nephew]	Buffalo Grove					
Shedden, Margaret Elise	Sep 21, 1996	Jeff City	Tn	Feb 5, 1905	91	Shedden, Joe [D]	Zirkle, Arthur P.		Jarnigan, Rachel Bruce, Carrie		Shedden, Glenn [Son]	West View	John & Linda				Churchman, Helen
Shedden, Ova Lee	Oct 28, 1972	Dandridge, Tn	Tn	Oct 26, 1895	77	Shedden, Wiley	Wheatley, Henderson		Dean, Sallie		Shedden, Hugh	Mt. Horeb					
Shedden, Tennie	Sep 19, 1945	Jeff Co	Tn	Jun 12, 1898	67	W	Dinwiddie, James	Tn			Shedden, Gene - Bettis, Dorothy	Mt. Horeb					
Shedden, Wiley E.	Sep 5, 1975	Allen Clinic	Tn	Oct 12, 1895	79	W	Shedden, Joseph		Dinwiddie, Tennie		Shedden, W.E.	Mt. Horeb					
Sheets, John	Jul 18, 1999	Morristown, Tn	Jeff City	Nov 8, 1924	74		Sheets, John W.		Dirt, Gertrude		Sheets, Tom [Brother]	West View	Huff, William Forrest				Sheets, Trudie Mae-[D]- Smith, Susan-Gwynn, Virginia - Phipps, Mary - Clay, Gladys
Sheets, John W. [Col]	Feb 1, 1951	Jeff Co	Tn	Mar 23, 1896	55	Ng	Sheets, Dan		Mc Crosey, Mattie Turner, Sarah M.		Sheets, Gertrude	West View Colored					
Shelton, Albert	Feb 8, 1955	Willie Pine	Tn	May 5, 1943	11		Shelton, J.A.		Keck, Isabelle		Shelton, J.A.	Lee - Cocke Co					
Shelton, Juanita Marnice	Oct 1, 1942	Jeff Co	Jeff Co	Sep 27, 1942	4d		Shelton, Oldy	Claiborne Co	Ellison, Jewell	Claiborne Co	Shelton, Oldy						
Shelton, Kathy Darlene	Jan 28, 1969	Knox Co		Jul 25, 1969	6m		Shelton, Jerry		Shelton, La Donna		Shelton, Jerry & Jewell	West View					
Shelton, Kevin Dewayne	Mar 27, 1972	Jeff Co		Mar 27, 1972					Mc Daniel, Shirley John	Tn	Shelton, Jerry & Shirley	West View					
Shelton, Olay Jr.	Nov 11, 1946	Jeff Co		Oct 27, 1946	14d		Shelton, Olay		Foster, Mary E.	Tn	Messer, Mrs. Howard - Shelton, Carl	Narcle's Grove					
Shely, Beulah	Dec 14, 1989	J.M.H.	Farmdreville, Tn	Sep 3, 1911	78	W	Stuart, Landon C.		Smith, Essie V.		Shirley, Ann Harrison	Jarrigan					

NAME	DDATE	DLOCAT	BLOCAT	BDATE	AGE	SPOUSE	FATHER	FRLOCAT	MOTHER	MRLOCAT	BY	BURIAL	VET	SON	DAUG	BROTHER	SISTER
Shepard, Mary Parolee	Jul 14, 1932	Jeff City	Tn	Jan 28, 1864	68	Ng	Norton, George	Tn	Roberts, Cornelia	Tn	Norton, C. - Shepard, R.M.	Shilo					
Shebert, Henry	Oct 15, 1959	Hamblen Co				W					Hatcher, R.M. - Hall, Mattie - Rogers, Brenda - Grass, Helm - Sherbert, M.M.	West View					
Sherbit, Della	Aug 11, 1952	Jeff Co	Tn	Apr 1, 1880	72	Ng	Eldridge, Black		Unk		Smith, Mrs Edgar	Providence - Dandridge, Tn					
Sherrod, James H.	Jul 1, 1982	Tn	Tn	Feb 18, 1918	64	W	Conry, Mabel				Sherbit, Henry	West View					
Sherrod, James Howard	Aug 23, 1942	Knox Co	Knox Co	Apr 27, 1873	69-4-1	Ng	Sherrod, Jonathan	Tn	Mc Millan, Ann	Tn	Cullon, Mrs Dan [Doug]	Dandridge					
Shields, George [Cpl]	Dec 24, 1960	E. State Hospital	Tn	Jun 6, 1887	73	W	Shields, George Sr.		Reed, Cindy		Shields, Clifford	Youngs Memorial					
Shields, James	Oct 18, 1941	New Market	Buncombe Co, Nc		6m-8d	S			Shields, Hattie K.	Knox Co	Jernigan, Milford [Uncle] & Father	Clokeys Chapel					
Shields, Thomas A.	Nov 15, 1993	Morristown, Tn	La Porte, Indiana	Aug 24, 1966	27		Murray, James Allen		Shields, Patricia A.		Mother	Jernigan, Milford City - Kingsbury, Indiana					
Shiffler, William Dorsey Jr.	Jun 28, 1945	Hamblen Co	Hamblen Co	Jun 28, 1945			Shiffler, W.D. Sr.	Claiborne Co	Evens, Leona	Claiborne Co	Shiffler, W.D. Sr [Father]	Lebanon - Hamblen Co					
Shillingburg, Mary Willa	Aug 15, 1990	Morristown, Tn	Chapmanvill & W. Va	Sep 24, 1910	79	W	Lowe, T.G.		Dingess, Louvena		Hunt, Anne [Sister]	Fairview - Chapmanville, W. Va					
Shipe, Helen Louise	Jun 2, 1994	Jeff City	Knox Co	Apr 19, 1922	72		Shipe, Woodfin Grady		Stevenson, Katherine		Bowman, Paul - Clanton, Ruth - Boruff, Margaret - Simpson, Evelyn - Walker, Wanda [Cousins]	J.M.G.					
Shipe, Katherine Zella	Jan 28, 1986	J.M.H.	Tn	Jan 5, 1912	96	Ng	Stevenson, Leonard		Hall, Martha		Shipe, Helen	J.M.G.					
Shipe, Woodfin Grady	Mar 24, 1971	Jeff Co	Tn	Jan 28, 1890	80	W	Shipe, Mack		Bates, Minnie		Shipe, Mrs. Kate & Helen	Memorial Gardens					
Shipley, Alice Gertrude	Jun 27, 1965	Knox Co		Feb 17, 1881	84	W	Martin, Robert B.		White, Mary Sue		Hull, Erwin - Fulton, C.E. - Huff, Mildred [Niv] [Daughters]	Fairview - Washington Co, Tn					
Shipley, Ira Wayne	Jan 1, 1946	Jeff Co		Dec 30, 1944	3d	Ng	Shipley, Thomas	Tn	Patterson, Azziee	Tn	Newman, George T.	Hebron	466				
Shipley, James	Sep 11, 1937	Straw Plains		Nov 25, 1892	44		Shipley, Tebe	Tn	Highsmith, Mattie	Tn	Bailey, Mrs. John	Straw Plains					
Shipley, Lilly June	Nov 6, 1976	Cape Guardian, Mo	Tn	Apr 24, 1920	56	Shipley, Jack	Brooks, Nyles		Householdwright, Grace Ann		Shipley, Jack	Hebron					
Shipley, Theodore Roosevelt	Jun26, 1983	Vet. Home - Mt. Home		Nov 1, 1904	58	Bible, Bernice	Shipley, Theodore L.		Keener, Ella		Shipley, Bernice	West View	WW 2				
Shires, John Hoke Jr.	Mar 14 1982	J.M.H.	Henrietta, Nc	Nov 1, 1904	68	Lindsey, Geneva	Shires, J.H. Sr.		Hughes, Ida Mae		Wife	J.M.G.	unk				
Shive, Pearl	Nov 25, 1994	Jeff City	Crosshill, Pa	Feb 15, 1923	71	Shive, Gerald E.	Gauker, Roy		Heidbach, Mary Alice		Husband	Cremated		Shive, Jane			
Shiverdecker, Helen Louise	Dec 5 1995	Knoxville, Tn	Brock, Ohio	Jul 28, 1921	74	Fischbach, Helen	Fischbach, Clarence		Jackson, Florence		Shiverdecker, Stephen [Son]	Gary [Ohio]- Bob-John			Price, Sharon [Ohio]		
Shiverdecker, Roscoe D.	Feb 27, 1993	Arsonia, Ohio		Jul 28, 1913	79	Fischbach, Helen	Shiverdecker, Dale		Lesper, Mary		Shiverdecker, Steve Brock - Greenville, Ohio [Son]	Brock - Greenville, Ohio		Gary-Bob-Steve-John	Price, Sharon		Mary - Trouscine, Dorothy
Shockley, Felix Ann	Apr 3, 1934	Jeff City		Mar 30, 1934	5d		Shockley, Dexter C.	Tn	Cleavinger, Extra Fay	Tn	Shockley, Dexter - Cleavinger, Joe	West View					
Shockley, P.W.	Nov 5, 1928	Tn		Dec 9, 1863	82-9-24	W	Shockley, E.		Coffin, Marta	Tn	Shockley, J.A.	Shilo					
Shorter, Cornelia	Jun 9, 1945	Grainger Co		Oct 12, 1995	81	W	Long, John		Wilson, Susan		Mc Daniel, Mattie	Sarah Swann					
Shorter, Edgar Graham	Jul 4, 1947	Hamblen Co		Feb 24, 1859	41-8-22	Ng	Shorter, William	Tn	Mc Anally, Cordia	Tn	Lynn, Emert	Lebanon					
Shorter, T.J.	Jan 11, 1931	Jeff City	Tn		71	Ng	Shorter, Berry		Long, Mary	Tn	Mc Dowell, Mattie	Sarah Swann					
Shortt, Delores Ann	Nov 30, 1994	Morristown, Tn	Morristown, Tn	Dec 26, 1935	58	W	Bacon, L.E.		Bush, Irene		Shortt, Teresa [Daug]	Hamblen Memorial		James			Wendell
Shoun, Irene	Sep 22, 1986	J.M.H.	Tn	May 26, 1900	86	W	Brooks, C.J.		Brooks, C.J.		Sisk, Freddie S. [Louisphire, Ky]	West View					

NAME	DDATE	BLOCAT	BLOCAT	DDATE	AGE	SPOUSE	FATHER	FELOCAT	MOTHER	MFELOCAT	BY	BURIAL	VET	SON	DAUG	BROTHER	SISTER
Shrader, Dylan Thomas	Apr 16, 1999	Knoxville, Tn	Knoxville, Tn	Apr 16, 1999			Shrader, Kevin		Cox, Jennifer		Shrader, Billy Joe & Tammy [G-P]-Cox, Harold & Martha-Wand, Faye & Tom[G-G-P]	Lebanon Baptist					
Shrader, James H.	Oct 7, 1953	Jeff Co	Tn	Dec 30, 1875	77	Ng	Shrader, George W.		Fox, Mary J.		Shrader, Mrs. Mary Hale	West View					
Shrader, Mary	May 14, 1967	Jeff Co	Tn	Dec 14, 1878	88	Shrader, James H. [D]	Hale, James	Tn	Ferguson, Sara		Nichols, Hattye-Haynes, Fern	West View					
Shrader, Mary Jane	Jan 10, 1931	Jeff Co	Tn	Jul 9, 1851	79	W	Fox, Branson		William, Mary		Shrader, James H.	Oakland					
Shrielsmon, Lisa	Feb 28, 1985	J.M.H.	New York	Apr 9, 1950	34	Christianson, Don	Beaumandt, Vivian				Merrick, Mrs. Asa - Jewish-F.H. (Portland, Maine)	Berkeley-Small-Rockland, Maine					
Shultz, Margaret	Oct 7, 1981	Knoxville	Tn	Jan 27, 1915	16	S	Shultz, P.M.	Tn	Hill, Sarah	Tn	Shultz, P.M.	Pleasant View					
Shupe, Ada V.	Oct 23, 1983	Linden, NJ	Toms Creek, Va	Dec 17, 1920	72	Fleming, John P.		Kiser, Alice		Tracy, Barbara I [Daug]	Oakland - Grainger Co		[Step] Shupe, J.R. [Vs]	Sexton, Sharon - [Steps] Miller, Linda - Davis, Wanda - Beddshaw, Renee - Shupe, Brenda	Harkiss [Fls] William [Vs]	
Silver, Ada	Mar 18, 1999	J.M.H.	Grainger Co	Nov 10, 1912	76	Silver, Marvin L. [Rev.] Ng	Bateman, Marion		James, Carrie		Silver, Marvin L.	Flat Gap					
Silver, Albert Listenberry	Jun 7, 1999	Jeff Co	Nc	Jun 6, 1899	80	Ng	Silver, John		Hicks, Mary V.		Silver, Leonard	Flat Gap					
Silver, John Listenberry	Nov 8, 1984	Jeff City	Knoxville, Tn	Jun 29, 1984	10		Silver, James D.		Ricks, Candace		Mother - Silver, Leonard & Robbie - Walkins, Carol - Rinne, Gaylord [G-Parents]	Lebanon Baptist					Susan
Silver, John Y.	Aug 7, 1970	Jeff Co	Nc	May 5, 1876	94	W	Silver, John		Hicks, Mary Victoria		Profitt, Bonnie - Churchamn, Mrs. Elmo	Flat Gap					
Silver, Marvin Leonard [Rev.]	Dec 15, 1990	J.M.H.	Henderson Co, Nc	Aug 31, 1907	83	W	Silver, John Young		Haney, Eliza Jane		Robeson, Drama Marvin	J.M.G.					
Silver, Mary Margaret	Jul 16, 1998	Knoxville, Tn	Old Fort, Nc	Jan 30, 1920	77		Hinchey, Myrtle	Nc			Silver, Jim [Nephew] - Shaner, Sandra [Niece]	Flat Gap				Leonard	
Silver, Mary V.	Aug 7, 1931	Jeff Co	Nc	Jun 1, 1852	79	W	Hicks, James M.	Nc	Green, Sarah	Nc	Silvers, John	Flat Gap					
Silver, Myrtle	Feb 22, 1984	Humana Hosp.	Nc	Nov 2, 1898	85	W	Hinchey, Robert Preston		Clevenger, Birsha		Silver, Miss Margaret Leonard	Flat Gap					
Silver, Reid Quinton	Jan 14, 1984	Jeff City	Nc	May 25, 1916	77	W	Silver, Weldie		Ogle, Lillie		Silver, Denise M. [Daug]	Lebanon Baptist		Keith	[Neice] Denison, Mary Ellen	Brook	Gonner, Mary Ellen
Silver, William Clayton	Aug 29, 1996	Dollerwal, Tn	Tn	Mar 25, 1937	51	Shackelford, Wanda	Silver, Marvin	Tn	Bateman, Ada	Tn	Mc Mahan - Burnsville, [Daug]	Mc Mahan - Burnsville, Nc	55-59				
Silvers, Eliza Jane	Sep 28, 1990	Tn	Nc	Nov 23, 1883	78-10-7	W	Silvers, J.Y.		Beteman, Ada	Tn	Silver, Wanda	J.M.G.	flat gap				
Silvers, John	Jul 5, 1934	Jeff City	W	Jan 1, 1844	90	Nc	Silvers, J.Y.		Wooly, Emma		Silvers, J.Y.	Flat Gap	flat gap				
Simmons, Elsie Culbert	Apr 19, 1981	New Jersey	New Jersey	Jul 11, 1887	83	W	Sibbald, Robert		Culbert, Margaret		Hallen, Mrs. Leslie	George Washington Memorial - Nj					
Simmons, Melvin W.	Dec 4, 1979	Jeff City	Nc	Jan 28, 1895	84	Sibbald, Elsie	Simmons, Oscar		Diddle, Carrie		Hallen, Mrs. Jane Maple Grove-Worcester, Ny	Flat Gap Maple Grove-Worcester, Ny	WW 1			Brook	
Simpkins, Cordelia	Jul 19, 1947	Grainger Co	Tn	Aug	adrt 79	W	Clevenger, James K.	Tn	Dyle, Ellen	Tn	Collins, Mrs. Taylor-Carroll, Cecil - Parker, Clarence	Mill Springs		Son-Charles E.			
Simpson, Charles Edwin	Sep 3, 1998	Jeff Co	Nc	Nov 15, 1906	89	Easley, Vesta	Simpson, Herbert		Parker, Sara		Simpson, Estcl-Sam-Wills	Flat Gap					
Simpson, Charles Herbert	Jan 18, 1957	Jeff Co	Sullivan Co, Tn	Apr 2, 1880	76	Ng	Simpson, Nathan		Nellies, Lydia		Simpson, Kenneth	West View	Joe-Charles E.				
Simpson, Gertrude	Jan 11, 1989	J.M.H.	Cleveland, Tn	May 9, 1903	86	Simpson, Jake [D]	Unk		Hallen, Lydia		Simpson, Kenneth	Eastview Memorial - Strawberry Plains					
Simpson, Infant Male	Apr 17, 1966	Jeff Co	Tn	Apr 17, 1966			Simpson, Michael Ray		Ballew, Donna Gale	Tn	Simpson, Michael	Memorial Gardens					
Sims, Lorena	Nov 7, 1981	Jeff Co	Tn	May 17, 1903	78	W [Twice]	Walker, Thomas Franklin	Indiana	Linss, Nancy Ellen		Briggs, Mrs. Doris	Sunderland					

NAME	DATE	BLOCAT	BLOCAT	BDATE	AGE	SPOUSE	FATHER	FRELOCAT	MOTHER	MFRLOCAT	BY	BURIAL	VET	SON	DAUG	BROTHER	SISTER
Sisk, William L. Lloyd	Oct 8, 1991	Sevierville, Tn	Jeff Co	Oct 11, 1937	53	Britton, Mary Ann	Sisk, Claude		Douglas, Eliza		Wife	J.M.G.	unk				
Sisse, Justin Russell	Apr 6, 1998	Jeff City	Greeneville, Tn	Dec 6, 1940	57	Sisse, David T.	Russell, John A.		Russell, Elizabeth		Husband	Andrew Johnson - Greenville, Tn		Turn-John			
Sizer, Mary Salter	Jan 2, 1942	Jeff City	Flushing, Ny	Sep 7, 1880	76-1-1	S	Sizer, William		Burnette, Maria	N.J.	Powers, Mrs. Ross				[Step] Leonard, Tina		
Sizer, Cora Myrtle	Jun 22, 1960	Knox Co	Tn	Sep 7, 1880	79	W	Bertia, W. W.		Riggs, Addie		Scott, Mrs. Henry - Howard, Edna Belle - Steen, Erwin & Fred	Ebenezer					
Sizer, Dorothy Kay	Dec 7, 1981	J.M.H.	Jeff City		31	Div	Sisen, James Carl		Friesis, Julia		Steen, Robert [Brother]	West View					
Sixen, Hubert A.	Nov 9, 1973	Knoxville, Tn	Tn	Feb 22, 1894	79	Norton, Mattie Lou	Sixen, Joseph M.		Inleblonger, Catherine		Steen, Carl-Mr. S. Hubert A.	West View					
Sixen, James Carl	Feb 4, 1990	Sebring, Fla.	Greenback, Tn	Dec 30, 1916	73	Friesis, Julia	Steen, Hubert A.		Coy, Maude		Steen, Clifford	West View	WW 2				
Sixen, Marshall H.	Jan 3, 1953	Jeff Co	Tn	Jul 23, 1884	68	Ng	Steen, Hale		Cortoell, Martha L.		Steen, Mrs. Flora [Wife]	Ebenezer					
Sixen, Matt Lou Norton	Nov 17, 1984	J.M.H.	Tn			Steen, Hubert A. [D]			Hodges, Mrs. W. A.		West View					
Sixen, Nettie Maude	Feb 18, 1946	Knox Co	Greenback, Tn	Oct 10, 1882	53	Steen, Hubert A. [Age-52] Ng			Elizabeth	Tn	Steen, Luta & James	West View					
Steen, William P.	Jul 26, 1981	Memphis, Tn	Tn	1961		Ng					Hodge, Mrs. R.K. - Steen, Mrs. Margaret	Oakland					
Steen, John Edgar	Jun 17, 1973	New Market, Tn	Tn	May 11, 1914	59	Jones, Margaret	Slagle, James H.		Ravenau, Sarah		Slagle, Mrs. Ollie [Wife]	Friends Station	WW 2				
Slagle, Joseph A.	Oct 2, 1947	Jeff Co		Sep 30, 1892	55	Ng	Slagle, William C.	Tn	Griffin, Louisha Ann	Tn	Friends Station					
Slagle, Mary Minerva	Apr 14, 1956	E. St. Hospital	Tn	Oct 25, 1880	75	S	Slagle, William		Griffin, Cynthia		Wilson, Mrs. Woodrow	Friends					
Slaton, Irene	Aug 27, 1983	J.M.H.	Tn	Nov 28, 1905	77	S	Slaton, Samuel		Pollard, Viola		Williford, Alma Ruth [Perry] - Glass, Bobbie - Hetherton, Faye - Millerd, Virginia	Flat Gap					
Slaton, Samuel H.	Nov 28, 1931	Jeff City	Tn	Aug 18, 1862	69	Ng					Birchfield, T. - Slaton, Bill - Williford, Mrs. Perry, Birchfield, Virginia - Slaton, Mrs. W. S.	Flat Gap					
Slaton, Viola Pollard	Dec 3, 1957	Jeff Co	Tn	Feb 18, -	101	W	Unk		Wickman, Elizabeth			Oakland					
Slaughter, Infant [Mayo]	Feb 20, 1927			Mar 1, 1944	0		Stallon, Y. William	Tn	Johnson, Effie Ogle		Slaton, Bill						
Slaughter, Evelyn Elaine [Mayo]	Jan 11, 1975	Knoxville, Tn	Tn		30	Div	Bellamy, James Lee		Ingram, Louise		Bellamy, Louise	West View					
Sliger, Vida	Mar 13, 1987	Jeff City	Ellijay, Nc	Jun 27, 1912	84		Lockford, Benjamin Allen		Asher, Dora Bell		Millgan, Virginia K. [Dana]	National - Chattanooga, Tn					
Sloan, Albert Russell	Mar 24, 1993	Knoxville, Tn	Rutherford Co., Tn	Jan 12, 1911	82	Deels, Lois	Sloan, Albert R.		Stubblefield, Emma		Sloan, Joe William [Son]	J.M.G.			Pemberton, Marcille & Jay - Johnson, Ann & Harry	Horace-Raymond	Sloan, Lucille -
Sloan, Albert Wayne	Mar 12, 1992	U.T.H.	Knox Co, Tn	May 3, 1938	53	Frazier, Valerie	Sloan, Albert R.		Deels, Lois		Wife	J.M.G.	unk				
Slover, Charles B.	Sep 23, 1949	Grainger Co.	Jeff Co	Dec 22, 1949	54-9-1	Ng	Unk		Slover, Elizabeth J.		Bellinger, Ed	Mill Springs					
Slover, Maggie	May 10, 1984	J.M.H.	Tn	Jun 6, 1892	91	W	Elodge, Maggie		Ferguson, Harriet		Winstead, Mrs. Velma	West View					
Slover, William Frank	Aug 4, 1977	Straw Plains	Tn	Oct 6, 1889	87	W	Elodge, Ashley W.		Brown, Cordla		Slover, Mrs. Frank	West View					
Smalling, Rose Alice	Mar 22, 1944	Hamblen Co	Jeff Co	Feb 13, 1877	67	W	Dukes, Alex	Tn	Cates, Mary	Tn	Hendrix, Relia - Dukes, Alex	Piedmont					
Smallman, Tennie Belle	Sep 25, 1942	Hamblen Co	Hamblen Co	Sep 7, 1881	61	Smallman, L.F.	Ivy, Patrick B.		Breeden, Mahala		Smallman, Glenn [Son]	Economy					
Smallwood, Paul Z.	Jan 28, 1995	Jeff City	Tn	Jan 28, 1905		Smallwood, William Earl			California	Tn	Link, Glenda Mae	Cumberland View - S. Pittsburg, Tn					
Smolcer, Berlis Underwood	Feb 3, 1979	Jeff City	Tn	Jun 8, 1893	85	W	Peppins, Amanda Jane	Hamblen Co	Cox, Helen - Underwood, Walter		Link, Martha	Mt. View					
Smolcer, Elvin Mae	Sep 18, 1989	Heritage Center	Greene Co, Tn	Jun 15, 1913	76	W	Wright, John		Beckner, Willie		Smith, Judd - James	J.M.G.					Goodson, Suzanne - Hoffman, Jane - Smith, Elizabeth

NAME	DDATE	BLOCAT	BLOCAT	BDATE	AGE	SPOUSE	FATHER	FBLOCAT	MOTHER	MFBLOCAT	BY	BURIAL	VET	SON	DAUG	BROTHER	SISTER
Smelcer, Enon Satolhell [M]	Jan 14, 1947	Jeff Co	Greene Co	Mar 9, 1879	67-10-30	Ng	Smelcer, James	Tn	Deleusk, Lanus	Tn	Smelcer, Mrs. E.S.	Colored					
Smelcer, Laura	Dec 31, 1925		Tn			W		Tn	Adams, Martha	Tn		Greene Co					
Smelcer, Loonie Albert	Oct 23, 1967	Greene Co. Tn	Tn	Aug 20, 1913	54	Ng	Smelcer, E.S.		Cobble, Nellis		Smelcer, Mrs. Elvie & Children	Memorial Gardens					
Smelcer, Nellie Elizabeth	Oct 4, 1950	Jeff Co	Tn	Oct 14, 1886	61	W	Cobble, L.M.		Maj, Laura		Smelcer, Edie & Loonie - Garry, Mrs.	Oakland					
Smith, A.M.	Feb 19, 1934	Straw Plains	Ng	Nov 4, 1954	79	Ng	Smith, William	Nc	Kerby, Susie	Tn	Smith, Frank, C.H. & R.H. [Sons]	Piney					
Smith, Adra Morris Lee	Jan 20, 1927		Tn			S	Cannon, Jettie	Tn	Smith, O.C.	Tn	Smith, O.C.	Cortner					
Smith, Alvin C. York [Pace-Offcer]	Mar 12, 1969	Knoxville, Tn	Jeff City	Feb 9, 1920	73	Smith, Agnes	Tate, Martha		Wife		Wife	West View					Cutting, Shelia
Smith, Alvin Harrison	Mar 20, 1940	Straw Plains, Tn	Tn	Oct 5, 1883	76	W	Henry, Pearl		Hubbard, J.S.		Wife	Beech Creek					
Smith, Arnusell	Mar 12, 1985	Jeff City	Knox Co	Jul 26, 1915	79	Ng	Smith, Dee		Medlett, Milford		Smith, Dan [Son]	Beech Springs		Doug Ed			
Smith, Archie Woodrow	Dec 11, 1983	Knoxville, Tn	Knoxville, Tn	Jan 7, 1914	79	Farrar, Elizabeth		Owens, Dora		Wife	Greenwood - Knoxville, Tn		David Bryan	Wiseman, Mary/Rachel Calloway, Opal		
Smith, Bessanna	Feb 10, 1931	New Market	Tn	Sep 6, 1910	20	S	Smith, Luther	Tn	Smith, Maud	Tn	Smith, Maud	Mill Sidge					
Smith, Boyd A.	Jan 5, 1980	Talbott, Tn	Tn		76	S	Smith, J.P.		Dyer, Mrs. W.E.		Dyer, Mrs. W.E.	Buck Creek - Hamblen Co					
Smith, Carl [Pandy]	Jul 28, 1987	J.M.H.	Tn	Jul 17, 1965	22	S	Smith, Carl R. Sr.		Moore, Sarah Adlaide		Higshins, Aislene S - Opis, Bob	Lebanon					
Smith, Carl L.	Sep 16, 1999	Knoxville, Tn	Jeff Co	Sep 1, 1917	82	Woods, Lucille	Smith, Sherman D.		Shorter, Allene		Wife	J.M.G.	42-46	Terry	Cox, Carlene- Byrd, Cheryl	J.G.	Day, Lorene - Webb, Dorothy
Smith, Carl Lilburn	Jul 6, 1962	Knox Co	Tn	May 12, 1901	61	Ng	Northern, Nora		McBliff, Olive B.		Wife	Mill Springs					
Smith, Cary Jordan	Sep 24, 1949	Knox Co	Va	Jun 22, 1881	68	Ng	Smith, Ballard		Northern, Nora		Wife	Highland Memorial - Knox Co					
Smith, Charlie Harrison	Sep 23, 1961		Tn	Oct 31, 1884	76	W	Smith, Archie Manoel		Price, Martha		Smith, Edd & Ralph - Morgan, Mrs. - Cole, Mrs.	Beaver Creek					
Smith, Cora Lee	Mar 9, 1971	Jeff Co	Va	Nov 15, 1883	87	W	Cole, Columbus Lee		Griffin, Nancy Melinda		Smith, Dr. Jane	Evergreen - Roanoke, Va					
Smith, Daisy	Jun 19, 1981	Jeff City	Tn	May 27, 1903	78	Smith, Frank		Whorton, Susan		Alley, Mack	Hills Union					
Smith, Della Bernice [Col]	Dec 28, 1944	Knox Co	Knox Co	Nov 17, 1896	58	W	Crockett, Jacob	Tn	Gaddis, Margaret	Tn	Fain, Sam - Williams, Mary	Colored					
Smith, Dorothy Lee [Col]	Jan 9, 1984	Dayton, Ohio	Tn	Nov 13, 1954	59	Smith, Jessie	Mills, Anderson		Fannie		Smith, Jessie [Dayton, OH]	West View					
Smith, Eugene	Jan 9, 1967	Greenville, Sc	Jeff Co	Dec 27, 1921	75	Talley, Mable Jean	Smith, Jessie		West Mae		Wife	J.M.G.	navy		Hicks, Faye- Brenda - Smith, Teresa		Hammond, Nina
Smith, Flora Merichla Beard Frazier	Dec 9, 1991	J.M.H.	Sevier Co	Jul 25, 1908	83	Smith, William H.	Brackins, Sara		Williams, Barbara [Daug]		New Market						
Smith, Frank Austin	Jan 17, 1965	Jeff Co	Tn	Feb 10, 1896	66	Ng	Cole, Andrew R.		Northern, Anna		Smith, George & Ruth - Smith, Alvin	Mill Springs	WW 1				
Smith, Frank Jr.	Jan 18, 1975	Dayton, Ohio	Tn								Jerome & Edward	West View	WW 1&2				
Smith, Frank P.	Mar 6, 1972	Jeff Co	Tn	Jul 10, 1897	74	Smith, Elizabeth	Smith, Thomas P.		Bevins, Anna		Smith, Elizabeth	Decatur - Decatur, Tn					
Smith, Frank Sr. [Col]	Dec 8, 1980	Jeff Co	Tn	Jul 30, 1871	89	W	Smith, James		Walker, Mary		Smith, Frank Jr.-Alvin- Jessie	West View Colored					
Smith, Freddy James Henry	Sep 4, 1944	Jeff City	Talbott, Tn	Nov 4, 1944	53	Marshall, Mary Ann	Smith, Fred D.		Helton, Alice	Tn	Wife	Sunderland		Fred 2nd; Scott- Lance-T.J.	Rogers , Rebecca		
Smith, G.A.	Apr 21, 1932		Tn	May 27, 1872	59	W	Smith, William		Walker, Pervilla		Moore	Ebenezer					
Smith, George Adam [Rev.]	Apr 9, 1979	Morristown, Tn	Tn	Jun 12, 1906	72	Ng	Smith, Warren		Northern, Lenar		Smith, Ruth-Pearl	Mill Springs					
Smith, Gilbert M.	Jun 3, 1940	Talbott	Tn	Mar 22, 1879	68	Ng	Smith, William	Tn	Priscilla	Tn	Wife & Children	Ebenezer					
Smith, Hazel Ruth	Jul 12, 1974	J.M.H.	Tn	Apr 4, 1909	75	S	Smith, William		Northern, Nora		Tate, Pauline	Mill Springs					
Smith, Henry H.	Feb 8, 1967	Strawberry Plains	Tn	Feb 8, 1898	69	W	Smith, Jim		Smith, Warren		Wife	West View					
Smith, Herbert C.	Apr 27, 1979	Knoxville, Tn	Tn	Aug 25, 1907	71	Ng	Smith, Toy		Watkins, Frankie		Smith, Alfred C. [Son]	Beaver Creek	WW 2				
Smith, Jack	Jun 9, 1970	Jeff Co	Tn	Oct 18, 1929	40	Hopkins, Edna Mae	Smith, Charlie		Nelson, Elizabeth		Smith, Mrs. Maria Trent	West View					
Smith, James [Col]	Dec 7, 1928		Va		63	Ng	Smith, Alex	Va	Smith, Mary	Va	Smith, James	Colored					

NAME	BDATE	BLOCAT	BLOCAT	BDATE	AGE	SPOUSE	FATHER	FRLOCAT	MOTHER	MTRLOCAT	BY	BURIAL	VET	WW 2	SON	DAUG	BROTHER	SISTER
Smith, James Alvin (Jack)	Jul 22, 1994	J.M.H	Tn	Apr 28, 1915	69	Deeta, Ruby	Smith, Charles J.P.		Smith, Rose		Elmore, Martha Sue - Lynn, Gary (Nephew)	Strawberry Plains - Sunderland						
Smith, James G.	Nov 7, 2000	Jeff City	Tn	Jul 9, 1916	84	W	Smith, James W.		Nelson, Elizabeth		Smith, Mrs. Mary Hammer	Lebanon						
Smith, James Walter	May 22, 1949	Gunfire, Ky		May 3, 1891	58		Smith, James W.	Va	Neeley, Anna	Tn	Jefferson Memorial	Jefferson Memorial						
Smith, Jennifer Anne	Mar 23, 1990	Hamblen Co	Tn	Mar 23, 1990	abt 73	W	Smith, Jim		Walker, Mary		Smith, Hugh [RV] & Rufus	Colored						
Smith, John [Curl]	Jan 25, 1946	Jeff Co	Jeff Co	May 9, 1889	73	Smith, A.P. [D]	Rankin, Edgar		Nix, Nora		Parker, Elsie - Grindstaff, Mrs. Georgia	West View						
Smith, Josie M.	Jan 2, 1963	Jeff Co	Tn	Mar 19, 1938	62	Smith, David	Bresson, Luther		Woods, Frances		Husband	Mt. Horeb						
Smith, Joyce Marie	Nov 25, 2000	Jeff City	Tn	Nov 6, ---	95	W	Hinkle, Henry		Branner, Mary A.		Dockery, Rex - Zirkle, Ben	Strawberry Plains						
Smith, Laura	Feb [14], 1952	Knox Co	Tn		52	Smith, Lee	Liddon, James		Carpenter, Eva		Smith, Lee - Ivy, Mary Lee - Cotter, Jessie L.	Annondale - Grainger Co						
Smith, Laura Dollie	Jul 18, 1959	U.T. Hospital	Tn	Sept 16, 1906	75	Ng	Parker, Henry		Mills, Mary		Smith, C.H.	Brott? Creek						
Smith, Lennie Belle	Apr 10, 1959	Jeff Co	Tn	Dec 25, 1883	70	Smith, Ralph H.	Burchfiel, George T.		Northern, Flora		Smith, Garyhal C.	Beaver Creek						
Smith, Lillian Lucille	Aug 19, 1990	Humana Hosp.	Grainger Co	Jan 29, 1920	80	W	Love, Marshall		Collier, Callie		Smith, Maryhal C.	Jefferson Memorial						
Smith, Mike Love	Jan 23, 1986	Jeff City	Tn	Sep 9, 1905	90	W	Nelson, Gilmore		Pendergrast, Rebecca		Smith, James G.	Sunderland						
Smith, Margaret Elizabeth	Aug 18, 1988	Hillhaven		Jul 3, 1899	84	W	Messimer, London		Ferris, Maude		Rogers, Ms. Lester	Jefferson Memorial						
Smith, Marie Monterey	Jul 24, 1974	Oak Ridge, Tn	Pa	Oct 23, 1891	66	W	Smith, John Henry		Lone, Mae		Wife	W						
Smith, Marshall Clarence	Nov 14, 2000	Knoxville, Tn	Ky	Jun 29, 1934	74	Evelyn P.	Carter, George M.		Newman, Sarah K.	Tn	Miller, Mrs. G.C.	J.M.G		unk				
Smith, Martha	Jan 21, 1990	Knox Co	Tn	Feb 19, 1865	90	W	Hubbard, Charles		Huff, Cora		Hubbard, J.S.	Piedmont						
Smith, Martha Jane	Oct 24, 1953	Knox Co	Tn	Sept 18, 1963	91	W	Ferguson, John Taylor		Ferguson, Sarah		Powell, William E. 3rd [Son]	Beaver Creek						
Smith, Martha Powell	Jun 2, 1999	Dandridge, Tn	Bristol, Va	Mar 28, 1908	78-8/25	W				Tn	Fieldhaven - Keith, Ky	Fieldhaven - Keith, Ky			Peek, Pat - Howard, Jane			
Smith, Mary [Curl]	Feb 7, 1926	Tn	Tn	May 10, 1907	85	W	Moore, Parthena		Walker, Sarah		Smith, Toy	Colored						
Smith, Mary [Curl]	Feb 1, 1936	Jeff City	Tn	Nov 11, 1906	abt 85	W			Ferguson, Sarah		Colored	Colored						
Smith, Mary Elizabeth	Nov 25, 1981	Jeff Co	Tn	May 10, 1907	74	Smith, Frank [D]	Hubbard, Sam		Huff, Cora		Crawford, Mary Ruth - Cates, Paul	Decatur - Decatur, Tn						
Smith, Mary Nancy	Oct 9, 1952	Jeff City	Tn	Nov 11, 1906	45	W	Hanna, Joseph		Ferguson, Sarah		Ball, Mrs. Bruce	Lebanon						
Smith, Mary Ruth	Apr 4, 1999	Talbott, Tn	Jeff Co	Jul 23, 1917	81	Burchfiel, James G.	Burchfiel, James H.		Burchfiel, Genevieve	Husband	Sunderland	Sunderland					Fred & Faye - Jim - Land Smith, Fred & Alice	Burchfiel, Eva (Tillie)- Helen - Hinchey, Lura Ett, & James R - [In-Law] Rogers, Mabelle - Messengill, Yvonne
Smith, Maude	Apr 3, 1989	New Market, Tn	Tn			Smith, George	Anderson, Sam		Snodgrass, Vida		Smith, George	Mills						
Smith, May	Jan 11, 1928	Tn	Tn	Aug 7, 1904	24-7/7	Smith, Jessie	Wish, Hickle	Tn	Wish, Mary	Tn	Wish, Hickle	Mills Springs						
Smith, Mildrie E.	Nov 7, 1989	Denton, Oh	Tn		73	Smith, Frank Jr			Hankins, Sallie		Smith, Frank Jr - Lauderback, Dana	West View						
Smith, Mossie	Jan 22, 1974	Jeff City	Va	May 15, 1884	69	Smith, Jim [D]	Williams, Alex		Clam, Alice F.		Satterfield, Kathryn - Smith, Elmer - James - C.F. Talley, Garron - Talla, Pauline	West View						
Smith, Nannie Bell	Mar 29, 1977	Jeff City	Va	Aug 7, 1904	72	W	Taylor, Benjamin Franklin		Clam, Alice F.		Smith, Elmer - James - C.F. Talley, Garron - Talla, Pauline	Mill Springs						
Smith, Nora	Mar 3, 1941	Mill Springs	Jeff Co		66-5/26	W	Smith, William		Hickman, Mellie	Tn	Smith, Carl [Son]	Mill Springs						
Smith, Nora Ann Belle	Jan 13, 1940	New Market		Jan 19, 1886	54	Ng	Dockery, James Mitchell		Smith, Mary	Tn	Husband & Children	New Market						
Smith, Octa Viola	Feb 8, 1952	Jeff Co	Tn	Jan 19, 1906	46	Smith, Henry [2 Neff]	Miller, William		Baker, Florence		Baker, Florence	Beaver Creek						
Smith, Olice	May 18, 1974	Talbott, Tn	Tn			W	McNeil, John		Bull, Ruth		Smith, Curl - LG - Day, Lorena - Wash, Dorothy S.	Mt. Pleasant						

NAME	DDATE	DLOCAT	BLOCAT	BDATE	AGE	SPOUSE	FATHER	FBLOCAT	MOTHER	MBRLOCAT	BY	BURIAL	VET	SON	DAUG	BROTHER	SISTER
Smith, Ora Irene	Sep 25, 1966	Tn	Tn	Jan 22, 1906	60	Smith, Valer [D]	Stipes, Robert	Sc	Tucker, Fannie	Sc	Stipes, W.E. - Lawson, Mrs. Mary - Smith, Bill	Strawberry Plains					
Smith, Pearl	May 28, 1946	Sc	Sc	Aug 19, 1894	51	Ng	Coley, Dan		Boggs, Katherine	Sc	Smith, Abe & John W.	Straw Plains					
Smith, Rachel Allyn	Sep 15, 1996	Knoxville, Tn	Shandong Province, China	Jun 4, 1916	80	Ng	Leonard, Charles A.		Corbett, Evelyn		Barr, Marilyn S. [Daug]	J.M.G.					
Smith, Richard Kenneth	Feb 3, 1996	Jeff City	Wellington, Ohio	Jul 27, 1926	69	Moore, Carole	Smith, Theodore		Hall, Ida		Wife	Milan, Ohio		James Lawrence [Nc] Vaughn [OH]- Michael [FT]- [Step] Trematore, David-Daniel [Ohio]	[Step] Ritzenthaler, Linda [Del.]	Larry [OH]	
Smith, Robert H.	Feb 25, 1965	Knox Co	Tn	Sep 15, 1883	81	W	Smith, Archie		Griffen, Nancy		Mc Daniel, Mrs. O.A. [Rev.] - Smith, Paul	Strawberry Plains					
Smith, Rose	Jul 16, 1975	Strawberry Plains	Tn	Apr 7, 1888	87	W	Smith, Jim		Jordan, Martha		Smith, Jack	Beaver Creek					
Smith, Ruby E.	Nov 24, 1999	Jeff City	Hancock Co., Tn	Mar 13, 1921	78	W	Davis, Wiley		Antrican, Eliza		Strawberry, Shirley [Daug]	Strawberry Plains				Gunn, Jackie - Elmore, Sue	
Smith, Sarah Elizabeth	Oct 25, 1984	Tn	Tn	Jul 22, 1886	78	Smith, Robert H.	Koontz, John		Smith, Mattie		Mc Daniel, Mrs. O.A. - Smith, Robert H.	Straw Plains					Smith, Martha [Cnc]
Smith, Sherman Daniel	Dec 9, 1950	Knox Co	Tn	Aug 18, 1889	61	Ng	Smith, George		Nabors, Margaret		Smith, C.L. - Colter, Mrs. - Carl	Mt. Pleasant					
Smith, Shelsley Kaye	Jun 6, 1989	Norfolk, Va	Tn	Nov 9, 1969	19	S	Smith, William E.		Rupe, Barbara		Smith, William E.	J.M.G.					
Smith, Stephen Decatur	Jan 7, 1967	Hamblen Co	Tn	Dec 18, 1882	84	Ng	Smith, John		Baker, Caroline		Carter, Mr. - Jaul [Les]	Jefferson Memorial					
Smith, Sue	Feb 1, 1986	Tn	Tn	Aug 17, 1903	82	W	Kincaid, J.A.		Riddle, Lullia		Jackson, Mrs. Cleo	Cedar Grove - Grainger Co					
Smith, Sylvanus [Col]	Feb 28, 1940	Ng	Ng	Dec 30, 1903	tn	Ng	Smith, Toy	Tn	Watkins, Fannie	Tn	Smith, Bennie-Toy-Herbert	Colored					
Smith, Toy [Col]	Mar 6, 1956	Granger Co	Ng	May 15, 1882	73	W	Smith, Jim		Walker, Jim		Smith, H.C.	West View Colored					
Smith, Valer S.	May 22, 1960	Jeff Co	Tn	Apr 2, 1883	77	Ng	Smith, James		Jordon, Josephine		Morgan, Ra-Mary-Smith, Bill	New Market					
Smith, Verlie M.	Feb 28, 1974	Hallmark Center	Tn	Aug 30, 1886	87	W	Hull, Henry		Lacy, Amanda		Carter, Mrs. Lois Smith	Jefferson Memorial					
Smith, W.G.	Feb 17, 1938	Tn	Tn	Mar 24, 1866	69	Ng	Smith, George		Nelson, Margaret		Smith, Frank A. [Knoxville]	Mill Springs					
Smith, Walter Mc Cown [Col]	Sept 2, 1942	Mill Springs	Jeff Co	Sep 5, 1884	57	Ng	Smith, John	Va	Walker, Mary	Tn	Smith, Della	Colored					
Smith, William [Col]	Feb 11, 1926		Tn	9-9-19	57	S	Smith, Walter		Fain, Della	Tn	Smith, Walter	Colored					
Smith, William Herman	Jul 16, 1983	Knoxville, Tn	Blount Co. Tn	Dec 17, 1900	92	Smith, Josephina	Mitchell, Nancy		Brown, Nancy L. [Daug]	42-44	Mc Olive-Knoxville, Tn	Beaver Creek	John D.	Pryor, Fay L. - Mc Daniel, Edna		[Sisters?] Brown, Mrs. James N. - Bales, Mrs. James T. - Williams, Mrs. Larry	
Smith, Wilma	May 10, 1927	Tn	Tn		1-1-21		Smith, Henry	Tn	Dockery, Ocsia	Tn	Smith, Henry	Beaver Creek					
Snider, Bettie L.	Jan 31, 1931	New Market	Tn	Nov 22, 1934	2m		Snider, R.P.	Tn	Pollard, Lola	Tn	Snider, R.P. - Mc Campbell, J.	Snider, R.P. - Mc Campbells Chapel					
Snider, George A.	Apr 18, 1931	Sevier Co	Tn	Sep 2, 1887	43	W	Snyder, Charles H.		Underwood, Francis	Tn	Mc Campbells Chapel	Mc Campbells Chapel					
Snodderly, Carl T.	May 9, 1992	J.M.H.	Union Co, Tn	Jun 4, 1928	63	W	Snodderly, Milliard E.		Settles, Francis W.		Pyle, Fran S. [Daug]	Strawberry Plains					
Snodderly, Frances Willard	Nov 13, 1995	New Market, Tn	Tn	Oct 31, 1896	87	W	Settles, Henry		Thomas, China		Snodderly, Bruce	Strawberry Plains					
Snodderly, John Bruce	Aug 21, 2000	Jeff City	Tn	Apr 17, 1924	76	Deeds, Annette	Snodderly, John		Ousby, Paralee		Wife	Strawberry Plains	unk				
Snodderly, Millard Elsworth	Dec 12, 1947	Jeff Co	Union Co, Tn	Sep 4, 1878	76	Ng	Snodderly, John		Ousby, Paralee	Tn	Snodderly, Mrs. Frances W.	Strawberry Plains					
Snodderly, Nathan Paul	Jun 8, 1995	Knoxville, Tn	Ft. Wayne, Indiana	May 14, 1957	38	Berry, Sherry	Snodderly, Doyle		Sliger, Audrey		Wife	Big Springs - Rutledge, Tn		Joshua P. - Jared M.		Doyle-David-Philip-Matthew-Jonathan-Matthias	Steck, Rebecca - Deats, Debra - Johnson, Martha - Howard, Rachel

NAME	DDATE	BLOCAT	BLOCAT	BDATE	AGE	SPOUSE	FATHER	FBLOCAT	MOTHER	MBRLOCAT	BY	BURIAL	VET	SON	DAUG	BROTHER	SISTER
Snodgrass, Wanda Mae	Oct 24, 1987	Home	Tn	Dec 13, 1930	56	Snodderly, Carl	Bramlett, Homer T.		Howard, Mary R.		Snodderly, Carl T.	Strawberry Plains					
Snodgrass, Schele Eugene	Jan 12, 1954	Columbus, Ohio	Tn		55	Reese, Virgie [Seperated]					Snodgrass, Dale-Eugene-Dorothy-Bobby-Jim-Johnny [Children]	Witts					
Snyder, Carrie Louise	Oct 17, 1981	Greeneville, Tn	Tn	Aug 14, 1917	64	W	Spencer, James		Cook, Sonia		Greene, Mrs. Jane G. [Illinois]	Shiloh					
Snyder, Frank Taylor	Aug 16, 1946	Jeff Co	Jeff Co	Nov 28, 1914	31	Div	Snyder, Tom	Tn	Brannam, Maude	Tn	Johnson, Mrs. Thelma - Burl & Emmett - Snder, R.P. - Mc Campbell, Gene	New Market					
Snyder, Jack	Aug 8, 1897	Piedmont															
Snyder, John A.	Aug 12, 1982	F.S.H.	Sevier Co	Sep 5, 1918	73	Hargus, Tennie	Snyder, John		Hickman, Jessie		Wilts	Oak Grove - Kodak, Tn					
Snyder, Maude	May 23, 1996	Sevierville, Tn	Jeff Co	Sep 15, 1916	81	Snyder Hugh M.	Carter, Daniel		Disil, Ethel		Husband	East View Memorial		Perry-Clayton [Cal]	Desk, Fay & Jeff -		Maples, Arlia
Snyder, Sherman Dick	Jul 19, 1996	Talbott, Tn	York, Pa	Mar 1, 1919	79	W	Snyder, Sherman		Dick, Naomi		Wife	Lebanon Baptist		Timothy 7 Carol			
Snyder, Thomas Samuel	Jul 9, 2000	Knoxville, Tn	Tn	Jan 16, 1922	78	Maples, Blanche	Snyder, John		Hickman, Jessie		Wife	Oak Grove - Kodak, Tn unk					
Snyder, Walter C. Sr.	May 30, 1987	S.M.M.C.	Tn	Mar 5, 1899	88	W	Snyder, Henry		Gilborth, Dorothea		Oak Grove - Sevier Co				Fortivis, Kay & John		
Sohnson, Mary E.	Jan 17, 1955	Jeff City	Tn	Apr 5, 1874	80	W	Pudley, George		Green, Nancy		Johnson, Clinton	Bethesda - Hamblen Co					
Solary, Laura Jane	Apr 29, 1996	Jeff City	Jul 24, 1924	Northville, MI	71	Salary, Herman	Lissenberger, Arthur W.		Hayes, Bina Henrita		Husband	Cremated		Honey, James	Lissenberger, John		Shietaz, Marge - Anderson, Marion
Solomon, John Wesley	Jul 12, 1945	Jeff Co	Jeff Co	Dec 7, 1870	74	W	Solomon, James	Tn	Riley, Sarah	Tn	Husband	Shady Grove					
Solomon, Laura	Apr 22, 1927	Tn	Tn		60+48	W			Helm, Deborah	Tn	Quarels, Mrs. Ralph - Marie - Webb	West View					
Sonnen, Susan Perdue	Oct 30, 1991	Gainsville, Fla.	Tn	Oct 4, 1950	41	W	Sonnen, John K.		Purdue, Virginia		Sonnen, John K. [Father]	J.M.G.					
Soord, Lula Druscilla	Dec 16, 1925		Tn		59.5-20	Soord, Unk	Bible, Elbert	Tn	Reed, Mary Jane	Tn	Bible, J.D. & A.S.	Bethel					
Spence, Mary Elizabeth	Apr 19, 1994	Jeff City	Huntington, W. Va	Oct 31, 1920	73	W	Daniels, Henry		Clinton, Minnie B.		Spence, Wetzel [Son - Calif.]	Community Gardens - Wayne, W. Va					
Spencer, Agnes Lorena	Jan 14, 1998	Jeff City	Grainger Co	Jan 29, 1921	76		Cockrum, Millard		Travis, Willie		Spencer, Jimmy [Son]	Shiloh		Ronald-Donald-J. Ralph			
Spencer, Anna	Aug 7, 1928	Jeff City	Tn		10+4 19		Spencer, George	Tn		Tn	Spencer, George						
Spencer, Edwin Bryan	Apr 7, 1981	Hamblen Co	Tn	Oct 17, 1996	24	S	Spencer, William H.		Bowlin, Wanda		Peoples, Mrs. Wanda - Spencer	Jefferson Memorial					Romines, Margaret
Spencer, Fred Roger	Feb 18, 1993	Knoxville, Tn	Morgan Co, Tn	Mar 22, 1920	72	W	Spencer, Liburn		Morgan, Nancy		Wife		44-45	Ronald-Donald-Jay-Fred		Henry-Lloyd-Layman	Eldridge, Julie
Spencer, Ira Belle	Feb 26, 1941	Dandgin, Tn	Tn		57.6-25	Spencer, M.C.			Link		James, Mrs. John [Dang]	Nance's Grove					
Spencer, Lonvill	May 2, 1994	White Pine, Tn	Dillort Co, Ky	Jun 18, 1925	68		Spencer, John		Adkins, Artie		Spencer, Robert L. [Son]	Spencer - Elliot Co, Ky					Parks, Alice
Spencer, Mack Cauley	Jun 19, 1949	New Market		May 17, 1879	70	W	Spencer, James		Craig, Maudlente		James, Mrs. John - Spencer, Earl & Hanson - Nox, Mack	Nance's Grove					
Spencer, Marshall Lee	Oct 5, 1987	Knoxville, Tn	Jeff City	Jul 27, 1947	50		Spencer, Charlie James		Smith, Stella Mae		Spencer, Lee Wade [Son]	West View	army				
Spencer, Mary Magdalene	Jun 15, 1960	Jeff City	Tn	Jan 2, 1939	21	S	Spencer, Charles J.		Smith, Stella		Spencer, Charles	West View				Eugene	
Spencer, Nancy	Nov 7, 1945	Grainger Co	Tn	Jan 7, 1888	57	Spencer, Lieb. E.	Morgan, Joe	Tn	Kuller, Eliza	Tn	Spencer, Lieb E. & Henry	Mill Springs					
Spencer, William Herman	Nov 13, 1978	Beckley, W. Va	Tn	Jul 15, 1920	58	Ng			Hyden, Ina Belle Borvlin		Spencer, Mrs. Wanda Henry	Jefferson Memorial	WW 2				
Spiws, Clarence A.	Jun 11, 1996	New Market, Tn	New Market, Tn	Feb 1, 1935	61		Spiws, Sam		Mc Farland, Mary Ruth		Haynes, Mary K. [Sister]	West View		Albon-Charles Edward	Anna Ruth	Ulysses Van-Walter E.	

NAME	DDATE	BLOCAT	BLOCAT	DDATE	AGE	SPOUSE	FATHER	FRLOCAT	MOTHER	MTRLOCAT	BY	BURIAL	VET	SON	DAUG	BROTHER	SISTER
Spiva, Josie Mills (Black)	Oct 12 1986	J.M.H.	Tn	Dec 25, 1883	92	W	Hodge, Pryor		Trotter, Lucy		Sunhall, Almeda M.; Spiva, L.C.-Sam; Erastus - Smith, Rebecca	West View					
Spiva, Luther W. [Col]	Apr 16, 1945	New Market	Waynesville, Nc	Jun 2, 1867	77	W	Spiva, Anthony	Nc	Barr, Elsie	Nc		Goods Chapel					
Spivey, Infant Male	Aug 25, 1944	Tn		Aug 25, 1944			Spivey, Clarence	Ga	Carr, Laura	Ga	Spivey, C.W.	New Market					
Spivey, Odessa Agnes	Apr 25, 1999	Jeff Co	Grainger Co	Feb 24, 1922	77		Kelley, Benjamin		Kelly, Elsie		Spivey, Bill & Pat [Son]	J.M.G.					
Spivey, Robert Earl	Jul 8, 1978	Jeff City	Alabama	Feb 7, 1927	51	Wall, Sara	Spivey, James E.		Wesley, Rose		Spivey, Mrs. Sara & Children	Jefferson Memorial	WW 2				
Spivey, Rose Wesley	Apr 10, 1990	Scrabble, Miss.			82	W					Wisecarver, Deborah [Sister, Ga] - Pete; F.H. [Scrabble, Miss] Hawkins, J.W. - Spradlin, Herbert [Godson, Alabama]	Greenwood					
Spradlin, Lula Ann	Jun 20, 1946	Jeff Co				W	England, Payne				Dinniard, Oscar	Greenwood					
Sproles, Elizabeth Faust	Aug 23, 1966	Strawberry Plains	Tn	Jun 20, 1889	77	W	Faust, Joseph Robert		Cox, Margaret		Leach - Anderson Co	Strawberry Plains					
Sproles, Mary	Aug 24, 1932	Tn	Tn	Dec 7, 1874	57	W	Hightower, A.	Sr	Howard, Harriett	Sr	James, Mrs. Edd	Strawberry Plains					
Sprinkles, Margaret Ray	Feb 5, 1928	Tn			35-7-55	Sprinkles, Robert	Fox, William E.	Tn	Zirkin, Ellen	Tn	Sprinkles, Robert	Dandridge					
Staines, Leonard C.	Sep 8, 1981	S.M.M.C.	Grainger Co	Nov 14, 1944	46	Reece, Margie	Staines, Leonard G. Sr.		Mitchell, Lou Ella		Staines, Margie R.	Richard - Grainger Co					
Staines, Leonard G. Sr.	Jul 15, 1989	Blaine, Tn	Tn	Dec 18, 1910	78	Staines, Lou Ella	Staines, John A.		Brewer, Mattie Lou		Staines, Mrs. Lou Ella	Richard - Blaine, Tn					
Staines, Lou Ella	Dec 14, 1994	Knoxville, Tn	Jeff Co	Jan 4, 1918	76	Staines, Lou Ella	Mitchell, Ellen		Mc Nish, Cordelia		Staines, Bobby Carol [Son]	Richard - Blaine, Tn		Larry James			
Staines, Virgil Jr.	Dec 24, 1978	Concord, Tn	Tn	Aug 7, 1927	49	Ng	Staines, Virgil Sr.		England, Ola		Staines, Mrs. Lois Ruth	Jefferson Memorial	WW 2				
Staines, William Arthur [Jack]	Mar 1, 1981	Maynardville, Tn.	Tn	Mar 26, 1916	64	Curl, Leota	Staines, John		Brewer, Mattie		Staines, Mrs. W.A.	Shiloh	WW 2				
Stalford, Mary Ida	Dec 24, 1945	Knox Co	Tn	Aug 21, 1874	71	Ng	Hargis, Bert		Dyer, Nancy	Tn	King, Floyd - Hargis, Tom	Friends Station					
Staines, Albert Lee	Mar 14, 1977	Jeff Co	Tn	Feb 10, 1903	74	Ng	Staines, Walter		Cromwell		Staines, Mrs. Velma	East Highland					
Stallings, Alma Louise	Jul 8, 1994	New Market, Tn	Tn	Aug 4, 1909	84		Staines, Samuel C.		Atchley, Bertha J.		Stallings, Ribbon-Sam [Nephews] - Moore, Jean - Pascchal, Alma - Holcomb, Marilyn [Nieces]	Pleasant Grove					
Stallings, Beatrice	Jul 6, 1998	J.M.H.	Tn	Aug 8, 1907	80	W	Hill, Joseph Benton		Walker, Ellie		Stallings, Sam E.	Pleasant Grove					
Stallings, Carolyn Florence	Oct 17, 1997	Jeff City	Jeff Co	Nov 6, 1939	57	Stallings, Samuel F.	Shackelford, Roy		Whitaker, Nannie Mae		Husband	Pleasant Grove		Freddi Jr.- Rodney	Chris, Sherri		
Stallings, Charles Anderson	Mar 1, 1977	New Market, Tn	Tn	Aug 14, 1895	81	Lee, Emma	Stallings, Walter		Cromwell, Elizabeth		Stallings, Mrs. Emma - Charles-Walter-Marvin-Davis, Mrs. Gertrude	Pleasant Grove					
Stallings, Charles Turner	Jun 30, 1997	New Market, Tn	Jeff Co	Apr 5, 1930	67	Poore, Anna Lynn	Stallings, Charlie A.		Hargis, Emma Lee		Wife	Pollard		Steve-Allen- Leon-David	Adams, Melinda - Roderick, Marlene	Marvin	Durkes, Gertrude
Stallings, Dalton	Jun 7, 1932	Strawberry Plains	Nc	Dec 14, 1844	87	Ng	Stallings, John		Key, Frankie	Nc	Stallings, S.C.	Piney					
Stallings, Elizabeth	Mar 13, 1933	New Market	Tn	Jan 5, 1876	57	W	Cornwell, Pstam	Tn	Rapass, M.	Tn	Stallings, Walter & Mack	Piney Grove					
Stallings, Emma Lee	Aug 1, 1978	Knoxville, Tn	Tn	Jan 21, 1909	69	W	John Lee		Hargis, Nora		Stallings, Walter [Son]	Piney Grove - Jeff Co					
Stallings, Mack Alexander	Oct 20, 1969	Strawberry Plains	Tn	Oct 20, 1897	72	Ng	Stallings, Walter		Cornwell, Sarah		Stallings, Rev. Roy J.	Strawberry Plains					
Stallings, Paul N.	Jun 21, 1994	Knoxville, Tn	Jeff Co	Mar 24, 1921	73	Underwood, Reba	Stallings, Mack		Koontz, Sally		Wife	Strawberry Plains		Joe	Cato, Candy & Carroll - Burchell, Cathy & Sherri - Cato, Andrea-Gina		

NAME	DDATE	DLOCAT	BLOCAT	BDATE	AGE	SPOUSE	FATHER	FRLOCAT	MOTHER	MFRLOCAT	BY	BURIAL	VET	SON	DAUG	BROTHER	SISTER
Stallings, Robert B.	Jan 5, 1971	Jeff Co	Tn	Dec 11, 1892	89	W	Stallings, Thomas		Hickman, Wallis Mae		Lindsey, Reba	West View					
Stallings, Ronnie Stevens	Jan 12, 1955	Jeff Co	Tn	Dec 13, 1954			Stallings, Carl		Carr, Margie		Stallings, Carl	Straw Plains					
Stallings, Sallie Mae	Nov 20, 1957	Jeff Co	Tn	Nov	56-11-		Koontz, W.M.		Romine, Rachie		Stallings, Mack & Children	Straw Plains					
Stallings, Velma Jo	Apr 17, 1977	Jeff Co	Tn	Jan 28, 1910	67	Stallings, A.L. Sr. [D]	Pollard, Jessie		Cate, Cynthia		Stallings, Gary M.-A.L. Jr.	E. Highland - Knox Co					
Stallings, Wallie [F]	Mar 3, 1954	Knox Co	Tn	Feb 24, 1885	69	Stallings, Robert	Hickman, Andrew J.		Shackleford, Mary E.		Stallings, Robert	West View					
Stallings, Walter A.	Feb 17, 1954	Jeff Co.	Tn	May 10, 1874	79	W	Stallings, Thomas		Glenn, Nancy		Bates, Mrs. J.E.	Piney Grove					
Stallings, Walter Alexander	Dec 8, 1990	New Market, Tn	Jeff Co.	May 29, 1903	57	Stiles, Faye	Stallings, Charlie A.		Lee, Emma		Stallings, Faye S.	Piney	unk				
Stalsworth, Arlis Licia	Mar 24, 1925		Tn			W	Hinshaw, Golden	Tn	Frogden, Margaret	Tn	Salsworth, Charles	Hinshaw					
Stalsworth, Clarence Edward	Aug 24, 1951	Tn	Tn	Aug 24, 1951	1h		Stalsworth, John		Bolden, Sylda		Stalsworth, John	Indian Ridge					
Stalsworth, J.C.	Mar 9, 1931	New Market	Tn	Jun 11, 1874	56	Ng	Stalsworth, Samuel	Tn	Coffer, Sue	Tn	Stalsworth, Mrs. J.C.	Indian Ridge					
Stalsworth, Martha Anne	Nov 25, 1948	Jeff Co	Tn	Nov 25, 1948			Stalsworth, Jake	Tn	Davis, Tressie Mae	Tn	Stalsworth, Jake	Indian Ridge					
Stalsworth, Maude Gertrude	Oct 20, 1943	Grainger Co	Grainger Co			Stalsworth, J.C.	Pate, John	Tn	Nicely, Anna	Tn	Denton, Willis - Nance, William [Doug]	Indian Ridge					
Stanley, Willie	Oct 8, 1980	Jeff City			60	Ng					Percy F.H. [Mt. City, Tn]						
Stansberry, Buddy Dwayne	Dec 22, 1978	U.T.H.	Tn	Nov 5, 1978	1		Stansberry, Lewis H. Jr.	Tn	Crowe, Patricia		Stansberry, Lewis	Jefferson Memorial					
Stansberry, Flora Margaret	Dec 21, 1948	Jeff Co	Tn	Jan 6, 1882	66-11-15	W	Wright, Columbus	Tn	Brown, Mary	Tn	Stansberry, L.R. & M.O.	Pleasant Grove					
Stansberry, Infant Female	Nov 23, 1948	Jeff Co	Jeff Co	Nov 23, 1948			Stansberry, Louis Herman		Ingram, Gladys Mae	Tn	Stansberry, R.H.	Mt. Pleasant					
Stansberry, Lisa M.	Dec 12, 1965	Knox Co	Tn	Dec 11, 1965			Stansberry, Thomas R.		Smith, Sherridine		Stansberry, T.R.	Horton View - Knox Co					
Stennett, Dewey Jackson	May 30, 1997	Talbott, Tn	Etowah, Tn	Dec 7, 1924	72	Norma Jean	Stennett, Samuel Dewey		Sims, Nettie Pauline		Wilie	J.M.G.	43-46	Len & Joy			Hotsington, Martha
Stennett, Nellie P.	Sep 21, 1980	Caro Inn	Whitfield Co, Ga	Aug 29, 1905	75	W	Sims, Robert		Howell, Maude		Stennett, Dewey - Lone F.H. [Dalton, Ga]	J.M.G.					
Stapleton, Birdie Jo	Jul 12, 1967	Jeff Co	Tn	Aug 4, 1882	74	Ng	Green, Samuel		Delord, Martha		Stapleton, R.C. & Children	Jefferson Memorial					
Stapleton, Dana Campbell	Oct 5, 1986	Hawkins Co, Tn		Jun 29, 1919	79	Stapleton, Dana	Stapleton, Robert C.		Green, Bertie J.		Stapleton, Phillip [Son]	J.M.G.					
Stapleton, Julia Marie	Aug 18, 1924	Knoxville, Tn	Hamblen Co	May 18, 1924	70	Stapleton, Dana	ink		Talley, Lucy		Husband			Larry N.-E. David & Janice- J. Phillip & Mary A.	Courtney, Mary F. & Dewey		
Stapleton, Robert Carnell	Aug 21, 1978	Jeff City	Tn	Sep 18, 1890	87	W			Trent, Mary		Stapleton, Danna	Jefferson Memorial			Danielsen, Brenda [BL] Cobble, Linda Dunsatton, Charlene [BL] - Anderson, Darlene		
Steele, Dorcas Irene	Mar 24, 1998	Morristown, Tn	Hamblen Co	Jul 28, 1928	69	W	Dixson, Samuel		Johnson, Leona		Steele, Arthur [Son]	West View					
Steele, Johnny Hobert	Nov 7, 1977	Jeff Co	Tn	Apr 25, 1952	25	S	Steele, Walter J.		Dixson, Irene		Steele, Walter	West View					
Steele, Walter Jefferson	Dec 18, 1989	J.M.H.	Wells Co, Nc	May 22, 1915	74	Dixson, Irene	Steele, John		Pelfer, Lora		Steele, Irena D.	West View	WW 2				
Stein, Nana Ethel Edmunds	Sep 17, 1985	J.M.H.	Tn	Feb 9, 1913	72	W	Collins, Marshall		Hubbard, E.		Edmunds, Von	West View					
Stennett, J.C.	Jan 30, 1984	Jeff City	Tn	Jul 27, 1968	65	Ng	Stennett, James Randolph	Tn	Yeerank, Edna	Tn		West View					
Stewart, David Randolph	Dec 6, 1986	Christian Co, Ky	Tn	Apr 18, 1934	50	W	Stewart, Leonard Randolph		Bell, Flora		Willie [Grace], Ky]	Greenhill					
Stewart, Mary Elizabeth [Col]	Jan 30, 1995	Dayton, Ohio	Tn	Mar 11, 1927	39	Div	Brooks, Anderson L.		Annie Mae		Stewart, James L. [Dayton, Ohio]- Bonnell, Mrs. -	West View					
Stiner, Infant Male	Apr 25, 1947	Jeff Co	Tn	Mar 25, 1947			Stiner, Billy				Stiner, Billy	West View					
Stinnett, George Walter	Apr 18, 1966	Jeff City	Tn	Dec 2, 1965			Mc.Ginnis, Lucy Lou	Tn	Mc Ginnis, Lucy L.	Tn	Stinnett, George	West View					

NAME	DDATE	DLOCAT	BLOCAT	BDATE	AGE	SPOUSE	FATHER	FEDLOCAT	MOTHER	MFRLOCAT	BY	BURIAL	VET	SON	DAUG	BROTHER	SISTER
Stinnett, George Washington [Dora]	Mar 8, 1992	S.M.H.	Jeff City	May 30, 1921	70	McGinnis, Lucy	Stinnett, James Calvin		Pendergrass, Mary	Tn	Wife Stinnett, Mrs. J.A.	West View	unk				
Stinnett, James A. [Dora]	Dec 31, 1940	Knox Co	Tn		40-7-25	Roach, Stella					Ward, Mrs. Leonard - Bradford, Clarence - Bailey, D.T. - Price, Birdie - Pinchum,	Flat Creek					
Stinnett, Mary	Sep 8, 1949	Jeff Co	Jeff Co	Oct 1, 1882	66	W	Pendergrass, Walter		Hansel, Harriet	Tn		West View					
Stiper, Lizzie	Apr 18, 1948	Jeff Co	Jeff Co	Sep 10, 1960	87-7-8	W	Miles, Randolph	Jeff Co	Harper, Cynthia	Jeff Co	Stipes, Jack - Morgan, Mrs. J.P. - McDaniel, James	Straw Plains					
Stipes, Alfred Samuel	Nov 1, 1944	Jeff Co	Hawkins Co	Dec 25, 1865	78	W	Unk		Dugnan, Ann	Tn	Stipes, Keith & Alford	Camp Branch - Alabama					
Stipes, Fannie	Aug 22, 1967	Knox Co	Tn	Jun 8, 1886	81	W	Tucker, Abner		Mary		Stipes, Will Edd	Chestnut Hill					
Stipes, Lottie	Oct 19, 1945	Jeff Co	Sc	May 30, 1864	81	W	Callaway, Thomas Henry	Sc	Hightower, Mary Jane	Sc	Stipes, Fred	Strawberry Plains					
Stipes, Mack Jr.	Nov 20, 1943	Jeff Co	Tn	Apr 15, 1900	43	S	Stipes, Mack Sr.	Tn	Calloway, Lottie	Sc	Stipes, Fred	Strawberry Plains					
Stipes, Myrtle Lee	Oct 28, 1984	Jeff Co	Tn	Sept 7, 1882	72	Stipes, Jack	Crowe, Tom		Collins, Nancy Jane		Stipes, Tom - McCall, Mrs. William B. [Chloe]	Straw Plains					
Stipes, William	Dec 13, 1938		Tn		35-3-2	Ng	Stipes, Mack	Tn	Calloway, Lottie	Tn		Strawberry Plains					
Stiplin, Theodore [Tee]	Jul 1, 1979	J.M.H.	Tn	Aug 11, 1910	68	S	Stiplin, Picket		Thornton, Mary		Stiplin, Tom	Chestnut Hill	WW 2				
Stokesbury, Sallie	May 15, 1961	Jeff Co	Tn	Jun 11, 1902	58	Stokesbury, Fred	Palmer, Victor W.		Campbell, Mary		Stokesbury, Harold & Fred	Jefferson Memorial					
Stokely, Mae	Oct 30, 1968	Cocke Co, Tn	Tn	Oct 22, 1890	78	Ng	Roberts, Joel L.		Lee, Jessie		Dawson, Gayle [Daug]	Union - Newport, Tn					
Stokely, John Huff	Mar 21, 1961	Morgan Co, Tn	Tn	Feb 5, 1883	68	Ng	Stokely, A.J.		Rosson, Sarda		Stokely, J.H. Jr. & Annie Huff Stokely [Daug]	Union - Cocke Co					
Stone, Roger S.	Sep 22, 1965	J.M.H.	New York	Mar 27, 1943	22	S	Stone, Roger W.		Schlitt, Janet		Stokely, J.H. Jr. & Guilford F.H. [Guilford, Conn.]	Alderbrook - New Haven, Conn.					
Stokesbury, Janna Pauline	Sep 28, 1991	U.T.H. Morristown, Tn	Scott Co, Tn	Jan 2, 1919	74	Stokesbury, W.C.	Marcum, John L.		Foust, Edith		Harvey, John S. [Daug]	J.M.G.	43-45	W.C. & Martha			
Stokesbury, William C. Sr.	Feb 13, 1994	Union Co, Tn	Tn	Jan 17, 1912	82	Stokesbury, W.C.	McFetchidge, Zettie		Harvey, Jan S. & Lyn [Daug]			J.M.G.					Stiner, Kate
Storms, Elizabeth	Aug 22, 1957	Axtell Residence Knoxville, Tn	Fulton, Ky	May 18, 1910	92	W	Dazle, Sam N.		Webb, Olivia P.		Adair, Mrs. W.F.	West View					
Stout, Gladys Elizabeth	May 18, 1979	Knoxville, Tn	Tn	May 2, 1925	53	Stout, Earl S.	Reters, Poncita		Wells, Glady		Stout, Earl S.	West View					
Stout, Howard Denver	Dec 2, 1946	Jeff Co	Carter Co. Tn	Feb 22, 1922	24	Ng	Stout, Sinkler	Tn	Snyder, Mary	Tn	Shady View Co. Johnson	Buffalo Grove					
Stout, Jeanette	Sep 30, 1992	F.S.H.	Knoxville, Tn	Jul 6, 1947	45	Stout, Denny J.	Alterman, William		Wells, Glady		Husband	West View					
Stracker, Kathryn	Mar 27, 1991	Aiken, Sc	Knoxville, Tn	May 3, 1907	83	Ng	Anderson, James T.		Jones, Maude		Johnson, Virginia [Sister] [Aiken, Sc]	West View					
Strand, Infant Female	Sep 28, 1960	Jeff Co	Tn	Sept 28, 1960		W	Strand, A.B.				Mr. Hope - Greene Co.	Russellville					
Strand, William Henry	Aug 31, 1967	Jeff Co	Tn	Aug 31, 1891	76	W	Harper, Ella		Strand, H.C. & J.T.		Mr. Hope & J.T.	Russellville					
Strange, Infant Male	Nov 6, 1949	Jeff Co	Tn	Nov 6, 1949		W	Strange, Dexter		Ward, Sallie		Strange, Dexter	Wesleys Chapel					
Striplin, Iowa	Feb 9, 1980	J.M.H.	Tn	Oct 19, 1917	70	S	Striplin, Picket		Thornton, Mary	Tn	Striplin, Tom	Chestnut Hill U.M.					
Striplin, Julia Ann	Mar 17, 1931	Jeff Co	Tn	Oct 4, 1855	75	Striplin, James [D]	Fox, Jemima		Fox, Jemima		Striplin, Tom	Birchfield [Service]					
Striplin, L.P. [M]	Feb 14, 1929	Jeff Co	Tn	Oct 4, 1864	73	Ng	Striplin, T.		Lagman, Julia A.		Striplin, Tom	Chestnut Hill					
Striplin, Mary Ella	Nov 7, 1978	Jeff Co	Tn	Mar 15, 1886	92	W	Thornton, Nicholas		Allen, Barbara Ann		Striplin, Thomas & Children	Chestnut Hill - Jeff Co					
Striplin, Thomas	Jun 3, 1994	Jeff City	Tn	Jul 16, 1915	78	Lewis, Ruby	Striplin, Picket		Thornton, Mary Ella		Wife	Narcost Grove				Woodrow	[Aunt] Thornton, Mary Klein
Strock, John Roy	Oct 30, 1978	Jeff City	Carlisle, Pa	Jun 8, 1882	96	Ng	Strock, George W.		Herman, Barbara		Osler, Mrs. Nell - Vaughn, Frank O. - Strock, J. Roy	Jefferson Memorial					
Strock, Magda Meyer	Sep 24, 1973	Jeff City	Germany	Oct 20, 1903	69	Strock, Dr. J. Roy	Meyer, William		Jeschke, Maria		Strock, J. Roy	Jefferson Memorial					
Shroup, Margaret	May 10, 1993	Jeff City	Jacksonville, Fla.	Jan 17, 1912	81	Strock, Dr. J Roy	Mayo, Charles H.		Powell, Viola K.		Bleauget, Margaret K. [Daug] [Fla]	Holly Hill - White March, Md					
Styles, Robert	May 19, 1961	Jeff Co	Tn	Sep 12, 1884	76	Ng	Stipes, John		Miles, Elizabeth	Sc	Stipes, Ralph	Strawberry Plains					
Sullivan, Britta Elizabeth	Aug 17, 1999	Lundsta, Sweden		Oct 28, 1921	77	Heligman, Thure E.			Janson, Anna		Heligman, Ann Kristine [Daug] - McCarty, Christine [Niece]	Cremated		[Br-Law] Crowe, Thomas	[Br-Law] Sullivan, Toni		

NAME	DDATE	DLOCAT	BLOCAT	BDATE	AGE	SPOUSE	FATHER	F/BLOCAT	MOTHER	M/F/BLOCAT	BY	BURIAL	VET	SON	DAUG	BROTHER	SISTER
Sullivan, Jessie Limline	Feb 23, 1987	J.M.H.	Mo	Jul 5, 1893	93	W	Arbuckle, James A.		Meadows, Martha A.		Hellgren, Mrs. Howard [Unreal]	N. Bellard - Wickliffe, Ky					Meade, Limline & Howard
Sullivan, William Z.	May 16, 1997	Wickliffe, Ky	Mo	Aug 25, 1918	78	W	Hellgren, Britta		Sullivan, William Z.		Hellgren, Ann Kristine [Dag]	J.M.G.		Karl - [Bri-Lee] Crews, Thomas			
Sunderland, Berta	Mar 4, 1971	Jeff Co	Tn	Sep 21, 1879	91	S			Carter, Ellis		Donelon, Margaret - Sunderland, Carl	Sunderland					
Sunderland, Carl R.	Nov 4, 1972	Jeff Co	Tn	Dec 19, 1886	85	W			Carter, Ellis		Formwait, John [M] - Sunderland	Sunderland					
Sunderland, Ella N.	Oct 28, 1941	Jeff City	Sullivan Co		87-5-22	W			Rockhold, Margaret	Tn	Sunderland, Berta	Sunderland					
Sunderland, Wendall	Dec 28, 1924		Tn		32-1-24	S			Carter, Ellis		Sunderland, Miss Berta	Sunderland					
Suwong, Margaret E.	Mar 13, 1932	Dandridge		Oct 5, 1914	16	S	Suwong, W.T.	Tn	Suwong, Mrs - Mc Nabb, Jim	Tn	Suwong, Mrs - Mc Nabb, Jim	Marysville, Tn					
Suwong, Rosa Mary	Oct 25, 1941	Dandridge	Tn	May 1, 1923	8	S	Suwong, N.F.	Tn	Mc Nabb, Estella	Tn	Magnolia - Maryville	Maryville, Tn					
Sutherland, A.W.	Jun 6, 1935	Jeff City	Canada	Sep 14, 1905	29	Ng	Sutherland, T.D.	Canada	Mc Nabb, Essie		Sutherland, Mrs. A.W.	West View					
Sutton, Joseph Jr.	Mar 28, 1968	Jeff City	Missouri	Sep 25, 1899	68	Div	Sutton, Joseph C.		Norris, Abbie Elizabeth		Brophy, Mrs. Corrine & Dick	Senaca - Mo					
Sutton, Ronald Kitfin	Oct 22, 1981	Knoxville, Tn	Tn	Dec 8, 1934	46	Walker, Patsy	Sutton, Alfred C.		Stinnett, Esther Lee		Sutton, Mrs. Patsy	Walker's Large - Cocke Co					
Swaggerty, William S.	Jun 1, 1990	Jeff Co	Tn	Jul 5, 1921	68	Walker, Helen M.	Swaggarty, Ira K.		Colls, Tavia		Swaggerty, Helen M.	Trentville - Straw Plains	WW 2				
Swan, Lena Campbell	Apr 21, 1940	Dandridge	Tn		abt 67	Ng	Campbell, William	Tn	Mitchell, Unk	Tn	Swan, Rascoe	Dandridge					
Swan, Roscoe Coaklin	Aug 20, 1945	Knox Co	Dandridge	1878	67	S	Swan, James Preston		Graham, Victoria	Nc	Swan, H.F.	Presby - Dandridge					
Swanberg, Julie	Apr 11, 1984	J.M.H.	New York	Sep 17, 1907	76	W	Swanberg, Oscar A.		Cleary, Nellie		Swanberg, Oscar A.	Cremated					
Swanberg, Oscar A.	Mar 8, 1988	J.M.H.	New York	Jun 15, 1906	81	W			Gahrke, Emilie O.		Swanberg, Roy [Weath. D.C.]	Billy-Winston-Eugene					
Swann, Bill	Dec 1, 1996	Knoxville, Tn	Tn	Jul 10, 1915	81	W			Moore, Lizzie		Wife	Hills Union					
Swann, Bobby Lee [M]	Mar 24, 1985	Chicago, Ill	Tn	Jun 7, 1948	36	Div			Richard, Nellie		Swann, Mrs. Nellie	Pleasant Ridge - Jeff Co			Collins, Linda Sue - Peters, Patty	Joe	
Swann, Calvin	Nov 21, 1995	Knoxville, Tn	Jeff Co	Sep 19, 1954	41	Morelock, Tammi	Swann, Robert L.		Wife - Richard, Mamie [G-Mother]		Wife - Richard, Mamie [G-Mother]	Pleasant Ridge - Talbott, Tn		Daniel-Matthew-Jared		Larry	
Swann, Carolyn Marie	Dec 17, 1949	Jeff Co	Tn	Dec 17, 1949	75	S	Swann, Robert Lee		Swann, Nellie		Swann, R.L.	Pleasant Ridge					
Swann, Charlie Lawater	Feb 7, 1960	Jeff Co	Tn	Apr 20, 1884	75	S	Swann, Robert		Nichols, Nancy		Fox, Mrs. Taylor	Hillcrest					
Swann, Dorothy	Jun 3, 1957	Jeff Co	Tn	Jun 27, 1902	54	Swann, John			Satterfield, Lillie		Swann, John	West View					
Swann, Freddie Delano	Oct 5, 1974	Knoxville, Tn	Tn	Sep 16, 1936	38	S	Swann, John		Thornton, Dorothy		Swann, Harner & James	West View					
Swann, Gertie Georgianne	Mar 17, 1953	Jeff City	Tn	Dec 29, 1887	65	Ng	Denton, William M.		Miller, Elizabeth		Swann, Juliette - Swann, W.R.	New Market					
Swann, Hugh Tinsley Sr.	Jan 5, 1977	Jeff City	Tn	Oct 24, 1903	73	Briggs, Hilda F.	Swann, James Preston		Clabo, Rachel		Swann, Mrs. Hugh T.	Jefferson Memorial					
Swann, John Sr.	Jan 1, 1974	At Home	Tn	Feb 14, 1896	77	W	Swann, William R.		Moore, Sarah		Swann, Homer & Brothers - Girt. & S.S.	West View	unk				
Swann, Lula	Nov 10, 1971	Jeff Co	Tn	Jan 24, 1889	82	Swann, William M. [D]	Henderson, Robert		Mc Mahan, Cory		Swann, Ray	Hillcrest					
Swann, Nellis Marie	Jan 29, 1993	Dalton, Ga	Jeff Co	Aug 21, 1931	61	Rickard, Curt	Smith, Mamie		Valdez, Evelyn [Sister]		Pleasant Ridge		Larry-Danny			
Swann, Ray	Jan 9, 1977	Knoxville, Tn	Tn	Dec 4, 1909	67	Ng	Swann, Will M.		Henderson, Lula		Swann, Mrs. Ray	Hillcrest				Earl	Knight, Inez - Fisher, Grace - Morgan, Mary E.
Swann, Walter B.	Mar 18, 1980	Tn	Tn	Oct 18, 1905	74	Dunton, Georginia [D]	Swann, James M.		Reeves, Elizabeth		Nichols, Mrs. Ray - Juliette & Genena	New Market					
Swann, William James	Jan 25, 1989	J.M.H.	Etowah, Tn	Aug 31, 1919	69	Connelly, Rebecca	Swann, William E.		Humphries, Minnie		Swann, Rebecca C. - VA.	West View	WW 2				
Swann, William M.	Mar 1, 1982	New Market	Tn	Apr 14, 1878	83	Henderson, Lula Mae	Swann, Robert		Nichols, Nancy		Swann, Ray [Son]	Hillcrest					
Swaringen, George	Sep 15, 1948	Jeff Co	Euphie, Ga	Jan 31, 1910	38	S			Miser, Mary		Miser, Mary	Char???, Ga					[Aunts] Knight, Inez - Walder, Evelyn

NAME	DDATE	DLOCAT	BLOCAT	BDATE	AGE	SPOUSE	FATHER	FRLOCAT	MOTHER	MFRLOCAT	BY	BURIAL	VET	SON	DAUG	BROTHER	SISTER
Swicegood, Hubert Hoyle Jr.	Nov 23,1986	V.A.- M. Home	Nc	Oct 27, 1955	31	Div	Betts, Joyce		Swicegood, Joyce B.		National - Salisbury, Nc	unk				
Swift, Laura Ellie	Apr 14, 1966	Rutledge, Tn	Nc	Sep 24, 187.	92-6-20	Swift, W.A.	Myers, Elizabeth		Davis, Frank - Hodges, Mrs. Edgar		Shiloh					
Swift, William Alexander	Dec 7, 1946	Grainger Co	Tn	Jun 16, 1946	76-5-21	Ng	Lampkin, Mary Frances	Tn	Kelley, Mrs. - Swift, Mrs		Shiloh - Grainger Co					
Sydnor, Frances	Mar 25, 1998	Richmond, Va		Jan 9, 1922	76	Ng	Charlen, James Crawford		Sydnor, Charles [Son - Va]		J.M.G.		James B. [R]	Greenberg, Nancy [Md]	Dwight [Tx]-James Crawford-Keith-Harold	
Tackett, Roy Winfred Jr.	Dec 14, 1995	Jeff City	Mingo Co. W.Va	Nov 20, 1924	71		Tackett, Roy W. Sr.		Walker, Cora Mae		Gillman, Barbara [Dau]	Highland Memorial - W.Va				
Talbert, Anna Ray	Dec 24, 1972	Jeff Co	Tn	Jun 5, 1896	76	Talbert, Jep	Dixon, E.R.		Bailey, Dora		Talbert, Jep	West View				
Talbert, John Mc Henry	Nov 8, 1925		Tn [D. Hamblen Co]			Ng	Talbert, Oscar		Dodson, Lucy		Talbert, W.O.	Sunderland				
Talbert, Mary H.	Dec 14, 1928		Tn			Ng	Taylor, Thomas	Tn	Murphy, Judith	Va	Talbot, W.O.					
Talkington, Billy Gene	Sep 11, 2000	Jeff City	Mo	Mar 24, 1926	74	Hutchison, Verle	Talkington, Harry O.	Tn	Moore, Wonsley ?	Tn	Wife	Memorial Park - Malden, Mo	WW 2			
Talbert, Frances June	Oct 5, 1994	Dandridge, Tn	Jeff Co	Jun 22, 1924	70	Talbert, Reece	Mills, Floyd		Perrott, Stella		Husband	West View		Ron & Judy	Laura - Howard, Karen	
Talbert, Jep J.	Sep 21, 1974	Jeff City	Tn	Mar 26, 1894	80	W	Talbert, Tom		Beck, Hester		Talbert, Reece	West View	WW 1			
Talley, James Frank Willie	Jun 3, 1982	Knox Co	Tn	Sep 15, 1907	44	W	Talley, Tom		Miller, Julia		Talley, Mrs. J. Frank	Batch				
Talley, Alpha	Aug 7, 1982	Hamblen	Tn	Oct 7, 1982	92	W	Shorter, Richard		Newly, Elizabeth [Doug]		Newly, Frankie - Moore, Agnes - James-Jack-Robert	West View				
Talley, Beecher Ivan	Oct 28, 1980	Jeff Co	Tn	Dec 4, 1898	55	Ng	Talley, J. Wiley		Hopkins, Mattie L.		Talley, Mary Combs	West View				
Talley, Bertie Bazil	Dec 18, 1996	U.T.H.	Tn	Apr 4, 1897	89	Combs, Mary	Talley, John		Benefield, Rena		Talley, John	West View				
Talley, Charles Henry	Aug 12, 1999	Jeff Co	Tn	Jan 22, 1877	92	W	Talley, Bill		Benefield, Ellen		Talley, Paul & John	West View				
Talley, Ethel	Jul 30, 1972	Cheatochobee, Fla	Tn			Talley, Harry E [R]	Edgar, Howard		Ely, Bob		Ely, Bob	West View				
Talley, Foster Alec	Aug 29, 1980	Jeff City	Tn	Jan 19, 1895	85	Bell, Maude	Talley, John C.		Benefield, Rena		Jefferson, J.C.	Jefferson Memorial				
Talley, Geneva Jane	Aug 19, 1989	U.T.H.	Tn	Jan 23, 1909	80	S	Talley, Henry		Acuff, Ann		Acuff, Ann	Mill Springs [Old Side]				
Talley, George Conley	Dec 28, 1968	Jeff Co	Tn	May 5, 1904	64	S	Talley, James Wiley		Hopkins, Mattie		Talley, Hollis & Frank	Mill Springs				
Talley, Gertrude	Dec 28, 1968	Hamblen Co	Cocke Co	Apr 11, 1900	31	S	Ballard, William		Reed, Zora		Talley, Vernon	West View				
Talley, Grace Ann	Nov 8, 1974	Knoxville, Indiana	Tn	Jul 22, 1921	73	Talley, Vernon	Houseright, James		Robinson, Clara		Talley, Paul & Doug	West View				
Talley, Harry E.	Feb 15, 1955	Jeff Co	Tn	Apr 21, 1901	59	S	Talley, Paul				Talley, Mrs. Ethel E.	West View				
Talley, Helen Ruth	May 21, 1983	J.M.H.	Tn	Dec 13, 1895	59	W	Thompson, Ellie				Talley, Gary & Jimmy Roger	Jefferson Memorial				
Talley, Hester Jane	Mar 1, 1983	Jeff Co	Tn	Jun 24, 1926	56	Div	Hayworth, Isaac		Beck, Frank		Lane, Mrs. Fred	Jefferson Memorial				
Talley, Hollis	Nov 17, 1996	Middlesboro, Ky	Tn	Nov 12, 1892	70	W	Hopkins, Mattie Lee		Wife		Batch	Batch				
Talley, Hubert Burton	Jan 30, 1942	Jeff City	Tn	Oct 2, 1913	83	S	Reynolds, Serah		Talley, Harry E.		Mill Springs		[Step] Engle, Scott	Glass, Linda & Charles - [Step] Young, Denise		Barker, Dorothy
Talley, Jack Beecher	Nov 17, 1972	Jeff Co	Tn	Dec 17, 1922	49	D	Talley, Beecher	Tn	Shorter, Myrna	Tn	Newley, Libby - Charles, Jack	Jefferson Memorial	WW 2			
Talley, James A.	Dec [12], 1934										Talley, Frank & Earnest					
Talley, James Frank	Aug 27, 1974	Knoxville, Tn	Tn	Sep 24, 1907	66	Purkey, Mary Kate	Hopkins, Mattie L.		Talley, Mrs. Mrs. Kate		Jefferson Memorial					
Talley, James Wiley	Nov 13, 1951	Jeff Co	Tn	Oct 5, 1874	77	Ng	Talley, William		Ballinger, Sarah		Talley, Hollis & Beecher	Mill Springs				
Talley, John Clifton	Apr 2, 1985	J.M.H.	Tn	Nov 13, 1912	72	W	Talley, Charles Henry		Arcutt, Lucicia		Arcutt, Mrs. Donald	Jefferson Memorial				
Talley, Lillie Mae	Apr 27, 1967	F.S.H.	Tn	Mar 8, 1917	70	Talley, Hollis	Cochran, T.M.		Carroll, Cora		Talley, Hollis	Mill Springs				
Talley, Lizzie	May 16, 1929		Tn		85-1-18	Talley, Hollis	Talley, James	Tn	Roach, Susan	Tn	Talley, H.L.	Mill Springs				
Talley, Lucy Viola	Sep 30, 1989	J.M.H.	Russellville, Tn	Jul 11, 1905	84	S	Talley, Joseph		Soloman, Louisa		Stapleton, Julia	J.M.G.				
Talley, Mary Mae	Sep 29, 1990	Jeff Co	Va	Mar 17, 1899	91	W	Combs, John C.		Moore, Emma E.		Talley, Ray - [Son]	West View				
Talley, Mattie Lee	Sep 16, 1963	Jeff Co	Tn	Jul 25, 1881	82	Talley, J. Wiley	Hopkins, John		Clevenger, --		Talley, Mattie-Frank-George	West View				
Talley, Maudie Ellen	Jan 13, 1988	J.M.H.	Hamblen Co	Jul 20, 1898	90	W	Bell, Sam		Norton, Mollie		Talley, J.C.	J.M.G.				

NAME	DDATE	BLOCAT	BLOCAT	BDATE	AGE	SPOUSE	FATHER	FBLOCAT	MOTHER	MFLOCATY	BY	BURIAL	VET	SON	DAUG	BROTHER	SISTER
Talley, Minnie	Jan 30, 1927		Tn		37-9-8	Talley, Ike	Ballinger, Marion	Tn	Griffith, Giulia	Tn	Talley, H.E.	Mill Springs					
Talley, Paul Arthur	Apr 1, 1983	Knoxville, Tn	Tn	Jul 12, 1906	76	W			Talbott, Lucilla		Shipley, Mrs Jack [Joyce]	Mill Springs					
Talley, Ruth	Feb 8, 1981	Jeff City	Tn	Jul 11, 1913	67	Talley, John C.	Swann, James P.		Alley, Bertie		Talley, John C.	Jefferson Memorial					
Talley, Sienna Florence	Jul 25, 1942	Jeff City	Va		abt 70	W	Benefield, Charles W.	Germany	Ford, Unk	Unk	Talley, Dooley-Basil-Vernon-Kelly-Moyers, Ruth-Everett-Vernon-Lowery, Kathy	West View					
Talley, Tina Melissa	May 31, 1965			May 31, 1965	S		Talley, Jimmie		Reulston, Barbara Jean		Reulston, Mrs. - Talley, Mrs.	Mt. View					
Talley, Vernon Lee Roy	Jul 27, 1996	Jeff Co			S		Talley, Jimmie		Reulston, Barbara Jean		Wills	Mt. View		Glenn			
Talley, William Anderson	Aug 3, 1944	Hamblen Co, Tn	Jeff Co	Jan 18, 1881	92	Smith, Lennora	Talley, John Calvin	Jeff Co	Reynolds, Sarah Jane	Jeff Co	Wills	J.M.G.			Owens, Glenda & James		Meyer, Ruth
Talley, William Robert	Nov 8, 1982	Knoxville, Tn	Benton, Tn	Jan 15, 1925	67	Ballinger, Minnie	Talley, Charles		Porter, Jewell		Hendrix, Linda [Doug]	Mill Springs		[G] Hendrix, John - Gless, Rick	Hunt, Kay - [G] Sellers, Deanna - Hunt, Jeannine		Johnson, Stella - Nelson, Arcella - Godfrey, Sylvi
Tarr, Edna Mabel	Jun 5, 1979	Jeff City	Tn	Apr 27, 1899	90	W	Linafton, —		Lonas, Mary		Tarr, Lonas	West View					
Tarr, H.L.	Jan 7, 1952	Jeff City	Tn	Feb 27, 1881	70	Ng	Tarr, James H.		Lonas, Mary		Tarr, Lonas	West View					
Tarr, Helen Elizabeth	Jan 28, 1948	Knox Co	Roane Co, Tn	Mar 6, 1900	18	S	Tarr, Alfred Hampton		Russell, Mary Louise	Polk Co, Tn	Tarr, Alfred H.	West View					
Tarr, Mary Bowlen	Feb 24, 1982	J.M.H.	Tn	Mar 24, 1857	81	W	Bowlen, Daniel A.		O'Dell, Frances		Collins, Mrs Carrie	West View					
Tarr, Mary Lonas	Apr 15, 1937	Jeff City	Tn		80	W	Lonas, James H.		Tate, Comfort Knox	Tn	Tarr, H.R. & H.L. [Sons] - Miller, Mrs. Helen	Tarr					
Tarr, William Tate	Nov 8, 1960	Knox Co	Tn	Feb 12, 1884	76	Ng	Tarr, James A.		Lonas, Mary		Tarr, Mrs. May B. Rivermead F.H. [Granger Park, Fla]	West View					
Tarro, Joshua Paul	Jun 22, 1976	Jacksonville, Fla		Jun 20, 1976			Tarr, Jack H.	Tn	Quarrels, Cathy		Tarr, Mrs. May B.	West View					
Tate, David T.	Jan 6, 1934	Hamblen Co	Monroe Co, Tn	Mar 31, 1861	72	W	Tate, David	Tn	Parsley, Mary		Parsley, Jim [Morristown]	Lebanon					
Tate, Dazzle Lewelle [Col]	Feb 11, 1945	Jeff Co	Tn	Jun 22, 1884	60	Tate, Will	Shears, Dan		Mc Croskey, Mattie		Tate, William	Colored					
Tate, E.K.	May 9, 1934	Granger Co	Tn	May 20, 1868	65	W	Tate, E.M.	Tn	Noe, Mary	Tn	Tate, William	Shilo					
Tate, Elizabeth W.	Aug 8, 1901	Morristown, Tn	Tn	Mar 5, 1901	87	W	Wolfenbarger, John		Nish, Susan	Tn	Nish-James E.-E.C. - Miller, Genova - Troutman, Frances	Shilo - Granger Co					Mc Nish, Elizabeth-Lange, Doretha-Miller, Genova-Troutman, Frances-Hinkle, Evelyn
Tate, Ernest Clay	Sep 22, 1993	Knoxville, Tn	Granger Co	Mar 4, 1921	72	Whitaker, Vivian			Wolfenbarger, Elizabeth		Wife	J.M.G.	43-45	William Ernest - Robert Clay	Musick, Margaret - Gentry, Linda	William N.	
Tate, Hollen Louise	Apr 5, 1931	Knoxville, Tn	Tn	Oct 6, 1930	5d	Ng	Tate, Dave E.	Tn	Churchman, Mary Jane	Tn	Tate, Mrs. J.N.	Shilo					
Tate, J.N.	Jan 17, 1935	Jeff City	Ng	Jul 26, 1870	64	Tn	Tate, David E.	Tn	Cunningham, Mollie	Tn	Tate, Mrs. J.N.	Shilo					
Tate, John	Aug 22, 1935	Jeff City	Tn	Abt 86	abt 86	Ng					Tate, Ernest C. & Children	Colored					
Tate, Katherine	Apr 8, 1976	Knoxville, Tn	Tn	Feb 6, 1922	54	Ng	Patterson, Henry		Fuller, Marcle		Jefferson Memorial	Jefferson Memorial					
Tate, Lou Ray	Feb 27, 1929		Tn		67-5-2 1	Tate, Knox	Ernest, N.W.	Tn	Hill, Emlay	Tn	Tate, N.E.	Shilo					
Tate, Mildred Marie	Oct 18, 1996	Jeff Co	Tn	Jun 13, 1934	2	Tate, Dave	Tate, Dave	Tn	Davis, Mae	Tn	Tate, Dave	Shiloh					
Tate, Sarah	May 10, 1959	Jeff Co	Tn		84	W	Lansdon, Dempcey		James, Victoria	Tn	Kinder, Mrs. Charlie - Tate, Dave	Shiloh - Granger Co					
Tate, Will J.	Dec 25, 1939	Jeff Co	Tn	Jul 19, 1900	39	Ng	Lansdon, Sarah		Lansdon, Sarah	Tn	Tate, Mrs. & Father	Shiloh					
Tate, William Andrew	May 15, 1946	Granger Co	Knoxville, Tn	Nov 10, 1872	73	Ng	Tate, William A.	Tn	Tate, Mrs. Sarah L (Jame)	Tn	Shiloh	Shiloh					
Tate, William Edward	Feb 14, 1989	Jeff City	Knoxville, Tn	Mar 14, 1906	82	Tate, Geneva	Tate, William W.	Tn	Sheets, Dossia L.	Tn	Tate, Mrs. Genova V.A.	J.M.G.	WW 2				

NAME	DDATE	DLOCAT	BLOCAT	BDATE	AGE	SPOUSE	FATHER	F.B.LOCAT	MOTHER	MF.B.LOCAT	BY	BURIAL	VET	SON	DAUG	BROTHER	SISTER
Talls, William Walter [Col]	Jan 22, 1953	Dandridge, Tn	Jeff Co	Sep 3, 1877	75	W	Talls, Talbot		Haskins, Susan Elizabeth		Talls, William E.	West View Colored		[Nephews] Wagner, Fred J, Harold			
Taylor, Callonia	May 8, 1999	Dandridge, Tn	Tn	Nov 18, 1910	88	W					Taylor, Mrs. Charles - Phillips, Alice Taylor [McH]	Piedmont	army		[Niece] Griffin, Dorothy		
Taylor, Charles Robert	Jul 22, 1967	Knox Co	Tn	Jan 7, 1909		Ng	Taylor, Bill		Woods, Ora		Mill Springs	Mill Springs					
Taylor, Edith Pearl	Sep 13, 1998	Jeff Foity	Brazil, In	May 14, 1945	22		Target, Elizabeth		Purdom, Lillian		Cremated	Cremated			Merryman, Marcia [Eal]		
Taylor, Elmer Wayne	Sep 5, 1983	J.M.H.	Ne	Mar 7, 1899	84	Swann, Margaret	Taylor, Earlee		Morgan, Martha		Taylor, Mrs. Margaret S.	Jefferson Memorial					
Taylor, Eugene Higgins	Jan 10, 1971	Harrison Co	Lincoln Co, Tn	Jul 11, 1908	62	Wagner, Callonia	Taylor, Walter Clayton		Reagan, Clara		Taylor, Carl & Callonia	Piedmont			Merryman, Marcia & Jack		
Taylor, Everett Charles	Mar 28, 1995	Jeff City	Indiana	Apr 3, 1904	90	Atkinson, Edith	Taylor, Charles		Tom, Lillie		Purdom, Lillian T. & John [Daug]	Cremated			Merryman, Marcia & Jack		
Taylor, Flora Brown	Jul 2, 1949	Jeff Co	Tn	Dec 2, 1881	67	W	Brown, William		Smith, Nettie		Taylor, Emily	West View					
Taylor, Harvey Lewis	Oct 18, 1984	Ne	Tn	Sep 23, 1915	69	Bradley, Elizabeth	Taylor, Henry		Gee, Bell		Taylor, Mrs. Elizabeth	Jefferson Memorial					
Taylor, Infant	Jan 13, 1935	Granger Co	Tn	Jan 10, 1935					Mitchell, Callita Mae	Tn	Taylor, A.C.	Indian Ridge					
Taylor, Infant	Jul 1-2, 1935		Tn				Taylor, A.C.				Taylor, A.C.						
Taylor, James A.	May 7, 1970	Jeff City	Tn			W	Taylor, James		Rader, Florence		Mayes, Helen	West View					
Taylor, Joe Evans	Jan 28, 1977	J.M.H.	Tn	Oct 2, 1920	56	Ng	Taylor, Walter Clayton		Renegar, Clara		Taylor, Mrs. Joe	Hillcrest					
Taylor, Kate S.	Aug 18, 1991	J.M.H.	Laivans, Sc	Nov 9, 1913	77	W	Griffin, Walter		Corbin, Minnie		Dukes, Pat [Daug]	West View					
Taylor, Laura E.	Oct 7, 1991	Jeff City	Tn	Feb 20, 1882	49	Taylor, George P.	Cox, M.P.	Tn	Simmons, Mary A.	Tn	National - Knoxville, Tn	West View					
Taylor, Leland Daniel	Aug 8, 1990	J.M.H.	Nashville, Tn	Aug 25, 1912	77	Howes, Helen	Taylor, Leland S.		Stoddard, Virginia		Taylor, Helen H.	J.M.G.					
Taylor, Margaret	May 13, 1988	J.M.H.	Tn	Oct 19, 1906	81	W	Abbey, Bertie		Nine, Robert [Father, Va]		J.M.G.					
Taylor, William	Nov -, 1987	Jeff Co	Tn	Aug 28, 1902	85-2-8	Ng	Taylor, Benjamin		Elam, Alice		Taylor, Mrs. Cira	Mill Springs					
Taylor, Willis Etha	Jan 9, 1998	Jeff Co	Tn	Dec 11, 1896	81	Ng	Huff, Marshall		Harrison, Cynthia		Taylor, James A.	West View					
Tamplin, Julia Samuel	Mar 4, 1918	Jeff City	Greene Co, Tn	Apr 18, 1918	78	Stapleton, Emma	Tamplin, John		Ellison, Mary		Mill	Ronald & Dean					
Terry, Fred G.	Dec 25, 1971	Jeff Co	Alabama	Jan 25, 1908	63	Spencer, Margie	Terry, Henry C.		Simmons, Mary A.	Tn	Terry, George	West View					
Terry, Marjorie	Apr 18, 1995	Harriman, Tn	Franklin, Tn	Feb 13, 1911	84		Terry, James S.		Jellen, Bertha (Lindsey, Mary Elizabeth)		Terry, James S. [Son]	West View			Bruce L.		
Tester, Harold Leon	May 1, 1962	Indiana	W. Va	Jul 22, 1912	79	Beaver, Mary	Tester, George		Dalley, Mary		Wife	J.M.G.					
Thacker, Thomas	May 11, 2000	Knoxville, Tn	Tn	Aug 28, 1920	79	Delbert, Vivian	Thacker, Avenial		Leadman, Willie M.		Wife	J.M.G.	WW 2				
Tharp, Herbert Franklin	May 9, 1980	S.M.H.	Union Co, Tn	Mar 15, 1920	70	Cox, Leona Lorena	Tharp, Burt Franklin		Bowers, Rowena		Tharp, Leona Lorena Cox	J.M.G.					
Tharpe, Helen Juanita	Dec 27, 1999	Dougherville, Ga	Dougherville, Ga	May 29, 1942	57	S	Tharpe, Herbert Franklin		Cox, Lorena		Johnston, Dorthy [Sister]	J.M.G.		Harold Fry, Wayne		
Thomas, Alice White	Jan 25, 1995	J.M.H.	Tn	Oct 1, 1900	84	W	White, Ross		Collier, Florence		Thomas, Hal-Bill	Mt. Horeb					
Thomas, Charles Ray	Dec 2, 2000	Jeff City	Tn	Mar 7, 1941	59	Corbett, Selma Jane	Thomas, Ollie H.		Chilton, Annie		Wife	J.M.G.	veteran				
Thomas, Claude H.	Jan 21, 1928		Tn		27-7-11	Ng	Thomas, U.N.	Tn	Fine, Susie	Tn	Thomas, U.N.	Dandridge					
Thomas, Cynthia [Col]	Jul 9, 1965	Knox Co	Tn	Jun 12, 1962	3		Thomas, James		Hodge, Lila		Thomas, John	West View Colored					
Thomas, Earl Lloyd	Mar 18, 1974	Jeff City	Tn	Nov 25, 1902	71	Mc. Dougal, Mrs. Edith	Thomas, James		Ramey, Sarah		Allen, Mrs. Lois - Tellico Plains, Tn	West View Colored					
Thomas, Euretha	May 1, 1989	Jeff Co	Tn	Nov 23, 1878	90	W	Wills, W.C.D.		Besler, Louise		Shipley, Ted - Bible, Willis	Locust Grove - Tn					
Thomas, George Alfred	Oct 24, 1938	Dandridge	Tn	Jun 14, 1918	18	S	Thomas, Taylor		Lane, Mary	Tn	Thomas, Taylor	Locust Grove - Granger Co					
Thomas, George F.	May 21, 1934	Dandridge	Tn	Dec 30, 1866	67	Ng	Thomas, Lowry		Taylor, Nancy	Tn	Thomas, Mrs. G.F.	Oak Grove					
Thomas, Glenn Preston	Feb 5, 1999	Lynchburg, Va	Knox Co	Sep 22, 1913	85	Solomon, Beaulah	Thomas, Ollie Herbert		Chilton, Annie		Thomas, Robert C. [Son]	Asbury		Clark M. [Md]		3	
Thomas, Hollis Ernestine	Dec 23, 1944	Jeff Co	Tn	Nov 30, 1944	21d	S	Thomas, Hal		Haynes, Mildred		Thomas, Hal - Haynes	Mt. Horeb				6	
Thomas, Hazel	Apr 10, 1926	Tn	Tn	Sep 15, 1930	0-5-1	S	Thomas, Will		White, Alice	Tn	Thomas, Will	Mt. Horeb					
Thomas, J.B.	Mar 25, 1931	Jeff Co	Tn	Sep 15, 1930	16m	S	Thomas, William		White, Alice	Tn	Thomas, William	Mt. Horeb					
Thomas, Jimmy Lewis	Mar 25, 1999	Knoxville, Tn	Sevier Co	Mar 1, 1935	64	Dalton, Bernice	Thomas, Jim		Thomas, Vina		Wills - Dalton, Velva [Mother-In-Law]	J.M.G.		Tim & Lisa Cobb, Paula & Chuck	West, Pam & Tim -	5	2

NAME	DDATE	DLOCAT	BLOCAT	BDATE	AGE	SPOUSE	FATHER	FBLOCAT	MOTHER	MFBLOCAT	BY	BURIAL	VET	SON	DAUG	BROTHER	SISTER
Thomas, John C.	May 7, 1927		Tn		78-1-0	Ng	Thomas, J.C.	Tn	Denton, Mary	Tn	Bible, Mrs. S.S.; Thomas, Mrs. J.C.; Thomas, Mrs. Della Lee [Wife]	Oak Grove					
Thomas, John Floyd	Mar 28, 1947	Jeff Co.	Tn	Apr 29, 1890	56-10-27	Ng	Thomas, John		Nichols, Katherine Aline		Thomas, Mrs. Della Lee [Wife]	New Market					
Thomas, Joseph David	Jun 9, 1979	Jeff City	Ga	Jul 9, 1969	9		Thomas, D.L.		Nichols, Katherine Aline		Thomas, D.L.	Piedmont					
Thomas, Kathy Dee	Jan 18, 1982	Blairsville, Ga	Nc	Sep 1, 1960	21	S	Thomas, D.L.		Nichols, Katherine Aline		Thomas, D.L.	Piedmont					
Thomas, Lillie Merris	Nov 20, 1998	Pigeon Forge, Tn	Rutledge, Tn	May 30, 1921	77	Thomas, Pershing	Roberts, John Butler		Edmonds, Nellie		Myers, Louise [Sister]	Granger Memorial			Couch, Emogene	J.W.	Hooper, Bertha - Floyd, Ruby - Mc Elhaney, Minnie
Thomas, Louise Mc Dougal	Jan 28, 1994	Dandridge, Tn	Arpone, Nc	Jul 28, 1905	88	Mc Dougal, Isaac [D]	Taylor, Della A.		Mc Carter, Mary Mc Dougal [Daug]		J.M.G.			Mc Dougal, Sam [In-Law] Mc Carter, Bob Lambertson, Phillip	Lambertson, Ruth - Price, Joyce & Charlie - [In-Law] Mc Dougal, Barbara	Frank-Clint	Lynn, Marie - Hiatt, Ann - Moses, Telma
Thomas, Margaret Ruth	Jan 20, 1992	Nashville, Tn	Tn	Jul 6, 1896	95	W	Vance, William Taylor		Kennedy, Margaret Jane		Thomas-Eldridge-Calhoun, Tn	Asbury					
Thomas, Mary Belle	Jan 20, 1937	Dumplin [Dumplin Springs]	Tn	Aug 5, 1871	65	W	Shurbert, Aaron	Sc	Belle, Maaey E.	Tn	Thomas, Taylor	Oak Grove					
Thomas, Milburn W.	Nov 3, 1939	Dandridge	Tn	May 27, 1882	57	Ng	Thomas, Lowery		Parks, Nancy	Tn	Thomas, Mrs. & Children	Dandridge					
Thomas, Robert D.	Jul 31, 1979	Jeff City	Tn	Jan 17, 1926	53	Rankin, Wanda	Thomas, Tolliver B.		Dodson, Josephine		Dodson, Josephine	Jefferson Memorial					
Thomas, Susan L.	Nov 4, 1987			Sep 30, 1967	20		Thomas, Charlene J. [Clayton, Nc]		Thomas, Charles [Uncle] - Thomas, Frank			Asbury					
Thomas, William Albert	Nov 19, 1900	Jeff City		Dec 19, 1896	63	White, Alice	Thomas, John A.		Fowler, Eliza		Thomas, Alice	Mt. Horeb					
Thomas, William Earl	Jan 25, 1964	Jeff City	Tn	Aug 24, 1913	50	Ng	Thomas, John Floyd		Templin, Della		Thomas, Mrs. Mae	West View					
Thomas, William Frankie	Aug 26, 1948		Tn	Aug 11, 1946	2		Thomas, William Earl	Tn	Collins, Lucy Mae	Tn	Thomas, William Earl	West View	WW 2				
Thomas, William Ray	Dec 21, 1997	Jeff City	Winchester, Ky	Apr 4, 1934	63	Reavis, Hilda	Thomas, Virgil Tutor		Oliver, Myrtie Ann		Wife - Godbee F.H. [Winchester, Ky]	Winchester					
Thompson, Arthur F. [Col]	Feb 21, 1954	Blount Co	Tn	Oct 13, 1865	60	Div	Thompson, Lem		Smith, Maggie		Thompson, Arthur Jr. - Jackson, Edna - Bralson, Lucy - Simpson, Maggie	West View Colored					
Thompson, Arthur Jr.	Jan 20, 1999	Jeff City	Tn	Jan 10, 1917	82		Thompson, Arthur Sr.		Bralson, Lucy [Sister]		Bralson, Lucy [Sister]	West View	41-45				Jackson, Edna
Thompson, Benjamin Luther	Dec 28, 1985	U.T.H.	Tn	Aug 12, 1983	2		Thompson, Gary W.		Fairman, Nancy J.		Thompson, Gary	Jefferson Memorial					
Thompson, Bettye Jane [Col]	Oct 9, 1971	U.T.H.	Tn	Feb 13, 1932	39	Thompson, Arthur Jr.	Donaldson, Ralph		Turner, Nellie		Turner, Mildred	West View					
Thompson, Carrie	Jul 6, 1996	Cocke Co., Tn	Tn	Feb 19, 1916	82		Link				Wingard, Beverly M. [Not Related]	Hopewell					
Thompson, Emogene	Sep 6, 1991	Athens, Tn	Tn	Jul 4, 1910	81	Thompson, Clyde E.	Maughon, Bill		Gurley, Helen		Thompson, Clyde E.	Cremated					
Thompson, Helen	Feb 8, 1999	Franklin, Nj	Tn	Sep 15, 1913	85	Thompson, Roy Edgar	Kovach, John		Jewel, Maria		Husband	Cremated		Robert J.	Schwenkfurth, Linda F. - Behr, Louise	Joseph	Gurley, Sophie
Thompson, Jack Bowen	Apr 5, 1987	Kox Co	Tn	Dec 12, 1930	36	S	Thompson, Arthur		Hodge, Clarinie		Simpson, Maggie - Bralson, Lucy - Civil, Thompson, Albert -	West View					
Thompson, Jeffery Walter	Jan 25, 1981	Knoxville, Tn	Tn	Dec 14, 1982	18	S	Thompson, Sam W.		Noe, Donna		Thompson, Sam W.	Jefferson Memorial					
Thompson, Paul	Feb 7, 1994	Jeff City	Yankton Co, Ne	Jan 12, 1957	72		Thompson, Nicholas		Thompson, Mae		Thompson, Carolyn [Daug]	Hamblen Memorial			Prigmore, Angela & James	Avril-Nickholas F.	Dockery, Hazel - Robinson, Ruth - Smith, Essie
Thompson, Queenie [Col]	May 29, 1958	Jeff City	Tn	Feb 8, 1958	65-3-21	Thompson, Arthur [D]	Hodge, Pryor		Hodge,		Bralson, Mrs. Herbert - Jackson, Edna - Simpson, Albert - Arthur Jr.-Willie-Jack Thompson, Mrs. Essie Moody	West View Colored					
Thompson, Theodore C.	Jun 5, 1957	Mt. Home, Tn	Ga	Jan 12, 1957		Ng	Thompson, V.H.		Phillips, Kathleen		Phillips, Kathleen	West View	WW 2				

NAME	DATE	DLOCAT	BLOCAT	BDATE	AGE	SPOUSE	FATHER	FBLOCAT	MOTHER	MBLOCAT	BY	BURIAL	VET	SON	DAUG	BROTHER	SISTER
Thompson, Willie Carter	Jan 30, 1995	Lafayette, Ind.	Tn	Jun 17, 1918	68	W	Thompson, Arthur Sr.		Hodge, Queenie		Thompson, Angela (Lafayette, Ind) - Thompson, Willie (Gary, Ind)	West View	WW 2				
Thompson, Philip David	Oct 4, 2000	Knoxville, Tn	Michigan	Jul 21, 1929	71	Sapulwala, Olga	Thompson, Harold	Tn	Snow, Jean		Wife	West View					
Thornton, Jack Jackson	Jan 5, 1940	Dandridge		Oct 17, 1893	46	Ng	Thornton, James B.	Tn	Francis, Nancy		Thorpe, Mrs. / Chestnut Hill	West View / Chestnut Hill					
Thorpe, Adaline	Mar 20, 1992	Jeff Co		Apr 17, 1856	75	W	Butcher, Jessie		Unk		Thorpe, A.H. & Brothers						
Thorpe, Georgia Dorothy	Aug 3, 1941	White Pine	Tn		31-6-23	Thorpe, Abe H.	Thorpe, Abe	Tn	Ramsey, Cordie	Jeff Co	Thorpe, A.H.	Flat Gap					
Thorpe, Virginia Pearl	Nov 22, 1942	Jeff Co	Jeff Co	May 27, 1938	4		Morris, Georgia		Morris, Georgia	Tn	Morris, Frank & Earl	West View					
Tiller, Clem Myrtle	Oct 1, 1998	Rossville, Ga.	Jellico, Tn	Feb 1 1906	92	Thorpe, Abe H.	Stanfield, Joseph		Stanfield, Sarah		Davis, Gerry (Dana)	West View					
Tiller, Jesse Alexander	Jan 6, 1958	Jeff Co	Tn	Sep 9, 1903	54	Stanfield, Myrtle	Tiller, Charles W.		Everette, Mary		Everette, Mary	West View					
Timmons, Forest Rhoten	Apr 21, 1974	Jeff Co	Tn	Apr 23, 1898	85	S	Timmons, George S.		Rhoten, Martha		Minns, George	West View					
Timmons, G.S.	Jan 4, 1929	Tn	Tn	Dec 20, 1848	80	W	Timmons, Gen. S.		Peck, Julia		Family	West View					
Timmons, Mattie Rhoten	Jun 7, 1931	Jeff City	Tn	May 15, 1899	82	W	Rimmons, Gen. S.	Va	Hampton, Alice	Tn	Tipton, Mrs. Stella	West View					
Tipton, George	Apr 7, 1955	Jeff City	Tn		56	Ng	Tipton, William				Tipton, Mrs. Stella - Demeterss, Mrs.	West View					
Tipton, Zoerel	Oct 16, 1951	Fortress Co, Tn	Tn	May 27, 1885	65-4-19	Ng	Tipton, William C.		Stephens, Mary E.		C.C. (Cedar Bluff, Va) - Curly, Mrs. Seldon	West View					
Tittle, Cecil	Nov 12, 1951	Jeff Co	Tn	Apr 2, 1905	47	Div	Tittle, Ephriam		Unk		Tittle, Old Grace & John A.	Wooden					
Tittsworth, Eva	May 24, 1963	Jeff Co	Tn	Nov 4, 1878	84	W	Mc Spadden, Alex		Chandler, Ellen		Tittsworth, Mary Kate - Nancy-Elizabeth - Francis (Children)	West View					
Tittsworth, Mary	Mar 9, 1946	Jeff Co	Jeff Co	Jul 29, 1871	84	W	Brannen, John F.	Tn	Brannen, Blanche	Tn	Maqus, Mrs. Walter - Tittsworth, H.H. - Mc Cown, Mrs.	West View					
Tittsworth, Mary Kate	Sep 28, 1998	J.M.H.	Tn	Mar 22, 1900	88	S	Tittsworth, B.M.		Mc Spadden, Eva		Tittsworth, Elizabeth	West View					
Tittsworth, Robbie Ross	Oct 14, 1987	Jeff Co	Tn	Dec 16, 1896	100	W	Ross, John Fath		Clark, Elizabeth		Formwalt, John M.	West View					
Tompson, Lizzie	Dec 29, 1935				51	Foy, Martha											
Toomey, John M.	Mar 5, 1997	Jeff City	Tn	Nov 30, 1945	94	W	Toomey, Glenn A.		Shell, Vivian R.		Wife	J.M.G.		John Mark- Samuel Scott			
Torbett, Fay	Oct 31, 1988	Hillhaven	Tn	Sep 17, 1894		W	Story, Charlie		Amanda		Whitlock, Robert R.	Greenwood - Knox Co				Glenn A.	
Tormey, Samuel	Aug 5, 1981	Jeff City	Ng	Ng	72	Ng	Tormey, David		Nancy		Tormey, Sam & James W.	West View					
Travis, David E.	Aug 22, 1981	Hamblen Co	Tn	Jun 22, 1912	80	W	Travis, Henry O.		Homer, Emma		Cox, Hazel (Sister)	J.M.G.					
Travis, Emma Elizabeth	Aug 2, 1981	Hamblen Co	Tn	Apr 20, 1896	75	Travis, Hu.	Homer, William				Travis, H.A.	Pleasant View					Keller, Pearl- Shearer, Mary
Travis, Henry Anvil	Apr 28, 1983	Hamblen Co	Tn	Jun 18, 1899	73	W	Travis, David E.		Pierce, Nancy E.		Elmer-Harwood- Keller, Nellie - Shearer, Mary (Mich.) - Cox, Hazel	Pleasant View					
Travis, Lela B.	Aug 6, 1992	Union Co, Tn	Nov 15, 1923	Nov 15, 1923	68	Travis, David E.	Becker, Pryor		Collins, Matilda		Husband	J.M.G.					
Treece, Edgar Jackson [Col]	Sep 16, 1963	Jeff Co	Tn	Jul 28, 1906	57	Ng	Treece, John		Chestnut, Lydia		Treece, Florence P. (Wife)	West View Colored / Rock Of Ages - Hamblen Co					
Treece, Garvin	Apr 3, 1956	Jeff City	Tn	Mar 6, 1855	78	W	Treece, John		Treece, Mrs. Lydia		Treece, Mrs. Lydia	Macedonia					
Treece, J.T.	Apr 9, 1933	Knox Co	Tn			W	Treece, William		Cos, Jane	Tn	Evans, Mrs - Miss Myrtal	Macedonia					
Treece, Lydia Chestnut [Col]	Apr 22, 1957	Jeff City	Tn		69	W	Treece, -		Cochrann, Hannah		Dyer, Mrs. Henry, Mills, Gertrude - Rufus	Macedonia					
Treece, Mrs. J.T.	Dec 28, 1927	Tn			63		Cooper, James	Tn			Children	Macedonia					
Trent, Charles Otto	Dec 13, 1965	Oben, Nc	Tn	Nov 26, 1902		Bailey, Maudie	Trent, C.O.				Trent, Mrs. C.O.	Strawberry Plains					
Trent, D.W.	May 4, 1965	Tn			96							Trent					
Trent, Frank [Col]	Jan 25, 1932	Tn					Unk					Colored					
Trent, Hazel Ruth	Sep 5, 1945	Jeff City	Jeff Co	Jun 4, 1944	1		Trent, C.O.	Tn	Bailey, Ollis Maudie	Tn	Trent, C.O.	Trent				Hall, Glenora- Forrest, Ruth Ann	
Trent, J.R.	April 21, 1935	Jeff Co															

NAME	DDATE	DLOCAT	BLOCAT	BDATE	AGE	SPOUSE	FATHER	FELOCAT	MOTHER	MFELOCAT	BY	BURIAL	VET	SON	DAUG	BROTHER	SISTER
Trent, James T.	Dec 27, 1953	Holston Valley	Hawkins Co	May 15, 1888	67		Trent, James		Cain, Ella		Trent, Mrs. Oma T.	Highland - Hawkins Co					
Trent, Lizzie [Col]	Jan 17, 1992	Jeff City										Colored					
Trent, Ollie J.	April 23, 1955	Jeff City															
Trentham, Arthur	Mar 24, 1999	Jeff Co	Tn	Mar 8, 1910	29	S	Trentham, N.U.	Tn	Trentham, N.U. [New Market]			Narro's Grove					
Trentham, Eda Mae	Sep 15, 1990	Evanston, Illinois	Sevier Co.	Nov 3, 1912	83	S	Trentham, N.V.		Trentham, Ollie		Narro's Grove - New [Brother]						
Trentham, Mary K.	Nov 9, 1933	Jeff City	Va	Jan 3, 1850	83	W	Collins, John	Va	Hartnenburg, Sarah		Narro's Grove - Farrar, Roy	West View					
Trentham, Newton Vanburen	Jan 5, 1961	Knox Co	Tn	Sep 20, 1885	75	Ng	Trentham, Rev. James		Link		Trentham, Rev.- Mc Carter, Mrs.	Narro's Grove					
Trentham, Ollie W.	Apr 26, 1970	Knox Co	Tn	Dec 10, 1887	82	Trentham, N.V. [D]	Williams, Simeon		Webb, Margaret		Webb, Margaret	Bethany - Sevier Co					
Trentham, Shannon Otis	Jul 24, 1976	Gatlinburg, Tn		Nov 16, 1893	82	W	Trentham, Isaac N.		Conner, Caldonia		Trentham, W.R.-J.C.- H.L. [Tessie]	West View					
Trentham, Walter Cleo	Jun 18, 1945	Knox Co	Sevier Co	Apr 6, 1924	21	S	Trentham, N.V.	Tn	Williams, Ollie	Tn	Trentham, N.V.- Green, Mrs. Charles	Narro's Grove					
Trentham, William R.	Apr 8, 1993	Mars Hill, Nc		Oct 8, 1925	67	Dotson, Jessie	Trentham, Shandon O.		Roekin, Iria Davis		Wife	Cremated		William Sidney- William Rodney	Strange, Anita - Proffitt, Melodie - Dudley, Carole - Nixon, Linda		Campbell, Helen - Owen, Joan - Taskersley, Margaret - Oliver, Betty
Trickett, Royce	Aug 7, 1982	Morristown, Tn	Pa	Dec 26, 1922	59	Mc Donald, Alice Muriel	Trickett, Grant L.		Roboy, Coletta		Wife	Stafford Memorial - Stafford Co, Va	WW 2				
Trotter, Douglas J.	Oct 12, 1984	Knox Co	Illinois	Jan 18, 1906	58	Ng	Trotter, Amos		Jordon, Grace		Trotter, Mrs. Geneva - Douglas Jr.- Garland, David - Reese, Will W. [Illinois]	West View		[G] Garland, David G. 3rd [D] Michael	Garland, Jane & David - [G] Garland Sarah - Trotter, Jill	
Trotter, Geneva M.	Apr 20, 1987	Johnson City, Tn	Jeff Co	Jun 8, 1904	92	Trotter, Douglas J. [D]	Moore, George		Bird, James	Tn	Trotter, Douglas & Brnoda [Son]	West View		[G] Garland, David G. 3rd [D] Michael	Garland, Jane & David - [G] Garland Sarah - Trotter, Jill	
Truitt, Bessie Lee	Jul 10, 1942	Granger Co	Hancock Co	May 28, 1925	17	S	Truitt, Fred	Tn	Moore, Laura	Tn	Mc Daniels, Albert - Truitt, George - Truitt, Fred	Shiloh					
Truitt, Stacy	Dec 13, 1977	Jeff Co	Nc	Aug 8, 1927	50	Goodwin, Leota	Truitt, Vincent		Jenkins, Rosie		Truitt, Mrs. Stacy & Children	Jefferson Memorial	unk				
Trumbotum, Mildred V.	Feb 18, 2000	Jeff City		Mar 7, 1917	82	Div	Vineyard, Loren		Schult, Ethel		Redfern, Cheryline K. [Daug]- Larch, Mrs. Lillian - Elizabeth-Carolyn [Daug]	Schult - Harrisburg, Il	WW 2				
Trusler, Albert James	Dec 27, 1966	Newark, Nj		Mar 27, 1916	50	Zoellush, Rose	Trusler, Albert Sr.		Ward, Susan		Jefferson Memorial					
Trusler, Rose Margaret	Nov 8, 1990	Essex Co, Nj		Sep 19, 1915	78	Zoelish, Daniel			Betts, Rose		Trusler, Carolyn [Daug]	J.M.G.			Missireo, Susan & Chuck	Walker, Anna
Tucker, Anna Louise	Dec 4, 1996	Knoxville, Tn	Laurens, Sc	Jul 24, 1919	77	Tucker, Edwin [D]	Solomon, William		Young, Robin [Daug]		Young, Robin [Daug]	Cremated		Kirk	Wender, Sara	
Tucker, Edwin George	Apr 17, 1993	Morristown, Tn	Thomas Co, Kansas	Jul 30, 1917	76	Solomon, Louise	Tucker, Hal E.		Lindquist, Winifred		Wife	Cremated			Wender, Saral	
Turlidge, Stephen Pimdoriske	Aug 1, 1999	Winston-Salem, Nc		Sep 16, 1959	39	Stapleton, Angela	Turlidge, Archer		Lundy, Dorothy		Wife- Stapleton, George & Dorothy [Parents-in-Law]	Cremated		Stephen [Buddy]	Marie	James-Harrison- Archer Jr.	
Turnell, Calvin Wayne	Nov 6, 1989	Shelton, Wash.		Sep 17, 1924	65	Etter, Emma	Turnell, Kenneth [Richmond, Va]		Turnell, Kenneth [Richmond, Va]		Cremated - Ebenezer	Cremated - Ebenezer					
Turk, William Graham	May 24, 1949	Tn	Tn		60-5 29	Ng	Turk, William		Smith, Lucy		Smith, Lucy	St. Lukas Presby					
Turk, Roger Lee	Sep 7, 1948	Knox Co	Jeff Co	Apr 5, 1948	5m	Ng	Turnell, Calvin W.	Tn	Elles, Emma Lou	Tn	Cross, Mrs. Calvin W.- Turnell, Calvin W.- Hall, Mrs. Albert	Ebenezer					
Turnbull, Emma Addie	Apr 11, 1966	Tn	Tn	Jan 19, 1891	75	W			Gibbon, Annie		Ledgerwood, Wilma	West View					
Turnbull, Mary	Mar 2, 1988	Scotland	Scotland	Jul 12, 1903	84	W			Livingstone, James		Ledgerwood, Wilma T.	Cremated					
Turnbull, William	Nov 3, 1986	Scotland		Jul 18, 1900	86	Livingstone, Mary M.	Turnbull, William		Christie, M.S.		Turnbull, Wilma T.	Cremated					
Turner, Byrda Hardin [Black]	Nov 8, 1993	Jeff City	Tn	Aug 11, 1905	88	Link			Link		Turner, Mildred D. [Daug-in-Law]	West View		[G] Donaldson, Jeremy [Ohio]			
Turner, Caleb Mack [Rev]	Oct 18, 1987	Tugelo, Miss.	Tn	Feb 1, 1915	72	Millard, Rose	Turner, Harry M.				Turner, Rose	Swahom Chapel Mt. Pleasant					
Turner, E.W.	Jan 31, 1931	Talbott	Tn														

NAME	DDATE	DLOCAT	BLOCAT	BDATE	AGE	SPOUSE	FATHER	FRLOCAT	MOTHER	MFRLOCAT	BY	BURIAL	VET	SON	DAUG	BROTHER	SISTER
Turner, Earl La Homes	Feb 19, 1984	Sweetwater, Tn	Tn	Feb 10, 1920	64	Reed, Frances	Turner, Harry	Tn	Trent, Alice	Tn	Turner, Mrs. Frances [Sweetwater, Tn]	Jefferson Memorial					
Turner, Flossie	Dec 17, 1933	Hamblen Co	Tn	Apr 8, 1920	313	Reed, Frances	Turner, Harry		Trent, Alice		Turner, J.H.	Pleasant View					
Turner, Fred [Buck]	May 16, 1989	Tunica Co., Miss.	Tn	Dec 31, 1922	66	Donaldson, Mildred	Workmen, Charles	Tn	Pascal, Florence	Tn	Turner, Mrs. Mildred	J.M.G.	WW 2				
Turner, Guy Edgar	Apr 12, 1984	J.M.H.	Tn	Feb 22, 1903	81	Phillips, Edith	Turner, Harry		Turner, Byrda H.		Erlinger, Mrs. Alger - Johnson, Ethel	Bretheren - Dandridge					
Turner, Harriet C.	May 23, 1948	Hamblen Co	Tn	May 28, 1870	77-11-25	W	Cox, William	Tn	Chaney, Sallie	Tn	Rines, Mrs. W.O.	Lebanon					
Turner, Harry Moore	Sep 11, 1947	Jeff Co	Hamblen Co., Tn	Nov	77	W	Turner, F.M.	Tn	Abard, Margaret	Tn	Turner, Case M.	Swaburn Chapel					
Turner, Horace Dewey	Feb 15, 1996	Talbott, Tn	Mo	Aug 19, 1898	87	W	Turner, R.P.		Hutton, Vivien		Turner, Keith D.	Sunderland					
Turner, James Hutton	Sep 6, 1926	Roanoke, Va			0-9-6		Turner, R.P.	Va	Hutton, Vivien	Va	Turner, R.P.	Roanoke, Va					
Turner, Mary Ellen	Sep 21, 1984	J.M.H.		Sep 17, 1903	81	Turner, Horace D.	Burnett, T.C.		Carter, Myrtle		Turner, Horace Dewey- Keith D.	Sunderland					
Turner, Ruby Frances	May 31, 1996	Knoxville, Tn	Hamblen Co	Dec 6, 1924	71	Reed, Edward			Rhea, Bonnie		Turner, Joy [Niece]	J.M.G.					
Turner, Thomas	Jan 22, 1936	Mossy Creek		Jan 22, 1936			Turner, Thomas		Hickey, Goldie Mai		Turner, Thomas [White Pine]						
Turner, William Pascal	Apr 10, 1946	Hamblen Co	Tn		78-3 10	Ng	Turner, James	Tn	Moore, Mary	Tn	Rines, Luzon - Turner, Boyd & Marshall	Lebanon					
Turner, Wilma Reed	Jan 23, 1990	Jeff Co		Jan 22, 1946	14	S	Turner, Earl		Reed, Frances		Turner, Earl	Jefferson Memorial					
Turpin, Jayne	Aug 5, 1990	Jeff Co	Jeff City	Mar 11, 1939	51	Div	Martin, Hal		Miller, Alice		Collins, Scarlett [Doug]	West View					
Turpin, Tammy Ray	Dec 7, 1957	Knoxville, Tn			6w		Turpin, William R.	Rutledge, Tn	Martin, Jayne	Rutledge, Tn	Turpin, W.R.	West View					
Tyler, Cecile	Jun 28, 1900	Rogersville, Tn		Jul 26, 1899	90	W	Walters, J.K.		Price, Ida M.		Miller, Mrs. Thomas E.	Bethesda - Hamblen Co					
Tyler, Henry	Dec 7, 1981	Tn	Tn	Aug 3, 1900	81	Tyler, Cecil	Tyler, John D.		Davis, Zenia		Tyler, Mrs. Cecil	Bethesda - Hamblen Co					
Umberger, Mary P.	Mar 13 1987	J.M.H.	Virginia	Nov 7, 1910	76	W	Pearman, Emmitt R.		Kemp, Laura V.		Umberger, Carlisle	St. Johns - Wytheville, Va					
Underwood, Agnes Lea	Aug 6, 1999	Morristown, Tn	New Market, Tn	Jan 7, 1912	87		Campbell, Stanford A.		Wisner, Nancy Jane		Underwood, Jean [Doug]	Piedmont					
Underwood, Amos	Jul 7, 1944	Tn	Tn						Rutledge. Tn		Miller, Ralph - Finchum, Jess	Lebanon					
Underwood, Bessie	Jun 17, 2000	Knoxville, Tn	Tn	Oct 18, 1916	83	Underwood, L.D.	Whitlock, James		Lee, Peggy Jane [Daug]		Lee, Peggy Jane- Finchum, Jess	Beach Springs - Kodak, Tn					
Underwood, Beulah	Mar 15, 1978	Jeff City	Tn	Nov 16, 1905	72	Ng	Bateman, Marion		Britt, Annie		Underwood, Fred A. & Children	Jefferson Memorial					
Underwood, Comfort Lonas	Feb 14, 1926	Tn	Tn		28-7-1		Lonas, W.A.	Tn	Lars, H.L.	Tn	Underwood, H.B.	Sunderland					
Underwood, Deborah Faye	Feb 28, 1961	Jeff Co	Tn	Mar 24, 1961		Underwood, Bert	Underwood, Marion		Cross, Marylin		Underwood, Marion	Jefferson Memorial					
Underwood, Elisha Edward	Jul 8, 1962	Jeff Co	Tn	Nov 20, 1881	80	Ng	Lee, Melikia Jane	Tn	Reed, Frances		Underwood, Fred- Frank-Jess [Sons]	Buffalo Grove					
Underwood, Flo	Jan 15, 1935	Jeff City	Tn	Dec 1, 1903	31	Underwood, Fred	Moore, R.E.	Tn	Lewis, William	Tn	Bateman, Beulah	Sunderland					
Underwood, Fred	Nov 24, 1935	Jeff City	Tn	Nov 24, ----			Underwood, Fred		Bateman, Beulah		Underwood, Miss Una Lee						
Underwood, Fred Agned	Dec 5, 1995	Knoxville, Tn	Va	Dec 25, 1906	78	W	Underwood, Elisha		Green, Gillis		Jefferson Memorial						
Underwood, Gillie Ann	Jul 8, 1964	Jeff Co	Va	Mar 18, 1885	79	Underwood, L.E. [D]	Combs, John L.		Whicker, Rachael		Carter, Mrs. Irvin - J.M.- Jim-Fred-Frank- William C. - Jett, Mrs.- Coffman, Mrs. - Marris, Mrs. -	Buffalo Grove					
Underwood, John Amos	May 6, 1956	Tn	Tn	Feb 12, 1882	74	Ng	Underwood, White		Pollard, Sarah		Underwood, Mrs. Lola	Oak Grove - Sevier Co					
Underwood, John Wendell	Jul 28, 1960	Jeff Co	Tn	Aug 7, 1911	49	Ng	Underwood, William		Fields, Maggie		Underwood, Harold - Wooten	Woolard	WW 2				
Underwood, L. Kaney	Apr 23, 1955	Jeff Co	Hawkins Co.	Sep 27, 1888	66	W	Underwood, James		Lee, Matilda Jane		Underwood, Walter - Cox, Mrs. Helen	Buffalo Grove					
Underwood, Louella Grace	Dec 13, 1953	Jeff Co	Sevier Co	Nov 15, 1893	60	W	Creswell, William		Dykes, Carolyn		Boyd's Creek - Sevier Co						
Underwood, Maudy Belle	Feb 6, 1948	Jeff Co	Tn		76-15-21	W				Finchum, Mrs. Jess		Finchum, Mrs. Jess	West View				
Underwood, Randall Dean	Mar 2, 1962	Jeff Co	Tn	Mar 1, 1962		W	Underwood, Marion		Cross, Marilyn		Underwood, Marion	Memorial Gardens					

NAME	DDATE	DLOCAT	BLOCAT	BDATE	AGE	SPOUSE	FATHER	FRELOCAT	MOTHER	MRELOCAT	BY	BURIAL	VET	SON	DAUG	BROTHER	SISTER
Underwood, Steve Owen	Oct 14, 1996	Knoxville, Tn	Knox Co	Jun 5, 1962	34	W	Underwood, James		Saxton, Mary G.		Cameron, Alice [Niece]	City - Crossville, Tn			Katy		
Underwood, Velma Gertrude	Oct 10, 1990	J.M.H.	Jeff Co	Feb 24, 1909	81	W	Wyatt, Alos		Long, Mary		Willie	J.M.G.					
Underwood, William Claude	Apr 22, 1957	S.M.H.	Tn	Oct 7, 1872	64	Ng	Underwood, Louis E.	Tn	Combs, Gillie Ann	Tn	Lowndey, Mrs. Frida V.	Hillcrest	WW 2				
Vaughn, Terry Alan	Aug 30, 1986	Cherokee Lake	Ohio	Jul 27, 1975	61-1-0	Gerdsen, Frida	Vaughn, John David		Wesley, Margaret May		Ebon, Margaret [Grandmother F.H. [Grove City, OH]		WW 2				
	May 6, 1987			Jun 10, 1986	20	S											
Van Dyke, Harley	Jul 23, 1957	New Market	Tn	Nov 7, 1874	73-2-16	W	Van Dyke, Harley	Tn	Lowery, Leslie	Tn	Van Dyke, Harley	Shady Grove					
Van Dyke, James Andrew Freeman	Jan 23, 1948	Knox Co	Jeff Co		16	W	Van Dyke, Peyton		Patterson, Martha J.	Tn	Bell, Birtie	Patterson's					
Van Dyke, James R.	Sep 17, 1992	J.M.H.	Jeff Co	Jul 28, 1913	79	W	Van Dyke, Freeman		Walker, Darcus		Willie	J.M.G.					
Van Hula, Nellie Roberts	Jul 8, 1960	Nashville, Tn	Tn		18						Burnett, Mrs. Lloyd	Sunderland					
Vance, Eleanor Alucella	Apr 27, 1950	Jeff Co	Tn	Oct 27, 1872	4	Ng	Vance, Paul		Drake, Thelma		Vance, Paul	New Market					
Vance, Hattie	May 18, 1927		Tn			Ng						Shiloh					
Vance, Manuard Graham [F]	Dec 27, 1991	F.S.H.	Jeff Co	Nov 15, 1986	93	W	Graham, James Rufus		Malooly, Mary Carolyn		Vance, Samuel G. [Son]	New Market					
Vance, Martha	Oct 22, 1923	New Market	Tn	Mar 13, 1873	93	Ng	James, J.C.	Tn	Pierce, Mary	Tn	Vance, Sam A.	Friends Station					
Vance, Mary Blake	Jul 12, 1925	St. Louis	Tn		10		Cobb, Martha E.	Tn			Vance, S.M.	New Market					
Vance, Robert	Sep 20, 1921	Jeff Co	Tn	Nov 10, 1866	66	Duggan, Nora	Vance, John D.		Matthis, Martha J.		Vance, Carl-Edward	New Market					
Vance, Samuel M.	Aug 23, 1953	Jeff Co	Tn														
Vandethoff, George	Jan 20, 1998	New Market, Tn	Morristown, Tn	Oct 4, 1919	78		Armstrong, Frank		Vandethoff, Iva		Vandethoff, Georgia [Dang]	Piedmont		Vandethoff, William			Prescott, Susan - Tassoo, Betty
Vanoman, Deborah Marie	Oct 24, 1958	Jeff City		Mar 29, 1877	87	W	Vanoman, Sherman B. Jr.		Singleton, Jeanita		Vanoman, S. Jr.	Lewisport - Ky					
Vanoman, Benjamin	May 2, 1964	Jeff Co	Tn		77-9-18	W	Varnell, John R.		Pierce, Margaret		Varnell, Ella	Wesleys Chapel					
Varnell, Daisy	Nov 12, 1957	Jeff Co	Tn		18	Varnell, Ralph	Newman, Sarah		Varnell, Ralph & Ella [Dang]			Wesleys Chapel					
Varnell, Oliver Bradley	Aug 28, 1954	Jeff Co	Tn	July 24, 1879	75	W	Varnell, John R.		Princo, Margaret		Varnell, Ben	Wesleys Chapel					
Varner, Sam	Oct 5, 1979	Knoxville, Tn	Tn	Sep 13, 1901	78	W	Varner, Lum		Denham, Emily		Branch, Joe	West View					
Vaughn, Daisy Lee Margaret	Nov 28, 1946	Cocke Co	Cocke Co	Oct 5, 1902	44	Ng	Lyle, Ben	Tn	Evans, Carrie	Tn	Vaughn, Rev. Lincoln M.	Pleasant Grove					
Vaughn, John D.	Mar 23, 1993	Jeff City	Trousdale Co, Tn	Jun 2, 1917	75	Holmes, Pauline	Vaughn, William Morgan		Kyle, Ada		Willie	Hermitage Memorial Nashville, Tn	42-45	R.C.-Eddie D.		Paul-James	
Venable, Marguerite	Oct 22, 1985	Tazewell, Tn	Nevada	Aug 6, 1892	93	W	Hamill, Robert		Wiseman, Elizabeth		Venable, B.W.	Oak Hill Memorial - San Jose, Cal.					
Vesser, James Howard	Mar 5, 2000	Jeff City	Tn	Oct 26, 1920	79	Layman, Imogene	Vesser, Warnie N.		Miller, Lucrecia		Venable, B.W.	J.M.G.	WW 2				
Vesser, Jimmie L.	Dec 22, 1968	Jeff Co	Tn	Jun 5, 1916	52	Ng	Vesser, Walter		Varnell, Bernice		Vesser, Mrs. Bernice	West View					
Vesser, Mandy	May 20, 1952	Jeff Co	Tn	Mar 25, 1893	59	Ng	Vesser, Mac		Vesser, Mac		Vesser, Mac	Balch					
Vesser, Mary Evelyn	Sep 16, 1955	Blount Co	Tn	Apr 4, 1950	5	Ng	Vesser, James		Slabby, Bernice		Vesser, James - Twilla	West View					
Vesser, Warnie N.	May 12, 1970	Jeff Co	Tn	May 24, 1886	83	W	Vesser, James		Anderson, -		Vesser, James - Twilla [Myrell, Mrs.]	Lebanon - Mt. Horeb					
Vesser, William C.	May 12, 1954	Jeff City	Tn	Nov 7, 1884	69	Ng	Vesser, James		Fusic, Priscilla		Vesser, Mary P.	West View					
Vest, Amanda B.	May 5, 1951	Jeff Co	Tn	Apr 1, 1875	76	Ng	Beeson, Bill		Funk, Priscilla		Vest, Peacoe	Hills Chapel					
Vest, Clarence Edgar	Dec 31, 1977	Jeff Co	Tn	Nov 1, 1897	80	Parks, Sara Elizabeth	Beeson, William		Beeson, Amanda		Vest, Mrs. C.E.	Jefferson Memorial					
Vest, Debora Lynn	Jan 11, 1962	Knox Co	Michigan	Aug 4, 1958	4	Vest, Edgar	Vest, James		Mc Million, Wilma Jean		Vest, Wilma Jean	Holston View - Knox Co					
Vest, Nella Elizabeth	Sep 10, 1989	S.M.H.	Tn	Dec 17, 1924	64	Vest, Edgar	Cockrum, Millard		Travis, Willie		Vest, Mrs. Clarence - Williamson, Mrs. Oney	J.M.G.					
Vest, Robert Henry	Feb 12, 1980	Jeff City	Tn	Jul 10, 1873	86	W	Vest, Alex		Carter, Nancy		Vest, Mrs. Clarence - Williamson, Mrs. Oney [W.Va]	Hills Union					
Vest, Roscoe	Mar 28, 1966	Jeff Co	Tn	Mar 23, 1911	55	Ng	Vest, Robert		Beeson, Amanda		Vest, Mrs. Roscoe	Hills Union					
Vest, Sarah Elizabeth	May 20, 1979	Jeff City	Tn	Sep 15, 1899	79	W	Parks, Albert		Palmer, Olisa		Vest, Mrs. Ruby	Jefferson Memorial					
Vineyard, Elmer Boyd	Aug 23, 1956	New Market	Tn	Oct 15, 1885	70	Ng	Vineyard, Sam S.		Cobner, Rebecca		Vineyard, Mrs. Elmer	New Market					
Vineyard, R.G.	Jan 5, 1940	Granger Co	Tn	Mar 17, 1864	75	Ng					Nance, William	Shiloh					
Vineyard, William Howard	Jul 22, 1994	Rutledge	Georgia	Nov 4, 1909	82	Kinsey, Thelma	Vineyard, William Samuel		Nance, Rosie		Wife	New Corrierth				Johnson, Kathleen-Kemp	
Vineyard, N.I.	Jul 8, 1992	F.S.H.	Tn	Feb 17, 1924	74	Ng	Vineyard, Samuel S.		West, Betty	Tn	West, Edgar	J.M.G.				Bennett, Doris - Corby, Elizabeth - Fielam, Ethel	Lewis, Shirley

NAME	DATE	B/LOC#	B/LOC#	DATE	AGE	SPOUSE	FATHER	F/B/LOC#	MOTHER	M/F/LOC#	BY	BURIAL	VET	SON	DAUG	BROTHER	SISTER
Vineyard, Ralph S.	Jul 18, 1972	Blaine, Tn		Sep 20, 1891	80	Moore, Stella	Vineyard, Gentry		Hall, Lida		Vineyard, Sally	Indian Ridge					
Voiles, James Monroe	Jan 6, 1980	Knoxville, Tn	Tn	Dec 23, 1914	65	Chumchwane, Mary Kate	Voiles, Roy		Bryant, Violet		Voiles, Mrs. Monroe	Jefferson Memorial	WW 2				
Voiles, James Theodford	Mar 14, 1983	J.M.H.	Tn	Feb 23, 1982	81	Ng	Voiles, Jake		Jefferson, Mattie		Voiles, Mrs. Mary E - Rebecca	Fairview - Greene Co, Tn					
Voiles, Lucy Pearl	Jan 18, 1970	Knox Co	Tn	Nov 23, 1906	63	Voiles, J.T.	Harmon, William		Melton, Vina		Voiles, J.T.	Fairview - Greene Co, Tn					
Voiles, Mary Kate	Dec 1, 1997	New Market, Tn		Oct 15, 1914	83		Churchman, Rufus Jackson		Johnson, Cornelia		Voiles, Jack [Son]	J.M.G.		Don	George		
Voiles, Robert L.	Dec 7, 1981	Knoxville, Tn	Tn	Jan 11, 1962	19	S	Voiles, R.C.		Walker, Irene		Voiles, R.C.	Jefferson Memorial					
Voiles, Toledo Willies	Dec 23, 1968	Jeff Co	Tn	May 4, 1909	59	Ng	Voiles, Sam		Spers, Mollie		Voiles, R.C. & Alonzo	Jefferson Memorial					
Wicks, John	May 6, 1928	Nc			79-9-	Ng	Wacks, William		Unk			West View					
Wacks, Minnie Cate	Jul 30, 1936	Tn		Jul 20, 1877	59	Ng	Mc Neln, John	Tn	Basketto, ---			West View					
Wagner, Fred P.	Mar 31, 1985	Knox Co	Tn	Sep 6, 1900	84	W	Wagner, L.L.		Hawkins, Susan Elizabeth	Tn	Griffin, Mrs. Sam E - Fred Jr.	Memorial Gardens	WW 1				
Wagner, L.L.	Jul 23, 1954	Jeff Co	Tn	Jun 30, 1968	86	W	Clagner, Jessie		Frencis, Martha		Clagner, J.R.	Piedmont					
Wagner, Rosie M.	Sep 22, 1985	Jeff City		Jul 30, 1906	88		Edmonds, Charles		Smith, Margaretta Elizabeth		Newman, Hazel & Alton [Daug]	Strawberry Plains		Luther Jr. & Alma-John & Jean-Jim & Carolyn			
Wagner, Ruby	Jan 17, 1982	Jeff Co	Tn	June --	86-7-14	S	Wagner, L.L.		Hawkins, Susan E.		Taylor, Mrs. E.H. - Ryner, Mrs. Sam	Piedmont					
Wagner, Stella	Dec 23, 1982	Jeff City		Jan 11, 1895	87	Ng	Curry, John		Gass, Zonia		Wagner, Fred-Fred Jr. - Griffin, Dorothy	Memorial Gardens	2701				
Wagner, Susan Elizabeth	Mar 7, 1983	Jeff City		Sep 30, 1875	87	W	Hawkins, L.H.		Keys, Emma		Ryner - Gertrude-Ruby- Cal-Fred	Piedmont					
Walker, Alice Rhoda	Jun 16, 1977	Va		Apr 15, 1887	90	W	Wyatt, William Frank		Meredith, Margaret		Walker, Leroy	Mt. Pleasant					
Walker, Andy [Cal]	Feb 8, 1957	Tn				Ng	Unk		Walker, Vinny	Tn	Walker, George Jr.	Jeff City					
Walker, Anthony Wade	Aug 8, 1962	Jeff Co	Tn	Aug 8, 1962	63	Ng	Walker, George Jr.		Clifton, Ruth		Walker, George Jr.	West View					
Walker, Callie Belle	Jan 1, 1944	Jeff City	Tn	Feb 2, 1960	69	W	Dixon, L.E.	Nc	Arnold, Valory	Nc	Walker, D.E.	West View					
Walker, Charles Alfred	Feb 17, 1992	J.M.H.	Jeff Co	Oct 2, 1902	89	W	Walker, David		Winstead, Sidney		Walker, Shirley [Daug]	Mt. View					
Walker, Charles R.	Jun 1, 1940	Jeff Co		Apr 18, 1904	36	Ng	Walker, W. Dave		Denton, Laura B.	Tn	County	Pleasant Hill					
Walker, Cora E.	Feb 7, 1951	Jeff Co	Tn	Nov 11, 1877	73	Ng	Dixon, Pleasant		Pennington, Margaret		Taylor, Mrs. Cecil	Perrin- Grainger Co					
Walker, David E.	Jun 30, 1949	Jeff Co	Tn	Jun 29, 1876	72	W	Walker, Porter J.		Noonkesser, Adeline		Perrin, Mrs. Donald [Lillian]	West View					
Walker, Donald Rudolph	Nov 2, 1966	Jeff Co	Tn	Apr 3, 1931	37	Ng	Walker, Charlie		Cox, Edith Inez		Walker, Mrs. Donald [Lillian]	Memorial Gardens	WW 2	Carroll & Linda- Jack & Suzanne			
Walker, Edward Ray	Jun 2, 1994	Knoxville, Tn	Tn	Jan 10, 1922	72	Welch, Zelma	Walker, Charlie		Bacon, Myrtle		Wire	J.M.G.					
Walker, Edward Roscoe	Nov 21, 1947	Jeff Co	Tn	Jan 3, 1885	62-10-18	Ng	Walker, Tom F.	Tn	Line, Nannie E.	Tn	Wyatt, Mrs. Alice	Mt. Pleasant					
Walker, Edward Sharp	Jul 17, 1981	Coopersville, Mich	Tn	Jan 6, 1941	40	Ng	Walker, Alfred		Dixon, Celie B.		Walker, Mrs. Ella Mae	Hillcrest					
Walker, Elmer Lee	Mar 31, 1991	Morristown, Tn	Jeff Co	Aug 30, 1915	75	Div	Walker, Dave E.		Morgan, Doris [Daug]	Tn	Morgan, Doris [Daug]	J.M.G.					
Walker, Frank William	Jun 8, 1977	J.M.H.	Tn	Aug 18, 1970	76-9-20	Ng	Gibbons, Ollie		Dixon, Cailoy		Walker, Mrs. Frank - Mrs. Callie						
Walker, Gregory Allen	Nov 24, 1995	Jeff City	Tn	Jul 7, 1965	30	Foust, Carolyn	Walker, Benjamine Fredrick		Gibbons, Emma Sue		Wife	Jefferson Chapel		Justin Tanner	Rebecca Scarlett		
Walker, Grover Keith	Oct 3, 1993	Knoxville, Tn	Jeff Co	May 29, 1941	54	Foust, Cornilyn	Walker, Charlie		Messangill, Kids		Wife	Community Chapel - Talbott, Tn		[Step] Brewer, J.R.-Danny	Boris, Donna [Ma]- Shelton, Dianna [Ma]	Davis, Henry - Walker, Fred-Stelly	
Walker, Ida Blanche	Feb 21, 1942	Jeff Co	Tn	Oct 3, 1922	19	Elder, Ruth	Jones, Edd	Tn	Young, Lucy		Wife	West View					
Walker, Infant Female	Jul 29, 1948	Hamblen Co	Tn	Jul 29, 1948	1 hour	Walker, Oliver	Walker, Oliver		Kyte, Freida	Tn	Walker, Allen [Jack]	West View					
Walker, J.C. [Frank]	Jul 26, 1973	Knoxville, Tn	Tn	May 25, 1898	75	Ng	Walker, Allen		Baldwin, Ann		Walker, Mrs. J.C.	Park Hill - Columbus, Ga					
Walker, James Charles	Dec 3, 1987	Talbott, Tn	Tn	Jan 30, 1902	85	Messangill, Mary Kate	Walker, Ed		Carter, Ora		Dobson, Juanita	Community Chapel - Talbott, Tn					West, Karen - Hatfield, Bonnie- Walker, Shirley- Dobson, Cloi [?]- Lord Walker, Iva

NAME	DDATE	DLOCAT	BLOCAT	BDATE	AGE	SPOUSE	FATHER	MOTHER	MFRLOCAT	BY	BURIAL	VET	SON	DAUG	BROTHER	SISTER
Walker, James H.	May 19, 1960	Jeff Co	Tn	Jun 25, 1879	80	W	Walker, William L.	Ballinger, Louisa		Taylor, Mrs. Cecil	Perrin Hollow - Grainger Co					
Walker, James Houston	Dec 7, 1943	Jeff Co	Jeff Co	Aug 12, 1866	77	Ng	Walker, Samuel	Maulay, Elizabeth Ann	Tn	Walker, Mrs. Sarah J.	New Market					
Walker, Jeb Stuart	Jun 4, 1950	Va		Apr 15, 1904	46		Greenlaw, Stella [B.Minn.]	Moore, Louella Progus		Hampton, Mrs. Ruby - Parrott, J.W.	Strawberry Plains	WW 2				
Walker, L.C.	May 16, 1992	Knoxville, Tn	Persia, Tn	Aug 29, 1923	68	Bishop, Minnie	Walker, R.M.	James, Rosa		Wife	Lebanon Church	unk				
Walker, Lee	Jan 8, 1989	New Albany, Ind.		Jun 29, 1939	49	Potts, Betty Lou	Walker, Elmer	Faulkner, Geneve E.		Walker, Betty Lou [Memphis, Tn] - V.A.	J.M.G.	unk				
Walker, Leroy	May 12, 1993	Jeff City	Jeff City	Aug 25, 1910	82	Ellison, Lottie	Walker, Edmond	Wyatt, Alice		Wife	Mt. Pleasant		James			
Walker, Luther Benjamin Sr. [Negro]	May 24, 1977	Jeff Co	Tn	Feb 7, 1907	70	Moore, Juna Marcella	Walker, John Mac Sr.	Whitls, Pearl		Walker, Mrs. Luther	Jefferson Memorial					
Walker, Margaret Lillian	May 21, 2000	Talbott, Tn	Tn	Jun 16, 1932	67	W				Walker, Donald Allen [Son]	J.M.G.					
Walker, Mark Anthony	Jul 13, 1990	U.T.H.	Knoxville, Tn	Jul 4, 1970	20	S	Walker, Tommy Louis	Matthews, Elaine		Walker, Tommy	Fain					
Walker, Marcella June [Black]	Jun 4, 1983	Jeff City		Feb 7, 1914	79		Moore, John	Vinson, Eva		Maxwell, Betty Ann [Daug]	J.M.G.		Luther B. Jr.	Lamieu, Joycelin - [Niece] Nelson, Mary K.: Webb, Marion		
Walker, Martha Jane	Dec 3, 1925		Tn		72-0-23	Walker, J.C.	Jallay, Charles	Rankin, Eliza	Tn	Walker, J.S.	Mt. Horeb			Long, Glenda - Lewis, Julie - Cameron, Alice		
Walker, Mary Kate	Nov 23, 1981	Cocke Co		Oct. 1919	62-1-4	W	Mullins, William Silas	Vinona, Ollie		Jefferson Memorial	Jefferson Memorial					
Walker, Mary Kate	Sep 9 1969	Morristown, Tn	Jeff Co	Sep 27, 1902	66	W	Massengill, George	Carter, Roe		Dobson, Juanita City - Lenoir City, Tn	Community Chapel - Talbott, Tn					
Walker, Mel V. Sr.	Sep 13, 1988	Jeff City	Tn	Jan 29, 1893	95	W	Walker, Tom	Lines, Nancy		Walker, M.V. Jr.	J.M.G.					
Walker, Mell Valentine Jr.	Dec 3, 1994	Loudon Co. Tn	Loudon Co. Tn	Feb 23, 1920	74	Hudson, Dorothy	Walker, Mell Sr.	Moore, Bernice		Wife	J.M.G.		Mell 3rd & Aran-Robert		Robert-James-Joe	Hawkins, Mary
Walker, Minnie	Jun 16, 1982	Morristown, Tn	Tn	May 2, 1900	82	Walker, William N. [?]	Hamilton, Joseph	Mc Crary, Mary		Creech, Mrs. Rose Mary	Mt. Pleasant					
Walker, Myrtle Jane	Jan 16, 1955	Jeff Co	Va	Jan 18, 1907	48	Walker, Charles A.	Fields, P.K.	Fields, Kate		Walker, C.A.	Mt. View					
Walker, Nadine K.	Jan 5, 1996	Strawberry Plains	Knoxville, Tn	Jun 2, 1923	72	Knight, Roscoe	Bolonger, Lucille			Husband	Fain - Jeff Co		Tommy & Elaine	Ray		
Walker, Nancy E.	Jan 6, 1927		Tn		63-6-11	Walker, Tom	Lynn, Alford	Cotter, Martha	Tn	Walker, E.R.	Mt. Pleasant					
Walker, Noel Lee	Oct 17, 1968	Jeffersonville, Indiana		Jul 17, 1966	s	Walker, Fred	Walker, Lee	Potts, Betty Lou		Walker, Lee						
Walker, Norma Jean	Nov 27, 1993	Louisville, Ky	Jeff City	Jan 23, 1960	33	Walker, Fred	Willings, Coy	Mc Haffie, Joyce Millis		Husband - Mc Haffie, Bob [Step-Father] - Kathryn [G-Parents]	Jernigan, Nina Rae [Daug]		Robby	Mc Haffie, Laura	Mc Haffie, Bobby - Willings, Ricky	Lamb, Robin
Walker, Ollie Mae	Feb 19, 1984	Jeff City	Talbott, Tn	Dec 11, 1912	81		Gibbons, John Ebb	Cameron, Mary Kate		Community Chapel - Talbott, Tn	Community Chapel - Talbott, Tn		Walker, Laura			
Walker, Pleasant Harvey	Sep 19, 1943	Knoxville	Knox Co	Apr 2, 1877	66	S	Walker, Charles Bliere	Best, Susan	Knox Co	Walker, J.C.- Balso, J.R.	Lynxhurst					
Walker, Porter William	Jul 9, 1960	Jeff City	Tn	Jan 31, 1884	76	Ng	Walker, Porter J.	Noorkessser, Adeline		Walker, Mrs. Georgia	West View					
Walker, Robert Lee	Feb 17, 1992	Talbott, Tn	Jeff Co	Jun 22, 1926	65	Div	Walker, Charles	Massengill, Kate		Walker, Eddie [Son]	Community Chapel	unk				
Walker, Ross Mae	Sep 17, 1994	Jeff City	Jeff Co	Dec 5, 1913	80	Walker, John A.	Lynn, Sidney	Stover, Nancy		Husband	West View					Hubbard, Maggie Lucille - Crye, Bershie Belle
Walker, Ruby Faye	May 31, 1999	Jeff City		Mar 13, 1937	2	S	Walker, Charlie Randolph	Cox, Edith	Tn	Walker, Charlie	West View			[In-Law] Walker, Raymond		Lamb, Maggie Lucille - Rhoads, Lucille - Lassiter, Ruth
Walker, Samuel	Dec 20, 1969	Jeff City	W. Va.		69-6-15			Elzers, Mrs. Gertrude		West View						
Walker, Sarah Victoria	Dec 18, 1924	Jeff City														
Walker, Selma	May 30, 1955	Jeff City	Tn	Sep 26, 1896	36	Walker, S.G.	Killian, Lawson	Rhinehart, Rhoda	Tn	Walker, S.G.	Mt. Pleasant					

NAME	DDATE	BLOCAT	BLOCAT	BDATE	AGE	SPOUSE	FATHER	FBLOCAT	MOTHER	MBLOCAT	BY	BURIAL	VET	SON	DAUG	BROTHER	SISTER
Walker, Thomas Franklin	Nov 22, 1942	Jeff Co	Tn	Sep 5, 1861	81	W	Walker, Thomas	Tn	Myers, ---	Tn	E.R.-W.N.-M.Y.-J.D. [Sore]	Mt. Pleasant					
Walker, Troy Butcher	Aug 25, 1983	Cherokee Lake	Tn	Oct 6, 1934	48	Div	Robinson, Bred		Davis, Vernie		Robinson, Becky	West View					
Walker, Viola [Col]	Feb 9, 1957	Knoxville	Tn			W					Walker, Ray						
Walker, Wiley David	Dec 11, 1944	Jeff Co.	Tn	Jul 13, 1872	72	W	Walker, Thomas	Tn	Lettson, Deliverance	Tn	Gunn, John & Mitchell	Sandy Ridge					
Walker, William	Oct 19, 1949	Hawkins Co., Tn.	Tn		74	W	Walker, William		Lettson, Deliverance		Miller, Mrs. France	Hills Chapel					
Walker, William Carl	Apr 9, 2000	Jeff City	Tn	Jul 15, 1924	75	Stephens, Dorothy S.	Walker, Charlie		Massengill, Mary		Wife	J.M.G.					
Walker, William Newton	Jun 28, 1998	Hamblen Co.	Tn	Nov 12, 1887	70	Walker, Minnie	Walker, Tom F.		Line, Nancy Ellen		Cresswell, Gene	Mt. Pleasant					
Wall, Jackson A.	Dec 21, 1957	Oak Ridge, Tn	Va	Oct 16, 1900		Ng	Wall, James		Murdock, Elizabeth		Breeden, Mrs. E. Cole [Sole]	Mt. Pleasant					
Wallen, Cecil B.	Mar 18, 1997	Dandridge, Tn	Taxwell, Tn	Dec 8, 1929	67		Wallen, Harvey		Spidinge, Bertha		Wallen, Stanley [Son]	J.M.G.		Michael Wayne			
Wallen, Ruby	May 7, 1979	Knoxville, Tn	Tn	Mar 21, 1931	47	Ng	Coffey, J.C.		Bunch, Nellia		Wallen, Cecil & Children	Garden Of Gethsemane - Jeff Co					
Walls, Carver	Apr 21, 1988	Morristown, Tn	Va	Jan 13, 1909	79	S	Walls, W.A.		Stevens, Delilah		Barr, Beatrice - Johnson F.H. [Dawsonville], Va.	Jefferson Memorial					
Walsh, Catherine Barbara	Aug 22, 1974	Jeff City	Tn	Sep 22, 1985	89	W	Garland, Jacob		Snyder, Eliza		Baer, Mrs. William W. - Franklin, Mrs. Edna Lilton	Jefferson Memorial					
Walston, Candy Michelle	Jun 13, 1989	J.M.H.	Tn	Jun 2, 1976	11	S	Walston, Donnie Sr.		Williams, Betty		Walston, Donnie Sr.	Sunderland					
Walston, Carolyn Jane	Apr 22, 1980	U.T. Hospital	Tn	Aug 21, 1952	7		Walston, Carroll Charles		Brown, L. Grace		Walston, Grace	Mt. View					
Walston, Carroll C.	Mar 13, 1982	Talbott, Tn	Tn	Jun 16, 1921	70	Brown, Grace	Walston, Noe		Harbin, Myrtle		Wife	Sunderland					
Walston, Ella J.	Oct 9, 1965	Jeff Co	Tn		63	Walston, Noah	Harbin, Jacob		Noe, Elizabeth		Woodburn - Knox Co	Sunderland					
Walston, Myrtle	Jun 17, 1954	Jeff Co	Tn	Jun 6, 1891	63	Ng	Harbin, Jacob		Noe, Elizabeth		Harbin, Joe - Morgan, Earl - Wells, Mrs. Coleman	Sunderland					
Walston, Noah	Aug 31, 1965	Jeff Co	Tn		79	Ng					Walston, Carroll & Raymond	Sunderland					
Walston, Noah Raymond	Dec 27, 1986	Knox Co	Tn	Dec 17, 1885	79	S			Hoskins, Myrtle		Walston, Carroll - Wisecarver, J.S.	Sunderland					
Walters, Hugh Lee Jr.	Oct 1, 1971	Morristown, Tn	Tn	Oct 1, 1971			Walston, Noah		Hull, Joyce Guy		Walters, Hugh Lee	West View					
Walters, Mary Margaret	Sep 4, 2000	Jeff City	Tn	Oct 29, 1921	78	Walters, Ed					Husband	West View					
Ward, Anna Ruth	May 17, 1983	Hamblen Co	Tn	Feb 8, 1928	65	W	Bacon, Walter S.		Bacon, Olive		Strader, Faye [Sister]	J.M.G.				Walter T.	Hodge, Doris - Berens, Gail
Ward, Dorcas	Jun 15, 1989	Jeff Co	Tn	Dec 18, 1871	98	W	Phillips, James		Taylor, Eva		Ward, Ray William - Franck, Mrs. Jessie	J.M.G.					
Ward, Lucy Eleanore	Dec 22, 1986	J.M.H.	Tn	Feb 15, 1921	65	Ward, Roy B.	Ellison, Charles L.		Purkey, Fannie Lou		Ward, Roy B. & Dorothy	West View					
Ward, Roy B.	Oct 14, 1983	Jeff City	Dandridge, Tn	Jan 21, 1908	85	S	Phillips, Charles L.		Phillips, Dorcas		Green, Dorothy [Niece]	West View	42-45				[In-Law] Ellison, Katherine
Ward, William R.	Jan 10, 1972	Jeff Co	Tn	Nov 7, 1914	57	S	Ward, Richard		Phillips, Dorcas		Ward, Roy-James - Franca, Mrs.	West View	WW 2				
Wardrop, Ada	Feb 12 1988	Knoxville, Tn	Walnut, Nc	Dec 21, 1892	95	Wardrop, J.E. Sr. [D]	Ramsey, Jasper		Allen, Lucy		Wardrop, J.E. Jr.	West View					
Wardrop, Jeter Edward Jr.	Jun 6, 1985	Nc		Jan 31, 1916	79	S	Wardrop, Jeter E. Sr.		Ramsey, Ada Kate		Wardrop, Jeter Edward 3rd [Son]	West View		Wardrop, James C. - Hamrick, Billy- James Jr.	Eade, Carolyn		Swafford, Doris - Collier, Elizabeth
Wardrop, Louise Eleanor	Feb 4, 1982	De Kalb Co., Ga	Tn	Sep 4, 1917	73	Wardrop, Jeter Jr.	Hotchkiss, ---		Russell, Lois		Wardrop, Royce [Son]	West View					
Wardrop, Ruth Hamrick	Feb 5, 1995	Knoxville, Tn	Tn	Jul 25, 1892	77	Ng	Lane, Abe Sr.		Rector, Lucinda		Wardrop, J.E. Jr.	West View					
Wardrop, Jeter Edward Sr.	Sep 1, 1999	Knox Co	Tn	Oct 13, 1886	98	W	Wardrop, E.C.		Rector, Lucinda		Wardrop, J.E. Jr.	West View					
Wardrop, Luther Adolphus	May 6, 1973	Alabama, Ga	Tn		57	W	Wardrop, Cornelius		Sims, Ora		Wardrop, Royce [Ga]	Jefferson					
Ware, James	Sep 26, 1975	U.T.H.	Tn	Jan 17, 1918	57	W	Ware, Joe				Massengill, Mrs. Addie Mae	West Memorial					
Warner, Shirley Clay	Apr 24, 1976	Jeff Co	Clothier, W. Va.	Apr 27, 1924	52	Robinson, Ethel	Warner, Henry		Workman, Addie		Workman - Clothier, W. Va						Davis, Agnes - Bernard, Eula Mae-Walton, Treva

NAME	DDATE	BLDCAT	BLOCAT	BDATE	AGE	SPOUSE	FATHER	FBLDCAT	MOTHER	MFBLDCAT	BY	BURIAL	VET	SON	DAUG	BROTHER	SISTER
Warren, Uretis Grant	Apr 10, 1955	Jeff City	Ne.	May 18, 1873	81	Ng	Warren, Joshua	Miss.	Bailey, Nancy	Warren, Mrs. U.	Underwood - Sevier Co Martin						
Warren, Annie L.	Nov 20, 1955	Knoxville	Miss.	Feb 14, 1885	70	W	Stillman, J.C.	Miss.	Surratt, Sarah	Warren, Mrs. U.							
Warren, Dolies	Aug 23, 1993	Knoxville, Tn	Jeff Co	Mar 25, 1914	79	W	Love, H. Marshall		Collier, Callie		Williams, Sheila [Daug]	J.M.G.			Ewing, Sandra Gail - [In-Law] Warren, Gary Clark		Bettis, Nina - Garrett, Bloodie - [In-Law] Love, Clarice
Warren, James Thomas	Jan 16, 1948	Knox Co Miss.	Alcorn Co, Miss.	Dec 5, 1884	63-1-12	Ng	Warren, John T.	Miss.	Stillman, Annie R.	Warren, Gladys	J.M.G.						
Warren, Loyd A.	Nov 17, 1931	Hodges Switch	Tn	Aug 13, 1912	19	Ng	Warren, John	Tn	Smith, Ethel	Warren, John	Narrod's Grove						
Warren, Martha	Apr 30, 1961	Hamblen Hall	Tn	Nov 14, 1865	95	Warren, [D]	Vincent, A.F.		Shackleford, Martha	Dyer, Jack - Mason, Sidney - Helm, Fred	West View					
Warren, Olin Grant	Jul 2, 1982	J.M.H.	Dundtown, Tn	Jan 25, 1911	81	Love, Dollies	Warren, Ulysses Grant		Peck, Sarah Jane	Ewing, Sandra Gail [Daug]	J.M.G.					
Warren, Robert Glenn	Oct 23, 1981	Knoxville, Tn	Tn	Jun 3, 1934	47	Clark, Gay	Warren, Olin G.		Love, Dollies	Warren, Mrs. Gay Clark	Jefferson Memorial					
Warren, Sara Jane	Oct 25, 1960	Jeff Foc	Ne		75-10-19	Warren, U.G.	Peck, John		Moreland, Sara	Russell, Adele - Olin	Underwood, Sevier Co					
Wrebum, James Harvey	Aug 20, 1949	Red Barn ?	Ne.	Jan 6, 1902	38	Ng	Swarlsen, William S.	Nc	Johnson, Mary M.	Nc	Young, Mrs. (Wife) Narod, G.H.	West View Colored					
Washington, George [Col]	Jul 5, 1929				64	Ng					Watkins, Louise - Humbard, Mrs. Ada	Wooders					
Watkins, Ada	Jan 28, 1955	Knox Co	Tn	Mar 19, 1912	43	Ng	Humbard, Sam R.		Elmore, Lillie		J.M.G.					
Watkins, Albert B.	Dec 12, 1991	S.M.M.C.	Jeff Co	Jan 31, 1917	74	Smith, Daisy	Watkins, Albert		May, Dora	Watkins, Lynn C. [Son]	J.M.G.	unk				
Watkins, Albert Milton	Mar 15, 1977	Jeff Co	Tn	Oct 11, 1889	87	Nce, Maude	Watkins, Isaac		Carter, Nancy E.	Watkins, Mrs. A.M. Thorpe, Margaret - Justin	Mt. Pleasant					
Watkins, Andrew J.	Aug 11, 1960	Jeff Co	Tn	Jun 29, 1867	93	W	Watkins, Rufus		Bruner, Margaret	Watkins, A.B. -	West View					
Watkins, Annabel	Jul 4, 1959	Jeff City	Tn	Dec 21, 1871	87-6-13	S	Watkins, James W.		Galbraith, Leanah	Watkins, Carrie	West View					
Watkins, Bob [Col]	Jan 4-5, 1930		Tn	Sep 21, 1876	94	S	Watkins, Temple		Galbraith, Leonna	Watkins, W.W.	West View					
Watkins, Carrie G.	Apr 11, 1971	Davidson Co		Dec 21, 1871													Huggins, Edith - Casper, Irene - Shirley, Kathleen [14]
Watkins, Cora	Jan 28, 1959	Jeff City	Hamblen Co	Feb 9, 1911	87		Rines, Oliver		Turner, Elizabeth	Harrell, Helen W.	West View			Fincham, Elizabeth		Ragat, May Smith
Watkins, Daisy	Mar 29, 1996	Knoxville, Tn	Talbott, Tn	Nov 2, 193	64	S	Smith, John William	Tn	Roberts, Eliza	May, Dirs Quarles [Niece]	J.M.G.		[Step] Watkins, Lynn			
Watkins, Dora Gail	Feb 8, 1965	Baptist H., Nashville, Tn	La		19	S	Me, Burney, Elbsi	Tn	Me. Burney, Elbsi	Watkins, Henry	Mt. Pleasant					
Watkins, Essie	Dec 15, 1983		Ky	Sep 17, 1895	88	Ng	Watkins, Will [D]		Ray, Mary	Watkins, W.W. [Nashville]	West View					
Watkins, Evelyn	Aug 10, 1942	Talbott	Tn	Nov 30, 1919	22	Watkins, A.B.	Pritchett, Rev. Rexell B.		Pout, Ella	Watkins, A.B. - Pritchett, R.B.	Brethren					
Watkins, Helen	Jul 10, 1948	Hamblen Co	Chester Co, Tn	Jun 224, 1898	50-0-16	Ng	Robinson, H.P.	Tn	Patterson, Lula	Robinson, J. Ed	Sunderland					
Watkins, Henry Eugene Sr.	Nov 21, 1975	Lake Charles, La	Jeff Co	Feb 22, 1919	56	Me. Burney, Elsiee	Watkins, Albert M.		May, Dora	Brown, W.S. [La.]	Mt. Pleasant	WW 2				
Watkins, Infant Male	Nov 18, 1961	Hamblen Co	Tn	Nov 18, 1961	.72-	S			Purtey, Arlene	Watkins, Wayne	Sunderland					
Watkins, Isaac Rence	Jan 1, 1961	Jeff Co	Tn	Mar 17, 1888	55-11-14	S		Tn	Carter, Nancy E.	Watkins, A.B. & W.R.	Mt. Pleasant					
Watkins, Jerry Clay	Jul 10, 1948	Hamblen Co	Jeff Co	Jul 26, 1891		Ng	Watkins, Isaac	Tn	Carter, Nancy E.	Watkins, A.B.	Sunderland					
Watkins, Lois June	July 10, 1948	Hamblen Co	Ball Co, Ky	Oct 5, 1926	21	Ng	Underwood, Eugene	Ky	Morgan, Myrtis	Morgan, Earl	Sunderland					
Watkins, Martha	Oct 1, 2000	Knoxville, Tn	Tn	Aug 2, 1947	53	Watkins, Lynn	Deele, Ira M.		Shirley, Ada Belle	Husband	Hebron					
Watkins, Martha Evelyn	Jul 22, 1976	Hamblen Co	Tn	Jun 18, 1929	47	Ng	Churchman, Clyde L.		Silvers, Edna	Watkins, Jasper R.	Hamblen Memorial					
Watkins, Maude Rice	Jul 12, 1995	Talbott, Tn	Tn	Feb 13, 1907	81	W	Nce, J. Alexander		Mc Cray, Mary	Northern, Mary	Mt. Pleasant					
Watkins, Raomae	Mar 26, 1993	Morristown, Tn	Corbin, Ky	Oct 13, 1921	71	Watkins, James F.	Robinson, Lonzo		Thomas, Rosie	Husband	Mt. Pleasant	army	Ronald R. & Sharon [Sd] - Homer, John	Watkins, Lonna - [Cti] Homer, Abigail	
Watkins, Robert Estes	Jul 11, 1948	Hamblen Co	Jeff Co	May 14, 1922	25	Ng	Watkins, Henry Clay	Tn	Robinson, Helen	Tn	Husband	Sunderland				
Watkins, Robert S.	Apr 7, 1985	Knoxville, Tn	Tn	Jan 15, 1906	77	Rines, Cora	Watkins, A.J.		Holis, Anna G.	Watkins, Mrs. Cora R.	West View					
Watkins, Robert Turley [Col]	Feb 20, 1990	Jeff City	Tn			S	Watkins, James M.		Harris, Mayme		Bassett, Lola	West View Colored	WW 1				

NAME	DATE	DLOCAT	BLOCAT	BDATE	AGE	SPOUSE	FATHER	FRLOCAT	MOTHER	MFRLOCAT	BY	BURIAL	VET	SON	DAUG	BROTHER	SISTER
Watkins, W. Britt	Apr 28, 1968	Tn	Tn	Jun 27, 1884	83	Bible, Wilma	Watkins, I.O.		Carter, Nancy E.		Watkins, W.B.Jr.	Mt. Pleasant					
Watkins, Wilma Nellie	Apr 17, 1982	Talbott, Tn	Tn	Jun 30, 1899	82	W	Bible, Abidge Wesley		Cox, Mrs. J.A.		Mt. Pleasant	Mt. Pleasant					
Watson, Alice Ann	Dec 22, 1947	New Market	Jeff Co			Watson, James F. [D]			Brasher, Nancy [?]		Atchley, Mrs. Pies	Nance's Grove					
Watson, Bryan Todd	Feb 19, 1968	Hamblen Co	Tn	Feb 19, 1968					Smith, Joyce Faye		Watson, Lawrence Edward	Memorial Gardens					
Watson, Fred	Oct 24, 1999	Strawberry Plains	Grainger Co	Aug 28, 1921	72	Shackelford, Ann	Watson, Walter		Hoffner, Ellis		Wills	Piney					
Watson, James Franklin	Oct 29, 1945	Jeff Co	Tn	Jun 4, 1868	77	Ng	Watson, Elishul	Tn	Pate, Julia	Tn	Atchley, Mrs. Pies J. - Watson, Guy & Mrs. J.F.	Nance's Grove					
Watson, Joe	Jan 5, 1940	Grainger Co		May 10, 1877	62	Ng	Watson, James		Smith, Sarah	Tn	Watson, Mrs. & Children	Central Point					
Watson, Kathy Diane	Mar 28, 1995	Jeff City	Jeff Co	Jan 16, 1959	36	Winstead, Bruce			Woods, Jane		Watson, Jerry [Husband]-Woods, Jim [Step-Father]- Owens, Beulah [Niece]-	Blue Springs Church - Rutledge, Tn		Lucas	Watson, Jane-Julie	Bobby-Eddie	Harrell, Patsy
Watson, Mae Owens	Jun 7, 1981	Jeff Co	Va	Nov 17, 1907	83	W					Johnson F.H. (Damascus, Va)	Sunrise					
Watson, Mrs. Samuel	Jan 3, 1931	Rutledge									Watson, Samuel	Sunrise					
Watson, Owner	Aug 10, 1907	Rutledge									Watson, Earnest	Sunrise					
Watson, Susie Jane	Jul 19, 1982	Knoxville, Tn		Aug 12, 1895	86	W	Weaver, John		Weaver, Mary R.		Ford, Charlie	Jefferson Memorial					
Watson, Wavie	Jul 26, 1959	Vanderbilt	Tn	May 6, 1898	61	Ng			Clark, Ellie		Combs, Mrs Emett [Betty]- Watson, Pryor	Shiloh					
Watson, West Edward	Oct 10, 1956	Jeff Co	Sevier Co	Apr 30, 1884	72	Ng	Watson, John D.		Evans, Annie		Watson, Mrs. Lillie Owerby	Shiloh - Sevier Co					
Watts, Forrest	Jan 31, 1976	Tn	Tn	Sep 4, 1912	63	W	Watts, Sam		Lane, Mary B.		Collins, Mrs. Shirley- Watts, Louise - Reed, Ethel Sue - Ray, Cecil	West View					
Watts, Ida Bell	Mar 28, 1955	Hamblen Co	Tn	Jan 24, 1981	74	W	Lane, Christopher		Cooper, Rebecca		Watts, Forrest	West View					
Watts, Infant Male	Jul 5, 1982	Jeff Co	Tn	Jul 5, 1982			Watts, Forrest		Watts, Ruby Mae		Rays Chapel - Cochie Co	Rays Chapel - Cochie Co					
Watts, Ruby Mae	Jul 10, 1975	U.T.H.		Feb 28, 1913	62	Watts, Forrest	Burchfield, John		Mc Gill, Josie		Watts, Forrest	West View					
Watts, Sam	Apr 4, 1940	Grainger Co	Tn	Aug 7, 1877	63-6-	Ng	Watts, Jake	Tn	Hance, Zylphia	Tn	Hubert & Forrest [Sons]	Pheat's					
Waugh, John E.	Mar 11, 1948	Nc	Nc	May 18, 1867	81-9-23	Ng	Waugh, Curtis	Nc	Shipping, Ann	Nc	Waugh, Mattie - Liner, T.	Hebron					
Waugh, Laura Ann	Dec 8, 1947	Jeff Co	Jeff Co	Jan 7, 1870	77-11-7	S	Waugh, Curtis		Shaping, Ann		Waugh, Mattie - Liner, Fred	Hebron					
Waugh, Mary	Jan 28, 1931	Tn	Tn	Aug 29, 1865	65	Waugh, J.E.	Bledison, B.M.	Tn	Hall, Tithia	Tn	Waugh, J.E.	Wesleys Chapel Friends Station					
Weaver, Mattie Keller	Feb 24, 1979	Jeff City	Va	Jun 27, 1889	89	W	Doane, William Penn		Keller, Amelda Jane		Mc Cowan, Dr. R.M.	Lebanon					
Weaver, Roy	Jan 3, 1926	Grainger Co	Tn	Aug 7, 1877	63-6-	S	Weaver, A.E.	Tn	Draper, Minnie	Tn	Carmichael, Walter	Fort Swoyrajdur ?					
Webb, Charles Franklin [Col]	Nov 17, 1956	Tn	Nc	Apr 15, 1900	56	W		Nc		Nc	Webb, Franklin [Chicago, Ill] & Lester	West View Colored					
Webb, Infant	Sept 24, 1934	Jeff Co	Tn	Sep 26, 1883	61	Ng	Webb, Charles				Webb, Mrs. Naomi	Jeff Co					
Webb, John Abraham	May 3, 1945	Jeff Co	Tn	Apr 25, 1944	89	W	Webb, Andrew	Tn	Walker, Nancy Jane	Tn	Webb, Mrs. John Abard, May Ann	Dandridge					
Webb, Lydia	Sep 5, 1933	Jeff City	Tn	Nov 26, 1907	27	W	Snodgrass, James		Watkins, Carrie	Tn	Mc Cowan, Dr. R.M.	Lebanon					
Webb, Naomi [Col]	Jul 2, 1935	Jeff City	Tn			Webb, Charles		Park, Pies		Brown, Sharon		J.M.G.					
Webb, Ronald Kenneth Jr.	Dec 12, 1996	U.T.H.	Illinois	Feb 20, 1970	16	S	Webb, Ronald K. Sr.		Brown, Sharon		Webb, Ronald K. Sr.	J.M.G.					
Webb, Floyd Jr.	Apr 17, 1981	Colorado	Tn	Dec 16, 1903	77	Ng	Weed, Floyd Sr.		Jensen, Blanche		Weed, Mrs. Dorothy R.	West View					
Weems, Maude Miller	May 9, 1973	Hamblen Co	Tn	Jul 19, 1886	86	W	White, A.W.		Collier, Florence		Davis, Stella - Weems, J.O.	Mt. Horeb					
Weisman, Warren L.	Oct 7, 1991	Lansdale, Pa	Tn	Aug 2, 1914	77	Easley, Martha Bat	Weisman, Warren Scranz		Leidy, Alveda		Wills	West View					
Welch, Andrew	Aug 31, 1965	Talbott, Tn	Tn	Jan 20, 1896	69	Ng	Welch, Jack		Smith, Alice		Welch, Lee						
Welch, Eugene Edward	Apr 11, 1983	Jeff City	New York	Jan 26, 1896	85	W	Welch, William		Seymour, Emma		Miller, Mrs. Joseph	Community Chapel St. Bernard - Lyon Mt. Ny					

NAME	DDATE	BLOCAT	BLOCAT	DDATE	AGE	SPOUSE	FATHER	FELOCAT	MOTHER	MER LOCAT	BY	BURIAL	VET	SON	DAUG	BROTHER	SISTER
Welch, Eva S.	Feb 13, 1980	Morristown, Tn	New York	Sep 3, 1897	82	Welch, Eugene	Jetts, Eugene		Miller, Joseph A.	Trundle, Argen	St. Bernard - Lyon Mt., Ny						
Welch, Fredie ?	Feb 15, 1970				71-8-29	Breeden, Nettie					Welch, Mrs. Nettie	Community Chapel					
Welch, Nola Francis	Dec 15, 1967	Jeff Co	Tn		71-8-5	W	Rickard, Sam		Welch, Martha		Welch, B.T.	Zion					
Welch, Robert James	Oct 14, 1945	Humana Hosp.	Ky	Aug 25, 1945	5m	W	Welch, Burl T.	Tn	Lewis, Lula Mae	Tn	Welch, B.T.	Community Chapel					
Wellbrock, Wilbert George	Oct 21, 1988	Talbott, Tn	Tn	Aug 12, 1916	72	W	Wellbrock, Joseph		Phagan, Katherine		Cox, Robert A. [R] - Jones F.H. [Ludlow, Ky]	Highland - R. Mitchell, Ky	WW 2				
Wells, Albert B.	Dec 5, 1987	Tn	Tn	Jun 11, 1881	86	Ng	Wells, Henry		Wells, Rushia - Clark, Mrs.		Wells, Rushia - Clark, Mrs.	Memorial Gardens					
Wells, Eugene	Feb 7, 1982	J.M.H.	Mc Donald, W. Va.	Jan 22, 1910	86	W	Wells, Samuel		Walker, Lora		Wells, Rebecca [Daug]	West View	unk				
Wells, Hattie Lee	Jun 11, 1944	Jeff Co	Tn	Dec 18, 1876	67	Wells, Dee	Bacon, Bud	Tn	Spoon, Anis	Tn	Wells, Dee	Pleasant View - Hamblen Co.					
Wells, Lois B.	Jun 9, 1984	Jeff City		May 13, 1923	71	W	Wells, Sam		Walker, Lora B.		Tatts, Geneva -Wells, Carl - Annobelle - Rebecca - Crossling, Alma [Nieces]	J.M.G.				Wells, Charles & Ethel	
Wells, Lora Bell	Mar 4, 1986	J.M.H.	Tn	Feb 17, 1886	100	W	Walker, Evans		Tatts, Alice		Wells, Lois	Jefferson Memorial					
Wells, Nora Virgie	Aug 13, 1985	Knoxville, Tn	Tn	Apr 7, 1909	76	W	Mills, Alice		Burnett, Annie		Crossling, Alma	Jefferson Memorial					
Wells, Ollie Jones	Jul 10, 1981	Strawberry Plains	Tn	Oct 15, 1883	77	Ng					Wells, Dee	Pleasant View					
Wells, Paul E.	Jul 21, 1982	Shelby Co., Indiana			59	W	Wells, Roscoe J.		Yeley, Clarence		Wells	Miller - Shelby Co. In					
Wells, Rushie C.	Apr 14, 1991	U.T.H.	Hamblen Co.	Jul 3, 1918	72	W	Wells, A.B.		Clark, Irene		Workman, Larry [Son] - Katherine - Rushie	J.M.G.					
Wells, Sarah Tennie	Jan 4, 1972	Knox Co	Tn	Dec 7, 1887	84	W	Clark, John		Cochran, Nancy		Cochran, Nancy	Jefferson Memorial					
Wells, Zebedee Will	Apr 2, 1982	Jeff Co	Tn	Jun 10, 1874	87	W	Wells, Henry A.		Phagan, Catherine E.		Coffey, Grace- Wells, Oscar-Buddy - Carver, Lewis [Margnason, Ne]- Butler, J.C.- Fincham, Raymond	Pleasant View					
Wells, Beulah	Mar 7, 1980	Tn	Tn	Sep 28, 1904	76?	W	Kelley, Walter		Martin, Mary Emma		Cornwell, Mrs. J.C.	Jefferson Memorial					
Wells, Edgar Allen	Jan 30, 1999	Mt. Home, Tn	Rutledge, Tn	Jan 20, 1924	75	West, Wallace Munsey, Alice Louise	Williams, Gertrude		Williams, Gertrude		Wife	Jefferson Memorial					
West, H.H.	Aug 4, 1943	Jeff Co		Jul 4, 1871	71	Ng					West, Mrs. H.H. & Adron [Sis]	West View					
West, James Walter	Feb 10, 1943	Grainger Co	Grainger Co	May 3	71	W	West, Marshall	Tn	West, Mary	Tn	West, W.H. [Brother]	West View					
West, Mary R.	Jan 23, 1992	Jeff City	Tn	Nov 29, 1912	61	West, J.O.	Grothen, Samuel		Stansbury, Reena	Tn	West, J.O.	Shilo - Grainger Co					
West, Mary Ruth	May 6, 1979	Knoxville, Tn	Tn	Nov 29, 1912	66	W	Cochram, Millard P.		Travis, Willie		West, William & C.R.	Hills Union					
West, Mary Shaver	Mar 29, 1956	Eastern State Hospital	Tn	Nov 23, 1872	83	W	Shaver, T.A.		Morgan, Mary Jane		Blanc, Mrs. Adrian	West View					
West, Nell Irene	Nov 16, 1990	Nashville, Tn	Grainger Co	Jan 10, 1920	70	W	Moody, Deistrick		Gilmore, Georgia		Miller, Frank L. Jr. [Son]	Buffalo Grove					
West, Orville Dean	Jun 14, 1995	Bean Station, Tn	Grainger Co	Feb 11, 1938	57	Burnett, Susie	West, Roscoe		West, Ethel		Wife	Rocky Summitt - Bean Station, Tn		Thomas Dean & Mindy	Trenholm, Kimberly & Daniel	Gale-Dennis	
West, Theodore Wallace	Aug 2, 1973	Jeff Co	Tn	Mar 22, 1901	72	Kelley, Beulah	West, Jacob		Greenlee, Mary		West, Mrs. Beulah- Ollie-Bernice	West View					Owens, Bernice - Carpenter, Bernice - Jo - West, Frances Jo - Reed, Onelia
Whaley, Aaron Crawson	Oct 13, 1984	J.M.H.	Tn	Nov 1, 1885	98	Mc Cartter, Inez	Rayfield, Katherine		Rayfield, Katherine		West, Mrs. Beulah- Ollie-Bernice- Whaley, Hugh	Jefferson Memorial					
Whaley, Angel Fay	Dec 16, 1984	New Market, Tn	Walker Mistake, Mich.	May 12, 1957	27	Whaley, Jeff	Cody, Tommy Sr.		Mc Kinney, Gladys		Huff, Tina Cody [Sister] - Mc Kinney, Myrtle [G- Mother]	Cottage Hill				Whaley, Lacey-Cassey [Nieces] Huff, Tomlika- Ashley-Dezerea	Tommy Jr.-Carroll- T.J.
Whaley, Gladys Nellie	Aug 26, 1992	Hamblen Co	Tn	Mar 10, 1950	42	Div	Gardner, Myrtie		Gardner, Myrtie		Cody, Tina [Daug]	Cottage Hill - New Market, Tn					
Whaley, Myrtie	Jan 13, 1961	Jeff Co	Tn		80-2-7	W	Mc Kinney, Charlie		Walker, Mary E.		Cody, Tina [Daug]	Mill Springs					[Aunts] Linser, Ann - Lewhrte, Ruby
Whaley, S.L.	Nov 2, 1946	Jeff Co	Tn	Jan 6, 1872	74	Ng	Simms, William	Tn	Lockhart, Mrs. William		Lockhart, Mrs. J.A.	Mill Springs					

NAME	DDATE	BLOCAT	BRLOCAT	BDATE	AGE	SPOUSE	FATHER	FELOCAT	MOTHER	MFELOCAT	BY	BURIAL	VET	SON	DAUG	BROTHER	SISTER
Wheeler, Geneva A.	Jul 29, 1999	Jeff City	Jeff Co	Oct 30, 1915	83	William, William	Wilson, Marie		Wheeler, Wayne [Son]		Gates, Eulaene - Stamdem, Carolyn - Mills, Juanita	Cate - Jeff Co			Roy		
Wheeler, Gerald	Sep 24, 1956	Blount ?	Tn	Apr 17, 1944	12		Wheeler, Cecil		Klepper, Paulina		Wheeler, Mrs. Cecil [Maryette]	White Pine					
Whitlock, Margaret Emily	Jan 2, 1956	Knox Co	Tn	Aug 18, 1918	37	Ng	Hinchey, Mattie		Whitlock, Hal & Mary Lou		Whitlock, Hal & Mary Lou	Piedmont					
Whitaker, Albert Jr.	Oct 14, 1986	J.M.H.	Tn	Sep 7, 1918	68	Acuff, Lorene	Phillips, Anna		Whitaker, Albert Sr.		Whitaker, Lorene Acuff Mrs.	Mill Springs	WW 2				
Whitaker, Christopher C.	Dec 13, 1954	Rock Valley, Tn		May 10, 1879	75	W	Whitaker, Elbert		Dilel, Sallie B.		Whitaker, Frank - Kerr, Mrs.	Piedmont					
Whitaker, Eleanor M.	Apr 11, 1993	Jeff City	Knox Co	Jun 21, 1920	72	Whitaker, James	Sherrod, Howard		Husband		J.M.G.	Piedmont		James S. & Nancy	Knight, Sylvia & William		English, Stella Maude - Culton, Marjorie - Shrader, Blanche
Whitaker, Fairy	Aug 2, 1945	Jeff Co	Jeff Co			Ng	Hodge, Sallie		Whitaker, J.J.		New Market						
Whitaker, Ruby Myrtle	Jun 11, 1947	Jeff Co	Jeff Co	Mar 27, 1902	45-2-14	S	Wooten, John	Tn	Whitaker, C.C.	Tn	Whitaker, Frank	Piedmont					
Whitaker, Susan K.	Aug 23, 1982	Jeff Co	Tn	Nov 30, 1892	89	Ng	Hawkins, Newton		Dye, Sallie B.		Whitaker, A.E.	Jefferson Memorial					
White, Agnes C.	May 3, 1999	Knoxville, Tn	Clincho, Va	Nov 23, 1917	81	White, Robert	Ramsey, Daniel Augustus		Reed, Susie		Temple Hill - Castlewood, Va			Culbertson, John & Teresa			Brooks, Esther - Riner, Edra - Edwards, Pansie - Ardinna, Josephine - Duncan, Margie - Cairns, Arhelus
									Ramsey, Hannah Victoria		Glass, Yotel [Dang] - Rhea, Lucille Austin - Luxenia [Sisters]						
White, Anagene Charlwood	Aug 23, 1990	Baldwyn, Miss.		Sep 17, 1921	68	W	Charlwood, Knowles S.		White, John R. [Son]		White, John R. [Son]	J.M.G.					
White, Charles	Sep 7, 1937	Strawberry Plains	Miss.			W			White, Mrs. Charles								
White, Charles R.	Jun 30, 1971	Strawberry Plains	Tn	Aug 28, 1945	25	Div	White, Ralph R.		Charlwood, Augenne		White, Ralph R. - Charlwood, Augenne						
White, Clenn E.	Nov 24, 1984	J.M.H.	Tn	Dec 23, 1923	60	Jernigan, Mary Lou	Knight, Josie		White, Roscoe		White, Roger D. [Bone - Tn] Janice - Mary L.						
White, Ellis	Jul 3, 1982	Jeff Co	Va	Oct 22, 1898	83	Ng	Brooks, William		Colley, Emma		White, Porter [Hus]	Mt. Horeb					
White, Frank Brownlow	Sep 28, 1967	Talbott, Tn	Tn	May 1, 1904	63	Ng	White, Res		Colley, Mary F.		Miller, Mary Jo	White, Pine					
White, Fred A.	Apr 21, 1990	Knoxville, Tn	Topeka, Kansas	Jul 6, 1919	70	W	Lamb, Barbara		White, John		White, Barbara L.	Mt. Horeb					
White, J.T.	Feb 14, 1931	Dandridge			41		White, Wmso		Feak, Ross		White, Mrs. J.T.	J.M.G.					
White, John Mack	Mar 16, 1977	Morristown, Tn	Tn	Mar 15, 1891	84	Frank, Ross	White, Marida		Colier, Florence		Ingram, Mrs. Ruby - White, Mrs. Ross B.	West View					
White, Louise S.	Feb 2, 1987	Strawberry Plains	Pa	Jan 20, 1898	88	W	Stewart, James		Keller, Ida		Callin, Mildred	Mt. Horeb					
White, Mary Florence	Jul 3, 1951	Jeff Co	Tn	Oct 6, 1862	88	W	Collier, James		Hamilton, Harriet		Masengill, Mr. Joe	J.M.G.					
White, Minnie	Apr 7, 1988	Hillhaven	Tn		99-5-9	W	Purkey, John F.		Shorter, Alice		Watkins Chapel - Hamblen Co						
White, Nancy Jane	Oct 2, 1996	Jefferson Co, Tn	Tn	Apr 5, 1924	72	White, Glenn	Cox, George		White, Boyd		Husband	J.M.G.	WW 2				
White, Porter Floyd	Sep 17, 1974	Jeff Co	Tn	Mar 15, 1899	75	W	Collier, Florence		Knight, Adlone		Husband	J.M.G.		James - Terry	Metcalf, Sue - Greene, Carolyn	Aefer	
White, Ralph Randolph	Mar 29, 1912	Knoxville, Tn	Miss.	Aug 25, 1912	68	Charlwood, Anagene	White, Res		Collier, Florence		Mt. Horeb						
White, Robert Jr.	Jul 16, 1985	Ireland		Jan 12, 1894	89	Stewart, Louise	Wright, Elizabeth		Rogers, Julia		White, Mrs. Ralph R.	Jefferson Memorial					
White, Ross Bell	Mar 19, 1980	Morristown, Tn	Kansas	Dec 10, 1895	83	W	Fault, Frank		Krouse, Emma		White, Mrs. Louise	Mt. Horeb					
White, Sallie Hudson	Mar 31, 1982	Jeff Co	Tn	Dec 1933	49-3-24	Ng	Hudson, Joe		Franklin, Margaret		White, Mrs. Fred	Mt. Horeb					
White, Samuel P.	Sep 7, 1952	Jeff Co	Tn	Jun 20, 1872	80	Ng	White, Abner		French, Mary		White, Frank	White Pine					
Whitehead, Henry Elmer	Dec 10, 1993	Hamblen Co	Tn	Mar 1, 1924	69	Graham, Grace	White, Abner		Franklin, Margaret		White, Mrs. Sina P.	Piedmont					
							Shutliz, Maggie				White	Pleasant Grove		Larry-Gary - [G] Jason-Patrick	[G] Whitehead, Kristi		Cooper, Cora - Travis, Winnie - Quinn, Cynthia - Cox, Naomi
Whitehead, James Robert	Apr 2, 1999	New Market, Tn	Widowen, Ky	Apr 20, 1944	54		Whitehead, Res C. Barnesh, Patrick Michael		Riner, Margaret E.		Shitehead, Helen M.						
Whitehead, Sally Ann	Feb 25, 1990	J.M.H.	Tn	Jul 21, 1913	76		Whitehead, Bruce E. Jr.		Weldon, Edna Mae		Husband						

NAME	DDATE	DLOCAT	BLOCAT	BDATE	AGE	SPOUSE	FATHER	FIELDLOCAT	MOTHER	MFELOCAT	BY	BURIAL	VET	SON	DAUG	BROTHER	SISTER
Whitlow, Mey Prieston	May 24, 1995	Jeff City	Nashville, Tn	Mar 27, 1922	73	Whitlow, Thomas Kemp Sr.	Prieston, Rufus A.		Lunn, Nannie Louise		Husband	Woodlawn - Nashville, Tn		Thomas K. Jr. - Jay Prieston	Daniel, Gloria		
Whitney, Charles Bruce	Apr 12, 2000	Jeff City	Sc	Jun 12, 1942	57	Tucker, Carole	Stokes, Mary O.				Wife	Cremated		Jay Prieston			
Whitney, Mary Olive	Aug 12, 1984	Beaufort, Sc	Sc	Sep 5, 1919	64	Whitney, Charles Sr.	Whitney, Charles B.		Walker, Dreka								
Whitt, Arthur Jr.	May 14, 1990	V.A. - Mt. Home, Rutledge, Tn	Sc	Oct 7, 1926	63	Swann, Juanita	Whitt, Arthur		Foster, Mollie Mae		Whitt, Grover & Glenda W.	Helton Springs Baptist - Rutledge, Tn	Korea			Swann, Julietta E. [D]	
Whitt, Velma Juanita	Jan 23, 1968	Jeff City	Jeff Co	Sep 15, 1910	87	Whitt, Arthur Jr. [D] - Nichols, Frank [D]	Swann, Walter B.		Denton, Georgia	Tn	Williams, Glenda [Niece]	New Market			Nichols, Infant [D]		
Whittaker, Arthur Ellis	May 3, 1969	Jeff City	Tn	Jun 20, 1892	76	W	Whittaker, George		Bishop, Elizabeth		Whittaker, James A. & Sisters	Memorial Gardens					
Whittaker, Bert M.	Nov 29, 1973	Jeff City	Tn	Nov 24, 1888	85	W	Whittaker, George		Wilson, Ruby		Whittaker, George Sr. & Sisters	Memorial Gardens					
Whittaker, Debra Gail	Jun 9, 1961	Jeff Co	Tn	Jan 27, 1955	6		Whittaker, Frank		Shanks, Betty		Wilson, Ruby	Friends Station					
Whittaker, Dennis Paul	Aug 2, 1985	J.M.H.	Tn	Sep 23, 1978	6		Whittaker, Dennis E.		Patton, Mary		Whittaker, Dennis E.	Cedar Grove - Jeff Co					
Whittaker, Ellis	Mar 18, 1962	J.M.H.	Tn	Mar 6, 1886	77	Whittaker, Bert	Rines, George		Dyel, Sallie		Whittaker, Bert	Buffalo Church					
Whittaker, Luther Frank	Mar 17, 1973	Jeff Co	Tn	June 22, 1913	59	Whittaker, Ruby	Whittaker, C.C.		Warren, Annie		Whittaker, Mrs. Ruby	Friends Station	WW 2				
Whittaker, Shirley	Jan 29, 1948	Grainger Co	Grainger Co	Feb 2, 1947			Whittaker, George				Whittaker, Bert	Shiloh					
Wickener, Arthur F.	May 12, 1984	Spring, Va.	Grainger Co	Nov 18, 1899	85	Cox, Lennie	Wickener, William		Brimmer, Cordelia		Wickener, Jack E.	West View	WW 1				
Wickener, Lennie [F]	Feb 20, 1984	J.M.H.	New York	Nov 9, 1899	84	Wickener, Arthur	Cox, Anderson		Oderholtez, Elizabeth		Wickener, Jack E.	West View					
Wigle, Wilhelmina Pauline Louise	Jan 12, 1988	Hillhaven	New York	Aug 18, 1894	93	W	Schuinesister, John		Moore, Bettie B.		Wigle, Vernon M. & Gerald E.	Highland Memorial - Knox Co					
Wilcox, Mae	May 31, 1946	Gatlinburg, Tn	Illinois	Apr 10, 1869	77	W	Burruss, William	Va	Donaldson, Nettie	Iowa	Moore, Belle B. [Gatlinburg]	West View					
Wilkerson, Andy Arce [Black]	Jan 10, 1980	Jeff City	Tn	Mar 12, 1909	70	W	Wilkerson, Luther		Reed, Cornelia		Donaldson, Nettie - Shirley Van	Jefferson Memorial					
Wilkerson, Booker Telford	Feb 3, 1970	Jeff Co	Tn	Jul 28, 1907	62	Hayworth, Flora	Wilkerson, Luther		Reed, Cornelia		Wilkerson, Flora	West View					
Wilkerson, Flora Hayworth	Apr 27, 1986	Anniston, Ala.	Tn	Mar 18, 1913	73	W	Hayworth, Samuel		Nance, Arlina		Jones, Arlina W. (Anniston, Ala.)	Garden Of Love - J.M.G.					
Wilkerson, Hattie Kelley	Sep 17, 1979	Knoxville, Tn	Tn	Jul 5, 1913	65	Ng	Thomas, George		White, Kelley		Wilkerson, Arce	Jefferson Memorial					
Wilkerson, Juanita	Sep 17, 1985	J.M.H.	Tn	Dec 25, 1899	85	W	Wilkerson, Luther		Reed, Cornelia		Wilkerson, Shelby	Jefferson Memorial	WW 2				
Wilkerson, Oscar M.	Nov 2, 1946	Jeff Co	Jeff Co	Oct 31, 1878	68	W	Wilkerson, R.L. Sr.		Newman, Mrs. Grace	Tn	Wilkerson, Mrs. Janina	West View					
Wilkerson, Robert Louis Jr. [Black]	Jul 25, 1984	Jeff Co	Jeff City	Jan 30, 1970	24		Williams, R.L. Sr.		Patricia		Father - Burden, S.H. [Daug]	[G-Parent]		Allen-Rex [G] / Aaron-Jimmy			Wilkerson, Patricia
Williams, Aaron Thomas	Jan 10, 1952	Hamblen Co	Tn	Jun 1, 1901			Grooms, E.H.				Grooms, Hazel	Pleasant View					
Williard, Bessie Viola	Sep 23, 1986	Brakeville	Tn	Dec 8, 1905	82	W	Wyatt, E.H.		Willard, Alice		Willard, Rex [Son]	Pleasant View					
Williard, Dola Faye	May 31, 1986	Knoxville, Tn	Jeff Co	Apr 18, 1927	69	Klevez, Janina Rella	Elmore, Linden		Cole, Demorius		Elmore, Sadie	Jefferson Memorial		Allen & Jean			
Williard, Edmund Earl	Jul 23, 1981	Jeff Co	Tn	May 31, 1926	55	W	Walker, Earl		Walker, Bessie		Walker, Earl	Jefferson Memorial		Lucian-Phillip		Lowery, Mildred - Hickman, Lucille	
Williard, Harold Conrad	Jun 20, 1984	Jeff City	Jeff City	Jul 2, 1928	66		Williard, Earl		Willard, Bessie		Jefferson Memorial	Jefferson Memorial					
Williard, Mamie	Dec 10, 1953	Knox Co		Jan 25, 1895	58	Williard, William	Wilson, Joe		Wagner, Belle		Wife	Hebron					
Williard, Rickey Lee [M]	Jul 15, 1958	Jeff Co	Tn	Jul 8, 1958		W	Williard, Bobbie Joe		Lowery, Virginia		Willard, Ray - Wheeler, Mrs. James R.	Willardtown					
Willard, Will W.	Jul 5, 1955	Knox Co	Tn	Apr 30, 1891	64	W	Williard, G.B.		Franklin, Louisa		Willard, Ray	Willard					
Williams, Alfred [Col]	Aug 5, 1949	Jeff Co	Tn		77-9/29	W	Moore, Thomas		Williams, J.J.		Williams, Arno	Colored					
Williams, Angeline [Col]	May 31, 1926	Tn	Tn	Jan 10, 1912	81	W	Winternute, Walter	Tn	Hipes, Margaret A. [Daug]	Tn	Husband	Hebron					
Williams, Annie A.	Oct 20, 1983	Memphis, Tn	Jan				Mitchell, Jennie		Mitchell, Jennie		Hipes, Margaret A. [Daug]			S. Donald [Val] - Walter E. [Pa]	John B.-Oval	John B.-Oval	Siebel, Ella - Kent, Mary
Williams, Barbara	Jun 15, 1996	Jeff City	Strawberry Plains	Jul 27, 1933	62	Williams, Larry	Beard, William Ahny		Cole, Flora Miranda		Husband	East View Memorial		Larry N. & Vickie-John T. & Leslie	Barry, Charlotte & John Collier, Katie & John	Bill	Brown, Violet & Norman - Bates, Grace & Joy
Williams, Barbara J.	Feb 12, 1996	Dandridge, Plains	Tn	Sep 29, 1947	48		Watson, Carroll		Brown, Grace		Mother	J.M.G.					
Williams, Casper [Col]	Jan 14, 1950	Jeff Co	Tn	Feb 5, 1882	68	Ng	Williams, Alex		Rommes, Sallie		Smith, Monnie	Colored			Donnie-Jeffrey		
Williams, Charles [Col]	Jun 24, 1961	Knox Co	Tn	Jun 6, 1908	53	Div	Williams, Alf		Smith, Jennie		Lauderbach, Dana	West View Colored					

NAME	DDATE	DLOCAT	BLOCAT	BDATE	AGE	SPOUSE	FATHER	FBLOCAT	MOTHER	MFBLOCAT	BY	BURIAL	VET	SON	DAUG	BROTHER	SISTER
Williams, Christopher Columbus Sr.	Jan 12, 1989	Jeff City		Jul 2, 1921	67	Hensley, Leona	Williams, Henry M.		Williams, Leona H.	Tn	Williams, Mrs. C.O.- Rex, Mrs. William A. [Kansas]	J.M.G.	WW 2				
Williams, Claude O.	Dec 28, 1944	Jeff Co.	Jasper, Mo	Dec 21, 1884	60	Ng	Williams, Charles T.	Wis.	Staton, Elizabeth A.	Illinois	Wife	Mt. Horeb					
Williams, Conford K.	Apr 23, 1928		Tn	Mar 4, 1869	37-10-26	Hayes, Sallie	Williams, Horace	Va	Tate, Mary	Tn	Williams, H.	Shilo					
Williams, Edd Spears	Feb 5, 1944	Sevier Co.		Mar 4, 1869	74	Hayes, Sallie	Williams, Houston	Tn	Hodge, Martha	Tn	Williams, Sallie	Dandridge					
Williams, Edward Wells	Apr 4, 1964	Jeff City	Mexico	Apr 30, 1905	88		Williams, Henry C.		Fletcher, Sara		Elnora, Carole M. [Doug] - [Bkgrnae, II.]	Cremated		[Nephew] Balzaczyk, Bob			
Williams, Fannie [Col]	Mar 21, 1968	Knox Co	Tn	Feb 20, 1896	72	Williams, Uriah	Murph, Tom		Godwin, Eliza		Williams, Uriah	Shiloh					
Williams, Horace Greely [Col]	Jul [8], 1989	Hamblen Co.	Tn	May 27, 1916	53	Ng	Williams, Horace G. Sr.		Ray, Nellie		Williams, Mrs. Ada C.	West View					
Williams, Hugh Doncey	Feb 15, 1993	Ringold, Ga.		Jul 27, 1915	77	Stockburger, Lois	Williams, Edwin R.		Smith, Zenobia A.		Wife	J.M.G.			Smith, Marilyn	J.C. Ray	
Williams, Hugh Hayes	Oct 7, 1939	Dandridge	Tn	Mar 10, 1909	30	Ng	Williams, Edd S.	Tn	Hayes, Sallie	Tn	Williams, Mrs. Adaline Brooks & Father	Dandridge					
Williams, Humbert Ellis John	Oct 15, 1995	Jeff City	Washington Co. Tn	Jul 4 1910	85	S	Williams, Joe Frank	Va	Crawford, Margaret	Tn	Williams, Dallas [Son] Kingdon, Mary	Cremated - Bethel Coll Church		Dallas-James- Williams, Margaret			
Williams, Infant	May 31, 1941	New Market	Jeff Co		1d		Williams, George		Knight, Mary	Jeff Co	Williams, George	Beth Car					
Williams, Infants	May 10, 1928		Tn		0		Williams, Lewis		Curl, Estell	Tn	Williams, Lewis	Shilo					
Williams, Jessie [Col]											Butler, D.L.						
Williams, Joseph	Jan 15, 1937			Mar 20, 1878	58	W	Williams, Andrew	Tn	Moore, Angeline	Tn	Williams, Henry & Richard	Jeff City					
Williams, Katherine	Feb 20, 1935	Hamblen Co		Jan 24, 1925	28d		Williams, A.T.	Tn	Law, Grace	Tn	Williams, A.T. [Talbott]	Pleasant View					
Williams, Lewis Jr.	Feb 18, 1980	Morristown, Tn	Granger Co	Jan 7, 1927	53	Roach, Irene			Williams, Mrs. Lewis		Williams, Mrs. Lewis	Hopewell					
Williams, Loura	Feb 8, 1946	Cocke Co	Tn	Mar 7, 1869	26d	S	Williams, Uriah	Va	Giles, Jane	Nc	Williams, Mrs. N.	Shilo					
Williams, Mabel	Nov 13, 1966	J.M.H.	Tn	Mar 21, 1913	75	W	Hurst, Rufe Sr.		Clevenger, Gypsy		Hurst, W Z. Sr.	Fairview - Greene Co. Tn					
Williams, Mae Ella [Black]	Oct 31, 1979	Jeff City	Tn	Feb 2, 1895	84	Williams, Casper	Bell, George		Smith, Maggie		Hall, Mrs. Margaret Jean	Jefferson Memorial					
Williams, Mary Catherine	Dec 22, 1945	Jeff Co.	Sevier Co				Sexton, Jacob	Union Co, Tn	Marshall, Jamica	Tn	Williams, Bert M.	Mt. Zion					
Williams, Melvin R.	Oct 2, 1971	Aiken, Sc				Faln, Isabel					Williams, Mrs. Melvin [Springfield, Va]	Hopewell					
Williams, N.	Aug 3, 1934	Nc			73						Williams, Mrs. N.	Shilo					
Williams, Nancy Free	Aug 25, 1971	Cincinnati, Ohio	Tn			Ng					Free, Nick - Bradford, Louise	Brethren					
Williams, Sarah	Sep 10, 1937	Granger Co	Tn	May 24, 1864	73	S			Giles, Jane	Nc	Williams, Lewis [Nephew]	Shilo					
Williams, Sarah Lewis	Nov 13, 1939		Tn	May 3, 1865	74	W	Williams, Joseph	Tn	Polk, Katherine	Tn	Williams, Lewis Children	Shilo					
Williams, Thurman [Col]	Jul 20, 1929		Tn		57-4-15	Ng			Romines, Sallie	Ky	Williams, C.W.	Colored					
Williams, Uriah H.	Mar 21, 1971	Knoxville, Tn	Tn	Jul 31, 1892	78	W	Williams, Nicholas		Lewis, Sarah		Williams, C.W.	Shiloh					
Williams, Walter P.	Apr 8, 1975	Knoxville, Tn	Va	Feb	331	Ng	Langston, Mary Lee		Fogarty, Ora		Hodges, Edward - Barrett - Wilson [Dang]	West View					
Williams, Willard	Feb 15, 1949	Jeff Co		Dec 12, 1917	36-9-10	Ng	Williams, George		Moore, Jane		Williams, Pauline	Nancy's Grove					
Williams, Nate [Col]	May 24, 1928		Tn	Sep 9, 1904	88	W	Williams, C.W.		Tate, John	Tn	Williams, C.W.	Colored					
Williamson, Albert G.	Mar 1, 1992	Rayton, Missouri				W	Tate, John	Tn			Hinton F.H. [Raytown, Mo] - Hinton, F.H.	West View					
Williford, Alex Hardine	Feb 3, 1960	Jeff Co		Feb 21, 1878	81	W	Williford, A.H.		Taylor, May		Williford, Muscott-Clark - Dawson, Leonard & Al??	Ebenezer					
Williford, Clark Dane	Apr 8, 1989	Hilltown	Jeff Co	May 15, 1913	75	Mc Carter, Margaret	Williford, A.H.		Reynolds, Hanna		Williford, Margaret	Ebenezer	WW 2				

Former Funeral Home Dandridge, Tennessee

NAME	DDATE	DLOCAT	BLOCAT	BDATE	AGE	SPOUSE	FATHER	F/LOCAT	MOTHER	M/FLOCAT	BY	BURIAL	VET	SON	DAUG	BROTHER	SISTER
Williford, Fate A.	Feb 11, 1967	Jeff City	Tn	Mar 11, 1905	61	Morrey, Zola Mae	Williford, Joseph		Lowery, Sally		Williford, Zol & Daughters - Denton, Jack - Walker, Donald	West View					
Williford, Hannah	Mar 28, 1957	Jeff Co	Tn	Nov 2, 1890	66	Williford, S.H.	Reynolds, William		Franklin, Julia		Williford, Donald Clark - Denton, Mrs. Leonard	Ebenezer					
Williford, Hillard	Mar 10, 1980	Jeff City	Tn	Oct 2, 1899	80	W	Williford, Joseph		Lowery, Susan		Walker, Mrs. Lillian	West View					
Williford, Joe	Mar 30, 1948	Coffee Co., Tn		66	W		Bradshaw, Rachael	Tn	Williford, Fate		West View						
Williford, Mary	Dec 26, 1955	Jeff Co	Tn	Nov 11, 1869	76	W	Mills, Robert		Link		Williford, Jake	Brethren					
Williford, Susan Lucille	Jul 7 1946	Jeff City		34	Williford, Fate [Age 36]	Putney, Robert J.	Jeff Co	Palmer, Emna Elizabeth	Jeff Co	Williford, Fate A.	West View						
Willocks, Teddy L.	Aug 17, 1986	Charlotte, Nc	Knox Co	Jul 7, 1912	64	W	Willocks, Willis		Emmert, Hannah		Charles, Rebecca & Andy [Daug]	Strawberry Plains		Benny & Irene			
Wills, Julia Emma	Sep 11, 1944	Jeff Co	Carter Co	Feb 1, 1855	89	W	Whalen, Michael	Ireland	Lacy, Elizabeth	Tn	Rhines, Mrs. W.H. - Anderson, Mrs.	West View				Bill-Fred-Gene-Max-Willard	Davis, Avis - Rogers, Aileen
Wills, Rev. L.M.	Feb 21, 1940	New Market	Tn	Mar 23, 1853	86	Ng					Hayes, J.H. [Admin]	New Market					
Willy, Carl Edward Sr.	Sep 27, 1985	J.M.H.		71	Gerlich, Augusta	Willy, Edward		Eigenhouse, Laura		Willy, Augusta	St. Marys - Bellona, Illinois					
Wilson, Annie Turh	Jan 10, 1941	Straw Plains	Illinois	Sep 9, 1914	1m-104	S			Bailey, Lucy			Piney					
Wilson, Cordelia	Jun 23, 1996	Houston, Tx		May 4, 1907	91	Wilson, Elbert		Whaley, Mary		Wilson, Basil David [Nephew]	Trantville				Woodrow	Payne, Eldora
Wilson, Estella	Feb 6, 1982	Knoxville, Tn	Tn	Jun 4, 1905	76	W	Gillespie, Thomas J.		Boyers, Sarah		Wilson, Charles [Son]	West View					
Wilson, Esta Elizabeth	Mar 9, 1982	J.M.H.	Tn			W	Appleby, Ben		Franklin, Hannah		Hart, Mrs. Ray Myers	Piedmont					
Wilson, Hoak Lee	Mar 2, 1943	Jeff Co		78	W	Wilson, Joe	Tn			Wilson, James L.	Shady Grove						
Wilson, Irene	Feb 10, 1974	Morristown, Tn	Tn	Jul 30, 1895	78	W	Card, Charles E.		Hixon, Louella		Wilson, Reid S.	Mont. Vista - Johnson City, Tn					
Wilson, James Ivan	Feb 13, 1943	Hot Springs, Nc	Jeff Co	Oct 17, 1910	32	Mum, Edith	Wilson, Edd		Dance, Eddie	Tn	Wilson, Edd & Mrs.	Piedmont					
Wilson, John Henry	Mar 4, 1959	Jeff Co	Jeff Co	Mar 8, 1899	68	Ng	Wilson, Jack		Hilliard, Carolyn		Wilson, Mrs. & Children	Straw Plains					
Wilson, John W. Sr.	Aug 15, 1945	Jeff Co	Blount Co	Dec 1, 1844	100-8-14	Ng	Fish, Luther	Tn	Hisle, Ellen		James, Mrs. Lee - Wilson, Harold & John	Strawberry Plains					
Wilson, Johnnie [F-Col]	Feb 17, 1966	Jeff Co	Tn			W	Fish, Luther		Rollins, Belle		Wilson, Cecil & Mrs.	Piedmont					
Wilson, Luther Daniel	Feb 27, 1955	Jeff Co	Tn			W	Wilson, Joe				Wilson, Estra	Piedmont					
Wilson, Major Charles Adair	Jun 3, 1944	Cocke Co	Dec 27, 1890	53	Ng		Fancher, Hettie	Tn	Wilson, Winford & Harriet	Tn	West View						
Wilson, Pirkle P. [M-Col]	Jun 19, 1956	Jeff City	Nc	Jun 8, 1904	51	Fain, Johnnie	Wilson, James				Fain, Johnnie	West View Colored					
Wilson, Willis Pearl	Apr 24, 1986	Morristown, Tn	Tn	Jun 6, 1895	70	W	Haskins, Willie		Puckett, Emma		Corpe, Hazel - Jones, Robert - Keller, Mrs. [Daug]	Strawberry Plains					
Winstead, Donald Eugene	Jun 23, 1996	Jeff City	Morristown, Tn	May 17, 1961	35	Gunter, Carol	Winstead, Eugene B.		Brooks, Mary Jo		Wife	Buffalo Grove			Kathrine-Christine-Danielle	Bobby-Chris-Scott	Kathy
Winstead, Mattie L.	Mar 19, 1947	Jeff Co	Jeff City	May 17, 1861	66-9-0		Gilliam, Joseph	Tn	Hamilton, Martha	Tn	Harrell, Pauline - Bass, Frank - Sherman - Winstead, Woodrow	Ebenezer					
Winstead, Sherman Ross	Jan 9, 1986	J.M.H.	Tn	Sep 6, 1910	75	Love, Velma	Winstead, Marion		Gilliam, Mattie		Winstead, Velma Love	WW 2					
Winstead, William	Nov 12, 1953	Hamblen Co	Tn	Feb 5, 1898	55	S	Winstead, Charlie		Green, Minerva		Arwood, Mrs. J.H. - Winstead, Charlie	Jefferson Memorial					
Winstead, Woodrow	Feb 24, 1990	Hamblen Co	Tn	Jun 18, 1915	45-5-17	S	Winstead, Marion		Gilliam, Mattie		Jarnigan - Hamblen Co	Ebenezer					
Winter, Herdon Struther	Sep 12, 1976	Dayton, Tn	Nc		61	Ng	Winter, David Herndon		Struther, Sarah		Winter, Park	West View					
Winter, Mary Frances	Mar 28, 1985	New Tazewell, Tn	Tn	Jul 28, 1917	67	W	Park, James Frank		Harrison, Pauline		Winter, Park S.	West View					
Wisecarver, J. Brice	Dec 13, 1988	J.M.H.	Tn	May 21, 1913	75	W	Wisecarver, John D.		Horton, Nora		Wisecarver, Charles B.	West View					
Wisecarver, Margaret Elizabeth	Jun 30, 1988	J.M.H.	Tn	Sep 2, 1920	67	Wisecarver, J. Brice		Brooks, Charles J.		Shannals, Blanche		Wisecarver, J. Brice	West View	WW 2				
Witt, Burgess Wilson	Aug 25, 1931	Jeff City	Tn	Feb 6, 1857	74	W	Witt, W.R.	Unk	Hancock, Mary	Unk	Wisecarver, J. Brice	West View					

NAME	DDATE	DLOCAT	BLOCAT	BDATE	AGE	SPOUSE	FATHER	FBLOCAT	MOTHER	MFBLOCAT	BY	BURIAL	VET	SON	DAUG	BROTHER	SISTER
Witt, Dan	Dec 27, 1932	Straw Plains	Tn	Dec 12, 1893	39	Ng	Bisby, John	Tn	Bisby, Emmiline	Tn	Witt, Mrs. Dan	Piney					
Witt, Emmiline	Nov 23, 1932	Straw Plains	Tn	May 31, 1861	71	Ng	Bisby, Hannah				Witt, Ron [Son]	Piney					
Witt, Henry E.	Jan 29, 1998	Jeff City	Jeff Co	Apr 4, 1909	88	Homer, Minnie	Witt, Frank		Branson, Martha		Witt, Ron [Son]	Strawberry Plains					
Witz, Sara Alpha	Nov 5, 1997	Knoxville, Tn	Bristo, Va	Jan 26, 1906	91		Rutherford, John Preston		Shoots, Sally		Witz, Paul R. [Son]	Hillcrest		[Br-Law] Hubba, Robert	[Step] Perez, Julie		[Br-Law] Rutherford, Jennie
Wolf, Charlie Eugene	Jan 18, 1996	Nashville, Tn	La Fette, In	Nov 26, 1922	73	O'Neil, Frances	Wolf, Charles Ray		Cripe, Helen		Wife	West View					
Wolf, Theodore R.	Jun 6, 1961	Jeff Co	Tn	Mar 24, 1899	62	Ng	Harvey, Laura		Riley, Ada Mae		Wife	Piney					
Wolfe, Jennifer Le Ann	Aug 6, 1979	U.T.H.	Tn	Aug 6, 1979			Wolfe, Jimmy C.		Collins, Ruby J.	Tn	Wolfe, Katie C. & Joe	Jefferson Memorial					
Wolfe, Katherine	May 7, 1984	J.M.H.	Tn	Oct 5, 1900	83	W	Cook, Thomas F.		Wolfe, Betty		Wolfe, Jimmy C.	Jefferson Memorial					
Wolfe, Kathleen Teresa	Oct 19, 1996	Knoxville, Tn	Chicago, Il	Apr 21, 1947	49	Wolfe, Jerr P.	Gerttis, Jacob		Conrm, Elenora		Husband	J.M.G.		Richard-Samuel			Smith, Helen
Wollard, Bertie Lee	Aug 22, 1991	J.M.H.	Jefferson, Tn	Dec 27, 1932	58		Eller, Joseph Pink		Rickard, Julia B.		Wollard, Alton [Husband]	Community Chapel - McCampbells [Wollard]		[Step] WilBanks, Robert			
Wollard, Carolyn M.	Sep 22, 1983	Jeff Co	Tn	Dec 19, 1941	21	S	Wollard, W. B.		Riley, Ada Mae		Wollard, Mrs. W.B. [Husband]	Wollard					
Wollord, John Edgar	May 15, 1948	Jeff Co	Tn	Aug 4, 1890	57-6-11		Wollard, John M.	Tn	Campbell, Elizabeth	Tn	Wollard, Mrs. Anna Lee	Wollard	WW 1				
Wombie, Luther John	Feb 13, 1987	J.M.H.	Miss.	Feb 5, 1909	78	Wombie, Dorothy	Wombie, John M.		Sheffield, Edna		Wombie, Dorothy Knapp	J.M.G.					
Wood, Anna B.	Dec 8, 1946	Hamblen Co	Tn	Jan 19, 1919	27-10-17	Ng	Seaborn, James Proul?	Tn	Burchfield, Daisy O.	Tn	Woods, H.G.	White Pine	WW 2				
Wood, Lloyd Alfred	Feb 28, 1985	J.M.H.	Tn	Mar 26, 1909	75	Melton, Mary Edith	Wood, P.A.		Palmer, Georgiann		Wood, Sanford & Brothers	Flat Gap					
Wood, Mira A.	Feb 3, 1927		Tn	May 4, 1842	84	Wood, P.A.	Wood, Lloyd		Edith, Mary E.	Tn	Wood, Carl & Lloyd	Cedar Grove					
Wood, Patsy Carolyn	Aug 12, 1942	Jeff Co	Tn	Aug 12, 1942		Ng	Wood, Powell			Knox Co	Wood, Mrs. Hazel Stinnett	Flat Gap					
Wood, Willie Clarence	Jan 13, 1987	Jeff Co	Tn	Mar 26, 1890	76	Ng	Wood, Powell					West View					
Woodard, Bertha	Feb 23, 1986	Alabama		Dec 8, 1900	85	W	Norris, Walter R.		Breedlove, Lucy		Woodard, John Frank	Maple Hill - Huntsville, Ala.					
Woodfin, Ralph William	Nov 21, 1997	Jeff City	Brevard, Nc	Nov 27, 1902	94	Hubbard, Hope [D]	Woodfin, Benson		Wilson, Beulah		Woodfin, James [Son-Covington, Ky]	Roselawn			White, Geneva - Voigt, Lois Jean [D]	Davis [Irenam, Sic]	
Woods, Bryan Allen	Mar 3, 1985	Jeff Co	Tn	Apr 30, 1985			Livesay, Martha		Marshall, Mrs. H.C. [Nashville] Malone, James		Mt. View					
Woods, Callie Lou	Mar 17, 1979	Knoxville, Tn	Tn	Apr 4, 1907	72	W	Volles, George A.		Wallace, Lucile		Woods, George W.	Flat Gap					
Woods, Clark Roger	Dec 25, 1992	Knox Co	Tn	Dec 13, 1951	1		Warwick, Louise		Warwick, Louise		Woods, Howard	Flat Gap					
Woods, Claude C. [Col]	Mar 11, 1955	Jeff Co	Tn	Apr 14, 1882	62	Ng	Woods, James		Melton, ----		Woods, Mrs. Ella	Community					
Woods, Harold B.	Sep 30, 1940	Knox Co	Tn	Dec 1, 1945		S	Woods, Lloyd		Woods, Lloyd		Woods, Howard	Flat Gap					
Woods, Infant Female	Dec 1, 1945	Jeff Co	Tn	Dec 1, 1945			Warwick, Louise	Tn	Wyrick, Louise	Tn	Woods, Howard	Flat Gap					
Woods, Infant Female	Feb 10, 1954	Jeff Co	Tn	Feb 10, 1954			Woods, Carl Sr.		Warwick, Mary Louise		Woods, Howard B.	Flat Gap					
Woods, James C.	Jan 30, 1989	F.S.H.	Tn	May 12, 1919	69	Cox, Juanita			White, Rosa		Woods, James C. - VA	Pleasant Grove	WW 2				
Woods, John J.	Jul 2, 1999	Knoxville, Tn	Jeff Co	Apr 30, 1923	76	Carrie	Fine, Myrtle		Woods, John G.		Pleasant Grove					
Woods, Martin Craig	Mar 25, 1991	U.T.H.	Jeff Co	Mar 25, 1991		S	Wood, Randy		Hurst, Gail		Woods, Randall [Father]	Swann/Atlanta		Larry S. & June		Bob-Bill	
Woods, Mary Jane	Mar 28, 1987	Jeff City	Hawkins Co, Tn	Aug 2, 1944	52	Woods, George	Depew, Martha				Husband	Mt. View					Lane, Ruth
Woods, Pamela Mae	Oct 13, 1964	Jeff Co	Tn	Oct 10, 1964		Woods, George	Vollies, Clyde		Cox, Juanita		Woods, Gary	Mt. View					
Woods, Ronald Dale	Sep 9, 1978	Jeff City	Tn	Mar 21, 1944	34	Livesay, Lorreene	Woods, Gary		Graham, Nancy	Va	Woods, Mrs. Lorreen	Pleasant Ridge					
Woods, Sarah M.	Mar 30, 1931	New Market	Va		70	W	Woods, James		Goodson, James		Woods, Jasper	New Market					
Woods, Tammy Dawn	Nov 26, 1984	Jeff Co	Tn	Nov 19, 1984			Goodson, James		Hill, Judy		Woods, Robert	Community Chapel					
Woods, Valeray Kimbrough Sr.	Oct 31, 1982	Jeff Co	Tn	Apr 9, 1919	63	Div	Woods, Herman		Trent, Mattie		Woods, Verley K. Jr.	Strawberry Plains					
Woods, William Hugh	Nov 9, 1957	U.T. Hospital	Tn	Sept 4, 1916	41	Ng			Finley, Eda Bell		Mowery, Mrs. Wayne - Foster, Mrs. - Grover & Harold - Woods, Mrs. G.C.	Mill Springs	unk				

NAME	DDATE	BLOCAT	BLOCAT	BDATE	AGE	SPOUSE	FATHER	FBLOCAT	MOTHER	MFBLOCAT	BY	BURIAL	VET	SON	DAUG	BROTHER	SISTER
Woolard, Cecil	Sep 28, 1952	Jeff Co	Tn	Sep 2, 1896	56	S	Woolard, Sam	Tn		Woolard, Mrs. Buford & Olyad		Woodard					
Woolard, S.R.	Aug 6, 1931	Jeff Co	Nc	Jun 13, 1867	74	Ng	Jones, Sarah	Tn	Jones, Sarah	Woolard, W.R. & Sam	Mc Campbells Chapel					
Woolard, E.E.	Apr 25, 1931	New Market	Tn	Feb 9, 1871	60	Ng	Woolard, Nathan	Tn	Bates, Rachel	Woolard, Clifford	Friends Station					
Wooten, Sallie Belle	Jun 19, 1947	Jeff Co	Tn	May 6, 1867	80-1-13	W	Hodges, Pharoah		Mc Bee, Sarah Louisa	Tn	Wooten, Ada	Friends Station					
Word, Lucy	Oct 12, 1985	Jeff City	Ga	Aug 3, 1885	99	W	Rogers, Joseph		Brooks, Margaret		Word, Joe	Oak Hill - Cartersville, Ga					
Workman, Angie	Oct 21, 1974	Jeff City	Tn	Oct 28, 1882	91	W	Cockram, George		Hill, Lula		Noe, Mrs. Mildred - Workman, Floyd	Sunderland					
Workman, Newton W.	May 13, 1939	Granger Co	Nc	May 15, 1939	93	Ng	Workman, William B.	Nc	Workman, Mary Frances	Workman, Mrs. Maude Young, Mrs.	Buffalo					
Wright, Ben A.	Aug [5] 1935															
Wright, Bertha	Apr 8, 1978	Jeff City	Gallatin, Tn	Dec 5, 1883	84	Wright, Dr. T.E. [D]	Mason, James W.		Durham, Minnie		Willis, David Mason	West View					
Wright, Billy Ray	Mar 28, 1984	Jeff City	Jeff Co	Jun 6, 1945	48	Glover, Martha	Wright, Frank		Rhinehart, Jessie		Willis	Swannpania		Clifton-Billy-Jamie-			
Wright, Carolyn Sue	Jul 21, 1982	Knox Co	Tn	May 15, 1951	1		Wright, Robert		Dempberry, Mary Jane		Wright, Robert	Lebanon					
Wright, Cas	Jun 15, 1951	Hamblen Co	Tn	Aug 22, 1934	16	S	Wright, James Oscar		Roberts, Mildred			Lebanon					
Wright, Frank	Jan 23, 1973	Knoxville, Tn	Tn		66-6-10	W	Wright, Oscar				Wright, Luther-Mrs. Frank - Hasbey, C.F.	Swannpania					
Wright, George A.	Dec 15, 1940	Jeff City	Tn			W					Wright, J.L. [Bro] - Cohorn, Sarah	Swannpania					
Wright, H. Laurie	Jan [11] 1954		Tn													
Wright, James	Nov 17, 1980	Jeff City	Dandridge, Tn	Aug 12, 1913	67	Div	Wright, James O.		Henry, Mollie		Wright, Rose-Frances - Massengill, Pearl	Swannpania	WW 2				
Wright, Jeffrey Robert	Jan 24, 1980	J.M.H.	Morristown, Tn	Oct 27, 1971	18	S	Wright, Thomas		Walker, Bobbie		Wright, Thomas	J.M.G.					
Wright, Jessie	Jan 28, 1928		Tn		26-2-15	Wright, John	Edwards, William		Prutt, Eliza		Wright, John - Jarnigan, F.	West View					
Wright, Jessie C.	Jul 25, 1934	Hamblen Co	Tn	Feb 10, 1915	19	S	Rhinehart, George	Tn	Henry, Mollie	Tn	Wright, Frank & Children	Swannpania					
Wright, Jessie Mae	Jan 8, 1966	Jeff Co	Tn	Feb 18, 1913	52	Wright, Frank	Lane, Emma				Wright, Frank & Children	Swannpania					
Wright, Katherine Virginia	Jul 12, 1933	Granger Co	Tn	Nov 1, 1932			Wright, Oscar	Tn	Roberts, Mildred	Tn	Wright, Oscar	Blackwell Branch					
Wright, Maggie Margaret	Jun 25, 1951	Tn	Tn	Feb 19, 1877	74	Wright, H. Lank	Lumbkins, Jefferson		Newman, Mollie		Wright, H.L.	West View					
Wright, Mary M. [Tilda]	Jun 25, 1906	J.M.H.	Tn	Jun 15, 1906	79	W	Edmonds, William		Prutt, Eliza		Malone, Betty	Flat Gap					
Wright, Mildred R.	Apr 3, 1963	Hamblen Co	Granger Co	Jan 12, 1891	72	Wright, Oscar [D]	Roberts, William		Phillips, Lucy		Brett, Chila, Mc Murry, James	Lebanon - Greenbrier					
Wright, Rose D.	Nov 10, 1996	Jeff City	Jeff Co	Jan 15, 1917	79	W	Wright, Oscar		Henry, Mollie		Wright, Frances [Sister]	Swannpania Baptist				Oscar	
Wright, Thomas Edward	Dec 11, 1994	Sumner, Co., Tn		Apr 7, 1885	84	Ng	Wright, Thomas	Sumner Co	Willis, Martha M.	Sumner Co	Willis, Martha M.	West View				Oscar	
Wright, Tom Henry	Dec 21, 1984	Jeff City	Tn	Aug 18, 1921	73	Ng	Wright, James Oscar		Henry, Mollie		Wright, Rose [Sister]	Swannpania				Oscar	Wright, Frances
Wright, Will	Jun 25, 1936	Jeff Colby	Tn	Feb 15, 1861	75						Wright, H.M.	West View					
Wright, William Alfred	Aug 15, 1963	Knox Co	Tn	Aug 1, 1906		S	Wright, Columbus		Brown, Mary		Wright, Clelia Standberry, L.R.	Pleasant Grove					
Wright, William W.	Feb 28, 1950	J.M.H.	Tn	Jan 12, 1891	66	S	Roberts, William		Phillips, Lucy		Wright, Oscar	Lebanon					
Wright, Willie [F]	Dec 2, 1959	Jeff Co	Tn		76	W	Backear, Jake		Sallie		Lindsey, Mrs. John - Wesley-Alford-B.J.- Isaac- Lindsey, Donald	Rocky Valley Baptist - Jeff Co					
Wyatt, Arch M.	Nov 3, 1966	Jeff Co	Va	Aug 16, 1884	82	Hill, Pearl	Wyatt, Frank		Meridith, Margaret		Wyatt, Mrs. Pearl H.	Memorial Gardens					
Wyatt, Charlce Faye	Mar 28, 1982	Jeff Co	Tn	Oct 11, 1944	7		Wyatt, Floyd James		Vesser, Lena		Wyatt, Floyd	West View					
Wyatt, Daniel Frank	May 26, 1905	Va			77-4	Wyatt, Rev. John F.	Wyatt, Martin	Nc	Love, Elna	Nc	Wyatt, Mrs. D.F.	Mt. Pleasant					
Wyatt, Flora Hurt	May 20, 1973	Va		Jun 12, 1899	73	W	Hurt, Henry		Cumbaugh, Margaret		Lawsons - Jeff Co	Jefferson Memorial					
Wyatt, Floyd James	Dec 21, 1981	Knoxville, Tn	Tn	Nov 18, 1911	70	W	Wyatt, Martin		Meddox, Annie		Wyatt, Mrs. Lena V.	West View					Mattox, Barbara Jean
Wyatt, John F.	Apr 18, 1982	Jeff Co	Va	May 20, 1892	69	Ng	Wyatt, Franklin		Meridith, Margaret		Wyatt, John F. Jr.	Jefferson Memorial				Charles-George-Luther-Franklin Dee-Jack-Clyde	

NAME	DDATE	BLOCAT	BLOCAT	BDATE	AGE	SPOUSE	FATHER	FELLOCAT	MOTHER	MFELLOCAT	BY	BURIAL	VET	SON	DAUG	BROTHER	SISTER
Wyatt, Pearl	Aug 10, 1975	Jeff Co.	Tn	Jul 21, 1885	90	Wyatt, Arch [D]	Hill, James B.		Malcolm, Margaret		Hawkins, Mrs. W.J. - Linden, Helen - Wyatt, J. McCoy	Jefferson Memorial					
Wylie, Minerva Belle	Apr 6, 1985	Jeff Co [Flee Ala]	Florence, Alabama	Jun 9, 1886	78	W	Wylie, D.P.		Dowdy, Emma		Richardson, Mrs. Raymond [Deborah]	Florence, Alabama					
Wyrick, Michael Duane	Oct 23, 2000	Kingsport, Tn	Mi	Jan 30, 1959	41	S			Wyrick, Peggy		Wyrick, Bill [Brother]	Strawberry Plains					
Wyrick, T.B.	Sep 13, 1941	Straw Plains	Knox Co	Jul 4, 1932	67-7-15	Bailey, Gertrude					Wyrick, Louise [Daug]						
Yarbrough, Velma Doreen	Mar 2, 1987	J.M.H.	Ky		54	W	Smith, Henry	Tn			Yarborough, Berlen; Carl Bros.	J.M.G.					
Yates, Fannie W.	Mar 31, 1929	Tn	Tn		54	W					Yates, George & Earnest	Shiloh					
Yates, John Jessie	May 10, 1926	Tn	Tn		78	S	Yates, Ord	Tn	Unk	Tn	Yates, Ord	West View					
Yates, L.L.	Jan 6, 1931			Dec 8, 1852	78	S	Yates, Anderson	Tn	Unk		Yates, Ord	Shiloh					
Yates, Minnie B.	Dec 23, 1932	Jeff City	Tn	Nov 4, 1872	60	Yates, Ord	Duff, W.H.H.	Tn	Vinyard, Naoma	Tn	Yates, Ord	West View					
Yates, Ord	Sep 18, 1945	Jeff Co	Granger Co	Jan 8, 1870	75	W	Yates, Ben	Tn	Rich, Elizabeth	Tn	Henry, Mrs. John	West View					
Yoder, Everett Wallace	Oct 23, 1982	J.M.H.	Nebraska	Mar 26, 1928	54	Mullendore, Patsy	Yoder, J.S.		Bales, Johanna		Yoder, Don - Baby / Carter, Bonnie Jean - Sims, C.J.	Jefferson Memorial					
Yoe, King [Col]	Jun 5, 1939	Granger Co	Tn	Jul 20, 1871	67	S	Yoe, Henry	Tn	Unk		Colored	Colored					
Young, Amanda T.	Jun 17, 1958	Jeff City	Ky	Feb 1, —	30-1-20	W	Turner, Andrew		Unk		Young, Bonnie Jean - W.B. & Johnny	West View					
Young, Charlova Michelle	Apr 13, 1971	Jeff Co	Jeff Co		60-4-16	S	Young, George		Young, George		Young, George	Bech					
Young, Cora Lee	Jun 10, 1947	Jeff Co	Jeff Co			S	Boatman, Cora Lee	Tn			Young, Jack	Shiloh					
Young, Fannie Elizabeth	Jan 15, 1997	Jeff City	Jeff Co	May 11, 1925	71	Solomon, George	Brown, Olney		Young, Riley	Tn	Young, Riley [Son]	Bech		George Rich- Doug	Robertson, Ellos - Leon, Janie & Danny - [B-Lee] Young, Gail-Rodie		Cox, Ardela
Young, Isaac George	Jan 25, 1958	Tn	Tn	Feb 27, 1880	77	Ng	Young, William		Young, Joe & Mack		Young, Joe & Mack / Young, Cora & Children	Mill Springs					
Young, Jack	Mar 25, 1960	Jeff Co	Tn	Feb 17, 1909	55	Ng	Young, West		Clevenger, Elizabeth		Shiloh	Shiloh					
Young, John F.	Feb 25, 1931	Knoxville	Tn	Feb 7, 1896	44	Ng	Clevenger, A.W.	Tn	Young, A.W.	Tn	Young, John F.	West View					
Young, Messine	Sep 20, 1966	J.M.H.	Tn	Dec 23, 1896	69	Young, Harvey [D]	King, Rufus B.		Merritt, Cornelia	Tn	Merritt, Virginia King	West View					
Young, Paul E.	Sep 11, 1929	Jeff City	Jeff City		15-2-24	S	Young, J.A.	Tn	Young, J.A.	Tn	Young, J.A.						
Young, Thomas [Col]	Feb 24, 1942	New Market	Jeff Co	Aug 7, 1963	80	W	Bradford, Simon	Tn	Young, Minerva	Tn	Moore, Wanda & Honeycutt, Lexia [Daug] - Murray, Charles - Young, Amanda	St. Luke Colored					
Young, William Halward	Mar 6, 1992	Jeff Co	Humana Hosp, Morristown, Tn	Mar 30, 1911	40	Ng	Young, I.G.		Young, Mrs. Halward		Young, Mrs. Halward	Mill Springs	U.S.A.F.				
Yount, George Marvin	Feb 3, 1990	Nc	Bowdon, Ga	Mar 23, 1921	68	Cavender, Mildred	Yount, Henry		Cavender, Ella		Mt. Pleasant - Talbott, Tn	Mt. Pleasant		Ricky		Kara [Gd]	
Zeller, Christopher Nicholas	Oct 23, 1999	Jeff City	Elyria, Ohio	Dec 28, 1950	48	W	Zeller, Gus John		Zeller, Christina N. [Daug]		Zeller, Christina N. [Daug]	White Pine	Army				
Zellers, Mary Kate	Dec 11, 1953	White Pine	Tn	Nov 12, 1875	78	S	Baker, Newton		Drinkell, Mrs. Jo Anna		Brookside - Elyria, Ohio	Hillcrest					
Zimmerman, Nellie Lucille	Sep 15, 1975	Jeff Co	Tn	Sep 17, 1919	55	S	Zimmerman, Frank		Franks, Ethel		Walden, L.C. - Whitlocks, Judy Teddy	Hillcrest					
Zirkle, Anna Katherine	Apr 7, 1987	New Haven, Ct	Millington, Tn	Jan 27, 1972	25	Zirkle, John W.	Zirkle, John W.		Engelbright, Eva		Father				[S] Zirkle, Anna Kathren-Laura Elizabeth-Sara Patrick		
Zirkle, Anna Lee	Apr 22, 1994	Jeff City	Wise Co, Va	May 6, 1913	80	Patrick, Orbin	Patrick, Orbin		Hill, Laura		Zirkle, John W. [Son]	West View		James W.			Weston, Mary Kathren-Lavan Pauline - Haynes, Alice Wyrick
Zirkle, Carrie	Jul 6, 1986	Jeff Co	Wise Co, Va	May 20, 1882	84	Bruce, William B.	Bruce, William B.		Gibson, Elvira		Sheddan, Mrs. Joe - Churchman, Mrs. Dan - Zirkle, Elvira / Albright, K. - Stephenson, Forrest	West View					
Zirkle, Cora Long	Mar 22, 1971	Hopkinsville, Ky		Jul 20, 1867	76	Long, —	Long, —				Zirkle, George - Fellers, Mrs. Will	Shady Grove					
Zirkle, Hallie M.	Dec 31, 1943	Dandridge	W			W	Fox, Campbell				Zirkle, Mrs. Pat & James						
Zirkle, James W.	Apr 19, 1982	Jeff City	Tn	Oct 14, 1903	59	Ng	Zirkle, John W.	Tn	Denton, Rebecca J.	Tn	Ashmore, Ollie	Jefferson Memorial		James W.	[S] Zirkle, Anna Kathren-Laura Elizabeth-Sara Patrick		Weston, Mary Pauline - Haynes, Alice Wyrick

NAME	DDATE	DLOCAT	BLOCAT	BDATE	AGE	SPOUSE	FATHER	FBLOCAT	MOTHER	MFBLOCAT	BY	BURIAL	VET	SON	DAUG	BROTHER	SISTER
Zinkle, John William	Aug 21, 1950	Jeff Co	Tn	Nov 4, 1867	82	Ng	Zinkle, William	Tn	Gaut, Mary	Tn	Zinkle, James W.	West View					
Zinkle, Joseph C.	Jan 22, 1954	Jeff Co	Tn	Sep 2, 1890	63	Ng	Zinkle, George		Wisdom, Florence		Zinkle, Mrs. Cora - Albright, Mrs. - Stephenson, Mrs.	Mt. Horeb					
Zinkle, Margret	Feb 16, 1932	Dandridge	1861	Nov 9, 1862	70	S	Zinkle, William		Gaut, Mary S.			Study Grove					
Zinkle, Ollie	Apr 29, 1962	Hamblen Hall	Tn	Feb 25, 1876	86	Zinkle, John W. [D]	Ashmore, James W.	Tn	Wisdom, Caroline	Tn	Zinkle, Mrs. James W.	West View					
Zinkle, Phillip Ray	Apr 127, 1985	Waco, Texas			67	Zinkle, Dorothy					Zinkle, Dorothy [Montgomery, Ala.]	Mt. Horeb					
Zuern, Joyce Elaine	Nov 19, 1951	Jeff Co	Ohio	Apr 5, 1923	28	S	Zuern, George A.		Jones, Jessie		Clannon, Mrs. Joe T.	West View					